WITHDRAWN

17-15

PEOPLE, POWER, AND POLITICS

People, Power, and Politics

AN INTRODUCTORY READER

Edited by

Lyman Jay Gould and E. William Steele

University of Vermont

Random House, New York

43264

To Ann and Ruth

First Printing

© Copyright, 1961, by
Lyman Jay Gould and E. William Steele

All rights reserved under International and Pan-American Copyright
Conventions. Published in New York by Random House, Inc., and
simultaneously in Toronto, Canada, by Random House of Canada, Limited.

Library of Congress Catalog Card Number: 61-9679

Manufactured in the United States of America

CONTENTS

CONSTITUTIONALISM

LAW

INSTITUTIONS

Preface

This is a book of readings. The selections have been chosen, the commentary written, and the entire volume organized for the purpose of introducing students to the study of political science. Chapter I deals with the current state of the discipline, first by considering the broad field in which the discipline operates—the social sciences—and then by delving into the scope and method of political science in particular. Chapter II is concerned with the prime physical factors that affect politics. Though we have subscribed to no particular school, and have sought throughout to avoid any kind of determinism, we have nevertheless recognized that political ideas and institutions are never wholly self-generative. Both in their substance and their operation, they always reflect that most crucial of all of the ingredients of politics, power. This, in turn, is rooted in the even more basic circumstances of population, geography, natural resources, and industrial capacity.

Of course these physical factors do not make up the entire political picture. Because men can rationalize, articulate, and—if they are truly gifted—synthesize, we must be fully aware of the important contribution made by theory, the ideological framework of the political process. Thus, Chapter III explores some of that theorizing, in which reason, faith, and passion are so frequently intertwined.

Chapter IV examines the formal and traditional devices of political life—constitutionalism, law, and the executive and legislative institutions. By contrast, Chapter V looks into other institutions, both public and private, that men have developed and the resulting nongovernmental devices that can be used for political achievement. The character and activities of these "mobilizers of political power" (the political party, the bureaucracy, business, labor, the military, the church, agriculture, students, and scientists) have already caused many competent observers to note a gradual move of the political process from the traditional "public" realm into a twilight half-public, half-private area. Chapter VI concludes the book by analyzing how the focus of power is successfully shifted. Since violent and nonviolent means are used in the transfer of power, both categories are discussed.

In compiling the material for this book, we have been motivated by several beliefs. We hold that it is imperative to study the political process as well as the formal institutional structure. Structure and process are the body and soul of politics; to ignore or to play down either of them in introducing students to political science seems to us unwarranted, unwise, and ineffectual. In addition, politics is not the monopoly of any one nation or culture. In our venture into the comparative approach we have aimed at pointing up both the universality and the variation inherent in politics, rather than at a detailed understanding of the political system of any country. Therefore we have not concentrated on painstaking analyses of a limited number of states but have used comparatively drawn illustrative materials which we felt would best achieve our purpose. Finally, there are few, if any, academic desert islands today. The student laboring in one discipline knows that he must be aware of descriptions, analyses, and insights that stem from the work done in other disciplines. Politics can be more fully understood only if this need is recognized. The readings reveal the editors' view that political scientists have no monopoly of political knowledge and insight. Thus, many of the selections are culled from the works of scientists, economists, labor leaders, corporation executives, journalists, professional revolutionaries, and those all too often maligned figures—the politicians themselves. One procedural point should be noted. We have been careful to indicate our editing by the insertion of ellipses. However, where the deletion involves a few words or a sentence topical rather than substantive in nature, the ellipses were omitted for the sake of style and clarity.

Each of the six chapters ends with a selective bibliography of the widest variety of reading selections consistent with the general nature of the subject matter. No periodical literature is listed; nor do we cite textbooks, except for a few which we feel have been acknowledged as unique contributions to political science. The omission of some desirable material was inevitable: in other areas, the paucity of material available is sadly evident. In our view, however, the bibliographies as they stand would make a useful and respectable library for a beginning student of political science.

At this point we want to acknowledge some of our debts. In a department blessed with a high degree of camaraderie, our colleagues have felt free to criticize, cajole, and confound us in our efforts. If we have sometimes failed to heed their advice, it was not due to their lack of ardor and conviction. We are indebted to all of them. A special word of gratitude is due Professor Raul Hilberg, of the Department of Political Science at the University of Vermont, who has not only given generously of his time but has been of invaluable aid in the selection of the readings relating to the German experience. Professor Robert Daniels, of the Department of History at the University of Vermont, suggested the treatment for the section on the Russian executive.

Professor Michael Reagan, of the Department of Politics at Princeton University, Professor David Spitz, of the Department of Political Science at Ohio State University, and Professor W. Ross Yates, of the Department of History and Government at Lehigh University, have been most helpful with perceptive criticisms and suggestions. If we have not followed through properly, the fault is ours. A special word of thanks is due Mr. Frank C. Mallory, Director of Medical Photography at the University of Vermont, who was most patient with the requests of "two outsiders." Our greatest debt, of course, is to the authors, editors, and publishers who so graciously granted permission for the use of their material.

The student is warned not to look forward to a set of neatly-packaged problems with solutions enclosed. Neither should he expect a manifesto calling him to the barricades. The study of politics is the study of conflict—conflict over information, over issues, and over values. We have not gone beyond trying to reveal some of these conflicts and organizing them into broad categories. As editors and teachers, we have had no desire to arrogate to ourselves the task of the individual reader to seek, to evaluate, and to choose. For this decision, we offer no apology. If the task is not easy for the student, this is as it was intended, for the willingness to make difficult choices is at once the ultimate responsibility and measure of man.

L.J.G.

E.W.S.

CHAPTER I

The Study of Politics

Progress in the sciences has not only yielded prospects of a more comfortable world, but has put into our hands a terrifying destructive potential. Debates over the morality of nuclear weapons, guided missiles, and nerve gas cannot alter the fact that these instruments of war *are* available. If there is to be a tomorrow in which to enjoy our new comforts, we must first make certain that our unprecedented technical progress does not prove self-defeating. This fact has lent to the age-old problems of man's relations with man an urgency they have never had before in history. For this reason—perhaps out of hope, perhaps out of necessity—the social scientist is moving ever closer to the political forefront.

Both governors and governed want answers. Like their counterparts in the other social sciences, political scientists are being more and more called upon for advice. An anxious society is even willing to aid financially those who, given time away from the classroom and an opportunity to think, might offer hope of some small accomplishments. This increased attention and support have flattered the political scientist, reinforced his native curiosity, and provided him with added incentive to undertake research. Moreover, the political science profession as a whole has been forced by these developments into considerable soul-searching. From this professional self-analysis have emerged two basic questions: What is the goal of the political scientist? How should he try to achieve it? Generally speaking, the profession is divided into two schools on these questions. If this fact suggests a certain schizophrenia in the profession, it also indicates something of the nature and complexities of the discipline of political science.

What is the goal of the political scientist? To one group it is the acquisition of knowledge about the political institutions and the political behavior of man. It is a search to discover the nature and meaning of the political environment; it is an obligation to communicate effectively to students and interested laymen the knowledge acquired. With this goal in mind, the political scientists of this first school have developed a commitment to cool, dispassionate analysis and a discerning eye for political change. Among this group, there is little, if any desire to pass judgment on what they observe and report. It is their aim to treat their subject matter with moral detachment. Their interests are clinical and descriptive, not evaluative or critical.

The second group also believes in the necessity for knowledge of the political environment, but sees the search as having a limited justification unless accompanied by prescriptions for future behavior and policies. This group does not depreciate the clinical efforts of its colleagues but maintains that it is not enough to know merely "how" and "why." Consideration, it feels, must also be given to the "should" and "ought."

It is this last point that causes trouble in a professional sense. Those who would avoid the "should" and "ought" have an honest fear of making value judgments in the course of what professes to be a scientific calling. They regard an emphasis on normative approaches as a threat to objectivity. They have seen too often what unfortunate effects inarticulate normative premises may have on scholarship. They believe that history shows all too many examples of the rejection or delayed acceptance of new knowledge because of entrenched dogma and superstition. Like the physical scientists, they therefore prefer to content themselves with the experience of discovery itself. In their capacity as scientists, that is, they believe the question of how the discovery is used to be outside their proper realm.

How Should the Political Scientist Try to Achieve His Goal?

One group sees the human environment as infinitely complex. Each aspect of that environment—social, psychological, and biological—may cast new light on man's political behavior. The large amount of quantitative data that is potentially available and must be investigated suggests to this group the necessity for carefully constructed concepts, frames of reference, and models which will reduce the information to manageable proportions. "Manageable" as used here means "that which can be ordered and classified and therefore be useful," "which lends itself to potential or real prediction." The logic of this methodological school demands a constant search for information from other disciplines. It has also led to the adoption of tools and techniques which these other disciplines have developed in interpreting their own data. Many of these tools and techniques are borrowed from the disciplines of mathematics and the physical sciences. They are adopted with gratitude and, frequently, with a sense of relief, because they represent a new communication process having a scientific objectivity which is absent in the more subjective, value-laden terminology of the older political language. For that reason, one today finds a sizeable body of work being done in political science, particularly in the fields of political parties, international politics, public administration, and even constitutional law, that bears the impact of this newer, scientific methodological school. Its common purpose is to reduce the data of its various fields to symbols with precise meaning.

The second school of thought prefers to choose its methods and techniques from the related fields of history and philosophy, which have contributed so substantially to the development of political science in the past. More specifically, this second group of political scientists approaches the study of the state and the phenomena of politics in a narrower and more formal sense. Highly institution-conscious, it is prepared to recognize that politics is something dynamic and constantly changing, but insists that what is involved is too complex, unique and interrelated ever to be analyzed completely, no matter how sophisticated the scientific concepts and symbols. It acknowledges that the scientific study of such subjects as technology, population, and human behavior may contribute a great deal to our knowledge. Yet it sees our political realities shaped to an even greater extent by ideas, men, and the events of history. While respecting the discoveries of the newer type of political study, this second group of political scientists continues to reserve its greatest enthusiasm for the brilliant insight, arrived at by the more traditional methods of reflection and intuition. The developing trend toward systematization through the building of scientific models and the creation of symbols, it sees partly as an artifice—an attempt to create "scientific objectivity" by merely applying new concepts and language to data which do not lend themselves to such treatment. In the last analysis most members of this second methodological school suspect that human political behavior is simply not susceptible to the precise and predictable tests of measurement that they ascribe to their more scientifically-minded colleagues.

While the resulting controversy is more than the proverbial tempest in the teapot, it would be incorrect to overemphasize the differences between the two groups. One should not suppose either that all the younger political scientists are on one side, with the older members of the profession on the other, or that the two methodological positions are mutually exclusive. On the contrary, members of the first group have no hesitation about drawing upon the researches and materials of the historico-philosophical school. The members of the latter have no intention of spurning the insights being yielded by the more consciously scientific type of work, whether in political science itself or any other discipline. Reasoned argument and discussion have thus not given way to an intractable fixity of belief by either group. Each, in fact, has profited by the other's skepticism and criticism.

Because of these differences of emphasis and viewpoint about the nature, scope, and limits of their discipline, political scientists often approach their subject matter with very different orientations, skills, and tools. In a sense, this is undoubtedly a disciplinary weakness. Yet in another sense, it is also a professional asset and, indeed, a social strength. For it indicates that political science—both the discipline itself as well as the men and women engaged in it—continues to be alive and growing.

The following readings illustrate and expand upon the problems involved. Professor Berle, an adherent of the qualitative approach, reminds all social scientists of the necessity of values and laments the growing emphasis upon scientific neutralism. Richard S. Leghorn, a physicist by training, is concerned with improving channels of information and communication. Leghorn's interest lies in the possibly prosaic, but extremely important task of facilitating the accumulation, storage, and availability of data. The selection by Professor Bailey examines methodology directly in the context of political science itself, reviewing and summarizing the various schools; in addition to its descriptive value, the article indicates that each methodological approach to the discipline may have a measure of professional validity. The article by Professor Neumann serves a dual purpose. It describes the so-called "power orientation" to the study of politics. At the same time, it is intended to remind the student that in subscribing to this approach, the present book, like every other treatment of a subject matter, is bound to start from its own biased premises, whether articulated or otherwise.

1 · COHERENCY AND THE SOCIAL SCIENCES *

Adolf A. Berle, Jr.

LORDS SPIRITUAL AND WORTHY
AND LEARNED MASTERS IN CONVOCATION:
 The salutation is here used not as a bit of exhibitionism, but as an element in a revolutionary plot. It was, in its time, the form used in addressing a convocation of Lords Spiritual and ecclesiastical worthies in medieval England. In time, taking action through such convocations became the right of degree-holders of certain universities. The plot hereby revealed is to ask that you as graduates of this great university school, with greater or lesser authority as your respective dignities and situations indicate, fulfill the responsibilities appertaining to you by giving guidance in a matter of serious, if non-temporal, concern.

This is not mere academic jesting. I wish it were. As will presently appear, the development of social science and in considerable measure with it the social development of the United States demands that a measure of order be brought out of its present semi-cognate anarchies. The life of Americans is likely to be affected by failure in the social science field. As a lawyer, I come within that field, and am aggrieved. I require consideration and remedy from my peers and superiors.

Let me begin by waiving a number of minor claims. I wish, for example, that social scientists would write and talk intelligible English —or indeed any current language. Each discipline, and too often each practitioner, claims a sacred right to invent a jargon of its own. The result resembles a sound-recording of the fall of the Tower of Babel taken on a matrix of solidified Hungarian goulash.

A second complaint is that no living being possesses, or could readily extract, any map of organization in this field. The definition of ethnology, for example, varies from Columbia to the University of Michigan, from Michigan to the University of Chicago, and thence all the way to the University of California. Under any one of two

* Dinner address given (June, 1957) to the Association of Princeton Graduate Alumni. Reprinted by permission of Adolf A. Berle, Jr.

or three department headings, one may find included analysis of the market for shaving cream, comparative statistics of skull measurements, voting habits of Erie County, or specialized application of genetics. At Harvard, elementary courses in history are relabeled "Social Science." One could carry out the list interminably. There ought to be some sort of agreement so that we know what we are talking about.

But let us not bother with small matters.

What I am really asking tonight is a body of philosophy; or, if that is impossible, at least a group of philosophers who work at their trade.

Social science should be a branch of learning and an intellectually causative field of study in American life. Through it, and from it alone, can come that skilled and orderly attack on a range of problems extending from the ridiculous (like mass media) to the fearful (like atomic warfare) which are transforming American life. Quite obviously we are leaving one era of politico-economic organization and are entering another, resplendent with possibilities, but glittering with a fierce advance reflection like that of sunlight on spear-points. The present is, as always, in the hands of the Lords Temporal who hold governmental and economic power. But the future turns on the leadership given by the teachers, the scholars, and the Lords Spiritual. The social scientists claim to hold the burden of analysis, discovery of cause and effect, preparation of tools of guidance and leadership. The plea here is that they assume the responsibility of their claim.

I speak here of the social sciences as a lawyer, in his true profession, has a right to do. The century has thus far dealt ill with my field. It early rejected the theory of "natural law" or, as it has come to be called, natural right. Worse yet, it asserted not only that there was not, but that there could not be, either any guiding revelation from religion or any guiding value-system from rationalist philosophy. It accepted, without protest, ideas proceeding from Germany, notably furthered by the great philosopher Max Weber. The social sciences were, in the accepted phrase, to be "neutral sciences." If brought to viability (not to say, perfection) they might assist men and society by telling them how things occurred and could be made to happen. But they could supply no guide as to whether anything *ought* to be done, or whether if done it would be good or bad.

Terribly, field after field fell into line. Historians promptly doubted whether we learnt anything from history. A solid group of them arose to assert that nothing ever could be learnt from history. Many of the most brilliant minds in my own profession, the law, discarded any theory that the law was attempting to bring rules of conduct (*lex*) into harmony with the rules of the good society (*jus*) which we call "justice." Instead, law was considered (and, in the second decade of the century, was taught at Harvard) as a means of social engineering.

Economics was perhaps the most advanced of the social sciences. Classically, however, this discipline assumed that the judgment of the market place represented a resultant of people's choices which, like the voice of the people, could be considered as the voice of God. Men like Ludwig Von Mises and Frederic Hayek stoutly maintain this view now; it is nominally the presently accepted doctrine. But the result of that reasoning is that whatever economically is, must be economically or somehow right, or at least, the best possible result. Actually, the human agonies of the decade from 1930 to 1940 led practically the entire Western world to turn from this in horror. This might have been tolerable had philosophy picked up the challenge: ethics and politics, the search for the good life and the good society, are traditionally the philosopher's task. But, since the late Hugo Muensterberg wrote his study of *The Eternal Values,* American philosophers have spent most of their time debating whether there is such a thing as cosmic order at all—let alone values within such a system. A few voices still cry in the wilderness: notably Professor Leo Strauss of the University of Chicago, whose volume *Natural Right and History* five years ago represented a desperate attempt to reverse the trend.

Certainly political mechanisms everywhere went to work to create economic systems giving effect to value systems as they were conceived. The results, of course, differed widely. Some were starkly horrible, like those achieved in Nazi Germany. Others, in many respects no less horrible, were more widely accepted because they professed—and perverted—a partly defensible value system: Stalinist Communism is an illustration. Others were humanitarian, like British democratic Socialism. Some were flexible and on the whole remarkably successful, like the American system of guided pluralistic economy today. Technically, the century of production, of mechanical liberation, of greatest technical domination of nature by man, shoved full steam ahead without other guidance save the instincts of the men temporarily in political power.

It is difficult for me to avoid connecting this philosophical lack with a surprising phenomenon. American intellectuals are, and will remain, predominantly liberal. But lacking any clear-cut body of philosophical doctrine in the social sciences, many of them accepted upstart political dogmas with remarkably uncritical minds. Some argued that any choate doctrine—Marxism, for instance—offered more hope than no doctrine at all: the "neutrality" concept. Others, unguided philosophically, swallowed a whole dogma because part of it seemed attractive. The second and third decades of this century should have been, and they were not, the golden age of social science applied either directly or through law, looking toward the formation of a really good society.

Now we are all conscious of the fact that the modern world, least of all modern America, does not want and will not tolerate any binding conscription of doctrine like that which bound the Middle Ages, or which now binds the Marxian world. In pleading for guidance we are not asking either for revelation from Mount Sinai or thought control from any group, be it court, council or congress. But I do submit that we are entitled to some working hypotheses; to the best guesses, if you like, that enlightened and disinterested scholars and observers can give us; more likely to several working hypotheses which may be discussed and evaluated so that choice can be made. This, it seems to me, is a demand those of us working in the mire and struggle of affairs can fairly make of the Lords Learned and Spiritual.

Many years ago, four philosophers were in the habit of meeting annually to consider the state of the universe: Henry Osborne Taylor, a historian, Alfred North Whitehead, a mathematical philosopher, William Morton Wheeler, a biological scientist, and Lawrence Henderson, a great doctor and teacher of medicine. At one of these conversations the writer was privileged to be a silent witness. The historian, Taylor, asked of the doctor, Henderson, "Why has medical science made such notable progress in the past generation, while the social sciences have made so little?" Henderson answered, "Medical science is always subject to the discipline of having to deal with a sick man on the bed or the operating table. There is no ivory tower in which it can hide. Its thinking may range over the whole relationship of the human personality to nature; but its answers must relate to the welfare of a patient who is sick and desires to be well." The subsequent discussion ranged to statistical methods (then, as now, very much in fashion). These derived validity in part from the idea that men, as individuals, were unpredictable, while the action of masses can be ascertained, charted and predicted. This is, at best, only approximate. No one has yet met a statistical norm, just as all of Communist theory has never provided the name and address of the "proletariat." Neither exists; both are abstractions. Abstraction is a method of working toward a result, but never is a result. This conversation has repetitively obtruded itself on the writer's thinking in the quarter-century since it occurred.

At present, social scientists are beginning to observe the emergence of a new phase in American economic life with sociological, psychological, and political implications which are only barely apprehended. Briefly, we are seeing the gradual transition (in historical time of course not gradual at all) of our vast country from a system of individual private possessory property (the norm a century ago) to a system of non-individual, non-statist, non-possessory economic and social power (a system of corporations, corporate insurance companies and pension trusts, of labor unions, professional guilds, and voluntary associations) which has concentrated economic power to a degree unknown in recorded history. We have seen that concentration of power producing benign results in many respects, with the result that the United States has a position of unparalleled opulence and an amazing minimum of economic misery. We have seen the new institutions of this non-statist power system detach themselves from their original fields of responsibility. Today the men principally in charge of the system are themselves asking for charters of responsibility and a place where account of their stewardship may be given, with resulting recognition for the splendor of their service or censure for failure to discharge their responsibilities.

American business and labor leaders and their associates alike secretly complain that they are unjustly dealt with. Theirs is the work; theirs the burden; theirs in considerable measure the achievements. Yet as their careers near their close, they have little to anticipate save a conventional and often ridiculous farewell dinner, an engraved wrist watch, a pension, and a politely concealed hope that they gracefully vanish from the discussion as soon as possible. So they do, and quite often from history as well.

What they are really saying, I think, is that they are entitled to be judged by someone more competent to give accolade or censure than their own public relations departments, to be esteemed by some more lasting measure than the size of their bank accounts, to be considered significant for better or worse as factors in their own time. They, like your orator (the word is used to mean one praying aid), are asking the Lords Spiritual and the scholars to define their field of responsibility and give some standard for performance—just as did old Emperor Charles, surnamed the Great, when he asked a like question of Pope Gregory in the year 800.

We may say that the twentieth century is making demands of the philosopher and the social scientist, comparable to those which the emergent feudal system made of the medieval Catholic Church eleven hundred years ago.

Perhaps our trouble is due to the fact that the social sciences, if they are unable to assume a philosophical burden, have not demanded of their mother faculty, Philosophy, that it get to work and do its job.

The late Oliver Wendell Holmes, a lawyer, used to meet with a philosopher, the late Morris Cohen, for the sole purpose of discussing just these matters. "We will twist the tail of the cosmos until it squeaks," he once wrote, and the philosopher met him on that ground. Judges and lawyers, like Lawrence Henderson's doctor, always deal with men under stress: philosophy translated into law must answer specifically. It may be—I am not competent to say— that Max Weber was right and that all the social sciences are merely neutral instruments. But to be put into action at all they must have a set of premises. The lawyer applying social science has to have some notion of his objective, just as the doctor must have his Aesculapian oath and his conviction that a well man is better than a sick one and, on the whole, that a live man is better than a dead one. Demand that philosophers provide at least a working hypothesis, I think, would provoke a response; if none were forthcoming, the social scientists might at least work up a tentative hypothesis of their own. Most of them, probably, have tacitly done this already and simply do not dare to admit it. The great and kindly economic tool-maker of our time, Professor Wesley Clair Mitchell of Columbia, firmly insisted that his tools were neutral, but their use was not. Our knowledge of the business cycle, our conception and tabulation of national income, our unparalleled though still incomplete statistical knowledge of American economy, is more due to him than to any one man. But he maintained that there must be some philosophical premise to guide their use or even to justify their construction. Else (he used to tell us) it would be as important to count the paving stones in Times Square as to calculate the productivity of the American economic system. Lacking other criteria, your social scientist must make his own. So unquestionably he does in fact, though as a rule he will commonly die rather than admit it. The time has thus come to drop the fiction of "neutrality."

Perhaps because of lack of philosophical premise, social scientists have been laid open to strange heresies. The most remarkable of these is the fallacy of the physio-scientific approach.

Here, a group of people working from surprisingly limited premises have been proposing themselves as having the key to great mysteries with which social scientists grapple. Cultural anthropologists and social psychologists, to name two, offered keys. No doubt their keys do open some doors. But too often, unhappily, the doors when opened were like the glittering gates rifled by Lord Dunsany's burglars in the belief that they were the gates of heaven. When they swung open, there was nothing behind.

We can sympathize even with these strange nestlings of the social sciences. There have always been soothsayers and magicians in the world. Powerful as well as humble men have always avidly sought guidance from men who claimed their esoteric knowledge gave them peculiar insight. King Nebuchadnezzar did that, and so does the New York Stock Exchange. If a cultural anthropologist can tell you what kind of people will buy soap and what kind of soap they like, or if a social psychologist will tell you what man will be successful as Vice President in Charge of Production, or if an economic analyst can tell you whether business will be better in the fourth quarter, there is a yearning to make this scholar, however honest, into a soothsayer—and the market for soothsayers is always good. Well, perhaps you are in an uncharted field, and your chances of guessing accurately by soothsayer's guidance are as good as by any other means. But, in our case as in any other, a claim to nonexistent knowledge debases the accuracy of scholarship.

Finally, we have had an odd perversion of the sound conception that social sciences must not be "compartmentalized" and that there must be "interdisciplinary" exchange.

The premise was accurate: any social science works in the presence of, and is modified by, one or more at least of the companion disciplines. Criminal law certainly works in a field in which penology is invariably present; corporation law, my own field, invariably works against a background of economics. So, it was rightly said, penologists and the criminal lawyers, economists and constitutional lawyers, must work together. . . . Now interdisciplinary work involves a sort of scholastic marriage, which (like any marriage) is subject to a certain amount of strain. Each of the individuals has to become at least amateur in the discipline of the other; and this is hard work. Because it was hard, people fell into the idea that mere parallel or associated studying would cause the same results: get someone to write an essay in the field in which you wish to write an essay and put the two together. Alas, in that business, one and one may or may not add up to two; as Whitehead observed, if the one is a match, and the other a keg of gunpowder, the results seem not to be two but an explosion. We have had few explosions in interdisciplinary work; too often we have merely had studies in which the parts did not fit, the gears did not mesh, the marriage was not comsummated, and the result was either sterility or monstrosity. A Lord Temporal passionately and poignantly seeking some guide to policy and action looks at this —and leaving social science to collectors, instead trusts his hunch or his intuition.

A wholly competent social psychologist recently proposed a research project to the writer. This was to be an analysis of certain methods used by our Communist opponents in given-type situations. Rightly and perceptively he considered that these would be illuminated if placed in the historical context of the institutions and backgrounds which brought them into existence; he was clear that the Communist methods in question were not strange magic but only an adaptation of old methods. As he was ignorant of the ethnology, history, and institutional background of the people involved, he proposed commissioning companion essays respectively from historians and sociologists. The writer asked how his colleagues could prepare such companion essays without knowing at least the data and premises of the social psychologist's thinking. Either they must learn some social psychology or he must learn some history. The fallacy was the fallacy that *two* limited approaches would necessarily produce a synthesis.

Let us leave over complaining, and soberly face the danger.

American civilization proudly affirms that it is humanist, devoted beyond all else to the maintenance and nurture of the free and creative individual. "What is man that thou art mindful of him?" is engraved on the hall which houses Harvard's Philosophy Department. But in this tangle of "neutral sciences" man is almost as denigrated as he is by Marxian or Nazi doctrine. Without that central concept, I do not see that the social sciences do more than offer (if they do) methods of manipulation. In "neutral" science men become fodder for a system or a machine, for IBM calculators or for psychologists' unchallengeable records; units in econometric calculus or specimens allowed to gambol in a living museum.

. . . Perhaps we should reject the all-inclusive claims of our social scientist Frankenstein-creators. Perhaps we should assign a field of sanctuary and immunity to the arts, in equal and uncompromising contradistinction to the sciences. Perhaps the dreams of humanity can be more highly sought, more splendidly apprehended, by means other than statistics, econometrics, social psychology, aptitude tests, calculated chances, descriptive equations. Just possibly we are merely children playing at the knee of the great humanities, and great insights, like great music, are born in realms which cannot in our time be called scientific. Perhaps, in a word, this convocation should direct that its social scientists should not take themselves quite as seriously as they seem to do. Could we, perhaps, ask them to cultivate the kindlier virtues of humor and humility? May we not insist that they grapple with the philosophers, so that their work may relate itself to the cause of good society and the good life?

2 · INFORMATION TECHNOLOGY *
Richard S. Leghorn

Gentlemen:

It is a pleasure and privilege to become better acquainted with you who serve as an important link between the investing public and American corporations, and to talk with you personally about the concepts and origins of Itek Corporation, a relatively new company with headquarters in the Greater Boston area. It is a most welcome opportunity to meet with you at such an early stage of our development to give you a progress report of the initial growth of our enterprise.

. . . . .

THE SWEEP OF SCIENCE

I am sure that your interest in Itek reflects the interest of the investing community in companies engaged in the business application of science and technology. As we know, the forward sweep of today's scientific and technological revolution has brought many changes in the production and sales emphasis of long-established companies. In these companies, which I will call product-based enterprises, science and technology have long been used to support the evolution of product lines. Today new companies, such as ours, based on entirely new concepts, are appearing on the scene, and some older companies are being recast along the new conceptual lines. In these, science and technology are joined more directly and immediately to problems of basic human needs, rather than solely through the product-improvement cycle. Science and technology are truly "busting out all over," and new organizational and management techniques are needed in research-based companies to harness the dynamics of science and technology to serve business and human purposes better.

In addition to piloting our way in this new environment dominated

* Condensation of an address given by Richard S. Leghorn, President of Itek Corporation (May, 1959) before the Boston Chapter of the Society of Security Analysts. Reprinted by permission of Richard S. Leghorn.

by research and development, at Itek we feel that we are also pioneering in a new business field. We specialize in information technology, especially the development of systems which cope with graphic forms of information—paper work, if you like, but also documents, maps, photographs, drawings, microcopies, and other graphic forms. To those of us who have spent many years in the field of information handling, the scope and nature of the Itek concept is clear. I am beginning to realize, however, that we need a basic explanation of our business if we are to achieve general understanding of what we do. So I am going to devote a little more time to telling you about our field of endeavor than about Itek Corporation itself.

Information Technology, the field in which Itek specializes, has hardly attained the stature of an industry. I assure you, however, that it will. And quite soon.

TODAY'S GREAT PROBLEM

Information Technology, defined in one way, is the creation of equipment and procedures by which information can be made available to those who need it, when they need it, where they need it. These processes may take the form of elaborate, highly complex devices, or they may be only well-developed work routines. Or, of course, a combination of the two. Whatever form these processes may take, the successful ones, technically sound and of proved economic efficiency, will solve one of the greatest problems facing science, education, government and business today—the problem of effective utilization of the vast and growing amounts of information that are created by men daily.

To keep this discussion as illustrative as possible, I would like to concern myself with only one phase of the problem—that of efficiently utilizing scientific information. I'm going further to confine my remarks to "published scientific information." Essentially, that means the documents produced by persons engaged in scientific endeavor which report the results of their research investigations.

As you may know, advances in science and engineering are built in substantial part on the published record of earlier work done throughout the world. There are 55,000 scientific journals published each year. They contain about 1,200,000 articles, each of significance to some branch of science. More than 60,000 different books are published each year. Annually, 100,000 research reports remain outside the normal channels of publication and cataloguing. Further complications arise from the fact that much important information appears in languages unfamiliar to the scientists, such as Russian and Japanese are to English-language workers.

Our scientists and engineers must have access to this rapidly increasing mass of scientific publications if we are to maintain and improve our position in the world's technological race. The situation has become critical.

Last December, the President of the United States, at the suggestion of the Killian Science Advisory Committee, directed the National Science Foundation to take the lead in bringing about an effective coordination of the various scientific information activities within the federal government.

As a result, action was taken to form a Science Information Service within the National Science Foundation. This Service will facilitate indexing, abstracting, and translating, plus other services leading to a more effective national pooling and dissemination of scientific information.

In January of this year, the National Science Foundation awarded a contract to Itek Corporation to carry out a program of basic research to develop methods and logical designs for mechanized systems which will help scientists search for what they need among the vast amounts of technical information I mentioned a moment ago. This project has important significance not only to Itek but to the scientific community and our country as well.

To further emphasize the scope and nature of the scientific information handling problem, let me quote two paragraphs from an article by Allen Kent, Associate Director of the Center for Documentation and Communication Research at the School of Library Science at Western Reserve University. This article appeared in the April issue of *Harper's* magazine.

He says: "Not long ago the director of a large engineering organization was chagrined to discover that his research staff had spent $50,000 and a year's time in repeating an unsuccessful design program for building military trucks that he himself had rejected ten years before. For a decade, the original research report had lain buried in the company library. . . ."

And here's another case: "In 1950, an article on the application of Boolean algebra to electrical circuits appeared in a journal of the Soviet Academy of Science, and though an English abstract was later published in *Mathematical Reviews,* it was not 'discovered' until five years later—after several teams of mathematicians in a variety of American industrial concerns had spent more than 15 man-years in unsuccessful attempts to solve the problem. . . ."

Put it this way: Over the years a tremendous store of information has been and will continue to be acquired. Not all of it is published in readily available form. A scientist about to engage in a research program must spend a great deal of valuable time searching with cumbersome and antiquated methods for reports that will tell him what has been done by others. Frequently, he never finds related work, and proceeds either to duplicate what has been done before, or to work without the stimulus of relevant knowledge.

THE SYSTEMS APPROACH

Now, basically, how do we go about correcting this condition? I think it is evident that there must be a systematic—a "systems" —approach. This system must cover the entire range of the problem, from source to final application. In this case, the source is the author. The author must be considered an integral part of the system, and the forms in which he produces his material must be adapted to overall systems needs.

The next function in the system is the actual publishing. Materials will increasingly be published in radically different forms; adapted to machine methods for handling, storage and searching. Present forms, such as journals, will continue for "awareness" type of reading, but the new forms will increasingly take over as the principal working tool.

The next system function is the information store—now commonly called the library. The volumes and machine techniques involved will require miniaturization. Micro-forms will some day dominate.

Throughout all these processes, provision must be made for coding, indexing, and abstracting so that rapid and pertinent retrieval, correlation, and analysis are possible. The system must be such that whenever a request for information is made to the system, the person making the request will be assured of getting the most relevant material available on the subject in which he's interested. Furthermore, the systems response must be so rapid that it will almost be as if the man and the information machine were talking to each other—the one asking a question, the machine providing an initial answer, the man rephrasing a new question, and so on until the requestor has rapidly searched out of the system the most pertinent information bearing on his problem.

Lastly, there are the transmission links in the system. The system must provide means for communicating with its customers, wherever located—to receive requests and transmit answers.

Let me summarize. An efficient scientific information system will be one that will begin with the author; speed the publication of his information, for both human and machine handling, and provide for efficient storage, rapid retrieval, and convenient use wherever the system's customers may be located.

APPLICATIONS EVERYWHERE

Now, although I have talked about scientific information systems, I would emphasize that entirely similar problems and solutions are relevant to practically all fields of human endeavor. The legal profession has a vast problem with cases and opinions. Medical records, engineering drawings, aerial reconnaissance, and military intelligence records represent other problem areas. And of course business and commercial intelligence, as security analysts well know, would be a welcome field for new information systems.

Specifically, where do the business opportunities lie for a company dedicated to the development of such systems? From our market investigations, let me describe certain areas of interest to us in more conventional business terms.

One, there is the field of office equipment. Plenty of mechanized office systems are available. IBM, Burroughs, National Cash Register, and many other good companies market them. However, these systems are generally concerned with numerical data. We are interested in the handling of non-numerical data and graphic forms—letters, charts, drawings, photographs, and the like.

Two, there's the publishing field. We see our future in this great area in two phases. The first will concern improvements that can be made in existing printing techniques. There have been few basic changes in publishing methods in 75 years, but economic pressures and recent innovations present substantial evidence of revolutionary developments during the next two decades. The great strides that have been made in photography, electronics, and other new arts will be reflected in printing and publishing. Secondly, there is the matter I spoke of when outlining the systems approach to information handling—publication in a form that can be readily machine-manipulated. As you probably know, the *New York Times* is now available in two forms: The regular, newsprint edition, and a microfilm edition. A new form, accommodating the coming filing and indexing techniques, would make the desired item in a file of this great newspaper available almost instantly through the new machine methods of storage and retrieval.

Our third area is the manufacturing business. First, let me point out that as a company we have no present ambitions in the field of automation known as process control. We are not thinking about devices which will control other devices, a field where other good companies are making substantial progress with computer equipment. We are thinking, for example, of the problems all manufacturers face with engineering drawings, which are their production intelligence. Also, there is the matter of quality control and inspection. These functions deal with graphic forms of information—our field.

Fourth, there is the field of communications. The technologies Itek has brought together are all, essentially, communications sciences, and, as I have pointed out, graphic information systems will increasingly involve transmission links.

The education field is another in which new graphic information systems will play an increasingly important role. Books and blackboards are well-known and venerable tools of the trade, but we are beginning to see the introduction of slides, films, and TV. These and other new forms will be designed on a systems basis, taking cognizance of the new teacher–actor–director on through publishing the new teaching forms and storing and displaying them to students, wherever and whenever they are needed.

A sixth market area of interest to Itek, and the one with which we are most identified today, is that of reconnaissance, both military and space reconnaissance, and related intelligence systems. This market is of steadily growing importance to our national security. In this age of civilization-obliterating weapons with speeds at velocity of escape from earth, further improvements in weapons systems—while necessary to maintain deterrence—can scarcely bring added security. Security will increasingly come from information systems—those involving intelligence, inspection, and the so-called "open" sources of information. Systems for warning against surprise attack will enhance and stabilize deterrence. Systems to prevent our country from being caught off guard by technological advances will be increasingly important, and there are many more.

PROGRESS IN SPACE

The matter of space exploration is the other governmental reconnaissance market of interest to us. For years to come, there will be ever-increasing effort put into probing the vast areas beyond the confines of this planet. The results of these efforts will be almost exclusively information.

I think that gives you an idea of the key markets we selected when we formed Itek Corporation. We are now working in about half of these target areas. In planning our enterprise, we knew we would need mastery of many technologies for a completely integrated approach to systems that would solve information problems in these market areas.

Graphic information systems require considerable optical know-how. Photophysics and photochemistry play a major role in miniaturization and reproduction. Many electronic techniques are involved, many related to the field of digital computers, such as memory devices, displays, and the like. The mechanical design problems in many cases are new and challenging and the logical sciences represent another critical area. We now have talents in all these technical areas involved in the industry of information technology.

. . . . .

A PATTERN FOR GROWTH

Perhaps the thing that has been responsible for our success and our growth as much as anything else is that from the beginning we have worked to a plan—a pattern for growth. While we have kept to our general plan, fortunately, we have been able to go much further in a much shorter time than we had expected. You might be interested in the key targets set in our original plan, and where we stand in relation to them.

Earlier I sketched for you the key markets we planned to enter. We are now in about half of these. I also mentioned the basic scientific and technical talents we planned to attract. Leading personnel in all of these fields are now with the company. A third aspect of our plan was to build a research-based company. To do this we recognized we would have to build in two phases. Because at first we did not have funds to support a substantial research program, we began by selling our research and development services to the government, largely the military. We believed that this should be our primary emphasis for our first two years—as indeed it has been.

Our major objective, however, was to create a research-based company in which the research program would be financed by the company itself so that we could control our own destiny.

We decided that for our chosen branch of industry Itek would have to achieve a sales volume of at least $50,000,000 annually if we were to support research in an amount sufficient to give the company a "self-regenerating" character. We also felt these sales should be at least two-thirds commercial.

I am pleased to report to you that we have successfully completed Phase I—the expansion of government-sponsored research and development activity—and that we are well along toward successful completion of Phase II. With the acquisition of Photostat Corporation, we have achieved our goal of one-third government business and two-thirds commercial business. With sales currently running at an annual rate of $30,000,000 we are well on our way to a $50,000,000 sales volume which we have set as the "threshold" size for a strong and viable research-based company in our field.

3 · NEW RESEARCH FRONTIERS OF INTEREST TO LEGISLATORS AND ADMINISTRATORS *

Stephen K. Bailey

"In the beginning God created the heaven and the earth." So begins the First Book of Moses, called Genesis.

"In the beginning was the word." So begins the Gospel according to St. John.

No exegesis is necessary to point out that, barring a cosmic simultaneity, either John or Genesis must be wrong. Did the act precede the thought or the thought the act?

This problem in cosmology, not to say metaphysics, is relevant here only because it indicates that theory and practice have posed

* Stephen K. Bailey, "New Research Frontiers of Interest to Legislators and Administrators," *Research Frontiers in Politics and Government* (Washington, D.C.: The Brookings Institution, 1955), pp. 1-22. Reprinted by permission of The Brookings Institution. The footnotes in the original version are omitted here.

a chicken-egg dilemma for a good many years. In retrospect, it is obvious only that John was a scholar and the author of Genesis a decision-maker.

The series of lectures that I am honored to introduce this evening is called "Research Frontiers in Politics and Government." The sponsors of this series, the directors of the Brookings Institution, have bravely assumed that the placing of longhairs and shorthairs in the same room would resolve Biblical dilemmas, or at least would settle the issue posed by Elihu Root, "Which comes first, the egghead or the chicken Colonel?"

• • • • •

Most thinkers about society are not pure scientists. As eclectic scholars and pamphleteers, they have frequently unleashed new worlds simply by describing, vilifying, or justifying old ones. What has seemed like new knowledge has often been, not discovery, but careful articulation, reinterpretation, or popularization of the known. When the Deuteronomic priests moralized the tribal sagas of ancient Israel, they placed new meaning on prior events and influenced mightily not only the course of subsequent history but their own times. In the area of social thought and action, creation precedes the word that precedes creation. No simple, articulated prior idea, for example, was responsible for the haphazard growth of cities in America, but this haphazard growth has stimulated research, theory, and value judgments that may have considerable impact on the further development of our urban communities. Social events, in short, run both ahead of and behind social thought. They frequently run behind in a somewhat perverse way. Lord Keynes made the point when he wrote in his *General Theory:*

> The ideas of economists and political philosophers, both when they are right and when they are wrong, are more powerful than is commonly understood. Indeed the world is ruled by little else. Practical men who believe themselves to be quite exempt from any intellectual influences are usually slaves of some defunct economist. Mad men in authority, who hear voices in the air, are distilling their frenzy from some academic scribbler of a few years back. I am sure that the power of vested interests is vastly exaggerated compared with the gradual encroachment of ideas.

Although it is perfectly obvious that new ideas about society are not a monopoly of professors, Keynes' statement suggests that the "academic scribbler" is more powerful than is commonly recognized.

Certainly in the long run, and I would maintain increasingly in the short run, the social scholar has much to offer the practical man of affairs.

The big trouble is that too many practical men of affairs expect the wrong services from the scholar. The scholar lives in a strange world, and the decision-maker often treats this world with patronizing contempt—sometimes with fear. I add the word "fear" because in one sense all scholars are potentially subversive. This is true whether or not the scholar consciously indulges in social criticism. A systematic description of the way in which our state legislatures actually function, for example, might so clash with present stereotypes and value expectations held by the public at large as to stimulate a widespread movement for change. Simple description might have been the only concern of the scholar, but the results of research might be pregnant with implications for reform. The reluctance of Congress to allow the Census Bureau to collect political statistics is in part, I believe, the result of an almost visceral fear that accurate knowledge about voting behavior might stimulate popular demands for certain kinds of change. The recent congressional investigations into the operations and policies of private foundations—barbaric and distorted as these investigations were—reflected in part a true understanding of the possible consequences of social science scholarship. At least since the days of Socrates, the life of reason has had its occupational hazards. The Burkian conservatism, which is now the toast of certain groups in this country, seems temperamentally and logically opposed to the application of reason where prescription might be challenged. What some people fear is not the clash of orthodoxies, but the challenge that reason hurls at all orthodoxies.

No matter what the political science professions might do to separate "policy-oriented" scholars from "scientific" scholars, even if this were desirable or possible, the problem would remain. In actual fact, the scholars who research on the run are probably less unsettling than their more systematic brethren. The scholar who marshals and interprets data to further a particular policy goal can be discounted almost immediately as a partisan operator. The institutionally detached scholar who simply reports and theorizes on what he sees, especially if he can prove it, can unintentionally undermine an entire culture. I need only mention Darwinism and Higher Criticism in the nineteenth century to make my point. In our own times, who can compute the possible long-run social impact of the simple discovery that Negro blood and white blood are chemically indistinguishable?

Some policy-makers not only fear the scholar—paradoxically, they think scholarship other-worldly and futile. Because the scholar cannot answer a specific operation problem in simple English, the decision-maker frequently assumes that the scholar knows nothing of practical value. There was a story going around Washington during World War II about a 26-year-old economist in the soap division of OPA who was buttonholed one day by the president of Lever Brothers. The president looked scornfully at the young scholar and said, "Young man, what can you possibly know about soap?" The economist looked the president straight in the eye and said, "Sir, I don't know much about soap, but I know a hell of a lot about price control."

Most scholars are better at the general formulation of issues than they are at the application of general knowledge to concrete circumstances. In fact, the pure scientist in any field is always on the prowl for species not sports, probabilities not sureties, recurring generalities not specific events. As my distinguished colleague, Marion Levy, has pointed out to me, no physicist worthy of the name would attempt to predict the exact speed with which a piece of chalk dropped from the top of Nassau Hall next Friday would reach the ground. All the physicist can do is to assume theoretical conditions, such as a perfect vacuum, under which the laws of gravity will operate on an object, and then to identify the kinds of variables in the real world that will modify this theoretical model.

The operator who asks the scholar to apply general theory to a particular situation is often asking either the impossible or the unreasonable. A carefully controlled sample survey, for example, might show that only one per cent of all barking dogs actually bite. This might be, for certain purposes, extremely useful information, even though the only real kindness to the postman is to tell him to beware of all dogs. A composite personality profile of 435 Congressmen might show that 82 per cent are low on a predetermined scale of neuroticism. For certain highly practical as well as theoretical purposes, this knowledge might be significant, even though the scholar could not at the moment tell an administrator going up for a budget hearing how many psychoneurotics are on the House Appropriations Subcommittee—or the implications thereof.

Cardinal Newman may have disclaimed the "distant scene" ("one step enough for me"), but the distant scene in the sense of general propositions is the stock in trade of the modern scholar. The practical utility of general propositions is frequently disclaimed by the decision-maker, but the decision-maker himself would be helpless without them.

The real hiatus between scholars and decision-makers is not that one deals with generalizations and the other with specifics. Every specific decision is based on a multitude of general working propositions. If, through experience, the decision-maker had not developed some general propositions in the sense of implicit assumptions about human behavior, he would be helpless whenever a new problem arose for solution. The differences between the scholar and the decision-maker are to be found in the respective environments in which they operate, the speed with which knowledge must be synthesized and applied, the degree of immediacy of value considerations, the degree of explicitness of assumptions and logic, and the nature of respective attitudes toward the use of language.

This last needs a few words of emphasis. Nonscholars accuse scholars of using big words—or worse, of using mathematical symbols. Language, verbal or mathematical, is both a precise tool and a shorthand for the scholar. For the decision-maker, on the other hand, language is often an artistic brush. In the uncertainties of a complex situation, a decision-maker may well use a phrase that is intentionally ambiguous. As ambiguities are the enemies of precise scholarship, the scholar attempts to delimit words and phrases to specific referents. Frequently, the scholar develops a new word or phrase because old words are imprecise or because a complex of simple words can be put more simply by the use of one complex word. The gobbledy-gook of scholarship is frequently carried to unnecessary extremes, but the science of botany would probably have progressed much more tortuously than it has if the vocabulary of the botanist had been limited to "green flowers, big flowers, fragrant flowers, and climbing flowers."

The real and justifiable criticism that practical men of affairs can levy against scholars is that the latter on occasion try to build superstructures of verbiage and mathematics on foundations of thin air. They then drape the superstructure with decorated panels of value interpretations and claim not only aesthetic and logical perfection but also functional perfection. In a book by John Palmer Gavit called

College, written in 1925, the author calls to account those "in the departments where subjects of study come nearest to pure guesswork, where men, bushwhacking around the edges of the inscrutable, pontificate about the week's gropings in the realm of the mind as if they had ultimate truth by the tail." As Professor Schattschneider says: "Political scientists should be modest because they have plenty to be modest about." The real danger is not that social scientists will be undersold to decision-makers. The real danger is that they will be oversold; and that their failure to perform according to immediate expectations will have the effect of discounting in advance the patient scratching that is the pre-condition of all great theoretical break-throughs.

. . . . .

Contemporary political science involves a spectrum of generalization. At one end of the spectrum are the describers of discrete events. At the other end are the conscious articulators or postulators of general systems—analytical and theoretical. New research frontiers exist at every point along this spectrum. If the spectrum is likened to a harmonica, political science has its share of virtuosos. The real divisions in political science, however, must be sought not along this spectrum but in schools of emphasis and approach of another sort. For the purpose of discussing new research frontiers, these schools can be categorized as historical, institutional, behavioral, and philosophical. Overlapping is constant, but differences in perspective are discernible.

HISTORICAL APPROACH

If history be defined as the selecting and structuring of prior events, all of us are historians. In truth we are little else. The so-called "insight" of the decision-maker—that most valued and seemingly mysterious of attributes—is history in use. Whatever the philosophers of history may decide, most decision-makers spend their lives betting on the proposition that the past has lessons and the new is never totally unprecedented.

In recent years a considerable number of political scientists have turned out case studies in administration and legislation. Most of these constitute historical writing at a low level of abstraction. By way of example, I refer to the Inter-University Public Administration Cases, to the many autobiographies and agency and service histories that have come from our governmental experience during World War II, and to some recent attempts to describe certain phases of congressional activity.

In my own limited experience in political and administrative life, I have found these historical studies of considerable utility. They have the effect of broadening experience vicariously, of limiting the totally unanticipated in any given decisional context, and of suggesting alternative means for accomplishing goals. Let me give an example. As mayor of Middletown, Connecticut, I was confronted by the problem of how to get a parking authority created. A parking authority with power to condemn land, to manage municipal parking facilities, and to finance itself could be created only by action of the state legislature. The state legislature was Republican. I was a Democratic mayor. In order to ensure favorable action in Hartford, I needed the support of local Republican leaders in Middletown. From the standpoint of personal political experience, this was an unprecedented situation. I remembered, however, in studying the course of a full employment bill in Congress, that Senator Murray had won the support of certain Republican senators by allowing them to offer needed amendments to the bill. This strengthened the bill and allowed the Republican senators to co-sponsor without loss of face. I used the same device in Middletown, and the parking authority went through the General Assembly in Hartford without opposition.

This is a homely and low-level example of what must go on every hour of the day in Washington. President Roosevelt did not need a political scientist to describe the reasons for the failure of Wilson to develop American support for the League of Nations, for Roosevelt had lived through the ordeal. But it is probably true that Roosevelt, in his conduct of the presidency, referred many times to the activities of Lincoln, Jefferson, and Jackson. Books are part of experience. I cannot help but feel that the patient scholarship of Leonard White in tracing the administrative growth of the federal government from the days of Washington to the present will have a high utility to legislators and administrators for generations to come. If nothing else, it is a source of comfort to the modern decision-maker to know that his respected ancestors had to deal with, and somehow overcame, many of the same kinds of issues he himself faces. Administrators and legislators go through a number of unnecessary frustrations because they have not read the minutes of previous meetings . . .

And we might add the wise words of Santayana, "He who does not know the past is doomed to repeat it." The past experience of mankind is always a new research frontier. Discoveries along this frontier, granted always the dangers of analogy, are often of immediate practical concern to decision-makers.

Much historical writing by political and other social scientists is consciously factual—granted always the unconscious biases that affect the selection and interpretation of data. In other cases, however, historical writing is highly impressionistic, philosophical, and value-laden. Whatever the dangers of this kind of scholarship, it is always with us on the frontiers of research, and often performs a highly creative function in its impact on decision-makers.

All decision-makers decide within a societal context. How they view their own culture and society in relation to other cultures and societies is a major determinant of policy. I speak here not only of the value framework to which I shall return in a minute. I refer to the importance of visualizing what really happened or is happening at a given time and place, and of judging the limits that prior events place on contemporary discretion.

A number of provocative studies have appeared in recent years on the subject of American foreign policy. In an important sense, these studies are on the frontiers of political science—notably, books like Charles Burton Marshall's *Limits of Foreign Policy,* George Kennan's *The Realities of American Foreign Policy,* Dorothy Fosdick's *Common Sense and World Affairs,* Chester Bowles' *Ambassador's Report,* and Louis J. Halle's *Civilization and Foreign Policy.*

All these studies attempt to create new images of America's place in the world, images to replace both the limitless concept of manifest destiny and the parochial concept of isolation, twin specters that America has inherited from another age and that have tended to bind cruelly our thinking about future options.

George Kennan is now working at the Institute for Advanced Study on a history of American-Soviet relations. Who can say what powerful forces will be released by such a book? If, through careful documentation and analysis, Kennan throws new light on the reasons for American intervention in Russian affairs in 1918-19, for example, a great deal of the diplomatic force of Soviet historical writing on this period may be effectively countered.

The construction of new images is not limited to the field of foreign policy. Gunnar Myrdal's thoughtful study of the Negro in

America is a case in point. Studies of this kind can have a high instrumental value by providing for the decision-maker a carefully constructed three-dimensional image of a social reality. Some of the great works on the American political scene like de Tocqueville's *Democracy in America,* Lord Bryce's *The American Commonwealth,* Wilson's *Congressional Government,* and Frederick Jackson Turner's *The Frontier in American Life*—all of them in their time on the frontiers of knowledge—created vivid images of the great American experiment and in the process became a part of the experiment itself.

The creation and refinement of these images is a continuing responsibility of political and other social scientists. Knowledge of these images can help the decision-maker in understanding his own society and in recognizing the limits that society sets on the effective discretion of public officials.

Beyond this, new historical writing can have a prophetic function —prophetic not in the sense of exact scientific prognostication, but prophetic in the Biblical sense: postulating the moral reality and the moral consequences of the choices before us. Arnold Toynbee's monumental *Study of History* is important not because it tells us what will happen fifty years from now but because it establishes a moral postulate that what we do can have an effect on what happens fifty years from now. In a recent speech closing the Columbia Bicentennial Celebration, Dr. J. Robert Oppenheimer stated that:

> In an important sense this world of ours is a new world in which the unity of knowledge, the nature of human communities, the order of society, the order of ideas, the very notions of society and culture have changed and will not return to what they have been in the past. What is new is not new because it has not been there before but because it has changed in quality.

Oppenheimer identifies the prevalence of newness, the changing scope and scale of change itself, the global quality of the world, and the massive character of the dissolution of corruption and authority in belief, in ritual, and in temporal order as evidences of the unprecedented. Toynbee's complementary corrective to Oppenheimer is that man in his long and tortuous history has often faced "newnesses"—"challenges" as Toynbee puts it—and that man's future has always been determined by his moral and intellectual responses to these newnesses.

In the kind of world in which modern decision-makers live, fraught as it is with bignesses, vastnesses, and statistical drifts, the postulate of faith that the future is really malleable, that individual choices really count, is of no small consequence. The assumption of classical economists that individual choice could have no effect on the market seems to have carried over into a great deal of fatalistic, if not nihilistic, twentieth-century political thinking. The prophetic service of Toynbee is his pointing out that history has always involved imperfect competition, and that the moral choices of men of power influence the market mightily.

INSTITUTIONAL ANALYSIS

Aside from hereditary influences, the greatest force that the past exerts on the present is institutional. Political science has been intrigued from Aristotle's day to the present with the institutional character of society—the legal framework and the social structures within which man functions as a social being. Like some huge invisible magnet, institutions condition, regularize, and to some extent polarize, human behavior.

Civilization as we know it is unthinkable without laws that establish regularized patterns of behavior and set the limits of nonconformity and official discretion in society. The laws may be, in the words of Thrasymacus, the "interest of the stronger," or they may be the product of the reasonably equitable distribution of advantages in an ethically oriented self-governing society. But one effect is constant: behavior is regularized by political sanctions. What the law is and what the law means are highly relevant considerations, not only to judges but to administrators and legislators as well. What the public at large, or particular groups or individuals, thinks the law is or means is also of high concern to decision-makers in government. Why are some laws difficult to enforce? Why is international law so difficult to create, not alone enforce? What confers and legitimizes the law-making function? Why do people obey? These questions have been at the heart of much political writing for centuries—and still are. Today the frontiers are being cleared by sociologists, social psychologists, and anthropologists, as well as political theorists and students of jurisprudence.

I have neither the time nor the competence to describe in detail the new scholarship in this area. I am concerned only to point out that the heritage and ubiquity of law give an enveloping institutional character to human behavior in our society and sensitize us to structure in all of our functional relationships. This is particularly true in large-scale organizations. The rules and procedures governing relationships in large-scale organizations, private and public, administrative and legislative, are not always legal in a formal sense, but they have many of the same purposes and consequences as law. What students of administration call "formal organization" is the pattern of expectations resulting from the conscious structuring of institutional energies. To use an elementary example, if we see Mr. X higher on an organizational chart than Mr. Y, we expect certain kinds of deferential relationships that would not ordinarily be present if Mr. X and Mr. Y were at the same level.

The past quarter-century has seen a vast extension of interest in, and knowledge about, formal institutional structures. With the growth of large-scale organizations in business and government, scholars in a variety of disciplines have addressed themselves to key questions of organizational practice and theory. I need only mention the names of Merton, Barnard, Dahl, Gulick, Macmahon, Appleby, Gaus, and Simon, to hint at the talents that have been concerned with research frontiers in this vast and exciting area. If students of administration had a tendency twenty years or so ago to place perhaps too much emphasis on static descriptions of formal structures, the 1940's saw a swing almost to the other extreme—the discounting of the importance of formal organization and the placing of heavy emphasis on informal, personal, and accidental factors in institutional behavior.

There is now a swing back—or a swing forward—a recognition among those working on the frontiers that organizations metamorphose organically, and that formal structures and informal human behavior interact to create a necessary institutional tension between responsibility and continuity on the one hand, and flexible adaptation on the other. Sociologists, anthropologists, psychologists, communications specialists, and political scientists are presently constructing theoretical models that should substantially increase our knowledge of institutional behavior—and particularly of the importance of formal structure. The significance of this theoretical work for practicing administrators should be obvious. Business and industry have already made considerable practical use of the work that has been done to date. . . .

Up to now most of the energies of scholars have been concentrated on bureaucratic organizations, but it is heartening to note that presidential nominating conventions are now being subjected to the elaborate scrutiny of political scientists and that Dr. George Galloway has recently returned from England where he studied the procedures of the House of Commons in relation to the procedures of the American Congress. All too little attention has been paid to the relationship of formal structures and formal procedures to the behavior and viability of democratic legislatures.

The ultimate importance of all this institutional research can best be suggested by a statement of Alfred North Whitehead on the subject of symbolism. Whitehead wrote that "those societies which cannot combine reverence to their symbols with freedom of revision must ultimately decay, either from anarchy or from the slow atrophy of a life stifled by useless shadows." The viability of large-scale institutions depends on their capacity to function efficiently and to adapt to new circumstances without dissolution of form. Increased sophistication about the impact of formal systems on institutional behavior may enormously increase the odds that man can successfully negotiate the turbid waters that run between the Scylla of bureaucratic rigidity and the Charybdis of tyrannical flux.

BEHAVIORAL SCHOOL

Complementing this emphasis on institutional structures is an increasing emphasis on what has come to be called the behavioral sciences. Granted formal organizational patterns, how do legislators, administrators, judges, and even voters actually behave? How do they decide? How do they solve problems? What forces—group and personal—actually impinge upon them and how do these forces operate? Why in two institutions with identical formal structure does one institution work efficiently and the other work inefficiently? What changes in institutional behavior can result from changes in leadership?

Many of the papers that follow in this series are specifically concerned with these questions. Tapping the resources and techniques of cognate disciplines, political scientists are experimenting with a wide variety of conceptual schemes and analytical tools to shed new light on human behavior in the context of politics and government.

Because the variables are manifold, because the jungle is dense, progress is maddeningly slow and tentative. But success here will have (as it already has had) an enormous impact on the decision-maker in government and in managerial enterprises of all kinds.

The fact is that today most decision-makers approach behavioral problems on a rule-of-thumb basis. They calculate anticipated reactions on the basis of what they call "common sense" or an "educated guess." If they do such and such, the resulting behavior of others will probably be such and such. When the result is not what they anticipated, they often search for devils, plots, and gremlins to explain their failures.

Employees are discontented. Salaries are raised. Employees are still discontented. Conclusion: employees are ingrates.

The field office is functioning inefficiently. A memorandum is sent from the central office giving instructions and clarifying previous directives. The field office still functions inefficiently. Conclusion: the field office staff can't read.

A legislative proposal is sent to Congress. Congress turns it down. Conclusion: Congress is the tool of selfish interests.

Many of the toughest problems in public life arise because we know so little about behavior that deviates from our stereotypes of anticipation. Students of administration speak of informal organization—behavior that does not square with the anticipations set by formal structure. What the behavioral sciences are postulating is that informal organization does have structure; that behavioral deviations from prescribed patterns of organizational process are not totally unpredictable; that a science of behavior is, within limits, possible.

As long as students of society assumed that all social activity was the result of the interplay of discrete, equally powerful, and unpredictable individuals, a science of behavior was patently absurd except at the level of vast societal aggregates. In terms of predicting the results of more limited interactions, the possible permutations and combinations of unpredictable forces were infinite. But if one assumes that for certain purposes, at least, human beings act and react according to group stereotypes rather than individual whim, the problem though difficult is theoretically manageable. The problem is transferred from the impossible task of predicting the vagaries of unpredictable parcels of energy inside the nucleus of the atom, to the possible task of describing and predicting molecular interaction.

It is at this point, however, that many decision-makers, practical men of affairs, theologians, and a number of suspicious fellow academicians get off the bus. Like the hill people in Tennessee during the Scopes monkey trial, the fearful and the suspicious chant, "Thank God we ain't got no education, thank God we ain't lawyers." Behavioral science seems to many to wish to kill the piano player and substitute perforated rolls, to substitute artificial insemination for love. There are some who believe that, in the field of human relationships, it can't be done. There are others, like Winston Churchill, who suspect it can be done, but who don't wish to be around on the day of victory. George Orwell was probably pleased that death took him before 1984.

The fear seems to stem from a feeling that leadership in a democracy must be unselfconscious and intuitive if we are to remain free; that conscious manipulation of others is a divine prerogative that can be usurped by man only with disastrous consequences. The fact that competing political regimes in this century have manipulated behavior for inhuman ends has led some people to conclude that a science of behavior is innately anti-democratic in its implications.

These fears are not without justification, but they are grossly overplayed, and they represent a tragic retreat from reason. Men have manipulated the behavior of other men since time immemorial. The evil has not been the manipulation, but the value context and the legal framework within which the manipulation has occurred.

Some social scientists, it is true, seem to underplay the supremacy of values. But in most cases, their fault is not callousness but sanguinity. They assume that behavioral knowledge will be used in a democratic society for democratic ends in a democratic way; that the widespread sharing of behavioral knowledge will itself be a counterforce to any attempt at monopolistic manipulation. Implicitly some of them go further. They assume that only if our chosen leaders refine and systematize their knowledge of human behavior can democratic societies consciously construct the kind of world that will square with their value premises.

Actually, the success of our democratic experiment to date has been due in large part to a primitive science of behavior: our inherited proverbs and maxims. In an unrefined state, rudiments of a science of behavior are discernible in much of our ethical and political literature.

Take the proverb "A soft answer turneth away wrath." Many administrators and legislators have found this a highly useful maxim in public life. My guess is that the proverb developed out of the accumulated experience of prehistoric man who found to his discomfort that blows and angry words were generally countered by blows and angry words. The idea was probably first articulated, or at least adumbrated, as a simple empirical statement: "If when provoked I hit someone my own size or larger, I am likely to be clobbered in return."

For most purposes and under most conditions this proposition is still highly scientific, although I for one do not intend to attempt an extensive validation. But there are obviously certain conditions under which the proposition is not true. The probability is less, for example (at least in this part of the western world) if a woman slaps a man. The probability slips still further if the slapper is supported by six plug-uglies and the slappee is alone. The probability slips to almost zero if the slappee is a marathon dancer whose partner is trying to keep him awake.

Legislative and administrative craftsmanship consists in large part of knowing when proverbs will and won't work. The folklore of politics is laden with artifices and public relations techniques that have worked under certain circumstances in the past and have become guides to future strategic and tactical decisions. In a huckster-conscious society, these techniques are useful and moral in the long run only if they are subservient to the top value premises of the society itself. Macaulay once wrote: "When will people learn that it is the spirit we are of, not the machinery we employ, that binds us to others?" Craftsmanship, in short, is not enough. That is why, in closing, I must emphasize once again the supremacy of values, for it is just here that scholars tend to be fuzziest and decision-makers in need of most help.

PHILOSOPHICAL APPROACH

The rival philosophies of our time have a superficial attractiveness because they offer pretty packages labeled "the good society." As long as the packages remain wrapped, the lonely crowd projects its own frustrated dreams into the hidden excelsior. The "great simplifiers" encourage the dreams, and do their best to hide the reality—to keep the labels bright and the packages unopened.

Americans, confronted by this marketing challenge, have reacted in a variety of ways. Some have concluded that America can win in the ideological struggle simply by wrapping a brighter package with fancier labels. Others have accepted the pessimistic position that our eighteenth-century labels have been tarnished by the years, and can never be burnished for twentieth-century display. Still others have contended that democracy means "no labels," but an infinite variety of packages available for common inspection and barter. A great deal of contemporary writing in political science seems to assume this last position. The real success of the American experiment, it is contended, stems not from a consistent philosophy, but from the interaction of a whole series of value myopias brought into focus by purely mechanical and institutional means.

Unfortunately, "unseen hands" and "countervailing powers" are not dramatic concepts from the standpoint of ideological export. Furthermore, I gravely doubt that the "good society" can ever be fashioned by ignorant armies that clash by night. Those who pretend to see the outline of the "good society" in the clash of pressure groups, the clash of governmental branches and levels, the clash of political factions, the clash of money, votes, and ambitions have in my estimation too low a view of man and too exalted a view of automatic stabilizers in our moral and political life.

Government in the last analysis is a supreme exercise of will and moral choice. The public interest, as Walter Lippmann points out in his new book *The Public Philosophy,* may be presumed "to be what men would choose if they saw clearly, thought rationally, acted disinterestedly and benevolently."

This is the real frontier of our epoch. All else pales into insignificance. Whatever the success of political science in describing institutions and refining our knowledge of behavioral uniformities, the administrator and legislator for decades and centuries to come must wrestle first with the toughest operating problem ever assigned to mankind: what is in the interest of the public? What Montaigne said four centuries ago is still relevant: "All other knowledge is hurtful to him who has not the science of honesty and goodness."

Omar Bradley has said the same thing in both an older and newer idiom: "We have too many men of science, too few men of God. We have grasped the mystery of the atom and rejected the Sermon on the Mount. . . . The world has achieved brilliance without wisdom, power without conscience. Ours is a world of nuclear giants and ethical infants. We know more about war than we do about peace, more about killing than we do about living."

This, then, is the everlasting frontier for administrators, legislators, and scholars. With all the impressive scholarship of modern social science, with all the tactical brilliance of our decision-makers, our social and political world is still "skirting the rim of hell." Together, we have somehow ignored—or at least failed to clear—the most important of frontiers: the frontier of the good life, the humane goal, the civilized means—what Lippmann calls *The Public Philosophy,* what others see at the heart of theology.

To this perennial frontier we must return—and we must assume that Kipling was talking to us, academicians and operators, as well as to "lesser breeds without the law" when he decried: All valiant dust that builds on dust, and guarding calls not Thee to guard;

> For frantic boast and foolish word,
> Thy mercy on Thy people, Lord.

4 · APPROACHES TO THE STUDY OF POLITICAL POWER *

Franz L. Neumann

ATTITUDES TOWARD POWER

Consciously or unconsciously, every student of politics has a specific attitude toward political power. It is this attitude which determines one's approach to all problems of political science. The valuative premises must be made clear so that objective analyses may be possible. The soul searching of the political scientist may be facilitated by a classification of the various attitudes exhibited in the history of political theory. The classification presented here is only suggested and is not meant to imply that there are no better and more convincing classifications.

1. For Plato and Aristotle, political power is more than a separate function of the organized community. It *is* the community. Political power is the total power of the community, distinguished from other relationships merely by its techniques. There is, in this view, no distinction between state and society, economics and politics, morals and politics, religion and politics, culture and politics. Man and citizen are equated. Every activity of the community and of its citizens is

* Franz L. Neumann, "Approaches to the Study of Political Power," *Political Science Quarterly,* LXV (June, 1950), 164-167, 171-177. Reprinted by permission of The Academy of Political Science. The footnotes in the original version are omitted here.

political. Only through political action can the citizen attain his fulfillment; only through politics does he become man.

2. To this, there is radically opposed what I shall call the Augustinian position. Politics is evil; political power is coercion, evil in origin and purpose. It is "unnatural" that man rule over man. Only at the end of history with the advent of the Kingdom of God can and will coercion be dispensed with. From this philosophy derive two radically different, and yet inherently related, attitudes: that of total conformism and that of total opposition to political power. If politics is evil, withdrawal is mandatory. Forms of government and objectives of political power become irrelevant. Salvation can be attained through faith, and the earthly life should be a mere preparation for it. Monasticism is the first consequence. By the same token, however, the demand for the immediate destruction of politics and the establishment of a Kingdom of God may equally be supported by the Augustinian premise. The Anabaptist movement was perhaps the most striking manifestation of the total rejection of society.

3. The radicalism of St. Augustine is, of course, "impractical." St. Thomas introduces what may be called a common-sense attitude toward political power. Power is not unnatural since hierarchic relationships already existed among the angels. Yet the attitude toward political power is not unambiguously positive. It is not only hedged in by many restraints but also, in some rather unclear way, subordinated to spiritual power operating indirectly through various levels of law.

4. It is this climate which·prepared the way for the liberal attitude. Its sole concern is the erection of fences around political power which is, allegedly, distrusted. Its aim is the dissolution of power into legal relationships, the elimination of the element of personal rule, and the substitution of the rule of law in which all relationships are to become purposive-rational, that is, predictable and calculable. In reality, of course, this is in large measure an ideology tending (often unintentionally) to prevent the search for the locus of political power and to render more secure its actual holders. Power cannot be dissolved in law.

5. Not to be confused with liberalism is the Epicurean attitude toward politics. In contrast to the Platonic-Aristotelian conception, politics is a separate business of society, clearly distinguished and distinguishable from all other activities. But it is a complete matter of indifference how it is organized, who exerts it, for what purposes it is used. Any power is justified which maintains that minimum

external order of society which permits the individual to go on with his life.

6. In its psychological consequences, Epicureanism is sometimes closely related to the anarchistic approach. To the anarchist, political power is evil, society good; hence it is possible to organize a society without politics. As in Augustinism, conformism or putschism may follow. Conformism: one should not dirty one's hands by participation in politics; putschism: one can establish an associative society at any time that man wills it.

7. Marxism shares with anarchism and Augustinism the belief that political power is not a natural but an historical phenomenon. In contrast to anarchism, and with Augustinism, however, it believes it to be a necessary historical phenomenon, but the necessity is limited (in contrast to Augustinism) to one historical phase through which mankind must pass before the classless society (a society without politics) can be established. The remedy against political power (again against the anarchists) is more and highly concentrated political power, skillfully used to smash political power (dictatorship of the proletariat). The Marxist thus has a positive approach to political power up to the establishment of a classless society.

8. Marx shares this positive approach with Rousseau. For the latter, political power is at once comprehensive and nonexistent. It is all-encompassing because the organized community (as in Plato and Aristotle) embraces all activities of man, economics, culture, religion; nonexistent because of the alleged identity of rulers and ruled in the general will. It is precisely this dual attitude toward political power which makes Robespierre's theory and actions understandable.

9. The liberal democrat shares with the total democrat a positive attitude toward political power which appears essentially as a rational instrument to be used for desired and desirable ends. Yet the fear of the liberal prevents him from accepting the total politicizing of life and causes him to insist on the separate character of political power. But the consistent liberal democrat is not, and cannot be, solely concerned with the erection of fences around political power. He is increasingly concerned with the potentialities of a rational use of political power.

This (or any other) typology of the attitudes toward political power enables us to discover contradictory statements often of a hypocritical or demagogic nature and to arrive at a consistent approach to the study of the power phenomenon. If a scholar or politician demands, in the same breath, the exclusion of dissenters from political participation and the inviolability of private property from governmental intrusion, we have before us a mixture of two attitudes: that of Plato–Rousseau, and that of liberalism.

The result is not a "new" attitude toward power but a propagandistic statement. Our typology of attitudes readily reveals that it contains contradictory positions. It is the duty of the critical student to remove such inconsistencies from his own thinking, to expose them when they appear in the statements of others, and to become aware of the premises of his own position.

. . . . .

ROOTS OF POLITICAL POWER

Three questions have to be faced in the analysis of the roots of political power: the conceptual framework has to be established; the institutional setting to be clarified; and the historical process to be understood which leads to a change in institutions and different attitudes toward power and to a different political behavior. For the ancient historians, this was no problem. Political power derived squarely from economic power, particularly from the control of land. Changes in ownership, the emergence of new modes of production, and so on, created new sources of political power and thus made for conflicts. Modern historians dealing with this period of history have not hesitated to restate the problem in the same way as the ancients stated it.

As we shall directly show, modern capitalist economy has rendered this whole subject problematical. And, despite the fact that the issue is so crucial, analysis has been hindered by senseless taboos. The older insights have been lost or hidden and are rarely brought fully into the open. Thus, the classical approach has been restated in modern times by Marx's interpretation of history (that this did not originate with him—and is not "Marxist"—he himself admitted). Yet since it is fashionable to reject Marxism root and branch—sight unseen, so to speak—the student precludes himself from a clear understanding of the relationship between economic power and political power.

The approach is facilitated by the establishment of certain categories of relationships.

1. The ancient conception. Here—and this follows already from what has been said—although the source of political power is eco-

nomic power, political power permeates all social activities and all spheres of life. The economic power position merely provides the motor of political power which then includes all power relationships.

2. The feudal conception. In the ideal–typical form, political power does not exist. It is merely a function of an economic power position: the ownership of land. From it flow judicial, military, religious, legislative, and administrative powers.

3. The capitalist conception. It is only in this period that a real problem arises: the independence of political power and yet its interconnection with economic power. Political power (the theoretical construction has been perfected by Hobbes) is a separate activity, carried out in a separate institution: the state. The state has the monopoly of coercive power which it exercises in a separate institutional framework. At the same time, however, this separate institution is intrinsically connected with society in the service of which it operates. It is this conception of political power that unites Locke and Hobbes, and distinguishes both from Rousseau. Both separate political power from social power; both connect them. Hobbes believes it necessary to maximize political power in order to serve society; Locke maintains that only by its minimization can society be served. Both, however, admit of exceptions. In Hobbes' theory, political power will be destroyed if it fails to serve its social function (the social contract lapses); Locke, through the institution of the prerogative and federative power, maximizes political power if it is necessary for the good of the commonwealth. What Hobbes and Locke did not clearly state is that the two are not only functionally but genetically connected; that is, economic power is the root of political power. The first systematic analysis of this relationship stems from St. Simon's analysis of the French Revolution and then spreads rapidly into French and English historiography and sociology.

From this general view of Hobbes and Locke it follows that whatever freedom society, and particularly economic activity, is to have, it has for the sake of maintaining a stable political order. There is thus no "pure" economic power and no "pure" political activity. Economics is as much an instrument of politics as politics is a tool of economics. The mythological conception of the laissez-faire state ought finally to be destroyed.

If this general view is accepted, the translation of economic power into social power and thence into political power becomes the crucial concern of the political scientist.

The Political Party

The single most important instrument for the translation of social power into political power is the political party. The reason for the supreme position of the party lies in the very nature of democracy. The party permits the presentation of particular and, quite frequently, very egoistic interests as national interests. At the same time, however, it prevents the total domination of national interests by particular interests. The function of the political party in democracy is thus ambiguous. The democratic process compels each social group to strive for mass support. Each group, therefore, must present its egoistic interests as universal. Politics in a democracy, the struggle for political power, thus becomes far more ideological than in any previous period in history. What was obvious for the ancients, and clear to the feudal system, becomes hidden in the democratic process. But the valuable side of this process must equally not be forgotten. The very need to appeal to social groups larger than the immediate interest group compels adjustment of various interests. Politics becomes more democratic.

Private Property

Social power, in turn, either is derived from private property or is against it. The legal meaning of private property comprises two radically different conceptions: power over an external piece of nature (or an absolute right) and power over other men derived from power over nature. It is only the second meaning of private property with which the political scientist is concerned: with proprietorship in the means of production. This type of property gives power—power in the labor market, in the commodity market, and in the political market of the state.

The three power functions of property are usually (and particularly in Europe where political and social life is more petrified than in the United States) institutionalized in three types of organization: for the labor market, the employer's association; for the commodity market, the cartel; for the political market, the territorial form of the chambers of commerce and the functional form of the trade associations.

As against property, the trade unions (in Europe) attempt to organize the labor markets and the political markets by the collective power of organized labor, sometimes in one organization, sometimes in several. Consumers' and producers' cooperatives, however, affect only slightly the power of property in the commodity market.

Studies of these organizations and the devices by which their power is translated into political power are vital to the political scientist. Large numbers of individual studies of pressure groups exist, but a really sophisticated, comparative analysis is still lacking. The translation of these economic power positions differs from country to country and from historical situation to historical situation. The relative strength of the competing economic groups is far more important for the analysis of political power than the study of the political institutions proper. There are countries (like Germany and England) where the agents and managers of the economic organizations enter parliaments directly; there are others (like the United States) where the influence is more indirect. There are countries (like Germany and England) where trade unions are political as well as industrial bodies; there are others (like France and the United States in certain situations) where they apparently abstain from politics.

The devices and forms for the translation of economic power into political power thus vary considerably and yet patterns are discernible which ought to be more sharply defined on a comparative basis. A high degree of knowledge of problems of social stratification and economic organization is thus indispensable for the political scientist.

The Ascendance of Politics and of Bureaucracies

The classical relationship between economics and politics changes. It now appears as if political power has begun to emancipate itself from its economic roots and, indeed, tends to become a base for the acquisition of economic power. In general, bureaucratization is believed to be the manifestation of that trend which culminates in doctrines of managerial rule: private and public managers eliminating property owners and parliaments. The trend toward bureaucratization has unquestionably two roots: the transformation of parliamentary democracy into mass democracy; and the transition of a predominantly competitive economy into a predominantly organized economy. While these trends are known and progress under our very eyes, they do not necessarily involve an assumption of political power by bureaucracies. The growth of the scope and number of bureaucratic structures may merely indicate that the social groups which rule now need more and more bureaucracies in order to cope with the exercise of political power. But the equation of a larger number of bureaucrats with increase of their power is due to the inability (or unwillingness) to distinguish sharply three different problems involved in what is called "bureaucratization"; namely, bureaucratic behavior, bureaucratic structure, and bureaucratic power.

Bureaucratic behavior (roughly equated here with routine performance as against initiative or creative performance) is, of course, spreading. No sphere of activity is exempted from it. Whether it is beneficial or not shall not be discussed here. We should merely remember the tremendous extent to which our comforts depend on routine performances. Moreover, it is untrue that the decisions of the bureaucrats (public or private) are exclusively routine decisions. Many, indeed, are creative ones, not derived from precedent or standing rules, but highly discretionary and thus essentially lawmaking in character. Finally, bureaucratic organization, that is, hierarchies where commands are channeled from above to below and responsibility goes from below to above, is not confined to public life. The facts are obvious.

Though the growth of bureaucratic behavior, with the increase in the number of bureaucratic structures, is a continuous process, it does not thereby follow that power (private or public) has shifted to the bureaucracies. No abstract answer can be given; only empirical investigations can reveal whether shifts in power have taken place. Such investigations are, unfortunately, rare.

The Soviet Union presents a clear-cut marginal case where political power not only has made itself supreme but has become the fount of whatever economic power positions exist. Nazi Germany, on the other hand, exhibited a transitional case. It is undisputed that the Nazi party rose to power with the financial and political assistance of German big-business leaders who doubtless hoped to use the party for the promotion of their own interests. But the party, once having achieved power, emancipated itself from business control, and its political power became autonomous. The party then went further and attempted to create economic power positions for itself. Clearly the new political power was seeking to give itself an economic power base. This, indeed, is the significance of the Goering combine, the expanding enterprises of the Labor Front and the S.S., and the acquisitions resulting from Aryanization and Germanization. The war, which made it inadvisable to carry out sweeping institutional changes, interrupted the process. But it is quite safe to assume that, had there been no war or had the Nazis been victorious, the Soviet pattern would have prevailed.

The reactions to the ascendant rôle of political power are, as a rule, hostile. Most notable is the attempt to ascribe this phenomenon to democracy. This is, of course, essentially correct. For, as we have indicated, the attitude of democracy toward political power is undoubtedly positive. Yet more is meant by that statement which by no means is a mere scientific one but has definite political undertones and overtones. It is implied that the growing political power will, by its inner dynamics, be abused and will ultimately lead to a totalitarian system. In this, modern criticism resumes the traditionalist critique not of political power but of democracy. Maistre and Bonald are resurrected. Proceeding from the shaky psychology of the essential evilness of man, they assert the inevitable transformation of democracy into mob rule, which, in conjunction with the modern trend of state interventionism, must culminate in totalitarianism. The remedy is some kind of aristocratic rule. A second reaction believes bureaucracy to be inimical to liberty and attempts to protect democracy by identifying it with individual liberty against the state.

Both reactions base themselves on what they call the tradition of Western civilization, the kernel of which is allegedly hostility to political power as expressed in constitutionalism. This is only a partial truth and, therefore, false. The tradition of Western civilization is more complex. Its richness was hinted at when we attempted to classify the various attitudes toward political power. Certainly, one may say that Rousseauism is a more important element in the political tradition of democracy than the essentially self-contradictory and arbitrary doctrines of Locke and of the natural law. That political power (whether democratic, aristocratic, or monarchic) can be abused is beyond doubt; but it is doubtful that abuses can be effectively checked by constitutionalism. The problem of modern democracy is much less the fencing of political power than its rational utilization and provision for effective mass participation in its exercise.

SUGGESTED READINGS

American Political Science Association, Committee for the Advancement of Teaching. *Goals for Political Science.* New York: Sloane, 1951.

Bailey, Stephen K., and others. *Research Frontiers in Politics and Government.* Washington, D.C.: Brookings Institution. 1955.

Brown, Everett S. *Manual of Government Publications.* New York: Appleton-Century-Crofts, 1950.

Catlin, George E. G. *A Study of the Principles of Politics.* New York: Macmillan, 1930.

Contemporary Political Science. UNESCO Publication No. 426. Liége: 1950.

Crick, Bernard. *The American Science of Politics, Its Origins and Conditions.* Berkeley and Los Angeles: University of California Press, 1959.

Easton, David. *The Political System: An Inquiry into the State of Political Science.* New York: Knopf, 1953.

Eulau, Heinz, Eldersveld, Samuel J., and Janowitz, Morris (eds.). *Political Behavior: A Reader in Theory and Research.* Glencoe, Ill.: Free Press, 1956.

Hyneman, Charles S. *The Study of Politics.* Urbana: University of Illinois Press, 1959.

Kaplan, Morton A. *System and Process in International Politics.* New York: Wiley, 1957.

Kaufmann, Felix. *Methodology of the Social Sciences.* New York: Oxford University Press, 1944.

Kirk, Grayson. *The Study of International Relations.* New York: Council on Foreign Relations, 1947.

Lerner, Daniel, and Lasswell, Harold D. *The Policy Sciences.* Stanford: Stanford University Press, 1951.

Schubert, Glendon A. *Quantitative Analysis of Judicial Behavior.* Glencoe, Ill.: Free Press and Michigan State University Bureau of Social and Political Research, 1959.

Van Dyke, Vernon. *Political Science: A Philosophical Analysis.* Stanford: Stanford University Press, 1960.

Waldo, Dwight. *Perspectives on Administration.* University, Ala.: University of Alabama Press, 1956.

————— *Political Science in the United States of America.* Paris: UNESCO, 1960.

Weldon, T. D. *The Vocabulary of Politics.* Harmondsworth: Penguin, 1953.

Wright, Quincy. *The Study of International Relations.* New York: Appleton-Century-Crofts, 1955.

Young, Roland (ed.). *Approaches to the Study of Politics.* Evanston, Ill.: Northwestern University Press, 1958.

CHAPTER II

The Physical Roots of Political Power

Political ideas, institutions, actors, and processes by no means exist in a vacuum. They are everywhere to a greater or lesser degree conditioned by certain major physical factors. The following selections spotlight the four most important of these underlying "conditioners": population, natural resources, geography, and industrial capacity. The significance of these factors as elements affecting a nation's political power would be difficult to exaggerate.

The subject of population has, since World War II, attracted more and more attention. Many countries have in this period undergone "population explosions" that have resulted in the most pressing and far-reaching social, economic, and political problems. To make matters worse, these vast and sudden population increases have occurred where it has been most difficult of all to cope with them: in the underdeveloped and newly emerging states of Asia, Latin America, and to a lesser extent, Africa. Coming on top of the already-existing tensions arising from demands for independence and social justice, mushrooming populations have created one of the most explosive and complex situations that the modern world has yet encountered. How to feed the constantly growing mass of humanity? How to accumulate the capital required for increased industrial productivity? How to provide sufficient social services to prevent political collapse altogether? These are questions that in a great many countries of today's

49

shrinking world are challenging the abilities of even the most competent political leaders.

Moreover, the problems of population do not arise only from the fact of growing absolute numbers. Hardly less relevant to politics is the matter of the distribution of population, even *within* a nation. Whenever there occur major shifts in population, as, for example, a change from predominantly rural to predominantly urban, the impact upon a country's political life is bound to be very considerable. Not only must political leaders reassess their strategies and tactics, they must also readapt the political process—from the structure and functioning of its institutions to the allocation of its human and physical resources.

A further and in some ways comparable set of problems results from shifts in the composition of populations in regard to age. For example, in those societies where population growth has in recent years been greatest, new drugs and improved prenatal care have at the same time greatly increased the proportionate number of the very young and the very old. Since the former group's productivity has not yet begun, and the latter's has already ended, the economic and social problems faced by the countries concerned are all the more acute.

Some students of politics and geography have seen such a strong and integral relationship between these two fields that they have sought to combine them into a wholly new and separate discipline, for which they have coined the word "geopolitics." The implication of this term is that political power is determined by certain geographical factors such as location, climate, topography, and water. The works of an American admiral, Alfred T. Mahan, and a British geographer, Sir Halford J. Mackinder, were designed to provide comprehensive plans, based on geographical factors, for illustrating the actual and potential development of political power in the nation-state system. Under the Nazi regime in Germany, a thriving institute of geopolitical studies, directed by General Karl Haushofer, devoted itself to blueprinting some of the strategies later employed by Hitler during the second World War.

Few political scientists would deny the important role that geography plays both in the motivation of political behavior as well as in the manner of its expression. Most of them, however, interpret the political implications of geography as conditioning, rather than determinative factors. In short, they believe that geographical considerations are important ingredients in political action but that the actual content and form of whatever actions are taken remain primarily a matter of the free choice of the human beings concerned.

The wealth of nations is measured not only in terms of the physical factors mentioned above. Countries are no less unevenly blessed with a whole range of natural resources whose presence or absence strongly affects not only their standard of living but their entire social and political life as well. The exploitation of such resources requires ingenuity, skill, patience, and maturity. In a world that places as high a value on material wealth and industrial skills as ours, it is not surprising that extensive natural resources and, especially, the capability of utilizing them, are matters about which nations care a great deal. Those who are endowed with these advantages understandably feel pride; those who are not are often envious and determined to rectify their inferior position. Moreover, natural resources and their utilization to increase productivity and raise standards of living also contribute very significantly to political power. A nation cannot resist aggression or embark on a war without a careful stocktaking of its natural resources and its industrial capacity. But as with the geographical factor, so with these other two elements of political power: *how* they come to be used is not something predetermined but an act of human will—political will.

All of these roots of political power clearly constitute limits within which politicians or statesmen may act. Even further limits are set by such additional circumstances of the political context as the prevailing governmental system, the existing body of trained manpower, the ideas that the society subscribes to, the quality of its diplomacy, and the nature of its particular traditions and customs. In view of this fact, it must always be recognized that the roots of political power are neither wholly physical nor wholly nonphysical; and that political power itself cannot ever be adequately understood in terms of any single-factor analyses.

No political leadership can afford to ignore the factors of population, geography, natural resources, and industrial capacity. They are part of the warp and woof of national and international politics alike. The final test of political wisdom is to evaluate the relative importance of these interrelated elements of power and so to combine them as to contribute the maximum possible to keeping the individual countries as well as the world as a whole free from hunger, disease, and war.

Population

5 · ANALYSIS OF THE POPULATION EXPLOSION *

Kingsley Davis

The increase of mankind has been so rapid, so overwhelming and utterly unprecedented in recent years that it is commonly referred to by scientists as a population explosion. We now number 2,750,-000,000, about twice as many as seventy years ago; and there is every sign that that number will double within another forty years. Moreover, the rate of increase is growing faster all the time. The world's population rose by 6 per cent per decade between 1850 and 1900; by 7 per cent between 1900 and 1930; by 10 per cent between 1930 and 1950, and by 17 per cent, on a decade basis, in the seven years since then. At present the number added to our globe each year is 47,000,000 (greater than the population of France), and before long it may be 75,000,000 annually.

This explosive human multiplication, unanticipated and unexampled in history, clearly cannot continue indefinitely. It would give us nearly 6,000,000,000 by the end of this century and nearly 13,000,-000,000 by the year 2050. How this growth is eventually stopped, and when, will play a tremendous role in human destiny.

Although a climax in population growth is approaching, nothing indicates that the peak has yet been reached. The total may climb faster in the next twenty years than it did in the last twenty. Even if the rate of increase begins to decline, centuries may pass before it falls to simple replacement level; and new billions will have been added to the human horde in the meantime. Unless a catastrophe in-

* Kingsley Davis, "Analysis of the Population Explosion," *The New York Times Magazine* (September 22, 1957), pp. 15, 77-79. Reprinted by permission of Kingsley Davis and *The New York Times*.

tervenes, we and our children will share the earth with a lot more people than we do today.

A strange fact is that in general it is the poorer and less developed regions, the regions least able to support additional millions, that are exhibiting the biggest demographic inflation. Briefly, according to the United Nations, the explosion is greatest in Latin America; next in Oceania, Africa, and most of Asia; less in the United States and Canada, and least in Europe, especially Western and Central Europe. The Latin Americans, for example, are multiplying more than four times faster than the people of Northwestern Europe; the people of East Asia more than three times faster.

In the past the greatest numerical increase occurred in the more successful nations—those that were expanding economically and raising their level of living. Now, however, it is primarily the peasant-agrarian countries, where poverty is most intense, that are ahead in the population marathon. Ceylon, Taiwan and Malaya; Paraguay, Costa Rica, Colombia and Mexico; Turkey and Syria—these are among the countries that have attained or are approaching a rate of increase that will double their numbers every twenty-three years. Our neighbor, Mexico, which now has 31,500,000 inhabitants, will have about 63,000,000 in 1980. The only industrial countries that have better than half of this rate are the new ones—such as Canada, the United States, New Zealand and the Soviet Union. The older industrial countries are far behind, despite their postwar baby boom.

The recent acceleration in world population growth is not due, as is often assumed, to rising birth rates. In advanced nations birth rates did rise after the depression, but for the most part they have slipped back to comparatively low levels.

The main factor is the revolutionary reduction in death rates in the underdeveloped countries, where most of the world's people live. And this spectacular drop has been gathering speed since 1935. Most notable is the case of Ceylon, where the death rate fell 34 per cent in a single year and 70 per cent in ten years. Other cases are similar: Since the Nineteen-Forties the average death rate in Puerto Rico dropped by 82 per cent in a single decade; in Cyprus by 64 per cent; in Trinidad by 45 per cent; in Mexico by 43 per cent, and in Jamaica by 30 per cent. As the United Nations shows in its latest *Demographic Yearbook,* the countries with the highest mortality have generally shown the most remarkable declines. This new achievement in death control is revolutionary not only because its speed has never before

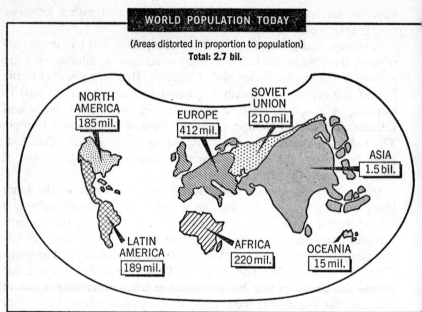

WORLD POPULATION TODAY

(Areas distorted in proportion to population)
Total: 2.7 bil.

NORTH AMERICA
185 mil.

EUROPE
412 mil.

SOVIET UNION
210 mil.

ASIA
1.5 bil.

LATIN AMERICA
189 mil.

AFRICA
220 mil.

OCEANIA
15 mil.

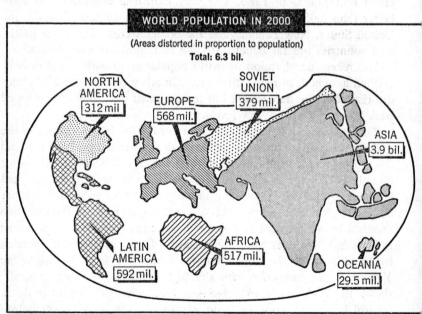

WORLD POPULATION IN 2000

(Areas distorted in proportion to population)
Total: 6.3 bil.

NORTH AMERICA
312 mil

EUROPE
568 mil.

SOVIET UNION
379 mil.

ASIA
3.9 bil.

LATIN AMERICA
592 mil.

AFRICA
517 mil.

OCEANIA
29.5 mil.

New York Times News of the Week in Review [December 6, 1959], p. E5.
Reprinted by permission of The New York Times.

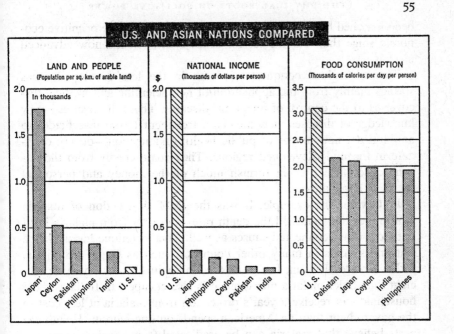

U.S. AND ASIAN NATIONS COMPARED

LAND AND PEOPLE
(Population per sq. km. of arable land)

In thousands

Japan, Ceylon, Pakistan, Philippines, India, U.S.

NATIONAL INCOME
(Thousands of dollars per person)

U.S., Japan, Philippines, Ceylon, Pakistan, India

FOOD CONSUMPTION
(Thousands of calories per day per person)

U.S., Pakistan, Japan, Ceylon, India, Philippines

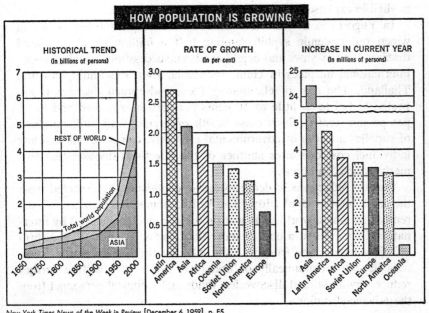

HOW POPULATION IS GROWING

HISTORICAL TREND
(In billions of persons)

REST OF WORLD

Total world population

ASIA

1650, 1750, 1800, 1850, 1900, 1950, 2000

RATE OF GROWTH
(In per cent)

Latin America, Asia, Africa, Oceania, Soviet Union, North America, Europe

INCREASE IN CURRENT YEAR
(In millions of persons)

Asia, Latin America, Africa, Soviet Union, Europe, North America, Oceania

New York Times News of the Week in Review [December 6, 1959], p. E5.
Reprinted by permission of The New York Times.

been matched but also because it is occurring at a more primitive economic stage than did the fastest death control in the now advanced nations.

The miraculous conquest of death in the less developed areas springs mainly from the application of new scientific and medical discoveries to the control of infectious diseases. These discoveries—new knowledge of diseases, new means of treatment (from insecticides to antibiotics), new modes of public health organization—do not originate in the underdeveloped regions. They come chiefly from the advanced countries, which furnish much of the money and personnel for their application.

In Ceylon, for example, it was the DDT destruction of malaria mosquitoes that smashed the death rate—not only from malaria itself but from other connected causes as well. This technique has achieved startling success in many other countries, such as Cyprus, Sardinia, India, Greece, Taiwan, Iran, and the Philippines. Not only more efficient than older malaria measures, it is also cheaper. In India a whole household can receive a year's protection from malaria at less cost to the government than an American spends on one haircut. Health experts believe that malaria can be eradicated from whole regions before the mosquitoes develop DDT immunity, thus making even the negligible expense of spraying unnecessary.

In Yugoslavia a WHO and UNICEF campaign utilizing penicillin wiped out endemic syphilis among half a million people. Related diseases such as yaws and bejel have been successfully attacked under international auspices in Haiti, Indonesia, Iraq, the Philippines and Thailand. The cost of eliminating these widespread diseases is expected to fall to as little as 10 cents per person examined and to $1 per person treated. Such mass health programs, with bulk purchase of supplies and use of governmental authority, can wipe out at a low individual cost one after another of the infectious diseases that formerly afflicted millions.

Further reductions in death rates can confidently be expected from the same international effort. The United States, for instance, is currently planning a world-wide war on malaria, to be managed by international agencies at a cost of more than half a billion dollars, a fifth of this sum to come from us. And whether the non-industrial countries develop economically or not, their death rates will be further reduced by additional discoveries, funds and technical personnel from the advanced nations.

If birth rates were dropping as fast as death rates, no acceleration of world population growth would be occurring. But birth rates in most countries have not declined. The recent baby boom has given the industrial nations—particularly the new ones—a greater increase than the experts anticipated. In the agrarian countries birth rates have remained high, largely because the amazing reduction of mortality has been accomplished with minimum disturbance to local customs and often without any rise in the level of living.

The old attitudes that encouraged prolific childbearing—necessary when death took most of the children before adulthood—thus persist even when high fertility no longer makes sense. The same industrial nations that have helped the poorer nations to get rid of diseases have done little to help them get rid of excessive reproduction. Actually, a sharp decline in mortality tends to raise the birth rate, because women are healthier, have fewer miscarriages and are less frequently widowed. For these reasons the birth rate in underdeveloped areas is currently about twice as high as it is in the advanced countries.

How will the acceleration of the earth's population growth and the spectacular increase among backward peoples affect future economic development?

Too often this question is misunderstood as simply the problem of getting enough food to feed the world's people. To do this requires economic expansion, and certainly such expansion is actually taking place; otherwise the huge population increase could not have occurred. But a rise in production that just matches the increase in human beings is not economic development. What brings prosperity is an increase in production per unit of human labor.

The product per unit is not enhanced by merely multiplying workers, but rather by adding things *to* human labor—fuels, hydroelectric power, machinery, rational organization. The task of economic development is therefore not to keep up with population growth but to get ahead of it. An increase in national income just sufficient to support ever more people at a near-subsistence level offers no solution to the problem of poverty; instead, it makes that problem bigger.

Poor people are more numerous today than ever before, because population is skyrocketing in the poorer countries. If two-thirds of the earth's population was impoverished a century ago and only one-third today, there would still be more poor people now than there were then. With many countries multiplying at a rate near 3 per cent per year, their economies must somehow move ahead at 4 or 5 per cent per year if poverty is to be reduced. This is no easy task when the ratio of people to resources is already excessive and the poverty so great that capital can hardly be accumulated for long-run industrial development.

In countries like India, Ceylon, Egypt, Pakistan, and Haiti, to mention only a few, per capita income has risen little if at all, despite a rise in national income. An economist, writing recently about Ceylon, had this to say: "The issue is plain: Any check to population growth will make economic progress more likely or speed it up. Continued or accelerated population growth will make progress slow down or stop. In one meeting of Government officials I attended, the problem of development was put as that of keeping the standard of living from falling—not of raising it."

A further consequence of tumbling death rates and surplus reproduction is the creation of the youngest populations ever known. The reason is that the greatest gains in saving lives are made among infants and children under 10 years of age. A swift drop in mortality therefore has the same effect as a sharp rise in fertility: It increases the proportion of children in relation to older age groups. In Algeria, for instance, 52 per cent of the Moslems are under 20 years of age, whereas in the United States only 37 per cent of the populace is under 20, and in France, 31 per cent.

Peasant-agrarian countries consequently have an excessive number of dependents for each person in his productive years. One of the ways of meeting this situation is to put children to work at an early age, a practice hardly conducive to education or to economic development. But in fact a great problem of these countries is to find jobs for the ever larger waves of youths that enter the working ages each year. If the young cannot find employment they naturally seek remedies for their plight. They are ready to follow any revolutionary leader who promises a quick, and preferably violent, way out.

A leader who rests his political career on the whims of these swollen cadres of youth is usually incapable of making solid economic improvements. He is driven to embrace the safest and most inflammatory of all issues—nationalism. He can persecute and expropriate the foreigners, the Jews, or the Christians. He can threaten war on neighboring states. He can play the Communists against the free world to get emergency funds for staving off calamity or for buying weapons. He is the unstable political offspring produced by the monstrous marriage between rapid population growth and national destitution.

Fortunately, not all impoverished or overpopulated countries are in irresponsible hands. In some there is a genuine attempt to make economic progress. In such cases, a government may ignore the population trend, but this policy entails a gigantic risk; for it assumes, first, that economic improvement will be possible despite the population avalanche and, second, that the economic gains will ultimately bring a drop in fertility and stop the runaway population growth.

The second assumption is probably correct; for if a country achieves a high level of living and becomes heavily urbanized, its better-educated people will plan their families and its birth rate will fall to something like a reasonable level. But the assumption that skyrocketing population growth will not obstruct economic development is so dubious that several governments have decided against the gamble of ignoring the population trend. They are striving to bring fertility control to their people in order to insure and hasten economic growth.

One industrial country that has officially decided to lower its birth rate is Japan. With a population that rose from 55,000,000 in 1920 to 91,000,000 today, with an area no bigger than Montana and with 617 persons per square mile, the Japanese do not think the number of people on their crowded islands has nothing to do with their economic future.

In 1948 the birth rate was 34 per 1,000, the death rate 12 per 1,000 and the resulting population growth sufficient to double the population in thirty-two years. In that year the Japanese Diet passed a law, backed by the five major political parties, legalizing abortions and sterilizations and setting up marriage-advice centers throughout the country. Subsequent liberalization and expansion of this law was accompanied by a semi-official nation-wide propaganda campaign for family planning, by the formation of a Population Problem Council under the Japanese Cabinet, and by the formation of private family-planning associations and publications. Increased emphasis was placed on contraception, with more than 800 Government-subsidized health centers and with some 30,000 birth control guidance officers.

The consequence has been an amazing drop in the Japanese birth rate. The 1955 figure was 19.4 per 1,000 and the birth rate now is substantially below that of the United States. The rate of population growth has already been cut in half.

Among less industrial countries, India has the boldest population policy. Nehru and a majority of his party have long held that avoidance of excessive population growth is essential to social and economic welfare for the Indian masses. The first Five-Year Plan, initiated in 1951, allotted 6,500,000 rupees for a program of research and education in family planning under the Ministry of Health. Under the second Five-Year Plan, 2,000 rural health centers and 300 urban centers are scheduled to be opened, with family planning an essential service of each center.

Several Indian states and cities have independently taken an interest in the subject; influential citizens are leading a strong birth control movement. Surveys have shown that Indian peasants as well as urbanites, pressed by poverty and by big families, yet aspiring to a better life, are not averse to the idea of birth control. One cannot expect the program to affect India's birth rate immediately, but Indian leaders are looking to the future.

The most recent and surprising convert to family planning is Communist China. Until 1953 the Chinese followed the standard Communist line that overpopulation is a vicious figment of the bourgeois mind. However, the census completed in 1954 gave mainland China a population of 583,000,000, some 15,000,000 more than the Chinese themselves had estimated and over 100,000,000 more than others had been estimating. Believing this huge population to be growing faster than the world average, the Chinese officials speedily did an ideological somersault, maintaining that "overpopulation" is still a myth but that the Communist program would fare better if population growth slowed down. Family planning was justified as conducive to maternal and child welfare.

The government, which had begun to spread the idea of birth control as early as 1953, stepped up its work in 1954 and 1955. Contraceptive supplies went on sale at Government-managed stores; a propaganda campaign was started. On March 5, 1957, the Communist party newspaper *People's Daily* carried an editorial saying that contraceptives should be widely and cheaply disseminated. Of late, a family-planning propaganda campaign has been intensively pursued throughout the country.

When the Population Commission of the United Nations had its eighth meeting in New York in 1955, the Soviet delegation firmly opposed the very idea of a national birth control policy. At the 1957 meeting, this position was changed. The Soviet delegate (the same man who was there in 1955) maintained that for *his* country no such policy should be adopted, but he said that other countries should be free to adopt whatever population policy they wished. This was an important shift in the Soviet line. What else could the Soviet delegate do with the example of Communist China and neutral India before him?

Officially, the United States and most other Western countries are more afraid of family limitation than the so-called backward nations. Such official silence, prompted by strong religious opposition to birth control, would be impossible if it were not for the fact that these nations are relatively prosperous and that their citizens limit the size of their families anyway. In some underdeveloped countries, such as Colombia and Peru and the Congo, the full effects of unrestricted propagation have not yet had time to manifest themselves. But in countries with extreme population pressure, responsible leaders cannot afford to adopt an ostrich attitude toward the population problem.

The American policy of improving the lot of the world's poorer peoples is seriously impeded by our official inability to aid them in their population control. A runaway inflation of people in the underdeveloped nations is not in our national interest.

6 · HOW THE WORLD FARES *

The problem of food is as old as the human race. It is likely that much of mankind in every generation has suffered from hunger or malnutrition, or both. Today, although more food is produced than at any previous time in history, we are still a long way from being able to provide enough good food for everybody. Indeed, the world food situation is perhaps more serious than ever before.

* From *Man and Hunger* (World Food Problems No. 2; Rome: Food and Agriculture Organization of the United Nations, 1957), pp. 4-9, 11-16. Reprinted by permission of the Food and Agriculture Organization of the United Nations. The footnote in the original version is omitted here.

PERCENTAGE OF ILLITERACY IN RURAL AND URBAN POPULATIONS OF SELECTED COUNTRIES*

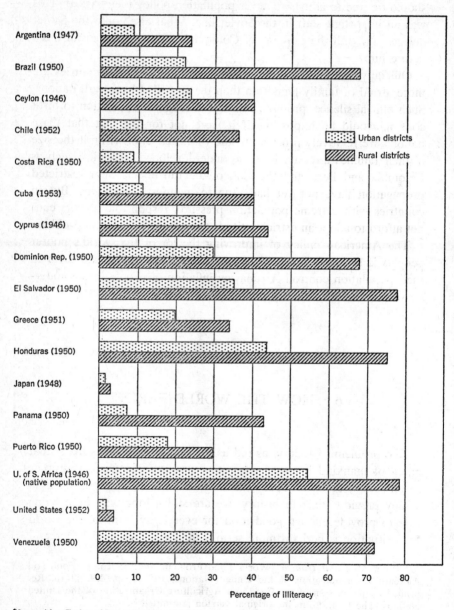

Percentage of illiteracy

*Reprinted from *The State of Food and Agriculture 1959* (Rome: Food and Agriculture Organization of the United Nations, 1959), p. 112. Reprinted by permission of the Food and Agriculture Organization of the United Nations.

AVERAGE LABOR TIME EXPENDED
PER 100 KILOGRAMS OF OUTPUT IN SELECTED COUNTRIES*

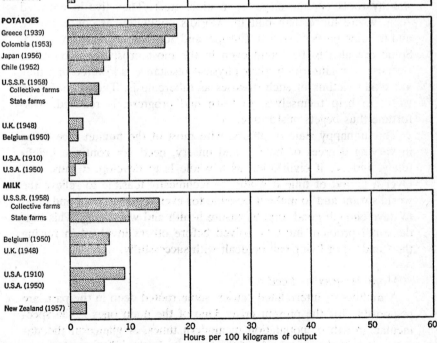

Hours per 100 kilograms of output

*Reprinted from *The State of Food and Agriculture 1959* (Rome: Food and Agriculture Organization of the United Nations, 1959), p. 125. Reprinted by permission of the Food and Agriculture Organization of the United Nations.

Haves and Have-nots

Today relatively high standards of living prevail in about 20 countries with a total population of around 400 millions. In these 20 countries, during the past century, the average length of life has increased from 35 to between 60 and 70 years, and thus a full generation has been added to the span of human existence. One thing which has helped to make this possible is that the people eat more and better food than people in other regions—animal products and fruits and vegetables needed for growth and health. They are also able to live in cleaner and more comfortable surroundings, and they are better clothed and sheltered. They tend to grow taller and stronger, and fewer of them die in childhood. Most of the people in this fortunate but comparatively small group are to be found in North America, in some parts of South America, in much of Western Europe, and in Australia and New Zealand.

But many more people never obtain enough good food for health and growth and full physical vigor. The people in this group eat mainly cereals (wheat, rice, maize, barley, and other grains) and starchy roots (potatoes, yams, manioc, etc.). They live in crowded Asia, where more than half the world's population is concentrated, and in some parts of Africa, Europe, and South and Central America. Some are also to be found even in the most prosperous countries. Because of malnutrition, their physical resistance is lowered and they are ready victims of such diseases as tuberculosis. Their capacity to work, to help themselves, to learn and progress, is reduced. Misfortune thus begets misfortune.

This unhappy state of affairs, with most of the human race living in varying degrees of hunger and misery, need not continue indefinitely. Indeed, if civilization as a whole is to develop, it must not. Over a period of time it would be technically feasible to relieve the world's want and to make it possible for every man, woman and child to have enough good food to ensure health and well-being. This fundamental problem must be solved before others involved in raising the standard of living can be dealt with successfully.

More Mouths to Feed

A number of interrelated causes, some rooted deep in the past, are responsible for the present crisis. One of the main ones is the spectacular growth of population in modern times. A glance at the statistics reveals the magnitude of the increase. In the 200 years between

1650 and 1850, world population doubled; in the 100 years between 1850 and 1950, it doubled again. The growth in the last half-century amounts to about 800 million people, or nearly 60 per cent in 50 years.

Increases in population seem to be most rapid in those regions where nutritional levels have always been low and where food problems are already acute. A part of the explanation is that in the least developed agrarian societies (the Far East, for example) both social tradition and practical necessity reinforce the ideal of the large family. As farm work must be carried on by simple methods, with few tools and generally without animal or mechanical power, possibilities for increasing agricultural production and food supplies are directly linked to the number of human hands available. In such circumstances the only way the farmer can feel secure is to guarantee his labor force within his own family. But the large family pattern, itself partly a defense against difficult living conditions, leads to overpopulation in agricultural areas, under-employment and low incomes, fragmentation of land holdings when they are transmitted from one generation to the next, and landlessness. These circumstances, in turn, often result in the overworking of the land itself and a deterioration in its productivity. Thus, levels of nutrition and standards of living in general are brought lower and lower as the population expands.

In more advanced countries, where industry and agriculture alike are further developed, social, cultural, and economic influences have often led to the acceptance of a smaller family pattern. The pressure of population on food supplies is therefore less heavy, and nutritional problems, by and large, are normally under control.

It seems certain that world population will continue to increase and with it the gravity of food problems in vast areas. There are approximately 2,650 million people living in the world today. In 1975, not 20 years away, it is estimated that there will be more than 3,000 million. What this means is that for every five plates of food provided now, an additional sixth plate will have to be provided by 1975. Even so, people would be no better fed than they are now, which is to say that by far the greater part of the world's population would still be subsisting on an inadequate diet. To improve nutritional standards on a wide scale, which is the real objective, a seventh plate of nutritionally important foods will be necessary. This is within the realm of possibility, but it will require a far greater effort than is now envisaged.

The Lag in Food Production

So far, food production in the world as a whole has not been able to keep pace with the ever larger requirements of the increasing population of the earth. As has been pointed out, food supplies are adequate for good nutrition in a few countries. There are even surpluses here and there. But these exceptional conditions are in sharp contrast with those in most of the world.

The reasons for the lag in food production are varied and complex. Among the main causes must be included man's long abuse of natural resources, which has destroyed or damaged the productivity of large areas. Destructive agricultural practices—such as stripping the earth of its natural cover of forest and vegetation and thereby exposing it to erosion by wind and water—have reduced once fertile lands to barren waste. These practices continue today in many places, partly through ignorance of the principles of conservation, partly through the pressing necessity to produce food for immediate needs, partly through resistance to any change in age-old methods of agriculture. This misuse of resources presents one of the greatest dangers for the future, as it can only lead to a further reduction in the possibilities for producing food.

Another cause of the lag in food production is the inefficiency of agricultural methods employed by most of the world's farmers. More than two thirds of the people of the world are engaged in agriculture, which is the world's largest primary industry, but in most agricultural territory, farming methods have remained nearly the same for many centuries. Those who work the soil plant their crops by hand and use primitive implements; they struggle to wrest sustenance from poor seed dropped in exhausted earth. Relatively few farmers are in a position to use modern methods and equipment and improved seeds which yield sturdy and plentiful crops.

Events as well as conditions and methods have played a part in shaping the present situation. In our own times, for example, the production of food, like most other human activities, was profoundly disrupted by the Second World War. Territories were laid waste; livestock, forests, farm buildings, farm machinery and food-processing facilities were destroyed; some of the prolific fishing grounds were closed and large numbers of fishing craft were converted to other purposes; and manpower for agricultural work was sharply reduced. Throughout history, wars have wreaked havoc and brought hunger in their train, but never before on such a scale.

These, then, are some of the circumstances which have given rise to the food problems confronting us today. In the following paragraphs are some details of the situation as it has developed in different regions during recent years.

The Early Postwar Period

The effects of the war varied from one region to another. Some of the more advanced countries emerged from the conflict with an abundance of food of all kinds. For example, food consumption levels in North America were maintained or even improved during the war period, and continued to rise afterward. But in the under-developed areas of the world, where the level of food production has always been low, the year or two immediately following the end of hostilities was a period of serious food shortages and widespread hunger. Thus, like a wedge, the war widened the gaps between the better fed and the worse fed nations.

Seen in relation to population, food supplies just after the war were inadequate everywhere, except in New Zealand and Australia, North America, and a very few parts of Latin America and Europe. Moreover, the nutritive quality of diets as well as the quantity of food available declined in the afflicted regions. The disastrous effects of famines were eased only by such emergency measures as the international allocation of food supplies, international help through the United Nations Relief and Rehabilitation Administration, UNICEF and similar agencies, and by systems of food rationing.

A few figures will help to indicate the situation in regions where difficulties were greatest. In Western Europe, the Union of Soviet Socialist Republics and North Africa, where physical destruction had been severe, agricultural production in 1946-1947 was one quarter to one third below the prewar level. In the Far East it fell about 10 per cent below the prewar level, which was already very low, and in Africa it dropped about 7 per cent. One consequence was that most people in these areas had to depend increasingly for their nourishment on cereals and starchy roots, as these foods can be produced quickly and in abundance at relatively low cost. Although they are valuable as sources of energy, such foods are comparatively poor in body-building protein and some other nutrients indispensable to health. Thus, a diet composed exclusively or too largely of cereals and starchy roots may lead to malnutrition and disease. In the early postwar years, the unduly high proportion of these foods in the total supply of a number of countries afforded clear evidence of dangerous nutritional unbalances.

Progress Toward Recovery

Recovery from the dislocations and devastations of the war was uneven. Five years after the war, the average food supply per person remained lower than before the war, and, due to increases of population in the areas where food problems were most serious, the percentage of people depending on inadequate food supplies had grown much larger. There were still no signs of the far-reaching changes in the entire scale of food production which must take place before there can be any general improvement in nutrition.

In Western Europe, recovery went forward faster than after the First World War. A partial restoration of agriculture in the first few postwar years, plus heavy food imports from the Western Hemisphere, brought average food intakes close to prewar levels in most countries. In Central, South and Eastern Europe, however, improvement was much slower. Even the consumption of cereals stayed under prewar levels in a number of countries, and livestock products remained scarce. The situation was much the same in many countries of the Near East.

In the Far East, progress was even less rapid. For a long period there was not enough rice, which normally provides most of the food supply of some countries in the region. Consumption of milk, meat, and eggs, already very low before the war, declined further. Only in the case of starchy roots was there an appreciable increase in production, but this development reflected the difficulties of the situation more often than a real agricultural advance.

Postwar shortages of food and other raw materials stimulated programs for the development of African territories, but nevertheless the production of staple foods like maize and root crops languished. Climatic difficulties resulted in frequent crop failures and acute shortage. In some territories a few years after the war, supplies were as much as 20 per cent below the estimated requirements.

Ten Years After War

The urgent need to produce more food after the war led to the establishment in many countries of plans and programs of agricultural development and to a large measure of international cooperation, notably through the Food and Agriculture Organization (FAO). Both literally and figuratively, the various efforts bore fruit: by 1954 per capita food production for the world as a whole had risen by about 30 per cent and was slightly above prewar levels. This world average, however, does not reflect the real situation of particular regions, some of which continued to suffer from severe shortages. Nevertheless, the advance provides a striking illustration of what can be accomplished when people and their governments work together to apply the remedies of modern science and technology to the world's old ills.

With the rise in production, the quality of diets showed a marked improvement in some regions. In Western Europe, for example, one of the most important developments during the past two or three years has been the increasing consumption of meat and other livestock products, which are valuable sources of protein. An illustration of the trend is provided by France. Statistically speaking, the average Frenchman in 1954 ate 17 kilograms more meat, and 50 kilograms more milk and dairy products, than he did in 1948. In the same period, the consumption of cereals and starchy roots gradually declined in Western Europe, as other foods became more abundant. In 1954, for instance, average per capita consumption of starchy roots in the Netherlands was 48 kilograms lower than in 1948, and per capita consumption of cereals was 9 kilograms lower. For the region as a whole, the average daily food intake, in quantitative terms, is near the estimated requirements and in some countries exceeds them.

Much the same can be said of North America. Consumption of cereals has fallen while consumption of meat, milk, and dairy products has increased. In the United States of America, for example, the average per capita consumption of cereals fell by 10 kilograms a year between 1948 and 1953, while in the same period consumption of milk and dairy products rose by 20 kilograms a year. Consumption of meat rose to a point well above the prewar average, and the average daily intake of protein is among the highest in the world. The quantities of food available are more than sufficient to meet the needs of the population. Indeed, the problem here has become one of surpluses rather than of shortages.

In New Zealand and Australia, food supplies in general have declined somewhat in recent years, but nevertheless remain, as before the war, ample for the needs of the population.

Average levels of food consumption in Latin America continue to be higher than before the war, but still below the estimated requirements for the greatly increased population. In some areas, because of the heavy proportion of cereals and starchy roots consumed, the quality of the diet is poor.

These are the relatively fortunate regions of the world. Malnutrition has not been eradicated from any of them (for example, protein deficiency, which affects young children in particular, is still a serious problem in some parts of Latin America, Africa, and Asia), but nevertheless they represent the brighter side of the food picture. Difficulties remain, but they seem less staggering than those of other regions of the world.

One of the regions where grave problems persist is the Far East. Here, food production per head remains below the prewar level and diets are generally deficient. It is true that consumption of cereals is approaching prewar levels, but consumption of animal foodstuffs, which have greater nutritional value, does not appear to have regained even the very low levels prevailing before the war. For example, in Ceylon the supply of meat dropped from the prewar level of eight kilograms a year per person to three kilograms in 1949-50, and in Indo-China supplies of meat and milk fell by more than 50 per cent. In the region as a whole in 1953-54, the average intake of protein from both animal and vegetable sources was less than 50 grams daily, or about half that during the same period in the United States of America and Oceania. It should perhaps be explained that such data, while useful as indicators of gross shortages and deficiencies, do not show differences in distribution within a population but only reflect inadequacies which would exist even if available supplies were distributed equitably among the population. As distribution is rarely equitable, it is safe to say that great numbers of people in the Far East had much less of such nourishing foods as meat and milk than the statistical averages would indicate. To bring the nutritional levels up to a point where even a barely adequate diet is possible for the growing populations of Far Eastern countries will be an enormous long-range task.

Little exact information is available on the food consumption of native populations in most of Africa, but it can be assumed that the situation is roughly similar to that in the Far East. It is known, for example, that protein malnutrition is widespread. In quantitative terms the average food intake, insofar as it is known, is generally below the estimated requirements (except in the Union of South Africa).

As in the case of Africa, statistics relating to food supplies and consumption are not readily available for many countries of the Near East. Such data as are available indicate that the situation has improved since the war, but that the average diet in many areas is far from being adequate for good nutrition.

World Problem: World Task

The foregoing details will perhaps serve to indicate, at least in broad terms, the food situation in different regions. In sum, millions upon millions of men, women and children cannot obtain enough good food to nourish themselves adequately. With all that it means in terms of human suffering, this is one of the most important facts of life in the world today.

The question is: What can be done?

It will be no simple task to procure even a partial solution of the problem, but a long and difficult process involving changes in the habits of vast numbers of people and in the way the world works.

The measures necessary to solve the problem of food cannot be carried out successfully by any one country or small group of countries: they can be accomplished only by the combined efforts of many nations. The efforts of each country must be supplemented by the knowledge, experience, and assistance of others. By its very nature, the problem of food is both national and international and action to solve it must also be both national and international. For hunger and malnutrition are no respecters of frontiers. They are to be found in every country of the world.

Geography

7 · GEOGRAPHY AND FOREIGN POLICY *

Nicholas J. Spykman

"La politique de toutes les puissances est dans leur géographie," conceded the man whose famous retort, "Circonstances? Moi, je fais les circonstances," indicates his contempt for any agency but the human will as the arbiter of human destiny. But since the Red Sea parted for Moses and the sun obligingly paused for Joshua, the human will has been unable to recapture the control over topography and climate exhibited by those forceful gentlemen, and it is probably safe to say that it was by Russian geography rather than by men that the diminutive Corsican was finally defeated. If he is still living, there is at Waterloo even today a loyal guide who asserts with unshakable conviction that neither genius nor skill but a swampy ditch gave that victory to Wellington.

Unfortunately for the political scientist with a fondness for simplification, but fortunately for the statesman striving to overcome the geographic handicaps of his country, neither does the entire foreign policy of a country lie in geography, nor does any part of that policy lie entirely in geography. The factors that condition the policy of states are many; they are permanent and temporary, obvious and hidden; they include, apart from the geographic factor, population density, the economic structure of the country, the ethnic composition of the people, the form of government, and the complexes and pet prejudices of foreign ministers; and it is their simultaneous action and interaction that create the complex phenomenon known as "foreign policy."

* Nicholas J. Spykman, "Geography and Foreign Policy, I," *The American Political Science Review*, XXXII (February, 1938), 28-41, 43-44, 46-50. Reprinted by permission of The American Political Science Association. The footnotes in the original version are omitted here.

It is the task of the social scientist to try to find in the enormous mass of historical material correlations between conditioning factors and types of foreign policy. This means that the study of diplomatic history must be supplemented by a search for the behavior patterns of states under different stimuli and in various international environments. Scientific method requires that the search operate by means of abstraction, and common sense warns that correlations found by means of such abstraction can by themselves be only partial, not complete, explanations of concrete historical situations.

Of the various factors that condition the foreign policy of states, there is no question that Napoleon indicated the most significant. War was an instrument of national policy in his time and still is today, and, in a world where groups struggle for power by means of war, policy becomes high strategy.

In such a world, the geographic area of the state is the territorial base from which it operates in time of war and the strategic position which it occupies during the temporary armistice called peace. It is the most fundamentally conditioning factor in the formulation of national policy because it is the most permanent. Ministers come and ministers go, even dictators die, but mountain ranges stand unperturbed. . . .

Because the geographic characteristics of states are relatively unchanging and unchangeable, the geographic demands of those states will remain the same for centuries, and because the world has not yet reached that happy state where the wants of no man conflict with those of another, those demands will cause friction. Thus at the door of geography may be laid the blame for many of the age-long struggles which run persistently through history while governments and dynasties rise and fall.

* * * * *

It should be emphasized, however, that geography has been described as a conditioning rather than as a determining factor. The word was chosen advisedly. It was not meant to imply that geographic characteristics play a deterministic, causal role in foreign policy. The geographical determinism which explains by geography all things from the fourth symphony to the fourth dimension paints as distorted a picture as does an explanation of policy with no reference to geography. The geography of a country is rather the material for, than the cause of, its policy, and to admit that the garment must ultimately be cut to fit the cloth is not to say that the cloth determines either the garment's style or its adequacy. But the geography of a state cannot be ignored by the men who formulate its policy. The nature of the territorial base has influenced them in that formulation in the past and will continue to do so in the future.

The nature of this base exerts a manifold influence on foreign policy. Size affects the relative strength of a state in the struggle for power. Natural resources influence population density and economic structure, which in themselves are factors in the formulation of policy. Location with reference to the equator and to oceans and land masses determines nearness to centers of power, areas of conflict, and established routes of communication, and location with reference to immediate neighbors defines position in regard to potential enemies, thereby determining the basic problems of territorial security.

The significance of size and location as factors in foreign policy cannot be evaluated, however, without a consideration of the modifying effects of topography and climate. Topography affects strength because of its influence on unity and internal coherence. Climate, affecting transportation and setting limits to the possibility of agricultural production, conditions the economic structure of the state, and thus, indirectly but unmistakably, foreign policy.

THE FACTOR OF SIZE

The comparative size of states, provided there is an effective political and economic integration of the area, is a rough indication of comparative strength and, as such, an element in foreign policy. Although in its abstract form as total surface area it does not give rise to specific objectives and gives no content to foreign policy, yet it is an indication of the power to resist pressure from other states and may affect the choice between war and diplomacy as instruments of national policy.

Throughout history, and especially during its earlier periods, an overwhelming majority of the strong states have been large states. Egypt, Babylonia, Assyria, Persia, and Rome were each in their turn the largest existing organized state, and by that token, the strongest. It is true that in certain periods small states like Athens and Venice and Holland, operating as sea-powers, could for a time, by means of the control of sea-routes, extend their sway over large areas of the world, but in land struggles they usually succumbed to the larger units and in sea struggles to units with broader bases, which meant larger territory. During the modern periods, great powers have again been large powers. . . .

Size is not strength but potential strength. It is strength insofar as size is equivalent to arable land and therefore to manpower, and, reasoning from this premise, most land powers have in the past followed a policy of territorial expansion. Since the Industrial Revolution, however, strength has become more and more identified with industrial strength. Raw material resources and industrial organization have therefore become the prerequisites of power whether by land or by sea. But size is still operative in the sense that the larger the area the greater the chances that it contains varying climatic ranges and varying topography, and therefore varied resources and economic possibilities.

Size is of primary importance as an element of defense, particularly if the vital centers of a country are far removed from the border. To reach Moscow, Napoleon forced an exhausted army across a space almost as vast as his own empire, only to find himself confronted by more silent space and his base of supplies hopelessly in the rear. More than a hundred years later, the anti-Communist campaigns of the White Russians and the Allies fruitlessly battered away their strength in the Russian border territories while the Communists, unperturbed, organized the vital centers of the country. A human foe exhibits the weaknesses and strengths common to the human race, and against him man can pit his skill and determination. Space simply is, and defeats by virtue of being. It can fulfill its defense function, however, only when the vital centers of a country are located away from the frontier. In a war between the United States and Canada, the vast reaches of Canada would afford far less protection than do the smaller stretches of United States territory, for the industrial and population centers of the former are concentrated on her southeastern border within easy reach of an invader, while those of the United States lie well behind the frontier.

• • • • •

The size of a state at any given time cannot be accounted for in terms of any one conditioning factor. It depends on technical, social, moral, and ideological development, on the dynamic forces within a state, on the political constellation of the past, and on the personality of individuals. But it has undeniably been conditioned by topographical facts. The effect of topography on size is admittedly less since man has learned to tunnel through mountains and throw bridges across great chasms, but until technological conquest is considerably more complete, topography cannot be disregarded.

. . . . .

The factors of topography which create barriers to expansion will, should these barriers be overcome, continue to operate as obstacles to effective defense and successful integration of the new territory with the old domain. . . . At this point must be mentioned the problem of effective control quite apart from the danger of aggression, because only with effective centralized control does large size become an element of strength rather than of weakness. Such control depends primarily on two factors: on the existence of an effective system of communication from the center to the periphery, and on the absence or the successful counterbalancing of centrifugal forces of separatism. On the establishment of a communication system, which is in turn one of the most effective means of counteracting separatist tendencies, the shape and topography of a state have a direct influence.

Obviously, the ideal territorial shape for a state is that of a perfect circle. Given such a configuration, the greatest possible area is enclosed within the shortest possible boundary, facilitating defense, and all parts of the area are equidistant from, and as near as possible to, a government located at the center of the circle. States that are long and narrow in shape—and this is particularly true for land powers—tend inevitably to disintegrate either by losing territory at the periphery where the centralizing influence of the government is least felt, or by splitting to reappear as separate states. Examples of the former tendency are to be found in the Ottoman Empire, which had lost effective control of all northern Africa and most of the Balkans before those areas were taken by other powers, and in the Arabian, Mongol, and Macedonian empires which preceded it.

A factor even more significant than shape in the establishment of centralized control over a given area is topography. On the height and configuration of mountain ranges, the depth and width of valleys, the direction of rivers, and the modifying effect of climate on all these features, will depend the ease of communication within a country. Where mountains like the Andes or the Scandinavian or Swiss ranges bar the way or cut the country into disconnected sections as in the Balkan peninsula, communication will be slow to be established and will remain expensive and infrequent; where marshes or deserts divide two parts of a country, road building will be difficult; and where river systems run parallel instead of converging, they offer no convenient means of communication to a centrally located government and tend to separate rather than to unite. Over those sections of the country with which it has but infrequent communication a government will have but slight control. Mountain distribution, the chief cause of the present ethnic distribution, has exercised on Switzerland a definitely decentralizing effect which is intensified by the river system. What is significant about this river system as a disunifying influence is not its direction, however, but the fact that all the rivers flow from the periphery outward, creating no network of communication within the country and tending to connect the peripheral sections more closely with foreign countries than with the central part of the homeland. For various political reasons this has not, in the case of Switzerland, resulted in actual political disunity. It has, however, been the cause of the cultural, linguistic, and economic decentralization that is such an outstanding characteristic of the Republic. . . .

Rivers can be, and often have been, however, the chief unifying influence, especially in early political organizations. The first states were without exception river states, centered around the Tigris and Euphrates and the Nile, and the French colonial empire in North America was established along the St. Lawrence and Mississippi valleys. . . .

From the beginning, governments have strengthened their control over territory by supplementing the natural means of communication and attempting to overcome the barriers posed by topography. The Incas unified their empire by roads, the Persians constructed a central highway from Sardes to Susa which interestingly followed practically the same route as the projected Berlin-to-Bagdad railroad about two thousand years later; the Chinese, the French, and the Russians supplemented their great rivers by a honeycomb of canals; and Rome retained contact with her distant empire by roads so well constructed that some of them exist today. Charlemagne built roads, and every forward step of the French kingdom toward centralization coincides with a step toward the perfection of communication within the country. In the period of reorganization after the Hundred Years' War, Louis XI established the first postal service; and at the beginning of the rapid national development that followed the religious wars, Sully planned his first great highway system.

It was the railroad, however, that made possible effective integration over wider areas. Before its development, few states located in conflict areas were able to maintain control over territories lying more than three hundred miles from the center of government. For this reason, large states have availed themselves of this instrument and have built lines for strategic and political reasons long before the economic significance of the outlying areas justified such construction. The railroads of France, Germany, and Russia radiate from Paris, Berlin, and Moscow. In the same way, the large continental powers have confirmed their unity by the development of their railroad systems. Transcontinental lines stretch across the United States, Canada, and Australia, and the Trans-Siberian and the Turk-Sib lines have brought Asiatic Russia within reach of the central government.

· · · · ·

Closely following the development of the railroads and interior waterways have come the airways which now cover every continent and which . . . are the most perfect means of retaining constant contact between a central government and distant parts of the country. In this connection, the efficacy of radio as a means of cultural and ideological centralization should not be forgotten.

Conversely, the decline of large empires has often been accompanied by a neglect of the communication system. The European and Asiatic states of the Middle Ages used the existing means without troubling to improve or develop them, and therefore remained small in size. Where large states did exist, such as the Caliphate and the Mongol Empire, they were political units in name only, with no actual control over the peripheral sections of their territory. . . .

Although the strategic and political problem of integrating and retaining overseas territories is entirely different from that presented by distant sections of contiguous territory, it is undoubtedly true that here also distance in relation to existing forms of communication played a role in the loss of American colonies to the British and Spanish mother countries. . . .

Topography, climate, and distance thus determine the ease of communication within a country and thereby greatly lessen or enhance the probability of the development of separatism. Sections cut off by mountains or deserts, or whose location in a river valley predisposes them toward economic identification with a foreign country rather than with other sections of the homeland, tend to develop local interests and a local policy and gradually to shake off the control of the central government. Regionalism will not lead necessarily to the actual severance of political connections unless it occurs on the periphery and in combination with ethnic differences. The regionalism which during the nineteenth and early twentieth centuries caused the disintegration of the Turkish and Austrian empires and resulted in the establishment of independent states throughout central and eastern Europe found its source in the existence of ethnic units rather than of topographically isolated areas, although topography played its part in the prevention of ethnic diffusions. When regionalism takes the virulent form of nationalism, as it did in these instances, it may break even a state like Austria-Hungary, which had an element of natural geographic unity as the basin state of the Danube.

Regionalism which falls short of separatism nevertheless creates difficulties in the formulation of a unified national policy, for the interests of different regions will inevitably conflict, and national policy will then represent a compromise between these conflicts. A paradoxical characteristic of regionalism is that economic regionalism may be one of the strongest elements in the unity of a country because of the interchange of goods which it fosters and still be an element of disunity in foreign policy because of the difficulty of incorporating into the foreign commercial policy the conflicting demands of various regions for protection, markets, raw materials, and capital.

Thus it appears that regionalism is a complex phenomenon, the result of many contributing factors, of which topography and climate are not the least important. . . . At the present time, technological progress, as manifested in railroad, steamship, and airplane development, has made it possible to overcome almost all the topographical elements in regionalism, and therefore to integrate effectively an area of almost any size. It is probably safe to say, then, that it is economic regionalism that exerts the most apparent influence on foreign policy.

It appears, therefore, that great size, especially if combined with favorable climate and productive soil, is a decided element of strength, but that such strength can become effective only after centralized control has been established over the entire area by the creation of an efficient communication system. If topography and climate lend their aid in the development of communications, the evolution from large state to strong state will be rapid. If topography and climate create barriers, the state must wait until the necessary elements of capital and technological skill are at hand to overcome the natural barriers by artificial means. . . . There is little escape from the conclusion that size means potential strength, and that with the diffusion of Western technology great size plus time and a will to power will almost inevitably mean actual strength. Unless the dreams of European Confederation should materialize, it may well be that fifty years from now the quadrumvirate of world powers will be China, India, the United States, and the U.S.S.R.

THE FACTOR OF LOCATION

Important as size may be, however, it does not exclusively determine the rank of a state in the hierarchy of world powers and may be less significant than location in determining its importance in international affairs and in defining its problems of foreign policy. The location of a state may be described from the point of view of world-location, that is, with reference to the land masses and oceans of the world as a whole, or from the point of view of regional location, that is, with reference to the territory of other states and immediate surroundings. The former description will be in terms of latitude, longitude, altitude, and distance from the sea; the latter will be in terms of relations to surrounding areas, distances, lines of communication, and the nature of border territory.

A complete description of the geographic location of a state will include not only both these points of view as facts of location, but an analysis of the meaning of those facts. The facts of location do not change. The significance of such facts changes with every shift in the means of communication, in routes of communication, in the technique of war, and in the centers of world power, and the full meaning of a given location can be obtained only by considering the specific area in relation to two systems of reference: a geographic system of reference from which we derive the facts of location, and a historical system of reference by which we evaluate those facts.

The geographic location of a state expressed, then, in terms of the facts and significance of its world and regional location is the most fundamental factor in its foreign policy. It can modify the significance of size and explain the historical importance of many small states. It conditions and influences all other factors for the reason that world location defines climatic zones and thereby economic structure, and regional location defines potential enemies and thereby the problem of territorial security and potential allies, and perhaps even the limits of a state's role as a participant in a system of collective security. . . .

Since the French dug a ditch near Suez, and the French and the Americans blasted a trench near Panama, the great land masses of the world consist of two islands, Eurasia and North America, which, because of navigation problems on the North Polar Sea, function as peninsulas, and three true islands, South America, Africa, and Australia. The world location of a state becomes therefore a question of its location with reference to these land masses. The fact that the greater land masses lie in the northern hemisphere, and that the largest land masses that do exist in the southern hemisphere lie in the tropics, has certain obvious implications. Politically and industrially, the northern hemisphere will always be more important than the southern, and relations between various parts of the northern hemisphere will have more influence on the history of the world than relations between parts of the southern hemisphere or between the two hemispheres. The location of a state north or south of the equator will therefore play a large part in determining the political significance of that state, the nature of its international relations, and the problems of its foreign policy.

Location with reference to the equator will largely determine climate, and the political activity of the world is for the most part centered in the temperate zones, although where ocean currents or other modifying influences alter the normal climatic conditions, the significance of location will be modified to that extent. On the European coast, which is warmed by the Gulf Stream, states can exist as far north as the polar circle, but the mouth of the Amur and the ports of Kamchatka and Labrador are closed by ice six months of the year. In general, however, history is made between the latitudes of 25° and 60°, and, because very little of the land mass of the southern hemisphere lies between these limits, history is made between 25° and 60° north latitude.

But the significance of world location does not become clear until it is expressed not only with reference to land masses but also in relation to oceans.

. . . . .

Location is therefore defined first in terms of the great land and ocean masses. But it should be remembered that this global frame of reference is different for each state because for each state it has a different focus, namely, the capital of that state. Every Foreign Office, whatever may be the atlas it uses, operates mentally with a different map of the world. This means that a given area in the world will have for two states which lie far apart an entirely different strategic and political significance. . . . It is responsible for the almost insurmountable difficulties which arise in attempts to achieve effective political cooperation between states with very different frames of reference. . . .

The facts of location do not change. Tarquinius Superbus from his peninsular kingdom surveyed the same sea as does Mussolini from his peninsular kingdom; McKinley signed the Platt amendment and Roosevelt abrogated it, but the geographic location of Cuba with reference to the United States remains unaltered. The significance of such facts, however, does change. The frame of reference previously described to serve for evaluating world location has both a geographic and therefore fixed, and a historical and therefore changing, aspect. It should also be remembered that the significance of a given location is both a factor in the foreign policy of a specific state and the result of the past history of that same state. Position on the North Atlantic is a factor in the foreign policy of the United States, and it is the development of the United States that accounts for the present significance of the Atlantic. The latter is a problem for the historians; the former a factual *datum* for the statesman.

Slow but irrevocable in effect are the changes in the significance of location which derive from shifts in the centers of culture diffusion and military power. From the beginning of history, Western civilization has developed around large bodies of water. Hellenic civilization was circumferential to the Aegean Sea, Roman civilization encircled the Mediterranean, and the Western civilization of the present surrounds the Atlantic. Location is important, therefore, in relation to the body of water which at a given historical period contains the source area of cultural diffusion.

The general direction in which civilization has moved through the centuries has been from a subtropical latitude northward to a cool temperate zone, and from east to west.

. . . . .

While shifts in centers of civilization and power occur only slowly, shifts in routes of communication may change the significance of location in a relatively short period of time. With the discovery of the sea-route to India, the old route through the Near East, the Mediterranean, and Central Europe was superseded. This, together with the discovery of America, made the Atlantic the scene of the world's most important activity, and the Mediterranean a minor inland sea. Venice yielded her place as queen of world commerce to Spain and Portugal. At the same time, the Baltic, formerly the center of northern European commerce, became cut off from the main trade routes. Nürnberg and Augsburg, which had prospered, sank into insignificance with Lübeck and the other Hanseatic cities, and Hamburg and Bremen, and even more the Netherlands and England, moved from the periphery of world trade to its center. As ships began to sail around the southern tip of Africa, Capetown came into prominence, only to lose its commercial significance in 1869 when the opening of the Suez Canal diverted trade once more into the Mediterranean, and the Near East regained its early importance, enhanced today because it is now the funnel for the air route from Europe to Asia. A large portion of the traffic which once flowed past the ports of Brazil and Argentina now flows through the Panama Canal, with benefit to Central America and the western coast of the United States, and to the corresponding detriment of the trade of the eastern coast of South America.

The construction of railroads as well as of canals may bring about a change in the significance of location. The opening of the Trans-Siberian railroad in 1901 dealt a deathblow to Kjachta, the former center of the Chinese tea trade, for the road was unkind enough not to include Kjachta in its itinerary, while Chita, Irkutsk, and other slumbering Siberian towns found themselves by the side of the road from Petrograd to Vladivostok. And the construction of the Turk-Sib railroad from Novo Sibirsk to the Moscow-Tashkent line placed in direct communication with the Pacific coast on one side, and with Moscow and Petrograd on the other, a district that had been practically isolated for centuries. . . .

It seems almost axiomatic that a country or section should benefit from a shift in communication or trade routes which places it on or near the line of traffic. Although this is true from an economic point of view, it is not necessarily true politically. If the country through which the route runs be weak, and the route of great significance, the section in question may well become a bone of contention among the great powers of the world and may pay for its advantageous location with its independence. Egypt was not strong enough or stable enough to be trusted with the defense of the Suez Canal and was forced to submit to British occupation. The isthmian canal in the New World was too vital a route of communication between the eastern and western coasts of the United States to be left in the hands of Colombia, and the state of Panama accordingly declared its independence. . . .

Some of the changes in routes already indicated and their effect on the significance of geographic location are the result of technological development in the means of communication. It was not until the development of the steamship that men could follow the great circle routes on the sea. With the development of the airplane has come the possibility of following the great circle routes overland to a greater extent than ever before. . . .

As such new routes of communication come into existence, new parts of the earth's surface will obviously gain, and other sections will decline, in importance. The future development of air transportation will mean that many now worthless and unclaimed bits of territory will become highly desirable. . . .

But the same geographic location will acquire a new strategic and political meaning with new means of communication even if it involves no change in route, for distance is defined not in miles but in hours, and therefore in concrete terms of movement possibilities. As we have progressed from the horse and cart through the railroad, the motor car, and tractor to the airplane and airship, and on sea from the sailing vessel through the steam and motor vessel to the hydroplane and airship, distances have grown consistently less. . . .

When the Greeks, after their victory over the Persians, stipulated that no Persian army should come nearer to the coast than the distance a horse could run in twenty-four hours, they provided a large degree of security for themselves. The same stipulation would today afford little security against a Turkish air attack from well behind the line that marked the cruising radius of the fleetest Persian steed. The English Channel, reinforced by the British navy, remained a barrier behind which the British felt secure even after the development of the swiftest ships. In terms of air transportation,

London is now no more secure from attack than if it were on the Continent.

It is the application of such technological development to the weapons of war that causes the quickest variations in the strategic, and therefore political, significance of a specific area. . . .

The preceding pages have provided an analysis of the ways in which geography conditions foreign policy. The influence of size has been indicated, as modified by climate, topography, and technological development, and the significance of location has been demonstrated as modified by shifts in centers of power, changes in routes of communication, and new inventions in transportation and warfare. . . . It is already clear that, whatever aloofness the student of international law may permit himself, the student of international politics must deal with geography as a basic reality.

Natural Resources and Industrial Capacity

8 · SELECTED TABLES

COAL
Production in Thousand Metric Tons

	World [1]	United States	U.S.S.R.
1946	1,181,300	536,837	114,295
1947	1,337,200	621,368	132,249
1948	1,382,000	592,911	150,012
1949	1,286,100	433,161	169,100
1950	1,394,200	505,319	185,225
1951	1,460,400	519,857	202,464
1952	1,434,000	457,590	215,009
1953	1,428,300	440,337	224,315
1954	1,393,700	379,154	243,681
1955	1,499,700	442,410	276,638
1956	1,576,000	477,085	303,946

NOTE: The figures relate to anthracite and bituminous coal (including semi-bituminous), but exclude lignite and brown coal.
[1] Excluding mainland China.
Source: United Nations *Statistical Yearbook 1958*.

LIGNITE
Production in Thousand Metric Tons

	World	United States	U.S.S.R.
1946	273,800	2,420	49,768
1947	290,000	2,607 *	51,000
1948	316,200	2,799	58,230
1949	355,400	2,805	66,407
1950	382,900	3,057	75,864
1951	415,500	2,986	79,464
1952	437,900	2,737	85,866
1953	468,100	2,586	96,107
1954	496,400	2,579	103,428
1955	537,600	2,872	114,621
1956	567,500	2,611	125,228

NOTE: The figures cover lignite and brown coal. The table does not include the United Kingdom (63.6 and 16.3 thousand metric tons in 1947 and 1948 respectively; other years negligible) and a few minor producers.
Source: United Nations *Statistical Yearbook 1958.*

CRUDE PETROLEUM
Production in Thousand Metric Tons

	World [1]	United States	U.S.S.R.
1946	375,700	234,323	21,746
1947	414,000	250,952	26,022
1948	468,200	273,007	29,249
1949	466,400	248,919	33,444
1950	522,900	266,708	37,878
1951	593,300	303,754	42,253
1952	623,300	309,447	47,311
1953	658,800	318,535	52,777
1954	689,300	312,846	59,281
1955	772,800	335,744	70,793
1956	839,800	353,698	83,806

[1] Excluding mainland China.
Source: United Nations *Statistical Yearbook 1958.*

CEMENT
Production in Thousand Metric Tons

	World [1]	United States	U.S.S.R.
1946	70,100 [2]	28,102	—
1947	81,300 [2]	31,994	—
1948	102,000	35,210	6,455
1949	107,700 [2]	35,939	—
1950	122,100 [2]	38,724	—
1951	149,000	41,824	12,070
1952	159,000	42,394	13,910
1953	176,000	45,001	15,961
1954	189,000	46,433	18,992
1955	214,000	52,993	22,484
1956	229,000	56,152	24,858

[1] Excluding mainland China.
[2] Excluding mainland China and U.S.S.R.
Source: United Nations *Statistical Yearbook 1954.*
United Nations *Statistical Yearbook 1958.*

PIG IRON and FERRO-ALLOYS
Production in Thousand Metric Tons

	World [1]	United States	U.S.S.R. [2]
1946	78,500	42,024	9,862
1947	98,200	54,559	11,223
1948	112,500	56,166	13,742
1949	115,200	49,820	16,389
1950	132,700	60,211	19,175
1951	148,500	65,746	21,909
1952	150,600	57,507	25,071
1953	166,000	70,036	27,415
1954	156,600	54,206	29,972
1955	188,800	71,906	33,310
1956	196,300	70,461	35,754

NOTE: The table does not include Switzerland (estimated production: 1954, 35.0; 1955, 53.5; 1956, 41.0 thousand metric tons).
[1] Excluding mainland China.
[2] Excluding ferro-alloys.
Source: United Nations *Statistical Yearbook 1958.*

CRUDE STEEL
Production in Thousand Metric Tons

	World [1]	United States	U.S.S.R.
1946	111,500	60,421	13,345
1947	136,100	77,015	14,534
1948	155,300	80,413	18,639
1949	159,700	70,740	23,291
1950	188,700	87,848	27,329
1951	209,900	95,435	31,350
1952	210,100	84,520	34,492
1953	232,800	101,250	38,128
1954	221,100	80,115	41,434
1955	266,300	106,173	45,271
1956	278,200	104,522	48,698

NOTE: The table does not include Switzerland (estimated production: 1955, 166; 1956, 171; 1957, 234 thousand metric tons), nor a few very small producers.
[1] Excluding mainland China.
Source: United Nations *Statistical Yearbook 1958*.

ALUMINUM
Production in Thousand Metric Tons

	World [1]	United States (Primary)	United States (Secondary)	U.S.S.R.
1946	690	371.6	252.3	—
1947	960	518.7	312.8	—
1948	1,130	565.6	260.2	—
1949	1,140	547.5	164.0	—
1950	1,300	651.9	221.0	—
1951	1,600	759.2	265.4	—
1952	1,810	850.3	276.3	—
1953	2,180	1,135.8	334.4	—
1954	2,470	1,325.0	264.9	—
1955	2,710	1,420.4	304.8	410 (est.)
1956	2,920	1,523.1	308.2	440 (est.)

NOTE: The table does not include 1956, Australia: 9.3; Brazil: 6.3; East Germany: 30.0 and Rumania: 10.0 thousand metric tons.
[1] Excluding U.S.S.R. and mainland China. Primary production only, excluding secondary (i.e., derived from scrap aluminum).
Source: United Nations *Statistical Yearbook 1958*.

ELECTRIC ENERGY
Production in million KWH

	World [1]	United States [2]	U.S.S.R.
1946	594,000 [3]	269,361	—
1947	658,000 [3]	307,310	—
1948	797,000	336,808	66,000
1949	769,000 [3]	345,066	—
1950	858,000 [3]	388,674	90,300 (est.)
1951	1,065,300	433,358	104,022
1952	1,151,300	463,055	119,116
1953	1,257,500	514,169	134,325
1954	1,360,400	544,645	150,695
1955	1,535,600	629,010	170,225
1956	1,677,900	684,804	191,653

[1] Excluding North Korea and some small producers.
[2] Net production (i.e., excluding station use) and excluding a relatively small amount of generation by commercial establishments.
[3] Excluding U.S.S.R., China and some small producers.
Source: United Nations *Statistical Yearbook 1952.*
United Nations *Statistical Yearbook 1958.*

MOTOR VEHICLES
Production in Thousands

	WORLD		UNITED STATES [1]		U.S.S.R.	
	Passenger Cars	Commercial Vehicles	Passenger Cars	Commercial Vehicles	Passenger Cars	Commercial Vehicles [2]
1946	—	—	2,148.7	940.9	—	—
1947	—	—	3,558.2	1,239.4	—	—
1948	4,620	2,010	3,909.3	1,376.3	20.2	173.9
1949	—	—	5,119.5	1,134.2	—	—
1950	8,170	2,310	6,665.9	1,337.2	64.6	321.7
1951	6,910	2,440	5,338.4	1,426.8	53.6	229.8
1952	5,960	2,260	4,320.8	1,218.2	59.7	243.5
1953	8,120	2,270	6,116.9	1,206.3	77.4	300.5
1954	1,960	2,250	5,558.9	1,042.2	94.7	353.8
1955	10,940	2,640	7,920.2	1,249.1	107.8	399.9
1956	8,970	2,570	5,816.1	1,104.5	97.8	367.0

NOTE: *Production:* the manufacture of vehicles either wholly or mainly from domestically produced parts. Vehicles shipped in "knocked-down" form for assembly abroad are included.
Passenger cars: road motor vehicles designed for the conveyance of passengers and seating less than eight persons. Taxis are included, but three-wheeled passenger vehicles are excluded.
Commercial vehicles: light and heavy trucks (lorries), wheeled tractors for road haulage, special vehicles (ambulances, fire-fighting apparatus, etc.) and buses. Off-the-road vehicles (industrial and farm tractors) and other construction machinery are excluded, as are three-wheeled commercial vehicles.
[1] Factory sales.
[2] 1948, 1951-1952: excluding buses and wheeled tractors. 1956: excluding wheeled tractors only.
Source: United Nations *Statistical Yearbook 1955.*
United Nations *Statistical Yearbook 1958.*

9 · SOME SOCIAL IMPLICATIONS
OF NATURAL RESOURCES *

Howard A. Meyerhoff

In a country as richly endowed with natural resources as the United States, it is difficult to persuade our statesmen or our politicians—or, for that matter, the public—that raw materials have been so vital in shaping our development and history that they must be a primary consideration in the determination of domestic and foreign policies. Even historians, whose function it is to view historical factors in proper perspective, have underestimated the resource factor in their struggle against the so-called economic interpretation of history. But our civilization is predominantly industrial and from the moment the industrial revolution started, certain key resources predetermined the destinies of nations, though many other factors have modified the rate and the quality of progress which individual peoples have made. A brief analysis of the ingredients of industrialism will support this premise, which is basic in the thesis that I have undertaken to develop.

The industrial revolution started in England, and it was some time before it spread to other countries. Its beginnings in England are complex, but several factors in its development can be isolated. Basically the "discovery" of coal as a substitute for water in the generation of power and as a substitute for charcoal in the manufacture of pig iron and steel gave the industrial revolution its technological start, but no less important was the presence of commercial deposits of coal and iron ore in the Midlands of England. The political integration of the country minimized such problems as labor and taxation, while geographic compactness made domestic transportation a negligible item of cost. The incentive to industrialize was the growing and populous Empire, served by the merchant

* Howard A. Meyerhoff, "Some Social Implications of Natural Resources," *The Annals of The American Academy of Political and Social Science,* 249 (January, 1947), pp. 20-22, 24-30. Reprinted by permission of Howard A. Meyerhoff and *The Annals of The American Academy of Political and Social Science.*

marine and policed by the Navy. Here was a market that offered the lure of endless profits with comparatively little competition.

There are six ingredients in this brief analysis: raw materials, technology, labor, transportation, markets, and protection; and they are still the basic factors in the complex industrial civilization of our day. Among them, however, raw materials have been the sine qua non of industrial expansion, and no national effort to industrialize has yet been successful where it has not been adequately supported by domestic or proximate supplies of fuel and iron. The early collapse of Italy and the exhaustion of Japan in the late war are definitive commentaries on the failure of the two most ambitious attempts to offset the inadequacy of native resources. The gravitation of industrial power to the comparatively few large deposits of coking coal demonstrates that, until atomic energy has actually achieved a greater diversity of application than is now in sight, industrial and political might are moored to the world's bituminous coal reserves. A sketch of the geography of coal and industry will make this point clear.

TO HIM THAT HATH . . .

In the United States the major industrial regions lie upon, or within easy access of, the two largest deposits of high-grade bituminous coal—the Appalachian and the Eastern Interior coal fields. Except for local centers of light industry, the remainder of the country is concerned with agriculture, pastoral activities, mining, and forestry. In Great Britain the manufacturing districts are localized on and near the coal seams of the Midlands and the Scottish Lowlands. In central Europe the dominant industrial position of the Ruhr made it the main target of bombing attacks. It is the major problem of postwar Europe, for its excellent coking coals, which extend into Belgium, the Netherlands, and northeastern France, make the Ruhr inevitably the economic hub of continental Europe. Coal has converted the Silesian and Bohemian basins into secondary centers of industrial activity while, similarly, in prewar Russia the coal of the Donets Basin made the eastern Ukraine and Rostov sections of Russia the industrial heart of the U.S.S.R. One of the principal objectives of the three five-year plans was the establishment of a second industrial area in and marginal to the newly developed bituminous coals of the Kuznetsk Basin in the West Siberia Region. Smaller industrial centers nourished by smaller coal mining developments have grown up in Manchuria, coastal China, the Calcutta district of India, and New South Wales in Australia, but elsewhere heavy industry either is nonexistent or maintains a precarious economic hold on a local market or a nationalistic dream of self-sufficiency, rather than on handy energy resources.

Large hydroelectric installations have in recent years modified the industrial pattern to a minor degree. Yet even here it is evident that "to him that hath shall be given," for the most ambitious programs of water-power development have been instituted in countries already endowed with supplies of industrial coal, or in those which have ready access to nearby coal in neighboring countries. Some of the latter have attempted to balance deficiencies in coal by full utilization of hydroelectric energy, but the effect is usually to extend the margins of the highly industrialized regions which are based upon coal rather than to increase the number of these regions. In Europe, for example, Italy has fully developed its water resources, and there are large power installations in France, Switzerland, Norway, and Sweden. When plotted in relation to central European industry, these developments appear in proper perspective as peripheral extensions of the Ruhr industrial area. The same is true of Canada, which ranks second to the United States in developed water power. Most of the power has been harnessed in the Saint Lawrence Lowland and the Laurentian Upland, marginal to the Lower Great Lakes industrial area.

More fortuitously, two of the world's greatest industrial nations— the United States and the Soviet Union—are its largest producers of oil and natural gas, but with these two exceptions, nature seems to have placed oil in out-of-the-way places where there is little interest in its production and use. Under these circumstances, nationals of the industrial countries have discovered and recovered it, and nearly all of it finds its way to the industrial areas for processing and consumption. The geography of oil production may reflect the whims of nature but the geography of oil consumption is essentially the geography of industrialization. Only a few enterprising districts have succeeded in building a partial industrial economy on local oil production, but even such communities as Los Angeles and Houston have no illusions of industrial self-sufficiency.

FROM HIM THAT HATH NOT . . .

What applies to oil applies with even greater force to the earth's commercial minerals, for they too must make their way to the sources of heat and energy to be processed. In the Midlands and in Alabama, coal and iron ore are neighbors; in the Ruhr, in the Donets Basin, and in the Calcutta district these two complementary raw materials lie within reasonable distances of each other; but in the remaining industrial areas the problem of bringing the two together has taxed man's ingenuity. Lake Superior iron ore travels far down the Great Lakes to Gary or Detroit or Cleveland or Buffalo, and even overland to Pittsburgh and Youngstown. Chilean ore moves through the Panama Canal to the furnaces at Sparrows Point, Maryland, where it meets ore from Cuba and Lake Superior and sometimes from Bilbao, Spain. And in western Siberia, magnetite from the southern Urals journeys 1,200 miles overland to Novosibirsk and Stalinsk in the Kuznetsk Basin, while coal makes the return journey to keep furnaces busy at both ends of the line. Only here is the normal movement of iron ore to coal reversed, and the exception has been made solely to reduce the all but prohibitive costs of long-distance rail transportation.

Not only does iron ore move to coal, but manganese, molybdenum, nickel, chromium, vanadium, tungsten, and the rarer ferrous alloys make the same journey, commonly from remoter parts of the earth. Nonferrous metals tend to follow suit, though for more complicated reasons. The smelting of copper, lead, and zinc is relatively inexpensive, but these metals find their readiest markets in the industrial centers. Bauxite moves to fuel for calcining or dehydration, but as a rule the alumina thus produced must go still farther to cheap hydroelectric energy for the final process of reduction to metallic aluminum. Like a magnet, coal draws metallic and nonmetallic raw materials to it because it furnishes heat, power, and by-product gas, as well as many of the raw materials employed in the chemical and synthetic industries.

We are, then, confronted by the spectacle of mineral raw materials, agricultural raw materials, population, and food being drawn in increasing quantities into a dozen industrial areas which are endowed with the most basic raw material of them all—bituminous coal. We may talk about the decentralization of industry, but man can do little more than decentralize the light industries. The heavy industries can be spread within very limited geographic districts, but hardly decentralized. Herein lies one of the principal social problems of our industrial era, although there are others with more far-reaching implications. The dozen industrial areas of the world are partially competitive, and their competitive activities are beset with domestic and international questions of vital economic and sociological import. Upon the successful solution of these problems depends the economic and political security of virtually every one of the world's peoples.

* * * * *

PRODUCTION MOVES TO LOW-COST AREAS

It makes little difference whether we touch oil, rubber, copper, nitrates, radium, or food, the historical trend has been the same. Production of raw materials or of finished goods moves to low-cost producing areas. High-cost producers survive only if the low-cost producers cannot meet world demand, or if their governments "protect" them by tariff or subsidy, and the domestic consumer pays the price. Thus Americans pay two cents extra for every pound of sugar to keep domestic beet and cane sugar producers in business; four cents a pound to keep American copper miners at work; and approximately as much to enable cotton producers to raise four to six million bales of cotton more than this country normally needs. But in general, the locale of production has followed the lure of low costs: rubber moved from Brazil to the East Indies; copra forsook the West Indies for the East Indies; quinine likewise changed hemispheres, as did cacao, despite the retention of a feeble hold in Ecuador and the Caribbean countries. Radium moved from Colorado to the Belgian Congo, and it may be on its way to the Arctic Circle in Canada. Nitrate production has partially deserted Chile for widely scattered synthetic plants, and rubber may now be headed in the same direction.

Some of these movements are worth a brief analysis. In the cases of rubber, copra, quinine, and other forest and agricultural products which were successfully introduced into the Malaysian–East Indian region, three vital factors were involved: capital, management, and labor. The history of rubber affords an illuminating example. Rubber was native to the Amazon Basin, where it grew without cultivation. The British and the Dutch transplanted it to Ceylon, Malaya, and Sumatra, but it was some time before the managerial genius of the Dutch evolved the plantation system of cultivation. Then followed the development of large plantations, kept scrupulously clean by cheap and abundant native labor. Brazilian producers, harassed by a scarcity of labor, could not emulate the Dutch system, nor could they match in quality the rubber which the Dutch and the British placed on the market. The demise of the industry in Brazil was rapid and so complete that the combined efforts of the United States, Brazilian, and Peruvian Governments and a corps of experts, backed by unlimited capital, were unable to revive it, even under the grim requirements of war.

LABOR

The moral of the story is clear. In the case of rubber and of other products requiring laborious cultivation and other manual operations, low-cost production depends upon labor when other factors are equal. Recognition of this fact was basic in Dutch colonial policy, and it was evidently the cornerstone of German military and administrative policy in the "New Order" of Europe and of Japanese policy in the "New Order" of the Far East. In a less spectacular way, it was the cheap and abundant labor available in the South that led so many textile manufacturers to abandon mills in New England and set up operations in the Carolinas, Tennessee, and Alabama. The same factor took the needle industry out of New York and into Puerto Rico, and when the wage-and-hour law equalized labor costs in Puerto Rico, the industry moved as far afield as China, Italy, and Czechoslovakia.

Labor is a primary resource to those who need it, but it has not yet achieved comparable importance to those who have it. Germany and Japan had a momentary vision of its importance en masse but no comprehension of the prerequisites to its successful exploitation. Mussolini, with one of the most crowded countries in Europe, was so obsessed by the stupid illusion of Italian self-sufficiency that the military significance of forty-five million Italians meant more to him than their economic and political value.

If the British have learned officially that manpower is an economic asset, they have scrupulously refrained from revealing the knowledge, although the industrialists of Britain have long exploited British labor. Conditions in the coal mining districts of England and Wales were publicized during the depression years, but somewhat less has been said about working conditions aboard ships of the much vaunted British merchant marine. Any disinterested study of the industrial situation will reveal that the British have been maintaining a favorable competitive position for British goods in world markets primarily at the expense of labor. Domestically, Labor governments have effected social reforms, but chiefly to counteract or partially offset the abuses and inadequacies of the British industrial system—if it can be called a system. Abroad in the Empire no policy can be discerned, but here too there has been local exploitation of labor by industrial interests. The mines of Africa are not a worker's paradise and plantation conditions in many of the colonies leave much to be desired, but in general the natives in the colonies are left to their own devices and to the vicissitudes of local conditions.

Only the Dutch have evolved a well-ordered administration of native labor in the colonies, but its admirable order and efficiency have not endeared the system or its administrators to the native population. . . .

In review, labor appears to be an unreliable factor if one is seeking low costs. The textile manufacturers who moved South found it impossible to hold wages at low levels, although it is true that wage differentials between North and South are still marked and are so well established that a rather idealistic National War Labor Board gave them formal recognition and sanction. But it is evident that the densely populated nations of the earth, like Italy, Germany, Belgium, the Ukraine, England, India, Java, China, and Japan, have a labor potential which will exert a critical influence on costs and world economy. Whether these labor pools be utilized for the production and processing of raw materials—mineral or agricultural—or for the use of the raw materials in manufacturing, the law of migration of work will inexorably operate. Any operation requiring a large amount of manual labor will migrate to these populous regions, and to those which also possess industrial fuel will go the raw materials that nourish, or draw nourishment from, coal and the heavy industry founded on coal.

* * * * *

TECHNOLOGY

Labor, however, is not the only factor involved in costs, and to some extent high labor costs can be counter-balanced by technological ingenuity and invention. At times inventive ingenuity has been charged with the high crime of creating technological unemployment, and the charge may soon be heard again as war-inspired devices, designed to save manpower, increase production with fewer employees. But over the years technology has revolutionized industry, and it is likely to repeat the performance. It has certainly revolutionized the sources of raw materials.

In the field of mineral raw materials, geographic exploration has turned up many a new deposit of ore, but not a few of them have remained unused for years, and even for decades, until technological discoveries enabled man to exploit them. The development of techniques whereby the low-grade copper ores became available to commercial processes of recovery; the application of electrolysis to the reduction of alumina to metallic aluminum; the design of more efficient equipment, like the boats and the loading and unloading facilities that handle Lake Superior iron ore; the uncanny selectivity of flotation in the concentration of ores of metals and even non-metals —these and many other equally familiar developments have transformed the mining industry and have freed us from dependence upon a comparatively small number of high-grade mineral deposits and a limited number of metals. Even so, mining, milling, and metallurgical progress has barely kept pace with an insatiable industrial demand that has called for larger quantities of a greater variety of metals during the past generation than the human race consumed in all preceding history.

Indeed, technology has been called upon, not alone to devise production facilities, but to "invent" raw materials. Currently the processing of wood bids fair to transform the industries based on forest products. Within a comparatively few years plastics have been produced more rapidly than names have been found to designate the many varieties. As if by magic, despite the cumbersome equipment employed, the air is made to yield nitrogen for nitrates, and coal is changed more readily to nylon than nylon is to a pair of precious stockings.

As applied to natural resources, technology has so altered the geography of raw materials as to precipitate social revolutions in many parts of the earth. We think of the profound effect of the discovery of gold at Sutter's Mill in opening up California and ultimately, with the construction of the first transcontinental railway, in binding the far-flung corners of this country into a closely knit national unit. But do we realize what the development of oil in the steamy Maracaibo Basin has done to and for Venezuela? or what the exploitation of oil may do in Saudi Arabia?

Not all the consequences of new developments are beneficent. For many years the nitrates of the Atacama Desert made Chile the most solvent of South American countries. Then, in 1913, Germany perfected the nitrogen-fixation process, freeing itself from dependence on Chilean nitrates as it waged World War I. The nitrate supply was a sore trial to all other contestants, all of which set out to develop their own nitrogen-fixation facilities as soon as the war was over. Copper saved Chilean economy for a time, but African copper and depression ended that, and the country has had hard times ever since. As a current example, following the bitter experience of highly localized and monopolistic production of rubber, the United States may develop synthetic rubber to the point of impairing the economy of the East Indies.

Technology brings changes that are both profound and kaleidoscopic. It transplants civilization to the wilderness and to the desert; it makes and breaks economies in regions and in nations with limited resources; it creates problems of obsolescence which wreck investments; it brings necessities and luxuries within reach of more people. It is an undiscriminating social force which, thanks to the atomic bomb, our politicians and statesmen are confusedly trying to direct and to control.

But we are dealing with technology as a factor in costs, and it must be evident that, like abundant labor, it causes the migration of industrial demand to the cheapest source of raw material. In following technological applications, industrial demand has migrated widely over the face of the earth, and its peregrinations should hold one important lesson: supplies of raw materials have no political or national affiliations—they are international. Freedom of access is vital, at least to the industrial nations. Freedom to supply native resources is equally vital to any non-industrial nation or colony, for the time to dispose of native resources, particularly in the mineral category, is at the figurative moment when industrial demand and technological developments give them their greatest cash value and their maximum utility value. The notion of conserving irreplaceable raw materials for some hypothetical future use is pointless in a world whose needs are changing rapidly, and particularly is this true in countries which lack the energy resources to process their own mineral resources.

Technology is thus leading industrial demand over the face of the earth, shopping for industrial raw materials in those places where, at each given stage of technological progress, they may be acquired most economically. Each major industrial region may seek the same raw material from the same region, just as the Midlands and the Ruhr sought high-grade iron ore from the Kiruna district of northern Sweden in the days before the war. No nation can supply all its needs at home, and in the competition for raw materials abroad the successful competitor will be the one that offers in trade the best-priced products, rather than the best price for local products. Again the need to stay in competition with the rest of the world is self-evident.

LAND

Although industry uses many irreplaceable raw materials, replaceable products are playing an ever-increasing role, not alone in feeding the human race, but also in providing it with industrial employment. Technology has greatly changed land use in such a variety of ways as to defy listing. Modern transportation has opened up remote regions and has led to specialization and regionalization of land use that was unthinkable one hundred years ago. Refrigeration has transformed the *tierra caliente* of Caribbean countries into banana plantations and, in combination with irrigation, has converted a desert such as the Imperial Valley into truck gardens. Mechanization has greatly enlarged the economic land unit for many crops and has encouraged —and has itself been encouraged by—migration of population from farm to city. Laboratory techniques have developed new uses for old products, new products from old crops, and new products from new crops. Experiment has evolved hardier or more prolific plants and animals, and chemistry coaxes higher yields from every acre, until the dismal predictions of Malthus seem remote in a far more populous world than the one in which he lived, though their theoretical validity may still be sound.

Through all the changes which have occurred, a clearly defined order can be discerned. The geography of forests, crops, and animals has steadily become a function of climate, which in turn is a function of latitude, precipitation, topography, and elevation. The result, though logical, borders on the phenomenal, for regions in different hemispheres have developed startlingly similar characteristics, and even their peoples show tendencies to evolve comparable habits and outlooks. The wheatlands of the Argentine are scarcely distinguishable from those of Canada; and the members of Roy Chapman Andrews' Third Asiatic Expedition so reacted to the wheat-raising country beyond the wall in north China that they named their first camp "North Dakota." The Gaucho of the Pampa has been likened to the cowboy of the Great Plains, and the sheep rancher of South Africa or Australia has much in common with the sheep rancher of Wyoming or Texas.

LAND CULTIVATION

There is a temptation for the geographer and the historian to conclude that these striking similarities in land use reflect the normal transition of any "new" country from the pioneer to the mature stage of development. The agricultural history of the central United States, which finds recent parallels in Canada, Argentina, and Australia, appears to support this view. In accordance with this interpretation, only countries in which land is cheap and population scant can afford to use land for extensive agriculture. As population increases there is—it is claimed—an irreversible trend toward intensive agriculture.

The interpretation cannot be convincingly supported. China, India, and central and eastern Europe, with their dense agricultural populations, evolved agriculturally before modern techniques were evolved. Only in the Ukraine has a serious effort been made to modernize the agricultural pursuits of the farming population, and much as one may question the arbitrary methods employed by the Soviet Government in "collectivizing" the farms, it must be concluded that mechanization, coupled with drastic reduction in the rural population, has definitely resulted in more effective use of land and of manpower. Perhaps no other government has the "nerve" and the power to take similar steps, but comparable results could be achieved in the Danubian Basin, and perhaps in Poland.

. . . . . .

A critical appraisal of the agricultural situation throughout the world leads inevitably to a revision of the dubious dictum that in a country with a growing population the land will be used more and more intensively. The fact is, land seeks the most economical use, and this means the highest yield of the most valuable crop with the minimum expenditure of manpower.

. . . . .

Plainly the renewable raw materials—food, agricultural raw materials, and animal and forest products—obey the same economic law that governs all other natural resources: production moves to regions of low cost. Production can be maintained elsewhere only by subsidy or tariff, or the inability of low-cost producers to meet the full demand. Insofar as domestic food supplies are concerned, proximity to market will ordinarily equalize costs with more distant competitors; but with foods for foreign markets and agricultural raw materials for industry, competition makes the cost factor paramount. . . .

SOCIAL SIGNIFICANCE OF ECONOMIC TRENDS

Our industrial civilization is founded on six major and seven or eight minor deposits of industrial coal. Two of the major deposits are in the United States, two are in the U.S.S.R., one is in Great Britain, and one is in the Ruhr and its environs. The minor deposits are domestically or regionally important chiefly to the nations which have them. The belated development of the Kuznetsk coal field of western Siberia and the belated modernization of the Donets mines, not to mention internal problems, have thus far kept the U.S.S.R. concerned primarily with domestic demand, but Soviet coal reserves are ample for the country to enter into international competition.

As of 1946-47, however, the United States, Great Britain, Germany, and Belgium have an energy potential in excess of domestic requirements, and at the moment this nation and Great Britain have industrial production facilities in excess of any conceivable domestic demand. These resources alone make them inevitable competitors for foreign raw materials and for foreign markets. Until war terminated all normal international trade, Germany was also in the competition and could have been a more formidable rival had she not been so preoccupied with rearmament. Given a chance to achieve complete industrial recovery, Germany and her neighbors will feature once more in international trade.

War has seriously depleted our mineral resources: our supply of high-grade iron ore is perilously low; we are no longer self-sufficient in bauxite; copper production can be maintained only if protected by a tariff totaling 50 per cent of foreign mining and refining costs; we never have had sufficient stocks of the ferrous alloys, tin, antimony and other lesser minerals; the adequacy of our oil production is in doubt. More and more we must enter the open market for raw materials, and our chief competitor and all our prospective competitors are nations that have never practiced freedom of access to raw materials.

. . . . .

10 · THE STRUGGLE FOR A HIGHER STANDARD OF LIVING *

Willem Brand

The problem of the development of the economically retarded areas is one of the most important questions which confronts the world today. Recognition of its central importance is evident in the continually growing stream of literature. It is perhaps even more evident in the emotional overtones that mark the reactions of representatives of underdeveloped countries whenever the problem is discussed. There is no gainsaying the reality of the desire of the peoples of underdeveloped countries for a more ample supply of material goods and services, a desire aroused by their better acquaintance with the mode of living in western Europe and the United States; but this is only one aspect of the problem. The leaders of these countries are also conscious of the fact that economic backwardness often signifies political weakness. Therefore, their striving for economic betterment is also motivated by their wish to meet the industrial countries on an equal footing. A growing awareness of their social and political backwardness also strengthens the desire for economic growth felt by the majority of the population.

. . . . .

Only in a few countries does it seem possible to expand the amount of arable land without a capital outlay far beyond domestic resources. By contrast, the presently advanced countries had only small populations when they embarked on their industrialization. England and Wales, in 1770, had a population of not much more than 7 million, the Netherlands in 1829 had 2.9 million, and the United States in 1840 less than 20 million. Thus, these countries would seem to have possessed an important potential for extending cultivated land to meet

* Willem Brand, *The Struggle for a Higher Standard of Living* (Glencoe, Illinois: The Free Press, 1958), pp. 331, 333-339, 341-342. Reprinted by permission of The Free Press. The footnotes in the original version are omitted here.

the more varied food needs of their growing populations, though the factor of population density, especially in the case of the first mentioned countries, cannot be considered apart from the ensuing industrialization and the trade pattern which developed. With regard to the increase of agricultural production on the area cultivated, the static institutional structure of the peasantry makes the rapid introduction of better techniques in backward countries a difficult task. Also, as far as other natural resources are concerned, many underdeveloped countries seem to be unfavorably placed, though knowledge on this point is naturally deficient.

Capital formation is hampered by the general poverty and the small size of the domestic market. These conditions do not attract resources into activities directed to the provision of local manufactures. Increase in population does not itself augment investment. Indeed, a certain amount of capital is usually absorbed in financing the increase. As a result of the high percentage of income spent on food, and the high income-elasticity of the demand for food, population growth tends to result in the consumption of surpluses if they arise.

· · · · ·

The occupational structures of many less developed countries also mirror the stationary character of their economies. Despite the industrial development which has taken place, and is in progress in such countries, the vast majority of the people remain bound to a meager subsistence type of living. In many cases, the percentage of workers in primary activities has been maintained at a high level over a long period, partly because of the higher birth rate in the rural areas compared with the urban centers. Low mobility of the rural worker (and the scant attraction seemingly exerted by higher remuneration in the cities) is probably more a result than a cause of this static situation.

The possibility of alternative employment is closely bound up with the "high food drain" which characterizes the economic structure. The transfer of labor from agriculture to industry, commerce and services, so characteristic of a progressive economy, reflects the fact that, given rising incomes, the demand for food products tends to approach a point of saturation. This tendency is not found in the backward countries because, at their poor level of living, the demand for food remains predominant. Moreover, the safety valve of international migration, which the industrialized European countries possessed when they entered their phase of rapid population growth, is available to very few underdeveloped countries.

The aspiration to higher living standards, particularly marked among the urban populations of many underdeveloped countries, forms another obstacle to capital formation. This is most evident among the well-to-do classes who imitate Western consumption patterns and consume the part of their income that might be applied to additional investment.

Since international trade in processed goods, which might widen the market and provide the advantage of increasing returns from "economies of scale," involves competition with the more efficient concerns of industrial countries, it offers little prospect of early success to most underdeveloped countries. Increased production of agricultural and mineral exports, stimulated by the ever-increasing need of the industrial countries for raw materials, continues to be one of the most important means of promoting economic growth. But this keeps the underdeveloped countries in a position which they consider inferior—"hewers of wood" and "drawers of water"—to that of their more fortunate neighbors.

Trying to break through this vicious circle, by raising tariff walls in order to stimulate the development of new industry, leads in the first instance to an increased burden upon local consumers. The technological and, even more, the organizational backwardness of the industrial sector results in such enterprises having, at least initially, high costs of production, by comparison with similar factories in industrialized countries. The argument that such protection is necessary in order to stimulate industrial entrepreneurship and train the required labor, has a certain validity. Protective tariffs, however, are not likely to give rise to progressive industrialization in undeveloped countries unless purchasing power in the internal market expands to the extent necessary for the development of the new activities on an economic basis. In practice, the result of high tariffs has often been the perpetuation of an inefficient industrial sector.

This brings us to the role of the state. In many industrial countries the government has taken an active role in constructing transport systems, establishing essential enterprises, creating conditions to attract immigrants, or facilitating the training of nationals abroad, and in general in helping to create an appropriate climate and environment for building up industrial leadership. Many underdeveloped countries are handicapped by the lack of a dynamic administrative class on which such a transformation greatly depends. Government machinery is often dominated by groups with a pre-industrial outlook and more or less feudalistic social traditions, who are afraid of the weakening of their own position which might result from changes in the economic system.

The struggle between the values of an industrial culture and those of a feudal one—which was, in Europe, settled to a large degree before the industrial revolution—is still at its height in some of the economically backward countries. It also helps to explain the political instability in those countries. Nevertheless, because of the absence of an indigenous managerial class and the paucity and inertia of local private investors, it is the state which has to lead the struggle for higher standards of living. Despite its weakness, the government is required to promote industrialization. Protective duties, cheap credits, tax exemptions, and a whole gamut of other measures to encourage private individuals to establish certain industries, as well as the erection of public service enterprises, can be used to create a dynamic economy. In many instances, however, the most important task of the state remains the creation of a new value system in which incentives and opportunities are given to those who, through technological and organizational knowledge, can contribute to a more dynamic economic structure. Since many of the sources of change have to come first from abroad, such stimulation depends, to a large extent, upon the willingness and ability of the local population to absorb innovations and learn from outsiders.

Granted that such pre-conditions for economic growth are accepted, it still seems likely that, because of their capital, enterprise, and skilled manpower, the advanced countries will continue to have a greater capacity for development than the backward countries. Thus, even if the latter make progress in their industrialization efforts, the disparity in scales of living is not likely soon to diminish. . . .

The industrial nations, partly because of a growing sense of social justice, seem genuinely to want to share in the responsibility for bringing poorer countries up to a higher level. They are confronted, however, with a heavy, and in many cases, thankless task. Extreme nationalism in many underdeveloped countries, aggravated in some cases by consciousness of economic backwardness, makes it improbable that private foreign capital, which is primarily motivated by the pursuit of gain, can adequately assist in this function. Though nowadays, most foreign capitalists are aware of their social responsibility toward the countries in which they invest, the limited purchasing power of the local market tends to direct their resources into activities geared to demand on the world market.

．．．．．

Because so much of the investment required to stimulate the growth process is not attractive to foreign private capital and will have to be initiated by governments, a more important role is reserved in our opinion for foreign public capital, under which we may also include foreign technical assistance. Recent experience indicates that most underdeveloped countries prefer such aid to be administered in an international framework, for they themselves wish to determine the purposes for which foreign capital and foreign technicians are required. On the other hand, it is necessary to the success of any economic development program that the growth investment should "stick," and become self-generating. Therefore, a certain degree of supervision is needed to make certain that the political and social obstacles which hamper development are removed or at least reduced.

．．．．．

A prominent factor in the development problem in its present world setting is the influence of the Soviet Union and other centrally planned countries whose recent growth is claimed by many to reveal the most efficient solution of the problem of developing backward countries. The results which the U.S.S.R. and some of the other countries have achieved in the industrial field prove that social reorganization can indeed increase the rate of capital formation and speed up the process of economic growth. That such a transformation demands major sacrifices and the use of drastic measures to smother ancient traditions which handicap economic development is usually granted, but the fact that the peasant class has generally been victimized in order to procure a food surplus to maintain increased numbers of industrial workers often goes unrecognized.

Nevertheless, to start with a clean slate—to do away with the conspicuous consumption and out-of-date customs and relationships of the feudal leadership that impede economic growth—has a strong appeal among certain groups in the underdeveloped countries where democratic influences have only begun to take root. Improvement of the scale of living, it is true, may perhaps have to be deferred to some distant future, but expansion of those sectors of production which represent economic might, such as iron, steel, and similar industries, seems to promise them the satisfaction of challenging the supremacy of the industrial countries.

It is perhaps no coincidence that only the western European countries, and those countries which can be considered offshoots of their civilization, have been industrialized democratically. Japan and the Soviet Union, by contrast, chose a dictatorial form of government at the start of their industrialization. It is probable that democracy as known in the West is, in part, the fruit of a higher living standard. But if this is so, it implies that, in order to help sustain democratic forms of organization, everything should be done to raise the level of living of the poorer nations. Foreign help is, in a sense, an alternative to ruthless planning and austerity, making possible gradual removal of the political and social obstacles hampering economic growth, while maintaining humanitarian values and individual freedom. That much more than financial aid is needed is obvious.

It is also necessary for the industrial countries to continuously adapt their economic structures to give the underdeveloped countries a chance to continue their economic expansion once it has started. Certain countries may require the opportunity to export manufactured goods in order to develop industrially in view of their unfavorable population-resource ratio. This would require an improvement in the skill of their workers and the efficiency of the industrial sectors. Even if this readiness on the part of the industrial countries does exist, it may be that the nationalistic élan which seems to be an indispensable element of economic growth, may cause the underdeveloped countries to turn toward totalitarian forms of government.

There are several conflicting tendencies. On the one hand, the speed with which the backward countries want to develop is likely to impose great social stresses. These, with the cohesion and discipline required for the transition, may bring autocratic leadership to the fore. On the other hand, the social expectations and immediate demands already existing in many undeveloped countries may prevent the emergence of political power to the neglect of welfare objectives. In any event, the challenge of world economic development is bound up with the struggle for the minds and attitudes of mankind. And in this struggle, economic matters, while important, are often secondary.

The magnitude of the differences in levels of living between the industrial countries and the underdeveloped countries indicates the possibilities for the latter to make better use of their resources. This process can be assisted by the knowledge and wealth of the advanced countries. Only when differences have been reduced to an acceptable minimum can one expect any modification in the political and social feelings that now influence the attitude of underdeveloped countries toward the West. Only the future will tell whether this is possible.

SUGGESTED READINGS

POPULATION

Castro, Josue De. *The Geography of Hunger.* Boston: Little, Brown, 1952.

Chandrosekhar, S. *Hungry People and Empty Lands.* London: Allen and Unwin, 1954.

Food and Agriculture Organization of the United Nations. *The State of Food and Agriculture.* Rome: Food and Agriculture Organization (Annual).

Frumkin, Grzegorz. *Population Changes in Europe Since 1939.* London: Allen and Unwin, 1951.

Hauser, Philip M. (ed.). *Population and World Politics.* Glencoe, Ill.: Free Press, 1958.

Hauser, Philip M., and Duncan, Otis Dudley. *The Study of Population.* Chicago: University of Chicago Press, 1959.

Parsons, Kenneth H., Penn, Raymond J., and Raup, Philip M. *Land Tenure.* Madison: University of Wisconsin Press, 1956.

Political and Economic Planning. *World Population and Resources.* London: Distributed by Allen and Unwin, 1955.

Spengler, Joseph J., and Duncan, Otis Dudley (eds.). *Demographic Analysis.* Glencoe, Ill.: Free Press, 1956.

———— *Population Theory and Policy.* Glencoe, Ill.: Free Press, 1956.

Taft, Ronald R., and Robbins, Richard. *International Migrations: The Immigrant in the Modern World.* New York: Ronald Press, 1955.

United Nations. *Demographic Yearbook.* New York: Statistical Office of the United Nations—Department of Economic and Social Affairs.

Woytinsky, Wladimir S., and Woytinsky, E. S. *World Population and Production.* New York: Twentieth Century Fund, 1953.

GEOGRAPHY

Boggs, S. Whittemore. *International Boundaries—A Study of Boundary Functions and Problems.* New York: Columbia University Press, 1940.

Fifield, Russell H., and Pearcy, G. Etzel. *Geopolitics in Principle and Practice.* Boston: Ginn, 1950.

Gobley, Y. M. *Political Geography and the World Map.* New York: Praeger, 1955.

Gyorgy, Andrew. *Geopolitics, The New German Science.* Berkeley and Los Angeles: University of California Press, 1944.

Jones, Stephen B. *Boundary-Making.* Washington, D.C.: Carnegie Endowment for International Peace, 1945.

Mackinder, Sir Halford. *Democratic Ideals and Reality.* New York: Henry Holt, 1942.

Moodie, A. E. *Geography Behind Politics.* London: Hutchinson's University Library, 1947.

Spykman, Nicholas J. *The Geography of Peace.* New York: Harcourt, Brace, 1944.

Stamp, L. Dudley. *An Economic and Regional Geography.* London: Blackwell, 1959.

Weigert, Hans W. *Principles of Political Geography.* New York: Appleton-Century-Crofts, 1957.

Weigert, Hans W., Harrison, R. E., and Stefansson, Vilhjalmur (eds.). *New Compass of the World.* New York: Macmillan, 1953.

NATURAL RESOURCES AND INDUSTRIAL CAPACITY

Almond, Gabriel A., and Coleman, James S. (eds.). *The Politics of the Developing Areas.* Princeton: Princeton University Press, 1960.

Cottrell, Fred. *Energy and Society.* New York: McGraw-Hill, 1955.

Dahl, Robert A., and Lindbloom, Charles E. *Politics, Economics, and Welfare.* New York: Harper, 1953.

Emery, Brooks. *The Strategy of Raw Materials.* New York: Macmillan, 1938.

Food and Agriculture Organization of the United Nations. *Production Yearbook.* Rome: Food and Agriculture Organization.

———— *Trade Yearbook.* Rome: Food and Agriculture Organization.

Frankel, Sally Herbert. *Economic Impact on Underdeveloped Societies.* Cambridge: Harvard University Press, 1953.

Hirschman, Albert O. *The Strategy of Economic Development.* New Haven: Yale University Press, 1958.

Hoselitz, Berthold F. (ed.). *The Progress of Underdeveloped Areas.* Chicago: University of Chicago Press, 1952.

Isard, Walter, and Whitney, Vincent. *Atomic Power: An Economic and Social Analysis.* New York: Blakiston, 1952.

Knorr, Klaus. *The War Potential of Nations.* Princeton: Princeton University Press, 1956.

Meier, Richard L. *Science and Economic Development.* Cambridge: Technology Press of Massachusetts Institute of Technology, 1956.

Mouzon, Olin T. *International Resources and National Policy.* New York: Harper, 1959.

Netschert, B. C., and Schurr, S. H. *Atomic Energy Applications, with Reference to Underdeveloped Countries.* Resources for the Future; Baltimore: Johns Hopkins Press, 1957.

Staley, Eugene. *The Future of Underdeveloped Countries.* New York: Published for the Council on Foreign Relations by Harper, 1954.

CHAPTER III

The Ideological Roots of Political Power

There is a strong tendency in our society to consider all theory—and even those who teach it—as highly impractical. Yet the fact is that there are few, if any, areas of human activity in which some type of theory, whether spelled out or implicit, does not play a part. Indeed, theory is deeply rooted in human nature itself. For it is a product, simply, of man's ability and need not merely to *do* but also to *explain what he is doing.*

It is possible to distinguish at least two types of theory. The one, which we shall call empirical, consists of rules and generalizations about what we have observed in the past, along with predictions as to what, on the basis of our past findings, we expect to observe in the future. The other type of theory, which we shall refer to as normative, is concerned less with what "is" than with what "ought" to be. The former type of theory is primarily *de*scriptive, the latter type, primarily *pre*scriptive.

To the extent that political theory is of this latter, prescriptive type, it constitutes an important element in political power. For whether or not a particular political theorist has any messianic intentions himself, his words, analyses, and exposition are bound to kindle in the minds of his audience fires of curiosity, imagination, and, not infrequently, even indignation. Indeed, as Max Lerner has said, ideas are in a very real sense weapons.

The ideologies treated in the following selections have had this capacity to move vast bodies of peoples, to stir discontent, and to bring about a reallocation not only of values, but of political power as well. Not all idea systems are treated in these selections; those chosen have represented to the editors of this book significant movements in the struggle for political power. Each ideology, furthermore, illustrates the wide range of thought and conclusions that may exist even within a given ideology.

Few ideologies have, in modern times, so persistently excited mankind to political action as nationalism. Few ideologies have on the surface of it seemed so simple and yet have been so throughly comprehensive. Nationalism is based on mankind's age-old yearning for political independence and self-determination. It has been a battle cry against tyranny and colonialism; carried to an extreme, it has degenerated into racism. The urge toward nationalism seems to illustrate the Biblical aphorism, that "he that giveth his life shall find it." In short, nationalism has elicited the overwhelming loyalty of the individual to a group end—the creation and preservation of national identity—and has frequently required the sacrifice of life to achieve it. The resulting paradox—the commingling of elements of creativity and destructiveness—has made nationalism one of the most pervasive and powerful ideologies in recent history. Because nationalism takes root in the political climates of all parts of the world, it assumes, more and more, the character of a universal in mankind's struggle on earth.

Capitalism, to many students of politics, has seemed an all-inclusive term that vaguely signifies adherence to a free-enterprise economic system, in which something called "the laws of the market-place" provides the most genuine beneficence possible in an imperfect world. Capitalism is more than an economic theory, however, just as it is, at the same time, something less than unchanging. It has never been as pristine as its most dedicated advocates have held; nor has it been as inhuman as its critical detractors have alleged. Few ideologies have blended dogma and pragmatism more thoroughly. Moreover, few ideologies have proven more difficult to describe and theoretically analyze. In part this has been because of capitalism's unique flexibility and adaptability, and in part, undoubtedly, because man persists in acting not merely as an economic being but also as a social and political being. It has not been easy either to defend or to criticize a system that so subtly changes its tone and tenor in accordance with a given situation; yet it continues to survive and command strong loyalties. Perhaps its durability persists because its supporters share a usually unarticulated but most important major premise: that freedom of choice, whether in the market place of ideas or of material goods, is an end in itself and a condition eminently worth preserving.

There is some reason to view fascism as a reaction to ideology, rather than as an ideology in itself. Its spokesmen reveal their distrust of reason and their advocacy of emotion. Fascism has appealed to people who are tired of the quest for "proximate solutions to insoluble problems," to borrow a phrase from Reinhold Niebuhr. It postulates as a prime end the sanctity and glorification of the state. Its advocates have solved the ends-means dichotomy by considering the ends all-important and thereby justifying whatever means that are necessary to achieve the ends. Fascism relies on emotional attachment to the symbols of power. Power has meaning only in its external manifestations. Demanding of the citizen total loyalty, fascism rejects the distinction between state and society and requires a scapegoat to arouse and to synthesize the passions of its adherents. This "scapegoat demand" gave one aspect of fascism, National Socialism, a racial orientation. In Mussolini's Italy, on the other hand, the scapegoat was liberalism. Wherever it has occurred, fascism has been a doctrine of despair. In its view of the world as a jungle populated by two-legged animals in uniform, war becomes an act of necessity.

Socialism has been treated in the following selections as a political theory that is not monolithic. Starting from one basic premise—the highly moral one of man's inhumanity to man—its roots have in the past century spread in several directions. For purposes of simplicity, the editors have chosen to treat socialism as either *revolutionary* or *evolutionary*. That is, the formulators of socialist thought have criticized from common ground and have envisioned a similar, if not identical, end product of society; but they have differed widely in their views as to the proper and most effective means whereby their similar goal is to be reached. One group has insisted upon the necessity of some measure of violent action; the other has believed that socialist aspirations could be achieved peacefully and within the framework of existing social, economic, and political systems. As a result of this difference of approach, and because there are considerable differences of view as to strategy and tactics even within each of the two principal schools of thought, the ideological label of socialism has long been a very general and inclusive one.

Whatever variety of socialism one may study, however, one has the advantage that its premises are unusually clear. In what it opposes, the theory is an attack on what Socialists regard as the exploitation of man by man. In what it advances, it places a great deal of faith in human "reasonableness." The blueprints of the various socialist theories differ, but all are designed to place the direction of man's destiny in society as a whole and to establish as the dominant theme of human governance the ideal that every decision shall be "for the public good."

Socialists are generally of one mind in their view that the state system under capitalism nurtures inequality: social, economic, and political. The revolutionary Socialists seek to do away with the existing state completely; the evolutionary Socialists seek merely to convert it into an instrument of the general will.

In the following selections, it should become increasingly clear to the student that ideologies involve at least three major ingredients: reason, faith, and passion. In people all over the world ideas are able to arouse and appeal to long-nurtured and brooding grievances. To many it matters not whether these ideas have landing gears or not; it is important only that they have wings. Each of the ideologies that are discussed in these pages has shown its capacity to make men militant in action. In their competition for the minds and hearts of men, they continue to be, as they have been in the past, the prevailing ideological roots of political power.

Nationalism

11 · THE NATURE OF NATIONALISM *

Hans Kohn

Nationalism as we understand it is not older than the second half of the eighteenth century. Its first great manifestation was the French Revolution, which gave the new movement an increased dynamic force. Nationalism had, however, become manifest at the end of the eighteenth century almost simultaneously in a number of widely separated European countries. Its time in the evolution of mankind had arrived, and although the French Revolution was one of the most powerful factors in its intensification and spread, it was not its date of birth. Like all historical movements, nationalism has its roots deep in the past. The conditions which made its emergence possible had matured during centuries before they converged at its formation. These political, economic, and intellectual developments took a long time for their growth and proceeded in the various European countries at different paces. It is impossible to grade them according to their importance or to make one dependent upon the other. All are closely interconnected, each reacting upon the other; and although their growth can be traced separately, their effects and consequences cannot be separated otherwise than in the analysis of the scholar; in life, they are indissolubly intertwined.

· · · · ·

Nationalism is first and foremost a state of mind, an act of consciousness, which since the French Revolution is becoming more and more common to mankind. The mental life of man is as much domi-

* Hans Kohn, "The Nature of Nationalism," *The American Political Science Review*, XXXIII (December, 1939), 1001, 1008-1016. Reprinted by permission of the American Political Science Association.

nated by an ego-consciousness as it is by a group-consciousness. Both are complex states of mind at which we arrive by experiences of differentiation and opposition, of the ego and the surrounding world, of the we-group and those outside the group. The collective or group consciousness can center around entirely different groups, of which some have a more permanent character, like the family, the class, the clan, the caste, the village, the sect, the religion, etc., whereas others are of a more or less passing character, e.g., schoolmates, a football team, or passengers on a ship. In each case, varying with its permanence, this group-consciousness will strive toward creating homogeneity within the group, a conformity and likemindedness which will lead to and facilitate concerted action. In that sense, we may speak of a group-mind and a group-action. We may speak of a Catholic mind and Catholic action, of an English mind and English action, but we may also speak of a rural mind or an urban mind, and of action of rural groups or urban groups. All these groups develop their group character. The character of an occupational group, as peasants, soldiers, civil servants, may be as clearly defined and stable as, or even more than, any character of a national group. Each group creates its own symbols and social conventions, is dominated by social traditions, which find their expression in the public opinion of the group.

Group consciousness is never exclusive. Men find themselves members of different groups at the same time. With the growth of the complexity of civilization, the number of groups of which men find themselves a part generally increases. These groups are not fixed. They have changing limits, and they are of changing importance. Within these pluralistic, and sometimes conflicting, kinds of group-consciousness there is generally one which is recognized by a man as the supreme and most important, to which therefore, in the case of conflict of group-loyalties, he owes supreme loyalty. He identifies himself with the group and its existence, frequently not only for the span of his life, but for the continuity of his existence beyond this span. This feeling of solidarity between the individual and the group may go, at certain times, as far as complete submergence of the individual in the group. The whole education of the members of the group is directed toward a common mental preparedness for common attitudes and common actions.

In different periods of history, and in different civilizations, we find different groups to which this supreme loyalty is given. The modern period of history, which started with the French Revolution, is characterized by the fact that in this period, and in this period alone, the nation demands the supreme loyalty of man, that all men, not only certain individuals or classes, are drawn into this common loyalty, and that all civilizations which up to this modern period have followed their own, and frequently widely different, ways are now dominated more and more by this one supreme group-consciousness, nationalism.

It is a fact often commented upon that this growth of nationalism and of national sectionalism happened in the nineteenth and twentieth centuries, just at the time when a growth of international relations, trade, and communications developed as never before; that local languages were raised to the dignity of literary and cultural languages just at the time when it seemed most desirable to efface all differences of language by the spread of world languages. This view overlooks the fact that it was this very growth of nationalism all over the earth, with its awakening of the masses to participation in political and cultural life, that prepared the way for the closer cultural contacts of all the civilizations of mankind, now for the first time brought into a common denominator, which at the same time separated and united them.

. . . . .

Nationalities are the product of the historical development of society. They are not identical with clans, tribes, or folk-groups— groups of men united by actual or supposed common descent or by a common habitat. Ethnographic groups like these existed throughout history, from earliest times on; yet they do not form nationalities; they are nothing but "ethnographic material," out of which, under certain circumstances, a nationality might arise. Even if a nationality arises, it may disappear again, absorbed in a larger or new nationality. Nationalities are products of the living forces of history, and therefore always fluctuating, never rigid. Nationalities are groups of very recent origin, and therefore of utmost complexity. They defy exact definition. Nationality is an historical and a political concept, and the meaning of the words "nation" and "nationality" has undergone many changes. The words used before the nineteenth century denoted something very different from the modern meanings in the age of nationalism. It is only in recent history that man started to regard nationality as a center of his political and cultural activity and life.

Nationality is therefore nothing absolute, and the greatest mistake, responsible for most of the extremities of today, is to make it an absolute, an objective *a priori* which is a source of all political and cultural life.

Nationality has been raised to an absolute by two fictitious concepts which have been accepted as having real substance. One holds that blood or race is the basis of nationality, and that it exists eternally and carries with it an unchangeable inheritance; the other sees the *Volksgeist* as an ever-quelling source of nationality and all its manifestations. These theories offer no real explanation of the rise and the role of nationality; they refer us to mythical, prehistorical pseudo-realities. Rather, they must be taken as characteristic elements of thought in the age of nationalism, and are subject themselves to analysis by the historian of nationalism.

Nationalities come into existence only when certain objective bonds delimit a social group. These bonds are most frequently used for the definition of nationality. None, however, is essential for the existence of a nationality. A nationality generally possesses several of these attributes; very few possess all of them. Usually, the following attributes are enumerated: common descent, language, territory, political entity, customs and traditions, and religion. A short discussion will suffice to show that none of these attributes is essential for the existence or definition of nationality.

Common descent seemed of great importance to primitive man, for whom birth was as great a mystery as death, and therefore surrounded by legends and superstitions. Most modern nationalities, however, are mixtures of different, and sometimes even very distant, races. The great migratory movements of history and the mobility of modern life have led everywhere to an intermingling, so that few if any nationalities can at present claim anything approaching common descent.

The importance of language for the formation and life of a nationality was stressed by Herder and Fichte. But there are many nationalities that have no language of their own, as the Swiss, who speak four different languages, or the Latin American nationalities, all of which speak Spanish or Portuguese. The English-speaking nations—Great Britain, the United States, Canada—or the Spanish-speaking nations of Latin America, are mostly of common or similar descent, speak the same language, and had until quite recently the same historical background, also traditions and customs very much akin to each other; yet they represent different nationalities, with frequently conflicting aspirations. Another example of the comparative irrelevance of objective criteria for their formation and continued existence is to be found in Norway and Denmark, where the people are most probably of common racial stock and speak almost the same language. Nevertheless, they consider themselves two nationalities, and the Norwegians set up their own language only as the result of their having become a nationality.

Customs and traditions were first stressed in their importance for nationalities by Rousseau. Each nation undoubtedly possesses its customs, traditions, and institutions; but these often vary greatly from locality to locality, and on the other hand tend in our times to become standardized all over the world, or at least over large areas. Customs and manners nowadays often change with great rapidity.

Religion was a great dominating force before the rise of nationalism in modern times. This is true of Western as well as Eastern Christianity, of Islam, and of India. The dividing lines were not drawn according to nationalities. Therefore the rise of nationalities and of nationalism was accompanied by transformations in the religious attitude of men, and in many ways the growth of nationalities has been helped or hindered by the influence of religion. Religious differences sometimes divided and weakened nationalities, and even helped to create new nationalities, as in the case of the Catholic Croats and the Orthodox Serbs. On the other hand, national churches have frequently been an important element in helping to arouse nationalism; and when conflicting nationalities were of different religions, religion often played a large part in the defense mechanism of the weaker nationality, as did Catholicism in Ireland and in Prussian Poland.

The most important outward factor in the formation of nationalities is a common territory, or rather the state. Political frontiers tend to establish nationalities. Many new nationalities, like the Canadian, were formed entirely because they comprised a political and geographic entity. Generally we may say that statehood or nationhood (in the generally accepted sense of common citizenship under one territorial government) is a constitutive element in the life of a nationality. The condition of statehood need not be present when a nationality originates, but in such a case (as with the Czechs in the late eighteenth century) it is always the memory of a past state and the aspiration toward statehood that characterizes nationalities in the period of nationalism.

Although it may be said in conclusion that some of these objective factors are of great importance for the formation of nationalities, the most essential element is a living and active corporate will. Nationality is formed by the decision to form a nationality. Thus the French nationality was born of the enthusiastic manifestation of will in 1789. A French nation, the population of the French kingdom, existed before, as also existed some of the objective conditions necessary for the formation of a nationality. But only the newly aroused consciousness and will made these elements active and effective, fused them into a source of immense centripetal power, and gave them a new importance and meaning. The English and American nationalities were constituted by covenants, by free acts of will, and the French Revolution evolved the plebiscite as a result of which membership in a nationality was determined, not by objective characteristics, but by subjective declaration. The foundation of the Swiss nationality was dramatized by Friedrich Schiller, in his *Wilhelm Tell,* according to legendary tradition, into the famous oath on the Rütli: "Wir wollen sein ein einig Volk von Brüdern." This mythical declaration, "We wish to be one single nation of brothers," was uttered at the birth of every nationality, be it that this birth happened, after a long pregnancy, in the enthusiasm of a revolutionary period, or be it that the awakening of the masses took years of ceaseless propaganda. Nationalities as "ethnographic material," as "pragmatic" and accidental factors in history, existed for a very long time; but only through the awakening of national consciousness did they become volitional and absolute factors in history. The extensive use of the word "nationality" must not blind us to the fact that the lack of this voluntary element makes what are sometimes called nationalities before the rise of modern nationalism something fundamentally different from nationalities at the present time. To base nationality upon "objective" factors like race implies a return to primitive tribalism. In modern times, it was the power of an idea, not the call of blood, that constituted and molded nationalities.

Nationalities are created out of ethnographic and political elements by nationalism breathing life into the form built by preceding centuries. Thus nationalism and nationality are closely interrelated. Nationalism is a state of mind, permeating the large majority of a people and claiming to permeate all its members, which recognizes the nation-state as the ideal form of political organization and the nationality as the source of all creative cultural energy and of economic well-being. The supreme loyalty of man is therefore due to his nationality, as his own life is supposedly rooted in and made possible by its welfare. A short discussion of the components of this definition will help to clarify the issues involved.

A state of mind of the large majority of the people: Even before the age of nationalism, we find individuals who profess sentiments very much akin to nationalism. But these sentiments are confined to individuals; the masses never feel their own life, culturally, politically, or economically, dependent upon the fate of the national group. Periods of oppression or danger from the outside may arouse in the masses a feeling of nationalism, as happened in Greece during the Persian wars and in France during the Hundred Years' War. But these sentiments pass quickly. As a rule, wars before the French Revolution did not arouse a deep national sentiment. In religious and dynastic wars, Germans fought against Germans and Italians against Italians without any realization of the "fratricidal" nature of the act. Soldiers and civilians entered the services of "foreign" rulers and served them, often with a loyalty and faithfulness which proved the absence of any national sentiment.

The nation-state as the ideal form of political organization: That political boundaries coincide with ethnographic or linguistic frontiers is a demand of recent times. Formerly, the city or the fief or a multilingual state held together by dynastic ties was the accepted form of political organization, and frequently was regarded as the "natural" or ideal form. At other periods, the educated classes as well as the masses believed in the ideal of a universal world-state, although on account of the technical and geographic conditions this ideal never approached realization.

The nationality as the source of cultural life: During most of historical time, religion was regarded as the true source of cultural life. Man was thought to become creative by his profound immersion in religious tradition and by his abandonment into the divine fountainhead of all being. At other times, the basis of man's education was steeped in the civilization of a class which spread beyond all national boundaries, like the civilization of knighthood in medieval Europe or of the French court in the seventeenth and eighteenth centuries. During and after the Renaissance, man's education was rooted in the soil of classical civilization. Education and learning, the formation of man's mind and character, were not bound by any national limits.

The nationality as a source of economic well-being: This phase of nationalism was, as well as the political, prepared by the period of absolute monarchy, with its mercantilism. But mercantilism never became more than a scheme imposed from above, trying to achieve a national unity which it in reality never approached, continuing in many ways the medieval confusion and disruption of economic life and leaving provinces, cities, and villages as centers of economic life. The purpose of mercantilism was to strengthen the state and its power in international politics. The system following mercantilism, in the period of laissez-faire, had as its aim the promotion of individual welfare. Economic nationalism brought about a neo-mercantilism, filling with life, as had been the case with the centralized state, the form erected by the monarchs. It is a much younger development than political or cultural nationalism, and it believes that the well-being of the individual can be achieved and secured only by the economic power of the nation. The close political and cultural identification of the individual with his nationality which took place at the end of the eighteenth and beginning of the nineteenth century, extended to the economic field during the latter part of the nineteenth century.

The supreme loyalty due to the nationality: The Austrian monarchy was generally accepted as long as man's supreme loyalty was due to the legitimate king; its existence became precarious with the shift of loyalty from the dynasty to the nationality. Only a very few centuries ago, man's loyalty was due to his church or religion; a heretic put himself out of the pale of society in the same way that a "traitor" to his nation does today. The fixation of man's supreme loyalty upon his nationality marks the beginning of the age of nationalism.

12 · IN DEFENSE OF AMERICAN IMPERIALISM *

Albert J. Beveridge

Mr. President, I address the Senate at this time because Senators and Members of the House on both sides have asked that I give to Congress and the country my observations in the Philippines and the far East, and the conclusions which those observations compel; and because of hurtful resolutions introduced and utterances made in the Senate, every word of which will cost and is costing the lives of American soldiers.

Mr. President, the times call for candor. The Philippines are ours forever, "territory belonging to the United States," as the Constitution calls them. And just beyond the Philippines are China's illimitable markets. We will not retreat from either. We will not repudiate our duty in the archipelago. We will not abandon our opportunity in the Orient. We will not renounce our part in the mission of our race, trustee, under God, of the civilization of the world. And we will move forward to our work, not howling out regrets like slaves whipped to their burdens, but with gratitude for a task worthy of our strength, and thanksgiving to Almighty God that He has marked us as His chosen people, henceforth to lead in the regeneration of the world.

PHILIPPINES COMMAND THE PACIFIC

This island empire is the last land left in all the oceans. If it should prove a mistake to abandon it, the blunder once made would be irretrievable. If it proves a mistake to hold it, the error can be corrected when we will. Every other progressive nation stands ready to relieve us.

But to hold it will be no mistake. Our largest trade henceforth must be with Asia. The Pacific is our ocean. More and more Europe will manufacture the most it needs, secure from its colonies the most it consumes. Where shall we turn for consumers of our surplus?

* Reprinted from the speech delivered by Senator Albert J. Beveridge (Republican-Indiana) on the floor of the Senate of the United States, January 9, 1900. *Congressional Record*, Vol. 33, Part 1, pp. 704, 711-712.

Geography answers the question. China is our natural customer. She is nearer to us than to England, Germany, or Russia, the commercial powers of the present and the future. They have moved nearer to China by securing permanent bases on her borders. The Philippines give us a base at the door of all the East.

Lines of navigation from our ports to the Orient and Australia; from the Isthmian Canal to Asia; from all Oriental ports to Australia, converge at and separate from the Philippines. They are a self-supporting, dividend-paying fleet, permanently anchored at a spot selected by the strategy of Providence, commanding the Pacific. And the Pacific is the ocean of the commerce of the future. Most future wars will be conflicts for commerce. The power that rules the Pacific, therefore, is the power that rules the world. And, with the Philippines, that power is and will forever be the American Republic.

. . . . .

THE WHOLE QUESTION ELEMENTAL

Mr. President, this question is deeper than any question of party politics; deeper than any question of the isolated policy of our country even; deeper even than any question of constitutional power. It is elemental. It is racial. God has not been preparing the English-speaking and Teutonic peoples for a thousand years for nothing but vain and idle self-contemplation and self-admiration. No! He has made us the master organizers of the world to establish system where chaos reigns. He has given us the spirit of progress to overwhelm the forces of reaction throughout the earth. He has made us adepts in government that we may administer government among savage and senile peoples. Were it not for such a force as this the world would relapse into barbarism and night. And of all our race He has marked the American people as His chosen nation to finally lead in the regeneration of the world. This is the divine mission of America, and it holds for us all the profit, all the glory, all the happiness possible to man. We are trustees of the world's progress, guardians of its righteous peace. The judgment of the Master is upon us: "Ye have been faithful over a few things; I will make you ruler over many things."

What shall history say of us? Shall it say that we renounced that holy trust, left the savage to his base condition, the wilderness to the reign of waste, deserted duty, abandoned glory, forgot our sordid profit even, because we feared our strength and read the charter of our powers with the doubter's eye and the quibbler's mind? Shall it say that, called by events to captain and command the proudest, ablest, purest race of history in history's noblest work, we declined that great commission? Our fathers would not have had it so. No! They founded no paralytic government, incapable of the simplest acts of administration. They planted no sluggard people, passive while the world's work calls them. They established no reactionary nation. They unfurled no retreating flag.

GOD'S HAND IN ALL

That flag has never paused in its onward march. Who dares halt it now—now, when history's largest events are carrying it forward; now, when we are at last one people, strong enough for any task, great enough for any glory destiny can bestow? How comes it that our first century closes with the process of consolidating the American people into a unit just accomplished, and quick upon the stroke of that great hour presses upon us our world opportunity, world duty, and world glory, which none but a people welded into an indivisible nation can achieve or perform?

Blind indeed is he who sees not the hand of God in events so vast, so harmonious, so benign. Reactionary indeed is the mind that perceives not that this vital people is the strongest of the saving forces of the world; that our place, therefore, is at the head of the constructing and redeeming nations of the earth; and that to stand aside while events march on is a surrender of our interests, a betrayal of our duty as blind as it is base. Craven indeed is the heart that fears to perform a work so golden and so noble; that dares not win a glory so immortal.

Do you tell me that it will cost us money? When did Americans ever measure duty by financial standards? Do you tell me of the tremendous toil required to overcome the vast difficulties of our task? What mighty work for the world, for humanity, even for ourselves, has ever been done with ease? Even our bread must we eat by the sweat of our faces. Why are we charged with power such as no people ever knew, if we are not to use it in a work such as no people ever wrought? Who will dispute the divine meaning of the fable of the talents?

Do you remind me of the precious blood that must be shed, the lives that must be given, the broken hearts of loved ones for their slain? And this is indeed a heavier price than all combined. And yet as a nation every historic duty we have done, every achievement we have accomplished, has been by the sacrifice of our noblest sons. Every holy memory that glorifies the flag is of those heroes who have died that its onward march might not be stayed. It is the nation's dearest lives yielded for the flag that makes it dear to us; it is the nation's most precious blood poured out for it that makes it precious to us. That flag is woven of heroism and grief, of the bravery of men and women's tears, of righteousness and battle, of sacrifice and anguish, of triumph and of glory. It is these which make our flag a holy thing. Who would tear from that sacred banner the glorious legends of a single battle where it has waved on land or sea? What son of a soldier of the flag whose father fell beneath it on any field would surrender that proud record for the heraldry of a king? In the cause of civilization, in the service of the Republic anywhere on earth, Americans consider wounds the noblest decorations man can win, and count the giving of their lives a glad and precious duty.

Pray God that spirit never fails. Pray God the time may never come when Mammon and the love of ease shall so debase our blood that we will fear to shed it for the flag and its imperial destiny. Pray God the time may never come when American heroism is but a legend like the story of the Cid, American faith in our mission and our might a dream dissolved, and the glory of our mighty race departed.

And that time will never come. We will renew our youth at the fountain of new and glorious deeds. We will exalt our reverence for the flag by carrying it to a noble future as well as by remembering its ineffable past. Its immortality will not pass, because everywhere and always we will acknowledge and discharge the solemn responsibilities our sacred flag, in its deepest meaning, puts upon us. And so, Senators, with reverent hearts, where dwells the fear of God, the American people move forward to the future of their hope and the doing of His work.

Mr. President and Senators, adopt the resolution offered, that peace may quickly come and that we may begin our saving, regenerating, and uplifting work. Adopt it, and this bloodshed will cease when these deluded children of our islands learn that this is the final word of the representatives of the American people in Congress assembled. Reject it, and the world, history, and the American people will know where to forever fix the awful responsibility for the consequences that will surely follow such failure to do our manifest duty. How dare we delay when our soldiers' blood is flowing? (Applause in the galleries.)

13 · THE "REAL" AMERICANS HOLD A CONVENTION *

Hale Champion

What Westbrook Pegler calls "my cell of the American resistance movement" held an aboveground meeting in San Francisco some weeks ago. The gathering, known as the Congress of Freedom and dedicated to "getting the U.S. out of the UN and throwing the UN out of the U.S.," was not enormously significant, but it had its moments.

There was, for instance, the following conversation in a small "symposium" studying the dangers posed to U.S. sovereignty by the International Labor Organization of the United Nations.

"I know this isn't directly on the subject matter," apologized the ever-courteous Merwin K. Hart. "But have you noticed that President Eisenhower isn't looking well lately? The change for the worse in the last three months has been quite remarkable."

His half-dozen fellow students of internationalist one-world treachery, most of them disturbed ladies of advancing age, were finding the technical going a little hard anyway, and seemed to welcome the diversion with open-mouthed gratitude.

"I've always understood he was physically the weakest in that family," noted one.

"I was told he has diabetes," declared a second.

This news galvanized a third woman. Her soft, sweet smile twitched once and was gone.

"Did you know that Washington, D.C., has fluoridated water?" she asked excitedly. "Did you? And that fluoridation is bad for diabetes?"

* Hale Champion, "The 'Real' Americans Hold a Convention," *The Reporter,* 12 (June 30, 1955), pp. 31-34. Reprinted by permission of Hale Champion and *The Reporter*.

This more-than-coincidence so impressed the assemblage that it turned briefly to a general discussion of the evils attendant on fluoridation ("Mass medication is the first step by the Communists . . ."). Once again, however, there was an interruption.

"I'm not so sure that's the President's trouble," said a woman who had been sitting pensively for the last ninety seconds. "It may be his conscience."

The conversation was now back on the Hart spur track, and the group began to discuss the most desirable alternatives to the disappointing Eisenhower. Hart himself expressed no preference as between Governor J. Bracken Lee of Utah, a man courageous enough to call for repeal of the Federal income tax, and Senator William F. Knowland, a leader with the fortitude to suggest that we might get out of the United Nations unless it does as we say. "Both very good men," he told the ladies.

There was a McCarthy murmur from one member of the group, but that was quickly squelched. As one of the anti-fluoridation spokesmen observed, "McCarthy has done very good anti-Communist work, but he has a funny voting record. He's voted for some pretty socialist bills—farm subsidies and things like that."

"COMMUNISM"

All this is not to say that the United Nations ("UN is just two letters in the word CommUNism") failed to get proper attention from the anxious delegates, both in such panel sessions and in the fiery evening speeches of the six-day meeting.

Robert T. LeFevre, the white-haired charmer who was executive director of the Congress (but is perhaps better known as the expurgator of "collectivism" and "internationalism" from the Girl Scout Handbook) drew a roar of approbation when he assailed the United Nations as "an incredible monster that must be knocked in the head."

George S. Montgomery, Jr., a New York corporation lawyer who was the keynote speaker, reviewed the now-familiar series of Executive agreements, Supreme Court opinions, and proposed UN covenants and conventions on which those who support the Bricker amendment rest their contention that the treatymaking power is being used both in and out of the UN to subvert our Constitution. High on the list of villains in the review were Supreme Court Justices Oliver Wendell Holmes and Felix Frankfurter and Presidents

Roosevelt, Truman, and Eisenhower. "Americans have turned their backs on their neighbors and their flag!" Montgomery cried. "The whole world is wallowing in moral disintegration."

Westbrook Pegler told how he had watched "that old meathead Stettinius" participate in the writing of the UN Charter, how baffled he was by what was going on, and how clear it all became when he learned later that "only Alger Hiss and his chums" knew what was really going on. "It was a trick backfield," complained the aggrieved Pegler. "I never did see the ball."

Freda Utley, ex-Communist and old China hand, decided that the United Nations, having been founded on principles with which she disagrees, was "conceived in sin."

Leora Baxter, a black-garbed former schoolteacher from Pasadena who blazes study trails for California's socially select Pro America chapters, was upset because the United Nations encourages the presence of "foreigners on our soil."

Suzanne Silvercruys Stevenson, the Belgian-born founder of the Minute Women of the U.S.A., Inc., came from Connecticut to tell the Congress that the United Nations grew from "the poisonous conspiracy of Alger Hiss, Molotov, and Harry Dexter White."

Joseph Zack Kornfeder, an ex-Communist expert witness, carefully explained how the Communists conceived the United Nations as an instrument of conquest, captured its machinery, and are busy using it to achieve world domination.

MORE UNMARRIED PREGNANCIES

The United Nations Educational, Scientific and Cultural Organization and other special agencies of the UN came in for comment too. C. O. Garshwiler, operator of the Educational News Service in the Los Angeles area (which has a high concentration of pioneers in anti-UNESCO work), had been informed that one UNESCO-influenced textbook on family life increased the unmarried-pregnancy rate in a moderate-sized California town by eighty per cent, and he has seen for himself that the first word in another textbook's index was "abortion." After listening to a shocked story from a northern California delegate about a seventeen-year-old girl who was being permitted to attend an "interracial summer camp," he could only conclude that "the parents must have been brainwashed."

"If they don't belong to the Communist Party, they're cheating the C.P. out of dues," he added cheerfully. Garshwiler was also an effervescent quizmaster, asking "the good ladies" whether they had heard this scandalous passage or detected the treasonous content in that one. As often as not they had.

Florence Fowler Lyons of the Los Angeles school system took a larger view of UNESCO's influence as "a glorified and perfected Institute of Pacific Relations," or, a moment later, as the UN "Espionage, Sabotage and Corruptive Organization," which is about "to deliver the United States into the icy, godless, ruthless arms of Communism." She demanded, and the Congress later endorsed her demand unanimously, that the Senate Internal Security Subcommittee begin an investigation of UNESCO and its American sponsors forthwith. She got the greatest single ovation of the Congress.

THE BRAINWASHING THEME

As indicated by the discussion of President Eisenhower's alleged disabilities, so small a topic as the United Nations, its agencies and sins, could not continually absorb all the animosities of those who made up the Congress.

Surprisingly, Dean Acheson and the twenty years of Democratic Administration proved less satisfactory than Eisenhower, Dulles, *et al.* At one point Myron Fagan, head of Hollywood's Cinema Educational League and a follower of Gerald L. K. Smith, called for the President's impeachment. And Hart, after denouncing the Democratic holdovers in the Republican Administration, called Ike "the biggest holdover of them all."

There were yet other matters that roused the delegates to "country-saving." Mrs. Mary D. Cain, buxom lady candidate for Governor of Mississippi and national chairman of her own organization, Individuals for Liberty, was aghast at the school-desegregation decision of "that smart-aleck Supreme Court." "If they come at us again, we might have to get out the old firearms," she told her fellow delegates in a sweet voice, smiling warmly at them. Her other favorite target was the Sixteenth (income-tax) Amendment. This "legalized thievery" will be the principal topic of the Congress to be held next year in Dallas.

A panel discussion of the UN Convention on genocide somehow turned to the threat of mental-health-clinic legislation being pushed in California and elsewhere by people concerned about mounting mental-illness figures. This provoked several repetitions of the word "brainwash," a favorite in the vocabulary of almost every vocal delegate. An elderly cane-thumping gentleman with a generous white goatee averred that "psychiatry is basically a denial of God." He expressed fear that under pending mental-health legislation in California, a number of his fellow delegates might be subject to arbitrary commitment. "They will knock on your door and say, 'Citizen, you are charged with being an American,'" he warned. "Then they will haul you away to the booby hatch."

Other frequent topics were the perfidy of clergymen who support the United Nations despite the omission of prayer at its founding; the duplicity of press, radio, and television ("The New York *Times* prints more flattering pictures of Chou En-lai than of Senator McCarthy"); the fraud of Social Security; the failure to unleash the avenging forces of Syngman Rhee and Chiang Kai-shek; and the betrayal of the American fliers in Red Chinese prisons. Captain Eugene Guild, president of the Fighting Homefolks of Fighting Men of Glenwood Springs, Colorado, demanded that the U.S. go to war if necessary to secure their immediate release.

THE EMERGENCE OF LE FEVRE

To bring together this collection of some of the nation's most vociferous crusaders and to keep them busy and relatively happy for most of six days was not easy, but it was done. Most of the credit belongs to executive director Robert T. LeFevre, a comparative unknown.

LeFevre has won powerful backing. As vice-president of Merwin K. Hart's National Economic Council, he presumably can tap the cash of those who have kept Hart so prosperously employed as a propagandist and lobbyist for decades. And although some other influential figures sent wires of regret instead of appearing, many gave their names to LeFevre for use on his National Advisory Committee list. Among the noteworthy names appearing there are those of Spruille Braden, former ambassador, and critic of the State Department from within; Mrs. Craig Carrier, president of the National Association of Pro America; Harry H. Hoiles of the Hoiles newspaper-chain family that employs LeFevre as an editorial writer on its Colorado Springs *Gazette Telegraph;* Herbert U. Nelson, secretary of the American Real Property Federation and the leader of the potent real-estate lobby in Washington; John Francis Neylan, San Francisco attorney; Lieutenant General A. C. Wedemeyer, retired from military service; Johnston M. Hart, public relations director of the Sun Shipbuilding

Company of Chester, Pennsylvania; and Colonel Alvin Owsley of Dallas, former national commander of the American Legion. Congratulatory wires also arrived at the Congress from Clarence Manion, former Dean of the Notre Dame University Law School and member of the Eisenhower team who got dropped; Dan Smoot, voice of H. L. Hunt's Facts Forum; Colonel Archibald Roosevelt; Brigadier General Bonner Fellers of For America; Admiral William Standley; and others.

Their confidence in LeFevre-managed ventures has some justification. Not only did he succeed in forcing Girl Scout officials to make forty textual changes in their handbook last year; he also effectively pressed his campaign against "one-worlders" on another front at roughly the same time. As executive director of the U.S. Day Committee, LeFevre put together the letter-writing and pressure-bringing effort that persuaded a number of governors and mayors to ignore the usual proclamation of UN Day and to declare a U.S. Day instead.

LeFevre's aptitude was nicely demonstrated on the final day of the Congress when a stream of resolutions poured in from the panels for consideration by the assembled delegates. They were far fewer than one would have expected. LeFevre had begun by claiming the Congress represented more than five hundred organizations. But when the voting delegates had been separated from the observers, there were fewer than ninety accredited voters, a heavy concentration of them from just a few organizations.

Most of the resolutions, treated as noncontroversial, were passed with casual unanimity. A sample was that asking that the American people observe Memorial Day as a "Day of Shame" for the failure of the United Nations and the Administration to secure the freedom of the Americans imprisoned in China. All the delegates were equally willing to urge that Americans observe the day by wearing black badges, flying flags at half staff, and sending postcards to the United Nations and the White House on which the word "shame" should be written.

BUDDHISTS AND OTHERS

However, a few people threw sand in the gears. Dr. V. Orval Watts, with only four or five supporters, twice attempted to change the language of resolutions to remove words and phrases which he said would offend non-Christians, pleading that the Congress not go on record as "just one segment of the religious movement in America." Watts said that in his long history of fighting the socialist and Communist planners, he had learned the need to get support from "many who are not Christians but Jews, for example." Delegates booed him, the man in the chair tried to cut him off, and indignant speakers popped up all over the auditorium.

"The real American movement consists chiefly of Christians," declared Dr. A. G. Blazey, a Washington, Indiana, physician.

"This Christian gathering should not deny Christ by supporting Watts," said Mrs. Frank Cunningham of Santa Monica, but should join in the "fight against Antichrist."

Watts had also used the example of the Buddhists in one argument, to which a fellow delegate retorted, "Let the Buddhists make their own resolutions!" Some of the other remarks were considerably less polite, and Watts, restrained but pale with anger, began to assail "the spirit of the Congress."

LeFevre acted swiftly and skillfully to avert disaster. First by hand and voice signals to the chairman, then by brief and adroitly phrased little speeches, he got control. He eased the situation for the tiny Watts minority by praising the profundity of their motives.

That done, and Watts and friends apparently mollified, LeFevre assumed the floor leadership of the majority, declaring that despite his great humility before Watts' scholarship, his own ultimate simplicity of approach led him to join with those who wanted to emphasize the importance of the Christian religion in making the United States the greatest country in the world today. The Watts motions were shouted down, and LeFevre and Christian nationalism triumphed.

14 · ON NATIONS AND PEOPLES *

Heinrich Himmler

THE 1941 ATTACK

In 1941 the Fuehrer attacked Russia. That was, as we can well see now, shortly—perhaps 3 to 6 months—before Stalin prepared to

* Speech of the Reichsfuehrer–SS Heinrich Himmler, at the meeting of SS Major-Generals at Posen, October 4, 1943. Nuremberg Document 1919-PS.

embark on his great penetration into Central and Western Europe. I can give a picture of this first year in a few words. The attacking forces cut their way through. The Russian Army was herded together in great pockets, ground down, taken prisoner. At that time we did not value the mass of humanity as we value it today, as raw material, as labor. What after all, thinking in terms of generations, is not to be regretted, but is now deplorable by reason of the loss of labor, is that the prisoners died in tens and hundreds of thousands of exhaustion and hunger.

. . . . .

A Slav is never able to build something. Not in the long run. . . . With the exception of a few phenomena which Asia produces every couple of centuries through a mixture (fortunate for Asia, but unfortunate for us Europeans) of two hereditary elements—with the exception, then, of an Attila, a Genghis Khan, a Tamerlane, a Lenin, a Stalin, this mixed people of Slavs is built on a subrace which has a few drops of our blood, the blood of a race of leaders, but which is itself not capable of self-government and the maintenance of order. It is capable of discussion, capable of debate, capable of subversion, capable of resistance to every kind of authority. But this cheap merchandise of humanity is as incapable of sustaining order today as it was 700 or 800 years ago.

. . . . .

It is basically wrong for us to infuse all our inoffensive soul and spirit, our good-nature, and our idealism into foreign peoples. This is true since the time of Herder, who clearly wrote "Voices of the Nations" in a state of drunkenness, thereby bringing on us, who come after him, such immeasurable sorrow and misery. This is true, for instance, of the Czechs and the Slovenes to whom we gave their consciousness of nationality. They were just not capable of it themselves; we had to discover it for them.

One basic principle must be the absolute rule for the *SS* man: we must be honest, decent, loyal, and comradely to members of our own blood and to nobody else. What happens to a Russian, to a Czech does not interest me in the slightest. What the nations can offer in the way of good blood of our type, we will take, if necessary by kidnapping their children and raising them here with us. Whether nations live in prosperity or starve to death interests me only insofar as we need them as slaves for our *Kultur;* otherwise, it is of no interest to me. Whether 10,000 Russian females fall down from exhaustion while digging an anti-tank ditch interests me only insofar as the anti-tank ditch for Germany is finished. We shall never be rough and heartless when it is not necessary, that is clear. We Germans, who are the only people in the world who have a decent attitude toward animals, will also assume a decent attitude toward these human animals. But it is a crime against our own blood to worry about them and give them ideals, thus causing our sons and grandsons to have a more difficult time with them. When somebody comes to me and says, "I cannot dig the anti-tank ditch with women and children, it is inhuman, for it would kill them," then I have to say, "You are a murderer of your own blood because if the anti-tank ditch is not dug, German soldiers will die, and they are sons of German mothers. They are our own blood." That is what I want to instill into the SS and what I believe I have instilled into them as one of the most sacred laws of the future. Our concern, our duty is our people and our blood. It is for them that we must provide and plan, work and fight, nothing else. We can be indifferent to everything else. I wish the SS to adopt this attitude to the problem of all foreign, non-Germanic peoples, especially Russians. All else is vain, fraud against our own nation and an obstacle to the early winning of the war.

RUSSIAN SOLDIERS ON OUR SIDE

It is self-explanatory in this war: better that a Russian should die than a German. If we are going to use Russians, that is all right if we mix them up with Germans in a ratio of 1:2 or 1:3. It is best to use Russians singly, then you can ride with them in a tank. A Russian with two or three Germans in a tank—wonderful—no problem. All you have to watch out for—you must not allow a Russian to meet with a Russian driver in a tank—then these fellows will conspire. If for any reason, you want to have companies composed only of Russians, then see to it, gentlemen, and that is not some sort of thought, it is an order, that you have in that company your spy apparatus, your "NKVD." Then you can sleep quietly. Aside from that —and that is one of the earliest reasons I have given—make sure that these subhumans always look at you, that they must always look their superior in the eye. That is just as with an animal. So long as it looks its keeper in the eye, that long it will do nothing. Be always clear about this: it is a beast. With this attitude we will be able to take advantage of the Russian. With that kind of attitude we will always be superior to him. Not so with any other attitude.

. . . . .

THE ITALIAN THEATER OF WAR

Now to Italy, the other theater of war. Let us be clear about this. The weakness of this people is in its blood, in its race. In examining this problem we must distinguish between that which is pleasant or unpleasant for us today, and that which may be pleasant or unpleasant in the future. Italy was a weak partner, starting in Greece and Africa right up to Russia. After all, there is no people which has not beaten up the Italians, from which the Italians have not had a thrashing. Italy is going to be—and this final result can be taken for granted—the pariah people of the world, because no one, no Albanian, no Montenegrin, no Frenchman, no American, no Englishman, no Russian, no German is going to respect them, for everywhere they were cowards as soldiers, as men. That is the most miserable judgment one can pronounce upon a nation and a race. One must therefore distinguish between what would be pleasant today and tomorrow. Had Italy been a real neighbor in the inner sense, it would have been very nice if it had remained strong. But with a permanently weak neighbor, who does not after all withstand anything, I must say the condition today is preferable. It is most preferable. At the moment, it is unpleasant. It came at a very bad time. Had this treason occurred three months later, then it would have been better for us. But in wartime one cannot select these things that way. Fate does not ask questions. It throws one a crumb. In anticipation of our great future, we should thank fate and the merciful God that it came the way it did.

Capitalism

15 · THE WEALTH OF NATIONS *

Adam Smith

This division of labour, from which so many advantages are derived, is not originally the effect of any human wisdom, which foresees and intends that general opulence to which it gives occasion. It is the necessary, though very slow and gradual, consequence of a certain propensity in human nature which has in view no such extensive utility; the propensity to truck, barter, and exchange one thing for another.

Whether this propensity be one of those original principles in human nature, of which no further account can be given; or whether, as seems more probable, it be the necessary consequence of the faculties of reason and speech, it belongs not to our present subject to enquire. It is common to all men, and to be found in no other race of animals, which seem to know neither this nor any other species of contracts. Two greyhounds, in running down the same hare, have sometimes the appearance of acting in some sort of concert. Each turns her towards his companion, or endeavours to intercept her when his companion turns her towards himself. This, however, is not the effect of any contract, but of the accidental concurrence of their passions in the same object at that particular time. Nobody ever saw a dog make a fair and deliberate exchange of one bone for another with another dog. Nobody ever saw one animal by its gestures and natural cries signify to another, this is mine, that yours; I am willing to give this for that. When an animal wants to obtain something either of a man or of another animal, it has no other means of

* Adam Smith, *The Wealth of Nations* (New York: Random House, Inc., 1937), pp. 13-16, 66-68, 78-80, 248-250. Reprinted by permission of Random House, Inc.

persuasion but to gain the favour of those whose service it requires. A puppy fawns upon its dam, and a spaniel endeavours by a thousand attractions to engage the attention of its master who is at dinner, when it wants to be fed by him. Man sometimes uses the same arts with his brethren, and when he has no other means of engaging them to act according to his inclinations, endeavours by every servile and fawning attention to obtain their good will. He has not time, however, to do this upon every occasion. In civilized society he stands at all times in need of the co-operation and assistance of great multitudes, while his whole life is scarce sufficient to gain the friendship of a few persons. In almost every other race of animals each individual, when it is grown up to maturity, is entirely independent, and in its natural state has occasion for the assistance of no other living creature. But man has almost constant occasion for the help of his brethren, and it is in vain for him to expect it from their benevolence only. He will be more likely to prevail if he can interest their self-love in his favour, and shew them that it is for their own advantage to do for him what he requires of them. Whoever offers to another a bargain of any kind, proposes to do this. Give me that which I want, and you shall have this which you want, is the meaning of every such offer; and it is in this manner that we obtain from one another the far greater part of those good offices which we stand in need of. It is not from the benevolence of the butcher, the brewer, or the baker, that we expect our dinner, but from their regard to their own interest. We address ourselves, not to their humanity but to their self-love, and never talk to them of our own necessities but of their advantages. Nobody but a beggar chuses to depend chiefly upon the benevolence of his fellow-citizens. Even a beggar does not depend upon it entirely. The charity of well-disposed people, indeed, supplies him with the whole fund of his subsistence. But though this principle ultimately provides him with all the necessaries of life which he had occasion for, it neither does nor can provide him with them as he has occasion for them. The greater part of his occasional wants are supplied in the same manner as those of other people, by treaty, by barter, and by purchase. With the money which one man gives him he purchases food. The old cloaths which another bestows upon him he exchanges for other old cloaths which suit him better, or for lodging, or for food, or for money, with which he can buy either food, cloaths, or lodging, as he has occasion.

As it is by treaty, by barter, and by purchase, that we obtain from one another the greater part of those mutual good offices which we stand in need of, so it is this same trucking disposition which originally gives occasion to the division of labour. In a tribe of hunters or shepherds a particular person makes bows and arrows, for example, with more readiness and dexterity than any other. He frequently exchanges them for cattle or for venison with his companions; and he finds at last that he can in this manner get more cattle and venison, than if he himself went to the field to catch them. From a regard to his own interest, therefore, the making of bows and arrows grows to be his chief business, and he becomes a sort of armourer. Another excels in making the frames and covers of their little huts or moveable houses. He is accustomed to be of use in this way to his neighbours, who reward him in the same manner with cattle and with venison, till at last he finds it his interest to dedicate himself entirely to this employment, and to become a sort of house-carpenter. In the same manner a third becomes a smith or a brazier; a fourth a tanner or dresser of hides or skins, the principal part of the clothing of savages. And thus the certainty of being able to exchange all that surplus part of the produce of his own labour, which is over and above his own consumption, for such parts of the produce of other men's labour as he may have occasion for, encourages every man to apply himself to a particular occupation, and to cultivate and bring to perfection whatever talent or genius he may possess for that particular species of business.

The difference of natural talents in different men is, in reality, much less than we are aware of; and the very different genius which appears to distinguish men of different professions, when grown up to maturity, is not upon many occasions so much the cause, as the effect of the division of labour. The difference between the most dissimilar characters, between a philosopher and a common street porter, for example, seems to arise not so much from nature, as from habit, custom, and education. When they came into the world, and for the first six or eight years of their existence, they were, perhaps, very much alike, and neither their parents nor playfellows could perceive any remarkable difference. About that age, or soon after, they come to be employed in very different occupations. The difference of talents comes then to be taken notice of, and widens by degrees, till at last the vanity of the philosopher is willing to acknowledge scarce any resemblance. But without the disposition of truck, barter, and exchange, every man must have procured to himself every necessary and conveniency of life which he wanted. All must have had the same duties to perform, and the same work to do, and there could have been no such difference of employment as could alone give occasion to any great difference of talents.

As it is this disposition which forms that difference of talents, so remarkable among men of different professions, so it is this same disposition which renders that difference useful. Many tribes of animals acknowledged to be all of the same species, derive from nature a much more remarkable distinction of genius, than what, antecedent to custom and education, appears to take place among men. By nature a philosopher is not in genius and disposition half so different from a street porter, as a mastiff is from a greyhound, or a greyhound from a spaniel, or this last from a shepherd's dog. Those different tribes of animals, however, though all of the same species, are of scarce any use to one another. The strength of the mastiff is not in the least supported either by the swiftness of the greyhound, or by the sagacity of the spaniel, or by the docility of the shepherd's dog. The effects of those different geniuses and talents, for want of the power or disposition to barter and exchange, cannot be brought into a common stock, and do not in the least contribute to the better accommodation and conveniency of the species. Each animal is still obliged to support and defend itself, separately and independently, and derives no sort of advantage from that variety of talents with which nature has distinguished its fellows. Among men, on the contrary, the most dissimilar geniuses are of use to one another; the different produces of their respective talents, by the general disposition to truck, barter, and exchange, being brought, as it were, into a common stock, where every man may purchase whatever part of the produce of other men's talents he has occasion for.

· · · · ·

What are the common wages of labour, depends every where upon the contract usually made between those two parties, whose interests are by no means the same. The workmen desire to get as much, the masters to give as little as possible. The former are disposed to combine in order to raise, the latter in order to lower the wages of labour.

It is not, however, difficult to foresee which of the two parties must, upon all ordinary occasions, have the advantage in the dispute, and force the other into a compliance with their terms. The masters, being fewer in number, can combine much more easily; and the law, besides, authorises, or at least does not prohibit their combinations, while it prohibits those of the workmen. We have no acts of parliament against combining to lower the price of work; but many against combining to raise it. In all such disputes the masters can hold out much longer. A landlord, a farmer, a master manufacturer, or merchant, though they did not employ a single workman, could generally live a year or two upon the stocks which they have already acquired. Many workmen could not subsist a week, few could subsist a month, and scarce any a year without employment. In the long-run the workman may be as necessary to his master as his master is to him, but the necessity is not so immediate.

We rarely hear, it has been said, of the combinations of masters, though frequently of those of workmen. But whoever imagines, upon this account, that masters rarely combine, is as ignorant of the world as of the subject. Masters are always and every where in a sort of tacit, but constant and uniform combination, not to raise the wages of labour above their actual rate. To violate this combination is every where a most unpopular action, and a sort of reproach to a master among his neighbours and equals. We seldom, indeed, hear of this combination, because it is the usual, and one may say, the natural state of things which nobody ever hears of. Masters too sometimes enter into particular combinations to sink the wages of labour even below this rate. These are always conducted with the utmost silence and secrecy, till the moment of execution, and when the workmen yield, as they sometimes do, without resistance, though severely felt by them, they are never heard of by other people. Such combinations, however, are frequently resisted by a contrary defensive combination of the workmen; who sometimes too, without any provocation of this kind, combine of their own accord to raise the price of their labour. Their usual pretences are, sometimes the high price of provisions; sometimes the great profit which their masters make by their work. But whether their combinations be offensive or defensive, they are always abundantly heard of. In order to bring the point to a speedy decision, they have always recourse to the loudest clamour, and sometimes to the most shocking violence and outrage. They are desperate, and act with the folly and extravagance of desperate men, who must either starve, or frighten their masters into an immediate compliance with their demands. The masters upon these occasions are just as clamorous upon the other side, and never cease to call aloud for the assistance of the civil magistrate, and the rigorous execution of those laws which have been enacted with so much severity against the combinations of servants, labourers, and journeymen. The workmen, accordingly, very seldom derive any advantage from the violence of those tumultuous combinations, which, partly from the interposition of the civil magistrate, partly from the superior steadiness of the masters, partly from the necessity which the greater part of the workmen are under of submitting for the sake of present subsistence, generally end in nothing, but the punishment or ruin of the ring-leaders.

But though in disputes with their workmen, masters must generally have the advantage, there is however a certain rate below which it seems impossible to reduce, for any considerable time, the ordinary wages even of the lowest species of labour.

A man must always live by his work, and his wages must at least be sufficient to maintain him. They must even upon most occasions be somewhat more; otherwise it would be impossible for him to bring up a family, and the race of such workmen could not last beyond the first generation. Mr. Cantillon seems, upon this account, to suppose that the lowest species of common labourers must every where earn at least double their own maintenance, in order that one with another they may be enabled to bring up two children; the labour of the wife, on account of her necessary attendance on the children, being supposed no more than sufficient to provide for herself. But one-half the children born, it is computed, die before the age of manhood. The poorest labourers, therefore, according to this account, must, one with another, attempt to rear at least four children, in order that two may have an equal chance of living to that age. But the necessary maintenance of four children, it is supposed, may be nearly equal to that of one man. The labour of an able-bodied slave, the same author adds, is computed to be worth double his maintenance; and that of the meanest labourer, he thinks, cannot be worth less than that of an able-bodied slave. Thus far at least seems certain, that, in order to bring up a family, the labour of the husband and wife together must, even in the lowest species of common labor, be able to earn something more than what is precisely necessary for their own maintenance; but in what proportion, whether in that above mentioned, or in any other, I shall not take upon me to determine.

· · · · ·

The real recompence of labour, the real quantity of the necessaries and conveniencies of life which it can procure to the labourer, has, during the course of the present century, increased perhaps in a still greater proportion than its money price. Not only grain has become somewhat cheaper, but many other things, from which the industrious poor derive an agreeable and wholesome variety of food, have become a great deal cheaper. Potatoes, for example, do not at present, through the greater part of the kingdom, cost half the price which they used to do thirty or forty years ago. The same thing may be said of turnips, carrots, cabbages; things which were formerly never raised but by the spade, but which are now commonly raised by the plough. All sort of garden stuff too has become cheaper. The greater part of the apples and even of the onions consumed in Great Britain were in the last century imported from Flanders. The great improvements in the coarser manufactures of both linen and woollen cloth furnish the labourers with cheaper and better cloathing; and those in the manufactures of the coarser metals, with cheaper and better instruments of trade, as well as with many agreeable and convenient pieces of household furniture. Soap, salt, candles, leather, and fermented liquors, have, indeed, become a good deal dearer; chiefly from the taxes which have been laid upon them. The quantity of these, however, which the labouring poor are under any necessity of consuming, is so very small, that the increase in their prices does not compensate the diminution in that of so many other things. The common complaint that luxury extends itself even to the lowest ranks of the people, and that the labouring poor will not now be contented with the same food, cloathing, and lodging which satisfied them in former times, may convince us that it is not the money price of labour only, but its real recompence, which has augmented.

Is this improvement in the circumstances of the lower ranks of the people to be regarded as an advantage or as an inconveniency to the society? The answer seems at first sight abundantly plain. Servants, labourers and workmen of different kinds, make up the far greater part of every great political society. But what improves the circumstances of the greater part can never be regarded as an inconveniency to the whole. No society can surely be flourishing and happy, of which the far greater part of the members are poor and miserable. It is but equity, besides, that they who feed, cloath and lodge the whole body of the people, should have such a share of the produce of their own labour as to be themselves tolerably well fed, cloathed and lodged.

Poverty, though it no doubt discourages, does not always prevent marriage. It seems even to be favourable to generation. A half-starved Highland woman frequently bears more than twenty children, while a pampered fine lady is often incapable of bearing any, and is generally exhausted by two or three. Barrenness, so frequent among women of fashion, is very rare among those of inferior station. Luxury in the fair sex, while it inflames perhaps the passion for enjoyment, seems always to weaken, and frequently to destroy altogether, the powers of generation.

But poverty, though it does not prevent the generation, is extremely unfavourable to the rearing of children. The tender plant is produced, but in so cold a soil, and so severe a climate, soon withers and dies. It is not uncommon, I have been frequently told, in the Highlands of Scotland for a mother who has borne twenty children not to have two alive. Several officers of great experience have assured me, that so far from recruiting their regiment, they have never been able to supply it with drums and fifes from all the soldiers' children that were born in it. A greater number of fine children, however, is seldom seen any where than about a barrack of soldiers. Very few of them, it seems, arrive at the age of thirteen or fourteen. In some places one half the children born die before they are four years of age; in many places before they are seven; and in almost all places before they are nine or ten. This great mortality, however, will every where be found chiefly among the children of the common people, who cannot afford to tend them with the same care as those of the better station. Though their marriages are generally more fruitful than those of people of fashion, a smaller proportion of their children arrive at maturity. In foundling hospitals, and among the children brought up by parish charities, the mortality is still greater than among those of the common people.

Every species of animals naturally multiplies in proportion to the means of their subsistence, and no species can ever multiply beyond it. But in civilized society it is only among the inferior ranks of people that the scantiness of subsistence can set limits to the further multiplication of the human species; and it can do so in no other way than by destroying a great part of the children which their fruitful marriages produce.

The liberal reward of labour, by enabling them to provide better for their children, and consequently to bring up a greater number, naturally tends to widen and extend those limits. It deserves to be remarked too, that it necessarily does this as nearly as possible in the proportion which the demand for labour requires. If this demand is continually increasing, the reward of labour must necessarily encourage in such a manner the marriage and multiplication of labourers, as may enable them to supply that continually increasing demand by a continually increasing population. If the reward should at any time be less than what was requisite for this purpose, the deficiency of hands would soon raise it; and if it should at any time be more, their excessive multiplication would soon lower it to this necessary rate. The market would be so much under-stocked with labour in the one case, and so much over-stocked in the other, as would soon force back its price to that proper rate which the circumstances of the society required. It is in this manner that the demand for men, like that for any other commodity, necessarily regulates the production of men; quickens it when it goes on too slowly, and stops it when it advances too fast. It is this demand which regulates and determines the state of propagation in all the different countries of the world, in North America, in Europe, and in China; which renders it rapidly progressive in the first, slow and gradual in the second, and altogether stationary in the last.

．　．　．　．　．

The whole annual produce of the land and labour of every country, or what comes to the same thing, the whole price of that annual produce, naturally divides itself into three parts; the rent of land, the wages of labour, and the profits of stock; and constitutes a revenue to three different orders of people; to those who live by rent, to those who live by wages, and to those who live by profit. These are the three great, original and constituent orders of every civilized society, from whose revenue that of every other order is ultimately derived.

The interest of the first of those three great orders, it appears from what has been just now said, is strictly and inseparably connected with the general interest of the society. Whatever either promotes or obstructs the one, necessarily promotes or obstructs the other. When the public deliberates concerning any regulation of commerce or police, the proprietors of land never can mislead it, with a view to promote the interest of their own particular order; at least, if they have any tolerable knowledge of that interest. They are, indeed, too often defective in this tolerable knowledge. They are the only one of the three orders whose revenue costs them neither labour nor care, but comes to them, as it were, of its own accord and independent of any plan or project of their own. That indolence, which is the natural effect of the ease and security of their situation, renders them too often, not only ignorant, but incapable of that application of mind which is necessary in order to foresee and understand the consequences of any public regulation.

The interest of the second order, that of those who live by wages, is as strictly connected with the interest of the society as that of the first. The wages of the labourer, it has already been shewn, are never so high as when the demand for labour is continually rising, or when the quantity employed is every year increasing considerably. When this real wealth of the society becomes stationary, his wages are soon reduced to what is barely enough to enable him to bring up a family, or to continue the race of labourers. When the society declines, they fall even below this. The order of proprietors may, perhaps, gain more by the prosperity of the society, than that of labourers: but there is no order that suffers so cruelly from its decline. But though the interest of the labourer is strictly connected with that of the society, he is incapable either of comprehending that interest, or of understanding its connexion with his own. His condition leaves him no time to receive the necessary information, and his education and habits are commonly such as to render him unfit to judge even though he was fully informed. In the public deliberations, therefore, his voice is little heard and less regarded, except upon some particular occasions, when his clamour is animated, set on, and supported by his employers, not for his, but their own particular purposes.

His employers constitute the third order, that of those who live by profit. It is the stock that is employed for the sake of profit, which puts into motion the greater part of the useful labour of every society. The plans and projects of the employers of stock regulate and direct all the most important operations of labour, and profit is the end proposed by all those plans and projects. But the rate of profit does not, like rent and wages, rise with the prosperity, and fall with the declension, of the society. On the contrary, it is naturally low in rich, and high in poor countries, and it is always highest in the countries which are going fastest to ruin. The interest of this third order, therefore, has not the same connexion with the general interest of the society as that of the other two. Merchants and master manufacturers are, in this order, the two classes of people who commonly employ the largest capitals, and who by their wealth draw to themselves the greatest share of the public consideration. As during their whole lives they are engaged in plans and projects, they have frequently more acuteness of understanding than the greater part of country gentlemen. As their thoughts, however, are commonly exercised rather about the interest of their own particular branch of business, than about that of the society, their judgment, even when given with the greatest candour (which it has not been upon every occasion), is much more to be depended upon with regard to the former of those two objects, than with regard to the latter. Their superiority over the country gentleman is, not so much in their knowledge of the public interest, as in their having a better knowledge of their own interest than he has of his. It is by this superior knowledge of their own interest that they have frequently imposed upon his generosity, and persuaded him to give up both his own interest and that of the public, from a very simple but honest conviction, that their interest, and not his, was the interest of the public. The interest of the dealers, however, in any particular branch of trade or manufactures, is always in some respects different from, and even opposite to, that of the public. To widen the market and to narrow the competition, is always the interest of the dealers. To widen the market may frequently be agreeable enough to the interest of the public; but to narrow the competition must always be against it, and can serve only to enable the dealers, by raising their profits above what they naturally would be, to levy, for their own benefit, an absurd tax upon the rest of their fellow-citizens. The proposal of any new law or regulation of commerce which comes from this order, ought always to be listened to with great precaution, and ought never to be adopted till after having been long and carefully examined, not only with the most scrupulous, but with the most suspicious attention. It comes from an order of men, whose interest is never exactly the same with that of the public, who have generally an interest to deceive and even to oppress the public, and who accordingly have, upon many occasions, both deceived and oppressed it.

16 · ON WAGES *

David Ricardo

Labour, like all other things which are purchased and sold, and which may be increased or diminished in quantity, has its natural and its market price. The natural price of labour is that price which is necessary to enable the labourers, one with another, to subsist and to perpetuate their race, without either increase or diminution. The power of the labourer to support himself, and the family which may be necessary to keep up the number of labourers, does not depend on the quantity of money which he may receive for wages, but on the quantity of food, necessaries, and conveniences become essential to him from habit, which that money will purchase. The natural price of labour, therefore, depends on the price of the food, necessaries, and conveniences required for the support of the labourer and his family. With a rise in the price of food and necessaries, the natural price of labour will rise; with the fall in their price, the natural price of labour will fall.

With the progress of society the natural price of labour has always a tendency to rise, because one of the principal commodities by which its natural price is regulated, has a tendency to become dearer, from the greater difficulty of producing it. As, however, the improvements in agriculture, the discovery of new markets, whence provisions may be imported, may for a time counteract the tendency to a rise in the price of necessaries, and may even occasion their natural price to fall, so will the same causes produce the correspondent effects on the natural price of labour.

The natural price of all commodities, excepting raw produce and labour, has a tendency to fall, in the progress of wealth and population; for though, on one hand, they are enhanced in real value, from the rise in the natural price of the raw material of which they are made, this is more than counterbalanced by the improvements in machinery, by the better division and distribution of labour, and by the increasing skill, both in science and art, of the producers.

* David Ricardo, *Principles of Political Economy and Taxation* (McCulloch edition; London: John Murray, 1888), pp. 50-57.

The market price of labour is the price which is really paid for it, from the natural operation of the proportion of the supply to the demand; labour is dear when it is scarce, and cheap when it is plentiful. However much the market price of labour may deviate from its natural price, it has, like commodities, a tendency to conform to it.

It is when the market price of labour exceeds its natural price, that the condition of the labourer is flourishing and happy, that he has it in his power to command a greater proportion of the necessaries and enjoyments of life, and therefore to rear a healthy and numerous family. When, however, by the encouragement which high wages give to the increase of population, the number of labourers is increased, wages again fall to their natural price, and indeed from a reaction sometimes fall below it.

When the market price of labour is below its natural price, the condition of the labourers is most wretched: then poverty deprives them of those comforts which custom renders absolute necessaries. It is only after their privations have reduced their number, or the demand for labour has increased, that the market price of labour will rise to its natural price, and that the labourer will have the moderate comforts which the natural rate of wages will afford.

Notwithstanding the tendency of wages to conform to their natural rate, their market rate may, in an improving society, for an indefinite period, be constantly above it; for no sooner may the impulse, which an increased capital gives to a new demand for labour, be obeyed, than another increase of capital may produce the same effect; and thus, if the increase of capital be gradual and constant, the demand for labour may give a continued stimulus to an increase of people.

Capital is that part of the wealth of a country which is employed in production, and consists of food, clothing, tools, raw materials, machinery, etc., necessary to give effect to labour.

Capital may increase in quantity at the same time that its value rises. An addition may be made to the food and clothing of a country, at the same time that more labour may be required to produce the additional quantity than before; in that case not only the quantity, but the value of capital will rise.

Or capital may increase without its value increasing, and even while its value is actually diminishing; not only may an addition be made to the food and clothing of a country, but the addition may be made by the aid of machinery, without any increase, and even with an absolute diminution in the proportional quantity of labour required to produce them. The quantity of capital may increase, while neither the whole together, nor any part of it singly, will have a greater value than before, but may actually have a less.

In the first case, the natural price of labour, which always depends on the price of food, clothing, and other necessaries, will rise; in the second, it will remain stationary, or fall; but in both cases the market rate of wages will rise, for in proportion to the increase of capital will be the increase in the demand for labour; in proportion to the work to be done will be the demand for those who are to do it.

In both cases, too, the market price of labour will rise above its natural price; and in both cases it will have a tendency to conform to its natural price, but in the first case this agreement will be most speedily effected. The situation of the labourer will be improved, but not much improved; for the increased price of food and necessaries will absorb a large portion of his increased wages; consequently a small supply of labour, or a trifling increase in the population, will soon reduce the market price to the then increased natural price of labour.

In the second case, the condition of the labourer will be very greatly improved; he will receive increased money wages, without having to pay any increased price, and perhaps even a diminished price for the commodities which he and his family consume; and it will not be till after a great addition has been made to the population, that the market price of labour will again sink to its then low and reduced natural price.

Thus, then, with every improvement of society, with every increase in its capital, the market wages of labour will rise; but the permanence of their rise will depend on the question, whether the natural price of labour has also risen; and this again will depend on the rise in the natural price of those necessaries on which the wages of labour are expended.

It is not to be understood that the natural price of labour, estimated even in food and necessaries, is absolutely fixed and constant. It varies at different times in the same country, and very materially differs in different countries.* It essentially depends on the habits and

* "The shelter and the clothing which are indispensable in one country may be no way necessary in another; and a labourer in Hindostan may continue to work with perfect vigour, though receiving, as his natural wages, only such a supply of covering as would be insufficient to preserve a labourer in Russia from perishing. Even in countries situated in the same climate, different habits of living will often occasion variations in the natural price of labour, as con-

customs of the people. An English labourer would consider his wages under their natural rate, and too scanty to support a family, if they enabled him to purchase no other food than potatoes, and to live in no better habitation than a mud cabin; yet these moderate demands of nature are often deemed sufficient in countries where "man's life is cheap," and his wants easily satisfied. Many of the conveniences now enjoyed in an English cottage, would have been thought luxuries at an earlier period of our history.

From manufactured commodities always falling, and raw produce always rising, with the progress of society, such a disproportion in their relative value is at length created, that in rich countries a labourer, by the sacrifice of a very small quantity only of his food, is able to provide liberally for all his other wants.

Independently of the variations in the value of money, which necessarily affect money wages, but which we have here supposed to have no operation, as we have considered money to be uniformly of the same value, it appears then that wages are subject to a rise or fall from two causes:

First, The supply and demand of labourers.

Secondly, The price of the commodities on which the wages of labour are expended.

In different stages of society, the accumulation of capital, or of the means of employing labour, is more or less rapid, and must in all cases depend on the productive powers of labour. The productive powers of labour are generally greatest when there is an abundance of fertile land: at such periods accumulation is often so rapid, that labourers cannot be supplied with the same rapidity as capital.

It has been calculated, that under favourable circumstances population may be doubled in twenty-five years; but under the same favourable circumstances the whole capital of a country might possibly be doubled in a shorter period. In that case, wages during the whole period would have a tendency to rise, because the demand for labour would increase still faster than the supply.

In new settlements, where the arts and knowledge of countries far advanced in refinement are introduced, it is probable that capital has a tendency to increase faster than mankind; and if the deficiency of labourers were not supplied by more populous countries, this tend-

---

siderable as those which are produced by natural causes."—p. 68. *An Essay on the External Corn Trade, by R. Torrens, Esq.*

The whole of this subject is most ably illustrated by Colonel Torrens.

ency would very much raise the price of labour. In proportion as these countries become populous, and land of a worse quality is taken into cultivation, the tendency to an increase of capital diminishes; for the surplus produce remaining, after satisfying the wants of the existing population, must necessarily be in proportion to the facility of production, viz., to the smaller number of persons employed in production. Although, then, it is probable, that under the most favourable circumstances, the power of production is still greater than that of population, it will not long continue so: for the land being limited in quantity, and differing in quality, with every increased portion of capital employed on it, there will be a decreased rate of production, whilst the power of population continues always the same.

In those countries where there is abundance of fertile land, but where, from the ignorance, indolence, and barbarism of the inhabitants, they are exposed to all the evils of want and famine, and where it has been said that population presses against the means of subsistence, a very different remedy should be applied from that which is necessary in long settled countries, where, from the diminishing rate of the supply of raw produce, all the evils of a crowded population are experienced. In the one case, the evil proceeds from bad government, from the insecurity of property, and from a want of education in all ranks of the people. To be made happier they require only to be better governed and instructed, as the augmentation of capital, beyond the augmentation of people, would be the inevitable result. No increase in the population can be too great, as the powers of production are still greater. In the other case, the population increases faster than the funds required for its support. Every exertion of industry, unless accompanied by a diminished rate of increase in the population, will add to the evil, for production cannot keep pace with it.

With a population pressing against the means of subsistence, the only remedies are either a reduction of people, or a more rapid accumulation of capital. In rich countries, where all the fertile land is already cultivated, the latter remedy is neither very practicable nor very desirable, because its effect would be, if pushed very far, to render all classes equally poor. But in poor countries, where there are abundant means of production in store, from fertile land not yet brought into cultivation, it is the only safe and efficacious means of removing the evil, particularly as its effect would be to elevate all classes of the people.

The friends of humanity cannot but wish that in all countries the labouring classes should have a taste for comforts and enjoyments, and that they should be stimulated by all legal means in their exertions to procure them. There cannot be a better security against a superabundant population. In those countries, where the labouring classes have the fewest wants, and are contented with the cheapest food, the people are exposed to the greatest vicissitudes and miseries. They have no place of refuge from calamity; they cannot seek safety in a lower station; they are already so low, that they can fall no lower. On any deficiency of the chief article of their subsistence, there are few substitutes of which they can avail themselves, and dearth to them is attended with almost all the evils of famine.

In the natural advance of society, the wages of labour will have a tendency to fall, as far as they are regulated by supply and demand; for the supply of labourers will continue to increase at the same rate, whilst the demand for them will increase at a slower rate. If, for instance, wages were regulated by a yearly increase of capital, at the rate of 2 per cent, they would fall when it accumulated only at the rate of 1½ per cent. They would fall still lower when it increased only at the rate of 1, or ½ per cent, and would continue to do so until the capital became stationary, when wages also would become stationary, and be only sufficient to keep up the numbers of the actual population. I say that, under these circumstances, wages would fall, if they were regulated only by the supply and demand of labourers; but we must not forget that wages are also regulated by the prices of the commodities on which they are expended.

As population increases, these necessaries will be constantly rising in price, because more labour will be necessary to produce them. If, then, the money wages of labour should fall, whilst every commodity on which the wages of labour were expended rose, the labourer would be doubly affected, and would be soon totally deprived of subsistence. Instead, therefore, of the money wages of labour falling, they would rise; but they would not rise sufficiently to enable the labourer to purchase as many comforts and necessaries as he did before the rise in the price of those commodities. If his annual wages were before 24l., or six quarters of corn when the price was 4l. per quarter, he would probably receive only the value of five quarters when corn rose to 5l. per quarter. But five quarters would cost 25l.; he would, therefore, receive an addition in his money wages, though with that addition he would be unable to furnish himself with the same quantity of corn and other commodities which he had before consumed in his family.

Notwithstanding, then, that the labourer would be really worse paid, yet this increase in his wages would necessarily diminish the profits of the manufacturer; for his goods would sell at no higher price, and yet the expense of producing them would be increased. This, however, will be considered in our examination into the principles which regulate profits.

It appears, then, that the same cause which raises rent, namely, the increasing difficulty of providing an additional quantity of food with the same proportional quantity of labour, will also raise wages; and therefore, if money be of an unvarying value, both rent and wages will have a tendency to rise with the progress of wealth and population.

But there is this essential difference between the rise of rent and the rise of wages. The rise in the money value of rent is accompanied by an increased share of the produce; not only is the landlord's money rent greater, but his corn rent also; he will have more corn, and each defined measure of that corn will exchange for a greater quantity of all other goods which have not been raised in value. The fate of the labourer will be less happy; he will receive more money wages, it is true, but his corn wages will be reduced; and not only his command of corn, but his general condition will be deteriorated, by his finding it more difficult to maintain the market rate of wages above their natural rate. While the price of corn rises 10 per cent, wages will always rise less than 10 per cent, but rent will always rise more; the condition of the labourer will generally decline, and that of the landlord will always be improved.

. . . . .

When wages rise, it is generally because the increase of wealth and capital have occasioned a new demand for labour, which will infallibly be attended with an increased production of commodities. To circulate these additional commodities, even at the same prices as before, more money is required, more of this foreign commodity from which money is made, and which can only be obtained by importation. Whenever a commodity is required in greater abundance than before, its relative value rises comparatively with those commodities with which its purchase is made. If more hats were wanted, their price would rise, and more gold would be given for them. If more gold were required, gold would rise, and hats would fall in price, as a greater quantity of hats and of all other things would then be necessary to purchase the same quantity of gold. But in the case supposed, to say that commodities will rise, because wages rise, is to affirm a positive contradiction; for we, first, say that gold will rise in relative value in consequence of demand, and, secondly, that it will fall in relative value because prices will rise, two effects which are totally incompatible with each other. To say that commodities are raised in price, is the same thing as to say that money is lowered in relative value; for it is by commodities that the relative value of gold is estimated. If, then, all commodities rose in price, gold could not come from abroad to purchase those dear commodities, but it would go from home to be employed with advantage in purchasing the comparatively cheaper foreign commodities. It appears, then, that the rise of wages will not raise the prices of commodities, whether the metal from which money is made be produced at home or in a foreign country. All commodities cannot rise at the same time without an addition to the quantity of money. This addition could not be obtained at home, as we have already shown; nor could it be imported from abroad. To purchase any additional quantity of gold from abroad, commodities at home must be cheap, not dear. The importation of gold, and a rise in the price of all home-made commodities with which gold is purchased or paid for, are effects absolutely incompatible. The extensive use of paper money does not alter this question, for paper money conforms, or ought to conform, to the value of gold, and therefore its value is influenced by such causes only as influence the value of that metal.

These, then, are the laws by which wages are regulated, and by which the happiness of far the greatest part of every community is governed. Like all other contracts, wages should be left to the fair and free competition of the market, and should never be controlled by the interference of the legislature.

• • • • •

17 · POOR LAWS *

Herbert Spencer

Pervading all nature, we may see at work a stern discipline, which is a little cruel that it may be very kind. That state of universal warfare maintained throughout the lower creation, to the great perplexity of many worthy people, is at bottom the most merciful provision which the circumstances admit of. It is much better that the ruminant animal, when deprived by age of the vigor which made its existence a pleasure, should be killed by some beast of prey than that it should linger out a life made painful by infirmities and eventually die of starvation. By the destruction of all such, not only is existence ended before it becomes burdensome, but room is made for a younger generation capable of the fullest enjoyment; and, moreover, out of the very act of substitution happiness is derived for a tribe of predatory creatures. Note further that their carnivorous enemies not only remove from herbivorous herds individuals past their prime, but also weed out the sickly, the malformed, and the least fleet or powerful. By the aid of which purifying process, as well as by the fighting, so universal in the pairing season, all vitiation of the race through the multiplication of its inferior samples is prevented; and the maintenance of a constitution completely adapted to surrounding conditions, and therefore most productive of happiness, is insured.

The development of the higher creation is a progress toward a form of being capable of a happiness undiminished by these drawbacks. It is in the human race that the consummation is to be accomplished. Civilization is the last stage of its accomplishment. And the ideal man is the man in whom all the conditions of that accomplishment are fulfilled. Meanwhile the well-being of existing humanity and the unfolding of it into this ultimate perfection are both secured by that same beneficent, though severe, discipline to which the animate creation at large is subject: a discipline which is pitiless in the working out of good: a felicity-pursuing law which never swerves for the avoidance of partial and temporary suffering. The poverty of the incapable, the distresses that come upon the imprudent, the starvation

* Herbert Spencer, *Social Statics.*

of the idle, and those shoulderings aside of the weak by the strong, which leave so many "in shallows and in miseries," are the decrees of a large, far-seeing benevolence. It seems hard that an unskillfulness which with all his efforts he cannot overcome should entail hunger upon the artisan. It seems hard that a laborer incapacitated by sickness from competing with his stronger fellows should have to bear the resulting privations. It seems hard that widows and orphans should be left to struggle for life or death. Nevertheless, when regarded not separately, but in connection with the interests of universal humanity, these harsh fatalities are seen to be full of the highest beneficence —the same beneficence which brings to early graves the children of diseased parents and singles out the low-spirited, the intemperate, and the debilitated as the victims of an epidemic.

There are many very amiable people—people over whom insofar as their feelings are concerned we may fitly rejoice—who have not the nerve to look this matter fairly in the face. Disabled as they are by their sympathies with present suffering, from duly regarding ultimate consequences, they pursue a course which is very injudicious and in the end even cruel. We do not consider it true kindness in a mother to gratify her child with sweetmeats that are certain to make it ill. We should think it a very foolish sort of benevolence which led a surgeon to let his patient's disease progress to a fatal issue rather than inflict pain by an operation. Similarly, we must call those spurious philanthropists, who, to prevent present misery, would entail greater misery upon future generations. All defenders of a Poor Law must, however, be classed among such. That rigorous necessity which, when allowed to act on them, becomes so sharp a spur to the lazy and so strong a bridle to the random, these paupers' friends would repeal, because of the wailings it here and there produces. Blind to the fact that under the natural order of things, society is constantly excreting its unhealthy, imbecile, slow, vacillating, faithless members, these unthinking, though well-meaning, men advocate an interference which not only stops the purifying process but even increases the vitiation —absolutely encourages the multiplication of the reckless and incompetent by offering them an unfailing provision, and *dis*courages the multiplication of the competent and provident by heightening the prospective difficulty of maintaining a family. And thus, in their eagerness to prevent the really salutary sufferings that surround us, these sigh-wise and groan-foolish people bequeath to posterity a continually increasing curse.

Returning again to the highest point of view, we find that there is a second and still more injurious mode in which law-enforced charity checks the process of adaptation. To become fit for the social state, man has not only to lose his savageness, but he has to acquire the capacities needful for civilized life. Power of application must be developed; such modification of the intellect as shall qualify it for its new tasks must take place; and, above all, there must be gained the ability to sacrifice a small immediate gratification for a future great one. The state of transition will of course be an unhappy state. Misery inevitably results from incongruity between constitution and conditions. All these evils, which afflict us and seem to the uninitiated the obvious consequences of this or that removable cause, are unavoidable attendants on the adaptation now in progress. Humanity is being pressed against the inexorable necessities of its new position —is being molded into harmony with them and has to bear the resulting unhappiness as best it can. The process *must* be undergone, and the sufferings *must* be endured. No power on earth, no cunningly devised laws of statesmen, no world-rectifying schemes of the humane, no communist panaceas, no reforms that men ever did broach or ever will broach can diminish them one jot. Intensified they may be, and are; and in preventing their intensification, the philanthropic will find ample scope for exertion. But there is bound up with the change a *normal* amount of suffering, which cannot be lessened without altering the very laws of life. Every attempt at mitigation of this eventuates in exacerbation of it. All that a Poor Law or any kindred institution can do is partially to suspend the transition—to take off for a while from certain members of society the painful pressure which is effecting their transformation. At best this is merely to postpone what must ultimately be borne. But it is more than this: it is to undo what has already been done. For the circumstances to which adaptation is taking place cannot be superseded without causing a retrogression—a partial loss of the adaptation previously effected; and as the whole process must sometime or other be passed through, the lost ground must be gone over again and the attendant pain borne afresh. Thus, besides retarding adaptation, a Poor Law adds to the distress inevitably attending it.

At first sight these considerations seem conclusive against *all* relief to the poor—voluntary as well as compulsory; and it is no doubt true that they imply a condemnation of whatever private charity enables the recipients to elude the necessities of our social existence.

With this condemnation, however, no rational man will quarrel. That careless squandering of pence which has fostered into perfection a system of organized begging; which has made skillful mendicancy more profitable than ordinary manual labor; which induces the simulation of palsy, epilepsy, cholera, and no end of diseases and deformities; which has called into existence warehouses for the sale and hire of imposter's dresses; which has given to pity-inspiring babes a market value of 9d. per day—the unthinking benevolence which has generated all this cannot but be disapproved by everyone. Now it is only against this injudicious charity that the foregoing argument tells. To that charity which may be described as helping men to help themselves it makes no objection—countenances it, rather. And in helping men to help themselves, there remains abundant scope for the exercise of a people's sympathies. Accidents will still supply victims on whom generosity may be legitimately expended. Men thrown upon their backs by unforeseen events, men who have failed for want of knowledge inaccessible to them, men ruined by the dishonesty of others, and men in whom hope long delayed has made the heart sick may, with advantage to all parties, be assisted. Even the prodigal, after severe hardship has branded his memory with the unbending conditions of social life to which he must submit, may properly have another trial afforded him. And although by these ameliorations the process of adaptation must be remotely interfered with, yet in the majority of cases it will not be so much retarded in one direction as it will be advanced in another.

18 · THE TRANSFORMATION
OF AMERICAN CAPITALISM *

Nothing demonstrates the strength of the American way of life and the adaptability of the American system better than the transformation of American capitalism. Fifty years ago American capitalism seemed to be what Marx predicted it would be and what all the

* Condensed and reprinted from the February 1951 issue of *Fortune* Magazine by special permission; © 1951, Time, Inc.

muckrakers said it was—the inhuman offspring of greed and irresponsibility, committed by its master, Wall Street, to a long life of monopoly. It seemed to provide overwhelming proof of the theory that private ownership could honor no obligation except the obligation to pile up profits. And it was the capitalism that millions of people abroad and many even at home, to the immense aid and comfort of the Communists, still think American capitalism is.

American capitalism today is actually nothing of the kind. What has happened is that it has changed and developed beyond the ability of the historians to catch up with it; that its transformation, perhaps because people rarely see in perspective what is occurring before their eyes, has escaped the full awareness of even most businessmen; that most of the popular books, the great books even, that have furnished Americans with their stereotypes about capitalism are now obsolete. American capitalism is all-pervasive and intimately bound in with the political system, and it has undergone a vast dispersion of initiative and ownership. What might be called the influence of Main Street has become vastly more important to it than the control of Wall Street, and it has thus been changed into something very different from the capitalism that flourishes in most other lands.

The transformation can best be understood by looking at what has happened to "Big Business," which once was supposed to have controlled the economy from its headquarters in Wall Street. The fact is that Wall Street no longer wields much power over Big Business, which in turn is far from being the most powerful sector of the economy. For economic power boils down to the ability to decide who makes what and who gets what and in what proportions, and business alone no longer decides this. "The class struggle in America," writes Professor Clair Wilcox in the *Harvard Business Review,* "is not a struggle between the proletariat and the bourgeoisie. It is a struggle between functional groups possessing concentrated power—a struggle to control the products of industry." These groups, as Professor Wilcox describes them, are Big Labor, Big Agriculture, Big Little Business, and Big Business. Of them all, Big Business, if only because it is subject to the most pressure, exercises its power with a strong and growing sense of responsibility. Out of the experiment and change of American life, observed by all but comprehended fully by few, capitalism has developed into something that neither Karl Marx nor Adam Smith ever dreamed of.

IT'S EITHER RIGHT OR WRONG

At the bottom of the change is simple morality, which has concerned the U.S. as it has concerned no other great nation in all history. "The American," H. L. Mencken once said, "save in moments of conscious and swiftly lamented deviltry, casts up all ponderable values, including the value even of beauty, in terms of right and wrong." Like the European who described moral indignation as suppressed envy, Mencken scorned it as the mark of the peasant; and the American's capacity for moral indignation *has* resulted in many "uncivilized" excesses like prohibition. But it has also made him the most omnivorous reformer in history. Karl Marx based his philosophy on the fatalistic assumption that what he described as the inherent defects of capitalism are above the will of men to affect them. It has remained for the history of U.S. capitalism, beginning as early as the 1870's, to show that the moral convictions of men can change the course of capitalistic development.

• • • • •

REFORM UNLIMITED

The American's moral indignation, naturally enough, did not burn with a steady flame. In good times he tended to overlook violations of his basic notions; in bad times he looked for something to blame things on, and demanded that something be done about them. During the 1920's popular demand for reform was almost nonexistent. For one thing, the scorn of some of the nation's most effective writers made preoccupation with moral issues unfashionable if not ludicrous. For another, business seemed to be doing fine, and seemed to deserve not reform but praise. As the immensely popular *Saturday Evening Post* demonstrated in almost every issue, as Herbert Hoover himself phrased it, "The slogan of progress is changing from the full dinner pail to the full garage."

The catastrophe of depression blasted this dream. The shocked and angry people, seeing their livelihood disappear, put the Right to Life above the other rights. Their natural tendency to blame the bust on those who only yesterday were taking credit for having started an eternal boom was strengthened by revelations such as those of the Pecora congressional investigation into Wall Street financial practices. So they embraced the latter-day Populism of the New

Deal, and demanded that something be done. Writers and intellectuals took up the cudgels. Some were merely inclined to condemn what they had for so long contemned, but many tried to find out how and why it had happened, and how to keep it from happening again.

Many of the ensuing reforms survived. Immediately after the Pecora investigation, Congress passed a law divorcing investment banking from deposit banking. And a year later it passed the well-intentioned Securities Exchange Act, which put the Stock Exchange under federal regulation, gave the Federal Reserve Board authority to limit speculative margins, required all officers and stockholders of big companies to report their dealings in their companies' securities, and created the Securities and Exchange Commission to watch over the investment market.

Other attempts at reform were less successful. NRA, for example, went to a well-deserved death. As for the famed Temporary National Economic Committee, much of what it investigated was beside the point by the time it was in print—and not only because of the impending war. Even while the committee was mulling over the power of big business, and the intellectuals were in full cry on the trail of finance capitalism, business initiative had been dispersed among hundreds of enterprises, business power in the aggregate had been largely yielded to the farmers and unions, and Wall Street had ceased to be a valid symbol of great power.

The decline of Wall Street actually began long before the reforms of the New Deal. It began when corporations grew rich and independent. The rights to their profits, of course, were by traditional economics vested in the stockholders. But their managers saw no point in paying, say, $20 a share in dividends on their stock when $10 was enough to sustain the company's credit rating. They also reasoned that it was *they,* and not the stockholders, who were directly responsible for the profits. So they began to hold back on the stockholders and put the money into corporate reserves. As early as 1905 the Santa Fe, under Edward Ripley, adopted the policy of a dollar for the stockholder, a dollar for the property. Owen Young of G.E. and others, some years later, further developed the idea of self-capitalization, arguing that the money plowed back would in the long run enhance the stockholder's equity. Whether it did or not, it enabled a large part of business to do its own banking.

· · · · ·

WHERE THE POWER LIES

The cataclysm of the depression, which forever broke apart the old business universe, also heaved up the bright new stars of the unions and the farmers. With between 14 and 16 million members in labor unions, labor leaders now enjoy the kind of industrial power that has not existed since the time of Morgan. To understand this power, simply translate it into terms of industrial power. Imagine that a single company has a complete monopoly on some widely used device like electric motors, and that it decides to raise prices simply because it feels it is not getting enough for the motors. When its customers protest, the manufacturer announces that he will close down three days a week and make his motors scarce enough to command a high price. Or imagine he complains to the White House, which "settles" the dispute by forcing companies to buy at a higher price.

Imagine this, and you imagine something that cannot and has not occurred in behalf of American industry, even in the palmy days of the trusts. Yet John Lewis put his miners on a three-day week to keep prices up, and a railway-union wage dispute was settled in the White House. It is true that labor is not legally regarded as a commodity (the Clayton Act altered the antitrust law to forbid that) and certainly cannot be strictly compared to an electric motor. It is moreover elementary humanity that labor should not be regarded only as a commodity. But the price of labor is as vital as the price of anything else to the 60-odd million wage earners (including union members themselves), and an unjustified rise in the cost of labor affects them precisely as an unjustified rise in the price of commodities does. And in the unions' ability to force a decision on who makes what and who gets what, labor patently exercises as much or more economic power than business can.

The political power of the farmer is perhaps hardly as formidable. Represented in Congress out of proportion to his numbers, the farmer has been championed by legislators and bureaucrats who have effectively insulated him from the law of supply and demand. By restricting output, fixing prices, and storing up surpluses at government expense, they have done for agriculture what a watertight cartel would do for a group of manufacturers of widely varying efficiency. They have not only saddled the public with high prices, they have, of course, tended to prevent American farming from becoming as efficient as it ought to be and can be. For they have spread a price umbrella over the farmers that has enabled the worst of them to do all right and the best of them to make fantastic and undeserved profits without necessarily encouraging any of them to become more efficient. The $23-billion farm industry, furthermore, is hardly comparable to any one industry; it is more comparable to all industry—to all industry cartelized, subsidized, and rigidified. In terms of deciding who makes what and who gets what, it is one of the most powerful blocs in American history.

And where, in this regrouping of U.S. economic power, do we find the sense of responsibility that ought to go with the power if the nation is to increase its productivity? Labor, with a few exceptions, does not yet show much of it, and agriculture shows even less. The only place it can be found in any force is in the individual business enterprise, which now has the initiative that might have remained in Wall Street had not the transformation taken place.

One of the two chief characteristics of big modern enterprise is that it is run by hired management. As Berle and Means put it, the power inherent in the control of the "active property"—the plant organization and good will—has superseded the power inherent in "passive property"—the stocks and bonds. Even companies whose owners are managers may be described as management-run. The Ford company, for example, behaves not as an organization solely dedicated to earning the maximum number of dollars for the Ford family, but as an organization dedicated first of all to its own perpetuation and growth.

The other chief characteristic of the big modern enterprise is that management is becoming a profession. This means, to begin with, that a professional manager holds his job primarily because he is good at it. Often he has begun at the bottom and worked his way up by sheer merit. Or more often he has been carefully and even scientifically chosen from a number of bright and appropriately educated young men, put through an executive-training course, and gradually insinuated into the activities for which he shows the most talent. Since even at the top he generally functions as a member of a committee rather than as a final authority, his talents are so well balanced that none of them protrude excessively. He lives on what he makes, and even when he is well paid he doesn't have much left after taxes. Generally he is gregarious, and usually he is not a colossal "personality." But if he is not a General MacArthur, neither is he a Mr. Milquetoast. And if he is expected not to give arbitrary orders, he is also expected not to take them. In most well-run big enterprises, an executive is by definition a man who would object officially to a policy decision he disapproved.

THE MANAGERIAL EVOLUTION

More important, the manager is becoming a professional in the sense that like all professional men he has a responsibility to society as a whole. This is not to say that he no longer needs good, old-fashioned business sense. He does, and more than ever. The manager is responsible primarily to his company as a profit-earning mechanism, and current talk about the corporation as a nonprofit institution is more than a little naive. Any self-respecting businessman would rightly suspect a colleague who allowed he was in business not to make money. The modern enterpriser *should* be in business to make money. His ability to make money is the prime measure of his company's efficiency. If it cannot prosper on the service it supplies to society, or if it cannot persuade society to pay it enough to prosper, it does not deserve to stay in business. Moreover, the good, efficient manager *likes* to make money, and it is mainly because he likes to make money that he does a first-rate job. As the Russians have discovered, when the profit motive does not exist it has to be invented.

But the great happy paradox of the profit motive in the American system is that management, precisely because it is in business to make money years on end, cannot concentrate exclusively on making money here and now. To keep on making money years on end, it must, in the words of Frank Abrams, Chairman of the Standard Oil Co. of New Jersey, "conduct the affairs of the enterprise in such a way as to maintain an *equitable and working balance* among the claims of the various directly interested groups—stockholders, employees, customers, and the public at large." Not all pundits have understood this vital point. In his romantic *Managerial Revolution,* for example, James Burnham described the trend accurately enough but conveyed the idea that somehow the corporate manager is destined to become the Western equivalent of a King Farouk or perhaps an unusually favored commissar. The corporate manager neither is, nor is becoming, anything of the kind. He is part of a group that enjoys power only so long as it does not abuse it—in other words, precisely so long as it does not exercise power the way men and groups of men used to.

. . . . .

Modern management exhibits a sense of responsibility to its employees not only to prevent or anticipate the demands of labor unions but for the simple, obvious, and honest reason that a satisfied, loyal group of employees is at least as much a capital asset as a modern plant or a vital piece of machinery. A few enlightened managers, as a matter of fact, have been taking such an attitude for years. It is now twenty-five years since General Electric, under Owen Young, introduced employee stock-buying plans and the idea of a "cultural" rather than a "living" wage.

Corporations today support a wide variety of material benefits. Some go in for stabilization of employment. ATF, Inc., for example, which recently bought into the furniture business, has succeeded in almost eliminating the highly seasonal character of the business. Some companies (Procter & Gamble, Nunn-Bush, Hormel) carry employment stabilization to the point of guaranteeing an annual wage. Others have developed forecasting techniques to anticipate trends and to stabilize employment by leveling out production.

Almost every important company now has a pension plan, or is in the process of getting one. Many, like Sears, Roebuck, combine pensions with savings plans, so that when an employee retires he takes with him a sizable capital sum. Then there is the profit-sharing approach, backed by the newly formed Council of Profit-Sharing Industries (276 members), with annual bonus distributions ranging up to 100 per cent of base wages. Finally, there is the "participation" school. Its purpose is to bring the worker into the enterprise system by giving him a share in productivity decisions and a cut of productivity profits. Since *Fortune*'s report, at least a dozen firms, including Stromberg-Carlson of Rochester, New York, have adopted a Scanlon participation plan. There is a growing tendency on the part of blue-chip management to regard a job in its company as a kind of employment package, complete with pensions, savings plans, and numerous "fringe benefits" such as severance pay, maternity leaves, hospitalization and medical insurance.

But material benefits, as Elton Mayo and others have demonstrated, are often not as important as job satisfaction—the feeling of having done a good job, and of having it recognized by people who know what a good job is. Related and equally important is the feeling of participating in the company, of being a kind of partner without, of course, fully being one. The problem of generating these attitudes in the worker—particularly in making him feel his "participation"—is tremendous, and it cannot be solved merely by the resolution to do something about it. In one of the Standard Oil affiliates, for example, management was stumped by a case of group dissatisfaction until the president of the company began to talk to the men informally about some of the problems that were plaguing him and his board. "The men showed an immediate and extraordinary interest, and that gradually revealed the source of their dissatisfaction," recalls Frank Abrams. "They had been 'left out of things.'" The point to be noted here is that not every president could have done that. This president obviously had the "something" it takes to put a man across with his employees. And the gradual cultivation of that something is one of the unfinished tasks ahead of management.

Taking everything together, management has done well by its employees. The problem indeed may be to prevent it from discharging its responsibility to its employees *too* well. For when a company distributes employee benefits that are not compensated by rising productivity, it must in the long run pass the cost increase on to the consumer. Obviously a company *can* be tempted to win employee cooperation easily, and a few producers and a single union can combine to gang up on the public.

THE FINAL RESPONSIBILITY

Thus far, however, it is the modern manager's sense of responsibility to his customer and the general public that gives him his best claim to being progressive. More goods at lower cost (and prices) is the basic principle of American industry, and even companies regarded as anything but socially minded have built themselves upon it. Many a chemical, for example, has been sold at a progressively lower price without the spur of competition, simply to encourage the market. And most modern managers do worry a good deal about the related subjects of prices, monopoly, and competition. Competition has come a long way since the time of Lord Dewar, who cracked that "competition is the life of trade, and competition is the death of profits." The alternatives today are not monopoly or all-out competition. The Darwinian concept of all-out competition has given way to the concept of a pragmatic or "workable" competition, which far from being the death of profits provides, as smart companies know, the soundest way to ensure their survival. Aside from its value as a foil to anti-trust, which can be exaggerated, healthy, workable competition provides a good check on how a company is doing. Take du Pont, which, though almost unique, may well set a precedent. Pursued by the hounds of anti-trust (unjustly, it maintains) du Pont spent over a year looking for a competitor willing to put $20 million into a cellophane plant. Having found one in Olin industries, it is building the plant for Olin and supplying the necessary technical assistance. And that is not all. Because du Pont was the only market source for sodium metal, it induced National Distillers to make the stuff. And recently it turned over its nylon patents to the Chemstrand Co.

Other companies have learned that a similar self-discipline is the best price policy in the long run. The recent furor about rolling back the prices of automobiles obscures the fact that the automobile companies had conducted themselves with a notable respect for public opinion. Had they let the law of supply and demand take its course in the sellers' market of the past four or five years they could have priced their cars much higher. Their dealers, it is true, sometimes did extract a premium from eager buyers. But it was the manufacturers' list prices that in the main determined the price level, and the auto makers' refusal to charge what the traffic would bear must be reckoned as an extraordinary example of the transformation of the capitalistic mind.

THE MANAGER AND PUBLIC OPINION

One of the most pressing concerns of almost every large company today is what people are going to think about it. Board meetings often turn into self-examination sessions, with managers defending or explaining their actions as if before accusing judges. At a recent board meeting of a large consumer-goods company, the president rose up and remarked that the foremen had in effect built up a block between management and labor, and that management was mostly at fault. Fully two hours were devoted to soul-searching and discussion. There was also the matter of closing an old mill in a small town. Not only was the specific situation explored thoroughly, but a whole history of other similar cases was brought up. This problem was solved, after a full hour's discussion, by the decision to move a storage plant into the town and so absorb nearly all the displaced employees. As one executive remarked, "At least half our time is taken up with discussing the repercussions of what we propose to do. And this is what the boys who write the books call the managerial revolution."

. . . . .

Nothing perhaps is more indicative of the corporation's awareness of its responsibilities than the growth of public-relations activities. Upwards of 4,000 companies now go in for public-relations "programs." Although many of them are hardly more than publicity campaigns, more and more managers understand tolerably well that good business public relations, as *Fortune* has defined it, is good performance publicly appreciated, because adequately communicated. Now the mere comprehension of a moral axiom, as all parents know, does not guarantee its observance. But its constant iteration does make the subject more and more acutely aware of its importance, and thus eventually influences his behavior. As Paul Garrett of G.M. has been saying for years, "Our program is finding out what people like, doing more of it; finding out what people don't like, doing less of it."

HOPE FOR THE FUTURE

All of which should not be interpreted to mean that business is already rolling us down the six-lane, high-speed highway to economic paradise. When this article speaks of modern managers, it speaks of the pace setters, and does not presume to imply that all other managers and all other companies are doing as well. Many still give precedence to the big, quick profit, and incline to regard the stockholder mainly as a convenient personification of that goal, labor as a lamentably sensitive kind of commodity, and the customer as the man who gets rolled. Like many a labor and agricultural leader, they try to increase their share of the national product regardless of their contribution to that product. What Professor Wilcox calls Big (or organized) Little Business, for example, is responsible for or protected by most of the fair-trade laws, licensing systems, local bidding laws, and other legal devices that maintain prices independently of the market.

Big Business, too, has something to answer for. Just how much power it has for example to fix prices and to what extent it uses or abuses that power are right now the subjects of much expert contention. Some economists maintain that "Oligopoly is by all evidence the ruling market form in the modern economy"—i.e., since the nation's corporate assets are concentrated in a relatively few companies, the market is one of a few sellers, who can administer prices. Other economists, attacking the statistics on which such conclusions are based, maintain that only 20 per cent of the national income is provided by unregulated oligopoly, and that an analysis of competition in terms of market realities, which nobody has yet completed, will show that the American economy is becoming more, not less, competitive. It is to be hoped that such an important analysis will be undertaken soon. But whatever its results, it is not likely to reveal that business, socially speaking, has yet attained perfection.

What counts, however, is that the business leaders *are* setting the pace, and *are* being followed. What counts is that the old concept that the owner has a right to use his property just the way he pleases has evolved into the belief that ownership carries social obligations, and that a manager is a trustee not only for the owner but for society as a whole. Such is the Transformation of American Capitalism. In all the world there is no more hopeful economic phenomenon.

Fascism

---

19 · THE DOCTRINE OF FASCISM *

Benito Mussolini

In the Fascist theory of history, man is such only by virtue of the spiritual process to which he contributes as a member of the family, the social group, the nation, and in his relation to history to which all nations have contributed. Hence the great value of tradition in records, in language, in customs and in the rules of social life. Apart

* Benito Mussolini, *The Doctrine of Fascism* (2nd ed.—translated by E. Cope; Firenze: A. Vallecchi, 1937).

from history, man is a nonentity. Fascism is therefore opposed to all individualistic abstractions based on eighteenth-century materialism; and it is opposed to all Jacobin utopias and innovations. It does not believe in the possibility of happiness on earth as conceived by eighteenth-century economic writers, and therefore rejects the teleological notion that at some future time the human family will secure a final settlement of all its difficulties. This notion runs counter to experience which teaches that life is in continual motion and undergoing a process of evolution. In politics Fascism aims at realism; in practice it desires to deal only with those problems which are the spontaneous product of historic conditions and which find or suggest their own solution. Only by experiencing reality and getting a firm hold on the forces at work within it, may man influence other men and nature.

Being anti-individualistic, the Fascist system of life stresses the importance of the State and recognizes the individual only insofar as his interests coincide with those of the State, which stands for the consciousness and the universality of man as a historic entity. It is opposed to classic Liberalism which arose as a reaction to absolutism and exhausted its historical function when the State became the expression of the consciousness and will of the people. Liberalism denied the State in the name of the individual; Fascism reasserts the rights of the State as expressing the real essence of the individual. And if liberty is to be the attribute of living men and not that of abstract dummies invented by individualistic Liberalism, then Fascism stands for liberty and for the only liberty worth having, the liberty of the State and the individual within the State. The Fascist conception of the State is all-embracing; outside of it no human or spiritual values may exist, much less have any value. Thus understood, Fascism is totalitarian and the Fascist State, as a synthesis and a unit which includes all values, interprets, develops and lends additional power to the whole life of a people.

No individuals or groups, political parties, associations, economic unions, social classes are to exist apart from the State. Fascism therefore opposes Socialism which rejects unity within the State, obtained by the fusion of all classes into a single ethical and economic reality, since it sees in history nothing more than the class struggle. Fascism likewise opposes trade-unionism as a class weapon. But Fascism recognizes the real needs which gave rise to Socialism and trade-unionism, when they are brought within the orbit of the State, giving them due weight in the corporative system through which widely different interests are coordinated and harmonized for the unity of the State.

Grouped according to their several interests, individuals form classes; they form trade unions when they are organized according to their various economic callings; but first and foremost they form the State which is no mere matter of numbers, the sum-total of individuals forming a majority. Fascism therefore opposes the form of democracy which entrusts the nation to a majority, debasing it to the level of the largest number; but, if the Nation be considered, as it should be, from the point of view of equality instead of quantity, as an idea, it is the purest form of democracy, the mightiest, because it is the most ethical, the most coherent, the truest, the expression of a people through the conscience and will of a few, if not indeed, of a single man, tending to express itself as the consciousness and the will of the mass, as of the whole group ethnically molded by natural and historical conditions into a nation, advancing, as a single conscience and a single will along the self-same geographically defined region, but a people, historically perpetuating itself; a multi-tude unified by an idea and imbued with the will to live, the will to power, a consciousness and a personality becomes a Nation. It is not the Nation which produces the State; that is an old-fashioned naturalistic idea which afforded a basis for nineteenth-century pub-licity in favor of national governments. It is rather the State which forms the Nation, by lending strength and power and real life to a people conscious of its own moral unity.

The right to national independence does not arise from any merely literary and idealistic form of self-consciousness; still less from a more or less passive and unconscious *de facto* situation, but from an active, conscious, political will, expressing itself in action and pre-pared to assert its rights. It arises, in short, from the existence at least *in fieri* of a State. Indeed, as the expression of a universal ethical will, the State itself creates the right to national independence.

A nation, as expressed in the State, is a living, ethical entity only insofar as it is progressive. Inactivity means death. Therefore the State does not only stand for Authority which governs and confers legal form and spiritual value on individual wills, but it is also Power which makes its will felt and respected beyond its own boundaries, thus affording practical evidence of the universal charac-ter of the decisions necessary to ensure its development. This implies

organization and expansion, potential if not actual. Thus the State
is equal to the will of a single man whose development cannot be
checked by obstacles and it proves its own universality by achieving
self-expression.

The Fascist State, as a higher and more powerful expression of
personality, is a force, but a spiritual one. It sums up all the manifestations in the intellectual and moral life of man. Its functions
cannot therefore be limited to that of enforcing law and order, as the
Liberal doctrine would have it. It is no mere mechanical device for
defining the sphere within which the individual may duly exercise
his supposed rights. The Fascist State is an inwardly accepted
standard and a rule of conduct, a discipline of the whole person; it
permeates the will no less than the intellect. It stands for a principle
which becomes the central motive of man as a member of civilized
society, sinking deep down into his personality; it dwells in the
heart of the man of action and of the thinker, of the artist and of
the man of science: soul of the soul.

Fascism, in short, is not only a lawgiver and a founder of institutions, but an educator and a promoter of spiritual life. It does not
merely aim at remolding the forms of life, but also their content,
man, his character and his faith. To achieve this purpose it enforces
discipline and makes use of authority, entering into the mind and
ruling with undisputed sway. Therefore it has chosen as its emblem
the Lictors' rods, the symbol of unity, strength and justice.

.　.　.　.　.

As far as concerns the future development of mankind, quite apart
from all present-day political considerations, Fascism does not on the
whole believe in the possibility or utility of perpetual peace. Pacifism
is therefore rejected as a cloak for cowardly supine renunciation as
against self-sacrifice. War alone keys up all the energies of man to
their greatest pitch and sets the mark of nobility on those nations
which have the bravery to face it. All other tests are substitutes
which never place a man face to face with himself before the alternative of life and death. Therefore all doctrines which postulate peace
at any price as their premise are incompatible with Fascism. Equally
foreign to the spirit of Fascism, even though they may be accepted
for their utility in meeting special political situations, are all internationalist or League organizations which, as history amply proves,
crumble to the ground whenever the heart of nations is stirred deeply

by sentimental, idealist or practical considerations. Fascism carries this anti-pacifist attitude into the life of the individual. (I don't care), *me ne frego,* scrawled on his bandages by a wounded man became the proud motto of the storm-troopers, and it is not only an act of philosophical stoicism, it sums up a doctrine which is not merely political; it is the evidence of a fighting spirit which accepts all risks. It stands for a new mode of life of the Italians. The Fascist accepts and loves life; he rejects and despises suicide as cowardly. Life as he understands it means the fulfilment of duty, moral improvement, conquest; life must be lofty and full, it must be lived for oneself but above all for others, both nearby and far off, present and future.

The demographic policy of the Regime is a consequence of these premises. The Fascist loves his neighbor, but that word does not stand for a vague and incomprehensible idea. Love of one's neighbor does not exclude necessary educational severity; still less does it exclude differentiation and rank. Fascism will have nothing to do with universal embraces; as a member of the community of nations it looks other peoples straight in the eyes; it is vigilant, on its guard; it follows others in all their activities and takes note of any change in their interests; and it does not allow itself to be deceived by changing and deceptive appearances.

Such a conception of life makes of Fascism the resolute negation of the doctrine underlying so-called scientific and Marxist Socialism, the doctrine of historic materialism which would explain the history of mankind in terms of the class struggle and of changes in the processes and means of production, to the exclusion of all else.

That the vicissitudes of economic life, the discovery of raw materials, new technique processes, scientific inventions, have their importance nobody denies; but that they are sufficient to explain human history to the exclusion of other factors is absurd. Fascism believes now and always in sanctity and heroism, that is to say in acts wherein no economic motive, immediate or remote, is at work. Having denied historic materialism, which sees in men puppets on the fringes of history, appearing and disappearing on the crest of the waves while the real directive forces move and work in the depths, Fascism also denies the immutable and irreparable character of class struggle, which is the natural outcome of that economic conception of history; above all it denies that class struggle is the principal agent in social transformations. Having thus struck a blow at Socialism in the two main points of its doctrine, all that remains of it is the sentimental aspiration, old as humanity itself, towards social relations in which the sufferings and sorrows of the humble will be alleviated. But here again Fascism rejects the economic interpretation of happiness as something to be secured through Socialism, automatically so to say, at a given stage in social evolution, when a maximum of material comfort will be assured to all. Fascism denies the materialist conception of happiness as a possibility, and abandons it to the economists of the mid-eighteenth century. This means that Fascism denies the equation: well-being—happiness, by which men are merely considered as animals, happy when they can feed and fatten, thus being reduced to a purely vegetative existence.

Besides Socialism, Fascism points its guns at the whole block of Democratic ideologies and rejects both their premises and their practical application and methods. Fascism denies that numbers, as such, may be the determining factors in human society; it denies the right of numbers to govern by means of periodical consultations; it asserts the incurable and fruitful and beneficent inequality of men, who cannot be leveled by any such mechanical and external device as universal suffrage. Democratic Regimes may be described as those under which the people are deluded from time to time into the belief that they are exercising sovereignty, while all the time real sovereignty belongs to and is exercised by other forces, sometimes irresponsible and secret. Democracy is a kingless Regime infested by many kings who are sometimes more exclusive, tyrannical and destructive than a single one, even if he is a tyrant. This explains why, although Fascism was Republican in tendency prior to 1922 owing to causes of expediency, that was abandoned before the March on Rome, considering that the form of government is no longer a matter of preeminent importance, and that the study of past and present Monarchies and past and present Republics shows that neither the Monarchy nor the Republic may be judged *sub specie aeternitatis,* but that each stands for a form of government expressing the political evolution, the history, the traditions and the psychology of a given country.

Fascism has outgrown the dilemma: Monarchy versus Republic, over which the Democratic regimes dallied too long, blaming all imperfections on the former and praising the latter as the ideal regime, while actual experience teaches us that Republics are inherently reactionary and absolutist, while some Monarchies accept the most daring social and political experiments.

Renan, who had pre-Fascist intuitions, remarks in one of his philosophic meditations: (Reason and science are the products of mankind, but it is chimerical to seek reason directly for the people and through the people. It is not essential to the existence of reason that all should be familiar with it; and even if all were to be initiated, this could not be achieved through Democracy which seems doomed to lead to the extinction of all arduous forms of culture and of all the highest forms of learning. The maxim that society only exists for the well-being and freedom of the individuals which form it, does not seem to conform with nature's plans, which only concern the species and readily allow the sacrifice of the individual. It is much to be feared that the last word of Democracy, thus understood, and let me hasten to add that it is susceptible of a different interpretation, would be a form of society in which a degenerate mass would have no thought beyond that of enjoying the ignoble pleasures of the vulgar).

So far Renan. In rejecting Democracy Fascism rejects the absurd conventional lie of political equalitarianism, the habit of collective irresponsibility, the myth of felicity and indefinite progress. But if Democracy be understood as a regime in which the masses are not driven back to the outskirts of the State, then the writer of these pages has already defined Fascism as an organized, centralized, authoritarian Democracy.

The keystone of the Fascist doctrine is its conception of the State, of its essence, its functions and its aims. For Fascism the State is absolute, individuals and groups relative. Individuals and groups are admissible insofar as they act in accordance with the State. Instead of directing the nation and guiding the material and moral progress of the community, the Liberal State restricts its activities to recording results. The Fascist State is wide awake and has a will of its own. For this reason it can be described as (ethical). At the first quinquennial assembly of the Regime in 1929, I said:

> The Fascist State is not a night-watchman, only solicitous of the personal safety of the citizens; nor is it organized exclusively for the purpose of guaranteeing a certain degree of material prosperity and relatively peaceful conditions of life; a board of directors could do that. Neither is it exclusive and holding itself aloof from the manifold activities of the citizens and the nation. The State as conceived and

built up by Fascism, is a spiritual and ethical entity for securing the political, juridical and economic organization of the nation, an organization which is an expression of the spirit in its origin and growth. The State guarantees the safety of the country at home and abroad, and it also safeguards and hands down the spirit of the people, elaborated through the ages in its language, its customs and its faith. The State is not only the present, it is also the past and above all the future. Transcending the individual's brief spell of life, the State stands for the inherent conscience of the nation. The forms in which it finds expression change, but the need for it remains. The State educates its members to citizenship, makes them aware of their mission, urges them to unity; its justice harmonizes their divergent interests; it hands down to future generations the conquests of the mind in the fields of science, art, law, human solidarity; it leads them up from primitive tribal life to imperial rule, the highest expression of human power. The State hands down to future generations the memory of those who laid down their lives to ensure its safety or to obey its laws; it sets up as examples and records for future ages the names of captains who enlarged its territory and of the men of genius who have made it famous. Whenever respect for the State declines and the disintegrating and centrifugal tendencies of individuals and groups prevail, nations are headed for decay.

20 · EIN VOLK—EIN REICH—EIN FUEHRER

EIN VOLK

–1–

A full Jewess, after the birth of her child, sold her mother's milk to a woman doctor, and concealed the fact she was a Jewess. With this milk, infants of German blood were fed in a children's clinic. The accused is charged with fraud. The purchasers of the milk have suffered damage, because the mother's milk of a Jewess cannot be considered food for German children. The impudent conduct of the accused is also an insult. However, there has been no formal indictment in order to spare the parents—who do not know the facts—unnecessary worry. I will discuss the race-hygienic aspects of the case with the Reich Health Chief.

(Minister of Justice Thierack to Adolf Hitler, April, 1943, Nuremberg Document 1656-NG.)

–2–

1. You SS men have been withdrawn from the front lines by order of the Fuehrer because you are the last sons. This measure has been taken because the people and the state have an interest in seeing that your families do not die out.

2. It has never been the nature of the SS men to submit to a fate without attempting to effect a change. It is your duty to see to it that you are no longer the last sons by producing as many children of good blood as possible.

3. Strive to guarantee the continuation of your ancestors and families within a year, so that you will again be able to do your share in the front lines.

(Order by Reichsfuehrer-SS and Chief of German Police Heinrich Himmler, Aug. 15, 1942, Nuremberg Document 2825-PS.)

–3–

During various visits to the penitentiaries, prisoners have always been observed who—because of their bodily characteristics—hardly deserve the designation human (*Mensch*); they look like miscarriages of hell (*Missgeburten der Hölle*). Such prisoners should be photographed. It is planned that they too shall be eliminated (*auszuschalten*). Crime and sentence are irrelevant. Only such photographs should be submitted which clearly show the deformity.

(Chief Prosecutor Oberlandesgericht in Bamberg, to Generalstaatsanwalt Helm in Munich, Nov. 29, 1944, enclosing summary of conference held under the chairmanship of Ministerialdirektor Engert on Nov. 16, 1944, Nuremberg Document 1546-NG. Engert was Chief of Division IV [Criminal Law-Procedure] in the Ministry of Justice.)

EIN REICH

HITLER DECIDES TO GO TO WAR *

Berlin, 10 Nov 1937

NOTES on the Conference in the Reichskanzlei
on 5 Nov 37 from 1615—2030 hours

Present: The Fuehrer and Reich Chancellor
The Reichsminister for War, Generalfeldmarschall v.
BLOMBERG
The C-in-C Army, Generaloberst Freiherr von FRITSCH
The C-in-C Navy, Generaladmiral Dr. h. c. RAEDER
The C-in-C Luftwaffe, Generaloberst GOERING
The Reichsminister for Foreign Affairs,
Freiherr v. NEURATH
Oberst HOSSBACH

The Fuehrer stated initially that the subject matter of today's conference was of such high importance, that its further detailed discussion would probably take place in Cabinet sessions. However, he,
the Fuehrer, had decided NOT to discuss this matter in the larger
circle of the Reich Cabinet, because of its importance. His subsequent statements were the result of detailed deliberations and of the
experiences of his 4½ years in Government; he desired to explain to
those present his fundamental ideas on the possibilities and necessities
of expanding our foreign policy and in the interests of a far-sighted
policy he requested that his statements be looked upon in the case
of his death as his last will and testament.

The Fuehrer then stated:

The aim of German policy is the security and the preservation of
the nation, and its propagation. This is, consequently, a problem of
space.

The German nation is composed of 85 million people, which, because of the number of individuals and the compactness of habitation,
form a homogeneous European racial body which cannot be found in
any other country. On the other hand, it justifies the demand for
larger living space more than for any other nation. If no political

* Nuremberg Document 386-PS.

body exists in space, corresponding to the German racial body, then that is the consequence of several centuries of historical development, and should this political condition continue to exist, it will represent the greatest danger to the preservation of the German nation (*Volkstum*) at its present high level. An arrest of the deterioration of the German element in Austria and Czechoslovakia is just as little possible as the preservation of the present state in Germany itself. Instead of growth, sterility will be introduced, and as a consequence, tensions of a social nature will appear after a number of years, because political and philosophical ideas are of a permanent nature only as long as they are able to produce the basis for the realization of the actual claim of existence of a nation. The German future is therefore dependent exclusively on the solution of the need for living space. Such a solution can be sought naturally only for a limited period, about one to three generations.

Before touching upon the question of solving the need for living space, it must be decided whether a solution of the German position with a good future can be attained, either by way of an autarchy or by way of an increased share in universal commerce and industry.

Autarchy: Execution will be possible only with strict National-Socialist State policy, which is the basis; assuming this can be achieved the results are as follows:

A. In the sphere of raw materials, only limited, but NOT total autarchy can be attained. . . .

B. In the case of foods, the question of an autarchy must be answered with a definite "NO.". . .

Permanently to counter the difficulties of food supplies by lowering the standard of living and by rationalization is impossible in a continent which had developed an approximately equivalent standard of living. As the solving of the unemployment problem has brought into effect the complete power of consumption, some small corrections in our agricultural home production will be possible, but NOT a wholesale alteration of the standard of food consumption. Consequently autarchy becomes impossible, specifically in the sphere of food supplies as well as generally.

Participation in World Economy. There are limits to this which we are unable to transgress. The market fluctuations would be an obstacle to a secure foundation of the German position; international commercial agreements do NOT offer any guarantee for practical execution. . . .

. . . As our exports and imports are carried out over those sea lanes which are ruled by Britain, it is more a question of security of transport rather than one of foreign currency, and this explains the great weakness in our food situation in wartime. The only way out, and one which may appear imaginary, is the securing of greater living space, an endeavor which at all times has been the cause of the formation of states and of movements of nations. It is explicable that this tendency finds no interest in Geneva and in satisfied States. Should the security of our food position be our foremost thought, then the space required for this can only be sought in Europe, but we will not copy liberal capitalist policies which rely on exploiting colonies. It is NOT a case of conquering people, but of conquering agriculturally useful space. It would also be more to the purpose to seek raw material producing territory in Europe directly adjoining the Reich and not overseas, and this solution would have to be brought into effect in one or two generations. What would be required at a later date over and above this must be left to subsequent generations. The development of great world-wide national bodies is naturally a slow process and the German people, with its strong racial root, has for this purpose the most favorable foundations in the heart of the European Continent. The history of all times— Roman Empire, British Empire—has proved that every space expansion can only be effected by breaking resistance and taking risks. Even setbacks are unavoidable; neither formerly nor today has space been found without an owner; the attacker always comes up against the proprietor.

The question for Germany is where the greatest possible conquest could be made at lowest cost.

German politics must reckon with its two hateful enemies, England and France, to whom a strong German colossus in the center of Europe would be intolerable. Both these states would oppose a further reinforcement of Germany, both in Europe and overseas, and in this opposition they would have the support of all parties. Both countries would view the building of German military strong-points overseas as a threat to their overseas communications, as a security measure for German commerce, and retrospectively a strengthening of the German position in Europe.

England is NOT in a position to cede any of her colonial possessions to us owing to the resistance which she experiences in the Dominions. After the loss of prestige which England has suffered owing to the transfer of Abyssinia to Italian ownership, a return of East Africa can no longer be expected. Any resistance on England's part would at best consist in the readiness to satisfy our colonial claims by taking away colonies which at the present moment are NOT in British hands, e.g., Angola. French favors would probably be of the same nature.

A serious discussion regarding the return of colonies to us could be considered only at a time when England is in a state of emergency and the German Reich is strong and well-armed. The Fuehrer does not share the opinion that the Empire is unshakable. Resistance against the Empire is to be found less in conquered territories than amongst its competitors. The British Empire and the Roman Empire cannot be compared with one another in regard to durability; since the Punic Wars the latter did not have a serious political enemy. Only the dissolving effects which originated in Christendom, and the signs of age which creep into all states, made it possible for the Ancient Germans to subjugate Ancient Rome.

Alongside the British Empire today a number of States exist which are stronger than it. The British Mother Country is able to defend its colonial possessions only allied with other States and NOT by its own power. How could England alone, for example, defend Canada against an attack by America or its Far Eastern interests against an attack by Japan. . . .

It must be established . . . that the Empire cannot be held permanently by power politics by 45 million Britons, in spite of all the solidity of her ideals. The proportion of the populations in the Empire, compared with that of the Motherland is 9:1, and it should act as a warning to us that if we expand in space, we must NOT allow the level of our population to become too low.

France's position is more favorable than that of England. The French Empire is better placed geographically, the population of its colonial possessions represents a potential military increase. But France is faced with difficulties of internal politics. At the present time only 10 per cent approximately of the nations have parliamentary governments whereas 90 per cent of them have totalitarian governments. Nevertheless we have to take the following into our political considerations as power factors: Britain, France, Russia and the adjoining smaller States.

The German question can be solved only by way of force, and this is never without risk. The battles of Frederick the Great for

Silesia, and Bismarck's wars against Austria and France had been a tremendous risk and the speed of Prussian action in 1870 had prevented Austria from participating in the war. If we place the decision to apply force with risk at the head of the following expositions, then we are left to reply to the questions "when" and "how." In this regard we have to decide upon three different cases.

Case 1. Period 1943-45. After this we can only expect a change for the worse. The re-arming of the Army, the Navy and the Air Force, as well as the formation of the Officers' Corps, are practically concluded. Our material equipment and armaments are modern, with further delay the danger of their becoming out-of-date will increase. In particular the secrecy of "special weapons" cannot always be safeguarded. Enlistment of reserves would be limited to the current recruiting age groups and an addition from older untrained groups would be no longer available.

In comparison with the re-armament, which will have been carried out at that time by the other nations, we shall decrease in relative power. Should we not act until 1943/45, then, dependent on the absence of reserves, any year could bring about the food crisis, for the countering of which we do NOT possess the necessary foreign currency. This must be considered as a "point of weakness in the regime." Over and above that, the world will anticipate our action and will increase counter-measures yearly. Whilst other nations isolate themselves we should be forced on the offensive.

What the actual position would be in the years 1943-1945 no one knows today. It is certain, however, that we can wait no longer.

On the one side the large armed forces, with the necessity for securing their upkeep, the aging of the Nazi movement and of its leaders, and on the other side the prospect of a lowering of the standard of living and a drop in the birth rate, leaves us no other choice than to act. If the Fuehrer is still living, then it will be his irrevocable decision to solve the German space problem no later than 1943-45. The necessity for action before 1943-45 will come under consideration in cases 2 and 3.

Case 2. Should the social tensions in France lead to an internal political crisis of such dimensions that it absorbs the French Army and thus renders it incapable for employment in war against Germany, then the time for action against Czechoslovakia has come.

Case 3. It would be equally possible to act against Czechoslovakia if France should be so tied up by a war against another State, that it cannot "proceed" against Germany.

For the improvement of our military political position it must be our first aim, in every case of entanglement by war, to conquer Czechoslovakia and Austria simultaneously, in order to remove any threat from the flanks in case of a possible advance Westwards. In the case of a conflict with France it would hardly be necessary to assume that Czechoslovakia would declare war on the same day as France. However, Czechoslovakia's desire to participate in the war will increase proportionally to the degree to which we are being weakened. Its actual participation could make itself felt by an attack on Silesia, either towards the North or the West.

Once Czechoslovakia is conquered—and a mutual frontier, Germany-Hungary is obtained—then a neutral attitude by Poland in a German-French conflict could more easily be relied upon. Our agreements with Poland remain valid only as long as Germany's strength remains unshakable; should Germany have any setbacks, then an attack by Poland against East Prussia, perhaps also against Pomerania, and Silesia, must be taken into account. . . .

Should Case 2 occur—paralyzation of France by a Civil War —then the situation should be utilized *at any time* for operations against Czechoslovakia, as Germany's most dangerous enemy would be eliminated.

The Fuehrer sees Case 3 looming nearer; it could develop from the existing tensions in the Mediterranean, and should it occur he has firmly decided to make use of it any time, perhaps even as early as 1938.

Following recent experiences in the course of the events of the war in Spain, the Fuehrer does NOT see an early end to hostilities there. Taking into consideration the time required for past offensives by Franco, a further three years duration of war is within the bounds of possibility. On the other hand, from the German point of view a 100 per cent victory by Franco is not desirable; we are more interested in a continuation of the war and preservation of the tensions in the Mediterranean. Should Franco be in sole possession of the Spanish Peninsula it would mean the end of Italian intervention and the presence of Italy on the Balearic Isles. As our interests are directed towards continuing the war in Spain, it must be the task of our future policy to strengthen Italy in her fight to hold on to the

Balearic Isles. However, a solidification of Italian positions on the Balearic Isles can NOT be tolerated either by France or by England and could lead to a war by France and England against Italy, in which case Spain, if entirely in white (i.e. Franco's) hands, could participate on the side of Italy's enemies. A subjugation of Italy in such a war appears very unlikely. Additional raw materials could be brought to Italy via Germany. The Fuehrer believes that Italy's military strategy would be to remain on the defensive against France on the Western frontier and carry out operations against France from Libya against North African French colonial possessions.

As a landing of French–British troops on the Italian coast can be discounted, and as a French offensive via the Alps to Upper Italy would be extremely difficult and would probably stagnate before the strong Italian fortifications, the center of all actions would be in North Africa. The threat to French lines of communication by the Italian fleet will to a great extent paralyze the transport of fighting personnel from North Africa to France, so that at its frontiers with Italy and Germany France will have at its disposal solely the metropolitan fighting forces. . . .

The date of our attack on Czechoslovakia and Austria must be made dependent on the source of the Italian–English–French war and would not be simultaneous with the commencement of military agreements with Italy, but of full independence and, by exploiting this unique favorable opportunity he wishes to begin to carry out operations against Czechoslovakia. The attack on Czechoslovakia would have to take place with the "speed of lightning" (*blitzartig schnell*).

Feldmarschall von Blomberg and Generaloberst von Fritsch in giving their estimate on the situation, repeatedly pointed out that England and France must not appear as our enemies, and they stated that the war with Italy would NOT bind the French army to such an extent that it would NOT be in a position to commence operations on our Western frontier with superior forces. General-oberst von Fritsch estimated the French forces which would presumably be employed on the Alpine frontier against Italy to be in the region of 20 divisions, so that a strong French superiority would still remain on our Western frontier. The French would, according to German reasoning, attempt to advance into the Rhineland. We should consider the lead which France has got in mobilization, and quite apart from the very small value of our then existing fortifications

—which was pointed out particularly by Generalfeldmarschall von Blomberg—the four motorized divisions which had been laid down for the West would be more or less incapable of movement. With regard to our offensive in a South-Easterly direction, Feldmarschall von Blomberg draws special attention to the strength of the Czechoslovakian fortifications, the building of which had assumed the character of a Maginot line and which would present extreme difficulties to our attack.

Generaloberst von Fritsch mentioned that it was the purpose of a study which he had laid on for this winter to investigate the possibilities of carrying out operations against Czechoslovakia with special consideration of the conquest of the Czechoslovakian system of fortifications; the Generaloberst also stated that owing to the prevailing conditions he would have to relinquish his leave abroad, which was to begin on 10 November. This intention was countermanded by the Fuehrer who gave as a reason that the possibility of the conflict was not to be regarded as being so imminent. In reply to the remark by the Minister for Foreign Affairs, that an Italian–English–French conflict be not as near as the Fuehrer appeared to assume, the Fuehrer stated that the date which appeared to him to be a possibility was summer 1938. In reply to statements by Generalfeldmarschall von Blomberg and Generaloberst von Fritsch regarding England and France's attitude, the Fuehrer repeated his previous statements and said that he was convinced of Britain's non-participation and that consequently he did not believe in military action by France against Germany. Should the Mediterranean conflict already mentioned lead to a general mobilization in Europe, then we should have to commence operations against Czechoslovakia immediately, If, however, the powers who are not participating in the war should declare their disinterestedness, then Germany would, for the time being, have to side with this attitude.

In view of the information given by the Fuehrer, Generaloberst Goering considered it imperative to think of a reduction or abandonment of our military undertaking in Spain. The Fuehrer agreed to this insofar as he believed this decision should be postponed for a suitable date.

(Signed) Hossbach

EIN FUEHRER

WHY WE MUST RULE*

With the year 1918 a whole system collapsed. That it had to come about was often predicted, as much by economic leaders as, especially, by Geheimrat Kirdorf. The revolution which the year 1918 brought us was only conditional. In any case it did not bring about the revolution such as in Russia, but only a new school of thought, which slowly initiated the dissolution of the existing order. Bismarck's statement: "Liberalism is the pacemaker of social-Democracy" is now scientifically established and proven for us. A given school of thought—thought direction—can unsuspectedly lead towards the dissolution of the foundation of the State. In our country also, a new direction of thought had gained ground which slowly led to internal disruption and became the pacemaker of Bolshevism.

Private enterprise cannot be maintained in the age of democracy; it is conceivable only if the people have a sound idea of authority and personality. Everything positive, good and valuable, which has been achieved in the world in the field of economics and culture, is solely attributable to the importance of personality. When, however, the defense of the existing order (*des Geschehenen*), its political administration, is left to a majority, it will go irretrievably under. All the worldly goods which we possess, we owe to the struggle of the chosen (*Auserlesenen*). Would we have had the present conditions in the Middle Ages, the foundations of our German Reich would never have been laid. The same mentality that was the basis for obtaining these values must be used to preserve these values. All values which make up the height of our culture originated from an entirely different mentality than that which seized its administration since 1918. The revolution is the first conclusion of a decade-old development of discord in our people. All over the world we experience this crisis of disunity. The people, however, react differently towards it, as for example in Russia and Italy. In the other countries, Germany included, this crisis, in its last possibilities and consequences, is not yet being recognized. Our people has not yet sufficiently recognized that there are two souls struggling for it. Our entire life is based upon

---

* Speech of Hitler to leading members of industry before the election of March, 1933. Nuremberg Document D-203.

common agreements. The smallest example of this is the family and it leads on up to the State. It is an impossibility that part of the people recognizes private ownership while another part denies it. Such a struggle splits the people. The struggle lasts until one side emerges victorious. When a man deserts his unit he can be punished. When, however, 15 per cent to 20 per cent disregard their oath of allegiance, the unit must fail as a military instrument. The same applies to a State, if 15 per cent of the people deny the State as a permanent recognized social order, no sound system can be set up for the general public. Therefore, it is impossible to maintain Culture, Art, Religion and Science, if a large percentage of the Nation refuses to abide by the thoughts which created such a Culture. Justice also can only be established upon generally recognized theories. Therefore, it can also be Bolshevistic, if it has to protect the Bolshevist cause. Such a condition of discord leads slowly but surely to agony, to the death of an ideology. No two ideologies can continuously live alongside one another. In such struggles the strength of a people eats itself completely up internally and therefore cannot act externally. It does not rest. This condition of attrition lasts until one party emerges victorious or the State itself dissolves, whereby a people loses its place in history. We live in such times now, when the die must be cast, and when we must decide whether we want to adopt a form of life that supports the State or to have Communism. The latter is also thinkable. It is often being said that Communism is the last step of humanity. I believe the very opposite; it is the origin of human development. It represents the most primitive form of human life. The deeper one delves into nature, the more alike becomes its achievements, they become as in Communism more and more homogeneous. The Communist principle does not hold water. It is not by chance that one person accomplishes more than the other. The principle of private ownership which has slowly gone into the general conception of justice and has become a complicated process of economic life, is rooted in this fact. The course which we have to take is clearly indicated. It is, however, not enough to say: We do not want Communism in (our) Economy. If we continue on our old political course, then we shall perish. We have fully experienced in the past years that Economics and Politics cannot be separated. The Political conduct of the struggle is the primary decisive factor. Therefore, politically clear conditions must be reached. As Economics alone has not made the German Reich so did politics not make economics. But each one built steadily higher upon the other. As a hand-in-hand working of Politics and Economics brought us to our height, so meant the working against one another, as we experienced it after the revolution, continuous downfall. As I lay in the hospital in 1918 I experienced the revolution in Bavaria. From the very beginning I saw it as a crisis in the development of the German people, as a period of transition. Life always tears up humanity. It is therefore the noblest task of a Leader to find ideals that are stronger than the factors that pull the people apart. I recognized even while in the hospital that one had to search for new ideas conducive to reconstruction. I found them in Nationalism, in the value of personality, in the denial of reconciliation between nations, in the strength and power of individual personality. On this basis I tried to reach an understanding between two souls struggling with one another within the German people. The struggle which I undertook was so much harder because it was conducted during a time when the law for the protection of the weak and decadent held true, a law under which every nation is doomed to perish. Of course, nothing is being accomplished by simple denial of such ways of thought, one has to offer new thoughts. If one rejects pacifism, one must put a new idea in its place immediately. Everything must be pushed aside, must be replaced by something better.

For forty years we are experiencing a continuous growth of Social Democracy. Bismarck said shortly before he retired: "If this keeps up, Marx must remain victorious."

The creative and decomposing forces in a people always fight against one another. In this struggle one side always gains ever greater heights than the other, and therefore I have been following the development of Social-Democracy with steadily growing concern and said to myself, we must come to a decision. I have repeatedly taken the occasion to point out to responsible people what dangers were threatening the German people. Time and again it was argued, amongst others, by von Seeckt, that at the present time this would mean civil war. And when, a few years ago, the number of Socialist seats went back a little, I was told triumphantly: "Look here, the danger is already over." They always comforted themselves with the hope that the Socialist movement would slow down by itself. The danger, however, cannot be overcome by such means. Human beings are nothing less but equal, and if human beings are not led, they drop back into the most primitive ancient state. It was this perception that moved me to found a new Nationalist movement, which after fourteen years of struggle has become a leading force in the German Reich. We must not forget that all the benefits of culture must be introduced more or less with an iron fist, just as once upon a time the farmers were forced to plant potatoes. For all this however, courage, and iron will and perseverance are essential.

We stand today facing the following situation: Weimar imposed upon us a certain constitutional order by which they put us on a democratic basis. By that we were, however, not provided with an able governmental authority. On the contrary, as I criticized Democracy before, Communism had to bore its way constantly deeper into the German people. The result was an ever increasing tension, by which also—and that is almost the worst—the courts did not remain uninfluenced. Two fronts have thus shaped themselves which put to us the choice: Either Marxism in its purest form or the other side. One cannot assume the point of view and say: The other side will gradually break through again. Such an attitude means defeat. When I wanted to act, I was advised to wait a while. But I did not agree to such tolerance. With the very same courage with which we go to work to make up for what had been sinned during the last 14 years, we have withstood all attempts to move us off the right way. We have turned down the favor (benevolence) of the Catholic Center Party (*Zentrum*) to tolerate us. Hugenberg has too small a movement. He has only considerably slowed down our development. We must first gain complete power if we want to crush the other side completely. While still gaining power one should not start the struggle against the opponent. Only when one knows that one has reached the pinnacle of power, that there is no further possible upward development, shall one strike. In Prussia we must gain another 10 seats and in the Reich proper another 33. That is not impossible if we throw in all our strength. Then only begins second action against Communism.

Now we stand before the last election. Regardless of the outcome there will be no retreat (*Rueckfall*), even if the coming election does not bring about a decision. One way or another, if the election does not decide, the decision must be brought about even by other means (*Eben auf einem anderen Weg fallen*). I have intervened in order to give the people once more the chance to decide their fate by themselves. This determination is a strong asset for whatever must possibly happen later. Does the election bring no result, well, Germany won't go to ruin. Today, as never before, everyone is under the obligation to pledge himself to success. The necessity to make sacrifices has never been greater than now. For Economy I have the one wish that it go parallel with the internal structure to meet a calm future. The question of restoration of the Wehrmacht will not be decided at Geneva, but in Germany, when we have gained internal strength through internal peace. There will, however, be no internal peace until Marxism is eliminated (*Erledigt*). Here lies the decision which we must go to meet, hard as the struggle might be. I put my life into this struggle day after day as do all those who joined me in this struggle. There are only two possibilities, either to crowd back the opponent on constitutional grounds, and for this purpose once more this election, or a struggle will be conducted with other weapons, which may demand greater sacrifices. I would like to see them avoided. I hope the German people thus recognize the greatness of the hour. It shall decide over the next ten or probably even one hundred years. It will become a turning point in German history, to which I pledge myself with glowing energy.

GOERING ON THE LEADERSHIP PRINCIPLE *

Dr. STAHMER: What is your attitude to the Leadership Principle?

GOERING: I upheld this principle and I still uphold it positively and consciously. One must not make the mistake of forgetting that the political structure in different countries has different origins, different developments. Something which suits one country extremely well would perhaps fail completely in another. Germany, through the long centuries of monarchy, has always had a leadership principle. Democracy appeared in Germany at a time when Germany was very badly off and had reached rock-bottom. I explained yesterday the total lack of unity that existed in Germany—the number of parties, the continuous unrest caused by elections. A complete distortion of the concepts of authority and responsibility had arisen, and in the reverse direction. Authority lay with the masses and responsibility was with the leader, instead of the other way about. I am of the opinion that for Germany, particularly at that moment of its lowest

* Excerpt from the Proceedings before the International Military Tribunal at Nuremberg, *Trial of the Major War Criminals Before the International Military Tribunal* (Nuremberg: Secretariat of the Tribunal, 1947), IX, 263-264, 418-419. Dr. Otto Stahmer was Defense Counsel for Hermann Wilhelm Goering. Mr. Justice Jackson was Chief of Counsel (Prosecution Counsel) for the United States of America.

ebb, when it was necessary for all forces to be welded together in a positive fashion, the Leadership Principle—that is, authority from above downwards and responsibility from below upwards—was the only possibility. Naturally I realize the fact that here, too, a principle, while thoroughly sound in itself, can lead to extremes. I should like to mention some parallels. The position of the Catholic Church rests now, as before, on the clear leadership principle of its hierarchy. And I think I can also say that Russia, too, without the leadership principle, could not have survived the great burden which was imposed on her by this war.

. . . . .

Mr. Justice JACKSON: You established the Leadership Principle, which you have described as a system under which authority existed only at the top, and is passed downwards and is imposed on the people below; is that correct?

GOERING: In order to avoid any misunderstanding, I should like once more to explain the idea briefly, as I understand it. In German parliamentary procedure in the past responsibility rested with the highest officials, who were responsible for carrying out the anonymous wishes of the majorities, and it was they who exercised the authority. In the Leadership Principle we sought to reverse the direction, that is, the authorty existed at the top and passed downwards, while the responsibility began at the bottom and passed upwards.

Mr. Justice JACKSON: In other words, you did not believe in and did not permit government, as we call it, by consent of the governed, in which the people, through their representatives, were the source of power and authority?

GOERING: That is not entirely correct. We repeatedly called on the people to express unequivocally and clearly what they thought of our system, only it was in a different way from that previously adopted and from the system in practice in other countries. We chose the way of a so-called plebiscite. We also took the point of view that even a government founded on the Leadership Principle could maintain itself only if it was based in some way on the confidence of the people. If it no longer had such confidence, then it would have to rule with bayonets, and the Fuehrer was always of the opinion that that was impossible in the long run—to rule against the will of the people.

Mr. Justice JACKSON: But you did not permit the election of

those who should act with authority by the people, but they were designated from the top downward continuously, were they not?

GOERING: Quite right. The people were merely to acknowledge the authority of the Fuehrer, or, let us say, to declare themselves in agreement with the Fuehrer. If they gave the Fuehrer their confidence, then it was their concern to exercise the other functions. Thus, not the individual persons were to be selected according to the will of the people, but solely the leadership itself.

Mr. Justice JACKSON: Now, was this Leadership Principle supported and adopted by you in Germany because you believed that no people are capable of self-government, or because you believed that some may be, not the German people; or that no matter whether some of us are capable of using our own system, it should not be allowed in Germany?

GOERING: I beg your pardon, I did not quite understand the question, but I could perhaps answer it as follows:

I consider the Leadership Principle necessary because the system which previously existed, and which we called parliamentary or democratic, had brought Germany to the verge of ruin. I might perhaps in this connection remind you that your own President Roosevelt, as far as I can recall—I do not want to quote it word for word—declared, "Certain peoples in Europe have forsaken democracy, not because they did not wish for democracy as such, but because democracy had brought forth men who were too weak to give their people work and bread, and to satisfy them. For this reason the peoples have abandoned this system and the men belonging to it." There is much truth in that statement. This system had brought ruin by mismanagement and according to my own opinion, only an organization made up of a strong, clearly defined leadership hierarchy could restore order again. But, let it be understood, not against the will of the people, but only when the people, having in the course of time, and by means of a series of elections, grown stronger and stronger, had expressed their wish to entrust their destiny to the National Socialist leadership.

Mr. Justice JACKSON: The principles of the authoritarian government which you set up required, as I understand you, that there be tolerated no opposition by political parties which might defeat or obstruct the policy of the Nazi Party?

GOERING: You have understood this quite correctly. By that time we had lived long enough with opposition and we had had enough of it. Through opposition we had been completely ruined. It was now time to have done with it and to start building up.

Mr. Justice JACKSON: After you came to power, you regarded it necessary, in order to maintain power, to suppress all opposition parties?

GOERING: We found it necessary not to permit any more opposition, yes.

21 · PERÓNISM AND INDIVIDUAL LIBERTY *

George I. Blanksten

If the café is sufficiently secluded and the *vino* is good, and if no stranger or other politically unreliable person is within earshot, Argentines may tell a story about two dogs, one Chilean and the other Argentine. The Chilean dog was disease-ridden and underfed, and left his native land to journey to Argentina. The Argentine dog was in good health and was well fed, but nevertheless traveled to Chile. The two animals met near Mount Aconcagua, along the rugged Andean frontier between Chile and Argentina. Like other travelers, they greeted each other and discussed their journeys. The Chilean dog said that he had heard that food was plentiful and of high quality in Argentina and that he was therefore traveling there in search of a good meal. Noting the excellent physical condition of the Argentine dog, the Chilean beast asked him why he was going to Chile. "Oh," said the Argentine dog, "I want to bark."

The story, and hundreds like it now circulating in Argentina, is indicative of a major aspect of the Perón regime. Civil liberty has virtually disappeared in the "new Argentina." Freedom of speech and action—once enjoyed by *porteños* and *provincianos* alike—has little place in the Argentina of Juan Domingo Perón.

. . . . .

Individual liberty was once guaranteed in Argentina by the Constitution of 1853. Perón's 1949 document, on the other hand, takes

* Reprinted from *Perón's Argentina* by George I. Blanksten by permission of the University of Chicago Press. Copyright 1953 by the University of Chicago. All rights reserved. The footnotes in the original version are omitted here.

a very different approach to the problem of freedom. The new constitution declares that "the state does not recognize the liberty to undermine liberty." This proviso, as interpreted by a highly placed *Peronista* theorist, means that "individual liberty should not be absolute." According to this official spokesman, the regime "advocates the suppression of abuses of liberty without arriving at the collectivist extreme of abolishing liberty outright in the name of the state or the race." Extreme individual liberty, it is held, vitiates the citizenry's ability to obey the laws. Hear another of the "new Argentina's" wise men: "States survive public disasters not so much because their rulers know how to govern as because their citizens know how to obey. . . . Many well-intentioned governments have fallen because of anarchy among the people, and others have achieved glory and fame because of the obedience of the governed." If this smacks of Mussolini's fascism, let it be noted that President Perón himself has said that "Mussolini was the greatest man of our century, but he committed certain disastrous errors. I, who have the advantage of his precedent before me, shall follow in his footsteps but also avoid his mistakes." And, according to Perón, the suppression of individual liberty was *not* one of Mussolini's mistakes. From the *Peronista* point of view, Mussolini was at his best when he observed that "nobody asks me for liberty, everybody asks me for bread."

Among the "new Argentina's" first steps in the suppression of individual liberty—or, as the *Peronistas* would put it, the organization of obedience—was the requirement that all persons in the country register with the police so that the authorities might at all times know where individuals were and what they were doing. An order published on August 11, 1943—just two months after the revolution—required that "all adult male Argentines must register before October 31 and keep police advised of any changes in address or status." The registration machinery has been elaborated and "improved" upon incessantly in the years since 1943: at length, on October 14, 1948, a National Registry of Persons, charged with keeping track of literally everybody in Argentina, was established within the Ministry of the Interior. The requirement of registration, of course, means that all persons in the country must carry with them at all times the necessary documentation certifying that their business with the police is in order. On occasion the number of required documents makes for an almost ludicrously large bundle of papers.

In November of 1948, the government classified and listed the various papers persons must carry with them at all times. The official list established seven types of documents: (1) An *identification booklet,* issued by the Federal Police, must be carried by every Argentine citizen and by each foreigner resident in the country for an indefinite period of time. (2) A *credential,* issued by the same agency, must be borne by every government official and by each journalist. (3) A *passport* must be obtained by any Argentine intending to travel abroad, and by almost every foreigner in the country. (4) *Certificates of retirement* must be carried by persons claiming pensions. (5) *Certificates of release* must be held by all former prisoners as evidence that their exodus from jail was legally accomplished. (6) A *certificate of good conduct* must be carried by each Argentine citizen as evidence that he is in good standing with the government. This document, popularly called a *buena conducta,* is a matter of extreme importance to the average Argentine today. When it is realized that a citizen loses his *buena conducta* if he is in trouble with the regime, the tremendous pressure exercised by this harmless-looking little booklet can be appreciated. Argentines must present their *buenas conductas* when they (*a*) return to the country after having been abroad, (*b*) apply for employment, (*c*) register as university students, and (*d*) marry. Some of these, it will be admitted, are important aspects of the day-to-day lives of all Argentines. He who has been in trouble with the police—whether the reason be his political opposition or any of a host of other considerations—and has therefore been deprived of his *buena conducta,* finds life difficult indeed. He may not legally obtain a job, he is deprived of an opportunity for higher education in the country,* and he must forego marriage and/or live in sin. The cost of being an anti-*Peronista* is high for the average Argentine citizen. "There are those who call this government tyrannical," President Fárrell once observed in the early years of the "new Argentina." "Yes, we are tyrants, but only against those who disturb order and oppose the progress of the nation." (7) The tally is completed by the *police certificates,* which must be carried by all foreigners who are in Argentina as tourists.

The everyday administration of the multifarious restrictions on civil and political liberties is entrusted to two government agencies— the super-secret *Control del Estado* and the Federal Police. Although there is some jurisdictional overlap between the two organizations,

---

* Of course, if he goes abroad for his schooling, he may not return to Argentina without his *buena conducta.*

the *Control del Estado* theoretically deals only with Argentine government employees, while the Federal Police handles everybody else in the country.

Very little has been published in English—or in Spanish, for that matter—about the dreaded *Control del Estado,* popularly referred to in whispers as the *Control.* Its work is treated with the utmost secrecy: not even its budget is published. The *Control* is essentially Perón's confidential political police force. Argentines compare it with the *Mazorca,* Rosas' notorious "private army of terrorists and thugs." Germans with Hitlerian experience—and there are many of these in Argentina—frequently compare the *Control* with the Nazi *Gestapo.* Regardless of where the analogies are sought, the *Control* is primarily a military organization charged with the political policing of Argentines, with special attention devoted to government officials and employees. This agency is under the direct supervision of Perón, and is attached, for budgetary and other administrative purposes, to the presidential office.

The *Control del Estado* administers a huge loyalty program or security check, endeavoring to guarantee unquestioned loyalty to Perón on the part of every official and employee of the national, provincial, and local governments. To be a *Peronista* is a major qualification for public office in the "new Argentina": all persons "not identified with revolutionary ideals or imbued with the precepts of social justice" were relieved of their government jobs in the early years of the regime. Since then it has been the function of the *Control* to assure the continuing loyalty of the holders of government office and the aspirants therefor. This has been a large-scale undertaking. . . . Although official figures are not published, there are approximately 1,000,000 government employees in Argentina.† These form, "with their respective families, an army of at least 4,000,000 citizens, or about one quarter of the population of the country." This army is terrorized, intimidated, and kept "loyal" by the *Control.*

The methods of the *Control* range from the most obvious and summary to remarkably subtle and indirect tactics. Government workers may be simply dismissed, or they may be investigated, jailed—even tortured—or driven into exile. On occasion the victims of the *Control* may be advised informally and indirectly that "justice" is about to fall upon them: if they make judicious and efficient use of this

† National, provincial, and local officials and employees are included in this figure.

short notice they may be successful in absenting themselves from the country in time to avoid the more direct measures of the *Control*. The work of this agency is conducted in the utmost secrecy and the Argentine press is forbidden to mention its operations. It is, therefore, somewhat difficult to document the *Control's* activities. The reader may, however, obtain some insight into these activities from the case presented below. This case was delivered to the present writer by two of the principal figures in the affair. They are here called "Suárez" and "Gómez": the names are fictitious—to protect the principals from further harm when the *Control* reads this book, as it surely will—but the remaining facts in the case are based on the personal accounts of these two unfortunate gentlemen.

Both Suárez and Gómez were disloyal in the sense that they disapproved of many of Perón's methods and much of his program. Both, however, desired employment, and were able to secure government jobs. It is generally true that "every man employed by the government has lost his . . . independence and is forced to be, or appear to be, a *Peronista* in order to live." This was the difficult situation of both Suárez and Gómez when they entered the government service; and it was not long before the *Control* became suspicious of their political unreliability. Suárez, a mature man of some reputation, became the chief of a division in one of the executive ministries; the younger Gómez was given a lesser position in the division headed by Suárez. They did not become acquainted with each other until after they had worked in the same office for some time.

Suárez was not only mature and reputable, but also a man of financial means. He bought stocks and, of course, was interested in the fluctuations of the stock market. It happened that the only Buenos Aires newspaper which carried market quotations was *La Prensa,* then the leading anti-*Peronista* daily. Primarily because of his financial interests, Suárez frequently bought *La Prensa*. He would, of course, read other parts of the paper in addition to the market quotations—occasionally he even looked at the editorials. Suárez felt that some of *La Prensa's* editorials made good sense. Once—once was enough—he made the tragic error of telling one of his government associates (let him be called Morales) that a particular *La Prensa* editorial was worth reading. In his capacity as a division chief, Suárez was a bureaucrat of some importance. Occasionally he was required to attend official functions and to sit on the platform with other government people while speeches were made. A frequent orator at such functions was Eva Perón. Suárez was probably less entranced by the late Evita's speeches than a government official ought to be: he felt that *la señora* was not very original in her thinking, and that when a man had heard two or three of her speeches he had heard all of them. Once, while Evita was making a speech—and once was enough for this, too—Suárez confided to the gentleman seated next to him on the platform that *la señora* seemed to say the same things every time she spoke.

One morning—or, as the Argentines like to put it, one nice day— Suárez received a telephone call from the secretary of Colonel Alvarez* of the *Control,* and an appointment was made for an interview. The very mention of the *Control* has a connotation of terror for most Argentine government workers, and it had this effect for Suárez as well. He faced his meeting with Alvarez with considerable apprehension, and was already making plans to leave the country when he called at Alvarez' office. The colonel proceeded to tell him that the *Control* had received *laudatory* reports of his work, and that Perón was considering giving him a more responsible government position. This remark put Suárez at his ease, and he freely answered the colonel's questions about the work of his division.

During the questioning, the colonel asked Suárez for an evaluation of Gómez, who worked in Suárez' division. The latter was generally complimentary with respect to Gómez, saying that he was a conscientious worker devoted to his job. Alvarez' manner stiffened suddenly, and he told Suárez that the *Control* had information to the effect that Gómez was a Bolshevik. This sudden change in the atmosphere of the interview caught Suárez unexpectedly. His reaction was a mixture of incredulity with sudden fear. He remained somewhat defiant, however, and told Alvarez that he knew of no evidence to the effect that Gómez was a Bolshevik, and asked whether any proof of that existed. Alvarez replied by placing a document before Suárez. It was an affidavit declaring that Gómez was a traitor to Argentina; at the foot of the affidavit was a space for the signature of Gómez' division chief. Suárez, of course, was the division chief; with an ominous gesture, Alvarez provided the pen for signature. Terrified but still defiant, Suárez announced that he would refuse to sign the affidavit in the absence of proof that Gómez was indeed a Bolshevik.

Alvarez then proceeded to produce the proof. The evidence was a record of *Suárez'* activities! It was duly noted that Suárez was an

* This name is also fictitious.

habitual reader of *La Prensa,* an anti-government organ. It was further stated that on one occasion—Alvarez cited the date—Suárez had told one Morales that a particular *La Prensa* editorial was worth reading. And—worse than that—the *Control* had evidence that Suárez had once (again the exact date was cited) told a colleague that Eva Perón's speeches were not very good. Q.E.D. Gómez was a Bolshevik. Suárez would please sign the affidavit. Perspiring and thoroughly terrorized, Suárez signed. The rest of the story is simple: Gómez was imprisoned, and Suárez fled to exile.

Let it be noted that the *Control del Estado* polices only one quarter of the population of Argentina. The remaining three-fourths is left to the Federal Police.

. . . . .

Like the *Control del Estado,* the Federal Police is essentially military in its organization and orientation. As now organized, the Federal Police contains five major units of significance here. (1) The division of *Federal Coordination* is Perón's counter-espionage group, and is charged with tracking down such agents of foreign powers as might be operating in Argentina. (2) The *Political Order* section maintains a running surveillance over all Argentine political parties and groups with the exception of the Communists. (3) The *Special Section* performs this function with respect to the Communists. (4) The division of *Social Order* maintains a watch over Argentine social clubs and societies lest they develop political overtones. (5) The *Labor Order* section polices Argentine labor organizations with a view to the preservation of their politically "correct" position.

. . . . .

The Federal Police is one of the most overworked agencies of the "new Argentina." With or without a state of siege there is ample ground for the arrest of Argentines whose ideas and activities are not consonant with Perón's. Since the revolution of 1943, the number of political prisoners held in Argentine jails has been greater than at any other time in the nation's history. The government, as might be expected, has never published the number of persons held in confinement. However, unofficial but well-informed estimates placed the number of political prisoners at 2,000 in August of 1944, 3,000 in October of the same year, and at *14,500* a year later. In what was described as a magnanimous gesture, Perón celebrated his first inauguration as president on June 6, 1946, by signing Decree No. 7, which ordered a general amnesty for political prisoners. A month later—on July 3—he signed Decree No. 1,515, rescinding the amnesty. It is typical of Perón's propaganda techniques that Decree No. 7 was given wide publicity by the newspapers of Argentina, whereas Decree No. 1,515 was not mentioned in the press.

It is characteristic of the "new Argentina" that many of the people who now spend significant portions of their lives in jail are criminals only in the eyes of a *Peronista*. The crimes of a high percentage of them are political activity, "contempt," or seeking employment after having lost their *buenas conductas*. Many of the prisoners are labor leaders, politicians, writers, publishers, and members of various professions. On December 11, 1950, the Córdoba Bar Association released a statement pointing with alarm to the large sector of the nation's legal profession then in prison.

The process of political arrest has become virtually ritualized in the "new Argentina." If the intended victim has strategically placed connections, he may be informed that his arrest is about to take place, and he may have time to escape to safety—usually Montevideo, Uruguay, or the embassy of some foreign state. If he does not have that much time, or if he lacks the strategically placed connections, then he may be surprised when the agent of the Federal Police calls upon him at home or at his place of business. The affair is usually quite gentlemanly, in the best Argentine tradition. The policeman announces that his superior officer desires to see the victim—the announcement is made much as though it were an invitation to join the officer at tea. The ritual then requires that the victim ask whether the message is an invitation or a command, and the policeman normally replies politely that it is his fond wish that it be regarded as an invitation, but if it is not so regarded he regrets that it will have to be considered as a command. The two then depart for the prison, and, upon their arrival, tea frequently *is* served. The reactions of many of the political prisoners to the intriguing experience of arrest and confinement range from anguish to an intellectual, semi-morbid interest in what is happening to themselves and to the world of the Argentines. . . .

. . . The practice of torturing political prisoners continues in Argentina. Torture was outlawed in the country in 1813, but it was resumed shortly after the revolution of 1943. The first reports of this were circulated in November of that year. Detailed exposés were published by the Communist leader Rodolfo Ghioldi in May of 1944, and by the exiled Radical Deputy Silvano Santander in February of 1945. In the latter year, 60 inmates of concentration camps in the Chaco were reportedly subjected to physical torture, and 200 released political prisoners jointly accused the Buenos Aires police of using methods of extreme torture. And on November 25, 1949, a documented account of the use of torture by Argentine police was submitted to the United Nations by the International League for the Rights of Man.

Very little has been published about the *picana eléctrica,* or electric goad, which is the contribution of the Argentine *Control del Estado* and Federal Police to techniques of modern physical torture. The *picana eléctrica* is an electric rod which was originally used in Argentina for the purpose of herding cattle. The rod, when touched against a sensitive part of an animal's body, delivers an electric shock which inspires the beast to move rapidly in the direction desired by the herder. When applied to sensitive sections of the human body, the *picana eléctrica* is also effective. It produces a painful, burning shock, and has been known to induce nervous disorders and sexual impotency. From the standpoint of the *Control del Estado* and the Federal Police, a major advantage of the *picana eléctrica* is that it leaves no bruises or identifying marks on the body of the victim, who therefore finds it difficult to prove later that he had been tortured.

· · · · ·

There is, in short, something of a dearth of individual liberty in Perón's Argentina. The nation lives in an atmosphere of intimidation, in an *ambiente* or political climate where habeas corpus comes and goes while the *Control del Estado* and the Federal Police are ever-present. Whether there is a state of siege or a "state of prevention and alarm" or "constitutional government," life is essentially the same. One dare not discuss politics in public lest "politics" turn out to be synonymous with "contempt," "treason," "sabotage," or "espionage." Those who do not fit in well with the "new Argentina" are strong candidates for political imprisonment and even for cruel physical torture. Argentines with short-wave radios able to pick up the *Voice of America* on occasion hear themselves included among the "free peoples of the world." Some of them find this difficult to understand; other Argentines simply shrug their shoulders and smile cynically. After all, their constitution *does* provide that "the state does not recognize the liberty to undermine liberty."

Evolutionary Socialism

22 · THE SOCIALIST TRADITION *

Alexander Gray

We are perhaps in a position to classify the various types of social-ism. If their differences can be carefully catalogued, what they have in common may also become apparent. It is not impossible that the different types of socialism represent different attempted answers to the same question. If so, what is that question? This exercise in classification is all the more necessary, because there prevails in the use of certain terms not a little confusion which it is now doubtless impossible to eradicate. In particular, one of the most important of all, "communism," has in fact changed its meaning with the passage of time, and has at different stages had very different associations.

Waiving, as irrelevant for our present purpose, certain movements which have socialist infusions, though they are themselves doubtfully socialist—such as the cooperative movement—the socialist systems which have been prominent in the last generation fall broadly into four groups. There is, firstly, anarchism; secondly, collectivism; thirdly, communism; and fourthly, there is the type represented by syndicalism and Guild Socialism, for which no convenient name is in existence. In the early days, Faguet suggested for the fourth type "appropriationism" which is an ungainly word, and, as things have developed, is now inaccurate. Perhaps we may call this fourth type "trade union socialism" which, as it happens, is more or less a trans-lation of "syndicalism" without, however, the associations which that word has acquired. As briefly as may be, how do these types differ?

Of anarchism little need be said. Strictly speaking, it is hardly

* Alexander Gray, *The Socialist Tradition: Moses to Lenin* (New York: Longmans, Green and Co., Third Impression, 1948), pp. 494-499, 503-506, 510-511. Reprinted by permission of Longmans, Green and Co. The footnotes in the original version are omitted here.

entitled to appear as a socialist system at all; and nothing is easier than to show, in the lecture room or on paper, that anarchism, so far from being a type of socialism, is the complete antithesis of most forms of socialism. An anarchist is a liberal who carries his distrust of the State so far that he desires to abolish it altogether. Yet in practice anarchism works out as an extreme form of socialism. It has its roots in that side of socialism which seeks for freedom; and as the State is the greatest of all tyrants, the State (if we may waive the Almighty) is the chief enemy. Having abolished the State, the work of the world will be carried on by voluntary associations—spontaneously hatched like mayflies and with something of the mayfly's delightful evanescence. Anarchism is rather the charming dream of an innocent child. It postulates the passing of all political bones of contention; the evaporation of all passion; the reign of reason. In the matter of the relation existing between anarchism and other forms of socialism, it is of extreme significance that the ultimate long-term ideal of the Marx–Engels–Lenin tradition, after the State has withered away, is a condition of anarchy, indistinguishable from other dreams of anarchism. If Marx and Lenin detested anarchism, it was not because they disapproved of the ultimate vision, but because the anarchists were so foolish as to imagine that the vision could be realised forthwith, as the result of a mere act of volition.

Collectivism and communism may conveniently be considered together. "Communism" is the word with the longer pedigree, as witness *The Communist Manifesto*; J. S. Mill's use of the word is also of interest. "Collectivism," as a word, is a much more recent arrival. Collectivism has gradually come to denote that type of socialism which concentrates attention on the side of production. At its purest it is seen in the Fabians. By the nationalization of industry all enterprise is ultimately vested in the State. The private capitalist goes; the critics suggest that State capitalism arrives. All, or nearly all, would ultimately become employees of the State, which, as the unquestioned monopolist in every industry, would be exalted to a place of peculiar power. But collectivism need not aim at equality: as there is a hierarchy and much inequality in the Civil Service now, so in the extended Civil Service which will be represented by the nationalized industries of the collectivist State, there will be grades and ranks, marked by appropriate differences of rewards.

Communism is much more elusive; but it may be seen, *inter alia,* in More's *Utopia,* and in the brief glimpse which Lenin allows his readers of a far-off distant paradise. Communism is the socialism of consumption: it is the socialism in which all, metaphorically speaking, eat out of a common pot, sharing as members of a family. It would be wrong to regard communism as involving distribution on an equal basis, for nothing is less equal than formal equality. Rather is it distribution according to needs. Assume—and it is an easy assumption—that in a world cured of its unreason, all men will be reasonable. Then, if reasonable, they will not take more than they require, and the problem of distribution can be solved by allowing all to take what they require "from the Halls." Collectivism then, we may say, is the socialism of ordered production, prompted by the desire for efficiency, not necessarily unduly revolutionary in the matter of distribution. Communism is the socialism of consumption, prompted by the impulse to equality and justice, and not unduly curious of how the goods are in fact being produced.

There the matter might rest, but for the confusion which has resulted in the last generation owing to the adoption of the word "communist" by the dominant party in Russia. For sufficient reasons, Lenin desired to change the name of his party; for quite plausible reasons, he selected a name honorably associated with Marx's earlier days. The result, however, has been anything but fortunate, for the communist party is in no way a communist party—yet. There is a long journey to be traversed before that stage is reached. There is, firstly, the dictatorship of the proletariat, which is a regime of rigorous repression, followed by a long process of the withering away of the State—a process the very beginning of which is necessarily, according to Stalin, indefinitely delayed. Then, when the State has finally withered away, we may expect communism. The communism of the communist party is thus postponed to almost as remote a future as it is possible to contemplate. It is rather important to realize this, because orthodox "bourgeois" labor parties have at times shown little inclination to be identified with "communism," and have in certain quarters been harshly criticized and misunderstood in consequence. Communism is a great ideal: it is the vision of the brotherhood of man at last realized, of mankind living as a family. Even if they are impractical, it is the communist and the anarchist who have the loftiest vision. When, however, the bourgeois Labour M. P. avoids too close contact with communism, it is not that he wishes to disown the poetic vision of an ultra-remote future: what disconcerts him is the dictatorship of the proletariat of the immediate present, in which the dictatorship is more prominent than the proletariat. Enough, however, to note here that in the commonest use of the word in the last generation, "communist" has, strictly speaking, been a misnomer.

The fourth general group corresponds to Faguet's "appropriationism," a word devised when this tendency was still at the elementary stage of "the Mine to the Miners," "the Railways to the Railwaymen," "the Sewers to the Scavengers," and so on. In this phase, it is best regarded as an attempt to find a plausible solution to the problem of property. For if the objection to the absentee landowner, the absentee mine-owner, the absentee shareholder generally, is that he is in fact an absentee-owner, doing nothing and living prosperously notwithstanding, it is a fairly obvious suggestion that justice will be done and the unjust rights of property extirpated, if the land is given to the peasant, the mine to the mine-worker, and generally the tools and instruments to those who in fact are doing the work. But syndicalism and Guild Socialism are a great deal more than such "appropriation" of the means of production by the workers concerned; indeed Guild Socialism would deny that it is appropriationist in this sense at all. Trade union socialism is best viewed as resulting from Marxian hatred of the class State, seen as a potent instrument in the class war, combined with an infusion from anarchist sources, suggesting that perhaps the State is not really necessary. Putting aside the State, can the working classes build up their own machine to displace the State, or—if the State may not be wholly displaced—to reduce the State to its proper and comparatively insignificant role? The answer is that in the one case there are the syndicates, the trade unions; in the other that there may be guilds, obtained by a slight refashioning of trade unions, and if something like a State is left, it need be but a shadow of its former self, with its functions delimited and defined. And thus a world arises in which the government, so far as the government is necessary, shall be upon the shoulders of the workers' organizations, and in these the workers will enjoy freedom from tyranny.

In the light of this classification of the four main types of socialism, it is not difficult to arrive at what is the central question of socialism. . . . Socialism and individualism are complementary in this sense, that socialism tends to place society first and to subordinate the individual, whereas individualism underlines the importance of the individual and only thinks secondarily of society. It is a question of the relative emphasis placed on the obvious right (or duty) of self-expression, and the equally ineluctable fact that there are others who make claims (and hampering claims) upon us. In short, the contrast between individualism and socialism springs from the eternal question of the relation of the individual to society. Now it has been sufficiently hammered into us in the last generation that we must not confuse society and the State; nor should we. But just precisely what the State is, and what should be the relation of the State to society are questions which are not easily to be answered. It is clear that here we touch on the core of socialism, and above all of modern socialism. Increasingly, as we approach Leninism, socialism merges into the general, fundamental, eternal questions of politics. Do we need a State? What is the State anyhow? Can we cunningly sidetrack the existing State, and arrive at something "functional"? Can we make use of the State, such as it is, and with its help fashion a better world? Or is there a canker at the heart of the State, of any State known to us, which makes it forever an enemy and an instrument of oppression, so that the only remedy is to "smash" it and replace it by something which will be, not a State in the ordinary sense, but—a dictatorship?—a State, born to wither away? These, in various combinations, are the problems that more or less lie at the heart of recent socialism. In its modern forms, socialism has largely become a dissatisfied and skeptical questioning of the theory of the nature and the functions of the State.

It was of the essence of the teaching of Aristotle on the subject that the State has a natural existence. In a too frequently quoted dictum: "As the State was formed to make life possible, so it exists to make life good." It may be that if we are so hardy as to ask whose life it is that the State exists to make good, we may get an answer which will deter us from quoting Aristotle to Lenin: for assuredly, Lenin would have been more interested in the many unconsidered slaves than in the few consecrated to the good life. Nevertheless on the inevitability, the naturalness of the State, the teaching of Aristotle is as relevant today as ever. The conditions necessary for anarchism, whether it be the straightforward, immediate anarchism of Godwin and Kropotkin, or the indefinitely postponed "statelessness" of the Marx–Engels–Lenin tradition which will come with the final withering away of the State, are so remote from actuality that anarchism must remain a doctrinaire and academic plaything. Not till the nature of man has changed, as Lenin expressly realized, shall we be ready for the ultimate withering-away of the State. Till then the State (or *a* State) remains.

With somewhat more hesitation, the same may be said of trade union socialism. The leading exemplars here are hybrids, the daughter or the granddaughter of anarchy, and, like other hybrids, they are deprived of the hope of posterity. In its attitude to the State, syndicalism is almost entirely anarchist; Guild Socialism somewhat less so. Alike they leave unanswered a multitude of questions of coordination and what-not, which for their answer would recall the State (or its equivalent) from the semi-limbo to which trade union socialism would consign it. Doubtless ideas with kinship to those of syndicalism and Guild Socialism will periodically recur to enliven and fertilize discussion; but with some assurance it may be said that the future of socialism does not lie in the direction of trade union socialism.

There remains as the central question of socialism today the choice between the pessimistic view of the State inherent in the Marxian tradition, and the more hopeful and optimistic attitude represented conveniently by Bernstein and the Revisionists, and by the Fabians. The Marxian view is that the State always has been, is now, and always will be an engine of repression; that in consequence nothing good can come out of it, or be achieved through it; that it is the instrument through which the dominant class exercises its domination; that accordingly it is necessary to "smash" it, and replace it by something entirely different. This is the socialism of revolution, according to which socialism can be realized only as the result of a revolution. The contrary view is that the State is not so black as it is painted; that it can in fact be used, as it has been used, to effect reform—and indeed, indefinitely and without any assignable frontier, including reform in the State itself; that, in consequence, revolution is not an ineluctable necessity, but on the contrary would probably be an uncertain gamble. This, in short, is evolutionary socialism, making use of the existing State and of the existing State machinery.

．　．　．　．　．

This class war is so much at the root of the Marxian view of the State and is so potent an influence in determining the shape of Marxian politics, that one last method of approach may be permissible in considering how far in these days the class struggle does or does not exist as an actual fact. Nowhere in the Marxian tradition is the class war so prominent as in the syndicalists, and it is of unusual interest to look somewhat more closely at the implications of certain of Sorel's pronouncements on the subject. Labriola may say with vigor that "the only reality we recognize is the existence of the class struggle"; yet it is obvious that, at least for the intellectuals, this "reality" fades away into a mere myth—one of those things which, even if untrue, are nevertheless good to think about. There is an illuminating sequence of paragraphs in the *Préface pour Colajanni* on this point. The Marxian theory of classes is, Sorel here remarks, an abstraction. Admittedly, the middle classes are not disappearing; and indeed, as he rightly observes, it is from the middle classes that most of the leaders of socialism come. What Marx did was to present the conflict of juridical ideas *"sous la forme de luttes engagées entre couples antagonistes."* Without this dichotomic division of society, it would have been impossible for socialist propaganda to get the revolutionary idea across to their public—*de faire comprendre l'idée révolutionnaire.* The class struggle is thus merely a picturesque and symbolic abstraction, the justification of which is to be found in its effectiveness for propaganda purposes.

· · · · ·

It may be that in all this class-war business, there is something that eludes us of Anglo-Saxon stock, and disqualifies us from passing judgment. It is wisdom to realize that we never understand our neighbors. Sorel laments that the English and the Americans alike have no proper comprehension of the class war. In the case of America his comment is extraordinarily suggestive. In America, he says, *la vie ouvrière* is not looked upon as a condition peculiar to any section of the people; but rather it is regarded as "a preparation, a school, a means of selection for everyone": the fundamental idea is that every citizen should regard himself as under obligation to pass through this apprenticeship. This may or may not be a valid analysis of the American situation; it is certainly a happy and healthy contrast to the squalor of the class war. And, be it noted, in no country is capitalism so fully developed. With regard to contemporary England, Sorel can merely record, rather ruefully, that "the English are distinguished by an extraordinary lack of understanding of the class war"; and there is a naive footnote in which he contrasts

English and French trade union leaders: "the English trade union leaders rapidly become gentlemen, without anyone blaming them for it." Assuredly, we do not understand the class war. . . .

The State, as we have known it in the last two generations, has been anything but the organ of a class. It has given surprising evidence of adaptability, and of power to give effect to changes considered desirable—to changes, moreover, that may be far-reaching in their scope and consequences. The State can be used; unless in the eyes of those to whom a violent revolution is in itself a desirable experience, there is no occasion to "smash" it.

. . . . .

By a process of elimination we are thus forced back to the use of the existing State and the machinery of the existing State. But, for the socialist cherishing socialist ideals, the question of how the existing State should be used is by no means simple; and very probably —and indeed most certainly—the answer given today would be very different from that which would have been given forty years ago. Then the answer was simple. The ideal then of orthodox socialists was the completely collectivist State, arrived at by nationalizing as rapidly as possible all the industries of the country, and putting each one under a Minister, sitting on an indefinitely elongated front bench. This vision has rather faded, partly under criticism, and partly under the pressure of changing events. For the difficulties of the completely collectivist State are enormous. The State would be the universal employer; everyone would be an employee of the State. Life would be a civil service examination, in which there would be no failures. There would be no outer limbo, into which to toss the incompetents and the insubordinate, in the hope that they would be brought to their senses by being left to fend for themselves for a time. Also the completely collectivist State would in practice be the "horridest tyranny." The State being everything, there would be nothing outside the State; and though this does not seem to have unduly perturbed some of the socialists of the unadulterated collectivist era, a later generation has begun to wonder whether there would be quite enough fresh air about such an arrangement. The State may be as tough a taskmaker as any ordinary capitalist, and in a world of "State capitalism," where there would not even be the satisfaction of changing one's boss, life might be even less pleasant than at present.

Here, however, as not infrequently happens in life, the great change in the attitude to complete undiluted collectivism is due to the fact that in this long controversy, each side has to a very considerable extent succeeded in convincing its opponents. It would probably not be true to say, in the well-worn phrase, that "we are all socialists now": Lenin would certainly not admit that we were. But what may plausibly be suggested is that much of what the socialists contended for forty years ago has passed into fairly general acceptance in the minds of the population at large. We would certainly, with but few exceptions, all be regarded as socialists —and indeed as dangerous socialists, past praying for—by the startled eyes of Sudre and Thonissen. On the other hand, the socialist has to a large extent been convinced by the arguments of his opponents, reinforced (perhaps oddly) by those of the anarchists, that unrelieved collectivism would be not merely an unlovely and stifling world, but that in fact it would not work.

. . . . .

The doubts regarding collectivism are based on the contention that a Government department is not an appropriate machine for running much of the business of the country, so long as Ministerial responsibility is maintained. There are few today who would openly or consciously suggest that Ministers should in normal times be freed from the shackles of Parliamentary responsibility; although it may be observed that all the halfway houses are in one sense devices for diminishing or sharing the Minister's responsibility. If anyone doubts, let him study the answers given in the House in reply to questions regarding the B.B.C. It is true that an irresponsible Government, should we choose that path, might in the short period be an efficient Government; it is significant that, in the Marxian theory, after the revolution the first stage in the building of socialism is a dictatorship. After all, the irresponsible Government can plan; and an organized and planned system of production has always been a large part of the socialist vision. It is important in these days to consider how far "planning" calls for irresponsibility: how far it can be fitted into the machinery of democratic responsibility.

Insofar as a planned economy is the antithesis of a competitive economy, it is primarily a socialist ideal; and the almost universal clamor for a planned economy today may very properly be cited as an illustration of the general acceptance of much that socialism has stood for. In any case he is a fool who does not plan, if the contrary means doing things without foresight and without calculation. Yet the present mania for planning has its dangers, and it may indeed be doubted whether "planning" as understood by the zealous, is consistent with our freedom and our liberties. It may indeed be a short cut to a dictatorship. Let no one delude himself that it is possible to have an economic plan in an isolated chamber, kept rigidly apart from the political life of the country. If we agree to adopt a plan, then either we may not criticize the plan, once it is adopted, in which case the plan becomes our dictator during its currency; or we may reserve the right to criticize and modify the plan, in which case the plan ceases to be a plan, as now understood in many quarters. One simple-minded enthusiast has spoken quite cheerfully of a long-term 75-years plan. Who are we to expect from our great-grandchildren a measure of respect and docility which we ourselves would never have dreamed of according to our own great-grandfathers? Can anyone seriously contend that, if somewhere round about 1875 a plan had been evolved by the greatest minds of the day, the subsequent years would have regarded it as sacrosanct, or —even with the best intentions—could possibly have lived within the blueprint? Democracy, the critic may say, means the right to change views with indefinite frequency: it also means the right to shake off the fetters forged by our fathers. Even under the name of Planning, we cannot bind our successors. Socialism in the next generation may be tempted to play planning as its long suit. It should be very sure that its plan is a servant liable to statutory notice, not a master concealing a hidden dictatorship.

23 · THE FABIAN SOCIETY
Past and Present*
G. D. H. Cole

The Fabian Society, in the words of its Constitution, "consists of Socialists." The same fundamental rule, to which all its members must subscribe, goes on to define this phrase by saying that the Fabian Society "therefore aims at the establishment of a society in which equality of opportunity will be assured and the economic power and privileges of individuals and classes abolished through the collective ownership and democratic control of the economic resources of the community." The rule adds that "it seeks to secure these ends by the methods of political democracy."

That, together with a profession of faith in equal citizenship open to persons "irrespective of sex, race or creed," is the whole basis of belief to which those who wish to join the Fabian Society are asked to subscribe. The words have been changed from time to time during the long life of the Society; but for some time past they appear to have given so much satisfaction that no one has even tried to alter or to enlarge upon them.

The Fabian Society was founded in 1884. Throughout nearly seventy years it has done its best to keep the conditions of membership wide enough to admit a large diversity of views. It insists on Socialism, and does its best to define Socialism in the broadest possible terms. In all other matters of faith and doctrine, it prefers to leave its members free. There is no Fabian "orthodoxy" on matters of controversy within the Socialist movement, save to the extent to which the brief statements quoted above are regarded as controversial. Up to a point, no doubt, they can be so regarded. They would exclude an anarchist, or anyone who does not believe in political democracy. But of genuine Socialists they are meant to exclude as few as possible. The Fabian Society is not a sect: within the limits set by its affiliation to the Labour Party, which it helped to found, it is open to all democratic Socialists.

* G. D. H. Cole, *The Fabian Society Past and Present* (Revised by Margaret Cole; London: Fabian Publications Ltd., 1952), pp. 1-6, 11-14. Reprinted by permission of The Fabian Society. The footnote in the original version is omitted here.

The Fabian Society was named, more than half a century ago, after a certain Roman general, Quintus Fabius Maximus "Cunctator" —which means "the Delayer." This may appear an odd way of naming a Society which has stood throughout its existence for Socialism, and has become famous throughout the world as a planner of Socialist policies and an inspirer of Socialist ideas. For, by and large, most people tend to think of Socialists rather as rushing in where more timorous angels fear to tread than as biding their time, as Fabius did against Hannibal, from whom he saved Rome. I doubt if anyone, founding a Socialist society nowadays, would think of calling it "Fabian." The name is a bit of history: it derives from the state of the British Socialist movement getting on for seventy years ago.

Let us remind you. In 1884, when the Fabian Society was born, there was no Labour Party in Great Britain. The beginning of the Labour Party was sixteen years ahead, and nine years were to pass before Keir Hardie founded its forerunner, the I.L.P. The only pebbles on the British Socialist beach in the Society's early days were Hyndman's Social Democratic Federation and William Morris's Socialist League, which shortly after the birth of Fabianism split off from the S.D.F.; and both these bodies, though they did good work for Socialism in their day and generation, were adepts at "rushing in." In the same year the S.D.F. rushed into the General Election to such purpose that two of its three candidates scored respectively 27 votes against 4,695 and 32 votes against 6,342. Such miserable polls, to say nothing of other circumstances, discredited the Socialist cause; and it was one object of the Fabians to call a halt to such tactics and to set on foot a campaign of Socialist education that would prevent similar fiascos for the future. The Fabian Society set out to spread a knowledge of Socialism; and its propaganda played no small part in preparing the way for the wider successes of the I.L.P. and for the coming of the Labour Party and its adoption of a broadly Socialist creed.

FABIAN FUNCTIONS

. . . . .

Practical Proposals
The truth is that the Fabian Society has always believed its mission to lie more in ideas than in organization. Throughout its long

life it has always, in greater or less degree, combined three functions. It has tried to think out practical proposals for the reformation of particular political, social and economic evils along broadly Socialist lines, and to enlist, in support of its particular schemes, those who have been in key positions for helping to carry them out and have not had their ears stopped by vested interest to the appeal of reason; and it has tried to make plain to ordinary people who are intelligent enough to care about the possibilities of a better social system the necessity of Socialism, and the best means of achieving it. All these things it has done to such extent as its resources have allowed, at various stages in its history. For example—before there was a Labour Party in existence Fabians, largely under the inspiration of Sidney Webb, had a good deal to do with persuading the Liberal Party to adopt a more advanced program of social reform—the Newcastle Program of 1892. It was again Sidney Webb who drafted, in 1918, the first comprehensive program ever put forward by the Labour Party—*Labour and the New Social Order.* Persons who had been converted by Fabian propaganda were largely responsible for the social legislation passed by the Liberal Government after 1906 —until Lloyd George, instead of acting on the Fabian-inspired proposals of the Minority Report of the Poor Law Commission, again the work of the Webbs, sent the Liberals haring off after social insurance on the German model. In later years, Fabians have contributed much that has gone to the making of each successive Labour program, and, since 1945, has been embodied in actual legislation and in administrative practice—though, of course, Fabian advice has not always been taken—or, indeed, been always right. At all times, Fabian lecturers and writers have been busy, as they were busy in the midst of war, telling people about Socialism in terms which bring it down from generalities to concrete practicable proposals. It is the Fabian view that the "good news" of Socialism needs putting squarely and realistically before everyone, in every class and group, who can be persuaded to listen to it.

"Permeation"

The second Fabian method, that of trying to convert those who hold the key positions, was called in the Society's early days by the name of "Permeation," and a good deal of mud was slung at the Society for trying to talk commonsense to anyone who had ears to hear instead of spending all its time speaking comfortable words to those who had been converted already. Naturally, the Fabian Society expected its ideas to get the warmest welcome from those who were already Socialists, and especially from the livelier elements in the working-class movement. But it saw no reason for confining its efforts to those who were easiest to persuade. Not that Fabian "permeation" ever really meant simply the conversion of a few leading officials or "high-ups." Far from it. The person whom the Fabian Society, on this side of its work, most wishes to convert is the man or woman who is in the best position for influencing others, either over a wide area or in his or her comparatively narrow group. Such persons may be Civil Servants or professional men and women or Trade Union or Cooperative leaders, local as well as national, or parsons with a loyal following in their own churches, or speakers with a gift for moving men, or local government or social service workers, or shop stewards. They may be businessmen who have realized the futility of capitalism, or scientists, or teachers in school or university—or students. They may, in effect, be anybody who is a real living person, trying to think for himself and not content to be merely a passive recipient of mass-propaganda or a feebly acquiescent victim of things as they are. The Fabian Society likes to regard each individual in its relatively tiny membership of a few thousands as a stone thrown into a pool, spreading rings of influence all round him.

WHO THE FABIANS ARE

The Fabian membership has always been small, not because the Society desires it to be small, but because reasoning has, and probably always will have, a limited appeal. The Fabian Society's essential appeal is to certain particular kinds of people, and not to all and sundry. It wants, of course, to influence as many people as it possibly can; and it has been, throughout its long history, an agent in converting to Socialism, directly or indirectly, very many times as many persons as have joined it. But it does not expect more than a small fraction of those to whom it appeals actually to join its ranks, or at any rate the ranks of the parent Society. Of course, the more who do join it the better it is pleased; and it seeks to enroll in its local Societies and groups many more than are likely to become national members of the parent body. This is partly because the effectiveness of its work depends on supplying its members with a great deal of literature, itself the product of a great deal of careful research. Such a service cannot be financed without a subscription that is bound to seem high to those who are used to small weekly payments. At one time large donations were a big help; but they have been very much reduced by the redistributive taxation policy which the Fabian Society was one of the first to advocate; and apart from some help from research founds and some from Trade Unions and Cooperative bodies, the Society has to rely nowadays on regular subscriptions of a few pounds at most. The Society has not and could not afford to maintain the organization necessary to collect weekly subscriptions from a membership scattered all over the country. It has to have an annual subscription—though under certain conditions this may be paid quarterly; and this limits its possible membership. A pound a year is not much more than fourpence a week; but it is apt to seem much more. In fact, our smaller subscribers contribute little to the Society's general expenses; they get back from it most of what they pay in the actual expenses of supplying them with literature and keeping them in touch with the Society's work. So the parent Society has to get larger subscriptions from all who can afford to pay them—and, of course, a good deal more money from somewhere, or it could not go on at all, or at all events could not carry on any effective research. The local Fabian Societies do not suffer under this particular handicap, and can therefore aim at a wider membership.

But, even in their case, there are reasons why the Fabian membership is likely not to become large, in comparison with that of other political bodies seeking to exert a widespread influence. The Fabian Society will never, in the nature of things, become a mass movement. It does not aim at mass-conversions or at mass emotional appeals. While recognizing their political necessity and value, it leaves them to others, within whose province they lie. Mass-appeal is a different art from research and education; and the Fabian Society prefers to get on with its own different job, which is to put the right equipment of ideas and information into the possession of that not inconsiderable body of persons (some hundreds of thousands at the least, if they could all be reached) who believe in the value of getting at the real facts and thinking hard about them, and are aware that, even if politics depend fundamentally on men's emotions, emotional appeals by themselves will not get far in practice, unless clear thinking comes to their aid when it is a question of translating desires and ideals into positive achievements.

This type of clear thinking is not a monopoly of any class of specialists, or of those who have received the benefit of any particular kind of education. Men and women who are prepared to use their brains for thinking lucidly about politics are found in all classes; and in all classes they are at present the exceptions. It is much easier for the educated as well as for the uneducated man, in the ordinary sense of the words, to live by the rule of prejudice and tradition than to think things out in an objective way. Indeed, in this respect the highly educated are often among the worst offenders, both because they are blinded by social prejudice and because, even when they are not, they are very apt to think unrealistically, and with much too little understanding of the wants and sentiments of ordinary people. Those who have missed the chance of higher education often offend also against the rule of reason, and with much better excuse. The educated obscurantist turns his back on the truth, because it offends his prejudices or seems to involve knowing things too mean for his mind. The uneducated man, on the other hand, is apt to be unable to get his aspirations into a shape in which they are realizable, and consequently tends to flounder about in generalities.

The Fabian Society consists, to a quite remarkable extent, of reasonable people—by which I mean people who believe in using their reason and in not allowing themselves to be the victims either of prejudice or of intellectual dilettantism or of muddled goodwill. It is bound to make fairly high demands of its members in these respects in order to be true to its essential function. Not, of course, that it requires that all its members shall be original thinkers, or exceptionally able persons. What it demands of them is not exceptional ability, but a kind of intellectual courage which will not let them run away from the facts of contemporary society, whether they are pleasant or not. It calls, not for high educational attainments, but for a positive state of mind which refuses to be satisfied with phrases or to take things for granted, and insists on having everything carefully examined again and again, in order to find out whether what once held good holds good still, and to seek new ways of dealing with changing situations instead of trying to meet them by the application of ancient formulæ that no longer fit the facts.

Fabian Standards

This means that the Fabian Society has, within the limits imposed by its resources, to set itself a high standard in both research and the propaganda which it bases on its research. It is appealing to people who *know*, whether about the hewing of coal or the drafting of forms; it cannot afford to be ignorant or silly. Nor, as it believes in reason and the use of reason in argument, is it prepared to tell lies or compound slogans which it knows to be false for the sake of producing some immediate emotional result. It can be said with confidence that during the whole of its history the Fabian Society has steadfastly endeavored, subject to human frailty,

(1) to check and counter-check the *facts* contained in its publications;

(2) to *argue,* fairly and fully, the case for any proposal which it puts forward, and not to put forward any case which it does not believe to be substantially true, merely because it would like to believe it true, or because it forms part of the recognized Socialist "orthodoxy";

(3) to check, by consultation with those who know, the practicability, under existing conditions, of any proposals which it makes—i.e., not to be visionary or foolish.

These three ambitions may sound modest. But they are not particularly easy to work out in practice. They involve a fairly high standard of accuracy and competence in work, and sometimes a measure of self-abnegation, which the Society has often in fact employed, in withholding from the public work which has seemed to fall short of this standard.

. . . . .

FABIANISM AND POLITICS

There are two reasons why the Fabian Society attaches particular importance to preserving this undogmatic attitude. We believe there is need, somewhere in the Socialist movement, for a body which is entirely free to think out and to give publicity to new ideas, even where they run counter to Socialist orthodoxies inherited from the past. Socialism is not a set of fixed dogmas, always ready to be applied irrespective of time and place. It is a set of principles, which need continual re-interpretation in the light of changing needs and conditions. There is always a danger of mistaking dogmas for principles, and of allowing policies and programs to become ossified; and this danger can be held off only by continual fresh thinking of an essentially objective sort. A political party can never be quite free to do this, because it has to act solidly in support of a united policy in order to achieve its ends. But the Fabian Society is not a political party, and its object is to influence others rather than to carry out its ideas in practice. It is organized for thought and discussion, and not for electoral action, which it leaves to other bodies, though it encourages its members, in their individual capacities, to play an active part in the work of these other bodies. It counts among its members a great many leading members of local Labour Parties, Trade Unions, Cooperative Societies, and other working-class agencies and a large number of Labour Members of Parliament and of Labour representatives on municipal and other local authorities; and it expects all its members to take an active part in the political work of the Socialist movement, in their several spheres. But as a Society it keeps itself apart from electoral affairs, and values its freedom from the day-to-day exigencies of party politics. Thought must be free if it is to remain alive; and thinking about politics and economics is the Fabian Society's special job.

The second reason is closely connected with the first. The chief body of opinion which the Fabian Society seeks to influence is the Labour movement. But it would be entirely fatal to our prospects if we, as a body of people who specialize in plans and ideas, were to produce a program of our own, separate from and in rivalry with the accepted programs of the Labour Party and the Trade Unions, and were to attempt to force our program down the throats of the millions whose lives it would vitally affect. It is legitimate and necessary for the Fabian Society continually to throw out ideas and suggestions for notice by those who have the task of formulating the official programs, and to hope that these ideas and suggestions will influence official policy. But our chance of exerting this constructive influence would be gone if we appeared to be pushing our own program against the official programs.

That is precisely what has happened to other Socialist bodies which have tried to act in this way. The I.L.P. and the Socialist League in turn got the reputation of trying to force their own particular medicines down the throats of the Labour Party and the Trade Unions. Many of the leaders of these bodies thereupon refused to have anything to do with them, and denounced them as groups of irresponsible persons who were trying to teach their grandmothers to suck eggs. It does not matter, for the present purpose, whether the policies advocated by the old I.L.P. and the Socialist League were right or wrong. Personally, I hold that they were largely right. The point is that they were put forward in such a way that there was no chance of their being listened to, and that any fool who got up and denounced them as the work of a bunch of superior intellectual idiots was certain of rapturous applause. The Fabian Society does not mean to fall into that error. It is not trying to push anything down anybody's throat. It simply researches and thinks, publishes the results of its thinking in speech and writing—and hopes for the best. It trusts to the wisdom of the common people to ensure that what it does well will in course of time pass into the general stock of Socialist ideas and policy, and that what it does badly will be set aside.

Fabians and the Labour Party

That has been the Fabian way ever since it helped to found the Labour Party fifty years ago. For all that time the Fabian Society has been affiliated to the Labour Party, and has never quarreled with it, even if again and again many Fabians have disapproved of something the Party has done. We have watched other Socialist bodies break their heads against a brick wall, and knock their brains out in the process. We, as a Society, have sat tight, leaving our individual members to make the running in support of this or that idea through the local Labour Parties or other bodies to which they belong, but refusing to commit the Society collectively on any internal quarrel—jealously guarding our independence of thought and seeing to it that our identity as a Socialist body is maintained. For though we are affiliated to the Labour Party and working in loyalty to it, let it be clearly understood that the Fabian Society is not simply a part of the Labour Party, but an independent body of persons organized for furthering the Socialist cause.

It is of vital importance that both our members and others who have dealings with us shall understand this difference. We cannot as a Society be simply a part of the Labour Party, because Socialism is not simply a political question. Socialism is a theory and a way of life: it is what some people call a religion and others an ethical creed. It involves political action for achieving many of its ends; and for this purpose there is need for a political party committed to a Socialist program. But Socialism involves much besides this—much that is not "politics" in any ordinary sense. The Fabian Society, when it wishes to act politically, acts as a part of the Labour Party. But this is not all it does, and in view of its special character, its nonpolitical work is fully as important as that part of its work which falls within the field of politics.

For example, the Fabian Society has among its members a good sprinkling of men and women from many different professions— doctors, teachers, industrial managers and technicians, and so on. It wants all these persons to face as Socialists the special problems of their own professions, and to work out, not merely how these professions ought to be organized in a Socialist Society, but what can be done in them now both to improve the immediate equality of their service to the community, and to lead on towards their re-organization on sounder lines. What Fabians are trying to do in these spheres of action is hardly politics at all—certainly not "party politics"; but it is of immense importance for creating in the key positions of society the states of mind and preparation that will make Socialism work, if and when the politicians succeed in establishing it. Nor is it of less importance in the immediate cause of human happiness and decency under the existing order; for every doctor, or industrial manager or teacher who becomes a convert to Fabian Socialism is one more man or woman holding a key position who appreciates that his job is to work in terms of fellowship and social equality with others, irrespective of class or status, for improving the quality of human life.

Policy-Making

A few examples of what the Society is doing in these fields of action will serve to illustrate what I mean. We try from time to time to get together those of our members who hold positions as managers or technicians in industrial concerns for discussion, both among themselves and with others, of the forms of management and control of industry that need to be established in a democratic society. We try to get them to understand the claims of the Trade Unions and our Trade Union members to realize the importance of the technical problems of management and administration. In this way we do what we can to build a bridge between the workers "by hand and brain" for the essential tasks of Socialist construction. Again, on the economic side, we are continually studying problems of incentives in a Socialist economy, taxation, distribution, raw materials, and the economic significance of scientific developments. On the political side, we work on the necessary reform of the machinery of government, and of local government; we examine the structure and working of political parties, and the vital question of how the people can be found and trained to run the democratic "Welfare State"; we try to think out what ought to be done and what can be done about our still highly undemocratic system of education. We try to discover how the State and local authorities and other organizations can enable the citizen to participate in the arts and to have more facilities for enjoying them; and we take up as many other problems of the same importance as we can find members equipped to study. These are only a few instances of the Society's efforts to enlist the help of the many specialists who are among its members, and to ensure that Socialists who have expert knowledge are given every opportunity of putting their wisdom and experience at the disposal of the whole Labour Movement.

We of the Fabian Society wish most heartily that we could do more than we are doing in these fields—especially since there is so much thinking that urgently needs to be done, both on the experience of Labour in office and the morals to be drawn from that experience, and on the future programs for Labour. But the task is not easy. Ever since 1939 it has been more and more difficult to get people together for discussion. Many Fabians are in Parliament, working no less hard as an Opposition than they did on the Government side; many more are coping with the heavy work of local government or in nationalized industries or services, so as to have all too little time left to meet the Society's calls upon them. If, in spite of all these difficulties, the Society's activities are today greater and more varied than they have ever been, that is no reason for our feeling satisfied; for the times have aroused in many more men and women a readiness to respond to the Socialist appeal and to perform prodigies of energy beyond what they would have deemed possible in normal times. We have to recognize that we have touched only a tiny fraction of those who would be ready to help us if we could get near to them and explain to them where we stand and what we want them to do. Our resources are so pitifully limited in relation to our opportunities that we are continually conscious of a dozen opportunities missed for every one that we are able to take. We can avoid this only to the extent to which our present members not only work for us, but also bring in others, and thus widen the range of what we can put in hand.

24 · A SOCIALIST'S FAITH *

Norman Thomas

With the end of World War II, my sense of the necessity of re-examining the nature of socialism and the case for it grew steadily stronger. The emotional climate surrounding socialism in the middle of the twentieth century was greatly different from that of the year 1900, when both the British Labour Party and the American Socialist Party came into being, or from that of the First World War period, when I was drawn to the Party.

The romantic period of socialist enthusiasm has passed. The word *socialism* has been defiled in Germany by Hitler's use of it, preceded by the adjective national. It was not cleansed by Stalin's appropriation of it to describe the character of his totalitarian state. Like other great words—democracy and Christianity, for instance—the terms socialism and socialist have lost clarity and precision of meaning. In the mouths of its enemies—and some of its ill-informed friends—socialism is usually equivalent to any and every form of collectivism. Often it becomes a description of all welfare legislation or the goal to which such legislation might take mankind.

For myself, socialism has always seemed primarily a doctrine and movement consciously concerned with the common good. Therefore, it requires planning. Social ownership seemed a tool, a means, not an end. I have changed somewhat my opinion of the amount of social ownership that is desirable. I have come to recognize that of itself it does not mechanically answer our economic problems and that democratic controls will not come automatically but must be thought out. Yet substantial social ownership in the socialist tradition is basic to a happy solution of problems of production and distribution.

We democratic socialists have been partially responsible for misunderstandings about socialism. We have not made our position clear in relation on the one hand to Marxism and on the other to a purely pragmatic welfare state.

* Norman Thomas, *A Socialist's Faith* (New York: W. W. Norton and Company, Inc., 1951), pp. 3-8. Copyright, 1951, by Norman Thomas. Reprinted by permission of W. W. Norton and Company, Inc.

All socialism owes a debt to Marx and has been greatly influenced by him. Yet in practice—and to some extent in theory or lack of it—democratic socialism in Britain and the Scandinavian countries is non-Marxist. The French and Italian socialists who repudiate communism are rather more insistent on their Marxist orthodoxy, which, however, gives them no sure and steady light to guide their course amid the wreckage of the postwar world. Marxism of the communist brand has had its authoritative interpreter in Lenin, and communist Marxism, or rather Leninist Marxism, is under the vigilant guardianship of the political hierarchy of the Soviet Union. Under that guardianship it has become a totalitarian philosophy to be interpreted in theory and practice by the rulers of an absolute police state.

By contrast democratic socialism when avowedly Marxist has suffered from several conflicting tendencies. Often it has defined itself too narrowly in terms of opposition to communism. In that process it has sometimes felt impelled to a sterile orthodoxy concerned to prove that its spokesmen, rather than Lenin, Trotsky, or Stalin, are true interpreters of the Marxist word. On the other hand, their common Marxist origin has often tended to paralyze socialist opposition to communism. Marxism has frequently made socialists apologetic about true democracy. The fairly easy surrender of large sections of former social democratic parties to the communists in Czechoslovakia, Rumania, and Poland cannot be wholly explained in terms of bribes and coercion. Surrender was at least made easier by the consideration, "Are not we Marxists, however we differ, constrained to stand together against a capitalist or non-Marxist world?"

The situation has been less bad in France and Italy, but I suspect that there also the necessity felt by socialists to profess a fairly orthodox Marxism has been a factor—though not the most vital—in the failure of democratic socialism to constitute that strong third force which might surely save their countries from communism or a new fascist reaction.

It is by no means my intention to add another book to the Marxist controversy. Yet no book dealing with socialism as it was, is, or may become, can ignore Marxism. For me the outstanding fact about it, despite its proven power, is its inadequacy for our time under any interpretation.

Marx told us how socialism in the inexorable dialectical movement of history would come to power; but he barely suggested how it would use power. He assumed the humanistic ends generally accepted in the nineteenth century. He claimed to be the exponent of a science. His followers have tended to treat his writings as inspired scriptures. Precedents for Marxist controversies are to be found in the realm of theology, not science. Imagine how science would have been handicapped if Einstein had felt compelled either to prove that he was only interpreting Newton or to make a frontal attack upon his eminent predecessor, to whom he and all other scientists owed so much. A sound development of socialist thinking in the fields of economics and politics has suffered scarcely less from its theological approach to Marxism. Both the strength and weakness of Marxism find parallels and illustrations in the history of religion rather than of science. The sense of certainty that Marx gave his followers is immensely valuable in social conflict. But the quality of that certainty is of the order of religious faith rather than of proof in a scientific laboratory.

The real greatness of Marx himself has been obscured in the current controversy. Part of that greatness lay in his capacity for patient research into the body of historical, political, and economic knowledge available to him. The sum total of our knowledge, notably in the areas of history and psychology, has been vastly expanded since his time. His own predictions have been put to the test of events, a test which they have met partially but imperfectly. A tremendous mass of literature on Marxism has been developed, but quite obviously no living and vital philosophy has been or can be derived from the conscious effort not to seek truth for its own sake, but to vindicate this or that Marxist doctrine. It was not in this spirit that Marx himself developed the doctrines which gave to the working class of the world so deep a sense of its own revolutionary destiny.

Fortunately for me, socialism and Marxism are not identical, and the American Socialist Party, while heretofore predominantly Marxist, has never insisted that applicants for membership should accept a detailed and infallible Marxist creed.

I had come to socialism, or more accurately to the Socialist Party, slowly and reluctantly. From my college days until World War I my position could have been described, in the vocabulary of the times, as "progressive." In my callow youth I even contemplated writing a book in support of progressivism as against socialism. Life and work in a wretchedly poor district in New York City drove me steadily toward socialism, and the coming of the war completed the process. In it there was a large element of ethical compulsion. Certainly I was no anti-Marxist when I joined the Party, but mine, like much English socialism, was non-Marxist. Later I went through various degrees of belief in Marxism. It was, however, when I was closest to that *ism*—in the early nineteen thirties—that I became most aware of a desire that there should be a synthesis such as Marx did not provide between economics, politics, and the knowledge that had been brought to us by the newer schools of psychology.

That synthesis for which I felt so keen a need then is not even now consciously sought in our great universities, where savants in various fields tend blissfully to go their separate ways in complete indifference to one another's theories or findings of fact. Philosophers, psychologists, physical scientists, economists, and sociologists, by their unrelated theories, exaggerate where they do not create the confusion of our times.

As the years have passed, my belief in the need for developing a more adequate socialist philosophy has increased. Marxism had its great insights, but today not one of its principal dogmas is maintained by Marxists of integrity without elaborate explanation and qualification.

No less an authority than Engels himself contributed to this situation. In a letter he wrote: "Marx and I are partly responsible that at times our disciples have laid more weight upon the economic factor than belongs to it. We were compelled to emphasize that central character in opposition to our opponents who, denied it, and there wasn't always time, place, and occasion to do justice to the other factors in reciprocal interaction in the historical process.". . .

No serious thinker coming with fresh mind to Marxism one hundred years after the *Communist Manifesto* would find in it a completely scientific explanation of life or even of economics and politics. Marxism's importance lies not in its finality as science or religion, but in its record through a century of extraordinary propaganda power over large masses of men. It did foretell the collapse of the older capitalist system. It did not foretell the specific manner of that collapse which it helped to bring about. It is the state religion of the mighty Soviet Union and the international communist movement. It is reverenced by many democratic socialists, who derive from it at vital points conclusions opposite to the communists.

Clearly the world ought to have some more adequate social philosophy. Any new synthesis of our knowledge and aspirations will owe much to Marx, but it will not be Marxist unless by a very loose use of the word.

I do not approach my own reexamination of socialism in the belief that I can produce for myself, much less for mankind, a philosophic substitute for Marxism. I doubt if any man of my generation can render such service. We have been too much involved in the failures of our tme, its loves and hates, its wars and confusions, its dreams and their strange and often ironic endings. But out of our experience and our thinking we may offer something of value to the younger folk who must shape the future. Meanwhile, I can testify that we have found abundant reason for faith in democratic socialism as the best basis for ordering the good society.

Revolutionary Socialism

25 · MEMOIRS OF A REVOLUTIONIST *

Peter Kropotkin

Our main activity was in working out the practical and theoretic aspects of anarchist socialism, and in this direction the federation has undoubtedly accomplished something that will last.

We saw that a new form of society is germinating in the civilized nations, and must take the place of the old one: a society of equals, who will not be compelled to sell their hands and brains to those who choose to employ them in a haphazard way, but who will be able to apply their knowledge and capacities to production, in an organism so constructed as to combine all the efforts for procuring the greatest sum possible of well-being for all, while full, free scope will be left for every individual initiative. This society will be composed of a multitude of associations, federated for all the purposes

* Peter Kropotkin, *Memoirs of a Revolutionist* (Boston and New York: Houghton Mifflin Co., 1899), pp. 398-403.

which require federation: trade federations for production of all sorts—agricultural, industrial, intellectual, artistic; communes for consumption, making provision for dwellings, gas works, supplies of food, sanitary arrangements, etc.; federations of communes among themselves, and federations of communes with trade organizations; and finally, wider groups covering all the country, or several countries, composed of men who collaborate for the satisfaction of such economic, intellectual, artistic, and moral needs as are not limited to a given territory. All these will combine directly, by means of free agreements between them, just as the railway companies or the postal departments of different countries cooperate now, without having a central railway or postal government—even though the former are actuated by merely egotistic aims, and the latter belong to different and often hostile states; or as the meteorologists, the Alpine clubs, the lifeboat stations in Great Britain, the cyclists, the teachers, and so on, combine for all sorts of work in common, for intellectual pursuits, or simply for pleasure. There will be full freedom for the development of new forms of production, invention, and organization; individual initiative will be encouraged, and the tendency toward uniformity and centralization will be discouraged. Moreover, this society will not be crystallized into certain unchangeable forms, but will continually modify its aspect, because it will be a living, evolving organism; no need of government will be felt, because free agreement and federation take its place in all those functions which governments consider as theirs at the present time, and because, the causes of conflict being reduced in number, those conflicts which may still arise can be submitted to arbitration.

None of us minimized the importance and magnitude of the change which we looked for. We understood that the current opinions upon the necessity of private ownership in land, factories, mines, dwelling-houses, and so on, as the means of securing industrial progress, and of the wage-system as the means of compelling men to work, would not soon give way to higher conceptions of socialized ownership and production. We knew that a tedious propaganda and a long succession of struggles, of individual and collective revolts against the now prevailing forms of property-holding, of individual self-sacrifice, of partial attempts at reconstruction and partial revolutions, would have to be lived through, before the current ideas upon private ownership would be modified. And we understand also that the prevalent ideas concerning the necessity of authority—in which all of us have been bred—would not and could not be abandoned by civilized mankind all at once. Long years of propaganda and a long succession of partial acts of revolt against authority, as well as a complete revision of the teachings now derived from history, would be required before men would perceive that they had been mistaken in attributing to their rulers and their laws what was derived in reality from their own sociable feelings and habits. We knew all that. But we also knew that in preaching reform in both these directions, we should be working with the tide of human progress.

When I made a closer acquaintance with the working population and their sympathizers from the better educated classes, I soon realized that they valued their personal freedom even more than they valued their personal well-being. Fifty years ago, the workers were ready to sell their personal liberty to all sorts of rulers, and even to a Cæsar, in exchange for a promise of material well-being; but now, this was no longer the case. I saw that the blind faith in elected rulers, even if they were taken from amongst the best leaders of the labor movements, was dying away amongst the Latin workers. "We must know first what we want, and then we can do it best ourselves," was an idea which I found widely spread among them—far more widely than is generally believed. The sentence which was put in the statutes of the International Association, "The emancipation of the workers must be accomplished by the workers themselves," had met with general sympathy, and had taken root in minds. The sad experience of the Paris Commune only confirmed it.

When the insurrection broke out, a considerable number of men belonging to the middle classes themselves were prepared to make, or at least to accept, a new start in the social direction. "When my brother and myself, coming from our little room, went out into the streets," Elisée Reclus said to me once, "we were asked on all sides by people belonging to the wealthier classes: 'Tell us what is to be done? We are ready to try a new start.' But *we* were not yet prepared to make the suggestions."

Never before had a government been as fairly representative of all the advanced parties as was the Council of the Commune, elected on the 25th of March, 1871. All shades of revolutionary opinion—Blanquists, Jacobinists, Internationalists—were represented in it in a true proportion. And yet, the workers themselves having no distinct ideas of social reform to impress upon their representatives, the Commune government did nothing in that direction. The very fact of having been isolated from the masses and shut up in the Hôtel de Ville paralyzed them. For the success of socialism, the ideas of no-government, of self-reliance, of free initiative of the individual—of anarchism, in a word—had thus to be preached side by side with those of socialized ownership and production.

We certainly foresaw that if full freedom were left to the individual for the expression of his ideas and for action, we should have to face a certain amount of extravagant exaggeration of our principles. I had seen it in the nihilist movement in Russia. But we trusted—and experience has proved that we were right—that social life itself, supported by a frank, open-minded criticism of opinions and actions, would be the most effective means for threshing out opinions and for divesting them of the unavoidable exaggerations. We acted, in fact, in accordance with the old saying that freedom remains still the wisest cure for freedom's temporary inconveniences. There is, in mankind, a nucleus of social habits—an inheritance from the past, not yet duly appreciated—which is *not* maintained by coercion and is superior to coercion. Upon it all the progress of mankind is based, and so long as mankind does not begin to deteriorate physically and mentally, it will not be destroyed by any amount of criticism or of occasional revolt against it. These were the opinions in which I grew confirmed more and more in proportion as my experience of men and things increased.

We understood at the same time that such a change cannot be produced by the conjectures of one man of genius, that it will not be one man's discovery, but that it must result from the constructive work of the masses, just as the forms of judicial procedure which were elaborated in the early medieval period, the village community, the guild, the medieval city, and the foundations of international law were worked out by the people.

Many of our predecessors had undertaken to picture ideal commonwealths, basing them sometimes upon the principle of authority, and, on some rare occasions, upon the principle of freedom. Robert Owen and Fourier had given the world their ideals of a free, organically developing society, in opposition to the pyramidal ideals which had been copied from the Roman Empire or from the Roman Church. Proudhon had continued their work, and Bakúnin, applying his wide and clear understanding of the philosophy of history to the criticism of present institutions, "built up while he was demolishing." But all that was preparatory work only.

The International Workingmen's Association inaugurated a new method of solving the problems of practical sociology by appealing to the workers themselves. The educated men who had joined the association undertook only to enlighten the workers as to what was going on in different countries of the world, to analyze the obtained results, and, later on, to aid them in formulating their conclusions. We did not pretend to evolve an ideal commonwealth out of our theoretical views as to what a society *ought to be,* but we invited the workers to investigate the causes of the present evils, and in their discussions and congresses to consider the practical aspects of a better social organization than the one we live in. . . .

For myself, placed as I was in such favorable conditions, I gradually came to realize that anarchism represents more than a mere mode of action and a mere conception of a free society; that it is part of a philosophy, natural and social, which must be developed in a quite different way from the metaphysical or dialectic methods which have been employed in sciences dealing with man. I saw that it must be treated by the same methods as natural sciences; not, however, on the slippery ground of mere analogies such as Herbert Spencer accepts, but on the solid basis of induction applied to human institutions. And I did my best to accomplish what I could in that direction.

26 · REFLECTIONS ON VIOLENCE *

Georges Sorel

Syndicalism in France is engaged on an antimilitarist propaganda, which shows clearly the immense distance which separates it from Parliamentary Socialism in its conception of the nature of the State. Many newspapers believe that all this is merely an exaggerated

* Georges Sorel, *Reflections on Violence* (Translated by T. E. Hulme and J. Roth; Glencoe, Illinois: The Free Press, 1950), pp. 133-135, 137-142, 144-147. Reprinted by permission of The Free Press and of George Allen and Unwin, Ltd. The footnotes in the original version are omitted here.

humanitarian movement . . . ; this is a great error. We should be misconceiving the nature of the movement if we supposed that it was merely a protest against harshness of discipline, against the length of military service, or against the presence, in the higher ranks, of officers hostile to the existing institutions of the country; these are the reasons which led many middle-class people to applaud declamations against the army at the time of the Dreyfus case, but they are not the Syndicalists' reasons.

The army is the clearest and the most tangible of all possible manifestations of the State, and the one which is most firmly connected with its origins and traditions. Syndicalists do not propose to reform the State, as the men of the eighteenth century did; they want to destroy it, because they wish to realize this idea of Marx's that the Socialist revolution ought not to culminate in the replacement of one governing authority by another minority. The Syndicalists outline their doctrine still more clearly when they give it a more ideological aspect, and declare themselves anti-patriotic—following the example of the *Communist Manifesto.*

It is impossible that there should be the slightest understanding between Syndicalists and official Socialists on this question; the latter, of course, speak of breaking up everything, but they attack men in power rather than power itself; they hope to possess the State forces, and they are aware that on the day when they control the Government they will have need of an army; they will carry on foreign politics, and consequently they in their turn will have to praise the feeling of devotion to the fatherland.

Parliamentary Socialists perceive that anti-patriotism is deeply rooted in the minds of Socialist workmen, and they make great efforts to reconcile the irreconcilable; they are anxious not to oppose too strongly ideas to which the proletariat has become attached, but at the same time they cannot abandon their cherished State, which promises them so many delights. . . .

Thus it cannot any longer be contested that there is an absolute opposition between revolutionary Syndicalism and the State; this opposition takes in France the particularly harsh form of anti-patriotism, because the politicians have devoted all their knowledge and ability to the task of spreading confusion in people's minds about the essence of Socialism. On the plane of patriotism there can be no compromises and halfway positions; it is therefore on this plane that the Syndicalists have been forced to take their stand when middle-class people of every description employed all their powers of seduction to corrupt Socialism and to alienate the workers from the revolutionary idea. They have been led to deny the idea of patriotism by one of those necessities which are met with at all times in the course of history, and which philosophers have sometimes great difficulty in explaining—because the choice is imposed by external conditions, and not freely made for reasons drawn from the nature of things. This character of historical necessity gives to the existing anti-patriotic movement a strength which it would be useless to attempt to dissimulate by means of sophistries.

We have the right to conclude from the preceding analysis that Syndicalist violence, perpetrated in the course of strikes by proletarians who desire the overthrow of the State, must not be confused with those acts of savagery which the superstition of the State suggested to the revolutionaries of '93, when they had power in their hands and were able to oppress the conquered—following the principles which they had received from the Church and from the Monarchy. We have the right to hope that a Socialist revolution carried out by pure Syndicalists would not be defiled by the abominations which sullied the middle-class revolutions.

. . . . .

The revolutionary Syndicates argue about Socialist action exactly in the same manner as military writers argue about war; they restrict the whole of Socialism to the general strike; they look upon every combination as one that should culminate in this catastrophe; they see in each strike a reduced facsimile, an essay, a preparation for the great final upheaval.

The *new school,* which calls itself Marxist, Syndicalist, and revolutionary, declared in favor of the idea of the general strike as soon as it became clearly conscious of the true sense of its own doctrine, of the consequences of its activity, and of its own originality. It was thus led to leave the old official, Utopian, and political tabernacles, which hold the general strike in horror, and to launch itself into the true current of the proletarian revolutionary movement; for a long time past the proletariat had made adherence to the principle of the general strike the *test* by means of which the Socialism of the workers was distinguished from that of the amateur revolutionaries.

Parliamentary Socialists can only obtain great influence if they can manage, by the use of a very confused language, to impose themselves on very diverse groups; for example, they must have workingmen constituents simple enough to allow themselves to be duped by high-sounding phrases about future collectivism; they are compelled to represent themselves as profound philosophers to stupid middle-class people who wish to appear to be well informed about social questions; it is very necessary also for them to be able to exploit rich people who think that they are earning the gratitude of humanity by taking shares in the enterprises of Socialist politicians. This influence is founded on balderdash, and our bigwigs endeavor—sometimes only too successfully—to spread confusion among the ideas of their readers; they detest the general strike because all propaganda carried on from that point of view is too socialistic to please philanthropists.

In the mouths of these self-styled representatives of the proletariat all socialistic formulas lose their real sense. The class war still remains the great principle, but it must be subordinated to national solidarity. Internationalism is an article of faith about which the most moderate declare themselves ready to take the most solemn oaths; but patriotism also imposes sacred duties. The emancipation of the workers must be the work of the workers themselves—their newspapers repeat this every day—but real emancipation consists in voting for a professional politician, in securing for him the means of obtaining a comfortable situation in the world, in subjecting oneself to a leader. In the end the State must disappear—and they are very careful not to dispute what Engels has written on this subject—but this disappearance will take place only in a future so far distant that you must prepare yourself for it by using the State meanwhile as a means of providing the politicians with tidbits; and the best means of bringing about the disappearance of the State consists in strengthening meanwhile the Governmental machine. This method of reasoning resembles that of Gribouille, who threw himself into the water in order to escape getting wet in the rain.

Whole pages could be filled with the bare outlines of the contradictory, comical, and quack arguments which form the substance of the harangues of our great men; nothing embarrasses them, and they know how to combine, in pompous, impetuous, and nebulous speeches, the most absolute irreconcilability with the most supple opportunism. . . .

Against this noisy, garrulous, and lying Socialism, which is exploited by ambitious people of every description, which amuses a few buffoons, and which is admired by decadents—revolutionary Syndicalism takes its stand, and endeavors, on the contrary, to leave nothing in a state of indecision; its ideas are honestly expressed, without trickery and without mental reservations; no attempt is made to dilute doctrines by a stream of confused commentaries. Syndicalism endeavors to employ methods of expression which throw a full light on things, which put them exactly in the place assigned to them by their nature, and which bring out the whole value of the forces in play. Oppositions, instead of being glossed over, must be thrown into sharp relief if we desire to obtain a clear idea of the Syndicalist movement; the groups which are struggling one against the other must be shown as separate and as compact as possible; in short, the movements of the revolted masses must be represented in such a way that the soul of the revolutionaries may receive a deep and lasting impression.

These results could not be produced in any very certain manner by the use of ordinary language; use must be made of a body of images which, *by intuition alone,* and before any considered analyses are made, is capable of evoking as an undivided whole the mass of sentiments which corresponds to the different manifestations of the war undertaken by Socialism against modern society. The Syndicalists solve this problem perfectly, by concentrating the whole of Socialism in the drama of the general strike; there is thus no longer any place for the reconciliation of contraries in the equivocations of the professors; everything is clearly mapped out, so that only one interpretation of Socialism is possible. This method has all the advantages which "integral" knowledge has over analysis, according to the doctrine of Bergson; and perhaps it would not be possible to cite another example which would so perfectly demonstrate the value of the famous professor's doctrines.

The possibility of the actual realization of the general strike has been much discussed; it has been stated that the Socialist war could not be decided in one single battle. To the people who think themselves cautious, practical, and scientific the difficulty of setting great masses of the proletariat in motion at the same moment seems prodigious; they have analyzed the difficulties of detail which such an enormous struggle would present. It is the opinion of the Socialist-sociologists, as also of the politicians, that the general strike is a popular dream, characteristic of the beginnings of a working-class movement; we have had quoted against us the authority of Sidney Webb, who has decreed that the general strike is an illusion of youth, of which the English workers—whom the monopolists of sociology have so often presented to us as the depositaries of the true conception of the working-class movement—soon rid themselves.

That the general strike is not popular in contemporary England, is a poor argument to bring against the historical significance of the idea, for the English are distinguished by an extraordinary lack of understanding of the class war; their ideas have remained very much dominated by medieval influences: the guild, privileged, or at least protected by laws, still seems to them the ideal of working-class organization; it is for England that the term *working-class aristocracy,* as a name for the trade unionists, was invented, and, as a matter of fact, trade unionism does pursue the acquisition of legal privileges. We might therefore say that the aversion felt by England for the general strike should be looked upon as strong presumptive evidence in favor of the latter by all those who look upon the class war as the essence of Socialism.

. . . . .

Neither do I attach any importance to the objections made to the general strike based on considerations of a practical order. The attempt to construct hypotheses about the nature of the struggles of the future and the means of suppressing capitalism, on the model furnished by history, is a return to the old methods of the Utopists. There is no process by which the future can be predicted scientifically, nor even one which enables us to discuss whether one hypothesis about it is better than another; it has been proved by too many memorable examples that the greatest men have committed prodigious errors in thus desiring to make predictions about even the least distant future.

And yet without leaving the present, without reasoning about this future, which seems forever condemned to escape our reason, we should be unable to act at all. Experience shows that the *framing of a future, in some indeterminate time,* may, when it is done in a certain way, be very effective, and have very few inconveniences; this happens when the anticipations of the future take the form of those myths, which enclose with them, all the strongest inclinations of a people, of a party or of a class, inclinations which recur to the mind with the insistence of instincts in all the circumstances of life; and which give an aspect of complete reality to the hopes of immediate action by which, more easily than by any other method, men can reform their desires, passions, and mental activity. We know, moreover, that these social myths in no way prevent a man profiting by the observations which he makes in the course of his life, and form no obstacle to the pursuit of his normal occupations.

. . . . .

The myth must be judged as a means of acting on the present; any attempt to discuss how far it can be taken literally as future history is devoid of sense. *It is the myth in its entirety which is alone important:* its parts are only of interest insofar as they bring out the main idea. No useful purpose is served, therefore, in arguing about the incidents which may occur in the course of a social war, and about the decisive conflicts which may give victory to the proletariat; even supposing the revolutionaries to have been wholly and entirely deluded in setting up this imaginary picture of the general strike, this picture may yet have been, in the course of the preparation for the Revolution, a great element of strength, if it has embraced all the aspirations of Socialism, and if it has given to the whole body of Revolutionary thought a precision and a rigidity which no other method of thought could have given.

To estimate, then, the significance of the idea of the general strike, all the methods of discussion which are current among politicians, sociologists, or people with pretensions to political science, must be abandoned. Everything which its opponents endeavor to establish may be conceded to them, without reducing in any way the value of the theory which they think they have refuted. The question whether the general strike is a partial reality, or only a product of popular imagination, is of little importance. All that it is necessary to know is, whether the general strike contains everything that the Socialist doctrine expects of the revolutionary proletariat.

To solve this question we are no longer compelled to argue learnedly about the future; we are not obliged to indulge in lofty reflections about philosophy, history, or economics; we are not on the plane of theories, and we can remain on the level of observable facts. We have to question men who take a very active part in the real revolutionary movement amidst the proletariat, men who do not aspire to climb into the middle class and whose mind is not dominated by corporative prejudices. These men may be deceived about an infinite number of political, economical, or moral questions; but their testimony is decisive, sovereign, and irrefutable when it is a question of knowing what are the ideas which most powerfully move them and their comrades, which most appeal to them as being identical with their socialistic conceptions, and thanks to which their reason, their hopes, and their way of looking at particular facts seem to make but one indivisible unity.

Thanks to these men, we know that the general strike is indeed what I have said: the *myth* in which Socialism is wholly comprised, *i.e.* a body of images capable of evoking instinctively all the sentiments which correspond to the different manifestations of the war undertaken by Socialism against modern society. Strikes have engendered in the proletariat the noblest, deepest, and most moving sentiments that they possess; the general strike groups them all in a co-ordinated picture, and, by bringing them together, gives to each one of them its maximum of intensity; appealing to their painful memories of particular conflicts, it colors with an intense life all the details of the composition presented to consciousness. We thus obtain that intuition of Socialism which language cannot give us with perfect clearness—and we obtain it as a whole, perceived instantaneously.

We may urge yet another piece of evidence to prove the power of the idea of the general strike. If that idea were a pure chimera, as is so frequently said, Parliamentary Socialists would not attack it with such heat; I do not remember that they ever attacked the senseless hopes which the Utopists have always held up before the dazzled eyes of the people. . . . But when it is a question of the general strike, it is quite another thing; our politicians are no longer content with complicated reservations; they speak violently, and endeavor to induce their listeners to abandon this conception.

It is easy to understand the reason for this attitude: politicians have nothing to fear from the Utopias which present a deceptive mirage of the future to the people, and turn "men towards immediate realizations of terrestrial felicity, which any one who looks at these matters scientifically knows can only be very partially realized, and even then only after long efforts on the part of several generations." (That is what Socialist politicians do, according to Clemenceau.) The more readily the electors believe in the *magical forces of the State,* the more will they be disposed to vote for the candidate who promises marvels; in the electoral struggle each candidate tries to outbid the others: in order that the Socialist candidates may put the Radicals to rout, the electors must be credulous enough to believe every promise of future bliss; our Socialist politicians take very good care, therefore, not to combat these comfortable Utopias in any very effective way.

They struggle against the conception of the general strike, because they recognize, in the course of their propagandist rounds, that this conception is so admirably adapted to the working-class mind that there is a possibility of its dominating the latter in the most absolute manner, thus leaving no place for the desires which the Parliamentarians are able to satisfy. They perceive that this idea is so effective as a motive force that once it has entered the minds of the people they can no longer be controlled by leaders, and that thus the power of the deputies would be reduced to nothing. In short, they feel in a vague way that the whole Socialist movement might easily be absorbed by the general strike, which would render useless all those compromises between political groups in view of which the Parliamentary régime has been built up.

27 · MANIFESTO OF THE COMMUNIST PARTY

Karl Marx and Friedrich Engels

A specter is haunting Europe—the specter of communism. All the powers of old Europe have entered into a holy alliance to exorcise this specter: Pope and Czar, Metternich and Guizot, French Radicals and German police spies.

Where is the party in opposition that has not been decried as communistic by its opponents in power? Where the Opposition that has not hurled back the branding reproach of communism, against the more advanced opposition parties, as well as against its reactionary adversaries?

Two things result from this fact:

I. Communism is already acknowledged by all European powers to be itself a power.

II. It is high time that Communists should openly, in the face of the whole world, publish their views, their aims, their tendencies, and meet this nursery tale of the specter of communism with a manifesto of the party itself.

To this end, Communists of various nationalities have assembled in London, and sketched the following manifesto, to be published in the English, French, German, Italian, Flemish, and Danish languages.

BOURGEOIS AND PROLETARIANS

The history of all hitherto existing society is the history of class struggles.

Freeman and slave, patrician and plebeian, lord and serf, guild-master and journeyman, in a word, oppressor and oppressed, stood in constant opposition to one another, carried on an uninterrupted, now hidden, now open fight, a fight that each time ended, either in a revolutionary reconstitution of society at large, or in the common ruin of the contending classes.

In the earlier epochs of history, we find almost everywhere a complicated arrangement of society into various orders, a manifold gradation of social rank. In ancient Rome we have patricians, knights, plebeians, slaves; in the Middle Ages, feudal lords, vassals, guild-masters, journeymen, apprentices, serfs; in almost all of these classes, again, subordinate gradations.

The modern bourgeois society that has sprouted from the ruins of feudal society, has not done away with class antagonisms. It has but established new classes, new conditions of oppression, new forms of struggle in place of the old ones.

Our epoch, the epoch of the bourgeoisie, possesses, however, this distinctive feature: It has simplified the class antagonisms. Society as a whole is more and more splitting up into two great hostile camps, into two great classes directly facing each other—bourgeoisie and proletariat. . . .

PROLETARIANS AND COMMUNISTS

In what relation do the Communists stand to the proletarians as a whole?

The Communists do not form a separate party opposed to other working-class parties.

They have no interests separate and apart from those of the proletariat as a whole.

They do not set up any sectarian principles of their own, by which to shape and mold the proletarian movement.

The Communists are distinguished from the other working-class parties by this only: 1. In the national struggles of the proletarians of the different countries, they point out and bring to the front the common interests of the entire proletariat, independently of all nationality. 2. In the various stages of development which the struggle of the working class against the bourgeoisie has to pass through, they always and everywhere represent the interests of the movement as a whole.

The Communists, therefore, are on the one hand, practically, the most advanced and resolute section of the working-class parties of every country, that section which pushes forward all others; on the other hand, theoretically, they have over the great mass of the proletariat the advantage of clearly understanding the line of march, the conditions, and the ultimate general results of the proletarian movement.

The immediate aim of the Communists is the same as that of all the other proletarian parties: Formation of the proletariat into a class, overthrow of bourgeois supremacy, conquest of political power by the proletariat.

The theoretical conclusions of the Communists are in no way based on ideas or principles that have been invented, or discovered, by this or that would-be universal reformer.

They merely express, in general terms, actual relations springing from an existing class struggle, from a historical movement going on under our very eyes. The abolition of existing property relations is not at all a distinctive feature of communism.

All property relations in the past have continually been subject to historical changes consequent upon the change in historical conditions.

The French Revolution, for example, abolished feudal property in favor of bourgeois property.

The distinguishing feature of communism is not the abolition of property generally, but the abolition of bourgeois property. But modern bourgeois private property is the final and most complete expression of the system of producing and appropriating products that is based on class antagonisms, on the exploitation of the many by the few.

In this sense, the theory of the Communists may be summed up in the single sentence: Abolition of private property.

We Communists have been reproached with the desire of abolishing the right of personally acquiring property as the fruit of a man's own labor, which property is alleged to be the groundwork of all personal freedom, activity and independence.

Hard-won, self-acquired, self-earned property! Do you mean the property of the petty artisan and of the small peasant, a form of property that preceded the bourgeois form? There is no need to abolish that; the development of industry has to a great extent already destroyed it, and is still destroying it daily.

Or do you mean modern bourgeois private property?

But does wage-labor create any property for the laborer? Not a bit. It creates capital, *i.e.,* that kind of property which exploits wage-labor, and which cannot increase except upon condition of begetting a new supply of wage-labor for fresh exploitation. Property, in its present form, is based on the antagonism of capital and wage-labor. Let us examine both sides of this antagonism.

To be a capitalist, is to have not only a purely personal, but a social *status* in production. Capital is a collective product, and only by the united action of many members, nay, in the last resort, only by the united action of all members of society, can it be set in motion.

Capital is therefore not a personal, it is a social, power.

When, therefore, capital is converted into common property, into the property of all members of society, personal property is not thereby transformed into social property. It is only the social character of the property that is changed. It loses its class character.

Let us now take wage-labor.

The average price of wage-labor is the minimum wage, *i.e.,* that quantum of the means of subsistence which is absolutely requisite to keep the laborer in bare existence as a laborer. What, therefore, the wage-laborer appropriates by means of his labor, merely suffices to prolong and reproduce a bare existence. We by no means intend to abolish this personal appropriation of the products of labor, an appropriation that is made for the maintenance and reproduction of human life, and that leaves no surplus wherewith to command the labor of others. All that we want to do away with is the miserable character of this appropriation, under which the laborer lives merely to increase capital, and is allowed to live only insofar as the interest of the ruling class requires it.

In bourgeois society, living labor is but a means to increase accumulated labor. In Communist society, accumulated labor is but a means to widen, to enrich, to promote the existence of the laborer.

In bourgeois society, therefore, the past dominates the present; in Communist society, the present dominates the past. In bourgeois society capital is independent and has individuality, while the living person is dependent and has no individuality.

And the abolition of this state of things is called by the bourgeois, abolition of individuality and freedom! And rightly so. The abolition of bourgeois individuality, bourgeois independence, and bourgeois freedom is undoubtedly aimed at.

By freedom is meant, under the present bourgeois conditions of production, free trade, free selling and buying.

But if selling and buying disappears, free selling and buying disappears also. This talk about free selling and buying, and all the other "brave words" of our bourgeoisie about freedom in general, have a meaning, if any, only in contrast with restricted selling and buying, with the fettered traders of the Middle Ages, but have no meaning when opposed to the Communist abolition of buying and selling, of the bourgeois conditions of production, and of the bourgeoisie itself.

You are horrified at our intending to do away with private property. But in your existing society, private property is already done away with for nine-tenths of the population; its existence for the few is solely due to its nonexistence in the hands of those nine-tenths. You reproach us, therefore, with intending to do away with a form of property, the necessary condition for whose existence is the nonexistence of any property for the immense majority of society.

In a word, you reproach us with intending to do away with your property. Precisely so; that is just what we intend.

From the moment when labor can no longer be converted into capital, money, or rent, into a social power capable of being monopolized, *i.e.,* from the moment when individual property can no longer be transformed into bourgeois property, into capital, from that moment, you say, individuality vanishes.

You must, therefore, confess that by "individual" you mean no other person than the bourgeois, than the middle-class owner of property. This person must, indeed, be swept out of the way, and made impossible.

Communism deprives no man of the power to appropriate the products of society; all that it does is to deprive him of the power to subjugate the labor of others by means of such appropriation.

It has been objected, that upon the abolition of private property all work will cease, and universal laziness will overtake us.

According to this, bourgeois society ought long ago to have gone to the dogs through sheer idleness; for those of its members who work, acquire nothing, and those who acquire anything, do not work. The whole of this objection is but another expression of the tautology: There can no longer be any wage-labor when there is no longer any capital.

All objections urged against the Communist mode of producing and appropriating material products, have, in the same way, been urged against the Communist modes of producing and appropriating intellectual products. Just as, to the bourgeois, the disappearance of class property is the disappearance of production itself, so the disappearance of class culture is to him identical with the disappearance of all culture.

That culture, the loss of which he laments, is, for the enormous majority, a mere training to act as a machine.

But don't wrangle with us so long as you apply, to our intended abolition of bourgeois property, the standard of your bourgeois notions of freedom, culture, law, etc. Your very ideas are but the outgrowth of the conditions of your bourgeois production and bourgeois property, just as your jurisprudence is but the will of your class made into a law for all, a will whose essential character and direction are determined by the economic conditions of existence of your class.

The selfish misconception that induces you to transform into eternal laws of nature and of reason, the social forms springing from your present mode of production and form of property—historical relations that rise and disappear in the progress of production—this misconception you share with every ruling class that has preceded you. What you see clearly in the case of ancient property, what you admit in the case of feudal property, you are of course forbidden to admit in the case of your own bourgeois form of property.

Abolition of the family! Even the most radical flare up at this infamous proposal of the Communists.

On what foundation is the present family, the bourgeois family, based? On capital, on private gain. In its completely developed form this family exists only among the bourgeoisie. But this state of things finds its complement in the practical absence of the family among the proletarians, and in public prostitution.

The bourgeois family will vanish as a matter of course when its complement vanishes, and both will vanish with the vanishing of capital.

Do you charge us with wanting to stop the exploitation of children by their parents? To this crime we plead guilty.

But, you will say, we destroy the most hallowed of relations, when we replace home education by social.

And your education! Is not that also social, and determined by the social conditions under which you educate, by the intervention of society, direct or indirect, by means of schools, etc.? The Communists have not invented the intervention of society in education; they do but seek to alter the character of that intervention, and to rescue education from the influence of the ruling class.

The bourgeois claptrap about the family and education, about the hallowed co-relation of parent and child, becomes all the more disgusting, the more, by the action of modern industry, all family ties among the proletarians are torn asunder, and their children transformed into simple articles of commerce and instruments of labor.

But you Communists would introduce community of women, screams the whole bourgeoisie in chorus.

The bourgeois sees in his wife a mere instrument of production. He hears that the instruments of production are to be exploited in common, and, naturally, can come to no other conclusion than that the lot of being common to all will likewise fall to the women.

He has not even a suspicion that the real point aimed at is to do away with the status of women as mere instruments of production.

For the rest, nothing is more ridiculous than the virtuous indignation of our bourgeois at the community of women which, they pretend, is to be openly and officially established by the Communists. The Communists have no need to introduce community of women; it has existed almost from time immemorial.

Our bourgeois, not content with having the wives and daughters of their proletarians at their disposal, not to speak of common prostitutes, take the greatest pleasure in seducing each other's wives.

Bourgeois marriage is in reality a system of wives in common and thus, at the most, what the Communists might possibly be reproached with is that they desire to introduce, in substitution for a hypocritically concealed, an openly legalized community of women. For the rest, it is self-evident, that the abolition of the present system of production must bring with it the abolition of the community of women springing from that system, *i.e.,* of prostitution both public and private.

The Communists are further reproached with desiring to abolish countries and nationality.

The workingmen have no country. We cannot take from them

what they have not got. Since the proletariat must first of all acquire political supremacy, must rise to be the leading class of the nation, must constitute itself *the* nation, it is, so far, itself national, though not in the bourgeois sense of the word.

National differences and antagonisms between peoples are vanishing gradually from day to day, owing to the development of the bourgeoisie, to freedom of commerce, to the world market, to uniformity in the mode of production and in the conditions of life corresponding thereto.

The supremacy of the proletariat will cause them to vanish still faster. United action, of the leading civilized countries at least, is one of the first conditions for the emancipation of the proletariat.

In proportion as the exploitation of one individual by another is put an end to, the exploitation of one nation by another will also be put an end to. In proportion as the antagonism between classes within the nation vanishes, the hostility of one nation to another will come to an end.

The charges against communism made from a religious, a philosophical, and, generally, from an ideological standpoint, are not deserving of serious examination.

Does it require deep intuition to comprehend that man's ideas, views, and conceptions, in one word, man's consciousness, changes with every change in the conditions of his material existence, in his social relations and in his social life?

What else does the history of ideas prove, than that intellectual production changes its character in proportion as material production is changed? The ruling ideas of each age have ever been the ideas of its ruling class.

When people speak of ideas that revolutionize society, they do but express the fact that within the old society the elements of a new one have been created, and that the dissolution of the old ideas keeps even pace with the dissolution of the old conditions of existence.

When the ancient world was in its last throes, the ancient religions were overcome by Christianity. When Christian ideas succumbed in the eighteenth century to rationalist ideas, feudal society fought its death-battle with the then revolutionary bourgeoisie. The ideas of religious liberty and freedom of conscience, merely gave expression to the sway of free competition within the domain of knowledge.

"Undoubtedly," it will be said, "religious, moral, philosophical and juridical ideas have been modified in the course of historical development. But religion, morality, philosophy, political science, and law, constantly survived this change.

"There are, besides, eternal truths, such as Freedom, Justice, etc., that are common to all states of society. But communism abolishes eternal truths, it abolishes all religion, and all morality, instead of constituting them on a new basis; it therefore acts in contradiction to all past historical experience."

What does this accusation reduce itself to? The history of all past society has consisted in the development of class antagonisms, antagonisms that assumed different forms at different epochs.

But whatever form they may have taken, one fact is common to all past ages, *viz.,* the exploitation of one part of society by the other. No wonder, then, that the social consciousness of past ages, despite all the multiplicity and variety it displays, moves within certain common forms, or general ideas, which cannot completely vanish except with the total disappearance of class antagonisms.

The Communist revolution is the most radical rupture with traditional property relations; no wonder that its development involves the most radical rupture with traditional ideas.

But let us have done with the bourgeois objections to communism.

We have seen above, that the first step in the revolution by the working class, is to raise the proletariat to the position of ruling class, to establish democracy.

The proletariat will use its political supremacy to wrest, by degrees, all capital from the bourgeoisie, to centralize all instruments of production in the hands of the state, *i.e.,* of the proletariat organized as the ruling class; and to increase the total of productive forces as rapidly as possible.

Of course, in the beginning, this cannot be effected except by means of despotic inroads on the rights of property, and on the conditions of bourgeois production; by means of measures, therefore, which appear economically insufficient and untenable, but which, in the course of the movement, outstrip themselves, necessitate further inroads upon the old social order, and are unavoidable as a means of entirely revolutionizing the mode of production.

These measures will of course be different in different countries.

Nevertheless in the most advanced countries, the following will be pretty generally applicable.

1. Abolition of property in land and application of all rents of land to public purposes.

2. A heavy progressive or graduated income tax.

3. Abolition of all right of inheritance.

4. Confiscation of the property of all emigrants and rebels.

5. Centralization of credit in the hands of the state, by means of a national bank with state capital and an exclusive monopoly.

6. Centralization of the means of communication and transport in the hands of the state.

7. Extension of factories and instruments of production owned by the state; the bringing into cultivation of waste lands, and the improvement of the soil generally in accordance with a common plan.

8. Equal obligation of all to work. Establishment of industrial armies, especially for agriculture.

9. Combination of agriculture with manufacturing industries; gradual abolition of the distinction between town and country, by a more equable distribution of the population over the country.

10. Free education for all children in public schools. Abolition of child factory labor in its present form. Combination of education with industrial production, etc.

When, in the course of development, class distinctions have disappeared, and all production has been concentrated in the hands of a vast association of the whole nation, the public power will lose its political character. Political power, properly so called, is merely the organized power of one class for oppressing another. If the proletariat during its contest with the bourgeoisie is compelled, by the force of circumstances, to organize itself as a class; if, by means of a revolution, it makes itself the ruling class, and, as such sweeps away by force the old conditions of production, then it will, along with these conditions, have swept away the conditions for the existence of class antagonisms, and of classes generally, and will thereby have abolished its own supremacy as a class.

In place of the old bourgeois society, with its classes and class antagonisms, we shall have an association, in which the free development of each is the condition for the free development of all.

• • • • •

POSITION OF THE COMMUNISTS IN RELATION TO THE VARIOUS EXISTING OPPOSITION PARTIES

The Communists fight for the attainment of the immediate aims, for the enforcement of the momentary interests of the working class; but in the movement of the present, they also represent and take care of the future of that movement. In France the Communists ally them-selves with the Social-Democrats, against the conservative and radi-cal bourgeoisie, reserving, however, the right to take up a critical position in regard to phrases and illusions traditionally handed down from the great Revolution.

In Switzerland they support the Radicals, without losing sight of the fact that this party consists of antagonistic elements, partly of Democratic Socialists, in the French sense, partly of radical bour-geois.

In Poland they support the party that insists on an agrarian revo-lution as the prime condition for national emancipation, that party which fomented the insurrection of Cracow in 1846.

In Germany they fight with the bourgeoisie whenever it acts in a revolutionary way, against the absolute monarchy, the feudal squire-archy, and the petty bourgeoisie.

But they never cease, for a single instant, to instill into the work-ing class the clearest possible recognition of the hostile antagonism between bourgeoisie and proletariat, in order that the German work-ers may straightway use, as so many weapons against the bourgeoisie, the social and political conditions that the bourgeoisie must necessarily introduce along with its supremacy, and in order that, after the fall of the reactionary classes in Germany, the fight against the bour-geoisie itself may immediately begin.

The Communists turn their attention chiefly to Germany, because that country is on the eve of a bourgeois revolution that is bound to be carried out under more advanced conditions of European civiliza-tion and with a much more developed proletariat than what existed in England in the seventeenth and in France in the eighteenth century, and because the bourgeois revolution in Germany will be but the prelude to an immediately following proletarian revolution.

In short, the Communists everywhere support every revolutionary movement against the existing social and political order of things.

In all these movements they bring to the front, as the leading question in each case, the property question, no matter what its degree of development at the time.

Finally, they labor everywhere for the union and agreement of the democratic parties of all countries.

The Communists disdain to conceal their views and aims. They openly declare that their ends can be attained only by the forcible overthrow of all existing social conditions. Let the ruling classes tremble at a Communist revolution. The proletarians have nothing to lose but their chains. They have a world to win.

Workingmen of all countries, unite!

28 · STATE AND REVOLUTION *

V. I. Lenin

THE FIRST PHASE OF COMMUNIST SOCIETY

In the *Critique of the Gotha Program,* Marx goes into detail to disprove Lassalle's idea that under Socialism the worker will receive the "undiminished" or "full product of his labour." Marx shows that from the whole of the social labor of society there must be deducted a reserve fund, a fund for the expansion of production, for the replacement of the "wear and tear" of machinery, and so on; then, from the means of consumption there must be deducted a fund for the expenses of administration, for schools, hospitals, homes for the aged, and so on.

Instead of Lassalle's hazy, obscure, general phrase ("the full product of his labor to the worker") Marx makes a sober estimate of exactly how socialist society will have to manage its affairs. Marx proceeds to make a *concrete* analysis of the conditions of life of a society in which there will be no capitalism, and says:

> What we have to deal with here [in analyzing the program of the workers' party] is a communist society, not as it has *developed* on its own foundations, but, on the contrary, just as it *emerges* from capitalist society; which is thus in every respect, economically, morally and intellectually, still stamped with the birthmarks of the old society from whose womb it emerges.

And it is this communist society—a society which has just emerged into the light of day out of the womb of capitalism and which, in every respect, bears the birthmarks of the old society—that Marx terms the "first," or lower phase of communist society.

The means of production are no longer the private property of

* V. I. Lenin, *State and Revolution.* From *Selected Works* (2 vols., Moscow: Foreign Languages Publishing House, 1951), II, 294-306.

individuals. The means of production belong to the whole of society. Every member of society, performing a certain part of the socially-necessary work, receives a certificate from society to the effect that he has done such and such an amount of work. And with this certificate he receives from the public store of articles of consumption a corresponding quantity of products. After a deduction is made of the amount of labor which goes to the public fund, every worker, therefore, receives from society as much as he has given to it.

"Equality" apparently reigns supreme.

But when Lassalle, having in view such a social order (usually called Socialism, but termed by Marx the first phase of Communism), says that this is "equitable distribution," that this is "the equal right of all members of society to an equal product of labor," Lassalle is erring and Marx exposes his error.

"Equal right," says Marx, we indeed have here; but it is *still* a "bourgeois right," which, like every right, *presupposes inequality*. Every right is an application of an *equal* measure to *different* people who in fact are not alike, are not equal to one another; that is why "equal right" is really a violation of equality and an injustice. Indeed, every man, having performed as much social labor as another, receives an equal share of the social product (after the above-mentioned deductions).

But people are not alike: one is strong, another is weak; one is married, another is not; one has more children, another has less, and so on. And the conclusion Marx draws is:

. . . with an equal performance of labor, and hence an equal share in the social consumption fund, one will in fact receive more than another, one will be richer than another, and so on. To avoid all these defects, right instead of being equal would have to be unequal . . .

Hence, the first phase of Communism cannot yet produce justice and equality: differences, and unjust differences, in wealth will still exist, but the *exploitation* of man by man will have become impossible, because it will be impossible to seize the *means of production,* the factories, machines, land, etc., as private property. While smashing Lassalle's petty-bourgeois, confused phrases about "equality" and "justice" *in general,* Marx shows the *course of development* of communist society, which is *compelled* to abolish at first *only* the "injustice" of the means of production having been seized by individuals, and which *is unable* at once to eliminate the other injustice, which consists in the distribution of articles of consumption "according to the amount of labor performed" (and not according to needs).

The vulgar economists, including the bourgeois professors and "our" Tugan among them, constantly reproach the Socialists with forgetting the inequality of people and with "dreaming" of eliminating this inequality. Such a reproach, as we see, only proves the extreme ignorance of Messrs. the bourgeois ideologists.

Marx not only most scrupulously takes account of the inevitable inequality of men, but he also takes into account the fact that the mere conversion of the means of production into the common property of the whole of society (commonly called "Socialism") *does not remove* the defects of distribution and the inequality of "bourgeois right" which *continues to prevail* as long as products are divided "according to the amount of labor performed." Continuing, Marx says:

> . . . But these defects are inevitable in the first phase of communist society as it is when it has just emerged after prolonged birth pangs from capitalist society. Right can never be higher than the economic structure of society and its cultural development conditioned thereby. . . .

And so, in the first phase of communist society (usually called Socialism) "bourgeois right" is *not* abolished in its entirety, but only in part, only in proportion to the economic revolution so far attained, i.e., only in respect of the means of production. "Bourgeois right" recognizes them as the private property of individuals. Socialism converts them into *common* property. *To that extent*—and to that extent alone—"bourgeois right" disappears.

However, it continues to exist as far as its other part is concerned; it continues to exist in the capacity of regulator (determining factor) in the distribution of products and the allotment of labour among the members of society. The socialist principle: "He who does not work, neither shall he eat," is *already* realized; the other socialist principle: "An equal amount of products for an equal amount of labor," is also *already* realized. But this is not yet Communism, and it does not yet abolish "bourgeois right," which gives to·unequal individuals, in return for unequal (really unequal) amounts of labor, equal amounts of products.

This is a "defect," says Marx, but it is unavoidable in the first phase of Communism; for if we are not to indulge in utopianism, we must not think that having overthrown capitalism people will at once learn to work for society *without any standard of right;* and indeed the abolition of capitalism *does not immediately* create the economic premises for *such* a change.

And there is no other standard than that of "bourgeois right." To this extent, therefore, there still remains the need for a state, which, while safeguarding the public ownership of the means of production, would safeguard equality in labour and equality in the distribution of products.

The state withers away in so far as there are no longer any capitalists, any classes, and, consequently, no *class* can be *suppressed*.

But the state has not yet completely withered away, since there still remains the safeguarding of "bourgeois right," which sanctifies actual inequality. For the state to wither away completely complete Communism is necessary.

THE HIGHER PHASE OF COMMUNIST SOCIETY

Marx continues:

. . . In a higher phase of communist society, after the enslaving subordination of the individual to the division of labor, and therewith also the antithesis between mental and physical labor, has vanished; after labor has become not only a means of life but life's prime want; after the productive forces have also increased with the all-round development of the individual, and all the springs of cooperative wealth flow more abundantly—only then can the narrow horizon of bourgeois right be crossed in its entirety and society inscribe on its banners: "From each according to his ability, to each according to his needs!"

Only now can we appreciate to the full the correctness of Engels' remarks in which he mercilessly ridiculed the absurdity of combining the words "freedom" and "state." So long as the state exists there is no freedom. When there will be freedom, there will be no state.

The economic basis for the complete withering away of the state is such a high stage of development of Communism that the antithesis between mental and physical labor disappears when there, consequently, disappears one of the principal sources of modern *social* inequality—a source, moreover, which cannot on any account be removed immediately by the mere conversion of the means of production into public property, by the mere expropriation of the capitalists.

This expropriation will create *the possibility* of an enormous development of the productive forces. And when we see how incredibly capitalism is already *retarding* this development, when we see how much progress could be achieved on the basis of the level of technique now already attained, we are entitled to say with the fullest confidence that the expropriation of the capitalists will inevitably result in an enormous development of the productive forces of human society. But how rapidly this development will proceed, how soon it will reach the point of breaking away from the division of labor, of doing away with the antithesis between mental and physical labor, of transforming labor into "the prime necessity of life"—we do not and *cannot* know.

That is why we are entitled to speak only of the inevitable withering away of the state, emphasizing the protracted nature of this process and its dependence upon the rapidity of development of the *higher phase* of Communism, and leaving the question of the time required for, or the concrete forms of, the withering away quite open, because there is *no* material for answering these questions.

It will become possible for the state to wither away completely when society adopts the rule: "From each according to his ability, to each according to his needs," i.e., when people have become so accustomed to observing the fundamental rules of social intercourse and when their labor becomes so productive that they will voluntarily work *according to their ability.* "The narrow horizon of bourgeois right," which compels one to calculate with the coldheartedness of a Shylock whether one has not worked half an hour more than somebody else, whether one is not getting less pay than somebody else— this narrow horizon will then be crossed. There will then be no need for society to regulate the quantity of products to be received by each; each will take freely "according to his needs."

From the bourgeois point of view, it is easy to declare that such a social order is "sheer utopia" and to sneer at the Socialists for promising everyone the right to receive from society, without any control over the labor of the individual citizen, any quantity of truffles, automobiles, pianos, etc. Even to this day, most bourgeois "savants" confine themselves to sneering in this way, thereby displaying both their ignorance and their mercenary defence of capitalism.

Ignorance—for it has never entered the head of any Socialist to "promise" that the higher phase of the development of Communism will arrive; whereas the great Socialists, in *foreseeing* that it will arrive, presuppose not the present productivity of labor *and not the present* ordinary run of people, who, like the seminary students in Pomyalovsky's stories, are capable of damaging the stocks of public wealth "just for fun," and of demanding the impossible.

Until the "higher" phase of Communism arrives, the Socialists demand the *strictest* control by society *and by the state* of the measure of labor and the measure of consumption; but this control must *start* with the expropriation of the capitalists, with the establishment of workers' control over the capitalists, and must be exercised not by a state of bureaucrats, but by a state of *armed workers*.

The mercenary defence of capitalism by the bourgeois ideologists (and their hangers-on, like Messrs. the Tseretelis, Chernovs and Co.) consists precisely in that they *substitute* controversies and discussions about the distant future for the vital and burning question of *present-day* politics, viz., the expropriation of the capitalists, the conversion of *all* citizens into workers and employees of *one* huge "syndicate"—the whole state—and the complete subordination of the entire work of this syndicate to a genuinely democratic state, to *the state of the Soviets of Workers' and Soldiers' Deputies*.

Actually, when a learned professor, and following him the philistine, and following him Messrs. the Tseretelis and Chernovs, talk of unreasonable utopias, of the demagogic promises of the Bolsheviks, of the impossibility of "introducing" Socialism, it is the higher stage or phase of Communism they have in mind, which no one has ever promised or even thought to "introduce," because it generally cannot be "introduced."

And this brings us to the question of the scientific difference between Socialism and Communism, which Engels touched on in his above-quoted argument about the incorrectness of the name "Social-Democrat." Politically the difference between the first, or lower, and the higher phase of Communism will in time, probably, be tremendous; but it would be ridiculous to take cognizance of this difference now, under capitalism, and only individual anarchists, perhaps, could invest it with primary importance (if there still remain people among the anarchists who have learned nothing from the "Plekhanovite" conversion of the Kropotkins, the Graveses, the Cornelissens and other "stars" of anarchism into social-chauvinists or "anarcho-trenchists," as Ge, one of the few anarchists who have still preserved a sense of honor and a conscience, has put it).

But the scientific difference between Socialism and Communism is clear. What is usually called Socialism was termed by Marx the "first" or lower phase of communist society. In so far as the means of production become *common* property, the word "Communism" is also applicable here, providing we do not forget that this is *not* complete Communism. The great significance of Marx's explanations is that here, too, he consistently applies materialist dialectics, the theory of development, and regards Communism as something which develops *out of* capitalism. Instead of scholastically invented, "concocted" definitions and fruitless disputes about words (what is Socialism? what is Communism?), Marx gives an analysis of what might be called the stages of the economic ripeness of Communism.

In its first phase, or first stage, Communism *cannot* as yet be fully ripe economically and entirely free from traditions or traces of capitalism. Hence the interesting phenomenon that Communism in its first phase retains "the narrow horizon of *bourgeois* right." Of course, bourgeois right in regard to the distribution of articles of *consumption* inevitably presupposes the existence of the *bourgeois state,* for right is nothing without an apparatus capable of *enforcing* the observance of the standards of right.

It follows that under Communism there remains for a time not only bourgeois right, but even the bourgeois state—without the bourgeoisie!

This may sound like a paradox or simply a dialectical conundrum, of which Marxism is often accused by people who do not take the slightest trouble to study its extraordinarily profound content.

But as a matter of fact, remnants of the old surviving in the new confront us in life at every step, both in nature and in society. And Marx did not arbitrarily insert a scrap of "bourgeois" right into Communism, but indicated what is economically and politically inevitable in a society emerging *out of the womb* of capitalism.

Democracy is of enormous importance to the working class in its struggle against the capitalists for its emancipation. But democracy is by no means a boundary not to be overstepped; it is only one of the stages on the road from feudalism to capitalism, and from capitalism to Communism.

Democracy means equality. The great significance of the proletariat's struggle for equality and of equality as a slogan will be clear if we correctly interpret it as meaning the abolition of *classes*. But democracy means only *formal* equality. And as soon as equality is achieved for all members of society *in relation to* ownership of the means of production, that is, equality of labor and equality of wages, humanity will inevitably be confronted with the question of advancing farther, from formal equality to actual equality, i.e., to the operation of the rule, "from each according to his ability, to each according to his needs." By what stages, by means of what practical measures humanity will proceed to this supreme aim—we do not and cannot know. But it is important to realize how infinitely mendacious is the ordinary bourgeois conception of Socialism as something lifeless, petrified, fixed once for all, whereas in reality *only* under Socialism will a rapid, genuine, really mass forward movement, embracing first the *majority* and then the whole of the population, commence in all spheres of public and personal life.

Democracy is a form of the state, one of its varieties. Consequently, it, like every state, represents on the one hand the organized, systematic use of violence against persons; but on the other hand it signifies the formal recognition of equality of citizens, the equal right of all to determine the structure of, and to administer, the state. This, in turn, results in the fact that, at a certain stage in the development of democracy, it first welds together the class that wages a revolutionary struggle against capitalism—the proletariat, and enables it to crush, smash to atoms, wipe off the face of the earth the bourgeois, even the republican bourgeois, state machine, the standing army, the police and the bureaucracy, and to substitute for them a *more* democratic state machine, but a state machine nevertheless, in the shape of the armed masses of workers who develop into a militia in which the entire population takes part.

Here "quantity turns into quality": *such* a degree of democracy implies overstepping the boundaries of bourgeois society, the beginning of its socialist reconstruction. If really *all* take part in the administration of the state, capitalism cannot retain its hold. And the development of capitalism, in turn, itself creates the *premises* that *enable* really "all" to take part in the administration of the state. Some of these premises are: universal literacy, which has already been achieved in a number of the most advanced capitalist countries, then the "training and disciplining" of millions of workers by the huge, complex, socialized apparatus of the postal service, railways, big factories, large-scale commerce, banking, etc., etc.

Given these *economic* premises it is quite possible, after the overthrow of the capitalists and the bureaucrats, to proceed immediately, overnight, to supersede them in the *control* of production and distribution, in the work of *keeping account* of labor and products by the armed workers, by the whole of the armed population. (The question of control and accounting should not be confused with the question of the scientifically trained staff of engineers, agronomists and so on. These gentlemen are working today in obedience to the wishes of the capitalists; they will work even better tomorrow in obedience to the wishes of the armed workers.)

Accounting and control—that is the *main* thing required for "arranging" the smooth working, the correct functioning of the *first phase* of communist society. *All* citizens are transformed here into hired employees of the state, which consists of the armed workers. *All* citizens become employees and workers of a *single* nationwide state "syndicate." All that is required is that they should work equally, do their proper share of work, and get equally paid. The accounting and control necessary for this have been *simplified* by capitalism to the extreme and reduced to the extraordinarily simple operations—which any literate person can perform—of supervising and recording, knowledge of the four rules of arithmetic, and issuing appropriate receipts.

When the *majority* of the people begin independently and everywhere to keep such accounts and maintain such control over the capitalists (now converted into employees) and over the intellectual gentry who preserve their capitalist habits, this control will really become universal, general, popular; and there will be no way of getting away from it, there will be "nowhere to go."

The whole of society will have become a single office and a single factory, with equality of labor and equality of pay.

SUGGESTED READINGS

[*NOTE: There is no substitute for primary sources. The student should begin any study of ideology with a reading of the original works. Thus Plato, Aristotle, Machiavelli, Locke, Smith, Marx, and company need no emphasis by way of special listing. Below are some useful commentaries.*]

GENERAL

Brinton, Crane. *Ideas and Men*. New York: Prentice-Hall, 1950.

Crawford, William Rex. *A Century of Latin American Thought*. Cambridge: Harvard University Press, 1944.

Gray, Alexander. *The Socialist Tradition*. London: Longmans, Green, 1946.

Hallowell, John H. *Main Currents in Modern Political Thought*. New York: Henry Holt, 1950.

Lindsay, A. D. *The Modern Democratic State*. London: Oxford University Press, 1943.

MacIver, Robert. *The Web of Government*. New York: Macmillan, 1947.

Mayo, Henry B. *Democracy and Marxism*. New York: Oxford University Press, 1955.

Meisel, James H. *The Myth of the Ruling Class*. Ann Arbor: University of Michigan Press, 1958.

Parrington, Vernon Louis. *Main Currents in American Thought*. Cambridge: Harvard University Press, 1944.

Sabine, George H. *A History of Political Theory*. New York: Henry Holt, 1950.

Schumpeter, Joseph A. *Capitalism, Socialism, and Democracy*. 2nd edition. New York: Harper, 1947.

Wolin, Sheldon S. *Politics and Vision*. Boston and Toronto: Little, Brown, 1960.

NATIONALISM

Cobban, Alfred. *National Self-Determination.* Revised edition. Chicago: University of Chicago Press, 1948.

Hayes, Carleton J. *Essays on Nationalism.* New York: Macmillan, 1926.

——— *The Historical Evolution of Modern Nationalism.* New York: R. R. Smith, 1931.

Kohn, Hans. *The Idea of Nationalism.* New York: Macmillan, 1944, 1951.

Madariaga, Salvador de. *Portrait of Europe.* New York: Roy Publishers, N.D.

Moon, Parker T. *Imperialism and World Politics.* New York: Macmillan, 1926. Reprinted 1947.

Royal Institute on International Affairs. *Nationalism.* New York: Oxford University Press, 1946.

Schumpeter, Joseph A. *Imperialism and Social Classes.* Translated by Heinz Norden; edited and with an introduction by Paul M. Sweezy. New York: A. M. Kelly, 1951.

CAPITALISM

Arnold, Thurman W. *The Folklore of Capitalism.* New Haven: Yale University Press, 1937.

Bell, Daniel (ed.). *The New American Right.* New York: Criterion Books, 1955.

Berle, Adolf A., Jr. *The Twentieth Century Capitalist Revolution.* New York: Harcourt, Brace, 1954.

Galbraith, John K. *American Capitalism: The Concept of Countervailing Power.* Revised edition. Boston: Houghton Mifflin, 1956.

Hacker, Louis M. *The Triumph of American Capitalism.* New York: Columbia University Press, 1946.

Robertson, H. M. *Aspects of the Rise of Economic Individualism.* Cambridge, England: Cambridge University Press, 1933.

Tawney, R. H. *Religion and the Rise of Capitalism.* New York: Mentor Books, 1947.

Wright, David McCord. *Capitalism.* New York: McGraw-Hill, 1951.

FASCISM

Blanksten, George I. *Perón's Argentina*. Chicago: University of Chicago Press, 1953.

Borgese, G. A. *Goliath, The March of Fascism*. New York: Viking Press, 1937.

Finer, Herman. *Mussolini's Italy*. London: Victor Gollancz, 1935.

Hilberg, Raul. *The Destruction of the European Jews*. Chicago: Quadrangle, 1961.

Neumann, Franz L. *Behemoth*. 2nd edition. New York: Oxford University Press, 1944.

Poliakov, Leon. *The Harvest of Hate*. Syracuse: Syracuse University Press, 1954.

Shirer, William L. *The Rise and Fall of the Third Reich*. New York: Simon and Schuster, 1960.

West, Rebecca. *The Meaning of Treason*. New York: Viking Press, 1947.

EVOLUTIONARY SOCIALISM

Blum, Léon. *For All Mankind*. Translated by W. Pickles. New York: Viking Press, 1946.

Buber, Martin. *Paths in Utopia*. Translated by R. F. C. Hull. Boston: Beacon Press, 1958.

Crosland, C. A. R. *The Future of Socialism*. New York: Macmillan, 1957.

Crossman, Richard (ed.). *New Fabian Essays*. New York: Praeger, 1952.

Durkin, E. F. M. *The Politics of Democratic Socialism*. London: Routledge, 1940.

Gaitskell, Hugh. *Socialism and Nationalization*. London: Fabian Society, 1956.

Ulam, Adam R. *Philosophical Foundations of English Socialism*. Cambridge: Harvard University Press, 1951.

REVOLUTIONARY SOCIALISM

Almond, Gabriel A. *The Appeals of Communism*. Princeton: Princeton University Press, 1954.

Crossman, Richard (ed.). *The God That Failed*. New York: Bantam Books, 1952.

Djilas, Milovan. *The New Class: An Analysis of the Communist System*. New York: Praeger, 1957.

Kelsen, Hans. *The Political Theory of Bolshevism*. Berkeley and Los Angeles: University of California Press, 1948.

Koestler, Arthur. *The Yogi and the Commissar*. New York: Macmillan, 1945.

McVicker, Charles P. *Titoism: Pattern for International Communism*. New York: St. Martin's Press, 1957.

Meyer, A. G. *Marxism: The Unity of Theory and Practice*. Cambridge: Harvard University Press, 1954.

Rossiter, Clinton. *Marxism: View from America*. New York: Harcourt, Brace, 1960.

Schwartz, Benjamin I. *Chinese Communism and the Rise of Mao*. Cambridge: Harvard University Press, 1951.

Venturi, Franco. *Roots of Revolution*. Translated by Francis Haskell. New York: Knopf, 1960.

CHAPTER IV

The Formalization of
Political Power

All governments are, in part, a recognition by men of a "law" of anticipated reaction. Most people, whatever their culture or tradition, wish for at least a minimum number of rules that will allow them to predict with some degree of certainty the results of their action in society. Obviously, however, such rules cannot be made, altered, or administered unless there first exist organs whose function it is to establish a framework for the desired order and predictability. These organs, which in their nature and form inevitably come to reflect the power relations that exist in the body politic, are generally three in number: constitutionalism, law, and institutions.

"Constitutionalism" refers here to the process of setting forth the general means and the broad ends of government, and of supplying, at the same time, a description of the institutional arrangements through which the tasks in question are to be performed. Constitutionalism is also a set of limitations on governmental action—an expression of man's determination not only to acquire order and predictability but to make certain that in doing so he does not forfeit, but preserves his freedom.

"Law" refers here to the body of rules which officially designated authorities employ to maintain certain agreed standards of conduct between man and man, and between man and the public at large in the course of everyday life.

"Institutions" refers here to the basic procedures of creating and administering law. They are established both to give government continuity and to permit it to adapt to change.

It should be clearly understood that political power may be formalized without constitutionalism. While law and institutions are essential to the formalization of political power, constitutionalism, though important, is not.

The selections on constitutionalism furnish the student with sufficient comparative material to permit certain conclusions to be drawn. First, the existence of a "constitution" in a state is no automatic guarantee that the government of that state will actually abide by the aims and procedures to which it is formally committed. It is therefore always advisable to distinguish between a state having a constitution and a state observing constitutionalism. Furthermore, one should be aware of the fact that the absence in a state of any single document which can be called "the constitution" does not necessarily prevent this state from observing constitutionalism. Great Britain is the prime example of that situation, just as most totalitarian states illustrate the reverse, that is, the formal possession of written constitutions but a consistent failure to observe the practices that give constitutionalism real meaning.

Secondly, constitutionalism is never a finished "product" nor a phenomenon peculiar to any particular nation. It is true that Great Britain and the United States first established many of the major constitutional patterns, but as the readings suggest, other nations, notably in Europe, have made their own important substantive and procedural contributions.

A third conclusion is that constitutionalism is not to be associated with any particular legal system or institutional arrangement. It may exist in a unitary or federal system; it may be operative in a state with heavy reliance on "code" law or in a state in which the "common law" heritage is strong; and it may be found under either presidential or parliamentary forms of government. Furthermore, there is no necessary correlation between constitutionalism and any particular economic system.

Finally, constitutionalism represents not only an explicit distrust of absolute power but also the ethical commitment by the citizen of a state to the idea that ends and means are a continuum, not a dichotomy. Under constitutionalism, *how* something is done is as important as the goal itself.

Law is neither fixed nor standardized in any universal sense. The variety of rules under which men live in their public capacities attests to this fact. The one universal aspect of law seems to be that *it is found* everywhere in some form or fashion. To illustrate the comparative character of law, the editors have chosen a group of selections which point out the universality of the existence of law and which, at the same time, show the national and regional variation among existing legal systems. The readings drawn from the works of the late Justice Holmes and of Professor Llewellyn note the close relationship of law to time, place, and circumstance, and offer the student an insight into the broader and deeper role that law plays in societal change.

The development of institutions is a testimony both to the fertility of man's imagination and to his practicality. Though never stemming entirely from any single source or idea, institutions always tend to begin as experiments and to become, in time, part of the very essence of the particular society and way of life they are serving. Executive and legislative institutions, for example, may in a particular society have originally been designed for the general purposes of initiating, formulating, and reviewing policy; with the passage of time, however, as they come to be shaped by a multitude of events, personalities, and accidents, their actual functions may change and only the façade of the original design may remain. It is hoped that the comparative character of the few institutional structures treated in this section will give the student some awareness of the fact that each nation's institutions are partly the cause and partly the result of the particular society's approach to the problems of political power.

One concluding observation deserves attention at this point. The twentieth century has seen the emergence of many new governments. Events in Africa and Asia indicate that this situation will continue. In the creation of these new governments, many observers have been struck by the fact that the new nations are not turning to the Anglo-American models alone as they seek to formalize political power. The new constitutions reveal more than an insistent demand for political order and predictability; they reveal an equally insistent urge for social and economic equality—equality not only before the law but also at the department-store counter, in the doctor's office, and at the factory pay window. This urge for equality raises a number of questions, not the least important of which is this: Will the demand for social and economic justice prove compatible with the desire for political justice? Can the former be satisfied without sacrificing the latter?

Constitutionalism

29 · GREAT BRITAIN *

Herbert J. Spiro

CONSTITUTIONAL HISTORY

England's roots as both a people and a state reach farther back in history than those of any other European political system. For the continuity of the state is the same as that of the Crown, which dates at least from the Norman Conquest in 1066 A.D. Continuity as a people goes much beyond that, but the same date is significant in this respect, too, because no important immigration has occurred since then, nor any successful invasion from outside the British Isles. Constitutional continuity was disturbed only once, during Oliver Cromwell's Protectorate of short duration; even then it was not broken, and was soon restored.

It should be noted at the outset that, strictly speaking, the continuity described above applies only to England, and not to the present political system, which is officially called "the United Kingdom of Great Britain and Northern Ireland." Ireland—sometimes parts of it and sometimes all of it—was won and lost over the centuries. Today Northern Ireland's status is a dual one: it has its own Parliament and it also elects members to the British Parliament. The rest of Ireland has a republican constitution and maintains a tenuous status within the British Commonwealth. Wales was added shortly after the Norman Conquest. Scotland was brought under the British Crown after its King James VI became England's James I, in 1603. Down to this day, Scotland has a legal system which differs from that of the rest of Great Britain, in that it is based on the

* Herbert J. Spiro, *Government by Constitution* (New York: Random House, 1959), pp. 111-118. Reprinted by permission of Random House, Inc. © Copyright, 1959, by Random House, Inc.

Roman law rather than the English common law. And yet the absorptive and adaptive qualities of English political processes have been such that these additions of land and people have never brought about quick, revolutionary change, but only slow, evolutionary modification.

These qualities of English politics are also suggested by two other facts. The first of these is the remarkable success achieved by British political procedures when exported by the British themselves to America, Asia, and Africa. Some of the former British colonies, to be sure, have experienced difficulties as newly independent nations in trying to make British processes work—Pakistan, for example, or Ghana. But none of them has encountered as much trouble as the former colonies of France, Italy, or the Netherlands.

The second evidence of the uniqueness of the British constitution is the fact that the success of British politics, at least since the eighteenth century, has generated so much "envy of less happier lands," in Shakespeare's phrase, that British institutions and procedures have become the most widely copied in the world, by far. The French constitutional monarchies of the nineteenth century were modeled on the British pattern. Constitutional monarchy elsewhere in Europe also attempted to emulate Great Britain, either directly or indirectly. The copying has not been confined to the institution of constitutional monarchy; indeed, the widespread adoption of the system of parliamentary procedure in use at Westminster is especially significant. The influence of this kind of borrowing on the procedures used by international assemblies, such as those of the League of Nations and of the United Nations, is really incalculable and, in terms of present world problems, may well turn out to be of much greater importance than other forms of imitation.

Only in the last hundred years has the Constitution of the United States become an export commodity that has been giving considerable competition to Great Britain in this "market." The Latin-American countries and others wanting either a popularly elected president or a federal system, or both, have generally followed the model of the United States. Swiss federalism provides a limited illustration of this. But so many of the subtler, and for that very reason more fundamental, features of American political processes are also adaptations of the British archetype that copying them sometimes merely amounts to second-hand borrowing from England.

But what *is* "the British constitution"? The standard answer to this question emphasizes the word *unwritten*. But this is not quite accurate. True, Britain has no single constitutional document as do all of our other systems except (British) Canada and Sweden. The Swedish constitution consists of four documents. Similarly, the British constitution could be said to consist of a series of documents. First in the series is Magna Carta (1215), in which King John's barons forced him to accept a number of restrictions on his power *and* on that of his heirs. Magna Carta was followed by others, among them the Petition of Right (1628), in which King Charles I assented to even more far-reaching concessions demanded by his Parliament. This was followed by the Bill of Rights (1689), which was passed by Parliament after the so-called Glorious Revolution of the previous year, and many of whose provisions were repeated in the Bill of Rights of the Constitution of the United States. The Act of Settlement (1701) did the same thing for the British Crown that the Act of Succession, a century later, did for the Swedish Crown. The Reform Acts of 1832 and 1867 extended the suffrage. The acts granting the suffrage to all men in 1918, and to all women in 1928, would also be considered constitutional. The Parliament Acts of 1911 and 1949 reduced the functions of the House of Lords. Some students of the British constitution would extend this list, and it is unlikely that all would agree as to which documents should be included.

This, then, is one reason why Britain is said to have an unwritten constitution.

In studying Sweden, we could distinguish between acts of the Riksdag that are, and those that are not, part of the Swedish constitution, because constitutional acts can be amended only if passed by two successive Parliaments with a general election intervening. This is not true in Great Britain, where any Parliament could make the most fundamental change—one which would certainly be considered constitutional in Sweden or the United States—by a simple majority of the House of Commons and of the House of Lords and with the assent of the Monarch. The remarkable phenomenon is that constitutional amendments, in this sense, have never been passed by such simple majorities or without full and prolonged debate of the issue. As a result, there seems to be only one method for deciding which documents should be considered parts of the British constitution: the measurement of their effective longevity as parts of the operative constitution of which people and politicians are conscious, and of the proportions of the debate that preceded their adoption. This test leaves certain difficulties, one of them being the second reason for calling the British constitution unwritten. Most of those institutions and procedures, which occupy the most prominent places in written constitutions, are not mentioned in the great constitutional documents that have just been listed; in fact, they are not mentioned in any law at all. Just think of the detail with which the United States Constitution defines the functions of the Congress and of the President, and relations between them. British constitutional documents, by contrast, do not define the functions of the House of Commons at all; they specify only a number of things which the House of Lords and the Monarch must *not* do; and they say very little about relations between the Monarch and the two Houses of Parliament. And the Cabinet, which is usually considered the keystone of the arch of British government, is mentioned nowhere at all, except for the Standing Orders of the House of Commons, that is, its rules of procedure. Nevertheless, the more important aspects of Cabinet government, especially the dependence of the Cabinet upon the confidence of Parliament, have been stably established since the eighteenth century. Since they are not written down in any Act of Parliament, they could be changed overnight. Yet no British politician would even think of proposing anything of the sort.

Parliament evolved slowly out of the Great Council that the medieval English Kings convened from time to time. When Edward I summoned the so-called "Model Parliament" in 1295, it was made up not only of barons, the clergy, and knights, but also of burgesses, i.e., townspeople. However, by contrast with Sweden, peasants were not represented. Toward the end of the 1300's, it had become custom for the barons and the upper clergy to meet in one assembly, the knights and commoners in another. The House of Commons began to originate grants of money, the levying of which had been the initial reason for adding commoners to the Great Council. Bills of petition to the King were coupled with grants of money, and the King, in order to get the money, would grant the petition in an Act, the first sentence of which, from the fifteenth century on down to the twentieth, has invariably read: "Be it therefore enacted by the King's most Excellent Majesty, by and with the advice and consent of the Lords Spiritual and Temporal, and Commons, in this present Parliament assembled, and by the authority of the same. . . ." Parliament's share in the government of the realm increased during the struggle between Henry VIII and the Roman Catholic Church. The ultimate outcome of this struggle was a national Reformation in England and the establishment of the Church of England with the King as its head.

In the seventeenth century, under James I and Charles I, the problem of the relation between King and Parliament arose and was settled by means of the Civil War (1642-49). The royal side lost, Charles was executed, and Oliver Cromwell ruled as Lord Protector under the Instrument of Government (1653), the only written constitution in Britain's history. By 1660, monarchy had been restored, in the person of Charles II. His successor, James II, reopened the issue of Catholicism, which led to the "Glorious Revolution" of 1688 and the definitive establishment of the "supremacy of Parliament."

When German-speaking Hanoverian Kings began to occupy the British throne, in 1714, active government gradually devolved upon the Cabinet, partly because George I and II did not speak English. Throughout the eighteenth century, constituencies for the House of Commons were very unevenly distributed, and there was a great deal of corruption through patronage dispensed by the Cabinet acting on behalf of the Crown. The struggle over reform lasted for more than a century and was not rewarded until passage of the Great Reform Act of 1832, which provided for a very limited extension of the suffrage and the greater equalization of constituencies. The last couple of years of the debate were accompanied by sporadic eruptions of violence. The King had to threaten to create enough new Whig peers to outvote Tory opponents of the reforms in the House of Lords, before the upper chamber capitulated. After this concession, Cabinets generally would not resign after losing a vote in the House of Lords, although they needed to win majorities there in order to pass bills. Except for the extension of the suffrage, still to a very limited electorate, no other changes truly constitutional in nature occurred during the remainder of the nineteenth century.

In 1909, a serious constitutional crisis—one which was widely recognized as such—began with the refusal of the House of Lords to pass the budget proposed by the Chancellor of the Exchequer, Lloyd George. Again the country seemed on the verge of violence and again the King was persuaded to threaten to pack the House of Lords. This made possible passage of the Parliament Act of 1911, which eliminated for practical purposes the Peers' former ability to obstruct passage of money bills voted by the Commons. But the Parliament Act went even beyond this by providing that the House of Commons could override the Lords' veto on ordinary bills by passing them in each of three successive sessions of Parliament during a period of at least two years. This had the effect of making amendment of the British "constitution"—whatever it may consist of—about as difficult as amendment of the Swedish Constitution. Subsequently, there were the final extensions of the suffrage already cited and, after the great victory of the Labour party in the election at the end of World War II, the elimination of the remaining electoral inequities, such as the double voting privilege of university graduates (each of the great English universities had until then elected one member to Parliament). The Parliament Act of 1949 reduced the delaying effects of the Lords' veto to one year. And in 1958, the House of Lords was once more reformed, this time in its composition rather than its functions, by adding members for life—nonhereditary "life peers"—including women peers for the first time in history.

Many other important changes have occurred since 1832, but whether they should be considered constitutional or not is a question we are not yet equipped to answer. There was, for example, the reform of the civil service in the middle of the last century, which did away with inefficiency, ignorance, and corruption by reducing the number of positions filled by patronage. At the beginning of the present century, the post of Prime Minister was filled by a member of the House of Lords for the last time, and it is now understood that only a member of the House of Commons may hold that position. The theory of the "mandate" was somehow introduced, according to which neither the Lords nor the Opposition would obstruct passage of a bill dealing with an issue on which the electorate had clearly expressed itself in the previous general election. And finally, there were the many economic changes, especially those transforming the right of private property, which were brought about by the Labour government after 1945. These have been referred to as an "economic and social revolution" and should, therefore, perhaps be included in any catalogue of constitutional changes.

CONSTITUTIONAL STRUCTURE

The House of Commons has more than six hundred members; they are elected from single-member constituencies by a plurality system. General elections follow the dissolution of the House, whose normal tenure is five years. The Monarch calls upon the parliamentary leader of the majority party to form a Cabinet. When no single party can command a majority, as happened frequently during the interwar years, the Monarch has some choice in the selection of the party to which this task is entrusted. The same procedure applies when the majority party does not have an obvious parliamentary leader. The Prime Minister then forms his Cabinet, which must have the support of a majority in the House in order to remain in office. If it loses a vote of confidence, the Cabinet can do one of two things: The Prime Minister can resign and let the leader of the Opposition form a Cabinet, which then similarly requires majority support in the House. (Sometimes, the incumbent leader of the majority party simply resigns in favor of another, as Anthony Eden did in favor of Harold Macmillan after the 1956 Suez Canal crisis.) Or he can ask the Queen to dissolve the House of Commons and thereby "go to the country" in a general election on the issue on which he suffered his parliamentary defeat. The Queen, according to present usage, has to grant the request.

A vote of confidence has not actually been lost in British politics since the end of the three-party system in the early 1930's. What has occurred is the informal loss of confidence in their Prime Minister by members of his own party, leading to his resignation in favor of another leader of the same party, as in the Eden case just cited and also in the resignation of Neville Chamberlain in favor of Winston Churchill in 1940. Since 1924, dissolutions of the House of Commons have occurred only at or after the end of its five-year term— the House elected in 1935 served until 1945, because no election was held during the war—or when the Cabinet felt that dissolution before that time would be to its electoral advantage. Thus, the slim Labour party majority resulting from the election of 1950 enabled the Conservatives to harass the Cabinet in Commons to such an extent that it dissolved the next year. (Labour lost the ensuing general election, however.) In 1955, the Conservative Cabinet got a dissolution one year before expiration of the five-year term, because it thought the time propitious—as indeed it turned out to be, for the Conservatives increased their parliamentary majority by twenty-four seats.

Constitutionally speaking, the Cabinet itself is the active part of the Queen's Privy Council. Its members, as Privy Councillors, take an oath to observe secrecy about the Cabinet's business. This provision facilitates the collective accountability of the Cabinet to Commons and helps to make it more of a collegial group than its Italian, German, and French namesakes. The Monarch's role is roughly equivalent to that of the presidents of these Continental countries, whose offices were modeled on that of the British King. But the Monarch has many advantages over them, not the least being deliberate preparation for, and uninterrupted service in, the office.

Since Britain has no clearly defined constitution, there is no place in her politics for the judicial review of legislation. However, this function is performed for many of the overseas members in the British Empire and Commonwealth by the Judicial Committee of the Privy Council. The membership of this body overlaps with the so-called Law Lords. Until 1958, the Law Lords were, except for Bishops of the Church of England, the only members of the House of Lords appointed for life, since all others inherited their titles. The Law Lords perform the judicial function of the upper house, which is the highest court of appeal. They are presided over by the Lord High Chancellor, who is also the presiding officer of the House of Lords in its parliamentary role and is also a member of the Cabinet. The Lord Chancellor, in other words, performs executive, legislative, and judicial functions, if one were to apply the categories of the American separation of powers to his office. The only office provided for by the Constitution of the United States with any degree of similarity is that of the Vice-President, as successor to an incapacitated President and as presiding officer of the Senate. The British model influenced the design of this American institution.

30 · THE AMERICAN CONTRIBUTION

A · JUDICIAL REVIEW

MARBURY v. MADISON *

[In pursuance of the act of Congress of February, 1801, President John Adams nominated William Marbury to be Justice of the Peace in the District of Columbia. The Senate confirmed the nomination,

* 1 Cranch 137, 173-180. (1803).

Adams signed the commission, the seal of the United States was affixed thereto, but John Marshall, then Secretary of State, failed to deliver the commission. Application was made to James Madison, Secretary of State under the new Jefferson administration, for the commission. Under instructions from President Jefferson, he refused to honor the request, claiming that the appointment was invalid unless delivery were made. Thereupon, acting under Section 13 of the Judiciary Act of 1789, Marbury asked the Supreme Court, in original jurisdiction, to issue a writ of mandamus to Madison forcing delivery of the commission. The following opinion of the Court was delivered by the Chief *Justice (John Marshall).]*

. . . . .

This, then, is a plain case for a mandamus, either to deliver the commission, or a copy of it from the record; and it only remains to be inquired,

Whether it can issue from this court.

The act to establish the judicial courts of the United States authorizes the Supreme Court "to issue writs of mandamus in cases warranted by the principles and usages of law, to any courts appointed, or persons holding office, under the authority of the United States."

The Secretary of State, being a person holding an office under the authority of the United States, is precisely within the letter of the description, and if this court is not authorized to issue a writ of mandamus to such an officer, it must be because the law is unconstitutional, and therefore absolutely incapable of conferring the authority, and assigning the duties which its words purport to confer and assign.

The constitution vests the whole judicial power of the United States in one Supreme Court, and such inferior courts as congress shall, from time to time, ordain and establish. This power is expressly extended to all cases arising under the laws of the United States; and, consequently, in some form, may be exercised over the present case; because the right claimed is given by a law of the United States.

In the distribution of this power it is declared that "the Supreme Court shall have original jurisdiction in all cases affecting ambassadors, other public ministers and consuls, and those in which a state shall be a party. In all other cases, the Supreme Court shall have appellate jurisdiction."

It has been insisted, at the bar, that as the original grant of jurisdiction, to the Supreme and inferior courts, is general, and the clause, assigning original jurisdiction to the Supreme Court, contains no negative or restrictive words, the power remains to the legislature, to assign original jurisdiction to that court in other cases than those specified in the article which has been recited; provided those cases belong to the judicial power of the United States.

If it had been intended to leave it in the discretion of the legislature to apportion the judicial power between the supreme and inferior courts according to the will of that body, it would certainly have been useless to have proceeded further than to have defined the judicial power, and the tribunals in which it should be vested. The subsequent part of the section is mere surplusage, is entirely without meaning, if such is to be the construction. If congress remains at liberty to give this court appellate jurisdiction where the constitution has declared their jurisdiction shall be original; and original jurisdiction where the constitution has declared it shall be appellate; the distribution of jurisdiction, made in the constitution, is form without substance.

Affirmative words are often, in their operation, negative of other objects than those affirmed; and in this case, a negative or exclusive sense must be given to them, or they have no operation at all.

It cannot be presumed that any clause in the constitution is intended to be without effect; and, therefore, such a construction is inadmissible, unless the words require it.

If the solicitude of the convention, respecting our peace with foreign powers, induced a provision that the Supreme Court should take original jurisdiction in cases which might be supposed to affect them; yet the clause would have proceeded no further than to provide for such cases, if no further restriction on the powers of congress had been intended. That they should have appellate jurisdiction in all other cases, with such exceptions as congress might make, is no restriction; unless the words be deemed exclusive of original jurisdiction.

When an instrument organizing fundamentally a judicial system, divides it into one supreme, and so many inferior courts as the legislature may ordain and establish; then enumerates its powers, and proceeds so far to distribute them, as to define the jurisdiction of the Supreme Court by declaring the cases in which it shall take original jurisdiction, and that in others it shall take appellate jurisdiction; the plain import of the words seems to be, that in one class of cases its jurisdiction is original, and not appellate; in the other it is appellate, and not original. If any other construction would render the clause inoperative, that is an additional reason for rejecting such other construction, and for adhering to their obvious meaning.

To enable this court, then, to issue a mandamus, it must be shown to be an exercise of appellate jurisdiction, or to be necessary to enable them to exercise appellate jurisdiction.

It has been stated at the bar that the appellate jurisdiction may be exercised in a variety of forms, and that if it be the will of the legislature that a mandamus should be used for that purpose, that will must be obeyed. This is true, yet the jurisdiction must be appellate, not original.

It is the essential criterion of appellate jurisdiction, that it revises and corrects the proceedings in a cause already instituted, and does not create that cause. Although, therefore, a mandamus may be directed to courts, yet to issue such a writ to an officer for the delivery of a paper, is in effect the same as to sustain an original action for that paper, and, therefore, seems not to belong to appellate but to original jurisdiction. Neither is it necessary in such a case as this, to enable the court to exercise its appellate jurisdiction.

The authority, therefore, given to the Supreme Court, by the act establishing the judicial courts of the United States, to issue writs of mandamus to public officers, appears not to be warranted by the constitution; and it becomes necessary to inquire whether a jurisdiction so conferred can be exercised.

The question, whether an act, repugnant to the constitution, can become the law of the land, is a question deeply interesting to the United States; but, happily, not of an intricacy proportioned to its interest. It seems only necessary to recognize certain principles, supposed to have been long and well established, to decide it.

That the people have an original right to establish, for their future government, such principles, as, in their opinion, shall most conduce to their own happiness is the basis on which the whole American fabric has been erected. The exercise of this original right is a very great exertion; nor can it, nor ought it, to be frequently repeated.

The principles, therefore, so established, are deemed fundamental. And as the authority from which they proceed is supreme, and can seldom act, they are designed to be permanent.

This original and supreme will organizes the government, and assigns to different departments their respective powers. It may either stop here, or establish certain limits not to be transcended by those departments.

The government of the United States is of the latter description. The powers of the legislature are defined and limited; and that those limits may not be mistaken, or forgotten, the constitution is written. To what purpose are powers limited, and to what purpose is that limitation committed to writing, if these limits may, at any time, be passed by those intended to be restrained? The distinction between a government with limited and unlimited powers is abolished, if those limits do not confine the persons on whom they are imposed, and if acts prohibited and acts allowed, are of equal obligation. It is a proposition too plain to be contested, that the constitution controls any legislative act repugnant to it; or, that the legislature may alter the constitution by an ordinary act.

Between these alternatives there is no middle ground. The constitution is either a superior paramount law, unchangeable by ordinary means, or it is on a level with ordinary legislative acts, and, like other acts, is alterable when the legislature shall please to alter it.

If the former part of the alternative be true, then a legislative act contrary to the constitution is not law; if the latter part be true, then written constitutions are absurd attempts, on the part of the people, to limit a power in its own nature illimitable.

Certainly all those who have framed written constitutions contemplate them as forming the fundamental and paramount law of the nation, and, consequently, the theory of every such government must be, that an act of the legislature, repugnant to the constitution, is void.

This theory is essentially attached to a written constitution, and, is consequently, to be considered, by this court, as one of the fundamental principles of our society. It is not therefore to be lost sight of in the further consideration of this subject.

If an act of the legislature, repugnant to the constitution, is void, does it, notwithstanding its invalidity, bind the courts, and oblige them to give it effect? Or, in other words, though it be not law, does it constitute a rule as operative as if it was a law? This would be to overthrow in fact what was established in theory; and would seem, at first view, an absurdity too gross to be insisted on. It shall, however, receive a more attentive consideration.

It is emphatically the province and duty of the judicial department to say what the law is. Those who apply the rule to particular cases, must of necessity expound and interpret that rule. If two laws conflict with each other, the courts must decide on the operation of each.

So if a law be in opposition to the constitution; if both the law and the constitution apply to a particular case, so that the court must either decide that case conformably to the law, disregarding the constitution; or conformably to the constitution, disregarding the law; the court must determine which of these conflicting rules governs the case. This is of the very essence of judicial duty.

If, then, the courts are to regard the constitution, and the constitution is superior to any ordinary act of the legislature, the constitution, and not such ordinary act, must govern the case to which they both apply.

Those, then, who controvert the principle that the constitution is to be considered, in court, as a paramount law, are reduced to the necessity of maintaining that courts must close their eyes on the constitution, and see only the law.

This doctrine would subvert the very foundation of all written constitutions. It would declare that an act which, according to the principles and theory of our government, is entirely void, is yet, in practice, completely obligatory. It would declare that if the legislature shall do what is expressly forbidden, such act, notwithstanding the express prohibition, is in reality effectual. It would be giving to the legislature a practical and real omnipotence, with the same breath which professes to restrict their powers within narrow limits. It is prescribing limits, and declaring that those limits may be passed at pleasure.

That it thus reduces to nothing what we have deemed the greatest improvement on political institutions, a written constitution, would of itself be sufficient, in America, where written constitutions have been viewed with so much reverence, for rejecting the construction. But the peculiar expressions of the constitution of the United States furnish additional arguments in favor of its rejection.

The judicial power of the United States is extended to all cases arising under the constitution.

Could it be the intention of those who gave this power, to say that in using it the constitution should not be looked into? That a case arising under the constitution should be decided without examining the instrument under which it arises?

This is too extravagant to be maintained.

In some cases, then, the constitution must be looked into by the judges. And if they can open it at all, what part of it are they forbidden to read or to obey?

There are many other parts of the constitution which serve to illustrate this subject.

It is declared that "no tax or duty shall be laid on articles exported from any state." Suppose a duty on the export of cotton, of tobacco, or of flour; and a suit instituted to recover it. Ought judgment to be rendered in such a case? ought the judges to close their eyes on the constitution, and only see the law?

The constitution declares "that no bill of attainder or ex post facto law shall be passed."

If, however, such a bill should be passed, and a person should be prosecuted under it; must the court condemn to death those victims whom the constitution endeavors to preserve?

"No person," says the constitution, "shall be convicted of treason unless on the testimony of two witnesses to the same overt act, or on confession in open court."

Here the language of the constitution is addressed especially to the courts. It prescribes, directly for them, a rule of evidence not to be departed from. If the legislature should change that rule, and declare one witness, or a confession out of court, sufficient for conviction, must the constitutional principle yield to the legislative act?

From these, and many other selections which might be made, it is apparent, that the framers of the constitution contemplated that instrument as a rule for the government of courts, as well as of the legislature.

Why otherwise does it direct the judges to take an oath to support it? This oath certainly applies in an especial manner, to their conduct in their official character. How immoral to impose it on them, if they were to be used as the instruments, and the knowing instruments, for violating what they swear to support!

The oath of office, too, imposed by the legislature, is completely demonstrative of the legislative opinion on this subject. It is in these words: "I do solemnly swear that I will administer justice without respect to persons, and do equal right to the poor and to the rich; and that I will faithfully and impartially discharge all the duties incumbent on me as . . . , according to the best of my abilities and understanding agreeably to the constitution and laws of the United States."

Why does a judge swear to discharge his duties agreeably to the constitution of the United States, if that constitution forms no rule for this government? if it be closed upon him, and cannot be inspected by him?

If such be the real state of things, this is worse than solemn mockery. To prescribe, or to take this oath, becomes equally a crime.

It is also not entirely unworthy of observation, that in declaring what shall be the supreme law of the land, the constitution itself is first mentioned; and not the laws of the United States generally, but those only which shall be made in pursuance of the constitution, have that rank.

Thus, the particular phraseology of the constitution of the United States confirms and strengthens the principle, supposed to be essential to all written constitutions, that a law repugnant to the constitution is void; and that courts, as well as other departments, are bound by that instrument.

The rule must be discharged.

JUSTICE SUTHERLAND ON JUDICIAL REVIEW *

Under our form of government, where the written Constitution, by its own terms, is the supreme law, some agency, of necessity, must have the power to say the final word as to the validity of a statute assailed as unconstitutional. The Constitution makes it clear that the power has been intrusted to this court when the question arises in a controversy within its jurisdiction; and so long as the power remains there, its exercise cannot be avoided without betrayal of the trust.

It has been pointed out many times, as in the Adkins Case, that this judicial duty is one of gravity and delicacy, and that rational doubts must be resolved in favor of the constitutionality of the statute. But whose doubts, and by whom resolved? Undoubtedly it is the duty of a member of the court, in the process of reaching a right conclusion, to give due weight to the opposing views of his asso-

* Reprinted from the dissenting opinion of Justice Sutherland in *West Coast Hotel Company* v. *Parrish*, 300 U.S. 379, 401-405 (1937).

ciates; but in the end, the question which he must answer is not
whether such views seem sound to those who entertain them, but
whether they convince him that the statute is constitutional or engender in his mind a rational doubt upon that issue. The oath which
he takes as a judge is not a composite oath, but an individual one.
And in passing upon the validity of a statute, he discharges a duty
imposed upon *him,* which cannot be consummated justly by an automatic acceptance of the views of others which have neither convinced, nor created a reasonable doubt in, his mind. If upon a question so important he thus surrender his deliberate judgment, he stands
forsworn. He cannot subordinate his convictions to that extent and
keep faith with his oath or retain his judicial and moral independence.

The suggestion that the only check upon the exercise of the judicial
power, when properly invoked, to declare a constitutional right superior to an unconstitutional statute is the judge's own faculty of self-
restraint, is both ill considered and mischievous. Self-restraint belongs in the domain of will and not of judgment. The check upon
the judge is that imposed by his oath of office, by the Constitution
and by his own conscientious and informed convictions; and since
he has the duty to make up his own mind and adjudge accordingly,
it is hard to see how there could be any other restraint. This court
acts as a unit. It cannot act in any other way; and the majority
(whether a bare majority or a majority of all but one of its members),
therefore, establishes the controlling rule as the decision of the court,
binding, so long as it remains unchanged, equally upon those who
disagree and upon those who subscribe to it. Otherwise, orderly
administration of justice would cease. But it is the right of those in
the minority to disagree, and sometimes, in matters of grave importance, their imperative duty to voice their disagreement at such
length as the occasion demands—always, of course, in terms which,
however forceful, do not offend the proprieties or impugn the good
faith of those who think otherwise.

It is urged that the question involved should now receive fresh
consideration, among other reasons, because of "the economic conditions which have supervened"; but the meaning of the Constitution
does not change with the ebb and flow of economic events. We frequently are told in more general words that the Constitution must be
construed in the light of the present. If by that it is meant that the
Constitution is made up of living words that apply to every new condition which they include, the statement is quite true. But to say, if

that be intended, that the words of the Constitution mean today what they did not mean when written—that is, that they do not apply to a situation now to which they would have applied then—is to rob that instrument of the essential element which continues it in force as the people have made it until they, and not their official agents, have made it otherwise.

· · · · ·

The judicial function is that of interpretation; it does not include the power of amendment under the guise of interpretation. To miss the point of difference between the two is to miss all that the phrase "supreme law of the land" stands for and to convert what was intended as inescapable and enduring mandates into mere moral reflections.

If the Constitution, intelligently and reasonably construed in the light of these principles, stands in the way of desirable legislation, the blame must rest upon that instrument, and not upon the court for enforcing it according to its terms. The remedy in that situation —and the only true remedy—is to amend the Constitution. Judge Cooley, in the first volume of his *Constitutional Limitations,* 8th ed., p. 124, very clearly pointed out that much of the benefit expected from written constitutions would be lost if their provisions were to be bent to circumstances or modified by public opinion. He pointed out that the common law, unlike a constitution, was subject to modification by public sentiment and action which the courts might recognize; but that "a court or legislature which should allow a change in public sentiment to influence it in giving to a written constitution a construction not warranted by the intention of its founders, would be justly chargeable with reckless disregard of official oath and public duty; and if its course could become a precedent, these instruments would be of little avail. . . . What a court is to do, therefore, is *to declare the law as written,* leaving it to the people themselves to make such changes as new circumstances may require. The meaning of the constitution is fixed when it is adopted, and it is not different at any subsequent time when a court has occasion to pass upon it."

· · · · ·

The people by their Constitution created three separate, distinct, independent and coequal departments of government. The governmental structure rests, and was intended to rest, not upon any one or upon any two, but upon all three of these fundamental pillars. It seems unnecessary to repeat, what so often has been said, that the powers of these departments are different and are to be exercised independently. The differences clearly and definitely appear in the Constitution. Each of the departments is an agent of its creator; and one department is not and cannot be the agent of another. Each is answerable to its creator for what it does, and not to another agent. The view, therefore, of the Executive and of Congress that an act is constitutional is persuasive in a high degree; but it is not controlling.

JUSTICE FRANKFURTER ON JUDICIAL SELF-RESTRAINT *

Even where the social undesirability of a law may be convincingly urged, invalidation of the law by a court debilitates popular democratic government. Most laws dealing with economic and social problems are matters of trial and error. That which before trial appears to be demonstrably bad may belie prophecy in actual operation. It may not prove good, but it may prove innocuous. But even if a law is found wanting on trial, it is better that its defects should be demonstrated and removed than that the law should be aborted by judicial fiat. Such an assertion of judicial power deflects responsibility from those on whom in a democratic society it ultimately rests—the people. . . .

But there is reason for judicial restraint in matters of policy deeper than the value of experiment: it is founded on a recognition of the gulf of difference between sustaining and nullifying legislation. This difference is theoretical in that the function of legislating is for legislatures who have also taken oaths to support the Constitution, while the function of courts, when legislation is challenged, is merely to make sure that the legislature has exercised an allowable judgment, and not to exercise their own judgment, whether a policy is within or without "the vague contours" of due process. Theory is reinforced by the notorious fact that lawyers predominate in American legislatures. In practice also the difference is wide. In the day-to-day working of our democracy it is vital that the power of the non-democratic organ of our Government be exercised with rigorous self-restraint.

* Reprinted from the concurring opinion of Justice Frankfurter in *American Federation of Labor* v. *American Sash and Door Company,* 335 U.S. 538, 553-557 (1949). The footnotes in the original version are omitted here.

Because the powers exercised by this Court are inherently oligarchic, Jefferson all of his life thought of the Court as "an irresponsible body" and "independent of the nation itself." The Court is not saved from being oligarchic because it professes to act in the service of humane ends. As history amply proves, the judiciary is prone to misconceive the public good by confounding private notions with constitutional requirements, and such misconceptions are not subject to legitimate displacement by the will of the people except at too slow a pace. Judges appointed for life whose decisions run counter to prevailing opinion cannot be voted out of office and supplanted by men of views more consonant with it. They are even farther removed from democratic pressures by the fact that their deliberations are in secret and remain beyond disclosure either by periodic reports or by such a modern device for securing responsibility to the electorate as the "press conference." But a democracy need not rely on the courts to save it from its own unwisdom. If it is alert—and without alertness by the people there can be no enduring democracy—unwise or unfair legislation can readily be removed from the statute books. It is by such vigilance over its representatives that democracy proves itself.

Our right to pass on the validity of legislation is now too much part of our constitutional system to be brought into question. But the implications of that right and the conditions for its exercise must constantly be kept in mind and vigorously observed. Because the Court is without power to shape measures for dealing with the problems of society but has merely the power of negation over measures shaped by others, the indispensable judicial requisite is intellectual humility, and such humility presupposes complete disinterestedness. And so, in the end, it is right that the Court should be indifferent to public temper and popular wishes. Mr. Dooley's "th' Supreme Coort follows th' iliction returns" expressed the wit of cynicism, not the demand of principle. A court which yields to the popular will thereby licenses itself to practice despotism, for there can be no assurance that it will not on another occasion indulge its own will. Courts can fulfill their responsibility in a democratic society only to the extent that they succeed in shaping their judgments by rational standards, and rational standards are both impersonal and communicable. Matters of policy, however, are by definition matters which demand the resolution of conflicts of value, and the elements of conflicting values are largely imponderable. Assessment of their competing worth involves differences of feeling; it is also an exercise in prophecy. Obviously the proper forum for mediating a clash of feelings and rendering a prophetic judgment is the body chosen for those purposes by the people. Its functions can be assumed by this Court only in disregard of the historic limits of the Constitution.

B · SEPARATION OF POWERS

THE FEDERALIST NO. 47

JAMES MADISON

To the People of the State of New York:

Having reviewed the general form of the proposed government and the general mass of power allotted to it, I proceed to examine the particular structure of this government, and the distribution of this mass of power among its constituent parts.

One of the principal objections inculcated by the more respectable adversaries to the Constitution, is its supposed violation of the political maxim, that the legislative, executive, and judiciary departments ought to be separate and distinct. In the structure of the federal government, no regard, it is said, seems to have been paid to this essential precaution in favor of liberty. The several departments of power are distributed and blended in such a manner as at once to destroy all symmetry and beauty of form, and to expose some of the essential parts of the edifice to the danger of being crushed by the disproportionate weight of other parts.

No political truth is certainly of greater intrinsic value, or is stamped with the authority of more enlightened patrons of liberty, than that on which the objection is founded. The accumulation of all powers, legislative, executive, and judiciary, in the same hands, whether of one, a few, or many, and whether hereditary, self-appointed, or elective, may justly be pronounced the very definition of tyranny. Were the federal Constitution, therefore, really chargeable with the accumulation of power, or with a mixture of powers, having a dangerous tendency to such an accumulation, no further arguments would be necessary to inspire a universal reprobation of the system. I persuade myself, however, that it will be made apparent to every one, that the charge cannot be supported, and that the maxim on which it relies has been totally misconceived and mis-applied. In order to form correct ideas on this important subject, it will be proper to investigate the sense in which the preservation of liberty requires that the three great departments of power should be separate and distinct.

The oracle who is always consulted and cited on this subject is the celebrated Montesquieu. If he be not the author of this invaluable precept in the science of politics, he has the merit at least of display-ing and recommending it most effectually to the attention of man-kind. Let us endeavor, in the first place, to ascertain his meaning on this point.

The British Constitution was to Montesquieu what Homer has been to the didactic writers on epic poetry. As the latter have considered the work of the immortal bard as the perfect model from which the principles and rules of the epic art were to be drawn, and by which all similar works were to be judged, so this great political critic ap-pears to have viewed the Constitution of England as the standard, or to use his own expression, as the mirror of political liberty; and to have delivered, in the form of elementary truths, the several charac-teristic principles of that particular system. That we may be sure, then, not to mistake his meaning in this case, let us recur to the source from which the maxim was drawn.

On the slightest view of the British Constitution, we must perceive that the legislative, executive, and judiciary departments are by no means totally separate and distinct from each other. The executive magistrate forms an integral part of the legislative authority. He alone has the prerogative of making treaties with foreign sovereigns, which, when made, have, under certain limitations, the force of legis-lative acts. All the members of the judiciary department are ap-pointed by him, can be removed by him on the address of the two Houses of Parliament, and form, when he pleases to consult them, one of his constitutional councils. One branch of the legislative de-partment forms also a great constitutional council to the executive chief, as, on another hand, it is the sole depositary of judicial power in cases of impeachment, and is invested with the supreme appellate jurisdiction in all other cases. The judges, again, are so far connected with the legislative department as often to attend and participate in its deliberations, though not admitted to a legislative vote.

From these facts, by which Montesquieu was guided, it may clearly be inferred that, in saying "There can be no liberty where the legislative and executive powers are united in the same person, or body of magistrates," or, "if the power of judging be not separated from the legislative and executive powers," he did not mean that these departments ought to have no *partial agency* in, or no *control* over, the acts of each other. His meaning, as his own words import, and still more conclusively as illustrated by the example in his eye, can amount to no more than this, that where the *whole* power of one department is exercised by the same hands which possess the *whole* power of another department, the fundamental principles of a free constitution are subverted. This would have been the case in the constitution examined by him, if the king, who is the sole executive magistrate, had possessed also the complete legislative power, or the supreme administration of justice; or if the entire legislative body had possessed the supreme judiciary, or the supreme executive authority. This, however, is not among the vices of that constitution. The magistrate in whom the whole executive power resides cannot of himself make a law, though he can put a negative on every law; nor administer justice in person, though he has the appointment of those who do administer it. The judges can exercise no executive prerogative, though they are shoots from the executive stock; nor any legislative function, though they may be advised with by the legislative councils. The entire legislature can perform no judiciary act, though by the joint act of two of its branches the judges may be removed from their offices, and though one of its branches is possessed of the judicial power in the last resort. The entire legislature, again, can exercise no executive prerogative, though one of its branches constitutes the supreme executive magistracy, and another, on the impeachment of a third, can try and condemn all the subordinate officers in the executive department.

The reasons on which Montesquieu grounds his maxim are a further demonstration of his meaning. "When the legislative and executive powers are united in the same person or body," says he, "there can be no liberty, because apprehensions may arise lest *the same* monarch or senate should *enact* tyrannical laws to *execute* them in a tyrannical manner." Again: "Were the power of judging joined with the legislative, the life and liberty of the subject would be exposed to arbitrary control, for *the judge* would then be *the legislator*. Were it joined to the executive power, *the judge* might behave with all the violence of *an oppressor*." Some of these reasons are more fully explained in other passages; but briefly stated as they are here, they sufficiently establish the meaning which we have put on this celebrated maxim of this celebrated author.

If we look into the constitutions of the several States, we find that, notwithstanding the emphatical and, in some instances, the unqualified terms in which this axiom has been laid down, there is not a single instance in which the several departments of power have been kept absolutely separate and distinct. New Hampshire, whose constitution was the last formed, seems to have been fully aware of the impossibility and inexpediency of avoiding any mixture whatever of these departments, and has qualified the doctrine by declaring "that the legislative, executive, and judiciary powers ought to be kept as separate from, and independent of, each other *as the nature of a free government will admit; or as is consistent with that chain of connection that binds the whole fabric of the constitution in one indissoluble bond of unity and amity.*" Her constitution accordingly mixes these departments in several respects. The Senate, which is a branch of the legislative department, is also a judicial tribunal for the trial of impeachments. The President, who is the head of the executive department, is the presiding member also of the Senate; and, besides an equal vote in all cases, has a casting vote in case of a tie. The executive head is himself eventually elective every year by the legislative department, and his council is every year chosen by and from the members of the same department. Several of the officers of state are also appointed by the legislature. And the members of the judiciary department are appointed by the executive department.

The constitution of Massachusetts has observed a sufficient though less pointed caution, in expressing this fundamental article of liberty. It declares "that the legislative departments shall never exercise the executive and judicial powers, or either of them; the executive shall never exercise the legislative and judicial powers, or either of them; the judicial shall never exercise the legislative and executive powers, or either of them." This declaration corresponds precisely with the doctrine of Montesquieu, as it has been explained, and is not in a single point violated by the plan of the convention. It goes no farther than to prohibit any one of the entire departments from exercising the powers of another department. In the very Constitution to which it is prefixed, a partial mixture of powers has been admitted. The executive magistrate has a qualified negative on the legislative body, and the Senate, which is a part of the legislature, is a court of impeachment for members both of the executive and judiciary departments. The members of the judiciary department, again, are appointable by the executive department, and removable by the same authority on the address of the two legislative branches. Lastly, a number of the officers of government are annually appointed by the legislative department. As the appointment to offices, particularly executive offices, is in its nature an executive function, the compilers of the Constitution have, in this last point at least, violated the rule established by themselves.

I pass over the constitutions of Rhode Island and Connecticut, because they were formed prior to the Revolution, and even before the principle under examination had become an object of political attention.

The constitution of New York contains no declaration on this subject; but appears very clearly to have been framed with an eye to the danger of improperly blending the different departments. It gives, nevertheless, to the executive magistrate, a partial control over the legislative department; and, what is more, gives a like control to the judiciary department; and even blends the executive and judiciary departments in the exercise of this control. In its council of appointment members of the legislative are associated with the executive authority, in the appointment of officers, both executive and judiciary. And its court for the trial of impeachments and correction of errors is to consist of one branch of the legislature and the principal members of the judiciary department.

The constitution of New Jersey has blended the different powers of government more than any of the preceding. The governor, who is the executive magistrate, is appointed by the legislature; is chancellor and ordinary, or surrogate of the State; is a member of the Supreme Court of Appeals, and president, with a casting vote, of one of the legislative branches. The same legislative branch acts again as executive council of the governor, and with him constitutes the Court of Appeals. The members of the judiciary department are appointed by the legislative department, and removable by one branch of it, on the impeachment of the other.

According to the constitution of Pennsylvania, the president, who is the head of the executive department, is annually elected by a vote in which the legislative department predominates. In conjunction with an executive council, he appoints the members of the judiciary department, and forms a court of impeachment for trial of all officers, judiciary as well as executive. The judges of the Supreme

Court and justices of the peace seem also to be removable by the legislature; and the executive power of pardoning in certain cases, to be referred to the same department. The members of the executive council are made ex-officio justices of peace throughout the State.

In Delaware, the chief executive magistrate is annually elected by the legislative department. The speakers of the two legislative branches are vice-presidents in the executive department. The executive chief, with six others, appointed, three by each of the legislative branches, constitutes the Supreme Court of Appeals; he is joined with the legislative department in the appointment of the other judges. Throughout the States, it appears that the members of the legislature may at the same time be justices of the peace; in this State, the members of one branch of it are ex-officio justices of the peace; as are also the members of the executive council. The principal officers of the executive department are appointed by the legislative; and one branch of the latter forms a court of impeachments. All officers may be removed on address of the legislature.

Maryland has adopted the maxim in the most unqualified terms; declaring that the legislative, executive, and judicial powers of government ought to be forever separate and distinct from each other. Her constitution, notwithstanding, makes the executive magistrate appointable by the legislative department; and the members of the judiciary by the executive department.

The language of Virginia is still more pointed on this subject. Her constitution declares, "that the legislative, executive, and judiciary departments shall be separate and distinct; so that neither exercise the powers properly belonging to the other; nor shall any person exercise the powers of more than one of them at the same time, except that the justices of county courts shall be eligible to either House of Assembly." Yet we find not only this express exception, with respect to the members of the inferior courts, but that the chief magistrate, with his executive council, are appointable by the legislature; that two members of the latter are triennially displaced at the pleasure of the legislature; and that all the principal offices, both executive and judiciary, are filled by the same department. The executive prerogative of pardon, also, is in one case vested in the legislative department.

The constitution of North Carolina, which declares "that the legislative, executive, and supreme judicial powers of government ought to be forever separate and distinct from each other," refers, at the same time, to the legislative department, the appointment not only of the executive chief, but all the principal officers within both that and the judiciary department.

In South Carolina, the constitution makes the executive magistracy eligible by the legislative department. It gives to the latter, also, the appointment of the members of the judiciary department, including even justices of the peace and sheriffs; and the appointment of officers in the executive department, down to captains in the army and navy of the State.

In the constitution of Georgia, where it is declared "that the legislative, executive, and judiciary departments shall be separate and distinct, so that neither exercise the powers properly belonging to the other," we find that the executive department is to be filled by appointments of the legislature; and the executive prerogative of pardon to be finally exercised by the same authority. Even justices of the peace are to be appointed by the legislature.

In citing these cases, in which the legislative, executive, and judiciary departments have not been kept totally separate and distinct, I wish not to be regarded as an advocate for the particular organizations of the several State governments. I am fully aware that among the many excellent principles which they exemplify, they carry strong marks of the haste, and still stronger of the inexperience, under which they were framed. It is but too obvious that in some instances the fundamental principle under consideration has been violated by too great a mixture, and even an actual consolidation, of the different powers; and that in no instance has a competent provision been made for maintaining in practice the separation delineated on paper. What I have wished to evince is, that the charge brought against the proposed Constitution, of violating the sacred maxim of free government, is warranted neither by the real meaning annexed to that maxim by its author, nor by the sense in which it has hitherto been understood in America. This interesting subject will be resumed in the ensuing paper.   PUBLIUS

JUSTICE HOLMES ON SEPARATION OF POWERS *

The great ordinances of the Constitution do not establish and divide fields of black and white. Even the more specific of them are found

* Reprinted from the dissenting opinion of Justice Holmes in *Springer* v. *Government of the Philippine Islands,* 277 U.S. 189, 209-211 (1928).

to terminate in a penumbra shading gradually from one extreme to the other. Property must not be taken without compensation, but with the help of a phrase (the police power) some property may be taken or destroyed for public use without paying for it, if you do not take too much. When we come to the fundamental distinctions it is still more obvious that they must be received with a certain latitude or our government could not go on.

To make a rule of conduct applicable to an individual who but for such action would be free from it is to legislate—yet it is what the judges do whenever they determine which of two competing principles of policy shall prevail. At an early date it was held that Congress could delegate to the courts the power to regulate process, which certainly is lawmaking, so far as it goes. With regard to the Executive, Congress has delegated to it or to some branch of it the power to impose penalties, to make conclusive determination of dutiable values, to establish standards for imports, to make regulations as to forest reserves, and other powers not needing to be stated in further detail. Congress has authorized the President to suspend the operation of a statute, even one suspending commercial intercourse with another country, and very recently it has been decided that the President might be given power to change the tariff. It is said that the powers of Congress cannot be delegated, yet Congress has established the Interstate Commerce Commission, which does legislative, judicial and executive acts, only softened by a quasi; makes regulations, issues reparation orders, and performs executive functions in connection with Safety Appliance Acts, Boiler Inspection Acts, etc. Congress also has made effective excursions in the other direction. It has withdrawn jurisdiction of a case after it has been argued. It has granted an amnesty, notwithstanding the grant to the President of the power to pardon. A territorial legislature has granted a divorce. Congress has declared lawful an obstruction to navigation that this court has declared unlawful. Parallel to the case before us Congress long ago established the Smithsonian Institution to question which would be to lay hands on the Ark of the Covenant; not to speak of later similar exercises of power hitherto unquestioned, so far as I know.

It does not seem to need argument to show that however we may disguise it by veiling words we do not and cannot carry out the distinction between legislative and executive action with mathematical precision and divide the branches into watertight compartments, were it ever so desirable to do so, which I am far from believing that it is, or that the Constitution requires.

C · FEDERALISM

FEDERALISM *

EDWARD S. CORWIN

Federalism in the United States embraces the following elements: (1) as in all federations, the union of several autonomous political entities, or "States," for common purposes; (2) the division of legislative powers between a "National Government," on the one hand, and constituent "States," on the other, which division is governed by the rule that the former is "a government of enumerated powers" while the latter are governments of "residual powers"; (3) the direct operation, for the most part, of each of these centers of government, within its assigned sphere, upon all persons and property within its territorial limits; (4) the provision of each center with the complete apparatus of law enforcement, both executive and judicial; (5) the supremacy of the "National Government" within its assigned sphere over any conflicting assertion of "State" power; (6) dual citizenship.

The third and fourth of the above-listed salient features of the American Federal System are the ones which at the outset marked it off most sharply from all preceding systems, in which the member states generally agreed to obey the mandates of a common government for certain stipulated purposes, but retained to themselves the right of ordaining and enforcing the laws of the union. This, indeed, was the system provided in the Articles of Confederation. The Convention of 1787 was well aware, of course, that if the inanities and futilities of the Confederation were to be avoided in the new system, the latter must incorporate "a coercive principle"; and as Ellsworth of Connecticut expressed it, the only question was whether it should be "a coercion of law, or a coercion of arms," that "coercion which acts only upon delinquent individuals" or that which is applicable to "sovereign bodies, states, in their political capacity." In Judicial

* Edward S. Corwin (ed.), *The Constitution of the United States,* 82nd Congress, 2nd Session, S. Doc. 170 (Washington, D.C.: Government Printing Office, 1953), pp. xi-xvi. Reprinted by permission of Edward S. Corwin. The footnotes in the original version are omitted here.

Review the former principle was established, albeit without entirely discarding the latter, as the War between the States was to demonstrate.

The sheer fact of Federalism enters the purview of Constitutional Law, that is, becomes a judicial concept, in consequence of the conflicts which have at times arisen between the idea of State Autonomy ("State Sovereignty") and the principle of National Supremacy. Exaltation of the latter principle, as it is recognized in the Supremacy Clause (Article VI, paragraph 2) of the Constitution, was the very keystone of Chief Justice Marshall's constitutional jurisprudence. It was Marshall's position that the supremacy clause was intended to be applied literally, so that if an unforced reading of the terms in which legislative power was granted to Congress confirmed its right to enact a particular statute, the circumstance that the statute projected national power into a hitherto accustomed field of state power with unavoidable curtailment of the latter was a matter of indifference. State power, as Madison in his early nationalistic days phrased it, was "no criterion of national power," and hence no independent limitation thereof.

Quite different was the outlook of the Court over which Marshall's successor, Taney, presided. That Court took as its point of departure the Tenth Amendment, which reads, "The powers not delegated to the United States by this Constitution, nor prohibited by it to the States, are reserved to the States respectively, or to the people." In construing this provision the Court under Taney sometimes talked as if it regarded all the reserved powers of the States as limiting national power; at other times it talked as if it regarded certain subjects as reserved exclusively to the States, slavery being, of course, the outstanding instance.

But whether following the one line of reasoning or the other, the Taney Court subtly transformed its function, and so that of Judicial Review, in relation to the Federal System. Marshall viewed the Court as primarily an organ of the National Government and of its supremacy. The Court under Taney regarded itself as standing outside of and above both the National Government and the States, and as vested with a quasi-arbitral function between two centers of diverse, but essentially equal, because "sovereign," powers. Thus in Ableman v. Booth, which was decided on the eve of the War between the States, we find Taney himself using this arresting language:

This judicial power was justly regarded as indispensable, not merely to maintain the supremacy of the laws of the United States, but also to guard the States from any encroachment upon their reserved rights by the general government. . . . So long . . . as this Constitution shall endure, this tribunal must exist with it, deciding in the peaceful forms of judicial proceeding, the angry and irritating controversies between sovereignties, which in other countries have been determined by the arbitrament of force.

It is, therefore, the Taney Court, rather than the Marshall Court, which elaborated the concept of Dual Federalism. Marshall's federalism is more aptly termed national federalism; and turning to modern issues, we may say without exaggeration that the broad general constitutional issue between the Court and the Franklin D. Roosevelt program in such cases as Schechter Corp. *v.* United States and Carter *v.* Carter Coal Co. was, whether Marshall's or Taney's brand of federalism should prevail. More precisely, the issue in these cases was whether Congress' power to regulate commerce must stop short of regulating the employer-employee relationship in industrial production, that having been hitherto regulated by the States. In Justice Sutherland's words in the Carter case:

Much stress is put upon the evils which come from the struggle between employers and employees over the matter of wages, working conditions, the right of collective bargaining, etc., and the resulting strikes, curtailment and irregularity of production and effect on prices; and it is insisted that interstate commerce is greatly affected thereby. . . . The conclusive answer is that the evils are all local evils over which the Federal Government has no legislative control. The relation of employer and employee is a local relation. At common law, it is one of the domestic relations. The wages are paid for the doing of local work. Working conditions are obviously local conditions. The employees are not engaged in or about commerce, but exclusively in producing a commodity. And the controversies and evils, which it is the object of the act to regulate and minimize, are local controversies and evils affecting local work undertaken to accomplish that local result. Such effect as they may have upon commerce, however extensive it may be, is secondary and indirect. An increase in the greatness of the effect adds to its importance. It does not alter its character.

We all know how this issue was finally resolved. In the Fair Labor Standards Act of 1938 Congress not only prohibits interstate com-

merce in goods produced by substandard labor, but it directly forbids, with penalties, the employment of labor in industrial production
for interstate commerce on other than certain prescribed terms. And
in United States *v.* Darby this Act was sustained by the Court, in all
its sweeping provisions, on the basis of an opinion by Chief Justice
Stone which in turn is based on Chief Justice Marshall's famous
opinions in McCulloch *v.* Maryland and Gibbons *v.* Ogden rendered
more than a century and a quarter ago. In short, as a principle capable of delimiting the national legislative power, the concept of Dual
Federalism as regards the present Court seems today to be at an end,
with consequent aggrandizement of national power.

There is, however, another side to the story. For in one respect even
the great Marshall has been in effect overruled in support of enlarged
views of national authority. Without essaying a vain task of "tithing
mint, anise and cummin," it is fairly accurate to say that throughout
the 100 years which lie between Marshall's death and the cases of
the 1930's, the conception of the federal relationship which on the
whole prevailed with the Court was a competitive conception, one
which envisaged the National Government and the States as jealous
rivals. To be sure, we occasionally get some striking statements of
contrary tendency, as in Justice Bradley's opinion in 1880 for a
divided Court in the Siebold Case, where is reflected recognition of
certain results of the War between the States; or later in a frequently
quoted dictum by Justice McKenna, in Hoke *v.* United States, in
which the Mann White Slave Act was sustained in 1913:

> Our dual form of government has its perplexities, State and Nation
> having different spheres of jurisdiction . . . but it must be kept in
> mind that we are one people; and the powers reserved to the states and
> those conferred on the nation are adapted to be exercised, whether
> independently or concurrently, to promote the general welfare, material
> and moral.

The competitive concept is, nevertheless, the one much more generally evident in the outstanding results for American Constitutional
Law throughout three-quarters of its history. Of direct pertinence in
this connection is the doctrine of tax exemption which converted federalism into a principle of private immunity from taxation, so that,
for example, neither government could tax as income the official
salaries paid by the other government. This doctrine traces immediately to Marshall's famous judgment in McCulloch *v.* Maryland, and

bespeaks a conception of the federal relationship which regards the National Government and the States as bent on mutual frustration. Today the principle of tax exemption, except so far as Congress may choose to apply it to federal instrumentalities by virtue of its protective powers under the necessary and proper clause, is at an end.

By the cooperative conception of the federal relationship the States and the National Government are regarded as mutually complementary parts of a single governmental mechanism all of whose powers are intended to realize the current purposes of government according to their applicability to the problem in hand. This is the conception on which the recent social and economic legislation professes to rest. It is the conception which the Court invokes throughout its decisions in sustaining the Social Security Act of 1935 and supplementary state legislation. It is the conception which underlies congressional legislation of recent years making certain crimes against the States, like theft, racketeering, kidnaping, crimes also against the National Government whenever the offender extends his activities beyond state boundary lines. The usually cited constitutional justification for such legislation is that which was advanced forty years ago in the above quoted Hoke Case.

It has been argued that the cooperative conception of the federal relationship, especially as it is realized in the policy of federal subventions to the States, tends to break down state initiative and to devitalize state policies. Actually, its effect has often been just the contrary, and for the reason pointed out by Justice Cardozo in Helvering *v.* Davis, decided in 1937, namely, that the States, competing as they do with one another to attract investors, have not been able to embark separately upon expensive programs of relief and social insurance. Another great objection to Cooperative Federalism is more difficult to meet. This is, that Cooperative Federalism invites further aggrandizement of national power. Unquestionably it does, for when two cooperate, it is the stronger member of the combination who usually calls the tunes. Resting as it does primarily on the superior fiscal resources of the National Government, Cooperative Federalism has been, at least to date, a short expression for a constantly increasing concentration of power at Washington in the stimulation and supervision of local policies.

The last element of the concept of Federalism to demand attention is the doctrine that the National Government is a government of enumerated powers only, and consequently under the necessity at

all times of justifying its measures juridically by pointing to some particular clause or clauses of the Constitution which, when read separately or in combination, may be thought to grant power adequate to
such measures. In spite of such recent decisions as that in United
States *v.* Darby, this time-honored doctrine still guides the authoritative interpreters of the Constitution in determining the validity of
acts which are passed by Congress in presumed exercise of its powers
of domestic legislation—the course of reasoning pursued by the Chief
Justice in the Darby Case itself is proof that such is the fact. In the
field of foreign relations, on the contrary, the doctrine of enumerated
powers has always had a difficult row to hoe, and today may be un-
qualifiedly asserted to be defunct.

As early as the old case of Penhallow *v.* Doane, which was decided
by the Supreme Court in 1795, certain counsel thought it pertinent
to urge the following conception of the War Power:

> A formal compact is not essential to the institution of a government.
> Every nation that governs itself, under what form soever, without any
> dependence on a foreign power, is a sovereign state. In every society
> there must be a sovereignty: 1 Dall. Rep. 46, 57. Vatt. B. 1 ch. 1. sec. 4.
> The powers of war form an inherent characteristic of national
> sovereignty; and, it is not denied, that Congress possessed those
> powers. . . .

To be sure, only two of the Justices felt it necessary to comment on
this argument, which one of them endorsed, while the other rejected it.

Yet seventy-five years later Justice Bradley incorporated closely
kindred doctrine into his concurring opinion in the Legal Tender
Cases; and in the years following the Court itself frequently brought
the same general outlook to questions affecting the National Government's powers in the field of foreign relations. Thus in the Chinese
Exclusion Case, decided in 1889, Justice Field, in asserting the unlimited power of the National Government, and hence of Congress,
to exclude aliens from American shores, remarked:

> While under our Constitution and form of government the great
> mass of local matters is controlled by local authorities, the United
> States, in their relation to foreign countries and their subjects or
> citizens, are one nation, invested with the powers which belong to
> independent nations, the exercise of which can be invoked for the
> maintenance of its absolute independence and security throughout
> its entire territory.

And four years later the power of the National Government to deport alien residents at the option of Congress was based by Justice Gray on the same general reasoning.

Finally, in 1936, Justice Sutherland, speaking for the Court in United States *v.* Curtiss-Wright Corporation, with World War I a still recent memory, took over bodily counsel's argument of 140 years earlier, and elevated it to the head of the column of authoritative constitutional doctrine. He said:

> A political society cannot endure without a supreme will somewhere. Sovereignty is never held in suspense. When, therefore, the external sovereignty of Great Britain in respect of the colonies ceased, it immediately passed to the Union. . . . It results that the investment of the Federal government with the powers of external sovereignty did not depend upon the affirmative grants of the Constitution. The powers to declare and wage war, to conclude peace, to make treaties, to maintain diplomatic relations with other sovereignties, if they had never been mentioned in the Constitution, would have vested in the Federal government as a necessary concomitant of nationality.

In short, the power of the National Government in the field of international relationship is not simply a complexus of particular enumerated powers; it is an inherent power, one which is attributable to the National Government on the ground solely of its belonging to the American People as a sovereign political entity at International Law. In that field the principle of Federalism no longer holds, if it ever did.

31 · LATIN AMERICAN CONSTITUTIONS: NOMINAL AND REAL *

J. Lloyd Mecham

If the drafting of democratic constitutions serves as preparation for practice in the art of popular government then, indeed, Latin Americans are well prepared. Since gaining independence the twenty re-

* J. Lloyd Mecham, "Latin American Constitutions: Nominal and Real," *The Journal of Politics,* 21 (May, 1959), 258-275. The footnotes in the original version are omitted here. Reprinted by permission of J. Lloyd Mecham and the Southern Political Science Association.

publics have essayed a grand total of 186 *magna cartae*, or an average of 9.3 each. A breakdown per country reveals the following: Argentina 4; Bolivia 14; Brazil 5; Chile 7; Colombia 6; Costa Rica 7; Cuba 2; Dominican Republic 22; Ecuador 16; El Salvador 10; Guatemala 5; Haiti 18; Honduras 10; Mexico 5; Nicaragua 8; Panama 3; Paraguay 4; Peru 12; Uruguay 4; and Venezuela 24. Today thirteen of the Latin American republics are governed by constitutions adopted since 1940, and only two antedate World War I. There seems to be no end to constitution making.

This points up an anomaly: on the one hand apparent devotion to constitutionalism as a cure for national problems, and on the other, lack of respect for constitutional mandates. Nowhere are constitutions more elaborate and less observed. Politically, Latin Americans seem to be unqualified optimists, for the long succession of constitutional failures has never dampened hopes that the perfect constitution—a cure-all for national ills—will be discovered eventually.

THE NOMINAL CONSTITUTION

Since it is the objective of the present inquiry to show how widely government in operation departs from constitutional mandate, we first note the constitutional norm, *i.e.,* a composite or average constitution of the Latin American republics.

The Composite Constitution

This constitution is a lengthy instrument of about 35 pages, in contrast to 13 pages for the Constitution of the United States. Cuba's constitution is the longest with 68 pages; Mexico and Venezuela tie for second at 54 pages each. The excessive length results in part from a distrust of government, particularly the executive; hence the elaborate provisions to prevent abuse of power.

The composite constitution contains no preamble. It sets about forthrightly to declare that the nation is sovereign, independent, and unitary or federal as the case may be; that the government is republican, democratic, and representative; that sovereignty is vested in the people who express their will by suffrage which is obligatory and secret for all citizens, male and female, over 20 years of age. No literacy or property tests are required. This is universal suffrage in its most liberal sense.

The guarantees of individual liberty, the familiar rights of man, are spelled out in great detail. These include: the freedoms of speech, press, assembly, and petition; equality before the law; *habeas corpus;* no unreasonable searches or seizures; due process; no retroactive penalties; and no capital punishment. Religious freedom is guaranteed, and all cults receive the equal protection of the state. The minute enumeration of the inalienable rights of the individual is inspired by a desire to erect a constitutional barrier to tyranny.

The effectiveness of this barrier is weakened, however, by provisions for the suspension of the individual guarantees in times of stress. This device is called "declaration of state of siege," a temporary annulment, by presidential decree, of all constitutional guarantees and privileges. This important presidential power is restricted only by the formality of securing congressional approval before the act if the Congress is in session, and after the act when that body is convened. The easy suspension of the constitutional guarantees is evidence of the fact that they are considerably less than absolute.

One of the most detailed and lengthy sections of the constitution deals with "social rights and duties," a recent addition to Latin American constitutional law. Conforming to contemporary conceptions of social justice, social rights and duties are enumerated *in extenso* under the subheads: labor, family, education, and the economic order.

Labor is declared to be both a right of the individual and a social obligation. The state recognizes a special responsibility to protect the worker. The labor section, a veritable labor code, guarantees maximum hours of work and minimum wages, equal pay for equal work without regard for sex, compensation for industrial accidents, special protection for women and children, annual holidays with pay, medical assistance, collective labor contracts, and the right to strike. A labor jurisdiction is established to which all controversies between capital and labor are to be submitted.

The social guarantees relating to the family are based on the principle that the family, motherhood, and marriage are under the protection of the state. It is the duty of the state to safeguard the social development of the family, to preserve its integrity, and to assume responsibility for neglected children. All children are equal before the law whether born in wedlock or not.

Education also receives special mention. It is the right of everyone to receive instruction and is the responsibility of the state to provide educational facilities. Primary education is obligatory; that provided by the state is free. Secondary and higher instruction imparted by the state is also gratuitous.

The guarantees relating to the economic order are inspired by considerations of social welfare and national consciousness. Thus, although the right to private property is recognized, its use and retention are conditioned by social need. Private property cannot be expropriated without just compensation. The subsoil belongs to the state which may make concessions for its exploitation. Many of the social and economic guarantees find their inspiration in the nationalistic aspiration to abolish or bring under greater control foreign enterprises.

The supreme powers of government are divided for their exercise, by application of the principle of the separation of powers, into the legislative, the executive, and the judicial. Two or more of these powers shall never be united in one person or group of persons, for by counterbalancing and checking each other they will prevent the establishment of a tyranny.

The legislative power is vested in a Congress composed of two houses, a Chamber of Deputies and a Senate. Both deputies and senators are chosen by direct popular vote, for terms of four and six years respectively. . . . In general both houses of the national legislature possess the same powers and perform the same functions. They are equal partners in the legislative process. Although each chamber possesses certain special powers these are of no particular consequence. . . .

The powers of the national government in the federal states of Latin America are considerably broader than in the United States. In addition to virtually all those powers delegated to the United States Congress, the Latin American federal Congress is authorized to enact general codes of civil, penal, procedural, and commercial law for the whole nation. The federal Congress is also authorized by express constitutional grant to enact necessary legislation dealing with labor, education, public health, and natural resources. Most significant of all these exceptional federal powers, because of its use to convert constitutional federalism into actual centralism, is that of intervention into the affairs of the states "for the preservation of the republican representative form of government." As with respect to the declaration of a state of siege, the president plays the leading role in intervention; the Congress ratifies the presidential initiative.

An interesting feature of the legislative branch found in the composite constitution, and of course unknown to the American Constitution, is the Permanent Committee of Congress. Composed of senators and deputies chosen by their respective chambers, this body functions during the recess of Congress. Its principal task is to keep a watchful eye over the executive branch of the government, and, in the event of gross abuse of power, to summon the Congress in special session. Here is another of the numerous paper barriers to dictatorship.

The executive power is exercised by the president with a council of ministers. The president is chosen by direct vote of the people (even in the federal states), serves for a term of four years, and is not eligible for reelection until after one term intervenes. There is no provision for a vice-president because this heir apparent might become the magnet for conspiracies against the constituted government.

The powers of the Latin American president are relatively greater than those of the president of the United States, for, in addition to the customary executive grants, he is authorized to directly initiate legislation in the national Congress, expel foreigners on his own authority, suspend the constitutional guarantees, and in federal states impose his will on state administrations by exercise of the power of intervention. His decree-making power is so broad as to be quasi-legislative in character; indeed, the constitution authorizes the Congress to delegate, in emergencies, extraordinary legislative powers to the president. Constitutional checks on dictatorship are thus cancelled out by contrary constitutional delegations. The end result is that dictatorships are possible within the terms, if not the spirit, of the Constitution.

. . . . .

The judicial system, independent and coordinate, is composed of a hierarchy of courts; a supreme court, appellate courts, and inferior courts or courts of first instance. . . . The justices are appointed and serve for limited terms. The Latin American countries base their legal system on the Roman Law and so do not make use of trial by jury. United States influence is discovered however, in the constitutional provision conferring on the supreme court the power to declare laws unconstitutional.

In addition to the regular courts there are a number of special courts, notably the administrative tribunals and the electoral tribunals. The former have jurisdiction over suits involving the infringement of private rights by public officials, and the latter have jurisdiction over all cases involving the application of the electoral laws. The members of the electoral tribunal are recruited from the regular judiciary.

In its organization of local government the composite constitution for the unitary state provides a highly centralized system as in France. . . .

Reflective of the prominence which the military assumes in the political life of the Latin American nations, a separate constitutional chapter is devoted to "the armed forces." In addition to national defense the military are assigned the role of "guaranteeing the constitutional powers." This provides a basis for political intervention despite the injunction that the armed forces are "essentially obedient and not deliberative." This is another of the numerous but ineffective constitutional word-barriers to the rule of force.

The constitution is easily amended. The proposed amendment must receive a two-thirds vote in two consecutive legislative sessions. The executive cannot object. This is meaningless, however, since the amendment would have little chance of adoption if the president opposed. There is no popular ratification of constitutional amendments; indeed, the original constitution itself was not popularly ratified.

Variations from the Norm

Such is an average Latin American Constitution. Of course there are many interesting departures from this composite instrument. Included in these exceptions to the rule are the following: the National Council of Government or plural executive in Uruguay; the unicameral congress in four of the Central American republics, also Panama and Paraguay; functional representation in the Senate in Peru and Ecuador, and modified parliamentarism or ministerial responsibility in Cuba, Ecuador, Guatemala, Panama, Peru and Uruguay.

. . . . .

The contemporary Latin American constitutions measure up quite well, compared with other world constitutions, as advanced instruments of democratic government. Latin American framers of constitutions are generally keen scholars of political theory and bring to the constituent assemblies a high level of competence. Nor can it be fairly held that this competence is purely theoretical. One need but read carefully the debates and proceedings of constitutional conventions to realize that they reflect not only an intimate acquaintance with the literature of political science and with constitutional development and trends around the world, but also with their own national deficiencies. Latin Americans are unsparing in self-criticism; thus there is little that a foreign political scientist can tell them of which they are unaware.

The Latin American's attitude toward constitutional law differs radically from that of the Anglo-American in that whereas to us the constitution is the fundamental law and must be observed, to the Latin American it is, in many respects, merely a declaration of ideal objectives. To us the constitution is almost sacrosanct, for we subscribe to the principle of a government of law; to the Latin American the constitution, generally a useful and convenient guide and program, must bend to the principle of a government of men.

THE OPERATIVE CONSTITUTION

The foregoing, in broad outline, is the composite "paper" constitution of the Latin American republics, together with certain distinctive variations. It is now in order to describe that constitution as actually operative. With the exception of Uruguay, and the doubtful addition of Costa Rica, Chile and Mexico, democratic government does not exist in Latin America. A majority of the countries are either undisguised personalistic dictatorships or pseudo-democracies. In either case the proud constitutional assertions that these are popular, representative, democratic states, and that all governmental authority derives from the people in whom sovereignty resides, are mere verbiage, or at best declarations of ideal aspirations.

Divergences in Actual Practice

Universal suffrage, provided by more than half of the constitutions, is actually exercised by only a fraction of those qualified, even in countries where voting is supposed to be compulsory. These few votes must then run the gamut of the "official count." It is a well-known fact that a requisite more important than honest voting is the honest poll of the votes. . . .

What shall we say about the observance of those fundamental guarantees of individual liberty: the freedoms of speech, press, assembly and conscience? What of the guarantees of domicile and all of the components of what we know as due process of law? Since from the earliest days of their independence, Latin Americans have been so profoundly engrossed in the constitutionalizing of an ever expanding enumeration of civil liberties, it seems that they should, by this time, have attained a status of sanctity and respect. This however is not the case. The guarantees are respected only at governmental convenience and by sufferance. The constitutions generously supply the executives with the means to be employed in emergencies, to suspend the guarantees. This device, known as "state of siege," is abused by overuse for it is the customary resort to overwhelm opposition and entrench dictatorship. It is ironical that democratic constitutions bestow so lavishly on the executive the means to destroy the feeble manifestations of democracy. With respect to the status of the individual guarantees, therefore, much depends on the attitude of the president.

A principle of the "paper constitution" which is transformed beyond recognition in the operating constitution is the separation of the powers. Theoretically the three powers—executive, legislative and judicial—are separate, coordinate, and equal. Numerous safeguards, many of which are found in our own constitutions, are provided to prevent wanton exercise of authority by any one of these powers. Because of the well-founded belief that it is the executive which will be most prone to irresponsibility and be acquisitive of power, the most numerous constitutional limitations are those imposed on the presidents. Despite all this, and responsive to the strong-man tradition in Latin governments, the executive overshadows the other two powers. Latin American governments are emphatically of the strong presidential type.

That the president is the dominant power in the government is never doubted. His supremacy derives from his dual position as constitutional chief executive and as extra-constitutional *caudillo,* chief or boss. From the earliest days of their independence Latin Americans have shown a strong disposition for *caudillos,* preferably for those with a military background, for the magnetic attraction of the man on horseback can always be expected to reinforce the lure of demagogues. The *caudillo* embodies the program of his political partisans; he is the platform of his pseudo-party. This is what is called *personalismo* in Latin American politics, which means placing emphasis on individuals rather than on public policies. The *caudillo* because of his hold on the popular imagination, but more significantly because of his control of the army, meets with docile acceptance. Neither the disguised dictatorship nor the pseudo-democracy is a government of laws, all are governments of men. One of the least effective of the constitutional checks on ambitious presidents is the no-reelection provision. *Caudillismo* and *personalismo* have transformed the constitutional office of the presidency beyond recognition.

. . . . .

The constitutions of the centralistic states give to the president and his Minister of Interior sufficient power to maintain a firm grip on local government. Therefore it is seldom necessary to resort to extraconstitutional means to impose the will of the executive on all strata of local government. In the federal states, however, the imposing of the will of the national government on the individual states and their subdivisions, resulting in the converting of theoretical federalism into actual centralism, is accomplished by violating the spirit, if not the letter, of the Constitution. This is the notorious interventionism, a common practice in all of the so-called federal states of Latin America: Argentina, Brazil, Mexico and Venezuela.

. . . . .

Equally as fictitious as Latin American federalism is the constitutional mandate that the army does not deliberate, *i.e.,* intervene in politics. Any practical discussion of Latin American politics which omits reference to the political role of the army would be sadly unrealistic, for the most significant feature of Latin American politics has always been the predominance of the military authority over the civil. It is an old story dating from the independence period when the possession of governmental authority became the prize of contesting arms. None of the countries has escaped the blight of military political intervention, and today the military are in control, openly or disguised, in most of the nations of Latin America.

. . . . .

Violence Institutionalized

One of the most patent facts of Latin American government, and certainly the best-known to Anglo-Americans, is recurring *revolution.* The term is a misnomer, for it usually refers to nothing more than a *coup d'état* or a *cuartelazo* (barrack revolt), the classic "substitution of bullets for ballots," the ousting of the "ins" by the "outs," or perhaps the enforcement of the principle of "alternability of public office." These are not popular movements, for relatively few people participate, outside the military. The rabble, of course, assembles in the main plaza to acclaim impartially each succeeding *caudillo*.

Since the great revolution for independence early in the nineteenth century there have been few authentic revolutions in Latin America, that is if we restrict the term to those deep-seated popular movements aimed at fundamental change in the political, social, and economic orders. Only a limited number of the demonstrations of force so common to the political scene are worthy of designation as revolutions; this, notwithstanding the crying need in most of the countries for a thorough revamping. What Latin America needs, paradoxically, is not less but more revolutions. Fundamental revolution may be the specific for the cure of chronic pseudo-revolution.

· · · · ·

Adjusting the Constitutions to Reality

In view of the considerable divergences of actual practice from the constitutional norm, the question arises: how can the fundamental charters of Latin America be regarded as "acceptable examples of the constitution maker's art" since they are merely nominal or paper constitutions? Does not the fact that they are observed in the breach prove their artificiality? No, this is not necessarily so, for the validity of the cliché that Latin American constitutions are "divorced from reality" needs to be examined.

It can be conceded that these constitutions are divorced from reality in that they ostensibly establish democracies on the insecure foundation of a citizenry lacking in the tradition of freedom and undisciplined in democratic processes. However, it should be recalled that Latin American constitution makers do not delude themselves that they are building upon achieved democracy, but rather are setting their nations upon the road to democratic achievement. When viewed in this light Latin American constitutions are actually in considerable harmony with reality.

The critics of these alleged "exotic" and "artificial" constitutions fail to develop their arguments to any reasonable conclusion. They appear to hold for the incompatibility of the Latin American and the democratic constitution. Yet it is a fair surmise that these very critics would be the last to argue for the abandonment of all democratic pretense in Latin American constitutions. This must mean then, that they believe that the materials for democratic government are at hand in Latin America, and all that is needed is a rational arrangement of these parts.

This we find impossible to accept. How indeed are these so-called artificial and exotic constitutions to be modified to conform to the realities of the Latin American scene and still retain their democratic character? What provisions which they do not already contain in profusion will curb *caudillismo,* the *cuartelazo,* and the rigging of elections? Who can suggest constitutional formulae which will broaden and strengthen the bases of popular government and usher in political, social, and economic democracy?

The simple truth of the matter is that there are no constitutional formulae which, however well-suited to any practical situation or peculiar environment, will of themselves inaugurate a democratic regime. The road to popular and responsible government is a long and difficult way. There are no easy short-cuts. Those requisites of a democratic society: fair play, tolerance, self-discipline, responsibility, human dignity, majority rule but respect for the minority, a spirit of compromise, and respect for the rule of law, are the qualities of a democratic citizen which have deep roots in his historical past. These qualities which are of the inner man and so cannot be legislated into existence have not unfortunately prospered in the soil of the Latin American's historical past. Nor after 140 years of tortured experience in self-government does the present status of democratic achievement in Latin America augur much improvement in the forseeable future.

32 · FUNDAMENTAL LIBERTIES *

Sir Ivor Jennings

THE PROTECTION OF MINORITIES

The fundamental principle of democracy is that government shall be carried on for the benefit of the governed, and, since it is con-

* Sir Ivor Jennings, *The Law and the Constitution* (London: University of London Press Ltd., 4th ed., 1952), pp. 239-251, 263-264. Reprinted by permission of the University of London Press Ltd. The footnotes in the original version are omitted here.

sidered that only the governed themselves can determine what is for their benefit, under their control. The object of most constitutions is to set up machinery by which the wishes of the governed may determine the nature of the government. It is never entirely successful. But even if it were it would leave unsolved one most important problem. The wishes of the governed mean at best the wishes of a majority of them. Yet the minority, too, is composed of excellent persons, perhaps more intelligent and certainly less orthodox. The problem of government, therefore, is not only to provide for government by the majority, but also to protect the minority.

It is not possible to prevent the government, supported by a majority, from interfering in accordance with law with the liberty and property of a minority. It is not desirable that the attempt should be made. But there are certain rights which are commonly recognized as essential for effective social life and which, being considered to be inherent in the idea of justice, should be protected even against the majority. Exactly what they are depends upon the state of opinion and the organization of society. If religion is militant, protection may be needed by those who profess a religious belief not accepted by the majority. If education is the passport to a full life, free education may be made compulsory. If the means of production are not equally distributed, the right to sustenance may be the most insistent of the demands made.

GOVERNMENT BY OPINION

There are some rights, however, which are inherent in a system of government by opinion. This system implies the right to create opinion and to organize it with a view to influencing the conduct of government. There can be no such system if minority opinions cannot be expressed, or if people cannot meet together to discuss their opinions and their actions, or if those who think alike on any subject cannot associate for mutual support and for the propagation of their common ideas. Yet these rights are those most likely to be attacked. For those in power can, *ex hypothesi,* continue in power only so long as they command the support of the majority. If a sufficient section of the majority is converted to the views of a large section of the minority, their right to govern is gone, and at the next general election they lose the attractions of office.

FUNDAMENTAL RIGHTS

The problem is not merely one of limiting the powers of the administration. Its solution involves limiting the powers of the legislature as well. For it is normally the majority of the legislature which claims to represent most closely the opinions of the majority of the population. It is therefore usually regarded as desirable not only that the ordinary law shall protect the right of free speech, the right of association, and the right of public meeting, but also that the powers of changing the law, whether by legislation or administrative regulation, shall be so restricted that these rights may not be interfered with.

With a written constitution, this is an end which in principle is fairly easy to accomplish. Certain "fundamental rights" are inserted in the constitution, and every institution of government is forbidden to change them. A fundamental right can then be limited or taken away only by constitutional amendment, and if the process is in any way difficult or formal, such a limitation becomes plain for all to see. Nearly all written constitutions contain such provisions, though with varying definiteness of expression. Nearly all of them, too, provide for freedom of speech, freedom of association, and freedom of assembly.

DIFFICULTIES

1 · Need for Special Machinery

Three difficulties at once suggest themselves. The first is that the protection may be very ineffective if there is no machinery for determining when a fundamental right is being infringed. In the United States of America this function was assumed by the Supreme Court. In countries which follow the French tradition this is regarded as a usurpation by the judicial authorities of a function which does not rightly belong to them. For the question is one between the legislature and the electorate which the courts are considered incapable of settling. But where the American precedent is followed, as it is in many countries, the consequence is to place upon the courts the duty of acting as guardians of fundamental rights.

2 · Changing Ideas of What Is Fundamental

The second difficulty is that what are regarded as fundamental rights by one generation may be considered to be inconvenient limitations upon legislative power by another generation. For example, the fifth and fourteenth Amendments to the Constitution of the United States prevented the United States Congress and the legislatures of the states from depriving any person of life, liberty, or property, "without due process of law." This has been used by the Supreme Court to limit very seriously the enactment of social legislation dealing with such matters as hours of labor, minimum wages, and workmen's compensation. This is due, perhaps, as much to the beliefs of some of the judges of the Supreme Court as to the framers of the Constitution. It is nevertheless clear that the provisions of a constitution drawn up before the development of modern industrial society are likely to lead to such complications.

3 · The Right Cannot Be Absolute

The third difficulty is that even the rights of free speech, of association, and of assembly cannot be regarded as being without limitation. They may be used not for creating opinion in order to turn out the government by lawful means, but to persuade a small minority to use force to coerce the rest of the population. In their extreme meanings, the rights conflict with the fundamental requirements of public order. National emergencies, too, may demand a limitation upon the rights of individuals which would not be permissible in ordinary times. Two consequences follow. The first is that limitations must commonly be placed upon the rights expressed in the constitution, thereby making them much less effective in practice. The second is that some special provision must be inserted or implied for times of emergency, thereby depriving a minority of its rights just when the majority is least capable of rational appreciation of the contentious nature of its own ideas and when, therefore, the minority stands most in need of protection.

FUNDAMENTAL RIGHTS IN ENGLAND

Since the United Kingdom has no such written constitution, there are no fundamental rights in this sense. If it is attempted to talk about such "rights" in England, it becomes at once apparent that the word is ambiguous. Certain "rights" were inserted in the American Declaration of Independence because they were regarded as natural rights of man. "We hold these truths to be self-evident, that all men are created equal, that they are endowed by their

Creator with certain inalienable rights; that among these are life, liberty, and the pursuit of happiness; that, to secure these rights, governments are instituted among men deriving their just powers from the consent of the governed, that, whenever any form of government becomes destructive of these ends, it is the right of the people to alter or to abolish it, and to institute new government, laying its foundations on such principles, and organizing its powers in such form, as to them shall seem most likely to effect their safety and happiness. . . ." Fundamental rights were therefore inserted in the constitutions of the states, and the First Congress of the United States proposed amendments to the Constitution of the United States, of which ten were accepted and became known as the American "Bill of Rights." Thus the "natural rights" became rights given or recognized by positive law. They are binding upon the Congress and are applied by the Supreme Court to determine the validity of legislation.

These rights were founded essentially upon English traditions, and, indeed upon the apologia of the Revolution settlement made by John Locke. The American Bill of Rights goes further than the British practice of the eighteenth century, for the American Revolution was a protest against the tyranny of George III and his ministers. In large part, however, it repeats the substance of English experience. The other famous set of political principles, or fundamental or natural rights, the French Declaration of the Rights of Man, promulgated by the Assembly of 1791, was also founded upon British traditions and experience, though molded by the political philosophy of the era that preceded the French Revolution. The Constitution of 1791, to which it was the preface, has long since rolled into the dust, yet French constitutional lawyers continue to recognize the validity of its principles, either as principles of natural law, or as essential principles of political action in a free and democratic country. In Great Britain, too, the validity of the essential principles of the American Bill of Rights or the Declaration of the Rights of Man remains almost uncontested. The immediate result of the French Revolution was to create a revulsion in England, and from 1789 to about 1820 there were few fundamental rights which were not denied in practice; yet Charles James Fox and his Whig successors, though in a hopeless minority, maintained the Whig tradition of the English Revolution, and received valiant support from men who drew their inspiration directly from the French Revolution itself.

During the later nineteenth century these principles were not only restored by the repeal of some of the repressive legislation, but extended both in theory and in practice. There are relics of the notorious legislation of the beginning of the last century, and there are other limitations both by common law and by statute law that many would prefer to see abolished. The principles themselves, however, are accepted by all democrats as being not only necessary to but also implied in free or democratic government. A state is free only because its citizens are free.

We must nevertheless be careful in using the word "rights." If it is meant that they are natural rights, or if they are accepted as part of the logic of free or democratic government, the word is used in a sense different from its meaning in the phrases "contractual right," "right to damages." It is a distinction between essential constitutional principles and rights actually conferred by statute law or common law. Some writers use the word "right" only as correlative to a duty imposed upon some other person by positive law. If I contract with B to pay him £300 for a motor car, I have a right to the car and I owe a duty to pay the price, while B has a right to the price and owes a duty to deliver the car. Either of us can go to a court to enforce his right. On the other hand, I may enter into a contract with B or any other person, but no person is bound to enter into a contract with me. I may enter into the contract simply because there are no legal restrictions on my doing so. Similarly, I may invite my friends to tea in my house and they may assemble on my invitation not because there is any "right of assembly" (though, possibly, each may have a contractual right against me), but because there is no law which prevents them from doing so. In this sense, the right of assembly is a liberty, a freedom from restriction. It arises from the tautologous principle that anything is lawful which is not unlawful. There is no more a "right of free speech" than there is a "right to tie up my shoe-lace"; or, if there is a right of free speech, there is also a right to tie up my shoe-lace. The question to be discussed in each case is the nature of the legal restrictions. The "right" is the obverse of the rules of civil, criminal, and administrative law. A man may say what he pleases provided that he does not offend against the laws relating to treason, sedition, libel, obscenity, blasphemy, perjury, official secrets, etc. He may form associations provided that he does not offend against the laws relating to trade unions, friendly societies, religion, public order, and unlawful oaths.

He may hold a meeting where and how he pleases so long as he does not offend against the laws relating to riot, unlawful assemblies, nuisance, highways, property, etc.

This principle of the illegality of illegal acts (for it is nothing else) is, too, the simple way of asserting what is called "the right to personal freedom." The right to personal freedom is a liberty to so much personal freedom as is not taken away by law. It asserts the principle of legality, that everything is legal that is not illegal. It includes, therefore, the "rights" of free speech, of association, and of assembly. For they assert only that a man may not be deprived of his personal freedom for doing certain kinds of acts—expressing opinions, associating, and meeting together—unless in so doing he offends against the law. The "right of personal freedom" asserts that a man may not be deprived of his freedom for doing *any* act unless in so doing he offends against the law. The last is the genus of which the others are species.

ESSENTIAL CHARACTERISTICS

The position is different where the "rights" are set out in a written constitution, for then they govern the restrictions, and restrictions which infringe the rights are not law. With us, the nature of the liberties can be found only by examining the restrictions imposed by the law. We shall proceed presently to examine the restrictions; but for the moment it is essential that three characteristics of the British system should be borne in mind. In the first place, the law can always be altered by Parliament, and it is likely to be altered in time of emergency, such as a war. A government with a majority in both Houses of Parliament can restrict liberty as it pleases. It must be remembered, however, that in normal times the free tradition is extremely strong in Great Britain, and that it is as noticeable in the House of Commons as elsewhere. There have been several recent examples in which the House, without distinction of party, has shown itself extremely critical of police action which had a suspicion of unfair tactics. There is nothing that the House does better than to protest against individual acts of oppression, whether legal or illegal. The proceedings on the Incitement to Disaffection Bill showed, too, that Parliament can in normal times be trusted to protest energetically against any substantial increase of restrictions. It must be emphasized that this is in normal times. In wartime and other times of national hysteria, the dissident minority can expect no more mercy or toleration from the House of Commons than from the government itself. Indeed, the experience of the war of 1914-18 and of what Mr. Lloyd George rightly called "the worst and nastiest House of Commons," that elected at Mr. Lloyd George's request in 1918, suggests that the government may on such occasions be more "liberal" than the government's majority. In such exceptional times the supremacy of Parliament is a very great danger, especially to minorities.

In the second place, Great Britain differs from many other countries, and especially from the dictatorships, in that most restrictions are imposed directly by the law itself. They are to be found for the most part in the criminal law. An act is, therefore, either a crime or not a crime, and it is not left to the Government or the police to determine whether it shall be a crime or not. There are important exceptions, but generally speaking the restrictions on fundamental liberties are to be found in the civil and, especially, the criminal law, and not in administrative powers. Dicey was thinking of fundamental liberties when he emphasized the absence in England of "discretionary or arbitrary powers." In relation to those liberties his analysis was in principle correct. It is part of the British tradition, which is to be found in the law, that if restrictions are to be imposed on the rights of free speech, association, and assembly, they should be imposed by the law itself and not imposed under police or other Government discretion.

In the third place, though the law itself gives few discretionary powers to the police and other Governmental authorities, there is in practice a very substantial discretion. If an act is a crime it is a crime, and the criminal is liable to punishment unless he can produce a pardon. Any person can lay an information against him, and the judicial process will then continue unless the Attorney-General enters a *nolle prosequi*. In practice, however, private persons do not lay informations in respect of breaches of the restrictions on liberty, and prosecution is undertaken by the police. At the same time, the police are under no obligation to prosecute, and in practice they exercise a substantial discretion. This is particularly true in respect of public meetings. Even where they have no powers to regulate processions and meetings, they in fact do so. They can prohibit a meeting in, say, Market Square, St. Albans, simply because the meeting will be an obstruction to a public highway, and therefore illegal. If their prior permission is obtained, it is reasonably certain that they will not prosecute for the offense, though it is no less an offense, and any other person could prosecute if he thought fit. Thousands of public meetings are thus held every week, in defiance of the law, simply because the police exercise toleration. In time of stress, however, the toleration disappears, and the very considerable restrictions upon fundamental liberty in England at once become apparent.

What these restrictions are can be determined only by examining those parts of the criminal and civil law which interfere with the accepted fundamental liberties.

· · · · ·

It may be, as is sometimes alleged, that English law is too strict or that the police discretion is not always and everywhere exercised impartially; but there is less danger where substantial powers are under the control of a democratic government than where they are under the control of a dictator. So long as there are free elections, it is always possible to compel the government to exercise its powers not too partially, for there is an opposition to draw attention to abuses and to persuade the electorate that because of those abuses, if not for other reasons, the government should be turned out. An opponent of a dictator is an enemy of the state; for the dictator is the state, and he can be dethroned only by revolution. The fundamental liberty is that of free elections, and the others, including some at least of their limitations, follow from it.

Law

33 · THE LIFE OF THE LAW *

Oliver Wendell Holmes, Jr.

The object of this book is to present a general view of the Common Law. To accomplish the task, other tools are needed besides

* Oliver Wendell Holmes, Jr., *The Common Law* (Boston: Little, Brown and Company, 1881), pp. 1-2.

logic. It is something to show that the consistency of a system requires a particular result, but it is not all. The life of the law has not been logic: it has been experience. The felt necessities of the time, the prevalent moral and political theories, intuitions of public policy, avowed or unconscious, even the prejudices which judges share with their fellow-men, have had a good deal more to do than the syllogism in determining the rules by which men should be governed. The law embodies the story of a nation's development through many centuries, and it cannot be dealt with as if it contained only the axioms and corollaries of a book of mathematics. In order to know what it is, we must know what it has been, and what it tends to become. We must alternately consult history and existing theories of legislation. But the most difficult labor will be to understand the combination of the two into new products at every stage. The substance of the law at any given time pretty nearly corresponds, so far as it goes, with what is then understood to be convenient; but its form and machinery, and the degree to which it is able to work out desired results, depend very much upon its past.

In Massachusetts today, while, on the one hand, there are a great many rules which are quite sufficiently accounted for by their manifest good sense, on the other, there are some which can only be understood by reference to the infancy of procedure among the German tribes, or to the social condition of Rome under the Decemvirs.

I shall use the history of our law so far as it is necessary to explain a conception or to interpret a rule, but no further. In doing so there are two errors equally to be avoided both by writer and reader. One is that of supposing, because an idea seems very familiar and natural to us, that it has always been so. Many things which we take for granted have had to be laboriously fought out or thought out in past times. The other mistake is the opposite one of asking too much of history. We start with man full grown. It may be assumed that the earliest barbarian whose practices are to be considered had a good many of the same feelings and passions as ourselves. . . .

34 · LAW AND CIVILIZATION *

Karl N. Llewellyn

When one turns his eyes from law outward, the first effect is to make law shrink into seeming insignificance. There is so much outside. And it so obviously bears in upon and changes and remodels law itself. After a further while—so to speak, as the eyes grow adjusted to the glare—one attains a truer picture. One perceives an interplay of causation between law and the world outside. One begins to suspect something of the nature of the interplay. It may have value for you, it may shorten the period of refocussing, it may indeed stir you to break the surface tension of the law and take a slow look around, if I sketch here some outline of what I think one comes to see when he sets out to survey law's relation to civilization.

By *civilization* I mean what anthropologists call *culture,* the whole set-up of society, including the ways in which we act and the ways in which we are organized, including our material and intellectual equipment and our ways of using both. As to law, you know roughly what I mean. But it is not workable to tie to a single meaning when dealing with primitive times and with our own as well. You would not have me deny the presence of law in a society merely because there were no state officials. There was an international law before League or U. N. Both law and state have grown, and grown gradually, and at times quite independently of each other. If we are to watch law's relation to civilization we must therefore watch law's development in civilization—and what we watch will be a different thing from time to time and place to place. The sole inescapable common element is dealing with disputes. The sole inescapable common focus is the relation between the *ways* of dealing with disputes and the other ways of living. Hence, when I am talking of a ruder culture, before the state and the state's courts, I shall be thinking in the first instance of established ways for settling disputes without resort to violence by the contending parties, or even for settling them by violence, but by violence bridled and curb-bitted. As the

* Karl N. Llewellyn, *The Bramble Bush* (New York: Oceana Publications, 1951), pp. 107-112, 114-118. Reprinted by permission of Karl N. Llewellyn.

state of culture concerned grows more advanced I shall be introducing other ideas commonly associated with this symbol *law*: e.g., the regular tribunal. As soon as a state appears upon the scene, the idea of action about disputes by the officials of the state will of course appear, and will be contrasted, say with the settlement of a strike by the mediation of a prominent citizen. And the other aspect of law, regulation by officials for greater convenience and safety and prevention of disputes, will play a part. And there will come in from the beginning the notion of some considerable regularity in anything that is done, some recurrence and predictability, and some conception that there ought to be recurrence and predictability: the ideas of precedent and rules—for these are aspects of any institution, legal or other.

If, then, I am treating law as a part of government, and especially as the dispute-adjusting machinery of government, and civilization as the *whole* of the ways in which we live together, and of the things that we do while we are living together, it would seem to be clear that law becomes for me a *part* of civilization, and the question of law's relation to civilization becomes a question like that of the relation of the nervous system to the human body. It is not a matter of something from outside being turned over to or compared with civilization. It is a question of what role law plays in the same civilization of which law is itself one of the vital parts.

I think we make the best approach to that if we distinguish first *law* from *order*. Without order there is no group life, there is no group. If the members of a group do not in some manner manage to live together, if their respective conduct is not to some degree oriented with reference to each other, if there is not some cooperation, some self-restraint, some specialization, and some predictability for each one as to how the others will act when they cross his path, you do not have a group. And the group becomes more a group and less an accidental accumulation of several individuals in one spot, precisely as this *order* becomes increasingly definite, increasingly certain, increasingly extensive. But is it not clear that to the exact extent that order *does* exist in the actions of the group, members' disputes are nonexistent. Disputes mean, precisely to the extent that they occur, an *absence* of achieved order. *Settlement* of disputes, in any fashion, means re-establishment of the old order, or as the case may be, a new establishment of a somewhat different order in the group. And order is, to ninety-five or ninety-nine per cent, a question of the existence of *ways* or patterns of action among the members of the group, and of the *organization* of those ways into the interlocking complex sets of ways we know as institutions—ways common to all, and ways of some complementary to ways of others. And settlement of disputes is, too, a question primarily of ways: ways called into play when the more normal ways of doing hit a snag.

Now between civilization and order the main relations seem to be these. Order is a part of civilization, if only because civilization is a method of group life, and group life without order is inconceivable. Moreover, it seems to be fairly clear that what we call a *high* degree of civilization, a *complex* structure of cooperation, an effective way of coping with the environment which gives some high assurance of survival to the group, is possible only on the basis of a very considerable degree of order. . . . So that it would appear some order, indeed a high degree of order, is a necessary basis for a complex civilization; a conclusion buttressed somewhat further by the fact that we know of no complex civilization which has arisen or survived without such order. . . .

On the other hand, *too high* a degree of order seems to paralyze change, to freeze a society into inability to cope with emergencies. This statement may of course be merely a repetition in one half of the sentence of what is already contained in the other. "Too high a degree of order" may mean nothing more than a situation in which change cannot be coped with. But I think there is more to the matter than that. I think that in a régime of almost *total* predictability men are likely to lose the elasticity of mind which is necessary to work out new adjustments. Without the unexpected to deal with, it is not easy to keep fit to meet the unexpected. So that I take it we want order enough to get on with, but free play and unpredictability enough to keep at least some minds in the community elastic. To which I suspect that most modern men (and certainly I) would add, free play enough, too, to keep life interesting.

It is the presence of this free play in society which makes one great need for law. *For in the realm of free play disputes arise.*

Before I come to that phase of disputes, I wish to look at one other. There is one type of dispute which arises, not because the social scheme admits of free individual action, but because some individual or group refuses to abide by the social scheme where it does not admit free action. By and large the *basic order* in our society, and for that matter in any society, *is not produced by law*. And one

of the most misleading claims that has ever been put forward for
law's contribution to civilization is the notion that it is law from which
the basic order flows. The basic order grows, I repeat, not from law,
but (at least every generation) *from the process of education*. With
that process law may have much to do. But the much is not too much.

. . . . .

But we know that for one reason or another, this learning process is
imperfect in some individuals; in some individuals, various native
desires, whether or not stirred by particular chance contacts that we
can trace, break through the accepted mold. While the child is in
the home, this goes by the name of naughtiness. When he gets out
of the home it goes by the name of badness, or queerness, and in
due course delinquency—or brilliance. When he becomes an adult,
we call it criminality on the one hand and greatness on the other. . . .

To sum up what I have said thus far: I conceive civilization as
based upon and containing a wide core of established order (which
we are the less conscious of because we breathe it like the air),
and a much smaller field of relatively free play. Here and there some
man, for some reason, attempts to break through the established core
of order. Moreover, within the field of free movement interests of
different individuals are in constant flux and clash. One man can
run free in that field, but two men, each running free, may bump.
In the field of free play disputes arise. Law did not create the order,
but law attempts to guarantee its continuance. Law does not create the
sphere of free movement, nor control very much of it, but the office
of law is to make sure as far as may be *that the clashes of interest
within that sphere run off without disturbing* the great core of order,
and in cases where the ordinary processes of bargain, competition,
wearing down, economic and social pressure, fail to produce a workable result, to offer machinery to settle particular disputes and give us
all a new foundation for getting on. Disputes between single individuals and between organized corporations (those business groups
that are so tightly organized that we can treat them as units), law
settles, chiefly through *courts,* when it is called upon. Disputes between wider, less organized groups or classes (such as the beet sugar
growers and the consumers, between factory workmen at large and
employers at large, between lumbermen and conservationists) law
is more likely to settle by sweeping regulation through the legislature.
Administrative officials—commissioners and mayors and police cap-

tains, serve now in the one capacity, now in the other, today passing on an individual case, tomorrow laying down a regulation in advance as to the method of assessing property taxes, or the rates that shall be charged for telephone services, or whether the traffic lights are to be enforced against pedestrians.

Seen thus, perhaps, law appears to be a tiny thing, an infinitesimal part of civilization. In a similar way, medicine may perhaps appear to be a tiny thing. Few of us are interested in the doctor while we are well, or until an epidemic threatens. But like medicine, law is needed desperately when it is needed at all. It operates upon the fringe. But that fringe is a fringe of high necessity. And also, as is the case with medicine, intelligent use of law is often capable of so arranging matters that this climax of need has no occasion to occur. Or, if I may have resort to another image, it is a safety-valve—a minor and unimportant feature of an engine, *most* of the time.

. . . . .

Perhaps, however, I have stressed too much the criminal side of law, the adjustment of the graver breaches of the peace. The mind moves too readily to the criminal court as the type of all law. We must not let it rest there. The work of most lawyers, of most courts and most legislatures, and most of the ordinary individual's contacts with the law, lie in a wholly different field, not on the criminal but on the *civil* side; in the adjustment of disputes and conflicts between individuals and groups which have no connection with the jails. Here, too, in the regulation of business, in the enforcement of contract, in the division of property, law plays a vital part in stiffening the order of society. Peculiarly with property and contract we find this stiffening. . . .

But in the civil field the law does more. No longer is the question exclusively: "This you must not do, and that you must!" "You must not kill, except in time of war. In time of war you must enlist, to kill." Ordering and forbidding has been the burden of the criminal law. But in the civil law, the law of *transactions,* the law of *business,* there is another aspect. Law there picks up and shapes and hardens, or sometimes even creates out of itself, a host of *devices for accomplishing* one's purposes. If a man wishes to dispose of his goods and land after death, he can do it by a will. If a man wishes to invest some assets in an enterprise without endangering the balance of his fortune, he can do it by way of a corporation. If a man wishes to make a loan for twenty years, and be sure that in spite of death and change of management he will retain a prospect of repayment, he can do it by means of a mortgage. If he wishes to procure use of land for five years without taking all the permanent hazards of its change in value, he can do it by a lease. The civil law is full of these devices to make it easier for people to accomplish what they want in their relations with other people; to make it easier for people to deal at long range, or over long time periods, and still have some moderate guaranty that the arrangements made will stand.

Nowhere in the field of contract does the law make arrangements *wholly* certain, or the guaranty of performance *wholly* solid. Law is no substitute for sense. Your bond may be a legal bond, but will be worthless if the corporation whose bond it is falls prey to footless management, or is engaged in footless enterprise. Your mortgage on a boom plot may be good in law and yet a piece of paper. But if the *thing* goes well, then law assures you that no mere change of management, no loss of your trusted friend by death, no severance of social relations by an intervening quarrel, will kill off your prospect of repayment. So that, through these devices to get men's purposes accomplished, law and legal rights serve the property system and the business structure of the community as a framework. Bones are not flesh. They are not blood. They are not, it may be, very much alive, but they serve to *hold up* (and to limit!) what is both flesh and blood and very much alive.

Thus far I have spoken chiefly of the law that *is* at any given time, taken in relation to the life of that time. I have referred to the fact that disputes arose out of the fact that some one man kicked over the traces. I might refer equally to those other disputes which arise because two parties disagree about the facts. Did you make the promise I claim you made, or did you not? Have you performed as you agreed? We are likely to differ on that. The bank has been robbed. Did John Smith do it? You and he will have different views on that. These are questions which must be settled. But they can be settled on the basis of the order of society *as it is*. It is important that they be settled right. But let me insist upon a thing too often overlooked. *It is more important still that they be settled*. Indeed, the settling of disputes of fact *right* instead of *merely settling them* is both a sign and a responsibility of the presence in society of enough surplus energy to spend some of it on more than the mere struggle for existence. Like the radio, silk stockings and the motor, it is a luxury which grows into a necessity—though fewer people are alive to its necessity.

One other phase of this difficulty of social invention I must get before you. It is common to all legal institutions, it is common indeed to all social institutions, but it shows up with peculiar clarity in the machinery for settling disputes. One machine will be constantly put to and used for several purposes—but the needs of the various purposes are not the same, and to accomplish one is to defeat another. If I have a just claim against you, it needs collection. Speed is the need. If I have a dispute upon the facts with you, it needs a hearing. Settlement is needed; but fairness counts for more than speed. If fairness is to be judged by a standard from the community and not by the special ritualists, a lay tribunal is called for. But if I have a dispute with you about the ritual, only a ritual expert can decide it, and it may call for an appeal to the most expert of them all. Now all of these types of case tend constantly to be drawn into the same tribunal, and no man knows *in advance* which type of case is up. Then sham disputes about fact and sham disputes about ritual defeat speed in the just collection. And the lay tribunal handling the facts works at cross-purposes with the official handling the rules. And the complex machinery makes possible the eternal dragging out of unjust claims. All of this, in the courts as in other social institutions, calls for conscious readjustment: to diagnose the various purposes a given piece of machinery serves; to refine and specialize the machinery to accomplish *each* of them; to devise a *sieve* to throw each type of problem to its proper specialized machine. This is one lesson of industrial technique, of factory management, for law. Some of the lesson we have learned, as when we specialize our courts, set up commissions, even set a jury off to try the facts. Yet we are far from adequacy here. This is an instance where the planning aspect of the law has lagged behind the folkways of self-maintenance.

There are, now, other disputes which arise within the fringe of free movement and which *cannot* be *settled* on the basis of society as it exists. Dairymen are threatened by the manufacture of a new filled cheese or milk in cans. It may be healthful; it is cheap. The filled cheese maker profits. The dairyman suffers—yet he claims that only he makes filled cheese possible—and he wants profits. Or the apple tree is killed by cedar rust. The only known protection is to cut down cedar trees. Apple growers want the cedar trees cut down. Those who have and love cedar trees do not. Someone is bound to suffer. Shall we do nothing and let the apple growers howl? Shall we cut down the cedar trees? Shall we have war? In the moving fringes of conflict of interest have we no machinery for adjustment? Again I wish to insist that the machinery we have, to wit, the *legislature,* and the use of that machinery for the purpose, is *not* a thing which can be taken for granted, is not a thing which every society has known. On the contrary, it has been by the slowest and most painful growth that we have moved an increasing body of disputes over into that field of orderly adjustment. I need only to remind you that in fifteenth-century England, and in a Rome more highly civilized by far, they fought their elections out by arms. Within the memory of living man the privilege of stuffing the ballot box in New York City was the prize of combat between gangs of thugs. And what of the revolutions in South America and Europe? Still, more often than not, a strike means violence on one side or the other or on both. This shifting of *readjustments in the order* of society to the sphere of order and of peace means a tremendous alteration in civilization. It means the growth as *part of the great core of order* in civilization, of machinery for working out the remodeling of the core itself. It represents the addition to the nervous system and the skeleton of the body politic, of the cortex of the brain. A machinery for taking in new conditions, and for finding new means of action, and of regulating action which will keep the whole from disintegration. Like the work of the cortex, the work of the legislature is partially stupid, partially disregardful of the facts, highly irrational too much of the time. Like the work of the cortex, however, the work of the legislature, with all its blundering, does manage to keep matters bearable. And if we can claim no more than that for our individual persons, it is not surprising that that should be the limit of the performance of all of us together.

If we try now to put together all of this, what does it come to? Law in any form is an achievement of painful, slow invention—and probably, like most inventions, dependent in first instance upon accident. Its more developed forms are the product of whole series of inventions—yet lag and lag far behind the technique of physical production. Law consumes energy in its creation, consumes energy in its operation. What does it offer in return? At first sight, nothing. Order exists without law. Order continues. Yet maintenance, upkeep, is also one problem of a plant; and law seems to be the maintenance department of this order which is in turn a precondition to civilization itself. As to tools, law has borrowed copiously from the rest of culture: language, logic, writing; and for the subject matter of its thinking it borrows the whole stock of practices, standards, ethics that make up the social, economic and religious phases of society. What is dominant in society, then, is dominant in law. If oppression is the keynote of society, then so of law. But even as to the oppressor, law accomplishes something that other phases of order may not. Law makes order *express*. It thus sets limits, some limits, even on oppression. Stop and consider: it is no slight thing to be sure that the oppression you are open to extends only to the more *established* forms. And law has through the years gone far to guarantee you that; to guarantee you against the free play of ingenuity in your tyrant. Law, then, maintains the order as it is. Yet "as it is" means with its play of change. And here we find law at work on change. It offers, in its machinery for dispute-adjustment—courts, legislatures, and administrators—simultaneously a machinery for authoritative *choice* among experiments. Thus limiting experiment; but concentrating it, within the fields thus limited. Thus, too, guaranteeing the continuance of such experiments as it accepts. Here then is a positive contribution to our civilization.

· · · · ·

Finally, I think it is to law that we owe the conception of *justice*. I am not wholly sure of this. There is a very remote chance that the matter runs the other way, that we owe law to the concept of justice. There is a greater chance that both are shoots of the same root. Still, I think law as a discipline may claim the concept. It should, if it can, for the concept marks a noble achievement. As legislation offers the wherewithal for readjusting that same order which brought forth the device of legislation, so justice and the law. . . .

35 · ENGLISH, AMERICAN AND CONTINENTAL JURISPRUDENCE *

Wolfgang Friedmann

A comparison between the two trends of legal thinking, method and practice which, in a very generalizing way, are described as Anglo-American and Continental jurisprudence, is certainly a matter of great importance. Legal theory cannot achieve its principal object, self-reflection, without rising beyond the limitations of one-sided legal training; the practitioner, when confronted with a conflict of laws, often has to compare the legal notions and institutions of different nations; a workable system of international law must blend the methods and outlook of different national legal systems. The present world crisis and struggle compels us to take stock of the assistance or obstacles which the different legal systems may present to international collaboration. On the other hand, closer political, military, economic and cultural links between the Western democracies make a better mutual understanding of legal institutions and ways of thinking a matter of practical urgency.

Between English and American law there are many and even fundamental differences. So there are between the principal Continental systems. Nevertheless, it is possible to oppose in a broad sense Continental and Anglo-American law to each other. Historical development emphasizes the outward difference. English law, through geographical circumstances and the continuity of political and social evolution, has largely developed on a line of its own, and in its turn formed the basis of American legal evolution. Although American law has become increasingly independent in its actual system of law as well as in the approach to legal problems, the common basis of both systems, the common law of England and a judicial theory built on a precedent system, still preserves a fundamental unity which is evidenced by the persuasive authority enjoyed by decisions of one country in the other, and by the continuous ex-

* Wolfgang Friedmann, *Legal Theory* (London: Stevens and Sons Ltd., 3rd Edition, 1953), pp. 353-356, 386-387. Reprinted by permission of Wolfgang Friedmann. The footnotes in the original version are omitted here.

change of legal ideas. On the other hand all Continental codifications, most of them less than half a century old, owe their inspiration to the principles of the Napoleonic codes; they are largely influenced by the reception of Roman law, and thus by a common background of legal notions and institutions as well as by similar conceptions of law-making and law interpretation. Moreover, there has been much conscious imitation and mutual influence between the various Continental codifications. The oldest of the present-day civil codes, the French Civil Code, has been kept in tune with the more modern codifications through the breadth of its principles as well as the creative work of the French judiciary and the academic lawyers.

The differences of principle between the English and American systems of law, as they stand today, might be summarized as follows:

(1) The supreme law in the United States is a written law, the American Constitution, which prevails over any ordinary statute. There is no supreme law in England, where the law-making power of Parliament is unlimited.

(2) Through the frequent need for interpretation of the Constitution, American judges have been faced much more than English judges with vital problems of public policy, in particular the conflict between vested right and social State policy. . . . The precedent problem has also gained a different aspect in American law through the flood of decisions from a Federal and 48 state jurisdictions, which leave a much greater choice to the judge. Finally, the rapid economic expansion of the United States, compared with the gradual evolution in England, made the strict attachment to precedent an even more difficult proposition. All these influences together may account for the very different aspect the precedent problem has gained in the United States as distinguished from England. American judges may be conservative, as the majority of the Supreme Court, which for many decades consistently opposed and invalidated social legislation in the name of natural law, or progressive, as the minority of that court and many other American judges, but in either case the attitude towards the binding force of precedent is a much freer one than in English law. . . .

(3) The need for systematization of the law has been felt earlier and more urgently in the United States, owing to the mass of legal material which threatened to become unmanageable. Apart from a certain number of actual codifications in different states, the unof-

ficial codification of the different branches of law has proceeded far. Subject to these differences, one may still speak of "Anglo-American jurisprudence."

The principal factors which have tended to direct the development of Anglo-American and Continental law into different channels are partly of a technical character, that is, related to the structure of the law, partly of a sociological character, that is, deriving from the function and scope attributed to the law by the social order.

It is the technical side which has hitherto been almost exclusively emphasized by jurists. We may classify the principal factors alleged to bring out these differences as follows:

(1) Continental jurisprudence has been decisively influenced by the reception of Roman law, Anglo-American law has not. Instead it is largely the product of gradual historical growth and therefore still shows considerable elements of feudalism. It is for this reason that Scottish law might be ranked with Continental rather than with the English system, because of the affinity in legal method and theory.

(2) All Continental systems are essentially codified; Anglo-American law is still based on the common law.

(3) From this follows a different approach to problems of legal interpretation. Judicial decisions in Continental systems are no primary source of law, but only a gloss on the law. On the other hand, in Anglo-American law, precedent is one of the principal sources of law.

(4) It is connected with the contrast of inductive and deductive approach that Continental systems, proceeding from general rules to individual decisions, establish general legal principles, whereas Anglo-American law centers around a decision of individual problems and builds up the principle, from case to case. Such principles as there are have been developed from a gradual adjustment to practical requirements.

(5) As a corollary to this difference in legal development, Anglo-American legal thinking gives a predominant place to the law courts, where Continental jurisprudence thinks of law, not only in terms of litigation but largely in terms of its general function.

(6) The dualism of common law and equity in Anglo-American law is unknown to Continental systems where equity is a principle of interpretation applied to any legal question, but not a special body of law.

(7) All Continental systems distinguish in substance and pro-

cedure between private law and administrative law. The former deals with legal relations between subjects, as equals, the latter with legal relations between public authority of all types and the subject. Anglo-American law rejects that distinction and adheres—at least in theory—to the principle of the equality of all before the law.

(8) The more abstract and generalizing approach to law of Continental jurisprudence has been conducive to the development of legal philosophy, whereas the pragmatic and empiricist character of Anglo-American law has had the opposite effect. Hence the preeminence in Anglo-American law of the analytical school of jurisprudence, compared with the infinite variety of Continental legal theories.

An examination of these principal points of difference reveals that they have either been very much exaggerated in the first place or have recently lost much of such importance as they may once have had.

. . . . .

From the discussion of every one of the principal factors which in the past have been alleged to constitute vital differences between Continental and Anglo-American jurisprudence certain conclusions emerge. Broadly speaking, the differences between the systems have either been eliminated, or have lost in significance to the same extent to which common social and political developments have affected countries living under the different systems of law, and as the need to face these problems has overshadowed the difference in legal technique. This teaches us one lesson which lawyers, in times of tranquility and stability, are only too apt to forget: that law is dependent on politics although there is great variety in the degree and form of this dependence. The basis of every legal system depends upon the principles which govern the social order of the country or countries in which it operates. The fact that countries like Britain and Germany both developed into highly industrialized and densely populated countries was bound eventually to have a bigger effect upon their law than the differences in legal tradition and technique, which undoubtedly existed. Notwithstanding all these differences they, like all other countries affected by the same developments, were compelled to produce an immense new body of social legislation, to increase administrative functions and authority, to make judges aware of the social and economic significance of the issues before them; they all had to create a new body of law based on social responsibility rather than individual fault, they had to protect the workmen against the dangers of modern industrial labor, the public against the risks of modern traffic, the consumer against the dangers of modern mass products.

Undoubtedly differences in legal tradition and technique have done much to make these developments occur with different speed and often in different forms. For example, Continental countries have less objection to comprehensive new legislation, whereas under the Anglo-American system courts and Parliament are rivals in the legislative process. But these differences are more and more becoming secondary in importance. Nor is it surprising that on the whole Anglo-American law should move more towards Continental methods rather than vice versa. In meeting new social problems, Continental countries were technically at an advantage because their legal systems are more the product of modern times and conditions. With the exception of the Napoleonic codes which—young in Anglo-American legal eyes—makes up for their comparative age by the breadth of their principles, all Continental codifications date from the latter half of the last or from the present century. They were conceived and framed in awareness of the modern need for rationalization of the law, and of the social significance of legal principles and administration of justice. Small wonder, therefore, that our discussion reveals a strong movement of Anglo-American legal development towards the Continental technique. It has not been our object here to go into actual legal reforms which bear out that thesis. But it is interesting to note that all the reports of the English Law Revision Committee, for example, have recommended changes in the law which would bring English law close to Continental systems. . . . It is certainly true of the general tendencies in legal development: of the movement from thinking in terms of procedure to thinking in terms of legal principles, of the increasing weight of statute law in relation to non-statutory law, of the growing interest in the theory of law. Anglo-American legal traditions, professional particularities and characteristics of race and temperament, have certainly given this development a form largely different from the Continental one. But the increasing pressure of social and economic conditions is bound to reduce the importance of these factors in the law, as it had done in other walks of life.

· · · · ·

36 · LAW OF A NEW TYPE *

Harold J. Berman

One of the most significant internal developments in the Soviet Union, marking a new phase in the Revolution, has been the elaboration during the past thirteen years of an affirmative theory of the socialist state and socialist law. All other states, it is now claimed, are instruments of class domination; the Soviet state, existing in a classless society, is a "new type of state" with a "new type of law," "essentially different from all types of law known to history."

Yet now that Soviet law has been proclaimed to be socialist law, law of a new type, and not merely (as before) an accommodation of the proletarian dictatorship to legal survivals of the bourgeois past, some of the most striking innovations of the first twenty years of the Revolution have been abandoned. In the name of socialism many elements familiar to capitalist systems have been reintroduced, and in the name of Soviet patriotism many institutions of the pre-revolutionary Russian past have been restored. From the Left, Trotsky, Koestler, and other former Communists have spoken of these changes since the mid-1930's as "The Great Betrayal"; from another standpoint, Timasheff, Sorokin and other Russian *émigrés* have viewed them as "The Great Retreat." "After long years of destruction and experimentation, feverish efforts were made to restore the situation which existed at the outbreak of the Revolution or even earlier," writes Timasheff.

Socialism has become Russian and respectable. Even the new Soviet legal theory is now the acme of respectability: Soviet law "recognizes no class distinctions"—it provides "equal justice for all"—it represents "the will of the whole people." Revolutionary legality has become strict legality.

In fact an American lawyer would not have too great difficulty in accommodating himself to the Soviet legal system as manifested in the positive law proclaimed by the state. He would find many basic

* Reprinted by permission of the publishers from Harold J. Berman, *Justice in Russia* (Cambridge, Mass.: Harvard University Press, Copyright 1950 by the President and Fellows of Harvard College), pp. 199-206. The footnotes in the original version are omitted here.

principles, precepts, doctrines, and rules of contract law, tort law, criminal law, family law, procedure, and various other branches of the legal tree essentially the same in the Soviet system as in the German, French, Swiss, Italian, English or American. This similarity is due in part to the fact that the Soviet state, for all its socialism, must meet fundamental social and economic needs similar to those that confront "capitalist" states; it also stems from the common Roman derivation of both Russian and Western law, from the impact of later Western legal developments on prerevolutionary Russia, and from the Soviet reliance on German, Swiss, and French law in the preparation of the NEP codes. The American lawyer would have to reconcile himself to the Marxist emphasis on economic integration and public control of business; and he would have to adjust to the strong Russian spirit of collective consciousness, universal service, and dedication to the mission of Moscow, as well as to the dynamic and energetic quality of Russian government. But he would have to make similar (though not so radical) reconciliations and adjustments were he to practice law in England, for example, which has its own strong historical tradition of community spirit, service, and mission, and which is now incorporating into that tradition a nationalization of the economy as well.

Of course our American lawyer in Moscow would be shocked at the extent to which illegal and extralegal activity is still accepted as normal; but that would hardly strike him as manifesting a new type of law, except in the most ironic sense.

Yet Soviet law, even apart from manifestations of revolutionary terror and Russian ruthlessness, is in fact quite different from the law of socialist England (or wartime America). The differences are not immediately apparent in the codes, statutes, decisions, and rules of positive law. They become apparent only if one looks to certain basic conceptions which underlie these external normative acts.

Here it is necessary to add a third dimension to our study. We have explained Soviet law, in the first instance, as a Marxian socialist response to the social and economic problems which have confronted the Soviet regime. To this analytical dimension we have added a historical dimension, explaining Soviet law in terms of inherited traditions and experiences as they have imposed themselves on the habits and memories of both the rulers and the people. Yet some of the most important aspects of Soviet law stand outside the categories "socialist" and "Russian"; they cannot be satisfactorily explained either by the logic of socialism or by the experience of Russian history or by both together. We are compelled, therefore, to approach our subject once more, from a quite different angle.

To understand a legal system it is necessary to distinguish between the official law proclaimed by the state and the unofficial law which exists in the minds of men and in the various groups to which they belong. Each of us has his own conceptions of rights, duties, privileges, powers, immunities—his own law-consciousness. And within each of the communities in which we live—the family, school, church, factory, commercial enterprise, profession, neighborhood, city, region, nation—there is likewise an unofficial and largely unwritten pattern of obligations and sanctions. The official law of the state, with its authoritative technical language and its professional practitioners, cannot do violence to the unofficial law-consciousness of the people without creating serious tensions in society. At the same time, official law is more than a reflection of popular law-consciousness; it also shapes it, directly or indirectly.

This distinction between official and unofficial law is essential to a full understanding of the peculiar blending of Marxist theory and Russian history into a "new type" of law. It was the prophecy of classical Marxism that once class domination is eliminated, and once the economy is publicly integrated and rationalized, it will not be necessary to put conflicting claims through the wringer of legal reasoning, judicial conscience, and precedents. Marx and Engels foresaw a classless society in which disputes would be settled by the spontaneous, unofficial social pressure of the whole community, by the group sense of right and wrong or at least of expediency. They saw a precedent for this in the condition of certain primitive peoples who have no positive law, no state, but instead punish aberrational behavior through informal, spontaneous group sanctions. As among primitive societies at the beginning of history, so in classless society at the end of history, they said in effect, control will exist only in the habits and standards of the whole people, in the *mores* of the good society. This moral consciousness implicit in the Marxist utopia is something less than law-consciousness in the sense in which that word has been used. Nevertheless the two go together. Both are psychological rather than official. One is the feeling of what one *ought* to do, the feeling of being morally bound; the other is the feeling of what one *has* to do, the *feeling* of being *legally* bound.

The idea of a society without official law goes down hard in a culture such as that of the West, where positive law tends to be treated not as merely one particular means of social control but rather to be identified with social control altogether, so that every social norm, or at least every norm tolerated by the state, is assimilated to positive law. Everything tends to be positively legalized or illegalized. There is no case which does not fall under *some* rule. But in Russia, where both law-consciousness and positive law remained rudimentary through the centuries, where whole spheres of life were left outside the realm of law, the Marxist vision found an echo in the hearts and minds of the people. The Russian revolutionaries were not primarily interested in creating, ultimately, a new legal order, in the external, positive sense; they were interested rather in creating, ultimately, a new sense of justice, as between man and man. They seized on the Marxist promise that, with the elimination of the bourgeoisie and the abolition of all survivals of capitalism, the community would come to be regulated like a family, like a kinship society, by customary standards, by unofficial law, rather than by positive law. This corresponded to the historic Russian ideal of the regeneration of man and to the Russian conception of a society based on love and on service, a society with a mission. Only now such a society was to spring from the materialist conception of history, from class struggle and the end of class struggle, rather than from Christian faith in the Kingdom of God and (in Dostoevsky's phrase) from the transformation of the State into the Church.

The Russian Marxist vision of the withering away of (official) law under socialism has now been abandoned for the foreseeable future. "Law—like the state—will wither away only in the highest phase of communism, with the annihilation of capitalist encirclement," wrote Vyshinsky in 1938. Only then "will all learn to get along without special rules defining the conduct of people under the threat of punishment and with the aid of constraint." Thus even with the achievement of communism in Soviet Russia alone, about which there is considerable talk, law will remain. Nevertheless, the withering-away idea has repercussions on the Soviet legal system as now practiced. For the element of Soviet socialist law which makes it "law of a new type" is its focus on law-consciousness, the law in the minds of men, and its deliberate attempt to shape and develop law-consciousness through the medium of official law.

LAW AS A TEACHER AND PARENT

Of course every system of law educates the moral and legal conceptions of those who are subject to it. In the *Digest* of Justinian it is explicitly recognized that the task of law is the moral improvement of the people. Thurman Arnold describes the judicial trial as a "series of object lessons and examples." "It is the way in which society is trained in right ways of thought and action, not by compulsion, but by parables which it interprets and follows voluntarily." Mr. Justice Brandeis was a leading exponent of the view that the courts should recognize the importance of their educational function.

Nevertheless, the educational role of law has not been traditionally regarded as primary. Law has been conceived primarily as a means of delimiting interests, of preventing interference by one person in the domain of another, of enforcing rights and obligations established by the voluntary acts of the parties insofar as that is compatible with the social welfare. It has been assumed that the persons who are the subjects of law, the litigants or potential litigants, know their own interests and are capable of asserting them, that they are independent adults whose law-consciousness has already been formed. In some cases this goes so far, under our adversary procedure, as to enable the judge to sit back as an umpire while the opposing lawyers do battle with each other. The subject of law in our system, "legal man," has been the rugged individualist, who stands or falls by his own claim or defense and is presumed to have intended the natural and probable consequences of his acts. To educate his legal conceptions is no mean task. It requires a very good judge even to try it. At best he will succeed in educating only indirectly, secondarily, by seeing that justice is done.

In the Soviet system, on the contrary, the educational role of law has from the beginning been made central to the concept of justice itself. Law still has the functions of delimiting interests, of preventing interference, of enforcing the will and intent of the parties—but the center of gravity has shifted. The subject of law, legal man, is treated less as an independent possessor of rights and duties, who knows what he wants, than as a dependent member of the collective group, a youth, whom the law must not only protect against the consequences of his own ignorance but must also guide and train and discipline. The law now steps in on a lower level, on what in the past has been a pre-legal level. It is concerned with the relationships of the parties apart from the voluntary acts by which their alleged rights and duties were established; it is concerned with the whole situation, and, above all, with the thoughts and desires and attitudes of the people involved, their moral and legal conceptions, their law-consciousness. Soviet law thus seeks not simply to delimit and segregate and define, but also to unite and organize and educate. The result is the creation of entirely new legal values within a framework of language and doctrine which otherwise appears conventional and orthodox.

It is apparent that the Soviet emphasis on the educational role of law presupposes a new conception of man. The Soviet citizen is considered to be a member of a growing, unfinished, still immature society, which is moving toward a new and higher phase of development. As a subject of law, or a litigant in court, he is like a child or youth to be trained, guided, disciplined, protected. The judge plays the part of a parent or guardian; indeed, the whole legal system is parental.

It should be understood that the words "parental" and "educational" as used in this context are morally neutral. The parent or guardian or teacher may be cruel or benevolent, angry or calm, bad or good. He may dislike the child. But he is responsible for the child's upbringing. To speak of "parental law" is therefore not so much to describe the state which proclaims and applies the law as to describe the assumptions which are made regarding the nature of the citizen and his relationship to the state. To say that under Soviet law the state has extended the range of its interests and its powers is not enough. The state has sought in law a means of training people to fulfill the responsibilities now imposed on them—and it has made this function of law central to the whole legal system. The conception of man presupposed in the procedural and substantive rules is thereby changed. Man is a child or youth to be trained and protected —protected not against the state itself, but against others and against himself.

"Parental law" may be implicit in the actual practice of socialism as such. It surely has deep roots in Russian history. Yet it is essential to isolate the parental features of Soviet law from both its socialist and its Russian background, for parental law is not restricted to socialism or to Russia. According to Karl Llewellyn, "our own law moves steadily in a parental direction."

37 · THE RULE OF LAW
IN THE ARAB MIDDLE EAST *

Richard H. Nolte

Trevelyan in his *History of England* sums up the celebrated stand of Sir Edward Coke against James I in these words:

> In essence, the quarrel was this: James and Charles held, with the students of Roman Law, that the will of the Prince was the source of law, and that the Judges were "lions under the throne," bound to speak as he directed them. Coke, on the other hand, in the spirit of the English Common Law, conceived of law as having an independent existence of its own, set above the King as well as above his subjects, and bound to judge impartially between them. . . .

The doctrine of the supremacy of law has been called the outstanding contribution of English civilization, transcending even Parliamentary democracy, Shakespearean poetry, and the industrial revolution. Events in recent years suggest that the question of the rule of law in the Islamic countries of the Middle East is of more than academic interest. Coups d'état, suspensions of constitutions, "treason trials," the establishment of authoritarian regimes, and the easy disregard of civil rights, give rise to doubt as to whether there is a rule of law in our sense in this area.

It can be shown that during the millennium of classical Islam and right down until recent decades there was a rule of law in the Middle Eastern area, albeit an imperfect one; and that the net effect of the importation of western concepts and methods (the "impact of the West") has been a negative one. To borrow Coke's metaphor, the ruler in classical Islam had lions under the throne in the form of his Islamic law judges. But he could not command them. He could leash them and unleash them, but they listened to the command of the Sacred Law which was beyond his control. Now, however, the ruler has equipped himself with powerful new lions borrowed from the West who are fully subservient to his command, and has also asserted

* Richard H. Nolte, "The Rule of Law in the Arab Middle East," *The Muslim World*, XLVIII (October, 1958), 295-300, 304-307. Reprinted by permission of *The Muslim World*.

his control over the Sacred Law itself. As a result, law in the Islamic countries of the Middle East has become largely the unchecked instrument of the state.

THE SACRED LAW OF CLASSICAL ISLAM

In Islamic theory, the Sharī'ah claims to regulate all the actions of men, public and private, social and individual. In theory, it makes no concession to Caesar, and asserts its authority over political man in all his acts of government as well as over private man in his prayers. This idea is summed up in the maxim: *Islām Dīn wa Daulah*: "Islam is religion and state."

Much more than a legal system properly speaking, the Sharī'ah is the comprehensive catalogue of God's commands and recommendations laid down for the guidance of men. How and what to eat, when to wash, what to wear, how and when to pray and fast—these and similar matters are treated on the same basis and with just as much meticulous concern as matters more strictly legal, such as marriage and divorce, or commercial transactions, or crime. Governing the whole range of man's relations with God and society, and in the absence of any organized Muslim church hierarchy, the Sharī'ah is incomparably the central institution of Islam.

Wider in scope than law in the western conception, Muslim law is also more complicated in its judgments. In western law, an act is either lawful or not lawful. Whether or not such an act is also decent, good, pious, ethical, moral, or in good taste is beside the point. Not so in Muslim law. The Sharī'ah considers a given act—depending on circumstances—to be mandatory (*farḍ* or *wājib*), commendable or recommended (*sunnah*), permissible (*ḥalal* or *jā'iz*), reprehensible (*makrūh*), or forbidden (*ḥaram*). The highly normative character of the Sharī'ah is a fact of the greatest importance in the history of Islam. For in setting up an eternal, unchanging, divinely sanctioned standard of human conduct, the Sharī'ah was the decisive factor, over the centuries, in creating a stable, unified, orderly and law-abiding Muslim community out of widely diverse peoples, and a social fabric that was proof for over a thousand years against invasions, revolts, civil wars, famines, and all other calamities and political vicissitudes. The Sharī'ah may truly be called the backbone of Muslim society.

The normative quality of Muslim law is not accidental. It is a product of the process by which the law came into being. Immediately after the death of the Prophet in 632 A.D., the Arabs exploded out of their inhospitable peninsula and began the sweeping conquests which in less than a century carried them to dominion over an area stretching westward through North Africa and Spain to the Pyrenees, and eastward through Persia and far into central Asia. During this period, generally speaking, there was no such thing as Muslim law. The religion itself was only commencing to be elaborated beyond its primitive beginnings; and if the Arab conquerors were Muslims, they were so at a time when the term hardly meant anything more than Arab.

But there was law, of course. The new empire had to be administered; and in the process, a body of administrative practice was built up which together with customary practice was to constitute the main raw material of the Sharī'ah. By and large, the Arab rulers of the first century and their governors followed a policy of empiricism in solving the host of new administrative problems. Where precedents arising out of their background of Arab customary law (e.g., the arbitral method of settling disputes) or introduced by Prophetic innovation (e.g., punishments for certain delicts; a modified law of divorce, marriage, and inheritance) seemed appropriate, they were followed. Administrative and legal habits, institutions and concepts which the conquerors found in the civilized organized areas of Byzantine Egypt and Syria and Sassanid Iraq and Persia were taken over in wholesale lots (e.g., tax methods, and the institutions of market inspector and complaints tribunal). Talmudic law and the canon law of eastern Christian churches made their contributions; and beyond doubt, there was in addition a good deal of improvisation.

Generally speaking, the Arab administrators of the first century of Islam were successful in evolving a corpus of administrative practice out of these kaleidoscopic origins which, if not entirely integrated and coherent, was none the less equal to the demands of governing a vast and turbulent empire and of securing the revenues from the subject cities and provinces necessary to support a large military organization and to prosecute almost continuous war.

In a natural delegation of authority, Arab governors began early to put the business of deciding disputes and assigning penalties into the hands of secretaries for legal affairs, or *qāḍīs,* whose role was initially similar to that of the magistrates in the recently displaced Byzantine administration. The "jurisprudence" of these early *qāḍīs* contributed much to the formation of the recognized body of administrative and legal habit which had developed by the end of the first century of Arab rule.

The Sharī'ah, the Sacred Law of Islam, began as a protest against the customs and habits of Arab society including this body of administrative practice. During the initial century, it is possible to identify two main tendencies. The one, already touched upon, involved the organization and administration of a new empire, and the imposing on it of an Arab stamp. The other tendency was an Islamic one; and toward the end of the first century it became dominant. In the vanguard of the Islamicizing tendency were groups of pious scholars in various cities of the empire who had begun to examine and criticize Ummayyad administrative practice and the customary practices of the people at large, using as criteria the precepts of the new religion. No doubt motivations of piety were reinforced by political and other considerations. In any case, the objective was reform. They began by criticizing popular and administrative practice piecemeal, and gradually went on to elaborate in more and more detail a system of things as they ought to be, as compared with what they were in fact. In this way, Muslim law acquired its decisively normative character.

As time went on and the Islamicizing tendency gained more and more the ascendency in the Arab empire, pious scholars began to progress from criticism of the existing state of affairs to the systematization and logical elaboration of their earlier efforts. Legal thought for its own sake became a motivation; and gradually the main outlines of the Sharī'ah took form. As it gained in definition and prestige, it began to have an influence on the practice of the governors and their qāḍīs. But the decisive step in this direction remained to be taken by the 'Abbāsids.

In 750 A.D., a little more than a century after the beginning of the Arab conquests, the Persian-based 'Abbāsid dynasty, promising to establish the reign of God upon earth and, riding the egalitarian appeal of Islam to the non-Arab masses of the empire, overthrew the Arab hegemony of the Ummayyads. Under the 'Abbāsids Muslim law came as close as it was ever to come, except for a time many centuries later under the Ottoman Turks, to establishing itself in fact as well as in theory over administrative and legal practice. The great innovation of the 'Abbāsids was to centralize the appointment of the qāḍīs, and to select them from the ranks of the pious legal scholars. Except insofar as the qāḍīs had hitherto applied in practice certain

Quranic rules about inheritance, divorce, and the like, this departure established for the first time a direct nexus between the Sacred Law and everyday practice: a substantial part of the practice was put into the hands of specialists who were required to make decisions in accordance with the Sharī'ah.

On the face of it, the Sharī'ah had captured, so to speak, the chief legal officers of the empire. A bridge had been thrown across the growing gulf between theory and fact, and a foothold secured to administrative practice. But to complete its victory, the Sharī'ah would have had to go on to establish its practical authority over the other administrative officers of the empire including the ruler himself. This, in spite of the theory and in spite of continuing efforts, it was never able to accomplish. Although comparatively complete in matters of worship, family law, and even commercial transactions and private affairs in general, the Sharī'ah was sketchy indeed when it came to public law; and this very fact is a measure of its failure to bring conduct of state under its sway. The Sharī'ah did supply some guidance in matters relating to the holy war (jihād), and to the collection and disbursement of certain taxes. It specified punishments for certain crimes, and it set out in general terms the public duties incumbent on the ruling authority such as defense of the frontiers and maintenance of the religion. But for the men who had to administer the Muslim empire, the Sharī'ah could not in its incompleteness and rigidity establish itself in practice as an all-sufficient law.

The wide gaps it left in its attempt to regulate the conduct of state continued to be filled by the administrative initiative of Muslim rulers and their lieutenants who were faced with the day-to-day necessities of government. A large and developing body of secular administrative practice thus remained outside the precincts of the Sacred Law and often in direct contradiction to it; and it was a practice which included, in fact if not in theory, all the functions of government—legislative, judicial, and executive.

Well aware of all this, Islamic legal theory sought to maintain the Sharī'ah claim to omnicompetence by bringing the ruler's administrative practice into the fold of Islam. But to do so, it had to make all the concessions. It was forced to recognize the wide discretionary authority (*siyāsah*) the ruler already had, and to regularize it in the name of "common sense" (*istiḥsān*), or "consideration of the public good" (*istiṣlāḥ* or *maṣāliḥ mursalah*), or simply "necessity" (*ḍarūrah*). In return, the ruler was exhorted to keep his administrative practice "sound," "religious," and "just"—within the bounds of the Law (*siyāsah shar'iyah*).

If the Sharī'ah failed to "capture" the ruler and his other administrative officials and was forced to recognize their practical autonomy, even its new monopoly over the *qāḍīs* was an incomplete one. For although the law they were thenceforth supposed to apply was the Sharī'ah which was held to be divinely established, eternal, and independent of the ruler's control and which was vested in legal handbooks and interpreted by a corps of jurists (*'ulamā'*) and jurisconsults (*muftīs*) equally beyond the ruler's control, the *qāḍīs* continued to rely upon the ruler for execution of their judgments. Moreover, the *qāḍīs* themselves continued to be appointed, paid, and dismissed by the ruler; and the latter retained his power to limit the competence of the *qāḍīs'* jurisdiction in time, place, and subject matter. Despite their Islamic propaganda, the 'Abbāsid rulers were not long content to suffer the existence of so important an institution independent of their authority; and they used the various powers confirmed to them by the Sharī'ah to cut down the role of the *qāḍīs*. If they could not control the Law, they could at least fence in its judges.

The restrictions imposed upon the Sharī'ah in action, however, were not solely due to the despotic tendencies of the 'Abbāsid rulers or of their successors since then. In some ways, the Sharī'ah was self-limiting. It bound the *qāḍī* in terms of procedure as well as of law, with the result that *qāḍī* justice became more cumbersome and was deprived of all initiative. One quick result of the latter fact was that competence in matters of crime was mostly taken away from the *qāḍī* and given to the police (*shurṭah*), another arm of the administration. Similarly, utilizing the earlier Sassanid institution, the 'Abbāsid caliphs reestablished administrative tribunals to hear complaints (*maẓālim*) about miscarriages of *qāḍī* justice and the oppressions of powerful men. Very soon, this "King's justice" was competing with the *qāḍī* courts, notably in matters of property right; and they thus constituted a further limitation of the *qāḍī's* function.

Nevertheless, it remains true that the *qāḍī* institution is one of the most vigorous ever developed by Muslim society. Although in most Muslim countries the *qāḍī's* jurisdiction and power have progressively been narrowed to the point that only matters of family law remain in his hands, the *qāḍī* courts are still an important part of their legal systems. In Saudi Arabia, the Sharī'ah is still the only official law and the *qāḍī* courts are still the only official courts, although it is interesting to note the recent formation in that country of a board of complaints reminiscent of the 'Abbāsid prototype. In Turkey on the other hand, and recently in Egypt, the *qāḍī* courts have been abolished.

. . . . .

THE IMPACT OF THE WEST

With this background in mind, we may now glance at the changes produced during the past century or so by the so-called "impact of the West." The term has become a cliché, but it stands as an accurate description of the rising tide of goods, tools, techniques, social institutions, ideas, and values from the West that has inundated the Middle East along with other areas of the world. Faced with the evident inferiority—often emphasized by military force—of its own cultural equipment in the face of this onslaught, Middle Eastern society has been quick to seize upon and utilize all these things in its effort to overcome its disadvantage and to acquire respectability in terms of the new western model. In a Toynbeean sense, this is the Herodian response to the challenge of the West; and the great new reformist and reconstructive social force in the Middle East is nationalism, with the nationalists (whose basically constructive purposes become destructive and extremist when too long thwarted) as the "creative minority."

The result has been a profound and accelerating social transformation in the Middle East, and nowhere have the changes been more drastic than in the field of law. Modern nation states with their separate constitutions and governments have risen from the remains of the Ottoman Empire. National sovereignty has replaced the multinational religious doctrine of the Caliphate. Western-type codes, courts, and legislation have dispossessed the religious courts and all but deprived the Sharī'ah of social effect in Turkey and Egypt, and elsewhere have thrust them far into the background. Even in an isolated and "backward" country like Saudi Arabia, the new complaints board and other administrative "committees" suggest that developments parallel to those in the other countries are to be expected there before long.

On the face of it, the Sharī'ah has been a major victim of western legal concepts and methods; but this deserves a closer look. If one considers all the law actually applied in a modern Muslim state as a circle or pie-chart, one can think of it as being divided into sectors. One sector would consist of secular municipal law, the positive law of the state (or *siyāsah* in the terminology of Muslim law). A second sector would be that part of the Sharī'ah still applied in practice (dealing typically with matters properly religious or akin to the religious such as marriage, divorce, inheritance, pious endowments, etc.), leaving the rest of the circle to customary law. The size of the Muslim law sector has varied with time and place, impinged upon as we have seen by the police, complaints, or marketplace jurisdictions set up by a given ruler. But in recent decades it has been far more drastically constricted by the expansion of the municipal law sector through executive decrees and legislated codes and statutes. For the first time, the Sharī'ah has been in competition with a rival system of law. The constricting tendency was carried to its logical conclusion in Turkey in the 1920's during the secular revolution under Ataturk, and also recently in Egypt where abolition of the religious law courts meant the banishment of the Sharī'ah in its entirety to the realm of religious ideal.

The ruling authority's power to do this, however, is conceded by the Sharī'ah itself through its acknowledgment of the ruler's right to limit the jurisdiction of the *qāḍī;* and while they may deplore it, the conservative scholars of the law (*'ulamā'*) undoubtedly prefer straightforward suspension, which leaves the Sacred Law intact as an ideal, to attempts to change the Law itself.

Others, however, both within and outside the ranks of the *'ulamā'* want to do precisely that. They want to establish (or as they say, reestablish) a thoroughgoing Sharī'ah rule of law. They begin with the premise that the Sacred Law is valid universally, for all time, and for all the activities of man. Noting that the law seems no longer adequate to the needs of modern society, they conclude that its original and essential principles have been obscured by the later additions of the scholars. They therefore call for a return to the "true" principles of Islam.

. . . . .

All these approaches to the problem of ancient law and modern need reveal the profound shift in assumptions that the impact of the West has produced in Muslim society. In the past, the ruler and all of society were regarded as operating within the framework of the unchanging Sacred Law. Now, they have moved outside and have no doubt about their competence and title to write their own sovereign law to meet changing necessity. Nowhere is this change of viewpoint more strikingly evident than among precisely those modernizing theologians who call for the reimposition *in toto* of a reformed Sharī'ah. They no longer seek, as their ancient predecessors did, to learn the will of God as a guidance for man. In going back into the past in search of more suitable precepts, they already know what they are looking for. The need of modern society is the platform on which they stand. The Law is to be redefined in terms of social welfare: ". . . the goal of the Law is only the welfare of men, and wheresoever lies the welfare of men, there is the Law of God," writes Shaikh Khallāf of Al-Azhar in a recent treatise. In their reworking of the classical theory, public welfare (*maṣlaḥah*) becomes the great new source of law by giving Islamic approval to the positive law of the state (*siyāsah*) by which it is served, insofar as the latter is *siyāsah shar'īyah* and does not violate any of the basic principles (as newly defined) of the religion.

Viewed in historical perspective, this may be taken as merely the latest phase in the long effort of Muslim theologians to find a satisfactory Islamic explanation for the changing realities of political rule and to cast the net of Islamic control over the ruler. Through their attempt to sanctify *raison d'état,* as it were, they may now succeed. But it seems clear that in the process Islam and its Sacred Law will have been altered, secularized, and weakened even as an ideal.

By thrusting the Sharī'ah far into the background, the influence of secular conceptions from the West has mostly dissolved the qualified rule of law imposed during the centuries of classical Islam. Never fully controlled, the ruler now appears to be fully uncontrolled from a Sharī'ah point of view. It remains to ask whether the modern Islamic states of the Middle East by establishing constitutions and bills of rights based on western models have been able to establish in fact the substitute rule of law thus implied. Few western observers and few politically conscious Middle Easterners would concede that they have, or that it is even possible to do so without educated populations prepared to insist upon it. . . .

It is not, it would seem, necessary to take too pessimistic a view of the present lack of a rule of law in the Middle East. Education is being extended with very great rapidity in the area, and with it goes the penetration of modern ideas and aspirations. If constitutions and bills of rights so far amount only to a sort of lip service to a popular ideal, at least the ideal is newly there, and popular. Implementation may come in time.

Institutions

38 · THE CONGRESSMAN AND HIS WORLD *

James MacGregor Burns

On entering the House of Representatives at Washington, Alexis de Tocqueville wrote over a century ago, "one is struck by the vulgar demeanor of that great assembly. Often there is not a distinguished man in the whole number. Its members are almost all obscure individuals . . . village lawyers, men in trade, or even persons belonging to the lower classes of society."

The young Frenchman sensed that the character of the Representatives told something of the nature of our representative system. His approach is still fruitful today. There is no "average" Congressman. Men and women of many types, reflecting the diversity of American life, make up the mid-Twentieth Century Congress. But what the biologist would call a *type genus*—the member of Congress who best typifies his family—can be singled out for study. He is a composite of those Senators and Representatives who year after year and despite changes in party control determine the make-up of Congress and the main direction it takes.

What is his background? How did he win office? In what does he believe? Why will he have national—even international—significance? For whom does he act?

TALE OF A LOCAL BOY

The Congressman was born 56 years ago in Boone Center, in the family dwelling a block off Main Street. His father, who was raised on a farm east of Boone Center and who as a young man had moved to town for a business career, owned and operated a hardware store.

* *Congress on Trial* by James MacGregor Burns. Copyright 1949 by Harper and Brothers. Reprinted by permission of Harper and Brothers. The footnotes in the original version are omitted here.

Once just a county seat and market center for the surrounding farms, Boone Center had grown rapidly during the last part of the century with the establishment of several factories on the east side. The Congressman grew up in a thriving business community. Although it became increasingly integrated with the national economy, Boone Center always kept something of the flavor of a country town grown big.

As a youth the Congressman went to grammar school and high school in Boone Center. He was president of his class and served on the debating team that won the state high school tournament (on the subject: "Resolved: That the farmer, rather than the businessman, is the main source of American progress"). He worked one summer in a brickyard—an experience he later made much of in campaign talks—although he undertook this stint at manual labor mainly as part of training for the school football team. Other summers he clerked in his father's store.

At the age of eighteen he left for the law school of the state university, 65 miles away. This was the farthest he had been from home, but he was not homesick because the university town was much like Boone Center, and he associated mainly with his old high school friends. Aside from the classics, his studies were almost exclusively in the field of "applied law," and were carefully adapted to the demands of the state bar examination. This examination he duly passed after his fourth year at the university. Boone Center, already an up-and-coming city of 35,000, seemed the most promising place to make a good living; actually, he had never thought seriously of settling elsewhere. For two years he worked in the office of a small law firm before he went into practice on his own. His first client was a realtor who had done business with his father. The young lawyer became a Mason, like his father, and developed a modest but successful practice, with emphasis on trial work.

In 1917 he enlisted in the Army, arriving in France during the late summer of 1918 as an infantry officer. He stayed overseas about a year. Shortly after resuming practice in Boone Center he became active in politics. He was one of the founders of the Bob Davis Post No. 11 of the American Legion. He joined the Elks and Kiwanians and became active in his church (Methodist). He married a Boone Center girl who had been in the class behind him in high school.

After serving as town committeeman of his party for a year, in 1924 he won nomination for assistant prosecuting attorney of the county. Nomination for this office by his party was tantamount to election. He cultivated the party leaders, and his rise in the political hierarchy was steady: county prosecuting attorney; member of the lower house of the state legislature; and, by 1934, member of the state senate. He rose in American Legion circles too, becoming chairman of the legislative committee of the state department and later state commander, taking a year out from his public career to serve in the latter capacity. He won something of a reputation as a liberal in Boone Center when he defended two local AFL building trades officials against charges of extortion.

He moved with his wife and three children in 1935 to a farm on the outskirts of Boone Center. An expert cultivator of good will, he joined the Grange and extended his contacts among the farmers in the region. His new home was, of course, still in his state senatorial district, and it was also in the same Congressional district as before. This Congressional district—the 9th—extended from the retail business section of his town east through part of the factory and working class region, and after making an unnatural hook north to include the Negro population of a Boone Center suburb, it marched east for thirty miles over broad rich farmland and small townships. The shape of the district resulted from the redistricting of the state by the legislature following the 1930 census; the 9th was gerrymandered so that the party in power, which happened to be the Congressman's, could be expected to prevail by a safe but not excessive margin. In 1938, with the death of the incumbent Representative, he was well enough established throughout the district to be the logical successor to the position. Being acceptable to the local party leaders, he was unopposed in the primary, and he won the election without great difficulty.

Today, in his sixth term in the House, the Congressman is in the business of politics, and he is an expert at the trade. He is honest, shrewd, friendly, unassuming, hard-working. He is exceedingly articulate. He knows how to be prudent and conciliatory when the situation so demands, and how to be stubborn. He has a thorough knowledge of the politics and of the business of his district, and of the ties between politics and business. He has an acquaintanceship numbered in the thousands. Although he is not well known outside of his state, the Congressman has been in the House long enough to become one of the more influential members. Because he has an increasingly important role in the formation of national policies, the ideas that move him are of concern to all America.

A CREDO FOR BOONE CENTER

The Congressman believes firmly that he is a moderate and a middle-of-the-roader. Although he lays no claim to being even a "little left of center," he has abandoned certain ideas that once dominated his thinking. Fifteen or twenty years ago, for example, he believed that the open shop was the American way—certainly the Boone Center way. Today he champions the labor unions in the city, especially if they are not overly influenced by "outsiders."

He accepts governmental activity in fields today that he would have denounced before the Great Depression: price support for farm products; minimum wage standards for workers; old age pensions. On the other hand, planning, governmental paternalism, and centralized power are repugnant to him. America, he feels, is still the land of opportunity for those with initiative and industry, as Boone Center and the 9th District have been for him.

A section of the preamble to the American Legion constitution sums up his political credo, and he likes to quote it at the climax of his speeches: "To combat the autocracy of both the classes and the masses. . . ."

Above all else the Congressman believes in Boone Center and the rest of the 9th District. An unashamed booster of the district, he is an expert on its products, its history, and its importance to the nation. He easily becomes sentimental about the "folks back home," and it is honest sentiment. The ancient question as to whether a member of Congress should act for the nation or for his district bothers him not at all. He simply equates Boone Center's well-being with the national welfare. "The people of the 9th District sent me here to represent their interests first," he often proclaims on the floor of the House, but he sees no real issue on that score.

Next to his district, the Congressman believes in his state and in his country. Disdaining the tactics of those he calls "flag-wavers," he nonetheless feels that more Americanism would help solve the problems facing America. He considers himself a "moderate internationalist," having voted for United States membership in the United Nations. He supports American participation in all international organizations, at the same time demanding that this nation retain her full sovereignty. He opposed the loan to Britain on the grounds that America should not bail out socialist governments, and he believes that loans should be made only to nations maintaining free enterprise systems. He is in favor of lower tariffs, but not for foreign goods competing with products of the 9th District.

Part of his Americanism is a latent hostility toward outsiders. Catholics, Jews, and Negroes form small minorities in his constituency, and the Congressman prides himself on his racial tolerance. Indeed, one of his best friends is a Jew. But there is a decided difference in his mind between racial minorities as individuals and as groups. He conceives of minority peoples, especially those in the great urban areas, as tending to harbor alien and un-American ideas. He feels that the amount of racial and religious discrimination in this country is exaggerated, and that the best way to handle the slight intolerance that exists is to ignore it. Making an issue of discrimination simply aggravates it. Incitement to racial and class feeling he vigorously opposes.

Considering that vote-getting is his trade, the Congressman has a curiously ambivalent attitude toward politics and parties. As a practical politician he knows that the daily negotiations and give-and-take are central to the democratic process. Yet he feels that some of the great issues of the day, such as foreign policy, should be kept out of the arena of political conflict. "Politics stops at the water's edge," is a favorite slogan of his.

He is especially critical of party politics in this respect. His own partisanship is a matter of form and little content. Boone Center people are Republican or Democratic nationally, but party ties bind them loosely in local affairs, and the congressional election is considered a matter of local concern. Sane and stable government is possible only if both parties follow a middle-of-the-road course, he believes, and nothing would be worse than a labor party arrayed against a party of business. Although Boone Center has an elaborate class system, he would hate to see politics conducted along class lines.

The Congressman is flatly against "big government." The huge bureaucracy he often pictures as an octopus seated in Washington with its tentacles reaching into every corner of the land. Knowing the many services rendered his constituents, he defends the work of a number of the bureaus, but he looks forward to the day when the trend toward more central government can be reversed. Just how the reversal is to be accomplished he is not sure.

The Congressman distrusts the bureaucrats as a group. They are experts in their fields, while he must be a political jack-of-all-trades.

They are theorists and technicians, while he would like to see more "practical" people in government, like himself. Worst of all, they exercise power without having earned the right to do so, he feels. He complains that none of them "could get elected dog catcher" in his home town.

"I am fearful of these experts," he once said on the floor of the House. "The brain trust has cost us money every time it went into action. In my opinion, it will take some farmers from county seats to do the job."

The Congressman is not a man of political principle. He spurns the national platform of his party because it contains provisions designed to appease or attract groups throughout the country in whom he has no interest. But he has no real substitute of his own for such a platform. He has only a bundle of symbols and a sheaf of special claims for Boone Center's organized interests. He believes in Americanism, Democracy, Justice, Freedom, and Patriotism, and he knows why Boone Center needs a new post office and why its industries should have more tariff protection and why World War II veterans should have a bonus.

But between the misty symbol and the special plea he takes no stand on the vital national issues on which the presidential elections are at least in part fought out—on taxes and spending, on housing and river development, on full employment and fair employment, on relief and reconstruction abroad, on health and social security. He is no broker of ideas. Indeed, one of his most effective vote-winning techniques is to evade taking positions on thorny problems in order not to alienate voters.

How the Congressman steers clear of matters of policy and principle and sails calm political waters as diplomatic agent of the 9th District in Washington offers at once a clue to the Congressman's tenacity in office and a lesson in American political mechanics.

DIPLOMATIC AGENT

Though he may not admit it even to himself, the Congressman's chief aim is reelection. To stay in office means to gain added power and prerogatives in Congress on the basis of seniority, and to become eligible ultimately for higher office—senator, governor, judge, cabinet member. If his reelection depended on successful exploitation of key national issues, the Congressman would be compelled to run on the record of his votes on those issues. But his success at the polls hinge largely on how effectively the Congressman has served as the 9th District's representative in Washington. Here his record is almost flawless. He has rarely faltered in his protection of the sovereign interests of his locality. Against the encroachments of Big Business, Big Labor, and Big Government he has defended the rights of small business, local unions, and the average man in his district. By seeming to protect the totality of the 9th District's interests against the outside world, the Congressman contrives to avoid the basic but perilous issues of national and world policy.

But if the Congressman has little responsibility to his constituents on matters of broad public policy, he has a very definite responsibility to two groups in the 9th District. One of these consists of the local party leaders—called "bosses" by their opponents—and the other of the organized special interest groups.

The party bosses in the 9th District are concerned almost wholly with patronage and favors. They are not evil or venal men; they know that without patronage their political dominion, centered in city, courthouse, and county machines, would soon crumble. Operating at all levels of American government, they extract from Washington jobs for their followers as postmasters, federal marshals, collectors of internal revenue, judges, and the like. In state and local governments an army of petty officials makes obeisance to the machine for its jobs.

The Congressman advanced smoothly up the ladder from assistant county attorney to his present position only because he never failed to cooperate with his party leaders on matters of patronage. He is fully aware that he needs their support more than they need his supply of federal patronage. For in the case of a falling-out and a show-down—an unthinkable occurrence for the Congressman—he could cut off only one source of their patronage; the bosses would survive to put an end to his political career in the next party primary, over which they exercise a tight grip.

The local party leaders, for the most part, have little interest in the Congressman's votes on national issues. Even when he deserts the national party platform on important legislation, it never occurs to the party leaders that they have any responsibility for that platform. Indeed, the party machine itself often has a bipartisan slant because of unwritten covenants with the other major party over matters of patronage.

In several cases, however, the local leaders are concerned as individuals, rather than as party officials, with the Congressman's position on certain national policies. A leader of one of Boone Center's wards, for example, is a large lumber dealer, and naturally he is interested in the Congressman's votes on such matters as price control, housing, and subsidies. Two of the county leaders operate large farms and have considerable influence in the Grange; they follow the Congressman's votes on farm bills with care.

The other dominant element in the 9th District—the cluster of organized interest groups—has no concern with patronage but a deep concern with national legislation. The most important pressure groups in the district are those of business, farmers, veterans, and labor, in that order. These groups in turn are made up of individual organizations. The farmers, for example, are divided into the National Grange, the American Farm Bureau Federation, the National Cooperative Milk Producers' Federation, and the Farmers' Union. The veterans divide into the American Legion, the Veterans of Foreign Wars, and World War II organizations. Special issue groups, such as Townsendites and Prohibitionists, take an active part in politics. And there are scores of fraternal, religious, national-origin, and occupational associations.

How many votes do these groups control? The Congressman wishes he knew the answer to this question. With a sharp eye for political margins, he perceives that some organizations lay claim to large memberships, like-minded on all issues, where actually the rank-and-file is small in number, divided, and irresolute. But he cannot be sure. He must feel his way cautiously. Whether or not the pressure groups deliver the votes, they are important media of communication with thousands of voters. The political apathy in his district is often so great that he is unable to "get to" the electorate. The various associations, with their meetings, newspapers, and radio programs, can help him make connections with many voters who might never attend a party rally or read ordinary campaign literature.

Naturally the Congressman tries to gauge the reality of vote-power behind the facade of propaganda. But his responsiveness to the pressure groups is not a matter of votes alone. Often the Congressman makes political decisions without any evaluation of the exact line-up of the various groups back home. He truly "votes his own conscience." If his position happens to coincide with that of the organized groups in his district, it is not simply because he is controlled by them. It is because he is one of them. He is a Legionnaire; he is close to the farmers and their interests; his roots are in the business class. He knows the leaders of the various organizations, and by and large he considers them "sound."

Even the Congressman, with all his political dexterity, cannot act for every one of the groups. To some extent he must choose sides. In practice he speaks for a coalition of groups representing small business, the owners of large farms, veterans of three wars, and skilled labor. He speaks for these groups partly because they are politically effective, partly because he lives in their political world. Thus the business organizations, the Grange, the Farm Bureau, the Legion, the VFW, and the American Federation of Labor carry weight in the congressional representation of the 9th District.

Since even these interests may come into conflict, the Congressman must be able to act for one of them without seeming to flout the claims of the others. Consequently, he moves quickly to confer legislative favors on one pressure group where he can do so without injuring another. He selects his ground carefully. A bonus for veterans, subsidies and price support for farmers, high tariffs for business, the prevailing wage for AFL crafts—such measures are well adapted to the Congressman's use, for not one of them is likely to antagonize the other groups. Tariff protection for the small industries of the 9th District is an especially effective campaign argument because it appeals to both business and labor. Higher farm prices are justified as leading to more spending by farmers in Boone Center's shops. Such measures may mean a higher cost of living for the consumers of the 9th District, but consumers do not make up one of the pressure groups that the Congressman must reckon with on election day.

The Congressman reflects a sense of solidarity in the 9th District that is not wholly artificial. Not only Boone Center but the whole district is essentially a trading and producing community. The operators of big farms, employing machinery and hired hands, must be businessmen as well as farmers. On the local scale there is little disharmony between them and the businessmen of the city. The traders in Boone Center, who were originally independent and self-contained, during the past half-century have increasingly become instruments of a nation-wide commercial system. At one time free agents, Boone Center factories are now units of a national industrial order. But the myth of the autonomous and footloose community still persists, and the Congressman loses few votes in the 9th District when he attacks Wall Street and Big Business. For the dominant forces in both city and country have been steeped in the ideas of a local pecuniary society operating on its own. Militantly conservative, the substantial citizens of the district produce on the local level a gloss which partially conceals latent conflicts between large and small business, between business and industry, between workers and employer, between farm owner and hired hand, between city and country, between producer and consumer.

The most serious threat to the Congressman's strategy lies in the dramatization of epochal national questions such as often dominate the political scene during presidential campaigns. The exploitation of key issues by a Roosevelt or a Willkie, by a Wallace or a Stassen, draws unorganized voters to the polls and disrupts the united fronts assumed by pressure groups around their narrow designs. Such issues induce members of even the most tightly organized groups to forsake their petty interests and to think and vote in terms of broad national policy.

In such a juncture the Congressman assumes the politician's protective coloration—he straddles. Refusing to accept the gauge of battle on the open ground of national policy, he retires into a defensive zone of evasion, subterfuge, and recourse to "red herrings." At all costs he shifts the debate away from his position on controversial public policy and focusses attention on his fight for the 9th District and its interests. Here he is on safe ground.

Against the injection of national issues into the local campaign the Congressman's best defense is the absence of a clear-cut record on those issues. On some important votes in the House there was no record as to how the members lined up. The Congressman was not obliged to take a position on some matters because the bills died in the Senate or in committee. When other bills came before the House he may have been unavoidably detained on business in his office or district, and thus unable to vote.

The most effective way to straddle an issue, he has discovered, is to vote on both sides of the question. On one occasion the Congressman voted to kill a bill by recommitting it; half an hour after the recommittal move, he cast his ballot for the legislation. In the case of the price control act of 1942 he advocated a series of crippling amendments, some of which favored manufacturers and farmers in the 9th District, but in the end he voted for the Act. On several occasions he supported measures in Congress only to take part later in "economy drives" that would have starved the agency enforcing the laws. These subterfuges have obvious advantages. In case he is questioned back home as to his stand on these policies, the Congressman can tailor his answer to fit the views of his inquirers and he can point to the record to back up his claims.

If the Congressman were a modern Machiavelli, his advice to freshmen in Congress on "How to Stay in Office" would be: (1) vote for the home folks first, especially for those who are well organized; (2) keep on good terms with the local party bosses; (3) stress your protection of your district's interests as a whole against the outside world; (4) as far as possible do not commit yourself on the important national issues that divide your constituents. But the Congressman is not Machiavellian, and if he gave such advice he would speak in terms of the importance of following a safe and sane middle way, of the dangers of extremism and centralization, of the need for protecting local rights and interests.

CONGRESSIONAL REALPOLITIK

The Congressman is a member of the House Committee on Banking and Currency. His is an excellent assignment, for this committee is one of the most powerful in the House, handling such matters as fiscal policy, housing, price control, and government lending. Of the fifteen members of his party on the committee, he stands eighth in seniority. The chairman of the committee has been in Congress for twenty years, two years more than the next ranking member. If affairs take their normal course, the Congressman can look forward to heading the committee in another ten years, provided he holds his seat continuously and his party controls Congress when the time arrives.

If the Congressman attains the chairmanship, he will be one of a small company of men exercising far-reaching powers over public policy. His understanding of the committee's subject matter, his political outlook, his ideas on national policy would be of vital concern to the nation. What would be the reason for his rise to such an important position? Not because the other committee members were impressed with his grasp of fiscal matters—whether they were or not, the committee as such has no part in the choice of the man who will be its chief. Not because the House wished to assign him responsibility in this field, for neither do the members of the House have a part in the selection of its committee chairmen.

Even if every other Representative opposed his elevation to the chairmanship he would still take his place, provided he had served enough time, under the inevitable and indisputable workings of the seniority rule. The persons who actually make this decision are the voters of the Ninth District in general and the local party leaders and organized interests of the district in particular—in short, those who send him back year after year to his seat in the House. In the last analysis the chairmen of the House and Senate committees are locally chosen.

Because the Congressman is thoroughly aware of this practical political situation, his main concern will be to retain the favor of the 9th District rather than attempt the role of national statesman. Any prestige he may gain throughout the country will be a secondary factor to achieving popularity at home.

In representing the 9th District at Washington the Congressman must deal with two separate power groups in the House—the party leadership and the committee leadership. The former, elected by the party members, stands for a different constellation of forces from the latter, which holds power simply because of longevity in office. On matters of party procedure and organization in the House the Congressman follows the party leadership. But on matters of public policy he must cooperate with the committee chairmen, for they in turn manage the legislation in which the Congressman is interested. Their capacity for expediting bills advantageous to the 9th District is surpassed only by their ability to thwart passage of those bills. The Congressman knows that they are important people to have on his side.

He defers to the party leadership in the House only when by doing so he will not run counter to the interests of his district or to the undertakings of key chairmen. He operates with a full sense of the allocation of power as it affects him and his constituents. The leaders often take a stand representing a middle position of the party membership, in effect assuming something of a national point of view. The Congressman does not take a national point of view unless it happens to coincide with the predilections of his district, because he is not responsible to a national electorate.

Least of all does he feel that he must conform to the national platform as adopted by his party in convention and interpreted by the presidential candidate. This program, he knows, was written to attract voters in the great industrial states, especially in those states holding the electoral balance of power. The Congressman must operate within an entirely different political context—that of locality. He often greets with suspicion the efforts of the presidential candidates to spell out national platforms in their efforts to win over great masses of votes. In 1940, for example, he differed with many of the forthright opinions of both Wendell Willkie and Franklin D. Roosevelt. And when his party's candidate becomes President, the Congressman feels no obligation to support his policies. He must come to terms with the Chief Executive only if the latter is able, through skillful handling of national issues and of his patronage power, to affect public opinion and political forces in the 9th District.

Thus the grand strategy of congressional politics requires that the Congressman keep in mind the immediate interests of his own district first, last, and most of the way between. Accordingly, most of his time is taken up not with matters of national policy but with doing odd jobs for the politicians, pressure groups, and average voters of the 9th District. He is part promoter, part errand boy. He spends hours each week acting in effect as counsel for business firms and other groups before federal administrative agencies. He must try to find jobs every year for hundreds of the home folks. He must deal with thousands of requests each month for aid in getting satisfaction from the agencies.

Letters and telegrams pour into his office with personal problems that take hours of his or his staff's time to solve. Many of his constituents visit him with requests for favors, many others telephone him. Most of the time, in short, he is immersed in trivia. He knows that satisfying these requests is the best insurance for reelection. He believes, moreover, that he must help humanize the often impersonal relationships between citizen and bureaucrat.

"There are Congressmen elected year after year," Walter Lippmann has written, "who never think of dissipating their energy on public affairs. They prefer to do a little service for a lot of people on a lot of little subjects, rather than try to engage in trying to do a big service out there in the void." The Congressman ideally fits this picture.

Given the political and human situations involved, it is not surprising that the Congressman finds little time to be a legislator. He takes his intellectual nourishment in snatches—half an hour at a committee meeting in the morning, a few minutes listening to debate in the House following a quorum call in the afternoon.

His briefcase bulges with elaborate reports from the administrative agencies, with briefs from interest groups, with independent studies, all of which he hopes to examine but which he will have time to skim at most. He is in steady retreat before the constantly rising burden of private business, the never-ending task of satisfying local needs and interests.

At times the Congressman has a sense of his own inadequacy in attempting to tussle with vast and intricate questions of international and domestic policy on the basis of such limited study. But he is reassured by the thought that common sense, of which he has a full store, can solve most of these problems.

The Congressman's world, then, is largely confined within the boundaries of the 9th District and is shaped by the business spirit and way of life of Boone Center. It is a world where old ideas and myths still survive, blurring the alignments that economic and political forces inevitably produce. As the champion of his world, the Congressman defends it against its real and imaginary adversaries outside. As the product of his world, he puts its imprint on congressional action.

39 · THE BRITISH PARLIAMENT

A · PARLIAMENTARY PROCEDURE *

Parliamentary procedure is based on forms and rules, many of which date back to the beginning of the sixteenth century and even earlier.

Each House has its own Standing Orders, but procedure is based more on custom and precedent than on the written orders, which merely supplement practice in each House. The system of debate is much the same in the two Houses, except that, in the House of Commons, the Speaker has a much greater measure of control. In the House of Lords, the office of Lord Chancellor could be held by a commoner, since the Woolsack on which the Lord Chancellor sits as Speaker is technically outside the precincts of the House. In fact, the holder of the office is always created a peer, but the office carries with it no inherent authority to check or curtail debate. Such matters are decided by the general sense of the House, and not by rulings of its Speaker.

* *The British Parliament* (British Information Services, I.D. 952—revised, February, 1959), pp. 11-15. Reprinted by permission of the British Information Services. The footnotes in the original version are omitted here.

In the Commons, the Speaker has the prime duties of interpreting the rules of procedure and of controlling debate. It is his responsibility to see that parliamentary time is used to the best possible advantage and, therefore, although he must carefully guard against abuse of procedure or any infringement of minority rights, he has power to limit unreasonable obstruction, and his rulings on points of order cannot be challenged at the time. It is the duty of the Speaker to allow or disallow a closure motion (i.e. a motion to curtail or end discussion so that the matter may be put to the vote) and generally to enforce the rules of debate of the House. In cases of grave and continuous disorder, he may even adjourn the House or suspend the sitting.

Voting in the House of Commons is carried out under the direction of the Speaker, and it is his duty to pronounce the final result. If an equal number of votes is cast, the Speaker must give the decisive vote; he does this (if possible) in such a way as to leave the question to be debated on another occasion, or, if this is not possible, to avoid changing the original text. He is free to vote according to the merits if he wishes. When a division is called, Members voting "Aye" go out of the chamber behind the Speaker's Chair, and pass through the lobby on his right, while those voting "No" go out at the other end of the chamber into the lobby on the Speaker's left. Members' votes are recorded at the farther end of each lobby by two tellers.

The procedure on voting in the House of Lords is similar to that in the House of Commons, but the Lord on the Woolsack (the Lord Chancellor or his deputy), or in the chair, has no casting vote. With the exception of questions relating to Bills and subordinate legislation, the House is governed by the principle that the question is decided in the negative, unless there is a majority in its favor. While the House is sitting judicially, the question is put in such a way that, if the votes were equal, there would be no interference with the order under appeal.

The Speaker has the responsibility of deciding whether a Bill is a Money Bill (i.e., a Bill dealing only with national taxation and finance, which comes within the terms of the Parliament Act, 1911); and who, in case of doubt, is the Leader of the Opposition. He is also responsible for such matters as the decision whether a *prima facie* case has been made against persons accused of breach of privilege;

the issue of warrants for elections to fill vacancies in the House; and the appointment of the chairmen of the standing committees.

A quorum in the House of Commons is 40 Members; no business can be transacted if, upon the appeal of a Member to the Speaker, it is found that a quorum is not present. A quorum in the House of Lords is three, but if, on questions relating to Bills and subordinate legislation, less than 30 Lords have voted, the Lord on the Woolsack or in the chair declares the question not decided, and the debate stands adjourned to a subsequent sitting.

All proceedings of either House are public, except on extremely rare occasions, and a verbatim record is published daily in the Official Reports, *Parliamentary Debates* (*Hansard*).

STAGES IN LEGISLATION

A Bill is a draft Act of Parliament, and the passing of Bills is one of Parliament's chief functions. Most legislation applies to Great Britain, or the United Kingdom, as a whole, but on some matters separate Acts are passed for England and Wales and for Scotland. The majority of Public Bills, i.e., Bills which have for their object some changes in the general law, are Government measures; they are drafted by a minister, with the help of his advisers, and, before being introduced, will have the support of the Cabinet. An unofficial Member of Parliament may also introduce a Public Bill. A Bill, printed by Her Majesty's Stationery Office on green paper, normally consists of the following parts:

1. A short title which is the name by which it will generally be known.
2. A long title which summarizes the various purposes of the Bill.
3. A preamble (nowadays rare in a Public Bill) which may contain a number of assertions about the desirability of legislating on a particular subject.
4. The clauses of the Bill, containing the main provisions.
5. The schedules, which contain detailed matters dependent on the provisions of the Bill, e.g., lists of parts of laws repealed in general terms by a clause of the Bill.

If a Government Bill provides for expenditure of public money, it must have a financial memorandum. With this is also published, where deemed necessary, an explanatory memorandum.

The Effective Stages

A Bill must pass through both Houses of Parliament, and may originate in either, unless it deals with finance or electoral law, when it is normally introduced in the Commons. In practice, however, Bills which are likely to raise much party political controversy are normally presented first to the Commons. The First Reading of a Public Bill is a formality. A Bill may be presented and read a first time as a result of the House agreeing to a motion for leave to bring in the Bill, or it may be presented on notice, without a motion for leave. Once presented, it is automatically ordered to be printed, and publication shortly follows. The further stages of the Bill are Second Reading; Committee; Consideration on "Report"; and Third Reading.

The first main occasion for the debate of a Bill is the Second Reading, when it is usually introduced by the appropriate minister or Member in charge of the Bill on the motion, "That this Bill be now read a Second time," and the debate is limited to a discussion of the principles of the measure. Detailed discussion, including criticism which could be met by minor alterations, is reserved for the Committee or Report Stages. Thus, the Opposition may decide not to vote against the Bill on the Second Reading, but to introduce various amendments in Committee.

In Committee of the Whole House

When a Bill has passed its Second Reading in the House of Commons, it is then ordered to be committed either to a "Committee of the Whole House" or to one of the regular Standing Committees formed for the purpose. There are normally six committees: A, B, C, D, and E, and the committee dealing with Scottish legislation.

The Committee of the Whole House was originally a device framed in early Stuart times for the purpose of conducting debates more informally while the Speaker was not in the Chair: the Mace, his symbol of authority, is taken from the table, and the Chairman of Ways and Means (who is also Deputy Speaker) or his deputy, the Deputy Chairman, presides over the Committee from the Clerk's chair. At present, the Committee of the Whole House is usually employed for discussing only the main financial Bills of the year, those which are of the highest constitutional or political importance, or those in which the committee stage is likely to be a pure formality.

Standing Committee

In almost all other instances, Public Bills in the House of Commons are committed to a Standing Committee, which, in recent practice, consists of either 35 or 45 Members. The personnel is composed partly of Members nominated for the duration of the Session and partly of specialist Members added for particular Bills. Members of a Standing Committee are chosen in proportion to the strength of the political parties in the House and are presided over by a member of a panel of chairmen chosen by the Speaker.

Standing Committees are held in the committee rooms on the upper floors of the House, hence occasional reference in subsequent stages of debate to work done "upstairs."

In committee, a Member may speak as often as he wishes in the same debate, instead of only once, as on other occasions. The object of the Committee Stage of a Bill is the amendment of its individual provisions, and the measure is dealt with clause by clause. An amendment may take the form of an omission, an addition, or a substitution.

Report and Third Reading

When it has passed committee, a Bill has still to be considered in two more stages in the Whole House. These are the Report Stage and the Third Reading. The Bill is formally reported to the House by the Chairman of the Committee, and the House then has an opportunity to consider the Bill as amended in committee, and to make any further amendments as may be necessary. The House may, at this stage, recommit a Bill in whole or in part to a committee. After the Report Stage, the Bill reaches its final stage, the Third Reading, before being sent to the other House.

A third reading debate deals with the Bill as agreed to in committee and on Report. Only verbal amendments can be made at this stage. (There is no such limitation on Third Reading debates in the Lords.) When the Bill passes its Third Reading in the Commons, an order is made that the Clerk of the House carry the Bill to the Lords and desire their concurrence. The Bill has now to pass a similar number of stages in the House of Lords. (If it has originated in the Lords, it must then go to the Commons.) If there is no disagreement between the two Houses, the Bill is now ready for the Royal Assent.

Amendments in the Second House

If the Second House amends the Bill, it must be returned to the House where it originated for the consideration of these amendments. On each of them a resolution is passed, "That this House doth agree (or disagree) with the Lords/Commons in the said amendment."

If the first House rejects the amendments made by the second House, a committee is set up to show the reasons for the disagreement, and a message embodying the reasons is sent to the second House. The amendments in dispute may then be dropped, or alternative ones adopted, and so the process continues until either agreement or a deadlock is reached. If such a deadlock arose, the Government might apply procedure laid down by the Parliament Acts, 1911 and 1949, by which a Bill which passes the Commons in two successive sessions becomes law, in spite of the House of Lords.

Money Bills

Also under the Parliament Act, 1911, the assent of the Lords is not essential, subject to certain conditions, in the case of Money Bills. A Money Bill, which must be endorsed by the Speaker to that effect, is defined as "A Public Bill which, in the opinion of the Speaker of the House of Commons, contains only provisions . . . dealing with the imposition, repeal, remission, alteration or regulation of taxation, or subordinate matters incidental to those subjects or any of them." The definition is a narrow one, so narrow that only about half the annual Finance Bills are certified as Money Bills under the Parliament Act. Money Bills certified by the Speaker are sent to the Lords at least one month before the end of a session, and if not passed within one month, unless the House of Commons direct to the contrary, they receive the Royal Assent without the consent of the Lords.

The Royal Assent

When a Bill is ready for the Royal Assent, this is given in the House of Lords. The Queen is represented by Lords Commissioners, who sit in front of the throne. At the bar of the House of Lords stands the Speaker, with other members of the Commons, and the Reading Clerk of the House of Lords reads out the commission which authorizes the assent to be given. The Clerk of the Crown then reads out the title of each Bill, and the Clerk of the Parliaments pronounces the formula of assent. This Royal Assent converts a Bill into an Act of Parliament.

Private Bills and Private Members' Bills

The most usual type of Bill is the Public Bill, described above. A Private Bill is one introduced in the interests of an individual, a company, a local authority, and so on, and deals with such matters as waterworks or railways, which might interfere with the private rights of individuals. In substance, a Private Bill goes through the same procedure as a Public Bill, but most of the work is done in committee where the promoters of the Bill must prove the need for the powers or privileges that they are seeking, and where any objections raised by opposing companies, authorities or private persons may be heard.

A Private Members' Bill is a Public Bill in that it concerns the whole of the community, but differs from the normal Public Bill in being introduced by an unofficial Member, and not by a Member of the Government. Notable examples of Private Members' Bill in the past are Samuel Plimsoll's Merchant Shipping Act, 1876; Sir Alan P. Herbert's Matrimonial Causes Act, 1937; and Miss Ellen Wilkinson's Hire Purchase Act, 1938. During the war, Government business took up all the time of the House, but, from 1949, Private Members resumed their traditional rights. At present 20 Fridays in each session are devoted to Private Members' Bills and Motions (alternately). In addition, a Member may introduce a Bill after question time on Tuesday or Wednesday under the "Ten-Minute Rule," i.e., one short speech of ten minutes proposing, and another opposing, the Bill are allowed, after which the question that leave be given to bring in the Bill is put.

B · PARLIAMENTARY CONTROL OF THE EXECUTIVE *

Although the Government, through its party majority in the House of Commons, exercises a far-reaching control over parliamentary time, in practice the time-table of the House of Commons offers many opportunities for a searching examination of Government

* *The British Parliament* (British Information Services, I.D. 952—revised, February, 1959), pp. 16-20. Reprinted by permission of the British Information Services. The footnotes in the original version are omitted here.

policy by the Opposition and by Private Members. It is estimated that in the period 1945-55, when the average parliamentary session was 158 days, the Government program occupied an average of 75 days (i.e., 47.5 per cent of the total time), the Opposition initiated business on 41 days (26 per cent), and Private Members on 29 days (18.3 per cent); 13 days (8.2 per cent) were devoted to business which, while it did not form part of the Government program, afforded no special opportunities of initiative to the Opposition or to Private Members.

One of the most important safeguards of the rights and interests of the ordinary citizen is the answerability to Parliament of ministers on all matters affecting public policy within their departmental spheres. Any Member, as representative of the ordinary citizen, may challenge the policy put forward by a minister, and the minister, in turn, must either defend or withdraw it. The main ways in which this challenge is made are through the general course of the debate on a particular Measure, through the cherished institution of parliamentary question and answer, in debates on the estimates on "Supply" days, when the minister is, in effect, asking for money to run that part of the nation's business which lies within the purview of his department, and through a debate on the adjournment.

In the general debate on a Bill, Members may object to its broad principles on the Second Reading, or, as regularly happens, may put forward amendments in detail during the Committee Stage. Even though a Government may have a large majority, it is possible for members of the Opposition to put forward, and by reasoned argument to secure, the incorporation of amendments of this kind. Thus both the Government and the Opposition collaborate in securing improvements to a given measure.

Question Time

Question Time in the House of Commons is one of Parliament's most valuable institutions. It provides many lively moments and is of wide general interest both to the Members and the public. It is a safeguard to the liberty of the subject, and a guarantee that the rights and interests of the humblest citizen are not neglected. Questions have as their chief object "the throwing of a searchlight upon every corner of the public service." They are serviceable as obviating the necessity, in many instances, of more extended debate, and are often arranged by the Government so as to give them an opportunity of making announcements.

Question Time begins just after 2:30 p.m. on the first four days of the week and goes on until 3:30 p.m. Questions are handed in writing to the Clerks at least two days before an answer is required; any Member, except ministers, the Chair and the Leader of the Opposition, may ask up to three oral questions a day.

To be in order, a question must be framed as a question, not a statement, be concerned with fact, not opinion, ask for information or action, be addressed to a minister who is officially responsible for the matter with which it deals, and be framed in accordance with the rules of constitutional usage and parliamentary etiquette. Thus, a question must be a genuine request for knowledge and not a speech, and should not contain any "argument, inference, imputation, epithet, or ironical expression." A minister has entire discretion, on grounds of public interest, to refuse answer to a question asked.

The Member asking the original question, or any other Member, is entitled, at the Speaker's discretion, to ask a supplementary question or questions arising out of the original question, and both in asking and answering questions the greatest ingenuity is used. But the Speaker keeps a careful watch to prevent too much time being devoted to one question, nor will he allow interrogation to develop into debate. If a Member wishes to proceed further with a question, he may give notice that, owing to the unsatisfactory nature of the reply, he will raise the matter on the adjournment at the earliest opportunity.

Any question which there has not been time to reach by 3:30 p.m. and which has not been postponed by the Member concerned, and any question which a Member has sent in for written reply only, receive a printed answer in the Official Report (*Hansard*). The answers are printed at the end of the account of the day's debate. Typewritten copies of the replies to any questions not reached and not postponed by 3:30 p.m. are sent on the same day, by the relevant department, to the Member asking the question.

In the House of Lords, a limited number of "starred questions" may be asked for information only; no debate may take place, and supplementary questions must be confined to the subject of the original question. Members of the House of Lords may also ask questions for written answer.

Committee of Supply

The normal way in which the policy of the Executive can be criticized in the House of Commons is in the Committee of Supply, a Committee of the Whole House whose business is to consider and vote State expenditure, such as the Estimates, Votes on Account, Votes of Credit, and so on. A certain number of days (usually 26) are put aside in every session for that business of Supply, and are called "Supply Days." In the main Estimates and other instances, the Opposition have the right to decide what subject shall be discussed. Thus Members of the Commons have time and opportunity to discuss and demand "the redress of grievances" and to criticize the actions of ministers, while the ministers feel obliged to reply. The discussion of Estimates enables the Opposition, choosing their own ground, to criticize the administration of affairs covered thereby, and often the debate takes place on a resolution to reduce the salary of the minister concerned or the Vote of the department by a nominal sum. In this way it is assured that no part of Government policy is free from the possibility of criticism by the representatives of the citizen.

Adjournment Debates

At the end of the parliamentary business of the day in the House of Commons a period of 30 minutes is set aside for discussion of any grievance for which the remedy does not require legislation. If more than one Member wishes to raise a subject on the Adjournment a ballot is taken, and the Member who is successful in the ballot has the first opportunity to put forward his case. If unsuccessful the first time, he may take part in further ballots.

Financial Control

Parliamentary control over Government expenditure is exercised mainly by the Select Committee on Estimates and the Select Committee on Public Accounts. The Select Committee on Estimates was originally set up in 1912 but was re-formed in 1929 with wider terms of reference. Under these terms it has been reappointed annually except during the war years. The committee's functions are to examine the Estimates of proposed Government expenditure, to suggest the form in which they should be presented, and to report whether there are any economies which could be made without altering the policy implied in the Estimates. It is customary for the committee to select each year a few aspects of expenditure for review. In practice, the Estimates for the current year are not affected, but the committee's recommendations may reinforce Treasury control of departmental expenditure and influence the nature of expenditure in succeeding years.

The accounts of each Government department and the reports on the accounts by the Comptroller and Auditor General are considered by the Select Committee on Public Accounts. This was set up in 1861 for the purpose of ensuring that expenditure was properly incurred in accordance with the way it was voted and with any relevant Acts of Parliament. These terms of reference have been widely interpreted by the committee, which investigates whether full value has been obtained for the sums spent by departments and examines cases in which the administration appears to have been faulty or negligent. The committee has, therefore, become a powerful instrument for the exposure of waste and inefficiency. It embodies its findings in reports which may be discussed in the House of Commons. Its recommendations are considered by the Treasury in consultation with departments and put into effect, so far as they are accepted, according to Treasury instructions. If the recommendations are not acceptable, a reasoned reply has to be submitted to the Public Accounts Committee, which may either accept the objections or return to the charge in subsequent reports.

Control of Delegated Legislation

With the ever-increasing scope of Government activity in the twentieth century, pressure on parliamentary time has become acute; as a result, the system of delegated legislation (mainly in the form of statutory instruments) has become generally accepted and there are few Acts of Parliament which do not contain provisions for its use.

In order to minimize the risk—inherent in the system—that delegated legislative powers might supersede or weaken parliamentary government, such powers are normally delegated to the Queen in Council or to authorities directly responsible to Parliament, i.e., to ministers of the Crown, to Government departments for which ministers are responsible, or to organizations whose legislation is subject to confirmation or approval by ministers who thereby become responsible to Parliament for it. Moreover, the Acts of Parliament by which particular powers are delegated normally provide for some measure of parliamentary control over legislation made in the exercise of these powers. There are cases in which a statutory instrument must be approved by either House of Parliament before it can have permanent operation ("affirmative resolution procedure"); and others in which either House of Parliament may secure the annulment of an instrument by a resolution passed within a certain number of days of the instrument being laid before it ("negative resolution procedure"). The Resolution, in the case of an instrument to be annulled after it has been made, takes the form of an Address to Her Majesty that the instrument be annulled (after which the instrument is annulled by Order in Council).

The House of Commons is aided in its supervision of delegated legislation by the Select Committee on Statutory Instruments, which has the advice of the Speaker's Counsel. While the Select Committee is not empowered to consider the merits of delegated legislation or the policy implemented thereby, it has the important function of drawing the House's attention to provisions of such legislation which (a) impose a charge on the public revenues, (b) are made under an enactment which excludes challenge in the law courts, (c) appear to make some unusual or unexpected use of the powers conferred by the statute, (d) would have retrospective effect where the parent statute does not provide for this, (e) have had their publication or their laying before Parliament unjustifiably delayed, (f) have not been notified in proper terms to the Speaker in cases where they come into operation before being presented to Parliament, or (g) call for elucidation of their form or meaning.

In the House of Lords, the Special Orders Committee examines orders which require an affirmative Resolution of the House or an Address to the Queen before becoming effective, or continuing in force. The committee does not report on the expediency of an order but reports its opinion as to whether the order raises important questions of policy or principle and how far the order is founded on precedent; and advises the House whether the order can be passed without special attention, or whether there ought to be a further inquiry before the House proceeds to a decision.

Parliament and the Nationalized Industries

Public corporations operating the nationalized industries are appointed by an appropriate minister and are responsible, to him and through him, to Parliament. Such ministers can give the corporations general directives, can call for information, and have extensive powers over the use of capital funds; but they do not normally use these powers to interfere in the day-to-day operation of the industries and have refused on grounds of public policy to answer questions on day-to-day administration.

In general, therefore, ministers may be questioned in Parliament on the general policies of the Government towards the nationalized industries but not on detailed matters of day-to-day administration, unless the Speaker rules them to be of sufficient public importance.

Debates on the nationalized industries may take place on the presentation to Parliament of the annual reports and accounts of the various public corporations; on motions by Private Members; on adjournment motions; or on Bills affecting one or more of the industries.

In order to ensure that parliamentary discussion of the nationalized industries is informed and effective, a House of Commons Select Committee on the Nationalized Industries was established in March 1957. The terms of reference of the Select Committee are to examine the reports and accounts of the nationalized industries established by statute whose controlling boards are appointed by ministers of the Crown and whose annual receipts are not wholly or mainly derived from money provided by Parliament or advanced by the Exchequer.

40 · THE WORKING OF THE JAPANESE DIET *

Hattie Kawahara Colton

Constitutional changes under SCAP impetus have given to the postwar Japanese National Diet a status and powers which it never before enjoyed. Under the 1947 Constitution the Diet is "the sole law-making authority of the state" and "the highest organ of state power." The national charter establishes a parliamentary system,

* Hattie Kawahara Colton, "The Working of the Japanese Diet," *Pacific Affairs*, XXVIII (December, 1955), 363-372. Reprinted by permission of the Institute of Pacific Relations. The footnotes in the original version are omitted here.

modified by the stipulation for judicial review. However, certain powers accorded to the prime minister and the cabinet establish the leadership status of the executive, among them the power to dissolve the lower House, to extend Diet sessions, to call emergency sessions, and, in the case of the prime minister, to appoint cabinet ministers. Moreover, the fact that the initiation and planning of policy essentially rest with the prime minister, the cabinet and the ministries tends to give them a predominating role over the Diet. Yet no government can be formed or carry through a legislative program without Diet approval. While only eight years have elapsed since the new system went into effect, a tentative evaluation of the problems of governmental leadership in the Diet may provide clues to the vitality of the democratic system that SCAP attempted to introduce in Japan.

Certain conditioning factors affecting the development of the postwar Diet must be noted. First, it must be remembered that until April 28, 1952, SCAP supervised not only the formulation of policies but also their handling in the Diet. Hence Japanese experience under the occupation may well be regarded as tipped in favor of the executive, since occupation rule tended to put a brake on independent Diet action. Many Japanese discount the value of the occupation period in stimulating Diet competence and habits of initiative.

The purge programs of 1946 and 1947 also affected the implementation of the new Diet system. The purge directives removed from political activity many politicians of the prewar era, particularly of the conservative parties, and forced the appearance of new elements in the Diet. Thus non-purgees, postwar newcomers from the bureaucracy and other sources, and Socialists, who were elected in significant numbers for the first time, formed the bulk of Diet members. Many of these legislators had little or no experience in the Imperial Diet. A consequence was a sharper break with the prewar institution than would otherwise have occurred. By the time the depurgees returned in 1952, the new Diet had been in operation for five years, mostly under the occupation; the depurgees had to adapt themselves to the changed Diet situation, as well as to try to regain power in their respective parties.

A third factor was the fact that responsibility for effectuating the new Diet powers and procedures fell primarily to Shigeru Yoshida and the Liberal Party, who, with the exception of the brief Socialist-Democratic interlude of 1947-48, headed the Japanese Government until December 1954. The Liberal Party stewardship has left its impact upon Diet management, procedure and operations.

The Diet channels through which leadership is exercised consist of the House of Representatives, the House of Councillors, and their respective internal organs: the speakership or presidency, the plenary sessions, and the standing and special committees. The lower House is the more significant because of its constitutional powers over the budget, treaties, and even ordinary legislation, as well as over the selection and tenure of the government itself, and decisive conflicts take place in that body rather than in the upper House. The role of the House of Councillors has tended to be that of delaying measures which it disapproves, rather than of effectively influencing the course of legislation.

Within the House of Representatives, the several agencies vary in importance. The Japanese speaker, somewhat like his counterpart in the British House of Commons, loses his party identification and is primarily a neutral presiding officer. Theoretically he is empowered to draw up the agenda for plenary sessions in consultation with Secretariat officials but, in effect, this responsibility has been surrendered to the House management committee. He can, however, personally extend the sessions of the Diet, which makes it advantageous for the party in power to control the speakership. Customarily, the speakership has gone to the majority or plurality party, and the vice speakership to the next ranking party. The loss of this post by a government party does not, however, necessarily signify a major defeat. . . .

Secondly, the plenary sessions, held at most only three times a week at the scheduling of the House management committee, are formal sessions, significant in that House votes are registered. Indeed, the most important function of the plenary sessions may well be the election of the prime minister and House officials. Government spokesmen generally make administrative speeches at the beginning of a Diet session and the opposition parties engage in interpellations, but these tend to be perfunctory and general. The lack of importance apparently attached to Government speeches is suggested by their brevity during the Governments of Yoshida, when they lasted anywhere from nine to twenty minutes. As for bills introduced in the Diet, they are usually referred to the appropriate committees without even a first reading. In attempting to overcome members' objections that they frequently have no idea of the bills being considered by the Diet, the House management committee may provide for an explanation by Government spokesmen in the plenary sessions before commitment to committee. Such a practice was instituted during the fifteenth and nineteenth Diet sessions in 1953 and 1954 concerning administration bills to correct so-called "occupation excesses." Free discussion periods, instituted by SCAP to help raise the calibre of Diet debate and at the time regarded hopefully by the Japanese press, have virtually been abandoned as unrealistic and artificial, although they might have been utilized by the Government to air current issues. In the sixteenth session in 1953, when the Socialists demanded the calling of a free discussion period to question the Government on its rearmament policy, it was decided not to revive this technique but to call a special meeting of the budget committee instead.

Thus the standing committees have developed into the main testing ground for a government's policies. It is here that the government must explain in response to interpellations the contents and purposes of bills, defend them against the opposition, and attempt to secure their approval. A favorable vote in committee virtually assures the passage of measures in plenary session. It is here, therefore, that the full resources of the Administration are brought to bear: the prime minister often appears, and cabinet members and officials from the ministries nearly always do; party tacticians maneuver against the opposition; and witnesses favorable to the government are called in the public hearings. Moreover, here the nature of the cooperation worked out between the government and the majority party and the results of any bargaining or negotiations with an opposition party are put to the proof.

Until the recent 1955 amendment to the Diet Law of 1947, which reduced the number to sixteen, there existed twenty-two of these standing committees, of which eighteen dealt with bills in various categories, three dealt with operations of the Diet, and one was designed to check on government expenditures. The most important of those dealing with bills is the budget committee, which examines, debates, and votes on all budget measures. A special urgency attaches to the work of this committee, owing to the nature of the Japanese fiscal year, and consideration of the budget is the first major order of business in any regular Diet session. Indeed, work on other committees is usually almost at a standstill, for the attendance of the prime minister and his colleagues precludes their fulfilling other obligations. Once the budget is out of the way, a government's projected legislative program will determine which of the other standing committees receives priority of attention.

One other committee deserves brief mention: the House management committee, which does not examine bills, but directs the operations of the House. Even to Prime Minister Yoshida, who was not too concerned about all aspects of Diet management, the importance of this committee was obvious, for after the 1952 elections, during the struggle within the Liberal Party against the Hatoyama forces, he always selected as its chairman a man from the "closers" group (*sokkin-ha*) within the party, and thereby kept under his control the direction of day-to-day tactics and maneuvers in the Diet. Such matters as the referral of bills without clearly defined jurisdictional designation to appropriate committees and the determination of the agenda of plenary sessions, which may involve questions of when decisions are to be taken, when committees are to be prodded for reports, and when sessions are to be held, are tactical moves which can be used to further a government's program.

Within the committees, too, control over the chairmanship, as well as over the steering group or directors (*riji*) and the membership, makes it possible to manage committee proceedings. Unlike the American system, however, the chairman of a Diet committee is the creature of his party and its leaders, designated by the party and dismissed as party considerations dictate. He presides over steering group and committee sessions, supervises the staff, represents the committee in its dealings with other committees, and reports decisions to plenary sessions. Since his position is the result of party patronage, the chairman is not an important figure in his own right; he is usually a so-called comer, a second bencher, or perhaps someone who needs a badge of position for his election campaign. . . .

Above all, the success of a government in securing the adoption of its legislative program depends upon the extent to which it is able to command support in the Diet. With a majority, a government can maintain control in the various stages of the Diet process. With only a plurality, it must rely upon the support of at least a part of another party or group, and it may lose the speakership and vice-speakership, despite the nominal importance of these positions. Moreover, it must share committee chairmanships with the other parties, with the number and choices dependent upon their strength in the House. . . .

Whether a government is supported by a majority or a plurality, one condition of effective leadership is the degree to which it coordinates its policies with those of its own party. While discipline in Japanese parties, enforced by expulsion, is stricter than in American parties, despite weaknesses that may be inferred by the schisms, factionalism, and boltings characteristic of the Japanese party scene, a government often faces the possibility of clashes between its proposals and the demands of party members. These may be motivated by legislators' commitments in their constituencies, or by the need for preparing for future election contests. Essentially, the task of coordinating such gaps rests with the prime minister, who is also the party president, although he may delegate the responsibility to the secretary-general or other party officials. In that case, it behooves the prime minister to see that acceptable persons be chosen as party officials, a fact which Prime Minister Yoshida often ignored, to the detriment of party harmony and governmental stability.

While each of Japan's parties possesses different policy-making organs, the policy research committee and the executive committee constituted the Diet policy groups within the Liberal Party, and Diet members' caucuses provided the forums through which party decisions were communicated to and usually automatically agreed to by Liberal legislators. Habituated perhaps by a relatively unopposed majority and the fact of SCAP initiative in policy between 1949 and 1952, Yoshida never fully exploited the potentialities of these party channels for the coordination of party and government policy. Until the acknowledgment in 1953 of Hatoyama's demands for prior clearance and acceptance of legislative proposals by the policy research committee and the executive committee, these party organs played no vital role in policy-making.

Besides party channels, a prime minister may also utilize cabinet posts as a means of assuring coordination of government and party policy. Yoshida, however, appointed intimates, his closest adherents, "purchased" leaders of blocs, and, in order to secure *Ryokufukai* (Green Breeze Society) support in the House of Councillors, included a member from that group in almost all of his cabinets, rather than influential party men. The selection of parliamentary vice-ministers during Yoshida's rule also tended to be a matter of giving honorary recognition or patronage to his loyal followers. The result of Yoshida's failures in party relations was a protracted fight within the Liberal Party in which support for Government policies became one of the pawns in the power struggle. In the end, the Yoshida Government managed to pass its major pieces of legislation—the budget bills of 1953-1954 and 1954-1955, and those bills designed to "correct" so-called "occupation excesses"; the anti-strike bill in the coal and electric power industries, revisions of the anti-monopoly law, the two education bills, and the police revision bill.

These were not accomplished, however, without amendments and concessions wrought by internal factions within the Liberal Party and the opposition Progressive Party, upon whose votes the Yoshida Government depended after the April 1953 elections. Fundamentally, while it can be said that a general consensus on policy exists between the two conservative parties as opposed to the Socialist parties, yet the differences between them and their various internal groups cannot be ignored. It should be noted, for example, that the Progressive Party extracted from the Liberal Government an increase in the budget of 1954-1955 as the price for their support—something which would have toppled governments in other countries—and precipitated a constitutional dilemma for the Government. In the twenty-second Diet session of 1955, the Liberal Party is essaying a role similar to that of the former Progressives *vis-à-vis* the Democratic Government, critical and demanding compromises that would incorporate their stands in law and policy.

Thus opposition tactics in the Diet in Japan's multiparty situation may assume various forms. Despite the basic conservative-Socialist confrontation, each party, equipped with policy-formulating organs and organized within the Diet for strategy and tactics, operates as an independent entity. To a government and party in power, therefore, the problem of dealing with opposition parties presents itself in multiple facets. A plurality government must constantly be aware of combinations on specific objectives by opposition parties, such as that which brought down the Yoshida Liberals in December 1954, however illogical from a policy standpoint such cooperation between a conservative party and the two Socialist parties might seem. For this reason among a number of others, the urgency of close cooperation, if not of actual merger, is compelling to conservative politicians today.

In the day-to-day business of the Diet, a government party encounters the maneuvers and tactics of the opposition parties that run the gamut from harassment through interpellations, deliberate delays by refusal to attend House management committee meetings or by stalking out of committee meetings so that no quorum is present, postponement of sessions of committees whose chairmanships they control, to exposures of alleged scandals and investigations of presumed malfeasance with the objective of discrediting the government in power. Frequently, both plenary and committee sessions are characterized by noisy catcalling, jeering, and general hooliganism. The postwar Diet has been described by one visitor as "the greatest theater in postwar Japan." There have been brawls and fisticuffs, ashtray throwing, tent-village sitdowns, and red-bannered demonstrations that have brought out police barricades. On the night of June 3, 1954, the House of Representatives engaged in a free-for-all riot, the result of a Socialist attempt to prevent another extension of the Diet to permit passage of the controversial police revision bill. Although the responsibility for its initiation may be placed on the Socialists, it is also true that the Government and the Liberal Party might have averted the incident by more astute management.

· · · · ·

Besides the problem of party relations, another challenge to the effective exercise of government leadership in the Diet has been the growth of collaboration between individual party members, especially conservatives, and officials in the ministries. The institutional framework for such cooperation is the standing committee system, which is generally organized to correspond with the ministries. Through continuous service on one committee or previous experience in the bureaucracy, Diet members of standing committees handling legislation have been able to develop close working relations with the officials of the ministries, particularly at the bureau and section levels. In the winter of 1952, such an arrangement resulted in the cabinet's having to increase the budget for 1953-1954 before its submission to the Diet. In this case, no consultation on basic budget policy appears to have taken place between the finance minister and the finance ministry on the one hand, and the policy research committee of the Liberal Party on the other. Without party commitment to the budget proposals, which party members wanted increased anyway, and with at least two ministries especially dissatisfied with their allotments, the bureaucrats combined with party members to frustrate the cabinet's plans.

The development of collaboration of party members and bureaucrats through the standing committees has been facilitated by the system of individual member legislation (*giin rippo*) provided for in the Diet Law of 1947 and patterned after the American system as a stimulus to legislative independence. Under this system, it is possible for a bill rejected by a ministry or by the cabinet to be introduced as an individual member's bill. The chances of its passage are fairly good, as the bill will probably be referred to the appropriate committee, one of whose members introduced it, and will be an item about which not too many legislators will be informed. There is relatively little likelihood that, once a committee reports the bill out favorably, it will be rejected in plenary session.

To the legislator, such cooperation with the bureaucrats has advantages when he in turn wishes support for his interests. Since many requests from constituents involve favors by the bureaucracy, it is to the Diet member's advantage to keep on friendly terms with government officials. Moreover, not only the individual legislator but whole parties or sections of parties face pressures from organized interest groups seeking legislation and favors in return for election funds and other kinds of support. During the past few years there has been an increase in the number of Diet members' associations representing various interests from textiles to shipbuilding that even cut across party lines, and testify to the activity and persistence of pressure groups in the Diet. When legislation is desired by these groups, the provision for individual members' bills makes possible their introduction, though at times it may be only a gesture.

Whatever the source, there has been an increase in the number of such bills introduced and passed, particularly during and after the thirteenth Diet session in 1952, when SCAP's supervisory eye was removed. Because these laws often require funds not appropriated in the budget, the system of individual member legislation may actually challenge a government's established policy, endorsed by the Diet in the passage of a budget bill, as well as threatening administrative control by the prime minister and the cabinet over the ministries.

The existence of such a threat is evident from two amendments to the Diet Law of 1947 passed on January 24, 1955. The first provided that individual members' bills may be introduced in either House but only with the approval of at least twenty members of that House. The second stipulated that all such bills requiring any outlay of funds must be supported by at least fifty members before introduction. While these amendments may help, the parties themselves need to establish controls so that individual members' bills requiring appropriations are introduced only after the approval of the policy research committee and other party organs.

Certainly the development of close working relations between legislators and bureaucrats is one that bears watching, against the background of a long Japanese tradition of executive-bureaucratic power and influence. It could lead to the establishment of habits of Diet dependence upon the bureaucracy which in practice might tend to destroy the Diet's basis for control of the administration.

In 1955, the new Diet system has by no means congealed but certain trends seem discernible. Power and influence are weighted in favor of the executive, although they are shared to a far greater extent with a freely elected Diet than was ever the case in prewar or wartime Japan. One factor which may have affected this situation has been the preponderance of conservative strength during the postwar years. The growth of socialism, however, may be expected to force a greater focus and emphasis upon the Diet and its problems, even on the specific questions of Diet organization, management, and strategy. The formation of a Socialist government would almost certainly lead to a conservative reappraisal of the Diet as a significant political arena. Responsible criticism, habits of independent inquiry, and debate of high calibre have not been noticeable in postwar Diets. Nonetheless, many problems in the Japanese Diet are no different from those in legislative bodies in the Western democracies, which during the twentieth century have been on the defensive against executive-administrative dominance. Measured against the history of oligarchical rule, the recent, although short, experience indicates that political power in Japan is no longer the special preserve of the few, to be wielded without popular controls. It seems likely that Japanese politics will continue to operate within the present governmental framework, despite discussions, particularly among conservatives, envisaging amendments to the Constitution to reduce Diet powers, local autonomy, and civil rights. Already there is a substantial body of Diet members in all parties, as well as a growing number of citizens, to whom no other constitutional system is familiar in practice.

41 · THE MAN AND THE INSTITUTION *

Louis W. Koenig

All executive posts are part institution and part man. Yet the Presidency differs from all other major political executives in the balance it strikes between the parts. Far more than the French Premier and substantially more than the British Prime Minister, an incumbent of the Presidency has opportunity for personal self-expression.

This is a mixed blessing. Minimum institutional development both helps and hinders the President's affairs. At the helpful end of the scale, he enjoys exceptional freedom of action in dealing with his Cabinet. He can, if he chooses, abstain from calling it into session. He can drastically reduce the measures which come before it and blithely ignore its strongest recommendations. The British Prime Minister, in contrast, must consult his Cabinet at almost every turn and through precisely delineated procedures.

But the minimum institutional development also works to the disadvantage of the President. He has, for example, strikingly fewer and far less consequential means than the British Prime Minister for eliciting his party's support, especially in the legislature. In consequence, the President suffers in his proposals to Congress defeats that are inconceivable in Great Britain. Witness Truman's Fair Deal and the very minor percentage of it which Congress got around to approving—though, to be sure, his recommendations in the field of foreign affairs were more favorably received.

The relationship between the man and the institution has been an enduring problem of the Presidency. The Founding Fathers, in their act of creating the office, were much preoccupied with it, being haunted by George III and his system of "personal government," with its blunders, extravagance, and corruption. As they sought through institutional means to diminish the hazards of the Presidential personality, several variations of a council were considered to share in

* Louis W. Koenig, "The Man and the Institution," *The Annals of the American Academy of Political and Social Science,* 307 (September, 1956), pp. 10-14. Reprinted by permission of *The Annals of the American Academy of Political and Social Science.* The footnotes in the original version are omitted here.

the President's decisional activity. Only after extended consideration was this general formula dropped. The electoral college was established presumably to "screen" the "safest" personalities from among the aspirants to office. Under the principle of the separation of powers, a strong legislature was established so that although the President might propose policy, Congress would dispose of it. The list of measures could be extended. Yet there were also strong forces at Philadelphia pushing for an executive of independent strength, and to a large degree these forces prevailed.

Throughout our 167 years of experience with the Presidency, the problem of the relationship between the man and the institution has reappeared in various forms. Today it deserves to be regarded as one of the central problems of the Presidency. The problem may be stated thus: How can the Presidency of the future, occupied as it will be with men of uneven talents, be continuously able to meet the challenges of the times? It is assumed that the military, diplomatic, and economic problems of the country will be of such urgency as to require a continuously effective executive.

The record of the Presidency raises a serious question concerning its capacity to provide continuous leadership of high caliber. Although there are the striking accomplishments of Washington, Jackson, Lincoln, Wilson, and the Roosevelts, there are, too, the disastrous failures of Buchanan and Coolidge. Are the institutional resources of the office of today strong enough to sustain the Executive when as a person he falters or falls short of the demands which are made upon him? Before facing this question, we must look more closely at the role of the man in the workings of the Presidency.

THE PRESIDENCY AS PERSONALITY

"What the presidency is at any particular moment," writes Corwin, "depends in important measure on who is President." Any Presidency is stamped primarily with the personality of its incumbent, above all with his "style"—his gesture, his articulateness, his values.

For one thing, the President has unlimited power to make proposals for action. He can, if he chooses, espouse any cause from simplified spelling to the soil bank. He is under various influences and pressures to utilize his freedom. He is elected by and responsive to a national constituency. He is the only figure in public life whose prestige and power make anything he says and does sure-fire material for the front page. His appearance on television commands a Trendex rating that will swamp the best of the entertainment world's professionals. Not only does the President have great opportunity to propose, he is *expected* to make proposals. Early in his administration, President Eisenhower, for example, was criticized by legislators of both parties for not coming forward more opportunely with a fully developed program of legislation.

The President also commands what are by far the best resources for action available in the governmental mechanism. In a classic description in the Federalist papers, Hamilton listed the prime qualities of the proposed Presidency as "energy . . . unity . . . Decision, activity, secrecy, and despatch." The Constitution and statutes confer upon the President powers of great scope in foreign, military, and domestic affairs. He has available immense financial resources and the skills and energies of millions of civil and military experts. He has what Corwin calls "plasticity of method," enabling him to indulge his special talents and policy predilections. The daring ingenuity of Franklin D. Roosevelt's foreign policy in the year or more just before Pearl Harbor strikingly illustrates the importance of this attribute.

The President works in the area of accommodation. He pursues the difficult quest for consensus among competing sections of the country, among economic, national, and racial groups. George Washington was quick to discern this phase of the Presidency when at the outset of his administration he said that the new government was to be one "of accommodation as well as a government of laws."

In the arena of accommodation the arts of influence and persuasion hold sway. These are infinitely more demanding upon the talents of the man who is President than are simple exertions of power. Most Presidents have, however, seen the problem of accommodation as one deserving of their best effort, as a prerequisite to winning re-election or keeping their party in power. Washington was solicitous of achieving a general acceptance of his administration in all sections of the country. William McKinley labored mightily to unite the sectional factions of his party. F. D. Roosevelt carefully established his electoral invincibility on a combination of big labor, southerners, city bosses, New Dealers, and independent voters.

Some Presidents have found their best opportunities for self-expression by taking on the role of moral and social censor of their country and their times. Franklin Roosevelt envisaged the Presidency as "preeminently a place of moral leadership," and his New Deal can rightly be interpreted as in large degree a moral crusade. The political genius of F.D.R.'s cousin-predecessor, Theodore Roosevelt, lay in capturing the attention of the country and shaking it out of its placid acceptance of the evils of the trusts, the waste of natural resources, and other abuses.

RECENT TRENDS

In the twentieth century, the crises of depression and war expand and enlarge the President's personal role. Crisis or emergency serves to unshackle the President from a great number of the usual institutional restraints to the gain of his personal freedom of action.

Thanks to technology, the President has become a household presence, friendly and familiar. This is strictly a phenomenon of the twentieth century. Nineteenth-century Presidents, because of the infancy of communications, could reach and shape public opinion on relatively few issues in the course of a four-year term. Theodore Roosevelt, the first President really to exploit the rallying of public opinion, had the enormous advantage of press services of nationwide circulation. Franklin D. Roosevelt perfected the press conference and mastered the radio with his forte, the Fireside Chat. President Eisenhower has derived inestimable strength and political security from his impact as a television personality.

Foreign affairs have given new scope to the play of the President's personality. Twentieth-century Presidents have operated in an era of personal diplomacy, witness Eisenhower at Geneva, Truman at Potsdam, F.D.R. at Yalta, Wilson at Versailles. The propaganda struggle with the Soviet Union requires the projection of a pleasing image of Presidential man. In the United Nations and in military alliances around the globe, the President operates in realms where his personality as much as any factor may determine the success of United States policy.

In domestic affairs, various forces serve to highlight the President's personality. With government so deeply involved in the concerns of business and labor as regulator, promoter, and mediator, the President is brought increasingly into personal competition with the leaders of private groups for public attention and support. The chief sources of competition and conflict in the administration of Harry S. Truman, apart from the men in the Kremlin, were John L. Lewis and railway union leaders A. F. Whitney and Alvanley Johnston. It was not uncommon for the President to be blazing away with all his cannon of political showmanship in struggling with these oligarchs for public support.

DANGERS OF PERSONALITY

Of the thirty-three men who have occupied the Presidency, at least several rank among the world's great statesmen, and six or more deserve ranking as "strong" Presidents. None of our Presidents has represented the more extreme forms of political vileness. No dictator or despot, no scoundrel or profligate has appeared. Yet as we well know, we have had men who pursued folly, were naive, indolent, or blind to reality while the storm clouds of tragedy gathered. The country might have been spared untold havoc and suffering had better men been in their place.

The present-day setting of the Presidency invites a return of this mediocrity to the office. Television puts a new premium on affability. The winsome grin and mellifluous tonality do wonders for the presidential candidate. The uncertainties of our nuclear age bring new mass stirrings of the father complex which makes anxious people overvalue the President as he appears and undercritical of him as he really is. These and other forces contribute to a major danger of the modern Presidency, that personality will become a substitute for policy. As a step toward reducing this danger, we must look at the institutional side of the Presidency. To what extent can the institutional resources of the office assure that we shall have a policy regardless of the kind of man who occupies the post?

USES OF INSTITUTIONALIZATION

"Institution" is a catch-all term which, as applied to the Presidency, includes the legal resources of the office; the practice, precedent, and protocol; the staff and the bureaucratic skills, physical plant, and finance; the place of the office in society and in the culture as a medium for confronting and responding to challenges and problems.

It is through the institution that the man is kept responsible. The discerning Washington saw this as a primary purpose of his office. Time and again his own contribution to the Presidency was directed toward establishing practice which would keep himself and his successors responsible. For example, in considering the procedure he should follow in making nominations to posts which required the advice and consent of the Senate, he made this comment:

Nominations ought to be made by written messages; so that the acts of the President and the Senate will stand upon clear, distinct, and responsible ground.

In various ways the institution provides help to the man. The authority which adheres to precedent and practice has worked to convert the achievement and advance of "strong" Presidents into an enduring legacy for their less gifted successors. Responsibility, we are told, is a great developer of men. The Presidency, with its superabundance of responsibilities, has prompted unexpected growth in more than one incumbent. Polk and Lincoln, to take two notable examples, grew strikingly in stature after brief exposure to the trials and tribulations of office.

CHANGES IN THE INSTITUTION

Like all institutions, the Presidency undergoes growth and change. The electoral college, after brief importance, becomes perfunctory. The Cabinet is a body of fluctuating fortunes. So extensive, however, are the institutional changes in the Presidency that we properly speak of the "modern Presidency" as dating from the era of Theodore Roosevelt.

Of the many elements of our latter-day Presidency, at least several are particularly important. One is the rise of a substantial Presidential staff. This can be traced from the creation of the Bureau of the Budget in 1921, through expansions of the White House staff from the era of F.D.R. on. The years since World War II have seen the rise of such agencies as the National Security Council, the Council of Economic Advisers, the National Security Resources Board (succeeded by the Office of Defense Mobilization). The Truman and Eisenhower administrations have also experienced a certain resurgence of the Cabinet. Approximately 1,200 people staff these agencies, some of them personal and political appointees, most of them career civil servants. They exist solely to serve the President, to see that he is adequately and currently informed, to assist him in foreseeing problems and planning future programs, and to ensure that matters for his decision reach his desk promptly and in condition to be settled intelligently and without delay.

Accompanying this growth of staff has been the establishment of certain more or less stated occasions on which the President is expected to present proposals of policy and programs to Congress. The chief of these are the Budget Message and document, the Economic

Report, and the special messages to Congress. The latter type of message has been used extensively by modern Presidents to supplement the more general State of the Union message by setting forth the President's plan for individual fields of policy.

STAFF ACHIEVEMENT AND PROMISE

It is generally agreed that the President's staff has played a central part in the Truman and Eisenhower administrations. Anthony Leviero of the *New York Times,* in the course of the Truman administration, observed that never before had a President relied so much upon collective advice in making his decisions. Leviero was referring particularly to the role of the National Security Council, the Council of Economic Advisers, and the White House staff. Nor is the staff to be forgotten in Sir Winston Churchill's comment crediting President Truman "with great and valiant decisions which make us, I think, all feel better today than we did two or three years ago." In the Eisenhower administration, the staff has played an even greater part, owing to the willingness of the President to delegate large amounts of authority. Something of the ability of the staff to sustain the Presidency was demonstrated in the smooth functioning of the executive branch during President Eisenhower's illness.

In both the Truman and Eisenhower administrations, the Budget Message, the Economic Report, and other messages have been extensively used as sources of policy proposals. The staff has processed great numbers of Executive orders, policy statements, executive-originated legislative proposals, and comment on proposed legislation. One of the chief uses of these several activities is the opportunity they afford the departments to set systematically before the President extended proposals of policy. This is to say, then, that the inaction of a Buchanan or of a Coolidge would nowadays be challenged by a variety of staff sources, that the President would be expected to come forward with policy on a considerable number of more or less stated occasions, and that, therefore, it would be far more difficult for a present-day Calvin Coolidge to count apples and serenely wear out his rocking chair while the country raced into economic doom.

Staffs, of course, are far from perfect. They can balk, dawdle, fall into excessive routine, and commit a hundred other sins. They ought to be studied and improved at every opportunity. Perhaps they will be if we are as alert to the burdens of the staff as we are to the burdens of the President.

42 · THE PRIME MINISTER *

Sir Ivor Jennings

THE OFFICE

The office of Prime Minister, like most superior offices, depends very much on what the holder makes of it, though it also depends on tradition and convention. The name itself is French, *premier ministre,* and, like many names in English politics, it was at first a term of abuse. Sir Robert Walpole, who held the office of First Lord of the Treasury from 1721 to 1742, denied the title; and in 1741 the Lords protested against the development of the office. It was, however, a necessary development. George I rarely attended Cabinet meetings not only because of his ignorance of English but also because of his ignorance of English affairs. One of the Ministers necessarily took his place. The effect of his absence must not, however, be exaggerated. Cabinet government had not yet been established and Walpole rarely summoned a full Cabinet because he preferred to work with a few influential Ministers. Walpole's authority depended less on his office than on his personality. George I decided to rely on the Whigs because they could be regarded as wedded to and in fact dependent upon the Hanoverian succession. Walpole was not, in the modern sense, leader of the Whigs, but he was the most influential of them. Even so, his position depended on the King's favor. He needed a majority in Parliament, as his defeat in 1742 and subsequent resignation showed, but in some measure he owed that majority to the King's support. He advised the King on the expenditure of his Civil List and controlled most of the royal patronage. Nor must it be forgotten that, since the King governed, it was unpatriotic to oppose the King's Government. Many might complain that the King chose bad advisers, or that his advisers gave bad advice, but many others would support the Government because they thought it proper to support the King.

Even so, the authority of Parliament increased during Walpole's long hegemony. George III held back the development for twenty years, but when Lord North was defeated in 1782 through the loss

---

* Sir Ivor Jennings, *The Queen's Government* (Harmondsworth, Middlesex: Penguin Books Ltd., 1957), pp. 132-140. Reprinted by permission of Penguin Books Ltd.

of the American colonies Parliament began to take control. It is significant that the attack was directed mainly against corruption and patronage. William Pitt won the election in 1783 because of the King's support, but thereafter the Prime Minister depended more on Parliament than on the King. He could still rely on "the King's friends" who would support the King's Minister whoever he might be, but more and more he became a party leader whose strength lay in the support of his party. After 1832 "influence" declined in elections because of the extension of the franchise and the disfranchisement of the smaller boroughs. Electors began to vote for parties and not for the nominees of patrons. Sir Robert Peel's manifesto to the electors of Tamworth in 1834 was in effect an appeal to the people to elect his "friends." The party label became one of the most valuable electioneering devices. Organizations were established to secure the registration of party voters and were converted into propaganda machines.

All these developments enhanced the prestige of the party leader, who was for all practical purposes a potential Prime Minister. The conflict between Gladstone and Disraeli, which began with the death of Palmerston in 1865 and ended with Disraeli's death in 1881, added to the power of the office. The party conflict was in large measure a personal conflict. The issue was not only whether the Conservatives or the Liberals should govern Britain but also whether Disraeli or Gladstone should be Prime Minister. The effect of the personal appeal varies according to the personality of the leader. The Labour Party has tended to personify the Party with a capital P and to place less emphasis on the leader. The Conservatives rely heavily on the leader, though less on Baldwin than on Churchill. Also, the leader may become a liability, like Lloyd George in 1922.

We have seen that the Queen's most important function is to choose a Prime Minister. Usually, she has no real choice. If a party wins the election its leader must become Prime Minister. Nor has she necessarily much of a choice when a Prime Minister dies or retires while his party retains a majority. Even if formally there is no second-in-command, one of the Ministers usually obtains pre-eminence, is "groomed" for the post over several years, and steps almost as of right into the post, like Neville Chamberlain in 1937. Even when there is a real choice, as in 1923 (resignation of Bonar Law) or in 1940 (resignation of Neville Chamberlain), it is narrowly limited by political exigencies. The Prime Minister is not merely the Queen's first Minister, nor only the head of the Government, but also a party leader, and the Queen must give the party a leader which it is prepared to follow. This will be apparent from a consideration of the Prime Minister's functions.

FUNCTIONS

The Prime Minister is, in the first place, the Queen's private adviser. Though the Queen no longer takes part in politics, she must still be consulted and she may still advise and warn. Her relations with the Prime Minister are therefore close. She keeps in touch with public affairs and requires explanation when matters seem to her to be going wrong. There are times when the prestige of her position may enable her to help. When it was thought wise to make an *entente* with France, Edward VII went to Paris so that his personal popularity might be used to develop a favorable public opinion. In 1921 George V was advised to initiate the movement which led to the settlement of the Irish problem. In 1940 and 1941 George VI made visits to bombed areas in order to maintain morale. The visits which the monarch makes to other parts of the Commonwealth (and the Queen herself was in East Africa when her father died) help to maintain close relations. These are outstanding examples, but it is essential to remember that the Queen is always part of the Government and that her actions are of the greatest importance in maintaining the unity which is characteristic of the British peoples. Disraeli had the imagination to realize the harm caused by Queen Victoria's withdrawal from public functions after the death of the Prince Consort in 1861, and gradually he reversed the tradition. The State opening of the Parliament, the Trooping of the Colour, the celebration of the Queen's Birthday, the launching of ships, the visits to industrial towns, the inspection of the armed forces, the patronage of worthy causes, the celebration of coronations and jubilees, and generally the Queen's social functions, are all part of the process of government on whose performance the Queen needs advice. Even her private life may be a matter of public importance, as Edward VIII showed. In the matter of that king's proposed marriage to the present Duchess of Windsor the Prime Minister's advice was decisive.

The existence of the monarchy generally enables us to avoid the problem which republics have always to face, that there are times when a party politician has to speak for the nation. If the national sentiment has to be expressed it is usually possible to advise the

Queen to express it. Coming from her, it carries no political implications when, if it came from one who was or had been a party politician, an element of controversy could not be kept out. Even so, there are times when functions of this kind have to be exercised by the Prime Minister. One example will suffice. Recently the University of Glasgow celebrated its five hundredth anniversary. At a dinner given by the University to the representatives of other universities, Commonwealth and foreign, the Prime Minister, Mr. Attlee, was the principal speaker. His speech was carefully phrased to avoid partisanship; and when he left early to catch the night mail to London, the whole audience, among whom probably four-fifths of those who had votes in the United Kingdom would quite cheerfully have voted him out of office, spontaneously rose to its feet. He was not merely a Labour Prime Minister: he was Prime Minister, the representative of the people of Britain. In the House of Commons, too, he is sometimes the representative of Britain when he rises to move a vote of congratulations or condolence.

The Prime Minister is essentially a party leader. Formally his position may differ according to his party. A Conservative Prime Minister is elected by and technically removable by a body consisting of the Parliamentary Party (all the Conservative Lords and Members), the adopted candidates, and the National Union of Conservative Associations: but the election is always unanimous and a motion to remove him from office would be evidence of such a serious division of opinion in the party that it would be moved only in the most extreme case. He is virtually in control of the Conservative Central Office, the central organization of the party. A Labour Prime Minister has, formally, no such strong position. He is merely leader of the Parliamentary Labour Party and *ex officio* a member of the National Executive Committee of the Labour Party. The difference is not very great in practice, for the essential function of a Prime Minister is to keep his party behind him. Even a Conservative Prime Minister, like Baldwin, may have to battle with dissident elements, while a Labour Prime Minister has always a left wing which wants to go somewhere more quickly, though it is not always sure where it wants to go. What the party has to do is to win the next general election, and on this subject opinions may differ. What is certain is that if the party splits it will lose the election. In the opinion of Disraeli, Peel's greatest defect was that he split his party in 1846, and so condemned it to long years of opposition. Gladstone split the Liberal Party in 1885 and (though he became Prime Minister again in 1892) the Liberals never had real power again until 1906. Lloyd George split the Liberal Party in 1916 and it never again obtained office. Ramsay MacDonald in 1931 condemned the Labour Party to fifteen years of opposition. The management of the party majority, both in Parliament and in the country, is therefore a fundamental task, to which he must direct much of his energy.

The problem in Parliament is different from the problem outside. In Parliament are a few hundred party members, of whom a hundred are members of the Government. Being politicians, they think highly of themselves, and, being peers and members, they have some reason for doing so. The new member, who roared like a lion in his constituency, tends to feel isolated in Parliament. Nobody bothers about him unless he makes himself a nuisance: he is expected to vote frequently and to speak rarely. The Government Whips look after him, and the Prime Minister controls the Whips. A Prime Minister like Churchill, who can joke with anybody, has a great advantage over a Prime Minister like Neville Chamberlain, who had consciously to unbend. Outside Parliament, the Prime Minister is less a person than a personality. Unless members of the Royal Family are present he is top of the bill. He is in fact much like a film star though, not being employed by a profit-making company, he has no publicity manager to see that he hits the headlines. Even so, he must if possible build himself a reputation. His hair style, his pipe, his cigar, even his umbrella or his bald head, may help. On the other hand, the management of the party cannot be carried out by theatrical gestures. It involves careful attention to the shifts of opinion, an almost intuitive understanding of the ordinary man's ways of thought, a capacity to tread warily through the web of intrigue which ambitious politicians weave about them, and in short a truly remarkable capacity for judgment. Of all recent Prime Ministers, Baldwin was perhaps the most successful in this sphere because he was wily as a party manager and yet appeared in public as the simple rustic: he combined the wisdom of the serpent with the innocence of the dove.

Next, the Prime Minister is chairman of the Cabinet. He must pick a team and keep it as a team. A team of politicians is probably the most difficult to handle because, though each of them knows that his political future depends on the success of the team, there will usually be a few who are anxious to become captain. It is never very easy to draw the line between personal ambition and anxiety for the public weal. Some would place Joseph Chamberlain among the political prophets; others would regard him as an ambitious politician who twice took the wrong turning. Whatever the explanation may be, he was an uncomfortable colleague even for a Gladstone or a Balfour. His contemporary, Sir William Harcourt, was almost as difficult. More recently there have been other examples —Lloyd George, Churchill (in Baldwin's Government), Cripps (before the war) and Aneurin Bevan. Even when the Cabinet contains no obstreperous member, it is not easy to secure rapid agreement on a wide variety of controversial issues. Public opinion helps, but it never quite knows where it is going, and Cabinets must frequently take unpopular decisions because the consequences of any other decisions would be even more unpopular.

Examples occur almost weekly. Frequently the choice lies between bad alternatives, the one preferred by one section of the Cabinet, the other by the other section. The Prime Minister may try to force his own opinion on the Cabinet, as Gladstone almost always did, and thereby run the risk of splitting the party. He may seek to persuade a minority or convince a majority. He may try to temporize, as Balfour had to do over Tariff Reform. He may compromise, like Aberdeen in 1856—though that is not a happy precedent, for the compromise led to the Crimean War which history now pronounces to be foolish. He may feel it necessary to give way to the majority even when he does not agree. The management of the Cabinet is certainly the Prime Minister's most difficult function, because it compels him to take difficult decisions not only on the substance but also on the tactics.

The Prime Minister is not, however, concerned only with Cabinet questions. He must keep an eye on what goes on in the Departments. Sir Robert Peel, who is regarded by many as the model Prime Minister in this respect—since he split his party in 1846 he can hardly be regarded as the model in all respects—knew everything of importance that was under discussion by his Ministers and intervened when he considered it necessary. Such close attention is no longer possible now that the functions of government have expanded so widely, but since any Ministerial decision may cause political controversy, the Prime Minister must at least keep one ear open. Usually, though, he exercises supervision through the eagerness of Ministers to consult him. His success depends upon his ability to give sound advice almost on the spur of the moment. With the Foreign Secretary he is in the closest contact, for foreign affairs are always on the agenda. His physical proximity to the Chancellor of the Exchequer—who lives next door in 11 Downing Street—permits of regular consultation. For the rest, his door must ever be open, his mind clear and his judgment rapid and efficient. If he is intellectually lazy like Baldwin or difficult of approach like MacDonald, he cannot exercise these functions properly.

Next, there is the function of managing the House of Commons. This is not quite the same as that of managing the party majority, for the House has a life and a tradition of its own. What is more, the relationship with the party is established in private, whereas the House has to be managed in public. The specific function of arranging the business of the House is nowadays generally left to another Minister, perhaps the Lord Privy Seal or the Lord President of the Council, who is given appointment as Leader of the House: but this delegation cannot deprive the Prime Minister of his function as leader of the Government. The problem is not that the Government runs the risk of defeat—for unless the party breaks up, or has no majority, or has a very small majority, the Government cannot be defeated—but that it runs the risk of being worsted in the argument. The House is "the finest platform in Europe," the only debating society in Britain whose debates are read, or at least glanced at, by millions. If a Government is to keep its majority in the country, it must consistently make a good case. It may win at every division but lose the next election. Moreover, the House is a temperamental body: it reacts forcibly to any neglect and soon causes its displeasure to be known. The Prime Minister ought therefore to be what is called "a good House of Commons man," a man who observes its traditions and knows how to handle it, a man like Baldwin or Churchill.

This by no means exhausts the list of functions. The Prime Minister advises the appointment of bishops in consultation with the Archbishop of Canterbury, the superior judges in consultation with the Lord Chancellor, Permanent Secretaries in consultation with the Permanent Secretary to the Treasury, etc. He advises the conferment of honors in the Prime Minister's list, those conferred "for political and public purposes." Continually, too, there is the problem of his own Ministry. Its composition is not fixed when he first compiles the list. Some holders of offices will succeed and some will fail;

some would do better in different offices; from time to time there will be vacancies due to death or resignation. The recent tendency, begun by Churchill and continued by Attlee, has been to make changes more frequently.

Though it has been necessary to list those functions under different headings, they nearly all hang together. All roads in the Constitution lead to the Prime Minister. From the Prime Minister lead the roads to the Queen, Parliament, the Ministries, the other members of the Commonwealth, even the Church of England and the Courts of Law. Among his colleagues he is said to be *primus inter pares,* first among equals, but it is doubtful if this has been true at any time since Gladstone became Prime Minister in 1868. Harcourt said that he was a moon among lesser stars, but the lesser stars—as they seem to the naked eye—have no connection with the moon: and the Prime Minister is much more like the sun among the planets.

It is obvious that no Prime Minister will exercise all his functions equally well, for they demand qualities too varied in type. Oddly enough, though, there are very few failures, for success in the House of Commons is usually a guarantee of success as Prime Minister. The great exception of the present century, Ramsay MacDonald, had made his mark on the platform, not in Parliament, and he had had no previous Ministerial experience before he became Prime Minister in 1924. He never learned to handle either the House or his colleagues. On the other hand, Baldwin, an obscure back-bencher until Bonar Law made him Chancellor of the Exchequer in 1922, was superb as a tactician, though too careless to control his team. Neville Chamberlain had little opportunity to show his skill, for he became involved in the preliminaries of the war and foreign affairs were not his *métier*. War administration requires qualities of a very different type, those of a Lloyd George or a Churchill.

43 · THE RUSSIAN EXECUTIVE

A · WHAT HAPPENED TO "COLLECTIVE LEADERSHIP"? *

MERLE FAINSOD

On April 19, 1959, two days after Khrushchev's sixty-fifth birthday, the Soviet press erupted in a rash of congratulatory tributes, the tenor of which evoked vivid memories of the Stalinist "cult of personality" condemned only a few years ago. Of the many messages which were printed, the most important came from Khrushchev's fellow members of the party Presidium, who saluted his career as a "model" and "example" of "devoted service" and referred to him deferentially as "senior comrade and friend, true disciple of Lenin, and outstanding leader of the Communist Party, the Soviet state, and the entire international Communist and workers' movement." While the reasons for the press delay in celebrating Khrushchev's birthday remain somewhat mysterious, the contents of the congratulatory messages came as no surprise. They had been foreshadowed by an outpouring of lavish tributes at the 21st Party Congress in the course of which delegate after delegate joined in praising Khrushchev's "Leninist firmness," "profound practical knowledge," "fatherly solicitude" and "tireless energy," as well as his "brilliant, comprehensive, and profound report."

At the 20th Party Congress Khrushchev had denounced Stalin's craving for flattery and his insistence on presenting himself as a superman who "knows everything, sees everything," and "can do anything . . ."; at the subsequent party gathering Khrushchev interposed no objections as one speaker after another offered effusive thanks for the personal guidance and initiative which Khrushchev had supplied in every sector of Soviet life from foreign policy and the development of guided missiles to cotton-growing in Tadjikistan. If these genuflections still represented a far cry from the heights of glorification witnessed during the Stalin cult, they left little doubt that Khrushchev had reached the summit of the Soviet power struc-

* Merle Fainsod, "What Happened to 'Collective Leadership'?" *Problems of Communism,* VIII (July-August, 1959), 1-10. Reprinted by permission of *Problems of Communism.* The footnotes in the original version are omitted here.

ture and that his position of undisputed leadership was universally acknowledged.

The image of Khrushchev's personal leadership which emerged from the 21st Congress was obviously modeled on that of Lenin. As Khrushchev himself put it in his secret speech to the previous congress:

> Lenin resolutely stood against every attempt aimed at belittling or weakening the directing role of the party in the structure of the Soviet state. . . . He tried to convince; he patiently explained his opinion to others. Lenin always diligently insisted that . . . the party statute be enforced, that the party congresses and the plenary sessions of the Central Committee take place at the proper intervals. . . .

Taking his cue from these precepts, Khrushchev sought to project himself as the true custodian of the Leninist tradition—a leader who maintains his contact with the masses, who embodies his authority in the party and its Central Committee, and who insists on rigorous observance of the Leninist norms of party life. It is in this sense, and perhaps in this sense only, that it was still possible for delegates to the 21st Congress to refer to collective leadership at all.

If by collective leadership is meant an equal sharing of authority by all members of the party Presidium, then collective leadership must clearly be regarded as a thing of the past. The proceedings of the last Congress provide unmistakable evidence that Khrushchev now towers high above all his associates. While future events may demonstrate that his position is not impregnable, the possibility that he will soon be dislodged by another cabal in the party Presidium seems remote indeed. The levers of power in the Soviet system appear to be firmly in his hands, and the charismatic qualities of popular leadership which he has displayed contribute to give his authority a secure base. At the present time it is difficult to discern the direction from which a challenge to his supremacy might arise.

Disorder and Forgotten Sorrow

What happened to collective leadership? A retrospective analysis of the struggle for the succession may help to shed light on the problems of collective rule. When Stalin died, no single member of the Presidium loomed as the clearly anointed heir with an unquestioned title to supreme power. In the first few days after Stalin's entombment, there were some signs that Malenkov aspired to Stalin's role. But the *Pravda* announcement on March 21, 1953, that Malenkov had been "released" from his duties as party Secretary "at his own request" seemed to indicate that his colleagues in the Presidium were making a determined and successful effort to dilute his power. At the same time the delicate problems attendant on the transition and the need to consolidate the authority of the new regime compelled the new rulers to submerge their differences in the interest of presenting a united front to the nation and to the world. In these circumstances, collective leadership emerged as the natural formula to describe the divided and uncertain distribution of power.

Its long-term stability was in question from the start. Collective rule may attain a degree of solidity when those who share power are bound together by common dangers, interests, and purposes which outweigh their individual interests, where no one of the group possesses the ability, ambition, or will to stake out a claim to supremacy, and where power is so dispersed within the group as to make it dangerous for any member to try to dominate the rest. On the other hand, the stability of collective leadership is obviously endangered when deep policy differences begin to divide the group and one or more members strike out for the additional increments of power which make them a real threat to their colleagues.

The legacy which Stalin bequeathed to his successors did not easily adapt itself to collective rule. In the absence of the Supreme Despot, power was precariously apportioned and distributed with no point of coordination short of the Presidium itself. Malenkov, as Chairman of the Council of Ministers, rested his authority on command of the administrative apparatus and on such informal connections as he retained in the party organization itself. Beria, as head of the MVD, had a formidable weapon in his hands. Molotov, as Foreign Minister and Old Bolshevik, enjoyed the prestige of an elder statesman, but lacked an organizational power base. Khrushchev, who succeeded Malenkov as senior party Secretary, identified his authority with that of the party functionaries, but in the first months of the new regime, he remained largely in the background. Bulganin as Defense Minister supervised the armed forces, but the degree of personal control which he exercised over them was unclear. With Stalin gone, the interrelationship of these plural power centers was, to say the least, ambiguous. Since party, police, and administrative controls overlapped and penetrated each other, it was difficult to envisage how a clash of wills and interests could be avoided.

Moves and Countermoves

The possibility of conflict was magnified by the issues which the collective leadership confronted. Should the Soviet ship of state continue to be steered on a Stalinist course, or should new departures in policy be ventured? Should the new regime strive for a detente in its relations with the outside world, and if so, on what terms and conditions? Should large-scale concessions be made to the desire of the populace for more consumer goods, or should heavy industry and armaments continue to enjoy top priority in planning future economic developments? With power dispersed in the ruling groups and ambitions unleashed, a complete harmony of outlook on questions such as these could hardly be anticipated. In a political system where opposition is outlawed, policy conflicts ordinarily lead to the suppression or elimination of one or another of the antagonistic forces. This deeply-rooted party practice augured ill for the stability of collective leadership.

The first challenge came from Beria. The very existence of a powerful secret police controlled by one member of the oligarchy posed a constant threat to his colleagues, and their fears were doubtless reinforced by the uses to which the secret police had been put in past party struggles. Even though the charge that Beria endeavored to use his subordinates in the police hierarchy to gain control of the party and administrative apparatus cannot be fully documented, the remark attributed to Khrushchev (by the French socialist Senator Pierre Commin) that Beria "was clearly preparing a conspiracy against the Presidium" has a ring of authenticity. It expressed the underlying concern which ultimately resulted in Beria's liquidation.

While the arrest of Beria in July 1953 eliminated one of the chief contenders for supremacy, it left the problem of control of the police still to be resolved. The appointment of Kruglov, a professional police officer, as head of the MVD and the strengthening of party controls over the police at all levels served both to downgrade the police and to neutralize its role in the power struggle. The decision in the spring of 1954 to transfer the political police from MVD jurisdiction to a newly organized Committee on State Security (KGB) under Colonel-General Serov marked another phase in the dilution of police power. By the same token these actions also served to underline the residual importance of control of the armed forces.

The designation of Khrushchev as First Secretary in September

1953 set the stage for his bid for supreme power. After Lenin's death Stalin had used his position as General Secretary to consolidate his control of the party apparatus and to extend his authority into other spheres. Khrushchev's associates in the Presidium undoubtedly were aware of the precedent, and one must conclude that they either underestimated Khrushchev or displayed excessive confidence in their capacity to contain such ambitions as he cherished. The series of moves which he initiated, beginning in the fall of 1953, to install his henchmen in leading party posts in Moscow, Leningrad, and other key areas could hardly fail to arouse concern among his colleagues in the Presidium; one can only surmise that at this juncture some of them, at least, saw an even greater danger in the ambitions and programs of Malenkov.

Malenkov vs. *Khrushchev*

The search for an explanation of the alignments of the early post-Stalinist period cannot be limited to moves on the chessboard of power. Important policy differences divided the ruling group, and while they are only faintly illumined by Soviet press comment, they are visible enough so that patterns can be discerned. During this period Malenkov and Khrushchev emerged as the major antagonists. In the area of foreign affairs Malenkov saw nuclear war as spelling "the destruction of world civilization," developed a thesis of peace based on mutual deterrence which minimized the danger of war, and called for improvement in relations with the United States through a process of patient negotiations. Khrushchev took a harder line. Speaking before the 10th Congress of the Czech Communist Party on June 12, 1954, he hailed a nuclear war as inevitably leading to a collapse of capitalism rather than of "world civilization." He accused reactionary capitalist circles of seeking a way out of their difficulties "by the preparation of a new war" and stressed the aggressive intentions of the imperialist camp. Similar views were expressed in a series of speeches delivered by Molotov, Kaganovich, Voroshilov, and Bulganin.

Malenkov's optimistic outlook on the prospects for peace found its reflection on the domestic scene in his identification with the consumer goods program. Here again it was Khrushchev who took the "hard" line. In calling for a reassertion of the priority of heavy industry and armaments, he drew on the support of the armed forces as well as on those members of the Presidium who shared his world outlook. The alignment on such new agricultural programs as the opening of the virgin lands was somewhat different. Here it was Khrushchev who was the innovator, while, if later testimony is to be credited, Malenkov was joined by Molotov and Kaganovich in conservative opposition.

These cross-currents suggest the danger of viewing the struggle for the succession as merely a series of maneuvers for power and place. Coalitions were cemented by principle as well as by calculations of advantage and fear. The opposition to the Malenkov program provided a powerful rallying point which reinforced the position of Khrushchev. The erosion of Malenkov's strength can be traced at least from the spring of 1954. In a speech on April 26, 1954, which represented a complete concession to the views of his opponents, he declared that a third world war "would inevitably lead to the collapse of the capitalist social system." It was not without significance that this speech of the Chairman of the Council of Ministers was addressed to the Council of Nationalities of the Supreme Soviet, while the greater honor of addressing the Council of the Union was reserved for Khrushchev.

Meanwhile, the battle over the priority of heavy industry *vs.* consumer goods continued to be fought. The conflict came into sharp focus with the appearance of a curious pair of editorials on December 21, 1954. *Izvestia,* the presumed organ of Malenkov, called for the increased production of consumers' goods; *Pravda,* the organ of Khrushchev, summoned "the Soviet people to direct their main attention to fulfilling plans for the further growth of heavy industry." The issue between Khrushchev and Malenkov came to a head at the meeting of the Central Committee in late January 1955. The published version of Khrushchev's speech to a plenary session on January 25, 1955, named no names, but its intent was unmistakable. Said Khrushchev:

> In connection with the measures lately taken for increasing output of consumers' goods, some comrades have confused the question of the pace of development of heavy and light industry in our country. . . . These pseudo-theoreticians try to claim that at some state of socialist construction the development of heavy industry ceases to be the main task and that light industry can and should overtake all other branches of industry. This is profoundly incorrect reasoning, alien to the spirit of Marxism–Leninism—nothing but slander to our party. This is a belching of the rightist deviation, a regurgitation of views hostile to Leninism, views which Rykov, Bukharin, and their ilk once preached.

The denouncement was not long in coming. On February 8, 1955, Malenkov "resigned" as chairman of the Council of Ministers, after signing a letter acknowledging his administrative "inexperience" and his past "guilt and responsibility for the unsatisfactory state of affairs in agriculture."

By previous standards, his punishment was mild indeed. Although demoted to the positions of Minister of Power Stations and Deputy Chairman of the Council of Ministers, he remained on the party Presidium.

The Shrinking Collective

The demotion of Malenkov opened the way to a reconstruction of the top leadership. Bulganin replaced Malenkov as Chairman of the Council of Ministers and at the same time yielded his post as Minister of Defense to Marshal Zhukov. Khrushchev remained First Secretary. Five Presidium members, Molotov, Kaganovich, Mikoyan, Saburov, and Pervukhin, served as First Deputy Chairmen of the Council of Ministers. Voroshilov, the senior member of the Presidium group, continued to discharge the protocol functions of head of state. At the July 1955 session of the Central Committee two new Presidium members were elected, A. I. Kirichenko, First Secretary of the Ukrainian Party, and M. A. Suslov, the senior Central Committee secretary after Khrushchev.

At this same session of the Central Committee, Molotov was marked out as the next candidate for demotion and disgrace. As was subsequently revealed, the chief subject of discussion at this meeting—which came soon after the "B&K" state visit to Belgrade—was the question of policy toward Tito. Khrushchev favored reconciliation and an attempt to recapture Tito for the Soviet cause; Molotov opposed concessions to Tito as unnecessary and dangerous. But Molotov's views found little support in the Central Committee, and from that point on, his influence sharply declined. The party theoretical journal, *Kommunist,* in its issue of September 1955, administered an added blow to his prestige as an Old Bolshevik when it published a strange letter of recantation signed by Molotov. In it he acknowledged that in a speech delivered some seven months earlier he had committed a major ideological error by describing the Soviet Union as only having constructed "the foundations of a socialist society" instead of adhering to the orthodox formula that the Soviet Union had achieved socialism and was now building communism. A further sharp rebuff followed in June 1956 when Molotov was replaced as Foreign Minister by D. T. Shepilov.

Meanwhile, Kaganovich was undergoing a similar process of downgrading. In March 1955 his authority in the industrial sphere was reduced when Mikoyan, Pervukhin, and Saburov joined him as First Deputy Chairmen of the Council of Ministers. His appointment as Chairman of the State Committee on Labor and Wage Problems in May 1955 was terminated in June of the next year, and in September 1956 he was transferred to the still lower post of USSR Minister of the Construction Materials Industry. Despite these humiliations, which were shared with Molotov and Malenkov, all three remained members of the party Presidium, where, it can reasonably be assumed, they continued to harbor their grievances and thoughts of revenge.

The Hard Climb to the Summit

The maneuverings which attended the 20th Party Congress marked a further stage in the development of the intra-Presidium struggle. The attack on Stalin and "the cult of personality," which was first launched by Mikoyan and then documented in detail in Khrushchev's secret speech, was interpreted at the time as an effort to bar the way to the emergence of another Stalin. Yet if we assume, as in the light of later events we must, that Khrushchev was determined to consolidate his authority, his secret speech can also be read as an effort to discredit his major opponents in the Presidium. In the process of attacking Stalin, he made a studied effort to dissociate himself from responsibility for Stalin's excesses, and to single out others—particularly Malenkov, Molotov, and Kaganovich—as having been tarred with the brush of their master's misdeeds. Conversely, he attempted to demonstrate—though somewhat lamely—that he and Bulganin had opposed Stalin's methods and policies. Despite the fact that Khrushchev had served as one of Stalin's proconsuls during the Great Purge, first in the Moscow party organization and after January 1938 in the Ukraine, he insisted that he had nothing to do with the purge, that it was engineered by Stalin and Yezhov, and that they alone were responsible for the liquidation of Postyshev, Kossior and other prominent party figures in the Ukraine whom Khrushchev both succeeded and, at the time, denounced. Even though the explanations were labored, their intent was unmistakable. Khrushchev was seeking to demonstrate that the party had nothing to fear from him, while it had a great deal indeed to fear from those who had been more intimately involved in Stalin's crimes.

Meanwhile, Khrushchev also moved to use his powers as First Secretary to extend his influence in the leading organs of the party. More than a third of the Central Committee members—53 out of 133 —and more than half of the candidate members of the Central Committee—76 out of 122—were newly elected at the 20th Congress, and in numerous instances their elevation in the party apparatus was directly traceable to earlier associations with Khrushchev. Five additions were made to the alternate membership list of the Presidium— Marshal Zhukov; Brezhnev, First Secretary of the Kazakhstan party organization; Mukhitdinov, the Uzbek First Secretary; Furtseva, head of the Moscow party organization; and Shepilov, editor of *Pravda*. All of them appeared to owe their appointments to Khrushchev, although both Marshal Zhukov and Shepilov were later to break with him. Khrushchev strengthened his hold over the Central Committee Secretariat through the appointments of Brezhnev, Furtseva, and Shepilov as party secretaries. In addition, a special Russian Republic Bureau of the Central Committee was established with Khrushchev as Chairman; of its ten members at least nine could plausibly be identified as part of Khrushchev's entourage.

The 20th Congress was followed by a series of blows directed at the Stalinist Old Guard. On June 2, 1956, Shepilov replaced Molotov as Minister of Foreign Affairs, and Molotov was moved to the lesser post of Minister of State Control. Soon thereafter, Kaganovich was demoted. By mid-1956 Khrushchev appeared to be riding high with no competitor on the horizon to offer a serious challenge.

But appearances were deceptive. The shock of Khrushchev's revelations at the 20th Congress opened up a Pandora's box of wholly unintended consequences. The Hungarian uprising in October and the political overturn in Poland threatened the Soviet satellite system with disintegration. All this gave powerful ammunition to Khrushchev's Presidium opponents who could now argue that Khrushchev's policies at the 20th Congress had placed the entire Soviet bloc in jeopardy.

During this period evidence accumulated that Khrushchev was in trouble. The delegation which was hastily dispatched to Warsaw on October 19 to discuss "topical problems" with the Polish Politburo included Molotov and Kaganovich, as well as Khrushchev and Mikoyan—a juxtaposition which seemed to point to a new correlation of forces in the Presidium. The break with Tito which followed the Hungarian events served to discredit Khrushchev's policy of reconciliation. Increasing difficulties on the industrial front, which were complicated by the need to buttress the shaky satellite economies, contributed to undermine Khrushchev's leadership. Significantly, at the Central Committee session in December 1956, which revised the industrial targets downward and sought to tighten the planning machinery, Khrushchev did not even deliver an address. The main speeches were made by Bulganin, Saburov, and Baibakov. At this session the Central Committee greatly broadened the powers of the State Economic Commission, which was charged with current planning. Pervukhin was designated chairman of the Commission and became something of an "overlord of overlords," exercising primary responsibility for the operation of the national economy. The effect of this move was to strengthen the authority of elements in the Presidium identified with the state, rather than the party machine. The scheme was approved by the Supreme Soviet on February 12, 1957.

The very next day Khrushchev launched a counterattack. Appearing before a specially summoned session of the Central Committee, he offered a plan which was designed to emasculate the Economic Commission, to strengthen the role of Gosplan as the supreme planning authority, to abolish a number of central ministries, and to devolve many of their operational responsibilities on new regional economic councils, or *sovnarkhozy*. The plan which Khrushchev espoused was clearly calculated to weaken the power of his ministerial competitors, to enlist support from local and regional managerial personnel, and to leave the field free for the party apparatus to become the primary integrating and centralizing force. This bold move by Khrushchev to consolidate his authority served to bring matters to a head.

Open Conflict

The question may well be raised why Khrushchev was prepared to throw down the gage to his opponents in February when he was not willing to do so in December. While the answer must be speculative, certain considerations appear to be relevant. By February, far more than in December, the unrest in the satellite empire appeared to be under firm restraint and less of a threatening factor. The bountiful harvest in the virgin lands provided a vindication of Khrushchev's agricultural program and strengthened his position. And perhaps most important of all, Khrushchev's readiness to act indicated that he counted on the program which he had devised to rally the party apparatus to his banner.

From this point on Khrushchev moved swiftly to consolidate his position. A law approved by the Supreme Soviet on May 10, 1957, established the regional economic councils, abolished the State Economic Commission and made Gosplan the dominant economic planning agency. By a decree of the Presidium of the Supreme Soviet a week earlier, I. I. Kuzmin, one of Khrushchev's subordinates in the Central Committee apparatus, had already been installed as Chairman of Gosplan and First Vice-Chairman of the Council of Ministers.

Meanwhile, Khrushchev's opponents in the Presidium were also gathering their forces. By June Khrushchev found himself in a minority in the Presidium. Malenkov, Molotov, and Kaganovich were joined in opposition by Bulganin and Saburov, making a total of six out of eleven full members of the Presidium; they also enlisted the support of Shepilov, an alternate member of the Presidium. The details of the cabal remain obscure, but judging by the special violence of the attack on Malenkov at the 21st Party Congress in January of this year, it is probable that he was the moving and organizing spirit. Despite previous disagreements with both Molotov and Kaganovich, he was able to find common ground with them in the effort to curb Khrushchev's bid for supremacy. Bulganin, Pervukhin, and Saburov were late comers to the conspiracy. Bulganin, in his speech at the December 1958 plenum of the Central Committee, abjectly confessed to having been not only an "accomplice" of the anti-party group, but as Chairman of the Council of Ministers its "nominal leader as well."

Pervukhin's participation was directly traceable to the dispute over industrial reorganization. As he put it in his speech to the 21st Congress:

> In the Central Committee discussion on the problem of reorganizing the management of industry and construction, I cast doubts on and objected to certain propositions in the suggested reorganization. My incorrect position in this most important matter and the discontent connected with it caused me to commit a gross political mistake; namely that I upheld the attacks of the anti-party group on Comrade Khrushchev at the sessions of the Central Committee Presidium which preceded the plenum in June, and consequently, as I later became aware, also attacks on his stand with regard to several problems of internal and foreign policy.

But he also added that "once the anti-party group openly put forth the question of a change of leadership in the Central Committee, I disagreed and did not support this request." Saburov similarly confessed at the 21st Congress to having manifested "political instability" prior to the June Central Committee meeting. Nevertheless, in a subsequent speech at the Congress Kuzmin took both Pervukhin and Saburov sharply to task for seeking to minimize their parts in the conspiracy, and Pervukhin was singled out as having played a particularly active role, together with Molotov and Shepilov, in resisting Khrushchev's plans for industrial reorganization.

The opposition group's attempts to unseat Khrushchev by confronting him with a hostile majority in the Presidium misfired. Khrushchev refused to resign and took his appeal to a hastily assembled special session of the Central Committee where, according to the official report, he received unanimous support, with only Molotov abstaining. The resolution of the Central Committee, which was published on July 4, centered its fire on Malenkov, Kaganovich, and Molotov, as well as Shepilov "who joined them." That the conspiracy had wider ramifications could be inferred from the fact that Saburov was dropped from the Presidium and that Pervukhin was demoted to alternate membership. In the resolution, the "anti-party group" was accused of having used "factional methods in an attempt to change the composition of the party's leading bodies . . ." and of having disagreed with and fought the party line on a number of issues, including industrial reorganization, agricultural policy and foreign policy. Malenkov, Kaganovich and Molotov were expelled from the Presidium and the Central Committee; Shepilov lost his posts as a Central Committee Secretary, Presidium alternate, and Central Committee member.

From Rout to Triumph

The reconstruction of the membership of the Presidium which followed the June plenum represented a striking triumph for Khrushchev. The Presidium was enlarged to 15 members. Marshal Zhukov was promoted from alternate to full membership, an action which seemed to imply that the Marshal had given full support to Khrushchev in the struggle against the "anti-party" group. The other new members of the Presidium—Furtseva, Aristov, Belyayev, Brezhnev, Ignatov, Kozlov, Kuusinen, and Shvernik—had all been closely associated with Khrushchev in his rise to power and were appropriately rewarded.

The treatment of the conspirators was far less harsh than might have been anticipated. All of them retained their party membership. Molotov was honorably exiled to Outer Mongolia as an ambassador; Malenkov was dispatched to manage an electric power station in Kazakhstan; Kaganovich was sent to the Urals to run a cement plant; and Shepilov was reported as occupying a teaching position somewhere away from Moscow. The other major participants in the conspiracy, who were not publicly identified at the time of the June plenum, suffered a series of retaliatory demotions. Pervukhin, after stepping down to an alternate membership in the Presidium, lost his position as a First Deputy Chairman of the Council of Ministers, became Chairman of the State Committee for Foreign Relations, and was then shifted to East Germany as ambassador. Saburov's disgrace was more complete. After losing his Presidium membership he became a Deputy Chairman of the State Committee for Foreign Economic Relations under Pervukhin, was subsequently moved from that post, and at the 21st Congress was identified merely as a "factory manager in Syzran."

The treatment of Bulganin followed a particularly curious course. After the June plenum he retained both his seat in the Presidium and his position as Chairman of the Council of Ministers. Although his public role as government spokesman declined greatly, he was not replaced as Chairman of the Council of Ministers by Khrushchev until March 27, 1958, remained on the Presidium until September 5, 1958, and was not formally linked with the anti-party group until Khrushchev's speech of November 14, 1958. His consignment to the relatively obscure post of Chairman of the Stavropol Economic Council completed his humiliation.

Meanwhile, Khrushchev also found it necessary to settle accounts with Marshal Zhukov. While it is at least possible that the Marshal had Bonapartist pretensions, it is more likely that the purge of the popular World War II hero was a prophylactic action taken to eliminate a potential rallying point of military discontent. The issue was precipitated by friction between the party's political apparatus in the armed forces and the more professionally-oriented officers who followed Marshal Zhukov in seeking to subordinate political indoctrination to combat training and military control. Even before the 20th Congress the Army newspaper *Krasnaia Zvezda* reported in its issue of January 25, 1956, that Marshal Zhukov—speaking at a party conference of the Moscow military district—had complained:

. . . certain efforts have been made to subject the official activity of commanders to criticism at party meetings. Such efforts are blameworthy. Our task is the comprehensive strengthening of the authority of the commanders, giving support to exacting officers and generals.

This doctrine proved unpalatable to Khrushchev. The Central Committee resolution of October 1957, approving the ouster of Zhukov from his positions as Minister of Defense and member of the Presidium and Central Committee, charged that he had "pursued a policy" of underestimating and curtailing party leadership of the Army and Navy. It reminded the armed forces of the paramount role of the party and called for an intensification of political work in the armed forces. The reorganization of the military high command in the wake of the Zhukov purge also involved the elevation of such Khrushchev protégés as Marshal Konev to top command responsibilities.

The consolidation of Khrushchev's authority was manifest in every sphere of Soviet society. His assumption of the chairmanship of the Council of Ministers in late March 1958 represented merely a formal recognition of the leadership which he already exercised in the area of governmental administration. His own party henchmen were increasingly moved into key control positions. The so-called Ukrainian contingent, who had formed part of Khrushchev's entourage during his long period of service in the Ukraine, forged rapidly ahead under Khrushchev's tutelage. This was also true of assorted functionaries in the Central Committee Secretariat who worked closely with Khrushchev as First Secretary. As early as February 1, 1956, the professional police officer S. N. Kruglov was replaced as MVD chief by N. P. Dudorov, a former Khrushchev associate in the Ukraine and a section chief in the Central Committee Secretariat. On December 26, 1958, *Pravda* announced that A. N. Shelepin, former head of the Komsomol, would succeed General Serov as KGB chairman, and it was not without interest that Shelepin's successor as Komsomol chief for a period was one V. E. Semichatnyi, who had earlier occupied a corresponding post in the Ukraine.

The published proceedings of the December 1958 plenum of the Central Committee provide particularly dramatic evidence of Khrushchev's supremacy. Almost every important speaker at the meeting was interrupted by Khrushchev with questions or comments, and the kowtowing to Khrushchev which took place left no doubt that homage was being paid to the leader. The speeches at the 21st Congress represented variations on the same theme and were sufficiently fulsome in their praise to suggest that Khrushchev was being lifted to a new pedestal.

What then has happened to collective leadership? In an interview with Henry Shapiro, chief Moscow correspondent of the United Press, on November 14, 1957, Khrushchev was asked, "When you speak of the collective leadership, do you mean the Central Committee or its Presidium?" Khrushchev replied:

> I mean the Central Committee of our Party. The Presidium is an executive body of the Central Committee. . . . The collective leadership consists not only of the members of the Central Committee. Collective leadership is exercised in our party from top to bottom. . . .

Those who accept Khrushchev's assurance that collective leadership still prevails in the Soviet Union may point to the undoubted fact that the party Central Committee assembles with considerable frequency and that local party organizations function with greater regularity than was true during the latter part of Stalin's reign. But it may be worth remembering that Stalin at one time was also lavish in his praise of collective leadership and that he too made effective use of the Central Committee in his march to supreme power. Khrushchev's style of governance has its own distinctive characteristics, but the swiftness with which he has moved to consolidate his authority leaves little doubt that he is now, not merely *primus inter pares,* but the new master of the Soviet state.

B · CRIMES OF THE STALIN ERA*

NIKITA S. KHRUSHCHEV

[Special report to the Twentieth Congress of the Communist Party of the Soviet Union; closed session, February 24-25, 1956]

Comrades! In the report of the Central Committee of the party at the 20th Congress, in a number of speeches by delegates to the Congress, as also formerly during the plenary CC/CPSU [Central Committee of the Communist Party of the Soviet Union] sessions, quite a

* Nikita S. Khrushchev, *The Crimes of the Stalin Era* (Annotated by Boris I. Nicolaevsky; New York: The New Leader, 1956), pp. S7-S9, S12-S14, S64-S65. Reprinted by permission of *The New Leader.*

lot has been said about the cult of the individual and about its harmful consequences.

After Stalin's death the Central Committee of the party began to implement a policy of explaining concisely and consistently that it is impermissible and foreign to the spirit of Marxism-Leninism to elevate one person, to transform him into a superman possessing supernatural characteristics, akin to those of a god. Such a man supposedly knows everything, sees everything, thinks for everyone, can do anything, is infallible in his behavior.

Such a belief about a man, and specifically about Stalin, was cultivated among us for many years.

The objective of the present report is not a thorough evaluation of Stalin's life and activity. Concerning Stalin's merits, an entirely sufficient number of books, pamphlets and studies had already been written in his lifetime. The role of Stalin in the preparation and execution of the Socialist Revolution, in the Civil War, and in the fight for the construction of socialism in our country, is universally known. Everyone knows this well.

At present, we are concerned with a question which has immense importance for the party now and for the future—with how the cult of the person of Stalin has been gradually growing, the cult which became at a certain specific stage the source of a whole series of exceedingly serious and grave perversions of party principles, of party democracy, of revolutionary legality.

Because of the fact that not all as yet realize fully the practical consequences resulting from the cult of the individual, the great harm caused by the violation of the principle of collective direction of the party and because of the accumulation of immense and limitless power in the hands of one person, the Central Committee of the party considers it absolutely necessary to make the material pertaining to this matter available to the 20th Congress of the Communist Party of the Soviet Union.

Allow me first of all to remind you how severely the classics of Marxism-Leninism denounced every manifestation of the cult of the individual. In a letter to the German political worker, Wilhelm Bloss, Marx stated: "From my antipathy to any cult of the individual, I never made public during the existence of the International the numerous addresses from various countries which recognized my merits and which annoyed me. I did not even reply to them, except sometimes to rebuke their authors. Engels and I first joined the secret society of

Communists on the condition that everything making for superstitious worship of authority would be deleted from its statute. Lassalle subsequently did quite the opposite."

Sometime later Engels wrote: "Both Marx and I have always been against any public manifestation with regard to individuals, with the exception of cases when it had an important purpose; and we most strongly opposed such manifestations which during our lifetime concerned us personally."

The great modesty of the genius of the Revolution, Vladimir Ilyich Lenin, is known. Lenin had always stressed the role of the people as the creator of history, the directing and organizational role of the party as a living and creative organism, and also the role of the Central Committee.

Marxism does not negate the role of the leaders of the working class in directing the revolutionary liberation movement.

While ascribing great importance to the role of the leaders and organizers of the masses, Lenin at the same time mercilessly stigmatized every manifestation of the cult of the individual, inexorably combated the foreign-to-Marxism views about a "hero" and a "crowd," and countered all efforts to oppose a "hero" to the masses and to the people.

Lenin taught that the party's strength depends on its indissoluble unity with the masses, on the fact that behind the party follows the people—workers, peasants and intelligentsia. "Only he will win and retain the power," said Lenin, "who believes in the people, who submerges himself in the fountain of the living creativeness of the people."

Lenin spoke with pride about the Bolshevik Communist party as the leader and teacher of the people; he called for the presentation of all the most important questions before the opinion of knowledgeable workers, before the opinion of their party; he said: "We believe in it, we see in it the wisdom, the honor, and the conscience of our epoch."

Lenin resolutely stood against every attempt aimed at belittling or weakening the directing role of the party in the structure of the Soviet state. He worked out Bolshevik principles of party direction and norms of party life, stressing that the guiding principle of party leadership is its collegiality. Already during the pre-Revolutionary years, Lenin called the Central Committee of the party a collective of leaders and the guardian and interpreter of party principles. "During the period between congresses," pointed out Lenin, "the Central Committee guards and interprets the principles of the party."

Underlining the role of the Central Committee of the party and its authority, Vladimir Ilyich pointed out: "Our Central Committee constituted itself as a closely centralized and highly authoritative group."

During Lenin's life the Central Committee of the party was a real expression of collective leadership of the party and of the nation. Being a militant Marxist-revolutionist, always unyielding in matters of principle, Lenin never imposed by force his views upon his co-workers. He tried to convince; he patiently explained his opinions to others. Lenin always diligently observed that the norms of party life were realized, that the party statute was enforced, that the party congresses and the plenary sessions of the Central Committee took place at the proper intervals.

In addition to the great accomplishments of V. I. Lenin for the victory of the working class and of the working peasants, for the victory of our party and for the application of the ideas of scientific Communism to life, his acute mind expressed itself also in this—that he detected in Stalin in time those negative characteristics which resulted later in grave consequences. Fearing the future fate of the party and of the Soviet nation, V. I. Lenin made a completely correct characterization of Stalin, pointing out that it was necessary to consider the question of transferring Stalin from the position of the Secretary General because of the fact that Stalin is excessively rude, that he does not have a proper attitude toward his comrades, that he is capricious and abuses his power.

. . . . .

When we analyze the practice of Stalin in regard to the direction of the party and of the country, when we pause to consider everything which Stalin perpetrated, we must be convinced that Lenin's fears were justified. The negative characteristics of Stalin, which, in Lenin's time, were only incipient, transformed themselves during the last years into a grave abuse of power by Stalin, which caused untold harm to our party.

We have to consider seriously and analyze correctly this matter in order that we may preclude any possibility of a repetition in any form whatever of what took place during the life of Stalin, who absolutely did not tolerate collegiality in leadership and in work, and who practiced brutal violence, not only toward everything which opposed him, but also toward that which seemed, to his capricious and despotic character, contrary to his concepts.

Stalin acted not through persuasion, explanation and patient co-operation with people, but by imposing his concepts and demanding absolute submission to his opinion. Whoever opposed this concept or tried to prove his viewpoint and the correctness of his position was doomed to removal from the leading collective and to subsequent moral and physical annihilation. This was especially true during the period following the 17th Party Congress, when many prominent party leaders and rank-and-file party workers, honest and dedicated to the cause of Communism, fell victim to Stalin's despotism.

. . . . .

Stalin originated the concept "enemy of the people." This term automatically rendered it unnecessary that the ideological errors of a man or men engaged in a controversy be proven; this term made possible the usage of the most cruel repression, violating all norms of revolutionary legality, against anyone who in any way disagreed with Stalin, against those who were only suspected of hostile intent, against those who had bad reputations. This concept "enemy of the people" actually eliminated the possibility of any kind of ideological fight or the making of one's views known on this or that issue, even those of a practical character. In the main, and in actuality, the only proof of guilt used, against all norms of current legal science, was the "confession" of the accused himself; and, as subsequent probing proved, "confessions" were acquired through physical pressures against the accused. This led to glaring violations of revolutionary legality and to the fact that many entirely innocent persons, who in the past had defended the party line, became victims.

We must assert that, in regard to those persons who in their time had opposed the party line, there were often no sufficiently serious reasons for their physical annihilation. The formula "enemy of the people" was specifically introduced for the purpose of physically annihilating such individuals.

It is a fact that many persons who were later annihilated as enemies of the party and people had worked with Lenin during his life. Some of these persons had made errors during Lenin's life, but, despite this, Lenin benefited by their work; he corrected them and he did everything possible to retain them in the ranks of the party; he induced them to follow him.

. . . . .

Comrades! We must abolish the cult of the individual decisively, once and for all; we must draw the proper conclusions concerning both ideological-theoretical and practical work. It is necessary for this purpose:

First, in a Bolshevik manner to condemn and to eradicate the cult of the individual as alien to Marxism-Leninism and not consonant with the principles of party leadership and the norms of party life, and to fight inexorably all attempts at bringing back this practice in one form or another.

To return to and actually practice in all our ideological work the most important theses of Marxist-Leninist science about the people as the creator of history and as the creator of all material and spiritual good of humanity, about the decisive role of the Marxist party in the revolutionary fight for the transformation of society, about the victory of communism.

In this connection we will be forced to do much work in order to examine critically from the Marxist-Leninist viewpoint and to correct the widely spread erroneous views connected with the cult of the individual in the sphere of history, philosophy, economy and of other sciences, as well as in literature and the fine arts. It is especially necessary that in the immediate future we compile a serious textbook of the history of our party which will be edited in accordance with scientific Marxist objectivism, a textbook of the history of Soviet society, a book pertaining to the events of the Civil War and the Great Patriotic War.

Secondly, to continue systematically and consistently the work done by the party's Central Committee during the last years, a work characterized by minute observation in all party organizations, from the bottom to the top, of the Leninist principles of party leadership, characterized, above all, by the main principle of collective leadership, characterized by the observance of the norms of party life described in the statutes of our party, and, finally, characterized by the wide practice of criticism and self-criticism.

Thirdly, to restore completely the Leninist principles of Soviet socialist democracy, expressed in the Constitution of the Soviet Union, to fight willfulness of individuals abusing their power. The evil caused by acts violating revolutionary socialist legality which have accumulated during a long time as a result of the negative influence of the cult of the individual has to be completely corrected.

Comrades! The 20th Congress of the Communist Party of the Soviet Union has manifested with a new strength the unshakable unity of our party, its cohesiveness around the Central Committee, its resolute will to accomplish the great task of building communism. (*Tumultuous applause.*)

And the fact that we present in all their ramifications the basic problems of overcoming the cult of the individual which is alien to Marxism-Leninism, as well as the problem of liquidating its burdensome consequences, is an evidence of the great moral and political strength of our party. (*Prolonged applause.*)

We are absolutely certain that our party, armed with the historical resolutions of the 20th Congress, will lead the Soviet people along the Leninist path to new successes, to new victories. (*Tumultuous, prolonged applause.*)

Long live the victorious banner of our party—Leninism! (*Tumultuous, prolonged applause ending in ovation. All rise.*)

C · RESIGNATION OF SOVIET PREMIER MALENKOV *

[*In an unexpected resignation statement, read to a joint meeting of both houses of the Supreme Soviet on February 8, 1955, Georgi Malenkov relinquished his post as premier of the Soviet Union. Defense Minister Nikolai Bulganin was named as his successor, and Georgi Zhukov became Defense Minister. The text of the resignation speech follows.*]

To the chairman of the joint meeting of the Soviet of the Union and the Soviet of Nationalities:

I ask you to bring to the notice of the Supreme Soviet of the U.S.S.R. my request to be relieved from the post of chairman of the Council of Ministers of the U.S.S.R. My request is due to business considerations on the necessity of strengthening the leadership of the Council of Ministers and the need to have at the post of the chairman of the Council of Ministers another comrade with greater experience in state work.

I clearly see that the carrying out of the complicated and respon-

* *Current History*, 28 (March, 1955), pp. 185-186. Reprinted by permission of *Current History*.

sible duties of chairman of the Council of Ministers is being nega-
tively affected by my insufficient experience in local work, and the
fact that I did not have occasion, in a ministry or some economic
organ, to effect direct guidance of individual branches of national
economy.

I also consider myself bound to say in the present statement that
now, when the Communist Party of the Soviet Union and the workers
of our country are concentrating special efforts for the most rapid
development of agriculture, I see particularly clearly my guilt and
responsibility for the unsatisfactory state of affairs which has arisen
in agriculture, because for several years past I have been entrusted
with the duty of controlling and guiding the work of central agricultural organs and the work of local party and administrative organizations in the sphere of agriculture.

The Communist Party, on the initiative and under the guidance of
the Central Committee of the C.P.S.U. [Communist Party of the Soviet Union] has already worked out and is implementing a series of
large-scale measures for overcoming the lagging behind in agriculture.

Among such important measures is, undoubtedly, the reform of
agricultural taxation, regarding which I think it opportune to say it
was carried out on the initiative of and in accordance with the proposals of the Central Committee of the C.P.S.U.

It is now evident what important role this reform played in the
task of developing agriculture.

Now, as is known, on the initiative and under the guidance of the
Central Committee of the C.P.S.U., a general program has been
worked out for overcoming the lagging behind in agriculture and for
its most rapid development.

This program is based on the only correct foundation: The further
development, by every means, of heavy industry, and only its implementation will create the necessary conditions for a real upsurge in
the production of all essential commodities for popular consumption.

It is to be expected that various bourgeois hysterical viragos will
busy themselves with slanderous inventions in connection with my
present statement, and the fact itself of my release from the post of
chairman of the U.S.S.R. Council of Ministers, but we, Communists
and Soviet people, will ignore this lying and slander.

The interest of the motherland, the people and the Communist
Party stand above everything for every one of us.

Expressing the request of my release from the post of chairman of the U.S.S.R. Council of Ministers, I wish to assure the U.S.S.R. Supreme Soviet that, in the new sphere entrusted to me, I will, under the guidance of the Central Committee of the C.P.S.U., monolithic in its unity and solidarity, and the Soviet government, perform in the most conscientious manner my duty and the functions which will be entrusted to me.

D · REORGANIZATION OF RUSSIA'S PRESIDIUM *

[*Reprinted below is the text of a resolution issued by the Russian Communist party on July 3, 1957, announcing that G. M. Malenkov, L. M. Kaganovich and V. M. Molotov have been ousted from the Presidium.*]

Resolution of the plenary meeting of the Central Committee of the Communist party of the Soviet Union on the anti-party group of G. M. Malenkov, L. M. Kaganovich and V. M. Molotov.

At its meeting of June 22-29, 1957, the plenum of the Central Committee of the Communist party of the Soviet Union considered the question of the anti-party group of Malenkov, Kaganovich and Molotov, which had formed within the Presidium of the Central Committee.

Seeking to change the party's political line, this group used anti-party fractional methods in an attempt to change the composition of the party's leading bodies, elected by the plenary meeting of the Central Committee of the Communist party of the Soviet Union.

This was not accidental. In the last three or four years, during which the party has been steering a resolute course toward rectifying the errors and shortcomings born of the personality cult and waging a successful struggle against the revisionists of Marxism-Leninism, both in the international sphere and inside the country, years during which the party has done appreciable work to rectify distortions of the Leninist nationalities policy committed in the past, the members of the anti-party group, now laid bare and fully exposed, have been offering constant opposition, direct or indirect, to this course approved by the twentieth party congress.

The group attempted in effect to oppose the Leninist policy of peaceful coexistence between states with different social systems, of

* *Current History*, 33 (November, 1957), pp. 304-308. Reprinted by permission of *Current History*.

relaxing international tension and establishing friendly relations between the U.S.S.R. and all the peoples of the world. They were against the extension of the rights of the union republics in the sphere of economic and cultural development and in the sphere of legislation and against enhancing the role of the local Soviets in the fulfillment of these tasks.

Thereby, the anti-party group resisted the party's firm course toward the more rapid development of the economy and culture in the national republics, a course insuring the further promotion of Leninist friendship between all the people of our country.

Far from understanding the party's measures aimed at combating bureaucracy and reducing the inflated state apparatus, the anti-party group opposed them. On all these points, it came out against the Leninist principle of democratic centralism being implemented by the party.

The group persistently opposed and sought to frustrate so vastly important a measure as the reorganization of industrial management and the setting up of economic councils in the economic areas, approved by the whole of the party and the people.

They refused to understand that at the present stage when progress in Socialist industry has assumed a tremendous scale and continues at a high rate, the development of heavy industry receiving priority, it was indispensable to find new, better forms of industrial management such as would bring out greater reserves and guarantee an even more powerful rise in Soviet industry.

The group went so far as to continue its struggle against the reorganization of industrial management, even after the approval of the above measures in the course of the countrywide discussions and the subsequent adoption of the law at a session of the Supreme Soviet.

With regard to agricultural problems, the members of the group showed lack of understanding of the new, pressing task. They would not recognize the necessity of increased material incentives for the collective farm peasantry in expanding output of agricultural products.

They objected to the abolition of the old bureaucratic system of planning on the collective farms and to the introduction of a new system of planning, such as would release the initiative of the collective farms in carrying on their economy, a measure which has already yielded positive results.

They drifted so far away from reality as to be unable to see the actual possibility of abolishing at the end of this year obligatory deliveries of farm produce by collective farmers from their individual plots.

The implementation of this measure, which is of vital importance for the millions of the working people of the U.S.S.R., was made possible by substantial progress in socially owned livestock breeding at the collective farms and by the advancement of the state farms.

Instead of supporting this pressing measure the members of the anti-party group opposed it. They carried on an entirely unwarranted struggle against the party's appeal, vigorously supported by the collective farms, regions and republics, to overtake the United States in the next few years in per capita output of milk, butter and meat.

Thereby, the members of the anti-party group demonstrated an overbearing attitude to the urgent, vital interests of the broad masses of the people and lack of faith in the enormous potentialities of Socialist economy in the country-wide movement now going on for a speedy increase in milk and meat production.

It cannot be considered accidental that Comrade Molotov, a member of the anti-party group, who manifested a conservative and narrow-minded attitude, far from realizing the necessity of making use of virgin lands, resisted the raising of 35,000,000 hectares of virgin land, an enterprise which acquired such tremendous importance in the economy of our country.

Comrades Malenkov, Kaganovich and Molotov put up a stubborn resistance to the measures which the Central Committee and the whole of our party were carrying out to do away with the consequences of the personality cult, to eliminate the violations of revolutionary law that had been committed, and provide such conditions as would preclude their recurrence.

Whereas the workers, collective farmers, our glorious youth, our engineers and technicians, scientific workers, writers and all our intellectuals unanimously supported the measures which the party was putting into practice in accordance with the decisions of the twentieth party congress, whereas the entire Soviet people had joined the vigorous effort to carry those measures into execution, whereas our country is going through a powerful rise in popular activity and a fresh surge of creative energy, the members of the anti-party group kept turning a deaf ear to this creative movement of the masses.

In the sphere of foreign policy, the group, in particular comrade Molotov, showed narrow-mindedness and hampered in every way the implementation of the new pressing measures intended to ease international tension and promote universal peace.

Comrade Molotov raised obstacles to the conclusion of the state treaty with Austria and the improvement of relations with that country which lies in the center of Europe. The conclusion of the Austrian treaty was largely instrumental in lessening international tension in general.

He was also against normalization of relations with Japan, while that normalization has played an important part in relaxing international tension in the Far East. He opposed the fundamental proposition worked out by the party on the possibility of preventing wars in the present conditions, on the possibility of different ways of transition to socialism in different countries, on the necessity of strengthening contacts between the Soviet party and progressive parties abroad.

For a long time, Comrade Molotov in his capacity as Foreign Minister, far from taking, through the Ministry of Foreign Affairs, measures to improve relations between the U.S.S.R. and Yugoslavia, repeatedly came out against the measures which the Presidium of the Central Committee was carrying out to improve relations with Yugoslavia.

Comrade Molotov's erroneous stand on the Yugoslav issue was unanimously condemned by the plenary meeting of the Central Committee of the party in July, 1955, as not being in line with the interests of the Soviet state and the Socialist camp and not conforming to the principles of Leninist policy.

Comrade Molotov repeatedly opposed the Soviet Government's indispensable new steps in defense of peace and the security of nations. In particular, he denied the advisability of establishing personal contacts between the Soviet leaders and the statesmen of other countries, which is essential for the achievement of mutual understanding and better international relations.

On many of the above points Comrade Molotov's opinion was supported by Comrade Kaganovich and in a number of cases by Comrade Malenkov.

The Presidium of the Central Committee and the Central Committee as a whole patiently corrected them and combated their errors, hoping that they would draw proper lessons from the errors, that they would not persist in them and would fall into step with the whole of the party's leading body. Nevertheless, they maintained their erroneous anti-Leninist position.

What underlies the attitude of Comrades Malenkov, Kaganovich and Molotov, which is at variance with the party line, is the certain fact that they were and still are shackled by old notions and methods, that they have drifted away from the life of the party and country, failed to see the new conditions, the new situation, take a conservative attitude, stubbornly cling to obsolete forms and methods of work that are no longer in keeping with the interests of the advance towards communism, rejecting what is born of reality itself and is suggested by the interests of the progress of Soviet society, by the interests of the entire Socialist camp.

Both in internal problems and in matters of foreign policy they are sectarian and dogmatic, and they use a scholastic, inert approach to Marxism-Leninism. They fail to realize that in the present conditions living Marxism-Leninism in action and the struggle for communism manifest themselves in the execution of the decisions of the twentieth party congress, in the steady carrying out of the policy of peaceful co-existence, the struggle for friendship among peoples and the policy of the all-round consolidation of the Socialist camp in better industrial management, in the struggle for the fullest possible advancement of agriculture, for an abundance of food, for large-scale housing construction, for the extension of the rights of the union republics, for the flourishing of national cultures, for the all-round encouragement of the initiative of the masses.

Seeing that their erroneous statements and actions were constantly rebuffed in the Presidium of the Central Committee, which has been consistently putting into practice the line set by the twentieth party congress, Comrades Molotov, Kaganovich and Malenkov embarked on a group struggle against the party leadership.

Entering into collusion on an anti-party basis, they set out to change the policy of the party, to drag the party back to the erroneous methods of leadership condemned by the twentieth party congress. They resorted to methods of intrigue and formed a collusion against the Central Committee.

The facts revealed at the plenary meeting of the Central Committee show that Comrades Malenkov, Kaganovich and Molotov, as well as Comrade Shepilov who joined them, having embarked on the path of fractionary struggle, violated the party statutes and the decision of the nineteenth party congress on party unity, drafted by Lenin, which says:

> In order to effect strict discipline within the party and in all Soviet work and to achieve maximum unity in eliminating all fractionary activity, the congress empowers the Central Committee to apply in cases of breach of discipline or of a revival or toleration of fractionary activity, all party penalties including expulsion from the party, and in respect of members of the Central Committee their reduction to the status of alternate members, or even as an extreme measure, their expulsion from the party.
>
> A precondition for the application of this extreme measure to members of the Central Committee, alternate members of the Central Committee and members of the Auditing Commission shall be the convening of a plenary meeting of the Central Committee, and all members of the Auditing Commission should be invited. If such a general meeting of the most responsible party leaders recognizes by a two-thirds majority the necessity of reducing a member of the Central Committee to the status of alternate member or his expulsion from the party, then this measure shall be carried out immediately.

This Leninist resolution makes it obligatory for the Central Committee and all party organizations tirelessly to consolidate party unity, to rebuff with determination every evidence of fractionary or group activity, to insure that the work is indeed carried out by joint effort, that it indeed expresses the unity of will and action of the vanguard of the working class, the Communist party.

The plenary meeting of the Central Committee notes with great satisfaction the monolithic unity and solidarity of all the members and alternate members of the Central Committee and the members of the Central Auditing Commission who have unanimously condemned the anti-party group.

Not a single member of the plenum of the Central Committee supported the group.

Faced with unanimous condemnation of the anti-party activities of the group by the plenary meeting of the Central Committee, in a situation where the members of the plenum of the Central Committee unanimously demanded the removal of the members of the group from the Central Committee and their expulsion from the party, they admitted the existence of a collusion and the harmful nature of the anti-party activities and committed themselves to complying with the party position.

Guided by the interests of all-round consolidation of the Leninist unity of the party the plenary meeting of the Central Committee of the party has resolved:

(1) To condemn as incompatible with the Leninist principles of our party the fractionary activities of the anti-party group of Malenkov, Kaganovich and Molotov and of Shepilov, who joined them.

(2) To exclude Comrades Malenkov, Kaganovich and Molotov from the membership of the Presidium of the Central Committee and from the Central Committee, to remove Comrade Shepilov from the post of secretary to the Central Committee and to exclude him from the alternate membership of the Presidium of the Central Committee and from the membership of the Central Committee.

The unanimous condemnation of the fractionary activities of the anti-party group of Comrades Malenkov, Kaganovich and Molotov by the Central Committee of the party will serve to further consolidate the unity of the ranks of our Leninist party, to consolidate its leadership, to promote the struggle for the general line of the party.

The Central Committee of the party calls on all Communists to rally still more closely around the invincible banner of Marxism-Leninism, to bend all their energies to the successful fulfillment of the tasks of Communist construction.

Adopted on June 29, 1957, by the unanimous vote of all the members of the Central Committee, the alternate members of the Central Committee and the members of the Central Auditing Commission, with one abstention, in the person of Comrade Molotov.

SUGGESTED READINGS

[*NOTE: The editors are convinced that all bibliographical listings result from some arbitrary selection process. Nowhere is this more evident than in the suggested readings that follow. American Constitutional Law, for example, is blessed with many and varied valuable studies. An all-inclusive listing is not feasible within the context of our suggested readings. Thus, arbitrarily, the editors have not included judicial biographies such as the classic study of Chief Justice Marshall by Beveridge or the more recent work on Chief Justice Stone by Professor Mason. Furthermore, specialized analyses of such areas as the "commerce clause," "the due process clause," etc., while invaluable, were sacrificed in the interests of giving the beginning student a broader introduction to the field.*]

CONSTITUTIONALISM

Adams, George Burton. *Constitutional History of England.* Revised by Robert L. Schuyler. London: J. Cape, 1941.

Beard, Charles A. *An Economic Interpretation of the Constitution of the United States.* New York: Macmillan, 1913.

Blanksten, George I. *Ecuador: Constitutions and Caudillos.* Berkeley: University of California Press, 1951.

Blaustein, Albert P., and Ferguson, Clarence Clyde, Jr. *Desegregation and the Law.* New Brunswick: Rutgers University Press, 1957.

Brown, Robert E. *Charles Beard and the Constitution.* Princeton: Princeton University Press, 1956.

Browne, Edward G. *The Persian Revolution of 1905-1909.* Cambridge, England: Cambridge University Press, 1910.

Cahill, Fred V., Jr. *Judicial Legislation.* New York: Ronald Press, 1952.

Callard, Keith. *Pakistan, A Political Study.* London: Allen and Unwin, 1957.

Carr, Robert K. *The Supreme Court and Judicial Review.* New York: Farrar and Rinehart, 1942.

Corwin, Edward S. *The Doctrine of Judicial Review.* Princeton: Princeton University Press, 1914.

——— *Total War and the Constitution.* New York: Knopf, 1947.

Crosskey, William W. *Politics and the Constitution in the History of the United States.* 2 volumes. Chicago: University of Chicago Press, 1958.

Curtis, Charles P. *Lions Under the Throne.* Boston: Houghton Mifflin, 1947.

Douglas, William O. *We the Judges: Studies in American and Indian Constitutional Law from Marshall to Mukherjea.* Garden City: Doubleday, 1956.

Emerson, Thomas I., and Haber, David. *Political and Civil Rights in the United States.* 2 volumes. 2nd edition. Buffalo: Dennis, 1958.

Fellman, David. *The Defendant's Rights.* New York: Rinehart, 1958.

Fitzgibbon, Russell H. (ed.). *The Constitutions of the Americas.* Chicago: University of Chicago Press, 1951.

Frank, John P. *Marble Palace.* New York: Knopf, 1958.

Gledhill, Alan. *The Republic of India; The Development of Its Laws and Constitution.* London: Stevens, 1951.

Greenberg, Jack. *Race Relations and American Law.* New York: Columbia University Press, 1959.

Haines, Charles G. *The Role of the Supreme Court in American Government and Politics 1789-1935.* Berkeley and Los Angeles: University of California Press, 1944.

Horn, Robert A. *Groups and the Constitution.* Stanford: Stanford University Press, 1956.

Jackson, Robert. *The Supreme Court in the American System of Government.* Cambridge: Harvard University Press, 1955.

Jennings, Sir William Ivor. *Constitutional Laws of the Commonwealth.* Oxford: Clarendon Press, 1957.

——— *Constitutional Problems in Pakistan.* Cambridge, England: Cambridge University Press, 1957.

——— *Dominion of Ceylon—The Development of Its Laws and Constitution.* London: Stevens, 1952.

———— *The British Constitution.* 3rd edition. Cambridge, England: Cambridge University Press, 1950.

———— *The Law and the Constitution.* London: University of London Press, 1952.

Konvitz, Milton R. *Fundamental Liberties of a Free People.* Ithaca: Cornell University Press, 1957.

Konvitz, Milton R., and Rossiter, Clinton (eds.). *Aspects of Liberty.* Ithaca: Cornell University Press, 1958.

Le May, G. H. L. *British Government 1914-1953.* London: Methuen, 1955.

Macmahon, Arthur W. (ed.). *Federalism: Mature and Emergent.* Garden City: Doubleday, 1955.

McWhinney, Edward. *Judicial Review in the English Speaking World.* Toronto: University of Toronto Press, 1956.

Rackman, Emanuel. *Israel's Emerging Constitution, 1948-1951.* New York: Columbia University Press, 1955.

tenBroek, Jacobus, Barnhart, Edward N., and Matson, Floyd W. *Prejudice, War and the Constitution.* Berkeley and Los Angeles: University of California Press, 1954.

Twiss, Benjamin R. *Lawyers and the Constitution.* Princeton: Princeton University Press, 1942.

Warren, Charles. *The Supreme Court in United States History.* 3 volumes. Boston: Little, Brown, 1922.

Wheare, K. C. *Modern Constitutions.* London: Oxford University Press, 1951.

LAW

Abraham, Henry J. *Courts and Judges.* New York: Oxford University Press, 1959.

Berman, Harold J. *Justice in Russia: An Interpretation of Soviet Law.* Cambridge: Harvard University Press, 1950.

Brierly, J. L. *The Law of Nations.* 4th edition. Oxford: Clarendon Press, 1949.

Buckland, William W., and McNair, Arnold D. *Roman Law and the Common Law.* Revised by F. H. Larsen. Cambridge, England: Cambridge University Press, 1952.

Cardozo, Benjamin N. *The Nature of the Judicial Process*. New Haven: Yale University Press, 1921.

Carpenter, William S. *Foundations of Modern Jurisprudence*. New York: Appleton-Century-Crofts, 1958.

Clagett, Helen. *Administration of Justice in Latin America*. New York: Oceana Publications, 1952.

Cohen, Morris R. *Law and the Social Order*. New York: Harcourt, Brace, 1933.

Eder, Phanor J. *A Comparative Survey of Anglo-American and Latin American Law*. New York: New York University Press, 1950.

Elias, T. Olawale. *The Nature of African Customary Law*. Manchester: Manchester University Press, 1956.

Frank, Jerome. *Courts on Trial*. Princeton: Princeton University Press, 1949.

———— *Law and the Modern Mind*. New York: Coward-McCann, 1949.

Friedmann, Wolfgang. *Legal Theory*. 4th edition. London: Stevens, 1960.

Hackworth, Green Haywood. *Digest of International Law*. 8 volumes. Washington, D.C.: Government Printing Office, 1940-1944.

Hurst, J. Willard. *The Growth of American Law: The Law Makers*. Boston: Little, Brown, 1950.

Hyde, Charles Chenly. *International Law*. 2nd revised edition. Boston: Little, Brown, 1951.

Kelsen, Hans. *Principles of International Law*. New York: Rinehart, 1952.

———— *The Communist Theory of Law*. New York: Praeger, 1955.

Khadduri, Majid. *War and Peace in the Law of Islam*. Baltimore: Johns Hopkins Press, 1955.

Lauterpacht, Hersh. *The Function of Law in the International Community*. Oxford: Clarendon Press, 1933.

Llewellyn, Karl N. *The Bramble Bush*. New York: Oceana Publications, 1951.

Maine, Sir Henry. *Ancient Law*. London: Everyman's Library, Dutton, 1917.

Mayers, Lewis. *The American Legal System*. New York: Harper, 1955.

Motwani, Kewal. *Manu Dharma S'āstra.* Madras: Ganesh, 1958.

Oppenheim, Lassa Francis Lawrence. *International Law.* Volume I: *Peace.* 8th edition edited by H. Lauterpacht. London, New York: Longmans, Green, 1955.

——— *International Law.* Volume II: *Disputes, War and Neutrality.* 7th edition edited by H. Lauterpacht. London, New York: Longmans, Green, 1952.

Plucknett, Theodore F. T. *A Concise History of the Common Law.* 3rd edition. London: Butterworth, 1940.

Pound, Roscoe. *An Introduction to the Philosophy of Law.* New Haven: Yale University Press, 1922.

Recaséns Siches, Luis, and others. *Latin American Legal Philosophy.* Translated by Gordon Ireland and others. Cambridge: Harvard University Press, 1948.

Robson, William A. *Civilization and the Growth of Law.* New York: Macmillan, 1935.

Rosenblum, Victor G. *Law as a Political Instrument.* New York: Random House, 1955.

Simpson, S. P., and Stone, Julius (with the collaboration of M. Magdalena Schoch). *Law and Society.* 3 volumes. St. Paul: West, 1948-1949.

Stone, Julius. *The Province and Function of Law.* Cambridge: Harvard University Press, 1950.

Vyshinsky, Andrei Y. *The Law of the Soviet State.* Translated by Hugh W. Babb. New York: Macmillan, 1948.

INSTITUTIONS

Arneson, Ben A. *The Democratic Monarchies of Scandinavia.* Revised edition. New York: Van Nostrand, 1949.

Bailey, Sidney D. *Parliamentary Government in Southern Asia.* London: Hansard Society, 1953.

Bailey, Stephen K., and Samuel, Howard D. *Congress at Work.* New York: Henry Holt, 1952.

Barker, Sir Ernest. *British Constitutional Monarchy.* London: Her Majesty's Government, Central Office of Information, 1955.

Burns, James MacGregor. *Congress on Trial.* New York: Harper, 1949.

Carter, Byrum E. *The Office of Prime Minister.* Princeton: Princeton University Press, 1956.

Corwin, Edward S. *The President: Office and Powers.* 3rd edition. New York: New York University Press, 1948.

Fenno, Richard F. *The President's Cabinet.* Cambridge: Harvard University Press, 1959.

Friederich, Carl J., and Brzezinski, Zbigniew K. *Totalitarian Dictatorship and Autocracy.* Cambridge: Harvard University Press, 1956.

Galloway, George B. *The Legislative Process in Congress.* New York: Crowell, 1953.

Griffith, Ernest S. *Congress, Its Contemporary Role.* New York: New York University Press, 1951.

Håstad, Elis. *The Parliament of Sweden.* London: Hansard Society, 1951.

Haynes, George H. *The Senate of the United States.* 2 volumes. Boston: Houghton Mifflin, 1938.

Herbert, Sir Alan P. *Independent Member.* New York: Doubleday, 1951.

Hobbs, Edward Henry. *Behind the President.* Washington, D.C.: Public Affairs Press, 1954.

Hyman, Sidney. *The American President.* New York: Harper, 1954.

Jennings, Sir William Ivor. *Cabinet Government.* Cambridge, England: Cambridge University Press, 1947.

———— *Parliament.* Revised edition. Cambridge, England: Cambridge University Press, 1957.

King, H. M. *Parliament and Freedom.* London: Murray, 1953.

Koenig, Louis. *The Invisible Presidency.* New York: Rinehart, 1960.

Laski, Harold J. *The American Presidency.* London: Allen and Unwin, 1940.

Lidderdale, D. W. S. *The Parliament of France.* London: Hansard Society, 1951.

Lipson, Leslie. *The American Governor: From Figurehead to Leader.* Chicago: University of Chicago Press, 1939.

Morris-Jones, W. H. *Parliament in India.* London: Longmans, Green, 1957.

Morrison, Herbert. *Government and Parliament: A Survey from the Inside.* London: Oxford University Press, 1954.

Neustadt, Richard E. *Presidential Power: The Politics of Leadership.* New York: Wiley, 1959.

Rossiter, Clinton. *Constitutional Dictatorship.* Princeton: Princeton University Press, 1948.

———— *The American Presidency.* Revised edition. New York: Harcourt, Brace, 1960.

Schubert, Glendon A., Jr. *The Presidency in the Courts.* Minneapolis: University of Minnesota Press, 1957.

Schueller, George K. *The Politburo.* Stanford: Stanford University Press, 1951.

Taft, William H. *Our Chief Magistrate and His Powers.* New York: Columbia University Press, 1916.

White, William S. *Citadel: The Story of the United States Senate.* New York: Harper, 1957.

Wight, Martin. *The Gold Coast Legislative Council.* London: Faber, 1947.

Wilson, Woodrow. *Congressional Government.* Boston: Houghton Mifflin, 1885.

Wise, G. S. *Caudillo: A Portrait of Antonio Guzmán Blanco.* New York: Columbia University Press, 1951.

Young, Roland. *The American Congress.* New York: Harper, 1958.

CHAPTER V

The Mobilizers of Political Power

Under any governmental system, citizens develop a habitual aware-ness of the harmonious and the discordant voices of the traditional government institutions that speak to and for them. Whether execu-tive, legislative, or judicial, the voices are given an added weight in the body politic because of the power vested in the governmental institutions. It has been to these traditional institutions that citizens have turned, not merely for authoritative expressions of policy but also for the active mobilization of political power.

It is doubtful, however, whether the mobilization of political power was ever strictly and narrowly confined to the traditional govern-mental institutions. From the very beginning of organized govern-ment, other institutions and groups have been operating as factors in political power. Today, however, we are much more cognizant of the growth and operative techniques of these important mobilizers of political power. Without due recognition of them, the understanding of the governmental process is both narrow and incomplete.

One type of mobilizers of political action embraces three insti-tutions long associated with governments: the political party, the bureaucracy, and the military. The association of these mobilizers of political power with the governmental process has been a rapidly changing one in this century. Each has assumed, in one or more parts of the world, new and diverse roles. Political parties, for example, have in the United States and many other countries become the major legal avenue to elective office. In the so-called "one-party" states, in contrast, the political party has come to be almost synonymous with government as a whole, its decisions becoming in effect, at least, decisions of the state itself. In still other countries, political parties have become highly efficient organizations for mobilizing large and significant bodies of "organized opinion," which they convert into government policy through what we have come to call "party government." In this latter circumstance, parties have become legally recognized as the official and loyal "opposition."

All modern governments have, to some extent, a corps of professional public servants equipped with specialized skills and a continuity of government experience. More and more, the members of this bureaucracy play significant roles in the decision-making process and in the mobilization of political power. Individual elective and appointed officials come and go, but the career employees continue in their posts. With the increasingly technical and complex administrative tasks facing government today, it is small wonder that the professional experts of the bureaucracy are consulted right and left in regard to almost every governmental and administrative matter that may come up. If they are politically adept, they may, in addition, develop virtually unassailable positions of political influence and prestige. The increasing importance of the bureaucracy as a mobilizer of political power is additionally noteworthy because the development seems to be occurring in all governments, irrespective of the political system under which they operate.

Organized force has been the traditional monopoly of governments. Professional military forces are, thus, an integral part of present-day government. The role of the services has not, however, been confined strictly to war and defense. In Latin-American countries, participation of the military in the political process has been a long-established practice. In other parts of the world the military role has taken on added significance. Even in the United States, with its long-standing constitutional policy of subordination of the military to civilian officials, there is increasing evidence that our military leaders are playing a more active part in the political process. The reasons are both complicated and technical. They stem, in part, from the increasingly difficult task of making a precise distinction between what is of "military" significance and what is of a "nonmilitary" nature. Here again, we have an example of the politically elective or appointive administrative superior facing a highly articulate and professionally competent group of career officers, all armed with information and data that are often incomprehensible to the nonprofessional soldier. Given the strong position of military preparedness of major powers all over the world, it becomes extremely risky to challenge the requests and evaluations of military leaders, even where nonmilitary implications of the decisions are recognized.

Each of these institutions has developed a more significant status in the past half-century. For each, this status has meant, in addition, the development of vested interests in their respective roles. Each increasingly has felt the compelling need, as an institution with a vested interest, to take a more active hand in mobilizing political power to protect its position.

The second type of mobilizers of political action includes a number of institutions ordinarily recognized for their private character. The editors have not intended to present an exhaustive list of such private institutions, but have selected only a few of the more familiar. Business, labor, church, agriculture, students, and scientists, as private institutions, have developed nongovernmental devices for achieving certain political goals of specific importance to their respective institutions. Each, in short, seeks to mobilize political power, and each has, to a greater or lesser extent, achieved success in various nations. It may be well to note at this point that these successes have afforded them the legitimate right to claim credit for bringing about nonviolent transfers of political power. Thus, in reading some of the following selections, the student should keep in mind that the selections are further illustrations of the "nonviolent" transfer of power in the sense that these institutions operate as pressure groups within the existing political structure.

Business is no stranger to the political scene. Fortified by wealth and organization, it has long played an important role not only in the field of economic productivity but also in the field of politics. However, its precise role varies from nation to nation. Within the American framework of government, business has historically relied on the more formal, institutional channels to advance its policies, endeavoring to channel governmental decisions in directions congenial to its interests. Elsewhere, particularly in totalitarian and corporate states, it has operated as an integral part of the governmental process. More recently, in the United States, business has shown signs of increasing advocacy of organized participation in politics. As business has viewed the developing role of the state, especially in welfare areas, it has more consciously sought to articulate its responsibilities—and opportunities—through participation by its management and its employees in political parties and government offices. Generally, it can be safely assumed that organized business in the United States seeks two goals in this area: (1) the "redirecting" of the welfare function away from the state to the business firms, and (2) the development of sufficient political strength at the polls and in government to offset what it regards as the growing power of organized labor.

Labor, unlike business, has only recently been able to rely upon any measure of financial resources to achieve political goals. It has depended on its numerical strength and its consequent ability to exert pressure at the polls. In some areas of the world, notably Europe, labor has sought to mobilize political power by organizing labor parties through which it has carried its program directly to the electorate. In the United States, labor has developed some close alliances with local, state, and national political party organizations, but it has thus far refrained from setting up a party of its own. Again, in the United States, its organizing successes since the 1930's have enabled some parts of the labor movement to acquire at least sufficient financial resources to aid favored candidates. These resources have also enabled labor to carry on, more effectively, campaigns for legislative proposals in which it has had an interest. In any event, organized labor is developing distinctive political positions and a philosophy about its role in the political process. It has also developed tools and techniques in the mobilization of political power which it feels are essential to its preservation.

In a number of nations, religious organizations have operated in the most direct relationship with the government. In some states, there is an officially established religion; in others, there is a rigorous separation between church and state. In few nations, however, have the organized religious groups been content to remain totally aloof from the activities of government. When actions of the state have challenged the religious precepts and teachings of the religious bodies, there have been organized protests. Governmental action, insofar as it deals with ethical and moral behavior, continues to command the attention of religious bodies. In areas of birth control, education, and social welfare, the churches take strong and definite stands, revealing their willingness to mobilize their membership to political action if simple protests fail to change policy.

In consdering agriculture as one of the more noteworthy mobilizers of political power, an important distinction should be made between "agrarian movements" and organized agricultural groups with vested interests which they seek to preserve. Much of the land-reform activity we are witnessing in many parts of the world stems from the desire of peasants to own land. Their leaders articulate this desire, but the basis of power is to be seen in the demand of the masses expressed through the leader. In many lands, this growing demand for land reform, though appearing to have no strong organizational framework, remains a powerful force in the political calculations of governmental leaders. It is fear of the eventual eruption of these masses (which may produce results that go far beyond that of land reform) that initially gives such a movement its power.

By contrast, the organized agricultural groups characteristic of the so-called "developed" nations resort to more sophisticated, "pressure group" tactics. Thus, in lieu of crude force, they tend to adopt the more indirect but effective devices employed by other mobilizers of political power. This is well illustrated by the selection on France's alcohol lobby.

The advent of the new and awesome weapons of destruction made possible by the harnessing of the atom has brought forth a relative newcomer to the ranks of the mobilizers of political power, the scientist. As a member of the professional group which split the atom, the scientist today is increasingly concerned with the many ramifications of his discovery. Geneticists have pondered the implications of radiation on present and future generations. Physicists and chemists, observing the potential destructiveness of modern weapons in this space age, have come to feel that they have a vested interest in the applications of their discoveries. Furthermore, scientists have been called upon to work with or for government, and have found that government employment has entailed a restriction on the exchange of scientific information. Thus two factors, the moral implications of the use of atomic weapons and the security restrictions, have led scientists and public to demand the participation of scientific experts in decisions relating to the atomic-energy program.

A great many American citizens are concerned about what they regard as the political apathy of students in the United States. Some teachers have gone so far as to suggest that today's American college students are becoming more and more "apolitical." Although this criticism may be partly justified, it must be remembered that silence alone is no sign of political indifference. Moreover, in many parts of the United States, students often lead local movements in protest over what they feel to be unjust practices or behavior.

One must not infer, therefore, that students are necessarily either unwilling or unable to mobilize political power effectively. Recent student-led uprisings and demonstrations against existing governments and their policies in such scattered areas as Seoul, Tokyo, and Ankara show that students may be very politically active indeed. In Latin America, moreover, students have by tradition set off the sparks that have ignited movements leading to changes of government.

Any descriptive analysis of the mobilizers of political power cannot but impress the student with the increasing complexity of politics and with the extraordinary variety of forces that operate in its processes. Indeed, politics as the art of the possible becomes more and more meaningful as one views the incredibly large numbers of vested interests that compete for money, for time, for recognition, and for policy. It is small wonder that in the cacophony that results from these voices, there often arises the demand for a leader. Indeed, whether addressed to a monarch or an apostle, an authoritarian or a democrat, this demand has been heard throughout history. Each generation must decide, in its own way, whether it wishes to issue the call or whether it is willing to live with the onerous responsibility of having to make its own hard choices.

Leadership

44 · THE HERO AS KING *

Thomas Carlyle

We come now to the last form of Heroism; that which we call Kingship. The Commander over Men; he to whose will our wills are to be subordinated, and loyally surrender themselves, and find their welfare in doing so, may be reckoned the most important of Great Men. He is practically the summary for us of *all* the various figures of Heroism; Priest, Teacher, whatsoever of earthly or of spiritual dignity we can fancy to reside in a man, embodies itself here, to *command* over us, to furnish us with constant practical teaching, to tell us for the day and hour what we are to *do*. He is called *Rex,* Regulator, *Roi*: our own name is still better; King, *Könning,* which means *Canning,* Able-man.

Numerous considerations, pointing towards deep, questionable, and indeed unfathomable regions, present themselves here: on the most of which we must resolutely for the present forbear to speak at all. As Burke said that perhaps fair *Trial by Jury* was the soul of Government, and that all legislation, administration, parliamentary debating, and the rest of it, went on, in "order to bring twelve impartial men into a jury-box"—so, by much stronger reason, may I say here, that the finding of your *Ableman* and getting him invested with the *symbols of ability,* with dignity, worship (*worth*-ship), royalty, kinghood, or whatever we call it, so that *he* may actually have room to guide according to his faculty of doing it,—is the business, well or ill accomplished, of all social procedure whatsover in this world! Hustings-speeches, Parliamentary motions, Reform Bills, French Revolutions, all mean at heart this; or else nothing. Find in any country the Ablest Man that exists there; raise *him* to the supreme place,

* Thomas Carlyle, *On Heroes, Hero-Worship and the Heroic in History.*

and loyally reverence him: you have a perfect government for that country; no ballot-box, parliamentary eloquence, voting, constitution-building, or other machinery whatsover can improve it a whit. It is in the perfect state; an ideal country. The Ablest Man; he means also the truest-hearted, justest, the Noblest Man: what he *tells us to do* must be precisely the wisest, fittest, that we could anywhere or any-how learn;—the thing which it will in all ways behove us, with right loyal thankfulness, and nothing doubting, to do! Our *doing* and life were then, so far as government could regulate it, well regulated; that were the ideal of constitutions.

Alas, we know very well that Ideals can never be completely em-bodied in practice. Ideals must ever lie a very great way off; and we will right thankfully content ourselves with any not intolerable ap-proximation thereto! Let no man, as Schiller says, too querulously "measure by a scale of perfection the meagre product of reality" in this poor world of ours. We will esteem him no wise man; we will esteem him a sickly, discontented, foolish man. And yet, on the other hand, it is never to be forgotten that Ideals do exist; that if they be not approximated to at all, the whole matter goes to wreck! Infallibly. No bricklayer builds a wall *perfectly* perpendicular, mathe-matically this is not possible; a certain degree of perpendicularity suffices him; and he, like a good bricklayer, who must have done with his job, leaves it so. And yet if he sway *too much* from the perpen-dicular; above all, if he throw plummet and level quite away from him, and pile brick on brick heedless, just as it comes to hand—! Such bricklayer, I think, is in a bad way. *He* has forgotten himself: but the Law of Gravitation does not forget to act on him; he and his wall rush-down into confused welter of ruin!—

This is the history of all rebellions, French Revolutions, social explosions in ancient or modern times. You have put the too *Un*able Man at the head of affairs! The too ignoble, unvaliant, fatuous man. You have forgotten that there is any rule, or natural necessity whatever, of putting the Able Man there. Brick must lie on brick as it may and can. Unable Simulacrum of Ability, *quack,* in a word, must adjust himself with quack, in all manner of administration of human things;—which accordingly lie unadministered, fermenting into unmeasured masses of failure, of indigent misery: in the out-ward, and in the inward or spiritual, miserable millions stretch-out the hand for their due supply, and it is not there. The "law of gravitation" acts; Nature's laws do none of them forget to act. The miserable millions burst-forth into Sansculottism, or some other sort of madness: bricks and bricklayer lie as a fatal chaos!—

Much sorry stuff, written some hundred years ago or more, about the "Divine right of Kings," moulders unread now in the Public Libraries of this country. Far be it from us to disturb the calm process by which it is disappearing harmlessly from the earth, in those repositories! At the same time, not to let the immense rubbish go without leaving us, as it ought, some soul of it behind—I will say that it did mean something; something true, which it is important for us and all men to keep in mind. To assert that in whatever man you chose to lay hold of (by this or the other plan of clutching at him); and clapt a round piece of metal on the head of, and called King,—there straightway came to reside a divine virtue, so that *he* became a kind of god, and a Divinity inspired him with faculty and right to rule over you to all lengths: this,—what can we do with this but leave it to rot silently in the Public Libraries? But I will say withal, and that is what these Divine-right men meant, That in Kings, and in all human Authorities, and relations that men god-created can form among each other, there is verily either a Divine Right or else a Diabolic Wrong; one or the other of these two! For it is false altogether, what the last Sceptical Century taught us, that this world is a steam-engine. There is a God in this world; and a God's-sanction, or else the violation of such, does look-out from all ruling and obedience, from all moral acts of men. There is no act more moral between men than that of rule and obedience. Woe to him that claims obedience when it is not due; woe to him that refuses it when it is! God's law is in that, I say, however the Parchment-laws may run: there is a Divine Right or else a Diabolic Wrong at the heart of every claim that one man makes upon another.

It can do none of us harm to reflect on this: in all the relations of life it will concern us; in Loyalty and Royalty, the highest of these. I esteem the modern error, That all goes by self-interest and the check-ing and balancing of greedy knaveries, and that, in short, there is nothing divine whatever in the association of men, a still more despicable error, natural as it is to an unbelieving century, than that of a "divine right" in people *called* Kings. I say, Find me the true *Könning,* King, or Able-man, and he *has* a divine right over me. That we knew in some tolerable measure how to find him, and that all men were ready to acknowledge his divine right when found: this is precisely the healing which a sick world is everywhere, in these ages, seeking after! The true King, as guide of the practical, has ever something of the Pontiff in him,—guide of the spiritual, from which all practice has its rise. This too is a true saying, That the *King* is head of the *Church.*—But we will leave the Polemic stuff of a dead century to lie quiet on its bookshelves.

45 · POWER AND PERSONALITY *

David Spitz

. . . . .

The *idea* of an authoritarian personality has a certain plausibility as an impressionistic or intuitive-apprehending if not scientific fact. Consequently, it may be said, refinements in testing techniques may in time enable us to verify such impressions and reduce them to demonstrable facts. They may help to isolate what is intrinsic to character structure from what is part of the total environment. But whether or not they succeed in doing so, it can be argued, the important fact remains that the authoritarian personality—however men may differ as to its definition—can in some measure be detected even now; hence, this awareness properly becomes, or should become, a guide to political action.

Now the possibility that refinements in testing techniques and in other devices will be achieved, is hardly to be contested. Nevertheless, two problems at least will still plague those who hope to demonstrate through such means the validity of a particular personality typology. One problem derives from the curious but not surprising fact that while the concept of the authoritarian personality has received much attention and can be held to rest on some "scientific" evidences, the concept of the so-called democratic personality hangs very much in the air, and is more likely to remain there. For however difficult the task of defining the authoritarian personality may be, the description of those character traits or attitudes

* David Spitz, "Power and Personality: The Appeal to the 'Right Man' in Democratic States," *The American Political Science Review,* LII (March, 1958), 90-96. Reprinted by permission of The American Political Science Association. The footnotes in the original version are omitted here.

that constitute the democratic personality is a most dubious and controversial—because unscientific—undertaking. The other problem stems from the fact that the line between the individual and the social cannot be effectively drawn. This, of course, was precisely the point on which Mill's otherwise admirable essay *On Liberty* floundered, and it is by no means evident that psychologists and sociologists since his time have succeeded in establishing a legitimate principle by which to differentiate that which is intrinsic to man from that which is inherited or acquired from society. I do not mean to imply by this that personality cannot be distinguished from culture; for the two, while not separable, are not the same. I argue only that the individual, be he conformist or rebel, is so much a product of his society that his attitudes, values, and behavior are always in some measure socially conditioned; they are always a reflection of his cultural environment. When we add to this the very great complexity, the continuing mystery, of personality itself, we see that no psychology can hope through an analysis of individual character alone to establish a particular typology of democratic and authoritarian personality.

Let us, however, set these objections aside. Let us grant, in the face of our ignorance of future events, that a meaningful distinction may be drawn between democratic and authoritarian personalities, and that adequate tests may be devised to tell us into which category our various political leaders or would-be leaders belong. Can we then really expect the eradication of oppressive rule?

The answer, I fear, must still be negative, and for two reasons preeminently. On the one hand, abuses of power are not simply a consequence of some psychological quirk or defect in the ruler; they are also the product of conflicting interests, of long-sustained prejudices, and of established traditions. On the other hand, the right man, once in power, is not likely always to remain the right man. Contrary assumptions, while not wholly false, are insufficiently true to warrant the high expectations that some men have placed in them.

Consider first the view that men who abuse power do so primarily (in some formulations of this theory, exclusively) out of evil intent or vanity or madness. The list of tyrants who meet this view is a long but not an exhaustive one; Attila the Hun and Hitler and others like them are known, after all, only because they were, even among tyrants, unusual men. But, more importantly, the abuses of power that disfigure democratic states are customarily of a different order.

They derive not merely from the caprice or malevolence of those who come to power, but also from the fact that those who rule, like the factions of the people who support them, tend all too often to pursue their own narrow or selfish interests; that rulers tend all too easily to identify the good of the whole with the material good of their class or of some special portion of the whole, such as their families and themselves. Thus, unless it can be shown that personality stands in some necessary—or even approximate (understanding by this a highly probable)—relation to policy, so that the right man will by virtue of his "rightness" act justly (*i.e.,* in a way that transcends particularity of interest) and the wrong man will by virtue of his "wrongness" act unjustly (*i.e.,* in a way that sacrifices the rights of the many, or even of the few, to greed and ambition), the appeal to personality is no solution to our problem.

This cannot be shown. There is no demonstrable relation between "democratic" or "authoritarian" personalities and policy such that authoritarian men will line up on one side, and democratic men on the other side, of each conceivable issue. The lines of ideological division do not respect those of personality, whether we look at a particular issue such as desegregation or at more general questions of domestic and foreign policy or even at the basic problem of the form of the state itself. Indeed, if the theory of the authoritarian personality is a valid one, it is precisely among authoritarians that the greatest ideological divisions are likely to occur; for here the driving force is said to be not ideology but ambition, the craving for power, and in this context policies will be supported or opposed not in terms of their relation to one's character structure but in terms of their utility as steps along the pathway to power. The shifting positions on policy questions taken by Communist political parties in all democratic states at the command of the rulers in the Kremlin, most strikingly at the time of the Nazi-Soviet pact and again at the demise and subsequent denuding of their "great leader Stalin," is a continuing illustration in point; as are too the autocratic methods sometimes employed by democrats in combatting those whom they deem to be authoritarians. On the other hand, persons of quite different dispositions may well behave in a more or less uniform manner, as is evidenced, for example, by the wide diversity of personality characteristics to be found in any political movement, including a democratic one.

In fact, to argue that there is a causal relationship between democratic personality and social role, is to imply that the specific undemocratic practices in this country—many and varied as they are —could all be eliminated merely by placing men with democratic personalities into positions of power. But this, surely, is a fanciful expectation. History is not made by the impact of personalities alone. A Carlyle may look to the ablest man in loyal reverence, and decry any institutional or other restraints that lesser men seek to put upon him. But politics in a democracy is more than a matter of heroes and hero-worship. Other influences are also at play: the individual must come to grips with the interests and traditions of parties and pressure groups no less than with the established organs of government; he cannot ignore social conditions and the power of non-political organizations; he must look to the will, however erroneous he may believe it to be, of the electorate which put him in power, and which can vote him out. He is bound, in a word, by historical, political, and economic forces that are not of his own making and that are often beyond his effective control. Consequently, even if the ruler should be the right man, the right personality, it does not follow that he can, in a democratic state, do what he conceives to be the right thing.

Nor should he be permitted to do so. If it is the business of a democratic state to give the people what they want, to satisfy their stated desires rather than their objective needs (*i.e.,* what some allegedly wise men conceive their needs to be), then it is the function of the government to meet, not to negate, that demand. This is why, in principle, all the people, and not just a few of them, are given political rights. They need those rights, as Mill said, not in order that they may govern, but in order that they may not be misgoverned. And for this purpose it is not the right or the outstanding man, not the so-called democratic personality, that is required, but the representative man—who is sensitive to the changing tides of public opinion and will faithfully seek to translate them into public policy. This is not to imply that a democratic leader ought never to attempt to mold or to change public opinion, that he ought never to be more than an effective recording device for the popular will. But it is to say that however much he may essay a leading role, he ought not, by and large, to act contrary to the judgment of his constituents. So long as he fulfills this role effectively, it is no proper concern of the public what manner of man he is. In this respect it is the part of wisdom to distinguish, so far as one can, the ruler's public life from his private character.

All of this is not to deny that evil or stupid men can cause great harm, and that those states are fortunate that can keep such men out of power. It is only to argue that since tyrannical policies are not necessarily the result of wrong or authoritarian character structures, those policies can neither be removed nor prevented by a remedy that looks to personality alone.

This conclusion is reinforced when we turn to the second of our two major objections to the relevance of the right personality: that the right man is also prone to do great harm. In part, this is because the temptations of power may sooner or later corrupt him, in which case he ceases to be the right man. But in part too, it is precisely because he is the right man that he may do wrong things.

For if the right man is "right" in the moral sense of the word, and is moved by his intelligence and good will to correct the injustices that exist about him, he is sometimes apt to resent those of lesser talents or firmness of character who disagree with him and who would impede his work. Rather than risk failure, rather than have to say later, as the utopian communist Wilhelm Weitling bitterly said: "If all had followed me as the children of Israel followed Moses out of Egypt, I would have succeeded," he may endeavor to silence or to override dissent and to impose his own right judgment. Unhappily, in a world of conflicting moral codes, the right man is right for himself and perhaps for some others, but not for all men; and for those whose judgment is at variance with his own his coercive rule is as wrong as it may, in a particular situation, be oppressive. This is not, let it be understood, to argue that it is impossible to obtain a "right" man (*i.e.,* right to those who so conceive him) as a leader in a democratic state, or that it would be undesirable to have such a right man rule. Nor is it to contend that such a right man could not, under any conditions, succeed both in remaining a right man and in ruling wisely. It is only to insist that such a right man *may,* in a particular set of circumstances, insist on having his own way (*i.e.,* the "right" way) even if this requires him to act contrary to the popular will or to violate basic democratic rights.

If, on the other hand, the right man is "right" in the democratic sense of the word, he is prone to respond affirmatively to the dictates of public opinion. But public opinion may bid him on occasion do an undemocratic thing, in which case he must choose between conflicting policies. As a right man, he wants to give the people what they want; but as a right man, he is committed too to the preservation of democracy itself. To remain loyal to the latter obligation is to defy public opinion and thereby to risk dismissal from public office. To accede to the public will is to repudiate his greater allegiance and thereby to retain public office only at the cost of ceasing to be the right man. In the first case, he is right but he may also prove ineffective; in the second case, he is neither right nor effective. In both cases, therefore, the appeal to the right man, to the leadership of (say) the democratic personality, provides no sure solution to the abuse of power.

I do not mean to carry this self-defeating perplexity too far. The fact that too many men would rather have power than be right does not necessarily imply that all right men will seek at all costs to retain power. Not all power corrupts all men. Some power, in fact, is requisite to the making of a man. Without some autonomy of action, without some delegation of power and the responsibility to administer that power wisely, a man may never grow out of the mentality of a child; he may remain always a dependent animal. And if experience is any guide, the histories of the British and the American democracies make it abundantly clear that, within a respected tradition and an institutional framework that renders rule neither permanent nor absolute, power does not necessarily corrupt; by affording opportunities, it enables many to rule moderately, and some to achieve greatness.

But the temptations of power, though resisted by some, overcome many more. The lure of glory, of pride, of material gain, no less than the conviction that given the power to implement his will one can achieve great things, the right things, for the whole of his people—all these combine to make the pursuit, and later the retention, of power a more than necessary thing. Good men may begin the quest reluctantly, but they rarely end that way. The game is too serious, the weapons too biting, the stakes too high, for them to remain in fact what they strive to appear to be—selfless and genteel servants or would-be servants of the body politic. Those who lack power yearn for what appears now to be well within their grasp, and the failure to achieve it but stimulates them to greater endeavors than before; while the actual conquest and enjoyment of power, despite its bitter fruits, is yet so sweet as to seduce those who possess it into thinking that they were destined for the offices they hold, or (what amounts to the same thing) that their achievements will be destroyed if they surrender their protective role. And always there are the *courtiers*—the flatterers and the sycophants, the profit-seeking groups and the glory-seeking adventurers—whose own possibilities of success are linked to that of the rulers and who are ready, therefore, always to praise their rulers' actions and to encourage their idolatry of themselves.

It is not, therefore, surprising that even good men should begin to think that their power should be commensurate with their goodness, and that this being (in their own eyes at least) unlimited, they should desire their power to be unlimited too. It is true that many have echoed D'Avenant's warning that "no one man ought to think of being omnipotent, unless he could be omniscient and omnipresent." It is true also that in this respect the American political system has heeded only too well Montesquieu's warning "that every man invested with power is apt to abuse it, and to carry his authority as far as it will go. . . . To prevent this abuse, it is necessary from the very nature of things that power should be a check on power." But those who look to the guardianship of a right man do so precisely because the power which was designed to check the abuses of a lesser power is seen to require a check on its own abuses in turn. And those who, while recognizing the impossible requirement of omniscience and omnipresence, insist nevertheless on omnipotence (or a near-omnipotence) in the hands of a right man, do so precisely because they are confident that the right man, because he is a "democratic" man, will not abuse his power.

Yet surely it is here, at the level of such absolute or near-absolute power, that the greatest danger of tyranny lies. For while power in itself may have no more than a tendency to corrupt, absolute power, as Mill and Acton said, corrupts absolutely. It gives its holders a new importance, a new set of habits. Finding themselves worshipped by others, they soon come to worship themselves. Finding that they can do as they like, they indulge in actions that previously seemed so improbable of achievement as to be put beyond the realm of serious contemplation. This is why it is foolish to assume, as the theorists of "democratic" personality are too often inclined to do, that a man out of power will remain the same man when in power. We must never forget, after all, that temptations come more often to him who is in power, and who can by his indulgence advantage the tempter, than to one who is out of power, and who can therefore indulge but give nothing in return. Or that the removal of restraints on the bad as well as the good parts of one's nature makes possible the release of inhibitions that may work to the detriment of the community.

What requires emphasis here, however, is not the corrupting effects of absolute power; for absolute power, even in the hands of the best, the most "democratic" man, is incompatible with democracy. What must be noted is the more relevant fact that even a limited grant of power works somehow in invidious ways to corrupt many of those who exercise it. It is, therefore, a wise political system that looks not only to the beneficent uses that good men will make of power but also to the unhappy consequences that might flow from power in the hands of those who were the wrong men before they achieved power or who became the wrong men after they obtained it.

Political Parties

46 · SOME PERSONAL EXPERIENCES
OF A CANDIDATE *

Stimson Bullitt

Each election year there is a minor change in the ways by which candidate and voter best can come in touch. A campaigner tries experiments or suffers from a time lag. As two means to approach the voters in person while running for Congress in 1954, I attended "coffee hours" and accosted people one by one in public places. I met about 9,300 (count kept by numbered bundles of folders) in five weeks, or about 1 in 65 of the district's population. The following observations were set down at the end of that campaign. They are

* From *To Be a Politician* by Stimson Bullitt. Copyright © 1959 by Stimson Bullitt. Reprinted by permission of Doubleday and Company, Inc.

consistent with my experience in half a dozen others before and after it, in two of which I ran and in the rest of which I campaigned for other candidates.

Most of the time it is delightful to sit in a big chair and stuff yourself with cookies while polite guests treat you as a universal expert. In the homes of supporters who had invited their friends and neighbors I submitted to questions but gave no set speech. Because no more effective engine has ever been invented to probe the nature of a candidate than free interrogation at close quarters, these meetings are an advantage to guests as citizens. And they tend to be uneasy though stimulating periods for the candidate; in the course of an hour some cherished prejudices are likely to collide. The voter may go away shaking his head at the thought of this menace to the Republic whom he has just met, while he still tolerates the others in the race. One does not use these meetings solely as an exercise in civics. In turnover they do not approach waiting in front of a mill through the half hour before the eight o'clock whistle. But each contact is more intensive where candidate and voter meet in a home, introduced by a mutual acquaintance, and where, instead of one greeting the other, who passes on, they actually converse. From this transient intercourse under these favorable conditions, if you are or later become a big shot, the voter may refer to you thereafter as a friend of his.

For successive personal contacts which are more superficial but can be made at a faster rate, you stand each day in supermarket parking lots and outside factory gates, or walk up and down the sidewalks in suburban shopping districts and force yourself upon your fellow citizens hour by hour. I went up to each person and said: "My name is Stimson Bullitt. I'm a candidate for Congress and I'm glad to meet you." If it was a man, I held out my hand at his belt buckle and waited to see if he would raise his hand to let me take it. Then I gave him or her a folder. If there was enough time, depending on the rate and volume of foot traffic, I asked his name. If a difficult name, I asked him to spell it or tried myself to do so and asked him if my effort was correct. Each person had a wall of indifference or suspicion to be assailed. At worst, one first is thought to be a panhandler or pickpocket and at best, a salesman. Perhaps a politican comes somewhere in between.

One makes the strongest impact in front of an industrial plant at dawn. The men one meets are impressed to find anyone out there to greet them so early, especially a member of a group they consider lazy and aloof. Also, the encounter becomes a common experience for them, a subject of conversation during the day with others in the plant who were not met.

The suburban shopping areas are better than downtown sections. The tempo is not as fast, and there are few offensive strangers to make the others shy. People are less hurried and less averse to being accosted. An easy place to work is a commuters' train or ferry. The captive audience takes its ease in security and comfort.

The most barren soil is the waterfront. Many are tourists, some are bums, and the rest recoil at your approach. A race track is another waste of time. A low proportion of the crowd votes regularly for any office except the Presidency. And like people on other intense group occasions, the spectators resent one who interrupts their close attention. Taverns are unprofitable. The bartender is the only person worth meeting. Sober customers think you are a drunk coming over to molest them. Drunks grab you and hold on. They make speeches. Some of them used to entertain themselves with heavy jokes about my name and guns. If you approach anyone as you come out of a bar, he flees.

The best situation for meeting people at random is a small group engaged in idle conversation. This may be on the sidewalk or in a restaurant booth or barbershop. The people are less afraid to be accosted by a stranger because they feel protected by each other. With friendly banter you can often generate a jolly mood, leaving you the subject of their conversation after you have gone.

There are a variety of handshakes—warm, cold, hearty, firm, flabby, moist. I discovered that my hand did not get tired or sore although my hands are small and not very strong. It was a surprise not to be squashed sometimes by some powerful bully. I was embarrassed to make a few jump with pain, presumably from sore hands.

The range of response was wide—hostile, indifferent, suspicious, friendly, enthusiastic, encouraging. Some were flattered to shake the hand of such an eminent person; others politely stated that they differed with me in politics. Sometimes a person would show several reactions, shifting from one to the other in a few moments of discourse.

Some turned away showing ill will because they recognized me as a person about whom they had read bad things in the papers. Some refused to touch me, then, when told I was a Democrat, reversed their attitude and shook hands with warmth. Everyone who asked, "Are you a Democrat or a Republican?" appeared to be a Democrat. It seemed that the Republicans who cared either knew, or preferred to learn by looking at the folder.

Since the Depression years the feelings among voters were strongest in 1952, and the 1946 campaign was next strongest.

A tiny few admitted they had voted Republican in 1952 and then had changed their minds. Statistically, some among the substantial number who asserted that they always had voted Democratic must not have told the truth. Some declared support for the Republican incumbent. Not one of the 9,300 said that he or she was for either of my Democratic opponents. One accepted my handshake, folder, and greeting in a neutral, noncommittal manner, then drove away in a truck with an opponent's sticker on its bumper. I smiled and pointed to it as he drove by, and he waved and smiled back.

Many would not look me in the face. Some would say they were too busy to stop. Some would ask what I stood for, as though they expected a speech then and there. A negligible few would ask where I stood on a specified issue. Another few themselves would advocate a measure. Some would refuse to give their names. Others were unfriendly and rude but still willing to tell their names. Some would say, "I voted for you before and you may have my vote this time, too." In the late stages some would say, "It may please you to know that I've already made up my mind to vote for you." While others would say just before turning away, "I've got my candidate picked out, and he isn't you."

Some thought it silly for me to ask to meet them but took a manner of tolerant amusement and willingness to go along with the game. A few thought I was the incumbent. Quite a number, mainly in the suburban shopping districts, thought I was running for the Legislature rather than for Congress. Some would ask, often in a mocking tone, "What are you going to do for us (me)?" A Navy Yard worker on a ferry sneered that if I was elected I never would be back again to see him. At a horse meat market in a Bremerton suburb, a customer said he was a welder by trade and fancied one day maybe he would be a candidate and thereby get some easy work. Out of every three hundred people, about forty would be friendly and one hostile. But the effect of the one to depress or upset would equal the lift from the forty.

A substantial number of older people remembered my father who lived in Seattle for ten years before his death in 1932. If there was any comment it was praise, often with tender and touching recollections of his character, courtesy, and charm. As always, such responses moved me with pride at being his son and discouragement at my inability to capture men's devotion as he had done.

Only a small minority commented on my stand on the issues, either from information received from TV talks or indirectly by word of mouth from others. In the late stages there were many comments on my name familiarity advertising. The TV spots (a clever cartoon) were by far the most often remarked upon, followed by mention of the ads in other media.

Among those recognizable as a class, the most courteous were the persons behind the counter. They treat you as one more customer. The most universally indifferent as a group were the scavengers, the poorest of the poor. Orientals, with a few educated and Americanized exceptions, ran a close second. Among those whom I took to be Jews, not one was indifferent. Negroes sometimes showed indifference, reserved hostility, coldness, and suspicion, but none was deliberately rude. All accepted my hand.

My impression was that some of the hostile and apathetic reactions were not personal to me or to Democrats in general but rather to politicians as such. To these persons politics appeared to represent frustration and futility. They seemed to feel that nothing good can come of politics, that much of their troubles and perplexity is caused by acts and omissions of government, and that they would rather not be reminded of this painful and mysterious fact about which they feel they can do nothing.

In addition to these baffled ones who were unwilling to assume responsibility, there were many others who were annoyed to be bothered about politics. It was not the loss of time they grudged but rather the drastic shift in state of mind. In this aversion to the intrusion of politics they are like combat soldiers who find inadequate their assumption when they enlisted that only others will be killed, and who thus resign themselves to die, preferring the feeling of certainty of a short life to the anxious hope of a long one; or like some shipwrecked persons on a raft who are said to jump overboard when they no longer can endure the doubt about their rescue. This insecure contentment of the soldier in the field is disturbed by talk of long-range plans for civil life, recalling things that he has banished from the surface of his mind, things he wants and fears will be denied him. It revives the problem which he had settled by renouncing one alternative. In this temper, many citizens resemble these men who are too close to death to ignore it as other young folk do.

In a restaurant on Queen Anne Hill, a man seated in a booth talked with me but failed to take my offered hand. I thought him rude until I realized that he was blind. In the same way two deaf mutes unwittingly misled me. On Market Street in the Ballard District, I met a woman who said she had washed my "didies," to use her word, when I was a baby. On the ferry, I met a man with whom I had been a Boy Scout. On Rainier Avenue, I talked with a man who had watched me box an exhibition with Jack Hammer at an Inglewood Golf Club smoker fifteen years before. In front of the campaign headquarters a woman said that she had voted for me last time and then added "in Kittitas County" (150 miles away). On Pacific Avenue in Bremerton, I ran into Bill Whitney who had won a four-round decision from me at Port Gamble. Many of those I met were attractive people of high quality, whom I hoped to have the chance to meet again, and some of whom I wished to know.

Three days after losing the primary, I ran into an acquaintance in the elevator of the building where we both work. He was well dressed and above average in advantages and education. He mentioned that we had met on a street corner about a month before. Then he asked, "Say, how's your campaign coming along?"

When the duty was tedious or frightening during the Second World War, I kept putting one foot in front of the other by recalling words of Marcus Aurelius: "Every moment think steadily as a Roman and a man to do what thou hast in hand with perfect and simple dignity, and feeling of affection and freedom and justice; and to give thyself relief from all other thoughts." In a campaign, under conditions which are comparable but call for less fortitude and more self-propulsion, a candidate may use another precept to keep himself bound to the task. When he has had enough of hunting strangers in the streets and is tempted to take refuge around the corner in solitude with a book or an ice-cream cone, he may think of the remark by Zatopek, the Czech distance runner. Before the 1948 Olympics, other athletes loitered by the playing fields much of the day, available for interviews, but Zatopek would be pulling on his sweat shirt as he stepped out of the car and onto the track around which he then would run for the afternoon. When a persistent reporter came puffing alongside and remonstrated with him for this habit, Zatopek turned his head and replied, "When I come to the track, I run."

47 · THE TWO-PARTY SYSTEM

E. William Steele

The two-party system is not a political invention patented by the United States and Great Britain. Yet there is some merit in viewing it in an Anglo-American framework. This is not because of any national pride or parochialism. The reason, rather, is that these two countries have had lengthy two-party experience.

To cite Great Britain and the United States as prime examples of the two-party system is, of course, something of an oversimplification. For the fact is that each of these countries has also had its third parties. From time to time, indeed, these have played rather significant roles. In Great Britain, moreover, the present Liberal Party remains a force of some importance, and there are those who believe that its prestige is actually increasing. Generally, however, both the United States and Great Britain have politically organized themselves in terms of two parties, each alternating with the other in a role of leadership and opposition. In both countries, party labels and party composition have changed from period to period. Yet the political contest has consistently remained *between* rather than *among* parties.

It would be an even more inaccurate and misleading oversimplification to assume that the two-party systems of Great Britain and the United States are closely analogous. For on the contrary, each system is quite unique and distinct in its own right. In fact, the differences between the two systems are so extensive that, aside from their both being two-party, rather than one-party or multi-party systems, they might seem to have very little in common at all.

Great Britain is a unitary state with a centralized, rather than a federal governmental system. British parties of course conform to this basic political arrangement. This means most importantly that they assume a national perspective and operate through a disciplined organization. Both the Conservative and the Labour parties are always sufficiently united so as either to govern as the party in power or to serve the political process as the Loyal Opposition. Parties govern and are judged by this capacity to fulfill that function.

The United States also has its two national parties. Yet because of the federal nature of the American governmental system, the character and direction of the two national parties are frequently determined by the fifty state party organizations. And though these unite for the purpose of selecting and supporting a candidate for the Presidency, each is at the same time endeavoring to elect a group of candidates whose official positions may have only the remotest connection with a Presidential election. In the United States, that is, the parties are engaged in providing leadership at numerous levels of government. In the aggregate, they are not committed solely to governing the nation.

An interesting indication of this difference may be seen in the political language of the two nations. The British speak of "the Conservative government," or "the Labour government." An American uses a party label before an institutional designation—e.g., "a Republican President," or a "Democratic Congress." The words "Republican" and "Democratic" lose their capital letters when they precede the word government.

There is another fundamental distinction between the two systems. It is one that concerns the question of the importance for them of ideology. American parties are strong in the loyalty they command from many of their supporters, as a political discussion with a Georgia Democrat or a Vermont Republican readily shows. Yet the loyalty in question is much less to principle, policy and program than is the case in British parties.

The American political parties represent broad national policy approaches that, at least from a long-range historical perspective, are clearly distinguishable. Yet in any given election the two approaches may be so broad as to make it possible for each of the parties to encompass and seek to represent virtually the entire range of existing political opinion. Thus, rather than being "all things to all men," the two political parties in the United States are "different things to different men in different places." In their basic orientation, American parties show little concern with philosophy or theory. Their temper is pragmatic, not programmatic.

To a great extent, therefore, the American political parties are best viewed not as ends in themselves, but, rather, as means by which individuals and groups seek political office. Their organizational effort may take any one of a multitude of directions, depending on the particular leadership, the times, the place, and the felt necessities of the situation. Call it an anachronism if you will, but American parties, their durable labels and traditional loyalties notwithstanding, are, in reality, highly flexible, volatile and chameleon-like.

This should, of course, come as no surprise. Viewed against the background of a federal system, the political parties in the United States might well be expected to be even more decentralized than they are. It is no mean accomplishment that the parties are able to unite their ranks throughout the states as consistently and successfully as they do for the Presidential contests. One major reason for this success lies in the fact that the parties are primarily avenues for political participation. In the race to gain supporters, all that is sought—and in most cases all that is given—is not an intellectual commitment, but an "X" in the appropriate column. And in American politics, all "X's" are equal, once they are legally inscribed on the ballot.

The competition for the "X's" is fiercely waged, but not as much on the basis of alternative programs as on the basis of alternative groups of politicians. That is, the political contests are built around men more than around what they represent. This is generally true both in state party contests in the United States and in the national elections, and implies that the party labels have acquired such an elastic quality that they can be stretched to embrace the widest variety of supporters. Here again, we have a paradox. For in reality, the two parties in the United States increasingly give evidence of having preempted the workable political field, thus making it difficult for a would-be third party to file much of a profitable claim. Barring a wide desire in the United States for some very fundamental social revolution, the two major parties would thus seem to be firmly in control.

In Great Britain, the two major parties alternate in bearing the responsibility of governing. The parties are organized and directed for this purpose. Even in opposition, the British political party maintains its own "shadow" Prime Minister and Cabinet. Obviously, the electorate is not unconcerned with the personalities of those they choose to represent them, but given the unitary character of the British political system, the electorate is also conscious that it is choosing a governing party. As a national party, first and foremost, the British political party can legitimately propose programs, and is just as legitimately expected to work with disciplined effort to see that the programs secure parliamentary approval and thus become government policy. In Great Britain, that is, appeals to party supporters ask for the endorsement of a program, with the implicit understanding that a centralized political organization will undertake to see that the program is enacted. One may, therefore, contrast the political party systems of the United States and Great Britain in the following terms: in the United States, the parties are expected to supply officials of government who are to be responsive to public needs and responsible to their constituencies; in Great Britain, the parties are expected to supply officials of government responsive to public needs, but responsible above all to their party's broad national program, rather than to their constituencies.

The formal structure of government, long standing traditions, as well as historical circumstance are all factors that help to explain the party systems of these two nations. There is, however, one additional factor that must be noted. In each of these countries, there has existed a wide area of consensus, of agreement both as to the ends of government as well as to its proper means. Someone once said that between England and the Revolution, there will always be an army of bowler hats. One might say with equal justification that between the United States and the Revolution there will always be Macys and Gimbels. Despite the sound and fury of campaigns, the alternating warnings of salvation or damnation, and such customary pre-election rhetoric as "We view with alarm . . ." or "We point with pride. . . ," the day after the elections sees the restoration of the characteristic American and British live-and-let-live political spirit. The losers greet the day with regret, but not with revolutionary plots.

It may be that this is a key to the "why" of the two-party systems in these two countries. Extremes can survive only in the language of politics, not in the governing of the nations. In societies without deep ideological divisions, the intellectual demand to distinguish more than two parties may be too much to ask, particularly when politics itself is seen not as the core of life, but merely as one of its peripheral activities.

The political parties in Great Britain and the United States have been able to accommodate the widest variety of opinion and—what we often forget—the greatest amount of indifference. They have provided a convenient way of synthesizing complex choices. One has done it within a system of party government, the other within a Presidential system that sometimes makes a mockery of party distinctiveness. But each nation has recognized that though the voters may commit themselves to one party rather than the other, and to one set of candidates rather than another, they regard *both* parties as basic and invaluable national possessions. As long as the parties, taken together, help to avoid the dangers of Hobbes's *Leviathan,* the field of partisan warfare will be theirs.

48 · MULTI-PARTISM *

Maurice Duverger

Multi-partism is often confused with absence of parties. A country in which opinion is divided among several groups that are unstable, fluid, and short-lived does not provide an example of multi-partism in the proper sense of the term: it is still in the prehistoric era of parties; it is to be situated in that phase of general development at which the distinction between bipartism and multi-partism is not yet applicable because there are as yet no true parties. In this category we can place many Central European countries between 1919 and 1939, most of the young nations in Africa, the East, and the Middle East, many Latin-American states, and the great Western states of the nineteenth century. However, some of these countries might be better classified in an intermediate category: in them there are to be found authentic parties possessing a minimum of organization and stability in juxtaposition to inorganic and unstable groups. In this case the line of demarcation between multi-partism and absence of parties is blurred, all the more so because vestiges of inorganic groups subsist inside many countries that have organized parties: in France, for example, that whole sector of opinion to the right of the Radicals is almost entirely without true parties and

* Maurice Duverger, *Political Parties: Their Organization and Activity in the Modern State* (2nd English edition translated by Barbara and Robert North; London: Methuen and Co. Ltd., 1959), pp. 228-238. Reprinted by permission of Methuen and Co. Ltd. and John Wiley and Sons, Inc. The footnote in the original version is omitted here.

consists rather of the fluid groups which are characteristic of an earlier phase of development.

In this sense multi-partism is fairly characteristic of Western Europe, Great Britain excepted but Ireland included. It is of course true that some of these states have had experience of the two-party system at some periods in their history: Belgium was dualist until 1894; contemporary Germany is very near to being dualist. Other states have had experience of single-party systems: Italy from 1924 to 1945, Germany from 1933 to 1945, Spain and Portugal at the present day. It may also be thought that the European multi-party system is to-day in peril and that its future is uncertain. None the less the multi-party system continues to hold sway throughout continental Western Europe; it seems too to correspond to the most general of her political traditions.

FORMATION OF MULTI-PARTISM

The typology of the multi-party system is difficult to establish: innumerable varieties can be imagined ranging from three parties to infinity, and within each variety innumerable patterns and shades of difference are possible. Post-Liberation tri-partism in France has nothing in common with Belgian traditional tri-partism; Scandinavian quadri-partism is fundamentally different from Swiss quadri-partism; the dispersal of the French Right means something quite different from the splitting of parties in pre-war Czechoslovakia or Republican Spain: each national organization seems to retain its own extraordinary and unique characteristics which prevent it from being classified in any general scheme. However, we can discover some traits that they have in common if we consider the ways in which multi-party systems come into being. In this connection we can construct a theoretical pattern which fits most of the facts if we take as our point of departure the idea that the two-party system is natural, and then consider this fundamental tendency to be subject to modification as a result of two different phenomena: internal divisions of opinion and their overlapping.

Take for example a two-party system like that in Britain in 1950. In the Labour party there was a fairly clear distinction between the moderates who supported the Attlee Government and a more radical, more extremist group which was sometimes at odds with ministers and which followed its own line on some important questions, notably foreign affairs. Inside the Conservative party the divisions were less clear because the party was restricted to the role of opposition: when it came to power the differences became more obvious, as in pre-war days. We may proceed to generalize from this particular example: inside all parties there are moderates and extremists, the conciliatory and the intransigent, the diplomatic and the doctrinaire; the pacific and the fire-eaters. The cleavage between reformers and revolutionaries in European Socialist parties at the beginning of this century was simply one particular instance of a very general tendency. In fact the sociological distinction between "radical" and "conservative" temperaments should be complemented by a second distinction contrasting the "extremist" temperament with the "moderate"; each is complementary to the other, for there are extremist conservatives and moderate conservatives, extremist radicals and moderate radicals (e.g. Jacobins and Girondins). So long as this second distinction is limited in its effects to the creation of factions and rivalries inside parties produced by the first distinction, the natural two-party system remains unchanged. If, however, the factions become exasperated and can no longer meet on common ground the basic tendency to dualism is thwarted and gives way to multi-partism. It was in this way that the split in Switzerland between Radicals and Liberals breached the original 1848 two-party system (Conservatives vs. Liberals) and created a three-party system that the Socialists later transformed into a four-party system. The same is true of France: the gradual formation of the Radical party split the Republicans, with the result that by the end of the nineteenth century there were three basic tendencies visible: Conservatives, Moderate Republicans (Opportunists), and Radicals. In Denmark and Holland the birth of the Radical party was the product of an identical tendency: a split over the opinions common to moderates and extremists. About 1920 there were many cases in Europe of an increase in the number of parties due to splits between Communists (revolutionaries) and Socialists (reformers).

Such splits gave rise to Center parties. There exists no Center opinion, no Center tendency, no Center doctrine separate in kind from the doctrines of the Right or of the Left—but only a dilution of their doctrines, an attenuation, a moderate doctrine. If an old Liberal party (on the Left in a two-party system) splits into Liberals and Radicals, then the former become a Center party. The same happens when a Conservative party divides into Moderates and Extremists. Such is the first method by which Center parties are created (the second is a consequence of "Leftism"). In theory an authentic Center party would presuppose that right-wing Moderates and left-wing Moderates, breaking away from their initial tendencies, had united to form a single party; in practice, however, the origin of the central party is of little account; its very position and the contradictory attractions that are exerted on its members produce inside it a fundamental cleavage: every Center party is by its very nature divided. An exception occurs when two Center parties coexist in a country: this was approximately the case in Denmark before proportional representation was set up—the Liberals represented the Right-Center and the Radicals the Left-Center; the attraction of the two extremes still proved stronger than the solidarity of the Moderates, for the Radicals co-operated with the Socialists and not with the Liberals, illustrating thereby a tendency which is very common in Scandinavia. In France the Radical-Socialists (Left-Center) alternated throughout the Third Republic between Central solidarity (which produced the "concentration") and Left-wing solidarity (which produced the Left-wing Cartel, the Popular Front, and so on).

"Overlapping" is a phenomenon however that seems to be more widespread than the "split." It consists in the non-coincidence of a number of different dualisms of opinion with the result that their combinations produce a multi-partite division. In France, for example, the old division of opinion "Clerical" *vs.* "Anti-clerical" does not correspond with the division between "West" and "East" or with that between "Freedom" and "Planning." By superimposing these bipartite divisions we can draw a diagram showing the main spiritual families in France: Communists (East, Planning, Anti-clerical); Christian Progressives (East, Planning, Clerical); Socialists (West, Planning, Anti-clerical); M.R.P. (West, Planning, Clerical); Radicals (West, Freedom, Anti-clerical); Right (West, Freedom, Clerical). Of course this classification is somewhat arbitrary and much oversimplified; none the less it corresponds on the whole to the main lines of cleavage in opinion as well as to the real division of parties (it gives too much importance to the Christian Progressives who are weak). The multi-party system in France is a result of the non-coincidence of the main cleavages in opinion.

Here we see the limits of the field within which the two-party system is natural. All antitheses are by nature dualist where they involve rivalry between two points of view that are diametrically opposed (always remembering however that either can be defended with moderation or with zeal); if, however, there are various sets of antitheses and these are largely independent of one another, then one can adopt a viewpoint in one field and still be relatively free to choose one's point of view in other fields. Multi-partism arises from

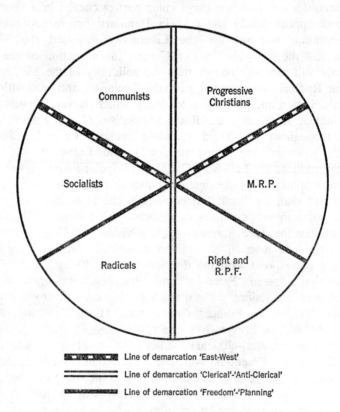

OVERLAPPING OF CLEAVAGES IN FRANCE

Communists

Progressive
Christians

Socialists

M.R.P.

Radicals

Right and
R.P.F.

Line of demarcation 'East-West'
Line of demarcation 'Clerical'-'Anti-Clerical'
Line of demarcation 'Freedom'-'Planning'

the mutual independence of sets of antitheses. It necessarily presupposes that the different sectors of political activity are relatively isolated and sealed off one from the other: the distinguishing characteristic of every "totalitarian" concept lies precisely in its establishment of a rigorous interdependence of all questions, with the result that an attitude to one necessarily involves a corresponding attitude to all others. Totalitarian ideologies may coexist, however, and produce a multi-party system on condition that they are not agreed upon the one supreme issue which determines for each of them the attitudes to be assumed on all other issues. If all Frenchmen were in agreement in holding that the antagonism East *vs.* West took precedence over all others, then there would be only two parties: Communists and Anti-Communists. If they all accepted as fundamental the rivalry between freedom and planning, there would be only two parties: Conservatives and Socialists. If on the other hand they thought that the Clerical *vs.* Anti-clerical issue was basic, as is still held in some corners of France, then there would be only two parties: Catholics and Free-thinkers (there was a trend towards this at the beginning of the century). It is on the contrary the very fact that some emphasize the Freedom *vs.* Planning issue, others the Clerical *vs.* Anti-clerical, and yet others the East *vs.* West that maintains multi-partism.

Very many antitheses can overlap in this way. First there are political antitheses proper, concerning the form or organization of the government, e.g. the Republican-Monarchist opposition, sometimes made more complex by subtle differences similar to those between Bonapartists and Royalists, or between Orleanists and Legitimists. Then there are social antagonisms: Aristotle noted, for example, in his Athenian Constitution, that there existed three parties, that of the port fishermen and sailors, that of the lowland agriculturists, that of the town workpeople; Marxism affirms in fact that social antitheses are fundamental and primordial in character. Next there are economic antagonisms illustrated by the controversy between planning and freedom, but this masks a more deep-seated social antithesis: tradespeople, industrialists, producers, and distributors defending freedom which favors them, the salaried classes, workers, clerks, and office workers supporting planning which protects them. There are religious antagonisms: the struggle between clerical and anti-clerical elements in Catholic countries (France, Belgium, Spain, Italy, etc.) where the ecclesiastical authorities have often preserved some political influence; the struggle between Protestants and Catholics in countries divided on religious questions—in Holland, for example, parties are primarily organized on this basis, the Anti-Revolutionaries (Conservative and Protestant) opposing the Catholic Conservatives, while the Christian Historical party was formed at the end of the last century in protest against the cooperation of the first two. There are national and racial antagonisms in states which comprise different racial and political communities: Czechs *vs.* Slovaks in the Masaryk and Beneš Republic; Serbs *vs.* Croats in the former Yugoslav kingdom; Germans, Hungarians, and Slavs at odds in the Habsburg Empire; Catalan and Basque independence movements in Spain; Irish movement in Great Britain before the independence of Eire; Sudeten movement in Czechoslovakia, and Alsatian independence movement in the German Empire and in the French Republic; antagonism between Flemings and Walloons in contemporary Belgium, and so on. There are diplomatic antitheses that are the reflections within states of international rivalries: Armagnacs and Burgundians, Guelphs and Ghibellines, Axis supporters and supporters of democracy, Easterners and Westerners. And finally there are the antitheses of history: like so many sedimentary deposits, new antitheses overlay old antitheses without destroying them, with the result that divisions of varying ages may coexist in the mind of the nation at the same point of time. In France, for example, the dispute between Monarchists and Republicans which was fundamental in 1875 no longer subsists today except amongst a very small minority of the population; on the other hand the division between "clericals" and "anti-clericals" which was dominant around 1905 still retains a large measure of influence in the provinces (and in the subconscious of Frenchmen) although for the most part events have made it obsolete; the Socialist-Liberal antithesis only really began to be important after 1940 and is only primordial so long as the economic situation is difficult (it has diminished somewhat since 1950-51); lastly, the East *vs.* West antagonism (Communists *vs.* Non-Communists), not born until 1947, is not always very clear: many workers, farm-labourers, and lower-middle-class people, who have no desire for a Soviet regime, vote Communist to show their discontent; moreover, the "neutralists" are in an intermediate position.

TYPES OF MULTI-PARTY SYSTEM

If we consider established multi-partism and not the methods of its establishment we can distinguish several varieties according to the number of rival parties, e.g. tri-partism, quadri-partism, poly-partism, but this classification is even more precarious than the preceding one. We shall therefore describe a few concrete examples instead of seeking out general explanations which would remain too theoretical. There are two chief cases of tri-partism which will re-pay analysis: 1900 tri-partism and contemporary Australian tri-partism. As we have seen, the fundamental dualism of opinion was transformed into tri-partism in England, Belgium, Sweden, Australia, New Zealand, etc., as a result of the development of Socialist parties at the end of the nineteenth and the beginning of the twentieth centuries. We might consider basing a system on this example and try to discover whether the tendency of the country to swing to the Left has not the effect of modifying in the direction of tri-partism the natural dualism of opinion. It is a fairly common occurrence that reformist or revolutionary parties become conservative once the reforms or revolutions they have fought for are accomplished: they move from the Left to the Right, leaving a gap which is filled by the appearance of a new left-wing party that in its turn evolves in the same way. Thus after an interval of twenty or thirty years the Left of one period becomes the Right of the next. The term "Leftism" can be applied to this constant drive. In theory the movement of the old Left party towards the Right should entail the disappearance of the old conservative party, with the result that the initial two-party system would be perpetually reborn (as in Anglo-Saxon countries). In practice parties are very long a-dying, their social structures tend-ing to persist long after they have lost their usefulness. The swing to the Left would therefore combine with the fundamental ten-dency to dualism to produce a tri-partism. Thus the tri-partite sys-tem "Conservatives–Liberals–Radicals" would be followed by a new tri-partism, "Conservatives or Liberals–Radicals–Socialists," and that by the tri-partism "Liberals–Socialists–Communists." Traces of such a tendency could be discovered in several countries, but it is combined with too many special phenomena for us to accord it any great weight. Since the old organizations often persist for a very long time, the swing to the Left increases the total number of parties instead of destroying one of them. The factors which led to the birth of the 1900 tri-partite system do not seem to offer the materials for any valid conclusion.

The contemporary three-party system in Australia has a social basis. The "Conservative–Labour" dualism which corresponds to the "middle-class–working-class" pattern is here modified by the separate political representation of the farming community by the Country party. The latter is the result of a marked effort to give the agriculturist a means of expression like that provided by Labour for the working class: the very fact that it has deliberately moulded its organization on that of the Labour party proves this. It is interesting to compare this example with the attempts made in certain People's Democracies to set up a multi-party system based on social considerations; in every case it ended in the same trinity, Workers', Peasants', and Liberal-Bourgeois parties. The increasing dominion of the Workers' party (Communist in practice) prevented the experiment, which might have been of interest, from bearing fruit. But the major difficulty of every Agrarian party comes from the perpetual conflict within it between Right and Left, springing from the variety of social strata among agriculturists: there exists no agricultural class, only a division between the agricultural proletariat and the agricultural proprietors, and a deeper division still between the smallholder and the large-scale farmer. Whence a natural difficulty in creating Agrarian parties, the inevitable limits to their expansion and their fairly general tendency towards the Right and conservatism: the smallholder and the agricultural worker prefer to join Socialist or Communist parties.

Agrarian parties are in consequence comparatively rare; in any case they have not become so widespread as Socialist parties. In some countries, however, their development has given rise to a quadri-partism which deserves mention, for the phenomenon involved is somewhat uncommon. The four-party system in question results from the addition of an Agrarian party to the Conservative–Liberal–Socialist tri-partism general in Europe about 1900. Such is approximately the present situation in the Scandinavian countries with which can be compared Switzerland and Canada. Why has the peasantry in these countries succeeded in creating and maintaining an independent political party whereas it has not succeeded elsewhere? The Scandinavian example can be associated with historical traditions. In the nineteenth century the antagonism "Conservative vs. Liberal" assumed in Scandinavia the form "town vs. country," the latter being more Left than the former, contrary to what happened elsewhere: it was a sign of a still elementary social structure resting upon a very limited industrial development (the first revolutions were Jacqueries). Thus a fairly powerful Agrarian party opposed the aristocrats and middle classes of the towns. However, the development of an urban Liberal party, then of a Socialist party, gradually drove the Agrarian party back toward conservatism, where it joined its former adversaries: at the end of the nineteenth century, the old Agrarian parties were tending to become Conservative parties pure and simple, either through the elimination of the old Right wing or by fusion with it. But a certain tradition of independent Agrarian policy remained and no doubt played some part in the reappearance of Agrarian parties when proportional representation encouraged multi-partism. In Denmark the decline of the Conservatives was arrested and the Left (*Venstre,* very moderate) was able to remain truly agricultural in character. A new Agrarian party, much more moderate than its nineteenth-century predecessors, was formed in Sweden in 1911 and in Norway in 1918. In fact the rural parties in these three countries today represent one fraction of right-wing opinion, in spite of the fact that their social basis is the lower and middle agricultural classes; it seems that agrarian civilization and the peasant's mode of living encourage political conservatism. The same might be said of the Swiss Peasant and Bourgeois party (which is not moreover entirely agrarian). In Canada, however, the Social Credit party is more progressive in outlook; in the United States the farmers established parties, quite strong locally (especially before the measures taken in their favor by Roosevelt in 1933) and markedly reformist. Some Agrarian parties operating in Central Europe between 1919 and 1939 displayed similar characteristics; they were based on Co-operatives and Trade Unions after the fashion of Labour parties; in Bulgaria in particular their organization was quite remarkable. From time to time a four-party system seemed to be emerging in these states, notwithstanding electoral manipulations and *de facto* dictatorships.

Over and above four parties classification is no longer possible. Separate consideration must be given however to *polypartism,* or the tendency to extreme multiplication of parties, which can be explained by general causes that are rather variable. There are several types of polypartism. One might distinguish a nationalist or ethnic polypartism, peculiar to countries divided into several traditional or racial groups: here racial antagonisms overlay the social and political, producing extreme complexity; "Twenty-five parties!" sadly noted Andrassy, Minister of Foreign Affairs in Austro-Hungary on the eve of the 1914 War, as he looked at the Viennese Parliament in which the rivalries between Conservatives, Liberals, Radicals, and Socialists were complicated by rivalries between Austrians, Poles, Czechs, Serbs, Croats, and so on. In the same way in Czechoslovakia there were in 1938 as many as fourteen parties, including one

Hungarian, one Slovak, and four German parties; among those which seemed to be active throughout the whole Republic some were in fact especially concerned with Bohemia or Slovakia. In the 1871-1914 German Reichstag places were occupied by a Polish, a Danish, and an Alsatian party. The Irish party played an important part in England towards the end of the nineteenth and the beginning of the twentieth centuries.

Furthermore it will be observed that there exists in many countries a right-wing tendency towards polypartism. In France, for example, since the beginning of the century, the Left has coalesced into two or three clearly defined parties whereas the Right is scattered into a swarm of small groups. In Holland religious divisions have the same effect in fundamentally dividing the Right and the Center, while the Left remains united in support of the Socialist party. Sometimes this right-wing polypartism is due to "Leftism": several of the present-day right-wing groups are nothing but old left-wing parties that have been driven to the Right by the pressure of new parties and that have not succeeded in completely absorbing the old right-wing parties. It also occurs as a result of the tendency of Conservative parties to split internally and to become dispersed into rival fractions. This is no doubt connected with the deeply individualist streak in the bourgeoisie, already frequently mentioned, and probably also with the fact that the most developed social class is naturally the most differentiated, which leads it to adopt a variety of political attitudes. The coincidence between party and class that is affirmed by the Marxists is valid only for primitive social classes that are undeveloped and undifferentiated; all progress in a class introduces into it diversities which tend to be reflected on the political plane and in the division of parties.

49 · MEMBERSHIP IN THE COMMUNIST PARTY *

Derek J. R. Scott

The rules provide (Rule 2) that "any toiler who does not exploit the labour of any other, who is a citizen of the Soviet Union, accepts the programme and rules of the party, co-operates actively in their realisation, working in one of the organisations of the party and fulfilling all the decisions of the party, may be a member of the Communist Party of the Soviet Union"; but the suggestion of a more restrictive admittance policy which we see in the constitution is in fact supported by the persistent practice of the party. The rules of the party themselves provided (5b): "The question of admittance of the party is considered and decided by the general assembly of the primary party organisation, the decision of which enters into force on confirmation by the district committee, or, in towns where there is no division into districts, by the town committee of the party." This process has to be gone through twice. Recruits are first admitted as probationary members or, in the party's terminology, "candidates," and only when they may be supposed to have acquainted themselves with the aims and methods of the party, as full members. Clearly this is something that one cannot just join by turning up at the meeting with an initial subscription in one's hands. A recent reiteration of the official doctrine on the point declares that "the party does not chase after quantity of accessions, understanding that its strength consists not in the quantity of members but, above all, in their quality. . . . The party regulates the business of admission with regard to the tasks which lie before it at this or that stage of activity." The principles on which the selection is made have therefore varied considerably from time to time in the party's history.

· · · · ·

By the time of the Eighteenth Party Congress of 1939 there were thus few motives for discrimination left. Stalin's power and the collectivization of agriculture were accomplished facts. The regime had at its disposal a managerial class of its own creation on which it felt

* From *Russian Political Institutions* by Derek J. R. Scott. © Rinehart & Company, Inc. Reprinted by permission of Holt, Rinehart and Winston, Inc., New York, and George Allen & Unwin, Ltd., London. The footnotes in the original version are omitted here.

it could rely. The traditional criteria of class origin had ceased to be significant in the new society where function alone—utility to the regime as manager, as maintainer of prestige, morale or security, or as exemplary worker in production or other approved purposes—was important. Consequently that congress abolished the social class categories regulating the entry of new recruits, and with them the short-lived sympathizers' groups. By the new rules all aspirants to party membership required three sponsors of three years' seniority in the party and were to serve for one year as candidates. The only special provision, apart from that concerning former members of other political parties, applied to persons between the ages of eighteen (the minimum age for candidate membership of the party) and twenty. Entry at such ages was restricted to members of the *Komsomol*. Any member of that organization might present the recommendation of its district committee as equivalent to the recommendation of one party member. These regulations remain unchanged. The period of the war of 1941-5, however, brought certain temporary concessions. A decision of the Central Committee of August 19, 1941 provided that soldiers should require only three sponsors of one year's standing, and another decision of three months later provided for those who had distinguished themselves in battle a reduced candidate stage of three months. Wartime concessions were allowed to continue until 1947, though they were less generously applied after the cessation of hostilities. There occurred a rapid rise in membership. This was not entirely a product of the circumstances of the war period. In the society as refashioned by Stalin recruitment to the party had obvious attractions for both recruit and regime; the advisability had been discovered of bringing all persons of importance within the party where in exchange for privileges and prospects they could be induced to accept obligations and a degree of supervision greater than could conveniently be imposed upon ordinary citizens, though it was realised that a watch must be kept for the arrant careerist. Early after the resumption of admissions, and repeatedly, local party organizations had to be warned against recruiting drives pressed as ends in themselves and to the neglect of individual fitness. Nevertheless recruitment went on apace, and during the war it seems that the party so far overcame its objections to seeking members as to persuade the officers and recipients of decorations to join, presumably in order that it might have the benefit of their prestige. At the beginning of the war the membership (with candidates) was just under 3,900,000.

By September 1947 it was 6,300,000, far higher than ever before, and in consequence of war casualties or other cause only some 2,000,000 pre-war members (i.e. about half) survived among this number.

This development gave rise to the expectation outside Russia that a weeding out of the unsuitable would follow, and some colour was lent to the supposition by authoritative hints of revision of the membership rules to be introduced at the Nineteenth Congress in 1952. In fact, no general purge has occurred, though there have been local checks, with expulsions, sometimes on a fairly large scale. There is evidence of this from Belorussia, Kirgizia, Esthonia and Moldavia up to 1952, and in 1948 the Georgian party, in reaction against previous over-generous recruiting, seems to have expelled more than it admitted. Some local party organisations apparently put a stop on all recruitment in this period, but this has been ruled incorrect. At the Nineteenth Congress Malenkov claimed that the party had since the war been applying a policy of restricting admissions and devoting more attention to training, and would continue to do so. But the only material change then made in the rules in this respect—and none was made in 1956—was the insertion of a provision limiting to one year the additional term which an unsatisfactory candidate could be required to serve. If thereafter he had still not justified himself he was to be expelled. Previously some aspirants had been allowed to cool their enthusiasm for the cause through protracted periods of probation. As usual the change of policy does not seem to have produced any immediate change of practice. In 1954 some party candidates in Armenia were reported to have remained as such for twelve years, and more than half of those in Georgia and Belorussia, as well as 45 per cent in the Ukraine and Lithuania, to have exceeded the official term. Some success, however, as well as the non-occurrence of the purge in the grand manner, is reflected in the proportions of the membership as announced at the 1952 and 1956 Congresses. At the former it was given as 6,013,259 full members and 868,886 candidates; at the latter it was 6,795,896 members and 419,609 candidates. The enlarged party seems to have come to stay, and the wartime recruits to have taken root and flourished—providing 21.6 per cent of the 1956 Congress delegates, with another 13.4 per cent for post-war recruits. The checking commission reported that since the previous Congress there had been a general recall and reissue of party cards, necessitated by the change in the party's name, but it does not seem that use was made of this occasion for a general critical review of members' records.

Over the country as a whole the full party members thus numbered 3.34 per cent of the population. On a very rough calculation from the particulars given by Aristov (in the report of the mandates commission) for the six largest republics by population outside the R.S.F.S.R. Georgia (with 4.75 per cent party full membership) and Azerbaidjan (with 3.82 per cent) were ahead, as in 1952. The others ranged between 2.8 per cent (Kazah) and 2.05 per cent (Uzbek). For all republics this represented a rise and apparently some levelling out. In 1952, when the proportion for the country as a whole was 3 per cent, the R.S.F.S.R. had 3.5 per cent, Georgia 4.4 per cent and Moldavia, at the other extreme, 1 per cent. The party is an institution of the whole Union, not in any significant sense "at home" in the R.S.F.S.R. and "in occupation" in the other republics. Nor is it a peculiar preserve of the Great Russians, from Russia proper or elsewhere. Non-Russian names predominate in the central committees of the republican parties and, as far as the evidence takes us, among regional first secretaries in the republics. Nevertheless, there are always a large number of Russians as well, while there is not a corresponding contingent of non-Russians in office in the R.S.F.S.R., and for most non-Russian first secretaries there seems to be a Russian in the almost equally powerful office of second secretary.

It is still, on the whole, a man's party. Aristov reported 1,414,456 women in the party—apparently including candidates—95,488 more than in 1952 and 1,080,635 more than in 1939. Even now the women do not hold many of the leading offices, though there are now a few of them serving as regional first secretaries and, latterly, a woman member of the Praesidium. They are more prominent in such lesser offices in the party's gift as those in the trade unions and the youth movement. That they should be in a minority is not surprising. The party is a party of active participants in politics, not one of supporters, and the most actively influential offices in the Soviet state are still held by men.

In general character the party seems to be, as it was becoming before the war, a form of co-optive aristocracy of the new society, representing primarily the managerial element of the system. In 1956 1,877,773 members and candidates had some form of specialist training of higher (university) or middle (secondary) standard. In all 2,651,745 had received higher or middle education, and another

2,127,862 partial middle education—making two-thirds of the whole membership available for posts of some influence. As early as 1936 it was stated that nearly 99 per cent of the factory managers were members, and the position was apparently similar in the higher ranks of the army. On the other hand, a report of 1939 indicated that the rural areas, with 65 per cent of the population, did not contain 20 per cent of the membership, and of these members only half were on the collective farms. Here there has been some change, partly because as a matter of policy recruiting has latterly been directed towards the rural population, and particularly the rural intelligentsia, and partly because of the intensification of the long-standing practice of posting urban communists to rural areas, mainly in the attempt to provide agriculture with managers capable of achieving the results which Moscow believes possible. By the Congress of 1956 the total rural membership had increased, but the balance within it was much the same. The rural districts, Mr. Khrushchev reported, had more than 3,000,000 party members and candidates, but less than half of them were working directly in the collective farms, the machine-tractor stations, or the state farms. There are some 87,000, 9,000, and 5,000 of these institutions respectively; each requires a head and a number of senior officials; most accounts which we have show at least the intention of filling these posts with communists, so that there is little room in the party ranks for the working peasant, though we have accounts from some farms where there are such members. A report from Smolensk region immediately after the congress mentioned one district where only seventy-four of 400 members were on the collective farms, though the region as a whole had shown a 20 per cent improvement since 1954, to 12,573 in the farms and stations out of 20,080 members and candidates. In the coal industry Mr. Khrushchev had similarly reported 90,000 communists, but only 38,000 of them working underground.

In the local soviets we have seen the party diluting its élite, which even now it has to some extent to limit in numbers in order to preserve its quality, with less satisfactory though still serviceable non-party material in the remoter places and less important posts for which considerations of economy and public relations require local recruiting. But, as we have suggested, the degree of dilution does not indicate the degree of party control. Nor perhaps do the same particulars indicate who is who in the party. Since the soviets, as distinct from the executive committees which are supposed to be answerable to them, do not ordinarily exercise much influence on the course of events, the members of the party assigned to serve in such bodies are not necessarily of more consequence socially or in their political influence than those engaged on the party's business in some other capacity which does not require them to stand for popular election. About party representation in the inner bodies, such as the Executive Committee, we have little direct information, but all the signs are that it is very high.

As in the Supreme Soviet, so also at the local level there is some interlocking of membership of party and state deliberative bodies. The first secretary of the party committee is normally a member of the soviet executive committee, and the chairman of the soviet executive committee is normally a member of the party bureau. An article of February 1956 declared that, in consequence, "in the recent past . . . leading workers of region and district spent almost their whole time at sessions. Scarcely had a meeting of the bureau of the regional committee of the party been concluded after several hours, and not infrequently after several days, when a meeting of the executive committee of the regional soviet began." It was claimed that this position was now somewhat eased by the reduction in the frequency of meetings in both types of body, but it seemed that it remained usual for the local leading officials to serve in both. They are, however, few in number and, in their executive functions, either in one hierarchy or in the other. To entrust office in the two systems into the same hand —to appoint, for example, the same person as both party secretary and soviet executive committee chairman—would not be consistent with the purposes which the two hierarchies serve, though the Yugoslavs in their Stalinist days appear to have overlooked this objection. Only at the very top has there been effective merging in the simultaneous tenure by the same person of office in the Praesidia of the party Central Committee and of the council of ministers. The effective cabinet, alone of all bodies in the Soviet structure, was not checked by a parallel body within the party structure but was merged with it. It is, however, now more common than it used to be for officials to move from one to the other in the course of their careers, and those who reach the top in the state structure seem usually to have held some party office at some time.

Bureaucracy

50 · PARKINSON'S LAW *

C. Northcote Parkinson

Work expands so as to fill the time available for its completion. General recognition of this fact is shown in the proverbial phrase "It is the busiest man who has time to spare." Thus, an elderly lady of leisure can spend the entire day in writing and dispatching a postcard to her niece at Bognor Regis. An hour will be spent in finding the postcard, another in hunting for spectacles, half an hour in a search for the address, an hour and a quarter in composition, and twenty minutes in deciding whether or not to take an umbrella when going to the mailbox in the next street. The total effort that would occupy a busy man for three minutes all told may in this fashion leave another person prostrate after a day of doubt, anxiety, and toil.

Granted that work (and especially paperwork) is thus elastic in its demands on time, it is manifest that there need be little or no relationship between the work to be done and the size of the staff to which it may be assigned. A lack of real activity does not, of necessity, result in leisure. A lack of occupation is not necessarily revealed by a manifest idleness. The thing to be done swells in importance and complexity in a direct ratio with the time to be spent. This fact is widely recognized, but less attention has been paid to its wider implications, more especially in the field of public administration. Politicians and taxpayers have assumed (with occasional phases of doubt) that a rising total in the number of civil servants must reflect a growing volume of work to be done. Cynics, in questioning this belief, have imagined that the multiplication of officials must have left some of them idle or all of them able to work for shorter hours. But this is a

* C. Northcote Parkison, *Parkinson's Law* (Boston: Houghton Mifflin Company, 1957), pp. 2-13. Copyright 1957 by C. Northcote Parkinson. Reprinted by permission of Houghton Mifflin Company.

matter in which faith and doubt seem equally misplaced. The fact is that the number of the officials and the quantity of the work are not related to each other at all. The rise in the total of those employed is governed by Parkinson's Law and would be much the same whether the volume of the work were to increase, diminish, or even disappear. The importance of Parkinson's Law lies in the fact that it is a law of growth based upon an analysis of the factors by which that growth is controlled.

The validity of this recently discovered law must rest mainly on statistical proofs, which will follow. Of more interest to the general reader is the explanation of the factors underlying the general tendency to which this law gives definition. Omitting technicalities (which are numerous) we may distinguish at the outset two motive forces. They can be represented for the present purpose by two almost axiomatic statements, thus: (1) "An official wants to multiply subordinates, not rivals" and (2) "Officials make work for each other."

To comprehend Factor 1, we must picture a civil servant, called A, who finds himself overworked. Whether this overwork is real or imaginary is immaterial, but we should observe, in passing, that A's sensation (or illusion) might easily result from his own decreasing energy: a normal symptom of middle age. For this real or imagined overwork there are, broadly speaking, three possible remedies. He may resign; he may ask to halve the work with a colleague called B; he may demand the assistance of two subordinates, to be called C and D. There is probably no instance in history, however, of A choosing any but the third alternative. By resignation he would lose his pension rights. By having B appointed, on his own level in the hierarchy, he would merely bring in a rival for promotion to W's vacancy when W (at long last) retires. So A would rather have C and D, junior men, below him. They will add to his consequence and, by dividing the work into two categories, as between C and D, he will have the merit of being the only man who comprehends them both. It is essential to realize at this point that C and D are, as it were, inseparable. To appoint C alone would have been impossible. Why? Because C, if by himself, would divide the work with A and so assume almost the equal status that has been refused in the first instance to B; a status the more emphasized if C is A's only possible successor. Subordinates must thus number two or more, each being thus kept in order by fear of the other's promotion. When C complains in turn of being overworked (as he certainly will) A will, with the concurrence of C, advise the appointment of two assistants to help C. But he can then avert internal friction only by advising the appointment of two more assistants to help D, whose position is much the same. With this recruitment of E, F, G, and H the promotion of A is now practically certain.

Seven officials are now doing what one did before. This is where Factor 2 comes into operation. For these seven make so much work for each other that all are fully occupied and A is actually working harder than ever. An incoming document may well come before each of them in turn. Official E decides that it falls within the province of F, who places a draft reply before C, who amends it drastically before consulting D, who asks G to deal with it. But G goes on leave at this point, handing the file over to H, who drafts a minute that is signed by D and returned to C, who revises his draft accordingly and lays the new version before A.

What does A do? He would have every excuse for signing the thing unread, for he has many other matters on his mind. Knowing now that he is to succeed W next year, he has to decide whether C or D should succeed to his own office. He had to agree to G's going on leave even if not yet strictly entitled to it. He is worried whether H should not have gone instead, for reasons of health. He has looked pale recently—partly but not solely because of his domestic troubles. Then there is the business of F's special increment of salary for the period of the conference and E's application for transfer to the Ministry of Pensions. A has heard that D is in love with a married typist and that G and F are no longer on speaking terms—no one seems to know why. So A might be tempted to sign C's draft and have done with it. But A is a conscientious man. Beset as he is with problems created by his colleagues for themselves and for him—created by the mere fact of these officials' existence—he is not the man to shirk his duty. He reads through the draft with care, deletes the fussy paragraphs added by C and H, and restores the thing back to the form preferred in the first instance by the able (if quarrelsome) F. He corrects the English—none of these young men can write grammatically—and finally produces the same reply he would have written if officials C to H had never been born. Far more people have taken far longer to produce the same result. No one has been idle. All have done their best. And it is late in the evening before A finally quits his office and begins the return journey to Ealing. The last of the office lights are being turned off in the gathering dusk that marks the end of another day's administrative toil. Among the last to leave, A reflects with bowed shoulders and a wry smile that late hours, like gray hairs, are among the penalties of success.

From this description of the factors at work the student of political science will recognize that administrators are more or less bound to multiply. Nothing has yet been said, however, about the period of time likely to elapse between the date of A's appointment and the date from which we can calculate the pensionable service of H. Vast masses of statistical evidence have been collected and it is from a study of this data that Parkinson's Law has been deduced. Space will not allow of detailed analysis but the reader will be interested to know that research began in the British Navy Estimates. These were chosen because the Admiralty's responsibilities are more easily measurable than those of, say, the Board of Trade. The question is merely one of numbers and tonnage. Here are some typical figures. The strength of the Navy in 1914 could be shown as 146,000 officers and men, 3249 dockyard officials and clerks, and 57,000 dockyard workmen. By 1928 there were only 100,000 officers and men and only 62,439 workmen, but the dockyard officials and clerks by then numbered 4558. As for warships, the strength in 1928 was a mere fraction of what it had been in 1914—fewer than 20 capital ships in commission as compared with 62. Over the same period the Admiralty officials had increased in number from 2000 to 3569, providing (as was remarked) "a magnificent navy on land." These figures are more clearly set forth in tabular form.

Year	Capital ships in commission	Officers and men in R. N.	Dockyard workers	Dockyard officials and clerks	Admiralty officials
1914	62	146,000	57,000	3249	2000
1928	20	100,000	62,439	4558	3569
Increase or Decrease	−67.74%	−31.5%	+9.54%	+40.28%	+78.45%

The criticism voiced at the time centered on the ratio between the numbers of those available for fighting and those available only for administration. But that comparison is not to the present purpose. What we have to note is that the 2000 officials of 1914 had become the 3569 of 1928; and that this growth was unrelated to any possible increase in their work. The Navy during that period had diminished, in point of fact, by a third in men and two-thirds in ships. Nor, from 1922 onward, was its strength even expected to increase; for its total of ships (unlike its total of officials) was limited by the Washington Naval Agreement of that year. Here we have then a 78 per cent increase over a period of fourteen years; an average of 5.6 per cent increase a year on the earlier total. In fact, as we shall see, the rate of increase was not as regular as that. All we have to consider, at this stage, is the percentage rise over a given period.

Can this rise in the total number of civil servants be accounted for except on the assumption that such a total must always rise by a law governing its growth? It might be urged at this point that the period under discussion was one of rapid development in naval technique. The use of the flying machine was no longer confined to the eccentric. Electrical devices were being multiplied and elaborated. Submarines were tolerated if not approved. Engineer officers were beginning to be regarded as almost human. In so revolutionary an age we might expect that storekeepers would have more elaborate inventories to compile. We might not wonder to see more draughtsmen on the payroll, more designers, more technicians and scientists. But these, the dockyard officials, increased only by 40 per cent in number when the men of Whitehall increased their total by nearly 80 per cent. For every new foreman or electrical engineer at Portsmouth there had to be two more clerks at Charing Cross. From this we might be tempted to conclude, provisionally, that the rate of increase in administrative staff is likely to be double that of the technical staff at a time when the actually useful strength (in this case, of seamen) is being reduced by 31.5 per cent. It has been proved statistically, however, that this last percentage is irrelevant. The officials would have multiplied at the same rate had there been no actual seamen at all.

It would be interesting to follow the further progress by which the 8118 Admiralty staff of 1935 came to number 33,788 by 1954. But the staff of the Colonial Office affords a better field of study during a period of imperial decline. Admiralty statistics are complicated by factors (like the Fleet Air Arm) that make comparison difficult as between one year and the next. The Colonial Office growth is more significant in that it is more purely administrative. Here the relevant statistics are as follows:

1935	1939	1943	1947	1954
372	450	817	1139	1661

Before showing what the rate of increase is, we must observe that the extent of this department's responsibilities was far from constant during these twenty years. The colonial territories were not much altered in area or population between 1935 and 1939. They were considerably diminished by 1943, certain areas being in enemy hands. They were increased again in 1947, but have since then shrunk steadily from year to year as successive colonies achieve self-government. It would be rational to suppose that these changes in the scope of empire would be reflected in the size of its central administration. But a glance at the figures is enough to convince us that the staff totals represent nothing but so many stages in an inevitable increase. And this increase, although related to that observed in other departments, has nothing to do with the size—or even the existence—of the empire. What are the percentages of increase? We must ignore, for this purpose, the rapid increase in staff which accompanied the diminution of responsibility during World War II. We should note rather, the peacetime rates of increase: over 5.24 per cent between 1935 and 1939, and 6.55 per cent between 1947 and 1954. This gives an average increase of 5.89 per cent each year, a percentage markedly similar to that already found in the Admiralty staff increase between 1914 and 1928.

Further and detailed statistical analysis of departmental staffs would be inappropriate in such a work as this. It is hoped, however, to reach a tentative conclusion regarding the time likely to elapse between a given official's first appointment and the later appointment of his two or more assistants.

Dealing with the problem of pure staff accumulation, all our researches so far completed point to an average increase of 5.75 per cent per year. This fact established, it now becomes possible to state Parkinson's Law in mathematical form: In any public administrative department not actually at war, the staff increase may be expected to follow this formula—

$$x = \frac{2k^m + l}{n}$$

k is the number of staff seeking promotion through the appointment of subordinates; l represents the difference between the ages of appointment and retirement; m is the number of man-hours devoted to answering minutes within the department; and n is the number of effective units being administered. x will be the number of new staff required each year. Mathematicians will realize, of course, that to find the percentage increase they must multiply x by 100 and divide by the total of the previous year, thus:

$$\frac{100\ (2k^m + l)}{yn}\ \%$$

where y represents the total original staff. This figure will invariably prove to be between 5.17 per cent and 6.56 per cent, irrespective of any variation in the amount of work (if any) to be done.

The discovery of this formula and of the general principles upon which it is based has, of course, no political value. No attempt has been made to inquire whether departments *ought* to grow in size. Those who hold that this growth is essential to gain full employment are fully entitled to their opinion. Those who doubt the stability of an economy based upon reading each other's minutes are equally entitled to theirs. It would probably be premature to attempt at this stage any inquiry into the quantitative ratio that should exist between the administrators and the administered. Granted, however, that a maximum ratio exists, it should soon be possible to ascertain by formula how many years will elapse before that ratio, in any given community, will be reached. The forecasting of such a result will again have no political value. Nor can it be sufficiently emphasized that Parkinson's Law is a purely scientific discovery, inapplicable except in theory to the politics of the day. It is not the business of the botanist to eradicate the weeds. Enough for him if he can tell us just how fast they grow.

51 · THE AMERICAN BUREAUCRACY—SOME ORGANIZATIONAL CHARTS

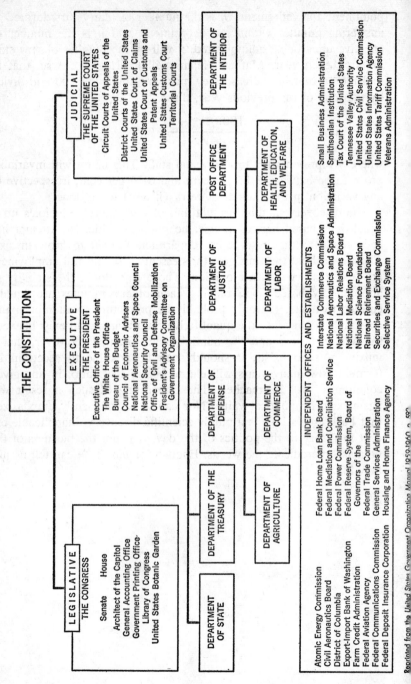

THE CONSTITUTION

LEGISLATIVE

THE CONGRESS

Senate   House

Architect of the Capitol
General Accounting Office
Government Printing Office
Library of Congress
United States Botanic Garden

DEPARTMENT OF STATE

DEPARTMENT OF THE TREASURY

EXECUTIVE

THE PRESIDENT

Executive Office of the President
The White House Office
Bureau of the Budget
Council of Economic Advisers
National Aeronautics and Space Council
National Security Council
Office of Civil and Defense Mobilization
President's Advisory Committee on Government Organization

DEPARTMENT OF DEFENSE

DEPARTMENT OF JUSTICE

DEPARTMENT OF AGRICULTURE

DEPARTMENT OF COMMERCE

DEPARTMENT OF LABOR

POST OFFICE DEPARTMENT

DEPARTMENT OF HEALTH, EDUCATION, AND WELFARE

JUDICIAL

THE SUPREME COURT OF THE UNITED STATES
Circuit Courts of Appeals of the United States
District Courts of the United States
United States Court of Claims
United States Court of Customs and Patent Appeals
United States Customs Court
Territorial Courts

DEPARTMENT OF THE INTERIOR

INDEPENDENT OFFICES AND ESTABLISHMENTS

Atomic Energy Commission
Civil Aeronautics Board
District of Columbia
Export-Import Bank of Washington
Farm Credit Administration
Federal Aviation Agency
Federal Communications Commission
Federal Deposit Insurance Corporation

Federal Home Loan Bank Board
Federal Mediation and Conciliation Service
Federal Power Commission
Federal Reserve System, Board of Governors of the
Federal Trade Commission
General Services Administration
Housing and Home Finance Agency

Interstate Commerce Commission
National Aeronautics and Space Administration
National Labor Relations Board
National Mediation Board
National Science Foundation
Railroad Retirement Board
Securities and Exchange Commission
Selective Service System

Small Business Administration
Smithsonian Institution
Tax Court of the United States
Tennessee Valley Authority
United States Civil Service Commission
United States Information Agency
United States Tariff Commission
Veterans Administration

Reprinted from the *United States Government Organization Manual 1959-1960*, p. 590

EXECUTIVE OFFICE OF THE PRESIDENT

```
                        THE PRESIDENT
```

- Bureau of the Budget
- The White House Office
- National Security Council
- National Aeronautics and Space Council
- Office of Civil and Defense Mobilization
- Council of Economic Advisers
- President's Advisory Committee on Government Organization

Reprinted from the United States Government Organization Manual 1959-1960, p. 593.

488

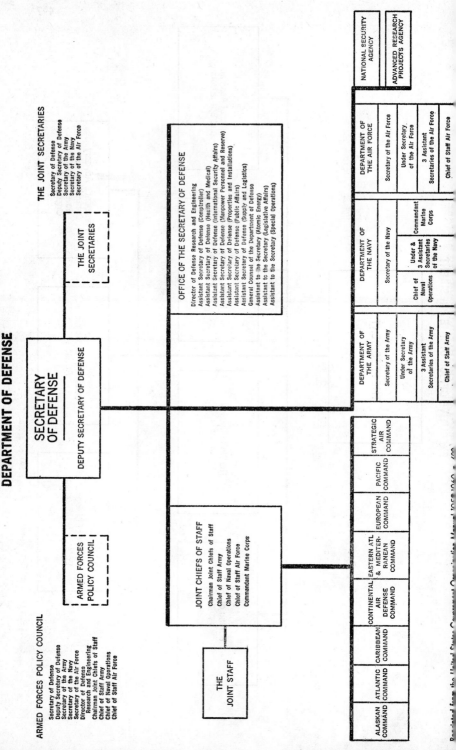

DEPARTMENT OF DEFENSE

SECRETARY OF DEFENSE
DEPUTY SECRETARY OF DEFENSE

ARMED FORCES POLICY COUNCIL
Secretary of Defense
Deputy Secretary of Defense
Secretary of the Army
Secretary of the Navy
Secretary of the Air Force
Director of Defense
  Research and Engineering
Chairman Joint Chiefs of Staff
Chief of Staff Army
Chief of Naval Operations
Chief of Staff Air Force

THE JOINT SECRETARIES
Secretary of Defense
Deputy Secretary of Defense
Secretary of the Army
Secretary of the Navy
Secretary of the Air Force

THE JOINT SECRETARIES

OFFICE OF THE SECRETARY OF DEFENSE
Director of Defense Research and Engineering
Assistant Secretary of Defense (Comptroller)
Assistant Secretary of Defense (Health and Medical)
Assistant Secretary of Defense (International Security Affairs)
Assistant Secretary of Defense (Manpower Personnel and Reserve)
Assistant Secretary of Defense (Properties and Installations)
Assistant Secretary of Defense (Public Affairs)
Assistant Secretary of Defense (Supply and Logistics)
General Counsel of the Department of Defense
Assistant to the Secretary (Atomic Energy)
Assistant to the Secretary (Legislative Affairs)
Assistant to the Secretary (Special Operations)

JOINT CHIEFS OF STAFF
Chairman Joint Chiefs of Staff
Chief of Staff Army
Chief of Naval Operations
Chief of Staff Air Force
Commandant Marine Corps

THE JOINT STAFF

ALASKAN COMMAND	ATLANTIC COMMAND	CARIBBEAN COMMAND	CONTINENTAL AIR DEFENSE COMMAND	EASTERN ATL. & MEDITER- RANEAN COMMAND	EUROPEAN COMMAND	PACIFIC COMMAND	STRATEGIC AIR COMMAND

DEPARTMENT OF THE ARMY
Secretary of the Army
Under Secretary of the Army
3 Assistant Secretaries of the Army
Chief of Staff Army

DEPARTMENT OF THE NAVY
Secretary of the Navy
Chief of Naval Operations
Under & 3 Assistant Secretaries of the Navy
Commandant Marine Corps

DEPARTMENT OF THE AIR FORCE
Secretary of the Air Force
Under Secretary of the Air Force
3 Assistant Secretaries of the Air Force
Chief of Staff Air Force

NATIONAL SECURITY AGENCY

ADVANCED RESEARCH PROJECTS AGENCY

489

DEPARTMENT OF HEALTH, EDUCATION AND WELFARE

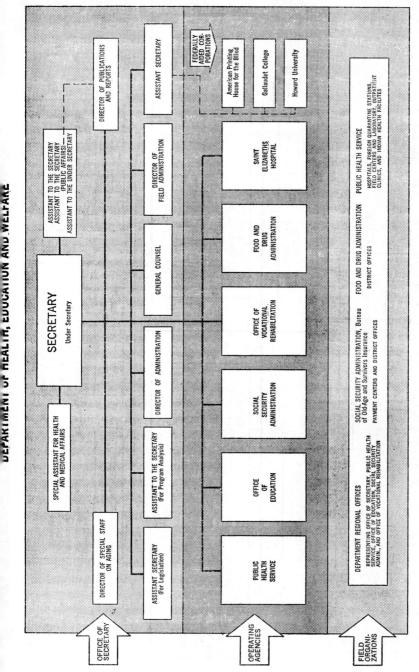

OFFICE OF SECRETARY

SECRETARY
Under Secretary

SPECIAL ASSISTANT FOR HEALTH AND MEDICAL AFFAIRS

DIRECTOR OF SPECIAL STAFF ON AGING

ASSISTANT SECRETARY (For Legislation)

ASSISTANT TO THE SECRETARY (For Program Analysis)

DIRECTOR OF ADMINISTRATION

ASSISTANT TO THE SECRETARY
ASSISTANT TO THE SECRETARY (PUBLIC AFFAIRS)
ASSISTANT TO THE UNDER SECRETARY

DIRECTOR OF PUBLICATIONS AND REPORTS

ASSISTANT SECRETARY

GENERAL COUNSEL

DIRECTOR OF FIELD ADMINISTRATION

FEDERALLY AIDED CORPORATIONS

American Printing House for the Blind

Gallaudet College

Howard University

OPERATING AGENCIES

PUBLIC HEALTH SERVICE

OFFICE OF EDUCATION

SOCIAL SECURITY ADMINISTRATION

OFFICE OF VOCATIONAL REHABILITATION

FOOD AND DRUG ADMINISTRATION

SAINT ELIZABETHS HOSPITAL

FIELD ORGANIZATIONS

DEPARTMENT REGIONAL OFFICES
REPRESENTING OFFICE OF SECRETARY, PUBLIC HEALTH SERVICE, OFFICE OF EDUCATION, SOCIAL SECURITY ADMIN., AND OFFICE OF VOCATIONAL REHABILITATION

SOCIAL SECURITY ADMINISTRATION, Bureau of Old-Age and Survivors Insurance
PAYMENT CENTERS AND DISTRICT OFFICES

FOOD AND DRUG ADMINISTRATION
DISTRICT OFFICES

PUBLIC HEALTH SERVICE
HOSPITALS, FOREIGN QUARANTINE STATIONS, FIELD CENTERS AND LABORATORY, OUTPATIENT CLINICS, AND INDIAN HEALTH FACILITIES

Reprinted from the *United States Government Organization Manual 1959-1960*, p. 610.

490

FEDERAL COMMUNICATIONS COMMISSION

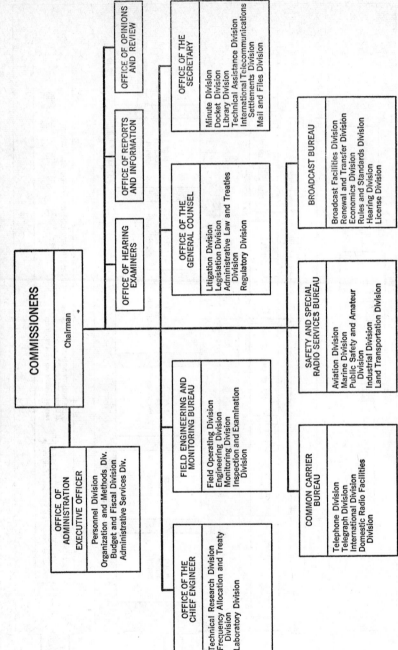

491

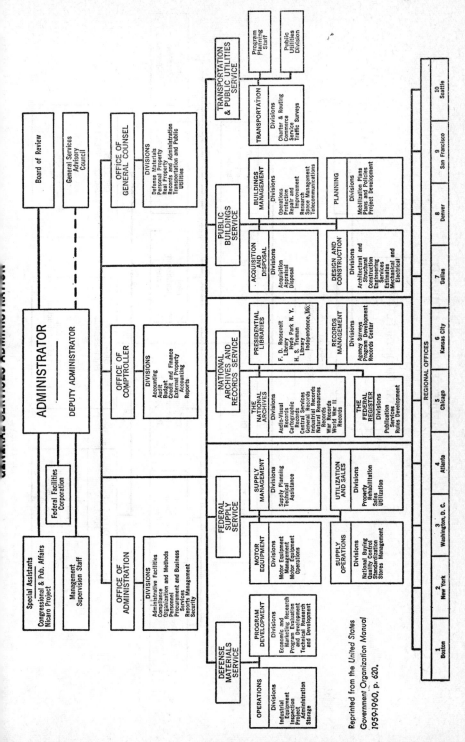

GENERAL SERVICES ADMINISTRATION

Reprinted from the *United States
Government Organization Manual*
1959-1960, p. 620.

492

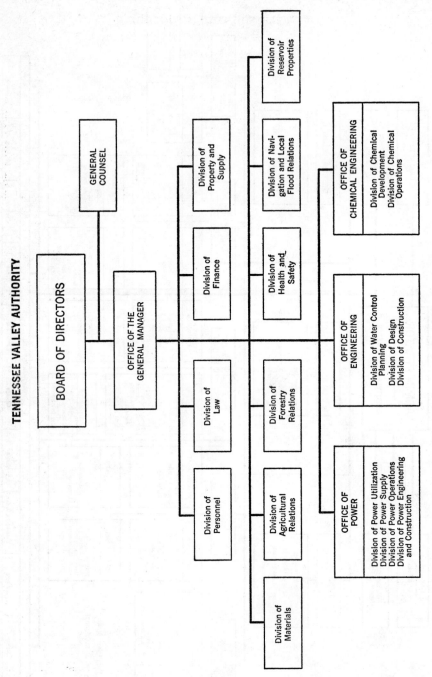

TENNESSEE VALLEY AUTHORITY

BOARD OF DIRECTORS

GENERAL COUNSEL

OFFICE OF THE GENERAL MANAGER

Division of Personnel

Division of Law

Division of Finance

Division of Property and Supply

Division of Materials

Division of Agricultural Relations

Division of Forestry Relations

Division of Health and Safety

Division of Navigation and Local Flood Relations

Division of Reservoir Properties

OFFICE OF POWER

Division of Power Utilization
Division of Power Supply
Division of Power Operations
Division of Power Engineering and Construction

OFFICE OF ENGINEERING

Division of Water Control Planning
Division of Design
Division of Construction

OFFICE OF CHEMICAL ENGINEERING

Division of Chemical Development
Division of Chemical Operations

Reprinted from the United States Government Organization Manual 1959-1960, p. 632.

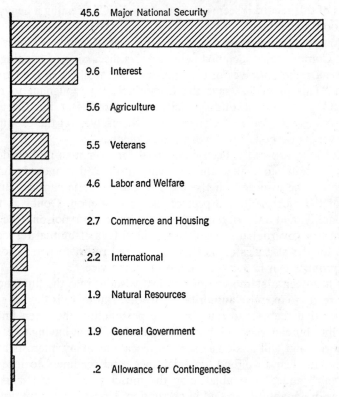

1961 EXPENDITURES BY FUNCTION
TOTAL $79.8 BILLION

45.6	Major National Security
9.6	Interest
5.6	Agriculture
5.5	Veterans
4.6	Labor and Welfare
2.7	Commerce and Housing
2.2	International
1.9	Natural Resources
1.9	General Government
.2	Allowance for Contingencies

Reprinted from the 1961 *Federal Budget in Brief,* p. 16.

52 · THE SCANDAL IN TV LICENSING *

Louis L. Jaffe

In recent months the air in Washington, New York, and Boston has been thick with rumors of political favoritism in the Federal Communications Commission. Some of them have been circulated by disgruntled losers, but the case against the FCC does not rest on these.

* Louis L. Jaffe, "The Scandal in TV Licensing," *Harper's Magazine,* 215 (September, 1957), pp. 77-84. © Copyright, 1957, by Harper & Brothers. Reprinted by permission of Louis L. Jaffe.

It rests on the record of the Commission's decisions in licensing television stations, and the reaction of the bench and bar. And on the basis of this record it seems clear that the FCC is dealing a heavy blow to good government.

Congress is becoming aware of this threat. Recently a House Antitrust Committee condemned behind-doors discussion of pending cases between representatives of the industry and members of the Commission. "This practice," says the Committee, "is repugnant to fundamental principles of quasi-judicial procedure." But the Committee neglects to mention that Congressmen themselves set the example by intervening on behalf of favored constituents.

Not long ago a TV license was sold for over nine million dollars. It is shocking to realize that a legally protected monopoly of such value can be awarded on the basis of bureaucratic caprice. But this is not the most serious aspect of the phenomenon. Doubt as to the rationality and integrity of administrative action poisons the wellsprings of government. Our democratic virtues of mutual respect, regard for the attitudes of our neighbors, and resort to persuasion and compromise can in such a situation become vices.

It has been a stereotype of political wisdom that the bureaucrat is ever ready to exercise authority arbitrarily. But there is the far greater danger that the second-rate, insecure personality who often finds his way into bureaucracy will become uncomfortable at having to exercise authority and will anxiously seek to placate as many interests as possible. This fear to offend, complaisance, and readiness to listen and be "fair" and "reasonable" clog the muscles of the will, and what begins in amiability can end in corruption. Undeniably there are great values in the widespread consent to government which our democracy produces. Nowhere in the world has government regulation made more brilliant creative contributions to society. But if the administrator is not disinterested, government will surely lose the credit which is a necessary condition for its moral leadership and creative initiative.

The trouble with the Communications Commission begins with the statute under which it operates. Originally it was passed to take care of a crisis: the courts had decided that the Secretary of Commerce was without authority to limit the number of broadcasters. As a result many programs could be broadcast at the same time on the same wave length, and their chaotic interference with each other threatened to destroy the usefulness of radio. Consequently, in 1927 power was conferred on the Radio Commission (later the FCC) to limit the number of broadcasters. But Congress gave the Commission no guides whatever to enable it to choose among rival applicants, or to regulate the performance of those who were licensed. The statute simply provided that a license should be granted to an applicant if "public convenience, interest, or necessity will be served thereby," and, very generally, that the Commission should "study new uses for radio, provide for experimental uses of frequencies, and generally encourage the larger and more effective use of radio in the public interests."

Perhaps Congress failed to see the difficult problems that were to arise in licensing and regulating broadcasting—a not unlikely assumption since the legislation was first adopted in 1927 and re-enacted in 1934. But the problems have since become glaringly acute, and though Congress has unceasingly criticized and investigated the Commission, it has not in all these years made a single contribution to policy, except through threats of committees and pressure exerted over the telephone.

A broad delegation of power to an administrative agency is not unusual. Both our railroad and public-utility commissions are authorized to fix the rates for services and otherwise regulate utilities. But when the utility legislation was passed, there was a precisely isolated problem, and the legislative attitudes for dealing with it were well understood, if not explicitly expressed. The Communications Commission, however, began life in a legislative vacuum.

WHO GETS THE PLUMS?

When faced with two applicants for the same broadcasting facility, therefore, the Commission had to devise some technique for determining which one should get the license. Furthermore, since by statute the license is good only for three years, each time its renewal is in question, the Commission is once again faced with the question of whether the licensee or some other entrepreneur should have the frequency.

The Commission decided that the choice should be made on grounds which were relevant to the effective use of the broadcast medium. Gradually it developed criteria which purported to enable it to choose, in the first instance, from among two or more applicants, and then to decide, at the end of three years, whether the licensee was entitled to a renewal.

In devising these criteria it was treading on treacherous ground.

What, indeed, are good radio and good TV? If the people want cakes and ale, does it lie in the mouth of a public authority to state that they shall have only so much cakes and ale and the rest physic? And if good radio can be defined, what kind of organizations and persons are best fitted to provide it? It takes little imagination to sympathize with the predicament of an agency which is called upon to answer such touchy and unprecedented questions without any guidance whatever from Congress, the authorized voice of the people.

Yet, up to a point, the Commission did not hesitate to grasp this thorny nettle. It started with the large concept that radio has public functions—of both entertaining and educating the citizenry; of providing a platform for the dissemination of the arts, the discussion of public questions, the propagation of news, and—somewhat more delicate—for religious observation and worship.

The Commission has not dictated precisely what the balance should be among the desirable and inevitable uses. It has done no more than announce that some balance there must be; and it has been persistently attacked for its hesitant timidity in enforcing this policy. But it must be recalled in its defense that it has no express statutory warrant for *any* policy in these areas; that in this country—as opposed to Britain with its governmentally produced radio—there is little or no tradition for controlling communications or for administering authoritative cultural or moral dispensations.

A more controversial and difficult task was the formulation of criteria for choosing among applicants. It is elementary and basic that the applicant must be decent and law-abiding, with sufficient intelligence and integrity to fulfill the public responsibility placed upon the broadcaster. He must also be required to make a tolerably concrete demonstration that his proposed program will have the necessary variety and interest, and that he has the means for delivering what he promises. The Commission has further indicated that an applicant whose management and proposed personnel are ultimately connected with the community and prepared to devote most of their time to a study of the community's needs will be preferred to an absentee owner.

Most controversial of all the Commission's criteria—and the one in which it is today foundering most dangerously—is the so-called diversification policy. It is a commonplace that the current trend is toward fewer and fewer newspapers and other outlets of communication. Many American cities are already one-newspaper towns. Newspapers were quite understandably interested in radio in its earliest beginnings, and have been successful in securing an important number of the most valuable AM and TV licenses. Furthermore, a newspaper licensee may own a number of newspapers, sometimes within a well-defined region, as well as a number of AM and TV stations—since the rules of the Commission which prohibit the ownership of more than seven AM and seven TV stations say nothing about other media.

The dangers of this concentration of communication facilities are obvious. A monopoly of channels of communication is a monopoly of the approaches to the mind of the citizenry. The lack of competition may produce a deterioration in the tone and extent of the service provided, and so ultimately of the cultural level of the community. And in those communities in which there are still two or more newspapers, a grant of a TV license to one may spell the doom of the other. Because a TV license is by its nature a monopoly, the profit is out of all proportion to the investment. The favored newspaper may offer special advantages to advertisers and readers below cost, and retrench its losses from its TV earnings. Ultimately its rival will be compelled to withdraw.

Because of these various considerations the Communications Commission has formulated a so-called policy of diversification. Thus, if two applicants are equal in other respects, the applicant who is not affiliated with other newspaper or communications media will be preferred. Some think the Commission should have a firm rule against ever granting a license to a newspaper. But whenever it has been suggested that the Commission was pursuing such a policy, there has been such strong protest in Congress that the Commission has been compelled to disavow the action.

These, then, are the purported criteria for making choices among competing applicants. They are, in my opinion, relevant criteria. They further important social and economic interests. They have secured the approval of the courts.

But they are unfortunately extremely imprecise, and they are capable of infinite manipulation. They can become—and, in my opinion, the record shows that they have become—spurious criteria, used to justify results otherwise arrived at.

It is, of course, obvious that a charge of this sort cannot be demonstrated with the kind of certainty that would be necessary to hang a man. But two cases decided by the Court of Appeals of the District of Columbia in the last year must cause any thinking man, any man who looks hopefully to government, acute discomfort.

THE CLARKSBURG AND MC CLATCHY CASES

The first is *Clarksburg Publishing Company* vs. *Federal Communications Commission*. In this case, the Clarksburg Publishing Company, a publisher of a newspaper in Clarksburg, West Virginia, protested the grant of a TV license to the Ohio Valley Broadcasting Corporation. If Ohio Valley's application were granted it would have direct or indirect ownership interests in two television stations serving Clarksburg. It already had similar interests in nearby radio stations. News Publishing Company, an affiliate, published morning, evening, and Sunday newspapers in Wheeling, fifty-eight miles away, and papers in eight other cities in West Virginia. Nine communities in West Virginia, including Wheeling, Parkersburg, and Fairmont— the third, fifth, and sixth largest cities, respectively—were completely dependent on Ohio Valley for their local daily newspapers.

Out of only nine cities in the state which have both morning and evening daily papers, Ohio Valley controlled both papers in three: Fairmont, Parkersburg and Wheeling. It also controlled six of the twelve single daily newspapers published in the state. The combined circulation of all daily newspapers published in the northern, north central, and eastern portions of West Virginia—where Ohio Valley Broadcasting Corporation interests predominated—was 191,922. Of this figure 121,005 represented the daily circulation of newspapers published or controlled by News Publishing Company.

Originally there had been a rival applicant for the TV license, and the two applications had been set down for a comparative hearing. Then the rival withdrew, after being paid $14,390 by Ohio—purportedly its out-of-pocket expenses in pressing the application. The next day an award was made to Ohio, without reference to the Commission's policy of diversification and without investigation of whether or not the payment to the rival applicant covered merely bona fide expense.

Clarksburg Publishing Company protested the grant of a TV license to so formidable a rival in the communications field, and asked for a hearing. This request was denied by the Commission. The Court, reversing the action of the Commission, found nothing in the record to justify the Commission's disregard of its own announced policy: "Nothing in the . . . record dispels the strong impression that, on the concentration of control issue alone, the grant would not be in the public interest." The matter was returned to the Commission for, at the very least, a hearing and a statement by the Commission justifying its departure from its announced standards.

Compare this with the actions of the Commission in the *McClatchy Broadcasting Case.* McClatchy was the owner of a chain of newspapers and radio stations in the Central Valley of California. It applied for a TV station in Sacramento. Another company, Telecasters, made a rival application. Initially Telecasters was permitted to amend its application to increase the height of its antenna so that its coverage might be equal to that proposed by McClatchy.

Following the usual Commission procedure, the hearing was conducted by a so-called trial examiner. The examiner found that McClatchy was superior to Telecasters in all respects except "diversification of control of the media of mass communication." He discovered, however, that McClatchy had never engaged in the practices frequently associated with monopolistic conduct in the public-information field, *e.g.,* cutthroat rate-slashing or personnel pirating. He noted also that there was a multiplicity of mass-communication media in the area to be served. He awarded the license to McClatchy. The Commission, reversing him, disagreed as to the relative superiority of McClatchy and Telecasters and then rejected McClatchy almost solely on the diversification issue.

McClatchy appealed to the Court of Appeals, which, holding that the Commission had acted within the legitimate area of its discretion, upheld the decision. But during the appeal curious things were happening. Immediately upon receiving its construction license, Telecasters petitioned the Commission to permit it to reduce the height of its antenna, and the Commission forthwith agreed. McClatchy protested and asked for a reopening of the comparative hearing. This the Commission denied. And all this time the case was on appeal! McClatchy appealed a second time, and the Court stated indignantly that it was "unseemly for the Commission without the knowledge or permission of the court to substitute another grant for that which is being judicially examined on appeal." It ordered the Commission to reopen the hearing.

Thus, in the *Clarksburg* case the Commission refused even to consider diversification; in the *McClatchy* case diversification became the controlling consideration.

A more recent decision awarding the immensely valuable TV

Channel 5 in Boston adds to this picture of contradiction. There were originally six applicants, four of whom held the course to the end. The winner was the Boston *Herald,* already the owner of a morning, evening, and Sunday newspaper, and licensee of an AM and TV radio station. The Commission, duly noting its diversification policy, nevertheless awarded the license to the *Herald.*

How did the Commission rationalize its action? The reason given was that the *Herald's* experience in operating its radio station assured a good TV performance. Is this not the very heart of contradiction? If, on the basis of its past performance, one already in the communications business is to be preferred, what room is there for the diversification policy?

A further feature of the case underlines the doubts raised by the decision. The *Herald's* chief newspaper rival, the *Globe,* after the close of the hearing, offered affidavits of its officers showing that the *Herald* had put constant pressure on it to merge the two newspapers, and when the proposals were refused said: "Wait until we get the television station and see what happens."

The *Globe* asked for a reopening of the hearing to present this evidence. The *Globe's* move came very late, it is true, but the information was quite unknown to the other applicants until the affidavits were filed. The Commission rejected the motions to reopen, partly because of their lateness, but also because the alleged behavior of the *Herald* was "magnified out of proportion" and its threats should be attributed to "pique"—thus cavalierly disposing of these serious charges without giving the parties even a chance either to prove them or to explore their relevance.

WHAT CAN BE DONE

These are not isolated instances. But by their striking character they cast a strong light on much that has been ambiguous, and bring into focus a pattern of administration which has been growing steadily more disturbing over the past few years. There is not space here to evaluate the whole performance, but enough has been shown, I think, to cause alarm. Standards are announced only to be ignored, ingeniously explained away, or so occasionally applied that their very application seems a mockery of justice.

There are, unfortunately, no immediate or easy remedies for the situation. The present modes of regulation and the existing structure of broadcasting are powerfully entrenched. It might have been possible at an earlier time to have taxed the monopoly profits of broadcasting; to have levied, for example, an annual license fee proportional to profit, and thus to have reduced the pressures for administrative irregularity. But the enormous investments which have been made preclude such a drastic revision of the legal structure.

Congress might, to be sure, clarify and reinforce the already developed licensing criteria, most of which are in themselves quite sound. Statutory enactment would somewhat strengthen the hand of the courts in reviewing and controlling wayward administrative activity. But it must be confessed that such legislation would not substantially narrow the range of administrative discretion. We must face the fact that the nature of the broadcasting problem does not lend itself to solution by formulas which would eliminate the need for official judgment.

In this it is like most government regulation today. Regulation assumes legislative determination only of the major policy conflicts, with a resulting firm declaration of the regulatory principles to be applied; a grant of sufficient discretion to find the best ways and means to adapt these policies to a constantly developing situation; and a well-informed, imaginative, *disinterested* bureaucracy operating in a *judicial* spirit.

Though Congress has been notably weak during the past few years in providing policy guides, strong administration would have in some measure filled the void. But in our administrative, as in our legislative, life, compromise, camaraderie, and trafficking are eating away at the fabric of the legal structure. This is a massive trend and can be fought only if there is a public opinion aware of this threat to effective government.

The challenge is a tremendous one. In our present context it will require an unwonted discipline and restraint in many quarters. We must re-establish the notion that commissioners when they have a case before them are quasi-judicial officers. Congressmen, high officials of the Administration, and party politicos must refuse to approach commissioners. The commissioners in their turn must close their doors and ears to everything except the record made openly before them. A litigant would not dare procure his Congressman to intercede with a judge. We must establish a tradition which makes the show of influence equally unthinkable in an administrative pro-

ceeding. It would be an important step in the building of such a tradition for Congress by statute to give authoritative expression to
these principles.

53 · THE CONTROL OF THE BUREAUCRACY— PUBLIC ADMINISTRATION IN THE SOVIET UNION *

Merle Fainsod

One of the salient outgrowths of modern totalitarianism is the bureaucratization of its power structure. The Leader who bestrides the
peak of the totalitarian edifice is the victim of his own limitations.
He cannot decide everything, and even when he exercises his power
to decide, he must depend on bureaucratic instruments to project his
will. Authority becomes institutionalized, and its fragments are distributed among the manifold sub-bureaucracies which collectively
contribute to the illusion of totalitarian omniscience.

The ways of bureaucracy elude totalitarian and nontotalitarian
labels. Bureaucracies everywhere generate their own special interests
and aspirations. They guard the expert knowledge which is the source
of their power and resist the encroachment of interlopers who seek
to invade their jurisdiction. They display what Soviet critics have
termed "a narrowly departmental approach" and build their loyalties
and hopes around the complex of concerns that have been entrusted
to their care. They develop their own routines and working habits
and are not easily persuaded to abandon them once they have become
established. The Soviet bureaucracy manifests many of the traits characteristic of bureaucratic behavior generally.

At the same time, Soviet totalitarianism also imposes its own peculiar requirements on the bureaucracy. Soviet public administration
exhibits attributes which sharply differentiate it from the administrative systems prevailing in Western constitutional democracies. Its

* Reprinted by permission of the publishers from Merle Fainsod, *How
Russia Is Ruled,* Cambridge, Mass.: Harvard University Press, Copyright, 1953,
by the President and Fellows of Harvard College. The footnotes in the original
version are omitted here.

scope is all-embracing. It seeks to organize the total experience of man in Soviet society. Every branch of the economy and every form of social expression, from art, music, and letters to sports and the circus, are subject to administrative regulation and direction. The totalitarian imperative drives to transform the nation into a hierarchy of public servants operating within a framework of disciplined subordination to state purposes.

Soviet public administration is one-party administration. The conception of the politically neutral civil servant who serves his successive political masters "with equal fidelity and with equal contempt" is utterly foreign to the Soviet scene. Soviet public administration is suffused with political content. Every field of administration, however technical, is regarded as a channel for the propagation of the Party line and the directives of the top leadership. As Stalin once put it, "not a single important political or organizational question is decided by our Soviet and other mass organizations without guiding directions from the Party." The Party itself is a creature of its high command. Functioning in this capacity, it permeates Soviet society, occupies the strategic positions of power in state administration, issues policy instructions which guide administrative activity, checks on their execution, and attempts to serve as an organ of continuous discipline and control.

In practice, this picture of monolithic unity is only imperfectly realized. Behind the totalitarian façade, the struggle of the elite formations of Soviet society for power and influence continues to find expression. The Party apparatus, the police, the army, and the administrative bureaucracy vie with one another for preferment, and the local and departmental interests of different sections of the bureaucracy exercise their counterinfluence on the Party. The public affirmations of unanimity on which all totalitarian regimes insist serve to obscure the diversity of interests which they can neither eliminate nor dare openly acknowledge. Although Soviet totalitarian controls drive some of the most vital interests in the society into a subterranean zone of illegality, other equally important concerns find partial and distorted articulation through the frequently camouflaged processes of bureaucratic representation and manipulation. The play of these pressures continues to operate within the limits imposed by the ruling priorities of the Party leadership. The monolithic control of the Party high command largely takes the form of enforcing its priorities and resolving the conflict which their execution generates.

The pressure from above is ruthless and unremitting, and evasion from below is resourceful and not unavailing.

Soviet public administration gives little weight to the rights of the individual. It is oriented toward a conception of state interests which every branch of government is dedicated to promote. The problem of erecting safeguards against the abuse of administrative power is therefore conceived differently from its counterpart in Anglo-American constitutional systems with their heritage of devotion to personal liberty. The safeguards that Soviet jurists stress are the state controls designed to insure efficient performance of official function. When Soviet lawyers speak of administrative responsibility, they have in mind a conception of state service which is embodied in the law, not a set of limitations to protect the individual from the administration. When state interests and individual interests clash, the duty of the Soviet administrator is always toward state interests. Soviet administrative law is built around the interests of the collectivity as interpreted by the Party leadership.

Soviet public administration replaces Western constitutional restraints on administration by a formidable proliferation of central controls of a variety and on a scale without parallel in the West. Despite efforts to strengthen executive authority in recent years, the typical Soviet administrator functions in an environment in which his every decision is subject to the possibility of check, recheck, and countercheck. The plan under which he operates must be approved by the State Planning Committee. His staff arrangements are controlled by standards established by the State Civil Service Commission. His financial transactions are subject to the scrutiny of the Ministry of Finance. The Minister of State Control maintains a check on his efficiency, enforces strict control over the expenditure of funds, and makes certain that he is fulfilling all government orders and decrees. The Procurator General watches the legality of his actions. The secret police of the Ministry of Internal Affairs (MVD) keeps him under constant observation to ensure his political reliability. The whole range of his activity, as well as that of the control organs, is always under careful surveillance by representatives of the Party. It is not too far-fetched to describe this complex network of controls as a system of power founded on cross-espionage and the institutionalization of mutual suspicion.

The insecurity developed by these arrangements engenders its own antidotes. In order to escape the unbearable burden of suspicion and distrust which the system imposes on those who are involved in it, both controlled and controllers sometimes form "mutual protection associations" and cover up for each other's sins and omissions in discharging the tasks for which they are held jointly responsible. The urge to find a peaceful sanctuary is deep-seated among Soviet administrators, and it comes into sharp conflict with the Hobbesian war of all against all upon which the ruling group relies in order to maintain its own security. The literature of Soviet administration is filled with criticism of administrators who enter into so-called "family relations" with the control organs that surround them. Despite the virulence of the denunciations, the phenomenon is recurrent, and it apparently registers a strongly felt need to erect barricades against the intrusive checks used by the regime to maintain the pressure of its power. The interstices of every totalitarian regime contain concealed pockets of effective bureaucratic resistance. The Soviet rulers engage in a ceaseless effort to stamp out this resistance and forge the bureaucracy into a pliable instrument of their will.

. . . . .

BUREAUCRATIC POLITICS IN A TOTALITARIAN SYSTEM

The Soviet bureaucratic structure is commonly visualized as a tightly centralized administrative hierarchy in which all initiative and decision-making power are concentrated in the top leadership and in which the lower officials serve as mere automatons to execute the will of the ruling group. While this stereotype performs the useful function of emphasizing the high degree of centralization which characterizes the Soviet system, it also distorts reality by ignoring the fluid play of bureaucratic politics that underlies the monolithic totalitarian façade.

The Soviet bureaucracy operates under the strain of constant pressure from above to accelerate the program of rapid industrialization to which the regime is committed. This program accords top priority to military needs and the expansion of heavy industry. Scarce resources are allocated in accordance with these dominating priorities. The "key sectors" which have been chosen for intensive development enjoy a preferential position in the Soviet economy, but no part of the Soviet bureaucracy is immune from the insistent and implacable demands of the leadership for maximum output and effort.

The "success" of the bureaucracy is judged by its ability to meet the demands made on it. Since the demands are great and the resources available to meet them are ordinarily limited, each sector of the bureaucracy is driven to fight for a plan which it can carry out and for an allocation of resources which will enable it to discharge its obligations. This struggle is in essence political. While it is broadly contained within the framework of the ruling priorities of the leadership, there is still considerable room for maneuver. The planning experts, whose precise calculus is supposed to define the tasks of the bureaucracy, are not divorced from the play of bureaucratic politics. Indeed, Gosplan is a focal point around which the battle for special treatment rages. The battle is waged by negotiation, by personal influence, and by invoking the assistance of the powerful. Each bureaucratic group is constantly engaged in an effort to mobilize as much political support as it can muster, right up to the member of the Party Presidium responsible for its performance.

Bureaucratic representation in the Soviet context expresses itself in a struggle for preferential advantage. Because each part of the bureaucracy operates with an eye to the feasibility of the demands which are made on it, it becomes an unwitting spokesman for the claims of that sector of Soviet life for which it is responsible. The dictates of survival compel it to mediate between two types of pressure, the drive from above to extract the last reserves of energy from the population and the resistance from below which seeks to tailor commitments to capabilities. In the process, Soviet administrators develop a certain agility in counteracting the squeeze in which they are caught, and the more powerful or influential manage, in some degree at least, to shift the viselike grip to other sections of the bureaucracy or the economy.

This crossfire of pressures occurs at every level of the bureaucratic hierarchy. Once a plan has been determined, the same ministry which has fought for a "reasonable" plan and "favorable" allocations for itself must resist the efforts of its own subordinate enterprises to carve out protected positions for themselves which will shift the squeeze to other enterprises in the ministerial domain. The enterprises, like the ministries, struggle with every means at their disposal to obtain plan quotas that will be easy to meet and to accumulate large reserves of supplies and other resources to facilitate plan-fulfillment. The responsibility of the enterprise is limited to its own performance, while the record of the ministry is the record of all the agencies subordinate to it. Thus the ministry finds itself in the position of being both driver and driven. The enterprise is in the same position with respect to its component parts.

The tensions generated by the industrialization drive set the stage for a steady tug of war between the central leadership and the bureaucracy. The leadership faces the constant problem of ensuring that the pressure which it exerts will be transmitted to the base of the bureaucratic pyramid and not be diffused and frustrated by bureaucratic manipulation and resistance. The ruling group has developed a variety of ingenious devices to make its control operative throughout the bureaucratic structure. It appeals to the self-interest of the bureaucratic elite by an incentive system which offers attractive bonuses and other large rewards for production in excess of plan. It combines positive incentives with negative controls which impose harsh penalties for failure. It pits one bureaucracy against another and relies on the rivalry between them to enforce its demands on both. It depends heavily on the separately organized Party and police hierarchies to control administration, and it supplements this type of surveillance and pressure by planning, financial, personnel, legal, and investigatory controls which are built into the administrative structure. It endeavors to prevent the growth of "family relations" between the controlled and the controllers by frequent shifts of personnel and by periodic campaigns against officials who cover up for each other's sins. It takes advantage of the activist's desire to move ahead in the Soviet system by stimulating pledges of "overplan" production and by encouraging denunciations of officials who evade the demands made on them. It seeks to protect the activists and careerists from retaliation by punishing "suppressors of criticism" who attempt to escape the controls which surround them by eliminating the critics in their own domain.

The essence of bureaucratic politics in the Soviet system consists in a search for a viable equilibrium between the pressures from above for maximal output and the inescapable limitations which factors of scarcity and human frailty impose. The successful Soviet administrator must be more than loyal and efficient. He must learn to manipulate the environment around him to meet the demands which are made on him. He cannot afford to be overscrupulous in obeying legal regulations if the price of conformity means failure to meet his set goals. He operates under an overriding compulsion to drive through to plan-fulfillment, and every expedient is justified which advances this transcendent purpose. In the Soviet Book of Acts, much is forgiven success, but nothing is forgiven failure.

Despite the remarkable skill with which some administrators manipulate the system for their own ends, the Soviet bureaucracy as a whole responds to the regime's inexorable demand for rapidly expanding industrial production. The pressure from above may be distributed unevenly as it is transmitted through the bureaucratic hierarchy, but it is distributed nonetheless. The administrators who fail to meet the expectations of the leadership disappear from the scene. The drivers and the manipulators survive.

The high-pressure system of Soviet administration imposes its costs. The administrators who drive are also driven, and the toll on their nervous energy and reserves of strength is great. The strain under which they operate is communicated to those below. The ultimate victims are not the administrative and managerial class, but the mass of collective farmers and unskilled and semiskilled workers who bear the major burden of the industrialization effort. The price of forced draft industrialization is the tensions and dissatisfactions which it inevitably generates.

The Party leadership attempts to protect itself against these consequences by both negative and positive measures. Its powerful instruments of surveillance and repression discourage any overt expression of disloyalty. It acts positively to build a labor aristocracy by reserving special rewards for its Stakhanovites and more productive skilled workers. It places great emphasis on attaching the loyalties of the new Soviet intelligentsia to the regime. It accords a privileged position to its bureaucratic elite and holds out the promise of rapid promotion for the most loyal and talented representatives of the younger generation. This conscious effort on the part of the regime to consolidate a subservient, but none the less privileged, layer of bureaucracy between itself and the Soviet populace represents an important aspect of its search for stability. The road which the regime has chosen to tread is that of primary reliance on a system of bureaucratic and police controls to engage the energies of the masses and to hold popular discontent in check. It builds its power on its elite formations and places its wager on their capacity to command that minimum degree of popular support which even a totalitarian dictatorship needs if it is to function effectively.

Business

---

54 · BIG BUSINESS—SOME STATISTICS ON SIZE

TWENTY LARGEST UNITED STATES INDUSTRIAL CORPORATIONS
Ranked by Sales—1958

Company	Sales[1] ($000)	Rank	Assets[2] ($000)	Rank	Net Profits[3] ($000)	Rank	Invested Capital[4] ($000)	Rank	Em-ployees[5]	Rank
General Motors	9,521,966	(1)	7,294,689	(2)	633,628	(1)	5,016,840	(2)	520,925	(1)
Standard Oil (N.J.)	7,543,571	(2)	9,478,693	(1)	562,475	(2)	6,457,204	(1)	154,000	(4)
Ford Motor	4,130,339	(3)	3,074,746	(7)	95,742	(16)	2,141,635	(8)	142,076	(6)
General Electric	4,120,770	(4)	2,420,939	(11)	242,943	(8)	1,310,987	(12)	249,718	(2)
United States Steel	3,472,177	(5)	4,632,837	(3)	301,558	(6)	3,113,986	(3)	223,490	(3)
Socony Mobil Oil	2,885,684	(6)	3,237,328	(5)	156,786	(9)	2,445,106	(5)	75,000	(17)
Gulf Oil	2,769,377	(7)	3,430,019	(4)	329,533[6]	(4)	2,441,297	(6)	56,000	(25)
Swift	2,645,389	(8)	584,936	(58)	10,048	(178)	377,366	(56)	64,300	(20)
Texas Co.[7]	2,327,939	(9)	3,111,527	(6)	310,168	(5)	2,283,742	(7)	52,515 *	(27)
Western Electric	2,173,352	(10)	1,337,422	(20)	85,936	(17)	887,540	(16)	128,290	(8)
Chrysler	2,165,382	(11)	1,337,509	(19)	(33,825)	(499)	691,280	(25)	95,846 [8]	(12)
Bethlehem Steel	2,005,937	(12)	2,195,046	(12)	137,742	(10)	1,626,622	(11)	143,024	(5)
Westinghouse Electric	1,895,699	(13)	1,411,508	(17)	74,773	(20)	870,319	(18)	114,652	(9)
Standard Oil (Ind.)	1,863,990	(14)	2,769,317	(9)	117,775	(13)	2,076,853	(9)	47,856	(35)
Armour	1,850,439	(15)	412,496	(85)	5,560	(289)	208,578	(102)	45,700	(40)
Du Pont (E.I.) de Nemours	1,829,250	(16)	2,804,230	(8)	341,249	(3)	2,488,599	(4)	85,886	(15)
Boeing Airplane	1,711,930	(17)	605,325	(57)	29,360	(69)	201,595	(104)	92,878	(14)
Shell Oil	1,665,989	(18)	1,648,271	(13)	116,563	(14)	1,239,779	(13)	38,572 *	(45)
Standard Oil of California	1,559,160	(19)	2,451,069	(10)	257,759	(7)	1,990,211	(10)	38,568	(46)
General Dynamics	1,511,456	(20)	651,182	(54)	36,729	(51)	274,884	(81)	92,900 *	(13)

[1] Net sales, including service and rental revenues for companies that derive at least 50 per cent of their revenue from manufacturing or mining, for fiscal years ending not later than January 4, 1959. Sales of consolidated subsidiaries included.

[2] Total assets employed in business net of depreciation and depletion, but including government securities offset against tax liabilities.

[3] Including special charges or credits, nonrecurring items of a non-operating nature are footnoted when they are 10 per cent of total profit or loss. Tax-loss carry-forwards are not footnoted. Figures in parenthe-sis are losses.

[4] Capital stock, surplus and retained earnings (i.e., net worth).

[5] Average employment for year unless followed by asterisk (*), in which case year end.

[6] Includes nonrecurring profit of $43,283,000.

[7] Name changed to Texaco, May 1, 1959.

[8] For United States plants only.

Courtesy of *Fortune* magazine; July-August 1959.

Ranked by Sales—1958

Company	Headquarters	Industry	Sales[1] ($000)	Assets[2] ($000)	Net Profits[3] ($000)	Employees
Royal Dutch/Shell	Britain-Holland	Petroleum Products	5,472,934	7,623,879	421,913	250,000
Unilever	Britain-Holland	Fats & Oils, Soap	3,525,015	1,926,104	130,988	283,055
British Petroleum[4]	Britain	Petroleum Products	1,675,198	1,589,174	173,383	100,000
Imperial Chemical Industries	Britain	Chemicals	1,295,496	2,027,396	64,380	112,108
Nestlé	Switzerland	Food Products	1,238,318 [A]	172,683 [C]	15,117 [C]	60,250
Philips' Gloeilampen-fabrieken	Holland	Electrical Equipment	946,053	1,099,571	64,161	174,000
Siemens	Germany	Electrical Equipment	794,524	667,619 [D]	19,881 [C]	179,000
Fried.Krupp	Germany	Iron & Steel	764,048	NA	NA	105,180
British Motor	Britain	Machinery, Coal Automobiles	742,000	338,443	25,812	67,700
British-American Tobacco	Britain	Tobacco	725,000 [A]	1,002,038	72,021	NA
Hawker Siddeley	Britain	Aircraft, Engineering	700,000	476,749	14,332	100,000
Dunlop	Britain	Rubber Products	680,400	464,016	13,401	94,000
Mannesmann	Germany	Coal, Iron & Steel	667,857	715,348	13,861	78,553
Volkswagenwerk[5]	Germany	Automobiles	647,381	245,546	79,426	47,916
Gutehoffnungshutte	Germany	Iron & Steel Machinery	647,381 [C]	39,865 [C]	2,231 [C]	71,782
Renault[5]	France	Automobiles	602,921	268,540 [B]	9,026	62,370
Gelsenkirchener Bergwerks-AG	Germany	Iron & Steel,	599,762 [A]	547,619	9,238 [C]	83,525
Fiat	Italy	Automobiles	596,800	1,040,473	26,610	79,930
Cie Française Des Pétroles	France	Iron & Steel Petroleum Products	595,238 [A]	404,534 [C]	33,005 [C]	4,000 [C]
Guest, Keen & Nettle-folds	Britain	Iron & Steel Engineering	585,190	493,300	31,053	71,750

[1] Sales are consolidated third-party sales for fiscal years ending no later than March 31, 1959.
[2] Assets are consolidated balance sheet totals.
[3] Profits are consolidated net profits after taxes and all deductions.
[4] 52 per cent government-owned.
[5] Government-owned.

[C] Includes intercompany sales.
[A] Fortune estimate.
[B] Previous fiscal year,
[C] Unconsolidated.
[D] Partly consolidated.

Courtesy of Fortune magazine; July-August 1959.

TWENTY LARGEST UNITED STATES LIFE-INSURANCE COMPANIES
Ranked by Assets—1958

Company	Assets[1] ($000)	Rank	Life Insurance in Force[2] ($000)	Rank	Employees[3]	Rank
Metropolitan (New York)	16,282,117	(1)	84,224,267	(1)	59,396	(1)
Prudential of America (Newark, N.J.)	14,731,773	(2)	70,524,192	(2)	59,000	(2)
Equitable Life Assurance (New York)	9,297,662	(3)	33,368,784	(3)	20,922 *	(3)
New York Life (New York)	6,707,203	(4)	20,669,934	(7)	16,274	(5)
John Hancock Mutual (Boston)	5,518,219	(5)	22,278,459	(5)	17,000	(4)
Northwestern Mutual (Milwaukee)	3,893,335	(6)	9,336,274	(9)	1,826	(31)
Aetna (Hartford)	3,550,966	(7)	21,492,907	(6)	5,953	(11)
Travelers (Hartford)	3,072,854	(8)	23,047,567	(4)	6,400	(10)
Mutual of New York (New York)	2,642,746	(9)	6,797,989	(12)	9,902	(6)
Massachusetts Mutual (Springfield)	2,215,066	(10)	6,737,482	(13)	4,443	(14)
New England Mutual (Boston)	2,023,812	(11)	6,068,199	(14)	3,376	(18)
Connecticut General (Hartford)	1,925,932	(12)	9,654,242	(8)	4,049 *	(15)
Mutual Benefit (Newark, N.J.)	1,780,882	(13)	4,503,344	(20)	3,082	(21)
Penn Mutual (Philadelphia)	1,725,216	(14)	4,653,878	(17)	3,166	(19)
Connecticut Mutual (Hartford)	1,435,666	(15)	4,000,868	(21)	2,619	(24)
Lincoln National (Fort Wayne, Ind.)	1,357,648	(16)	9,184,921	(10)	3,120	(20)
Bankers Life (Des Moines, Iowa)	973,877	(17)	3,272,654	(22)	2,239	(26)
Western & Southern (Cincinnati)	906,010	(18)	4,529,960	(18)	7,641 *	(8)
Provident Mutual (Philadelphia)	836,380	(19)	2,301,383	(29)	1,538	(36)
Phoenix Mutual (Hartford)	825,208	(20)	2,077,093	(33)	1,966 *	(28)

Courtesy of *Fortune* magazine; July-August 1959.

[1] Total assets employed in business as of December 31, 1958.
[2] Face value of all life policies outstanding.
[3] Average employment for year, including full-time agents. Figures followed by an asterisk (*) are year end.

TWENTY LARGEST UNITED STATES COMMERCIAL BANKS
Ranked by Assets—1958

Bank	Assets[1] ($000)	Rank	Deposits ($000)	Rank	Capital Funds[2] ($000)	Rank	Earnings[3] ($000)	Rank
Bank of America (San Francisco)	11,290,853	(1)	10,307,561	(1)	601,453	(3)	77,019	(1)
Chase Manhattan Bank (New York)	8,329,982	(2)	7,386,097	(2)	631,408	(2)	55,648	(3)
First National City Bank of New York	8,088,144	(3)	7,127,811	(3)	747,775	(1)	60,274	(2)
Manufacturers Trust (New York)	3,654,045	(4)	3,257,856	(4)	221,504	(11)	20,506	(10)
Chemical Corn Exchange Bank (New York)[4]	3,593,568	(5)	3,174,003	(5)	295,838	(5)	27,073	(5)
Security-First National Bank (Los Angeles)	3,362,150	(6)	3,087,330	(6)	222,792	(10)	21,130	(9)
Guaranty Trust of New York[5]	3,174,582	(7)	2,638,018	(9)	418,877	(4)	30,297	(4)
Bankers Trust (New York)	3,127,665	(8)	2,779,133	(7)	268,262	(7)	22,038	(7)
First National Bank of Chicago	3,025,592	(9)	2,705,882	(8)	261,958	(8)	NA	
Continental Illinois National Bank (Chicago)	2,857,982	(10)	2,555,171	(10)	261,278	(9)	23,394	(6)
Mellon National Bank & Trust (Pittsburgh)	2,145,679	(11)	1,834,249	(11)	277,598	(6)	21,292	(8)
Irving Trust (New York)	1,991,230	(12)	1,774,870	(12)	137,094	(15)	13,453	(14)
Hanover Bank (New York)	1,957,712	(13)	1,713,003	(14)	172,015	(13)	14,087	(13)
National Bank of Detroit	1,946,927	(14)	1,766,261	(13)	147,982	(14)	15,120	(12)
First National Bank of Boston	1,897,453	(15)	1,652,889	(16)	175,376	(12)	18,210	(11)
American Trust (San Francisco)	1,826,742	(16)	1,673,330	(15)	116,637	(17)	11,039	(16)
Crocker-Anglo National Bank (San Francisco)	1,691,915	(17)	1,526,989	(17)	117,833	(16)	11,578	(15)
Cleveland Trust	1,470,967	(18)	1,348,256	(18)	107,206	(18)	10,696	(17)
California Bank (Los Angeles)	1,205,486	(19)	1,111,864	(19)	68,185	(29)	6,546	(29)
First Pa. Banking & Trust (Philadelphia)	1,197,764	(20)	1,069,984	(20)	91,176	(20)	7,875	(21)

[1] Total resources as of December 31, 1958.

[2] Capital, surplus, and undivided profits.

[3] Net operating earnings after taxes.

[4] Merged with New York Trust (Assets in 1958: $1,001,086,000) to form Chemical Bank New York Trust Co. approved by stockholders of both banks, July 8, 1959.

[5] Merged April 24, 1959, with J. P. Morgan (assets in 1958: $982,560,000) to form Morgan Guaranty Trust Co. of New York.

Courtesy of *Fortune* magazine; July-August 1959.

513

55 · THE RESPONSIBILITY OF BUSINESS
IN PUBLIC AFFAIRS *

William C. Stolk

Having been in the sales end of business most of my life, your invitation to be here today is not only an honor but a real treat. There could be no greater pleasure for a salesman than an invitation to sell his bill of goods before several hundred fine customers and equally fine prospective customers—without interruption.

. . . . .

This I would do if it were not that I have become so deeply concerned—as have many other businessmen,—with the ominous outlook facing our country. If things continue to go the way they have, there is real reason for serious doubt that we, as a nation, *have* a glorious future in store for us.

I came here to sell—but not containers. If any businessman has not already been sold, he needs to be sold on the absolute need and urgency to participate in public affairs. My goal today is to convince you of the need for your participation in this vital area and for your help in encouraging, stimulating and helping your managers, your business associates, and your friends to do likewise.

We, as businessmen, have been working vigorously and conscientiously to increase productivity, cut costs and provide a firm basis for a constantly improving standard of living. But people in increasing numbers are discovering that while we have been busy developing, financing, producing and marketing new products and services, powerful forces have been working at least as diligently to develop, finance, produce and market ideas that are seriously undermining our political and economic system.

Standards are being lowered, ideals are being downgraded, character is being weakened, and our Constitution is—in effect—being rewritten. The Freedoms now becoming popular are: Freedom from

---

* A talk given by William C. Stolk, President, American Can Company, at the 45th Mid-Year Meeting of the Chemical Specialties Manufacturers Association, May 20, 1959. Reprinted by permission of William C. Stolk.

Care; Freedom from Effort; Freedom from Responsibility; and Freedom to Get without having to Give.

The public is being hoaxed into believing that the nation can consume more than it produces, that our standards of living can be increased by restricting output and reducing hours of work, and that the "good life" is a life of irresponsibility.

Efforts are being made to convince the public that the way to have booming prosperity in this country, improve living standards, and withstand the threat of annihilation by Russia is to forget the balancing of the budget, maintain existing tax rates, increase government expenditures, hamstring business incentive and initiative, build a larger and more powerful central government, and move farther and farther along the road toward Socialism.

Some politicians in government, in labor unions, in our two great political parties, and—sad to say—even in our educational institutions have been promoting concepts, ideas, and legislative actions which will surely rob the public of a substantial part—if not ultimately all—of its bank savings, Series E bond savings, life insurance protection, pension rights, and other property values.

These same politicians are promoting the idea that business is suspect; that *big business is particularly bad;* that anything which is good for an employer could not be good for an employee. They are coldly contriving to break down public confidence in and respect for business—particularly big business. This despite the fact that business, and business alone, makes possible the goods and services used by consumers, the income used by tens of millions of people to support their families, and—both directly and indirectly—the great bulk of government income.

To my mind, we businessmen, individually and collectively, have become much too refined for this day and age. We have striven too hard to seek universal acceptability for ourselves, as well as for our products.

We have devoted too much effort toward attempting to find areas where we can agree with other business managers, with labor leaders and with government. We have made too little effort to think about, and speak out on, areas of disagreement with labor leaders, with government, and even among ourselves. We must not, of course, confine ourselves to the purely negative exercise of saying "we are against what you are for." But in order to make clear to everyone what we stand for and why, we cannot avoid taking an open position against schemes that are designed to overturn the things we seek to advance. For example, as we speak out to support and promote the continuance of a free competitive market for goods and services, we have to oppose the ideas of those who want to see all business management directed by some combination of federal bureaucracy and union "trusteeship."

Business managers have assumed that, in the area of public affairs, their responsibilities to society are adequately discharged by making a financial contribution, once every two years, to the party of their choice and by contributing to the support of business organizations which take stands on legislative issues. This may have been adequate in the dim past—but certainly not in the recent past, and assuredly not now.

You and I and other businessmen, as *corporate executives,* must give more personal attention to our unique opportunity to exercise the *art of leadership*—to fulfill our unique responsibility as *managers of human resources.* As corporate executives we have great opportunity to demonstrate and promote sensible ideas and constructive actions for the common good. Let me be specific: I believe that the economic realities, and the social and political principles, that have operated to achieve success for the American Can Company as a corporation, are the same realities and principles that have operated to achieve success and prosperity for every employee—in our business, in your business, and for every citizen.

As corporate executives, you and I stand at the head of groups of employees who can and will judge, first-hand, whether *our* management ideas make sense and deserve *their* agreement and support. When our own people learn first-hand from us what we stand for—and when they decide for themselves that they agree with us—we will have accomplished our principal duty of leadership as corporate executives.

This, however, is not the end of our task.

You, and I, and other businessmen—*as individuals*—MUST, in order to be good leaders and good citizens, become politically sophisticated. We MUST, *as individuals,* personally participate in the job of helping to select, nominate, and elect able people to public office.

If we fail to do so, we can look forward with certainty to the day when the corporation will become obsolete and the government will become absolute.

Because we—in the American Can Company management—are so strongly convinced of this, we decided some months ago to do something about it.

We decided we were not going to be passive and thus be a party to permitting our country to be led, unobstructed, into intellectual, moral and financial bankruptcy by a relatively few, highly vocal people—people who are either selfish, shiftless, power-hungry, well-intentioned but misguided, or proponents of another kind of political and economic system.

Here, briefly, is what our company is doing in an effort to help preserve and strengthen our economic and political institutions.

We at American Can Company have laid out a four-part program. Some of the parts are already in action, others are in the make-ready stage. Let me emphasize that no part of our program is a one-shot project or a temporary campaign. All four parts are designed for long-term action, from now on. We wish we had started them years ago.

Part one is to inform, equip and encourage everyone in our management organization to lead out, and speak out, on the business facts that have a direct bearing on the economic and social well-being of our own company, our own people, and of the nation. And by "everyone in our management organization" I mean our people at every management and supervisory level from the front office to the shipping dock.

Part two of our program is to make sure that every employee, and his family and his neighbors, gets from us, both face-to-face and in writing, a continuous flow of facts and viewpoints to round out his understanding and make it possible for him to reach judgments based on all of the truth rather than only part of it. We are constantly on guard not to *underestimate* our people's intelligence, or *overestimate* the amount of information they already have.

The *third part* is to give our managers the opportunity to study political processes and learn the art of practical politics. Our purpose here is to give our managers, and through them all employees, genuine encouragement to participate actively in personal politics— on their own time and at their own expense, in their own precincts and wards, through the party of their individual and personal choice.

The *fourth part* of our program is to give elected officials, through our management organization, our management views on important national issues as they come up for consideration in pending legislation.

The first two parts of this program do not require anything different in the way of organization structure or operating techniques. This is not to say, however, that these parts will operate by themselves without careful planning and constant attention, from the chief executive on down. Several months ago I tried to summarize this area of our current program to our entire management organization, in the following three sentences:

1. Let us extend our principles of sound and successful management to provide an increasing initiative to lead out and speak out, in our plants and offices and in our communities, on the affairs that control the welfare of our business and the economic, social and political climate in which we live.
2. Let us take constant stock of our management decisions and actions, to be sure that our practices and actions are always consistent with our principles.
3. The task remaining, then, is to exercise both personal and corporate leadership, in talking and writing to people to get them to think straight—to make the right choice under sometimes difficult circumstances.

The third and fourth parts of our current program—encouraging personal political action, and putting our management viewpoint on national issues on record with Congressmen—are brand new activities in our company. I want to take a few moments to describe how we are going about serving our apprenticeship in these new ventures.

Our decision to participate much more actively and aggressively in public issues and personal politics was made some months in advance of the 1958 elections, although not in time to make an effective contribution to a better understanding of the major issues involved. We did, however—through a personal letter sent to the home of each one—urge our 50,000 employees to register and vote.

During the second half of 1958, we also sent a series of letters to all of our top management people explaining the purposes of the program and soliciting their support. We asked 153 of these men—managers in plants and offices across the country—to act as official spokesmen for our company and establish direct relationships with the 153 Congressmen and 52 Senators representing the areas in which our facilities are located.

This group was asked to make themselves known to their legislators, to invite them to their plants and offices, and to discuss subjects of mutual interest. In addition, we wrote to the Senators and Congressmen telling them of our new policy of taking a much more active interest in public affairs, of our desire to be of service to them, of our plan to provide our employees with an increasing body of economic facts, and of our intent to speak out on important issues and to study legislative results.

It would be heart-warming to you and even inspiring, to read the substantial number of replies received from Members of Congress which expressed warm approval and enthusiastic endorsement of our purpose. These letters were about evenly divided among Republicans, Democrats, liberals and conservatives.

We are not yet well-enough equipped or experienced to be articulate on all important national issues before this session of Congress. So as a practical matter we are limiting ourselves this year to such critical matters as a balanced budget and sound fiscal policy, the encroachment of government controls over business, and an effective labor law. On each of these, we have considered the problem and have taken a company stand on what we believe is right and what we think Congress should do.

These positions are documented in detail based on our analysis of the need to favor or to oppose proposed legislative actions. They are being given to every one of our top management people. Our positions are also being made known to middle management and all other employees through our normal communication channels.

The 153 managers selected as spokesmen for the company are asked to study these carefully formulated views, and then to make their conclusions known to their legislators. We, of course, expect that all of the others in top management, acting as responsible managers and public-minded citizens, are also studying our views and communicating their analyses to their Congressmen—on an individual and personal basis. We hope that eventually all fifty thousand employees, their families and their friends, will join us in articulate support of the same objectives.

Needless to say we appreciate that, to the extent corporate managers confine their communication of ideas to legislators, their influence is limited. We want and expect our managers also to express themselves, on important issues to their management associates, to other employees, and in public. We want and expect them to help others to understand the fundamentals of sound business, sound government and to enlist their support in working toward the common good.

We expect to be successful in helping our employees to gain an understanding of the kinds of legislation which will further the interests of themselves and their company, as well as the welfare of the country. But we know that we, as managers, cannot stop there. Management must also offer employees an opportunity to learn how to translate knowledge into forceful and constructive action.

For this reason we are currently testing out, at several of our facilities, a course designed to provide citizens with a basic understanding of the art of practical politics. This is a course prepared by the U.S. Chamber of Commerce which brings together twelve to twenty people for a two-hour discussion, once a week, for nine consecutive weeks. It is expected that those taking the course will be sufficiently well informed to exert a healthy and beneficial influence on politics in their precincts and wards.

How fast and how far we can go in offering this opportunity to an ever-increasing number of our employees will be determined on the basis of the results of our tests.

Nevertheless, we are firmly convinced that if our political and economic system is to survive—perhaps, even, if our nation is to survive —a very much larger number of citizens must actively work to aid in the selection of good candidates for public office, to nominate them, and to elect them. This being so, management has a definite responsibility to help provide its employees with opportunities for political education. We, in the American Can Company, are fully committed to bearing our fair share of this responsibility.

The payoff from all this educational effort will come only if and when knowledgeable people actually support the cause of good government with their own personal effort—using their own time and money. Thus a vastly increased number of people must be encouraged, stimulated, and urged to work in their own precincts and wards for good government, through the party of their individual and personal choice. We intend to provide this incentive.

This is really all we *should do*. Because the decision to work or not work to promote the cause of good government must, of course, be left to the individual's personal conscience.

In conclusion I want to quote Thomas Jefferson. He said "I know of no safe depository for the ultimate powers of society but the people themselves; and if we think them not enlightened enough to exercise their control with a wholesome direction, the remedy is not to take it from them, but to inform their discretion through education."

If and when your management, our management, and other business managements are well on the way toward discharging these important responsibilities to our employees, our companies, and our country, in the field of public affairs, the people will, we can be sure, become enlightened, and—as Thomas Jefferson phrased it—exercise their control with a wholesome direction.

56 · THE I. G. FARBEN CASE *

Paragraphs 103 through 110 of the indictment charge the defendants with the plunder and spoliation of the principal dyestuffs industries of France by means of the so-called Francolor Agreement. The proof fully sustains the charges outlined in this portion of the indictment. In utter disregard of the rights of the French, Farben, acting principally through the defendants von Schnitzler, ter Meer, and Kugler, proceeded with methods of intimidation and coercion to acquire permanently for Farben a majority interest in a new corporation, "Francolor," which was organized to take over the assets of the French concerns. The facts may be briefly summarized as follows: Three of the major dyestuffs firms of France, prior to the war, were Compagnie Nationale de Matières Colorantes et Manufactures de Produits Chimiques du Nord Réunies Établissements Kuhlmann, Paris (referred to hereinafter as Kuhlmann); Société Anonyme des Matières Colorantes et Produits Chimiques de Saint Denis, Paris (referred to as Saint Denis); and Compagnie

* Reprinted from the Decision and Judgment of the United States Military Tribunal in "The I. G. Farben Case." *Trials of War Criminals before the Nuremberg Military Tribunals* (Washington, D.C.: United States Government Printing Office, 1952), VIII, 1147-1150.

Française de Produits Chimiques et Matières Colorantes de Saint-Clair-du-Rhône, Paris (referred to as Saint-Clair-du-Rhône). These three firms had cartel agreements with Farben, including the so-called Franco-German Cartel Agreement, entered into in 1927; the so-called Tri-Partite Agreement, or the Franco-German-Swiss Cartel, concluded in 1929; and the so-called Four-Party Agreement, to which German, French, Swiss, and English groups were parties, entered into in 1932. Under these agreements, a basis of cooperation between the more important producers of dyestuffs on the European Continent had been laid. But in planning for the New Order of the industry, Farben had contemplated and recommended complete reorganization of the industry under its leadership.

Immediately after the French armistice in 1940, Farben conferred with representatives of the occupying authorities and other governmental agencies and deliberately delayed negotiations with the French to make them more receptive to negotiations. In the meantime, Farben's influence with the German occupation authorities was used to prevent the issuance of licenses and to stop the flow of raw materials which would have permitted the French factories to resume their normal prewar production in keeping with the needs of the French economy. When the French plants were unable to resume production and their plight became sufficiently acute, they were forced to request the opening of negotiations. Farben indicated its willingness to confer. A conference was held on 21 November 1940 in Wiesbaden, at which representatives of Farben, the French industry, and the French and German Governments were in attendance. The meeting was under the official auspices of the Armistice Commission. Patently the French knew that they were forced to ascertain in the so-called negotiations what the future fate of the French dyestuffs industry, then at the mercy of the occupying Germans, might be. The meeting of November 21, 1940 was held in this atmosphere. The defendants von Schnitzler, ter Meer, and Kugler were in attendance as principal representatives of Farben. At the outset of the conference the French industrialists were frankly informed that the prewar agreements between Farben and the French producers, which the French wished to use as a basis in the negotiations, must be considered as abrogated owing to the course of the war. Farben's historical claim to leadership, founded upon alleged wrongs traced back to World War I, was asserted as additional reason. In a most high-handed fashion, the German representatives informed the French that the course of events during the preceding year had put matters in an entirely different light, and that there must be an adjustment to the new conditions. A memorandum read by von Schnitzler was presented to the French representatives, in which Farben demanded a controlling interest in the French dyestuffs industry. The German demands, set forth in the Farben memorandum, were vigorously supported by Ambassador Hemmen, who pointed out the grave danger to the French dyestuffs industry if its future should be relegated to settlement by the peace treaty rather than through the medium of the "negotiations." It is clear that this conference was in no real sense the opening of negotiations between parties free to deal with each other without compulsion. It was rather the perfect setting for the issuance of the German ultimatum to the French dyestuffs industry, which was to be subjected to Farben's control.

The French industry was faced with an unenviable alternative: it could pursue the path of collaboration and surrender, recognizing the plight created by the situation in the light of Farben's demands, or, if it chose to resist, it entailed the risk of perhaps more severe treatment at the hands of the occupying authorities or of future governmental commissions appointed for handling the matter in connection with the negotiation of a treaty of peace. The French feared the exercise of the power of German occupation either to take over the plants completely or to dismantle and cart them away to Germany, in keeping with the pattern that had been established for military occupation by policies of the Third Reich. Notwithstanding these dread alternatives, the French were outspoken and vigorous in their resistance to the German demands. They were, however, astute enough not to break off negotiations completely.

On the following day, November 22, 1940, a second conference was held between representatives of Farben—including von Schnitzler, ter Meer, Waibel and Kugler—and representatives of the French group, with no government officials in attendance. Farben's demands for majority participation and absorption of the French dyestuffs industry were forcefully made at this conference. The French continued their protests. They refused to accept the proposals, but still without breaking off negotiations. In view of the situation, they stated that they would report the matter to the French Government for counsel and advice. They were advised by their government not to break off negotiations because such a step might have serious repercussions. Postponement and delay in the negotiations were in complete harmony with Farben's plan to force the French group into submission. Subsequently a French counterproposal was presented to Farben representatives on January 20, 1941 at a meeting in Paris. This proposal represented the limits beyond which the French hoped not to be compelled to go. It was proposed that there be created a sales combine with a minority interest in Farben, the French holding the majority of the shares. This proposal was rejected by Farben. It did not satisfy the claim to leadership. It became increasingly clear, as the negotiations progressed, that this was a matter which would be settled entirely on Farben's terms. Farben's demand was for outright control of the French dyestuffs industry by 51 percent participation in the stock of a new corporation, Francolor, which was to be formed to take over all of the assets of Kuhlmann, Saint-Clair, and Saint-Denis. Reluctantly the French accepted in principle the German demand for consolidation of French dyestuffs production in a new company with German participation, but they still protested against, and held out against, Farben's demand for the majority interest. The evidence establishes that, in this regard, they even received support from French governmental authorities. But the French industry's plight was too desperate.

Finally, on March 10, 1941, the Vichy government gave its approval to the plan for the creation of the Franco-German dyestuffs company, Francolor, in which Farben was to be permitted to acquire a controlling 51 percent stock interest. This decision of the Vichy government was announced by the defendant von Schnitzler to the French representatives at a conference on that date. After confirmation of the fact that the officials in charge of economic questions for the French Government supported the position taken by Farben, the French industry was forced to give in. Final agreement was reached at a subsequent conference on March 12, 1941, attended by representatives from the French and German industries involved and by representatives of Military Government in Occupied France.

The Francolor Convention was formally executed on November 18, 1941. It was signed by the defendants von Schnitzler and ter Meer on behalf of Farben. By this convention Farben permanently acquired the controlling interest in the French dyestuffs industry, and paid therefor in shares of IG's stock, which could not be realized upon by the French as they were prohibited by terms of the convention from transferring the shares except among themselves. A decree entered by a French court on November 3, 1945 declared the legal nullity of the transfer of the shares of stock in Francolor to Farben. The transaction, although apparently legal in form, was annulled by virtue of the Inter-Allied Declaration of January 5, 1943 and French decrees based thereon.

The defendants have contended that the Francolor Agreement was the product of free negotiations and that it proved beneficial in practice to the French interests. We have already indicated that overwhelming proof establishes the pressure and coercion employed to obtain the consent of the French to the Francolor Agreement. As consent was not freely given, it is of no legal significance that the agreement may have contained obligations on the part of Farben, the performance of which may have assisted in the rehabilitation of the French industries. Nor is the adequacy of consideration furnished for the French properties in the new corporation a valid defense. The essence of the offense is the use of the power resulting from the military occupation of France as the means of acquiring private property in utter disregard of the rights and wishes of the owner. We find the element of compulsion and coercion present in an aggravated degree in the Francolor transaction, and the violation of the Hague Regulations is clearly established.

57 · THE RED EXECUTIVE *

David Granick

The Red Executive has come far since the days of the Revolution. Today he is a college-educated engineer with a sound technical and administrative background, and he bears little resemblance to the flamboyant Party director of the early days whose credentials were years in Tsarist prisons, escapes from exile, and oratory exercised in stirring the masses. But the present-day Red Executive is also no throwback to the bourgeois plant manager of the late twenties and early thirties who, for all his education, was distrusted as an enemy of the Revolution and a potential saboteur. Today's executive com-

* From *The Red Executive,* by David Granick. Copyright © 1960 by David Granick. Reprinted by permission of Doubleday and Company, Inc.

bines sound training with the political assurance and power which permit him the freedom to make creative use of this training.

The Soviet manager may not live well when judged by the standards of his American counterpart, but he does quite satisfactorily compared to the ordinary Soviet citizen. He is given powerful monetary incentives to turn in a first-rate job. Yet never in his life will he have any certainty of tenure in his post. No civil service rules or old-school tie protect him; his superiors show a marked impatience with failure. This impatience, it is true, is now tempered more with common sense than was the case in the past. No longer, as often occurred during the mid-1930's, do production lapses lead swiftly to charges of sabotage and to a forced-labor camp. Nevertheless, blunders can result in swift demotion. The executive ulcer rate is high.

The Russian manager is a man with power, but he is no independent decision-maker. He is an organization man, filling a slot in an industrial bureaucracy which has lines reaching to the very heights of Soviet power. His production goals, his costs, and even his industrial research objectives are set for him. Moreover, he must establish and maintain successful contact with the members of other powerful bureaucracies—and in particular with that of the Communist Party.

But if the manager's goals are established for him, their achievement is his personal responsibility. No excuse exists for failure. Often, the drive to meet quotas will force him into illegal activities; this cannot be helped. It is a basic part of his task to determine what is necessary in order to "succeed"; in this sense, the Red Executive is very much an independent businessman.

The Soviet manager is oriented to production. Volume of output is the acid test of his work. Marketing is no problem; finance is a trivial concern. But the purchasing department is the rock on which the factory organization stands, for supply shortages lead to production shortages. A good procurement man is above price.

Although the situation is now in the process of change, raw materials and machinery are still the items of greatest scarcity to the Russian manager. It is these which are his bottlenecks. Labor, of course, is also a problem—but a labor-saving device is not nearly as valuable to him as is one which saves materials or which permits more production from a machine. Thus, the Soviet manager tends to emphasize in his daily work different problems and different shortages than does the American company president or even the plant superintendent.

Well trained, well disciplined, politically conscious and active, the Red Executive seems a figure permanently established in the seats of the mighty. There is no justification for picturing him as a man in conflict with the Communist Party official, the two uneasily sharing power for the moment. Rather, the industrial manager and the Party secretary are old classmates, neighbors, and colleagues, seeing the world from the same perspective.

Neither the Red Executive nor his Party-official colleague is any longer the revolutionary of the 1920's to whom ideology was everything. Both are men well established in the second most powerful country in the world, with enormous personal stakes in world stability and in peace. When Marx in the *Communist Manifesto* appealed for world revolution, he addressed himself to the worker who had "nothing to lose but his chains." The Red Executive and the Party administrator have a great deal more to lose—and they know it well. Their attitude toward world revolution and other threats to peace must inevitably bear the imprint of this knowledge.

Labor

58 · POLITICS AND THE UNITED STEELWORKERS OF AMERICA*

Mr. ABEL. Mr. Chairman and members of the committee, my name is I. W. Abel. I am secretary-treasurer of the United Steelworkers of America. I am also secretary-treasurer of the administra-

* Reprinted from the testimony of I. W. Abel, given on December 11, 1956, before the United States Senate Special Committee to Investigate Political Activities, Lobbying, and Campaign Contributions, Senator John L. McClellan, Chairman.

tive committee of the United Steelworkers of America Political Action Committee.

The Steelworkers Union welcomes your invitation to appear here today to testify about our political activities and to present certain recommendations for improvements in legislation governing Federal elections.

Our union has always operated on the assumption that we have a prime obligation to keep the general public, as well as our membership, fully informed regarding our activities.

We, of course, have been very careful to comply scrupulously with all laws requiring the filing of financial and other information designed to disclose the nature of our activities to the public, the filing of non-Communist affidavits, and registration of certain of our representatives with respect to lobbying and similar activities. In addition, we voluntarily have followed the practice of sending all Congressmen and many State, local, and community leaders copies of our semiannual audit reports, which are certified by the leading auditing firm of Main and Company, certified public accountants.

In line with this policy also, we have extended full cooperation to this committee's investigators and have made available to them whatever records and information they requested.

The United Steelworkers of America celebrated its 20th anniversary this year. From the birth of its predecessor, the Steel Workers Organizing Committee, in 1936, and the establishment of the United Steelworkers of America as an international union in 1942, we have grown to an organization with a present membership of about 1,250,000. There are some 2,800 local unions, chartered by the international union, in the United States and Canada. The international union is affiliated with the American Federation of Labor and Congress of Industrial Organizations.

The constitution of the international union sets forth three principal objects of the organization. The first object is to unite in this industrial union, regardless of race, creed, color, or nationality, all workers in the steel, iron, aluminum, nonferrous metals and allied industries. The second object is to establish through collective bargaining adequate wage standards, shorter hours of work, and improved conditions of employment for these workers.

The third object is as follows:

> To secure legislation safeguarding the economic and social welfare of the workers in the industry, to protect and extend our democratic

institutions and civil rights and liberties and thus to perpetuate the cherished traditions of our democracy.

Thus, in addition to organizing the workers in our jurisdiction and improving their working standards and conditions through collective bargaining, it is a major and fundamental purpose of the steelworkers to achieve legislation and enforcement of democratic rights for the benefit not only of our members but of all citizens. Our constitution recognizes that the interests of our members can be affected by legislative and other governmental action as by gains made through collective bargaining. Our constitution also recognizes that governmental action which is in the interest of the public at large is likewise in the interest of steelworkers.

Laws providing for the right to organize, old age and disability security, minimum wages, maximum hours, industrial safety and health standards, unemployment compensation, workmen's compensation, housing, schools and hospitals are but a few examples of the tremendous impact of legislation on the well-being and security of workers and the public.

In the 20 years of our existence, we have been active on the Federal and State levels in supporting the great economic and social reform legislation enacted in this period and in opposing legislation directed against labor or conveying special advantages on the privileged few. This activity has been and continues to be an important function of this union.

We in the United Steelworkers of America learned long ago that achievement of the legislative goals and enforcement of the democratic rights envisioned by our constitution and detailed by our conventions, is inextricably intertwined with the election of liberal legislators and executives.

Conversely, we know from experience that election of reactionary officials not only negates chances for forward looking legislation, but poses grave threats to the rights and legitimate activities of the labor movement.

The admittedly antilabor Taft-Hartley law, which President Eisenhower has stated can be used to destroy labor unions, and the employer-inspired State "right to work" laws unloosed by Taft-Hartley, are sharp reminders of the dangers inherent in political inactivity on the part of labor unions and their members.

Of necessity, therefore, we have had to take an active role in politics and we are justly proud of the role we have played.

Foremost in our political activity has been our effort to educate our members and neighbors as to the issues involved in election campaigns and the importance of exercising their fundamental democratic rights as citizens to register and vote.

In addition, we have encouraged our local unions to conduct registration and get out the vote drives.

Finally, we have given support to candidates sympathetic to our goals.

I wish to emphasize that the political policy of the steelworkers union always has been strictly nonpartisan. We have studiously avoided endorsement or support of any political party.

On the contrary, we have judged each candidate on his record and individual merits and have given our support, irrespective of party affiliation, to those candidates who showed promise of carrying out our programs.

The CHAIRMAN. May I interrupt to inquire there, as I understand it, it is the general policy of your organization not to be affiliated with a party as such, but to cross party lines?

Mr. ABEL. That is right.

The CHAIRMAN. Or irrespective of party lines, to choose the candidates of your choice, those whose views you think most likely coincide with your own and the policies of your organization?

Mr. ABEL. That is correct, sir.

The CHAIRMAN. Proceed.

Mr. ABEL. We believe our political activities have served, in a measure, to revitalize and strengthen our democratic institutions. There is no more fundamental obligation in a representative democracy than the obligation of a citizen to vote, and to vote intelligently. A disinterested and uninformed electorate bears the seeds of minority rule and tyranny which are all too prevalent in many parts of the world.

To the extent that we have succeeded in educating our members and friends to vote as informed citizens, to that extent have we made them better citizens and succeeded in preserving and furthering our representative form of government.

The importance which the steelworkers' union places on political action is illustrated by the following excerpts from the policy statement on this subject adopted by our recent convention in Los Angeles:

Political action is the lifeblood of democracy.

No government can adequately understand and meet the needs of all of its citizens unless it is truly representative of all of the people.

It has been forcefully demonstrated in the past that when the citizens of our country fail or are denied the right to take an active part in the political life of our Nation on a local, State, and National level the big business and special privilege groups take over.

The United Steelworkers of America has consistently urged its membership and all other Americans to meet their obligation of good citizenship by registering to vote and by voting. . . .

To assure effective participation by our union in the field of political action we call upon the political action committee of the United Steelworkers of America to continue and expand its work of political education, its aid to campaigns for registration of voters, and efforts to elect an administration, a Congress, and State and local governments sympathetic to the needs of our members, the ideals of our union, and all of the people of the United States.

We call upon each local union to cooperate fully with our political action committee and to seek voluntary contributions from our members to finance the work which is necessary.

We pledge cooperation of the United Steelworkers of America to the committee on political education of the AFL–CIO and we support its work and objectives.

Political activities of the steelworkers' union are administered by the political action committee of the United Steelworkers of America, which was formed in 1955.

Prior to that time, administration of our political activities was coordinated through the political action committee of the Congress of Industrial Organizations. The international union transmitted to CIO–PAC individual voluntary dollar contributions collected by the local unions from members and friends. Only these voluntary moneys were used by CIO–PAC to support the campaigns of various candidates for Federal offices, following enactment of the Taft-Hartley Act in 1947 with its restrictions on union political expenditures.

In addition, the international union made contributions from its treasury to a separate political-educational fund maintained by CIO–PAC. These educational moneys were used for education materials, registration, and get-out-the-vote drives, and to support candidates for State and local offices in States which placed no restrictions on union political expenditures.

Since 1955 the political fund-raising and disbursing activities of the international union have been carried on by the steelworkers' political action committee. The union's international officers are the administrative officers of the steelworkers' PAC.

Funds and accounts of steelworkers' PAC are separately kept and are carefully segregated from the international union's treasury account. There are two separate funds and accounts: (1) An individual voluntary contribution account and (2) an educational account.

The voluntary account is made up of individual contributions, mostly of $1 each, by members and friends. Campaigns for voluntary contributions are carried on by our local unions.

In advance of a voluntary-contributions campaign, the steelworkers' political action committee distributes books of cash receipts to our local unions. For each voluntary dollar that is contributed by an individual, a separate receipt is given to the contributor and a record of the contribution is kept in the receipt book.

Contributions and the supporting receipt books are sent by the local unions to the steelworkers' political action committee, which deposits the money in the voluntary account and preserves the receipt books in its files. Any voluntary moneys received by steelworkers' PAC which are not supported by receipts are, for the sake of extra caution in complying with the law, placed in the educational account instead of the voluntary account.

Steelworkers' PAC normally retains in the voluntary account only half of the voluntary moneys sent in by the local unions. The other half is returned to the respective local unions which, in turn, transmit all or a portion thereof to the respective State or local CIO–PAC organizations and retain any remainder for their own political activities.

Moneys in the steelworkers' PAC voluntary account, and only such moneys, are used to make contributions in support of candidates for Federal office and for State office in any State which restricts political expenditures from union treasuries.

Not 1 cent of the union-dues money is used to support any such candidates.

In addition, contributions are made from this account to the similar voluntary account maintained by the AFL–CIO committee on political education—COPE.

The steelworkers' PAC educational account is made up of contributions from the treasury of the international union and any voluntary moneys which are not supported by receipt books. These moneys are used for political-education purposes and to support candidates for State and local offices in States which place no restriction on union political expenditures.

Contributions also are made from this account to the similar educational account maintained by COPE.

I wish at this juncture to make a few observations regarding administration of these funds, which deserve emphasis.

Both the voluntary and educational accounts are audited and certified each year by Main and Company, certified public accountants.

All requirements of the Corrupt Practices Act, as amended, including the filing of periodic reports with the Clerk of the House of Representatives, are strictly complied with.

Indeed, as we have seen, we go out of our way to be sure that only voluntary moneys, which can be supported by records in our files of receipts issued to the individual contributors, are used in connection with Federal election campaigns.

From the reports which we have filed, copies of which have been made available to the committee staff, it is evident that the political expenditures of steelworkers' PAC, representing as it does 1,250,000 members, are of negligible proportions compared with the political expenditures of just a handful of wealthy families.

Numerous suggestions have been made for reforms in the laws governing Federal elections. I should like to comment briefly on several of these suggestions.

At the founding convention of the AFL–CIO just 1 year ago, cognizance was taken of certain outmoded election laws and practices which impair the effective functioning of our form of democratic self-government. The United Steelworkers of America is in accord with the suggestions made by the AFL–CIO for modernization of these laws and practices, and we commend these suggestions, as follows, to the members of this committee:

> The President and Vice President of the United States should be elected by direct popular vote. The electoral-college system has outlived its usefulness and should be abolished.
>
> We believe, further, that a uniform primary law should be adopted

by each State in order to permit direct and open primaries and to afford each person who desires it the opportunity to place his candidacy before the voters.

We believe, further, that a uniform registration system for each State, designed to facilitate rather than hinder free voting, should be adopted. All poll taxes should be abolished, and legalisms and technicalities which have done much to hamper voting should likewise be done away with.

．　．　．　．　．

The CHAIRMAN. Is not your educational campaign actually a political education campaign?

Mr. ABEL. Certainly, and we make no denial of it and we don't try to hide it, but corporations do.

The CHAIRMAN. I am not sure they all do. There may be some.

Mr. ABEL. Many.

The CHAIRMAN. The point is that all of the political education fund that you have, or this educational fund or most of it, is used for the purpose of educating your members and your friends to your political views, or to the political view of your union, and, therefore, to have them vote accordingly?

Mr. ABEL. That is correct, sir.

The CHAIRMAN. So in its actual essence the educational fund is purely a political fund?

Mr. ABEL. That is right.

Senator GOLDWATER. Mr. Abel, I have one point there. You say you believe that the union should be allowed to spend organizational money or dues money for the direct support of candidates.

How would you answer the members of your union who might not agree with your selection of the candidate?

As an example, say you picked a Republican and a group of your members were Democrats and they did not want to back that Republican, how would you answer the moral question they put to you, the propriety of using their money to support someone they are against and will vote against and work against on the outside?

Mr. ABEL. Senator, those are some of the hazards that go with being a union official or representative, just the same as your being a Senator representing your State. There are many, many things that we must make decisions on and engage in that all of our members don't look with favor on. We try to represent the thinking of the membership to the best of our ability and, of course, we assume the responsibility for any errors that we may make in that representation.

We, too, of course, are subject to the scrutiny by the membership periodically just the same as the United States Senator or Member of Congress. We stand for election. We stand on our record.

Senator GOLDWATER. I appreciate that, but my whole and entire interest in this field has been just what I have expressed to you. We find for instance on the whole the union movement is fairly representative of both parties. I think the Democrats are in a majority by possibly 60 to 40 or something like that.

But, nevertheless, a rather large segment of unions is represented by the Republican Party. Historically, the unions have been against Republicans, not entirely, but historically they have.

What recourse has the Republican member who has to pay his dues to keep his job? What recourse does he have to the union who spends that money of his against his political wishes.

I think it involves a question of morals.

Mr. ABEL. You see, as I said, there are many phases of our activity in which we encounter that same problem. As an example, we negotiate a wage increase. There are those who prefer a percentage application and there are those who prefer the flat across-the-board application. We are the ones that have the responsibility for making a decision and we have to make a decision.

It is the same when we get into the political activities; just the same as engaging in a strike.

Senator GOLDWATER. I do not think that would be apropos because I think the man joins the union basically for that kind of service and protection. He expects you to protect him at the bargaining table. He expects you to be concerned about his wages and his working hours.

I do not think a man joins a union organization for political advantage.

Mr. ABEL. Senator, as I pointed out earlier in the statement, our constitution provides certain activities for us to engage in. One, as you recall, provides for securing legislation safeguarding the economic security and social welfare of the workers in the industry, to protect and to extend our democratic institutions and civil rights liberties and thus to perpetuate the cherished traditions of our democracy.

Now, that is one of the principles set forth in our constitution for which we are organized.

Now, you accomplish those things in the field of political activity. There again we have to exercise the best judgment we know how to better achieve this objective set forth in the constitution.

Senator GOLDWATER. I am not trying to argue your responsibility in having to choose correctly to try to satisfy all your members. I do not think that can even be done when you make your decisions at the bargaining table.

I am not arguing that point. I think you have a good statement in your constitution. I believe that civil rights and liberties are something that all of us should protect.

My basic concern in the whole field is the fact that political liberties of some American workers are jeopardized when the union takes dues money and spends it for political purposes.

Now, I have never heard inferred that your union has done that. I have attacked one specific union in this field, but I do not like to hear you in your responsible position suggest that you would like to do that because you get again into the moral question of whether it is right or wrong.

It is not whether it is legal or not. Is it right or wrong to take a man's money that in many cases was collected under compulsion, whether we like that word or not, and it is spent at the will of a group of people at the top whether or not he agrees with it.

Mr. ABEL. Let me point this out. Maybe it will help clear up the problems you present.

In our union, and I think you will find it is pretty generally true of trade unions, we operate under a very democratic procedure. Our particular union so far as our day-to-day operations are concerned, is governed by what we term a wage policy committee, that is made up of representatives from the mills and plants. They formulate and establish policies on a day-to-day basis.

In addition to that, every two years we convene a national convention and there we engage in debate on the broad overall objectives of the union and the desires and the needs of the membership and we adopt policies, programs, both in the economic field as well as the legislative and political fields.

The portion of the statement I have presented here, which I did not read, spells out to a great degree the action of our national convention held in Los Angeles in September, the objectives of our union in the field of legislation and political action.

Those things are derived through democratic action and through majority rule. I mean the membership themselves through their elected delegates from the local unions adopt these programs by vote and after thorough discussion, so we do operate from a rule of the majority of the membership and we are guided very much by the wishes and the wills of the membership.

Believe me, we are just as sensitive to the wishes of the membership as a United States Senator or Congressman is to the wishes of his constituents.

In other words, it is another phase of democracy.

Senator GOLDWATER. I agree with you that your conventions are conducted in a democratic manner. I am not arguing that point, but there is a little bit of difference between your organization having a convention and passing your opinion on candidates or issues and say, the organization to which I belong, NRDGA. They do the same thing on economic matters.

If I do not agree with them, I quit. That does not affect my ability to work. If I belong to the steelworkers' union and I live in a State that is not protected by the right-to-work laws, if I quit the union I have to make up my mind to go to some other place or get some other job in some other skill and move from the State.

It is quite a decision to make. Say 40 per cent of your membership is Republican, and you decide to back a Democrat candidate. There is not much that 40 per cent can do about it. They can raise Cain with themselves and raise Cain with you, but if they want to work they will stay members of the union.

That is the moral point I get to.

Mr. ABEL. By the same token perhaps there are members of ours, in our union, who don't agree with our activities in the field of civil rights and don't agree with the expenditures we may make toward the achievement of the program of the union in the field of civil rights. But that does not hamper us from doing what we can, what we think is right and proper to establish and protect civil rights in this country for our own membership and the general public.

Senator GOLDWATER. I have argued, too, that the very act that we are discussing is a violation of civil rights when you impinge upon the political freedom of an individual, which may not amount to a

lot of money; it may only amount to 50 cents a month that comes
out of his dues for political purposes. It is part of his donation that
goes against his will. That is the point I wish to make.

59 · THE NEED FOR UNION POWER *

Mr. HOFFA. Senator, I have made a statement in front of this
committee, to the newspapers, and I make it again, that it is my firm
belief that it is my responsibility as president of this international
union to be able to associate in a council the transportation unions of
America, so we will not be harassed by employer combinations,
so we will not be placed in a position of secondary boycott, so we
will not be placed in a position of blackmail picketing, not placed in
a position of organizational picketing, not caught in a squeeze on
economic matters at negotiations, but rather, we will have enough
sense, I hope, to be able to piece together a transportation council
that will be able to exchange views and ideas on the economics of
this country and to be able to discuss between ourselves the matter
of wages, hours, conditions, pensions, welfares, et cetera, for the
common interest of transportation workers, as such, in the United
States.

· · · · · ·

The CHAIRMAN. Senator Goldwater.

Senator GOLDWATER. Mr. Hoffa, you have discussed with Senator
Mundt your nebulous plans for a council of all transportation unions?

Mr. HOFFA. Yes, sir.

Senator GOLDWATER. In your opinion, would this council have the
power to call a nationwide strike of transportation?

Mr. HOFFA. No, sir. At no time would we take away from our
membership the right to vote whether or not they wanted to accept
or reject the employer's contract, and we would not get into a
nationwide strike.

* Reprinted from the testimony of James R. Hoffa, President, The International Brotherhood of Teamsters, Chauffeurs, Warehousemen, and Helpers
of America, given on July 14, 1959, before the United States Senate Select
Committee on Improper Activities in the Labor or Management Field, Senator
John L. McClellan, Chairman.

Senator GOLDWATER. Could the council at any time utilize power to place the entire transportation industry in a secondary boycott position in order to force—in order to gain objectives for any one particular segment of the transportation industries?

Mr. HOFFA. Let me answer that by saying it may, Senator. Unfortunately for this country, the U.S. Government has apparently recognized the right of employers to band against them and be able to subsidize each others' strikes out of their pockets. If this is going to be the practice of employers of the United States—of combining themselves into an industrywide combination to where they may be able to buy out, if you please, their responsibility of negotiating a labor contract on fair terms, by knowing that they will receive the same profit they made the same period last year without a strike— then it would be conceivable that the American transportation units may have to find themselves in a position that employers hoping to be able to pay each other's debt have common expiration dates where there will be no profits to destroy and defeat organized labor in transportation or any other industry.

This could conceivably happen if you permit by law, as you are now doing, the formation of councils to be able to buy out each others' strikes, as newspapers do in this country in almost every city, as the airlines now do, as I see the railroads are trying to do, as I hear now, by the grapevine, the truckowners are trying to do, and I understand the steel companies are trying to do.

If this is the new, modern method of democracy in the United States for employers, then the same democracy ought to prevail for workers in America to be able to protect their own interest by having enough common sense and businesslike attitude to sit down and recognize the cost factor of a strike, to be able to circumvent and offset a strike; if not, use a combination sufficient to make that strike as limited as possible.

Senator GOLDWATER. Of course, the union movement today has that same right if they wanted to do it; in the secondary boycott and application of it you have pretty much that same phenomena occurring.

Mr. HOFFA. That is absolutely correct.

Senator GOLDWATER. You may think it is incorrect, but the power behind it is correct and the power of management in trying to help each other during the course of a strike, I suggest to you, Mr. Hoffa, has come about by the power of unions.

Mr. HOFFA. No, sir; I do not agree with you at all. I will show you, sir, back in 1932, if you please, when we could hardly get our head above water, the employers had organizations in existence the same as they have today and they worked together to defeat organized labor and tried to defeat us on the very first contract we had and had to finally strike the entire car-hauling industry of Michigan and the freight industry to keep each other from working to destroy our organization.

Senator GOLDWATER. I will not argue with you on that point because I have said many times in the early 1930's it was proper in my opinion that the Federal Government endow the labor movement with power to meet the other side of the table.

Mr. HOFFA. This was the employer. They didn't give us that power.

Senator GOLDWATER. I recognize that. I said it was proper for the Federal Government to give the labor movement these powers to balance management at the bargaining table.

Now, my question is getting to the same question I asked you nearly two years ago: It seems from this same subject, that the union movement in this country is no longer a weakling, no longer a fledgling, it is a powerful institution.

In my opinion, and I think in your opinion, you can sit down at the bargaining table with probably more cards in your hands in most cases than can management. You might not agree with me, but that is my opinion.

I asked you back in 1957, in August, after prefacing my question with remarks similar to the ones I have made, namely, the accumulation of power in the union movement, the ability to strike, which by the way we should never take away from the union movement, and I asked this question:

> Because of those facts would you think it wise, too, that the Congress consider placing unions under antimonopoly or under antitrust laws the same as we place the large corporations of this country?

You answered:
> I certainly do not.

Now, I thought that at that time I asked you that question. I evidently asked you this question after the meeting or I might have dreamed that I asked it, but I made a hypothetical situation which I will read to you again and I want to ask you this question once more:

If a person or a union has absolute control and, say, just to make it a hypothetical question, one man or small group of men have absolute control over the wage scales of an entire industry such as the trucking industry and the wrong group are heading it, could not that group do as much damage to the consumers of this country as, let us say, for example, X corporation who would control all of the acetate yarn production of the country?

Now, that was my hypothetical situation.

Mr. HOFFA. What was my answer, sir?

Senator GOLDWATER. Well, you made a mistake in your answer. You recognized me as a Senator from Nebraska and I thanked you for the compliment.

I wanted to ask you if your union or your council or your combination, whatever you want to call it, ever reaches a place where you can restrain trade in this country to the damage of the public?

Do you think that the Government should have controls over that restraint the same as they have in corporations in business?

Mr. HOFFA. No, sir; I do not. Now, or in the future, for two reasons: One, a worker in the industry that he has chosen to work in has only two things to offer: One, his time; the other his physical well-being. He may have lost an arm, he may have lost a leg, or a combination of both; he would have no place to go to work anywhere in the United States and probably would be too young to draw any sort of benefits from the Federal Government or the State.

If there comes a time in America when you are saying in effect that if organized labor becomes officially organized to match industry, then organized labor must be contained and organized labor must find itself regulated by law to where it will not be able to exercise its original intent of exerting economic pressure when it becomes necessary on employers to accept improvement in contracts, be willing to sign pension, welfare, vacations, et cetera.

Now, I say to you, Senator, I have had experience in this labor movement as long as most old men have had. I can individually remember the years of 1932, 1933, 1934, 1935, 1936, up to 1937, and all during those years we were battered around and beat by the employers all over these United States.

Finally we conceived the idea of a Central States Drivers' Council for the entire Middle West. I think now of the question of Nebraska, what we had there, and after the very first contract was signed in 1937 with the industry in the Middle West, the State of Nebraska employers thoroughly organized in the American way, American plan, defied the unions to get a contract signed in Nebraska even though their representatives had sat in and negotiated that contract.

(Members of the select committee present at this point in the proceedings: Senators McClellan, Ervin, Mundt, Goldwater, and Curtis.)

Mr. HOFFA. It became necessary at that time to picket the roads leading into and out of Nebraska.

Maybe you will recall it, Senator Curtis.

Those drivers belonging to our union, recognizing the substandard wages in Nebraska, recognized and respected those picket lines.

After a long, bitter fight, we were successful in getting the Nebraska employers to sign our contract. Since then—and I may say also, Senator Mundt, in your neighborhood it became necessary during the time of war, if you please, that the Government take over a hundred-and-some-odd trucklines because the employers refused to comply with the War Labor Board decision, and the Government operated the trucks at a deficit to the extent that you had to pass a special law in Congress to subsidize and pay the losses of those concerns.

I maintain, Senator, that you cannot apply the principle of profit to the American human being. He has nothing in his pocket. He has nothing in the bank, when it comes to comparing him to the smallest executive, or to a president of a corporation.

So I suggest that rather than try to hamstring the American labor movement that we recognize that the worker, out of sheer necessity, based upon the construction of large corporations today, must have the right of combinations, of organizations, to be able to assist each other to get for them what they are entitled to without the restraint of trying to say that the human body is subject to the same corporate structure of an industry who has stockmarkets, shares on the stockmarkets, who sells it to widows, to everybody concerned, trust funds, et cetera.

But the worker has no stocks, no bonds, no dividends. He has his hands, his feet, his eyes. Therefore, I suggest to you not to try to entrap him into a situation of anti-monopoly that will destroy organized labor and place him back in the year 1932-33.

· · · · ·

Senator GOLDWATER. Am I to believe that your position today is the same as it was two years ago; namely that you feel that the labor movement in this country should have absolutely no restraints placed on it, even when the actions of the labor movement can do damage to the public?

Mr. HOFFA. I would like to say, Senator, and I have no right to speak for the steel unions and I am doing something I normally don't do, but it happens to be in the public eye and in their mind today— I would like to say that the steel corporations of America have brought about a greater discomfort to industry and to the American public than any union could ever do by increasing capacity production to the extent that they can stock warehouses, that they can stock manufacturers, and then they can come to the bargaining table and arrogantly say, "This is what you will do or you will get nothing; go on strike."

If this is to be the democratic system of America, then I say to you, sir, in all due respect, that we must recognize the combination of organized labor, the combination of the ordinary worker, both in politics and in unionization; that we have a common enemy, and that common enemy has no right to expect to have the power to destroy our organization by locking us out and starving into submission individuals who have no money in the bank, who have very little limited credit when their paycheck is cut off, but, rather, sun themselves in Florida and elsewhere, saying that, "This is what you will do or else."

If this is the answer to the American worker, then I say to you the American worker will surprise industry and surprise all of the politicians in America, because they will not stand for it, nor will they stand to be destroyed by antitrust.

Senator GOLDWATER. That didn't answer my question. You can answer it "yes" or "no."

Do you believe that at any time, regardless of how powerful unions become, there should never be any restraint placed on them by the Federal Government, regardless of what this power can do to the country?

Mr. HOFFA. My opinion is the answer is "No." There should be no restraint on unions as long as they are complying with the current city, State, and Federal laws.

Senator GOLDWATER. Well, you are above the Federal law, you know, in some instances.

Mr. HOFFA. No, sir; that isn't true.

Senator GOLDWATER. You are above State laws in some instances.

Mr. HOFFA. I have read your statements, sir, and you have made speeches all over this country, and it absolutely is not true. We are subject to every law in the United States, whether it be from an ordinary scuffle on the street to any other law.

Senator GOLDWATER. How about the injunctive processes?

Mr. HOFFA. We are subjected to it more than anybody in America.

Senator GOLDWATER. Not until you do damage, though.

Mr. HOFFA. No, sir; that is not true. I have had injunctions served on me by the mere announcement in the newspaper that there was going to be a strike. I have seen the Steelworkers recently called in by the President of the United States, in all due respect to him, and have urged them not to go on strike, but, rather, that they should delay their negotiations to try and work out their problems.

But ultimately and eventually, and you know it, there is a section in the Taft-Hartley law, that without a strike those workers for 60 days could be required not to strike.

You also know full well, sir, that if there is a strike any one little justice of the peace, circuit-court judge, can sign an injunction, prior to going on strike, limiting the number of pickets in front of an establishment, or restricting the strike entirely if they desire to do so.

Then it becomes a matter of appeals, which takes weeks, months, and money.

Senator GOLDWATER. I will still stand by my interpretation that you can't have injunctive processes applied to you until you do damage to persons or property. I wish you would agree.

Mr. HOFFA. I wish you would sit in my office. I would like to hire you for a lawyer. I have hundreds of cases to the contrary, sir.

60 · LABOR IN POSTWAR EUROPE *

Adolf Sturmthal

The time is probably approaching when the history of European labor during and after World War II ought to be written. Indeed,

* Adolf Sturmthal, *The Tragedy of European Labor 1918-1939* (New York: Columbia University Press, 1943; second printing with a new preface, 1951), pp. vii-xviii. Reprinted by permission of Columbia University Press. The footnotes in the original version are omitted here.

there is some danger in delay; memories fade (and memories are probably at this time the only record of much of this history), and in the fast-moving kaleidoscope of the postwar scene history is no doubt being assiduously rewritten to fit later insights and necessities. Pending this major piece of history writing, however, a few significant trends perhaps deserve immediate, though brief, attention.

The end of hostilities in Europe has been followed by a major attempt to unify the trade-union movement in those countries in which it has traditionally been split according to political philosophies. This effort was the result of a number of factors: the Socialist-Communist division, sharply accentuated by the Russo-German pact of 1939, had lost a good deal of its acerbity after June, 1941, when the Communists once again changed their "line" and became the most enthusiastic advocates of resistance to Hitlerism; under the Nazi occupation the labor groups—Socialists, Communists, and Catholics—coöperated wholeheartedly in the "Resistance"; after June, 1941, the Communists developed a new stage in their United Front policy, which was intended to bring about the merger of all anti-Nazi unions, clearly in the hope of dominating the united organizations; lastly and less significantly, the German Labor Front, despite its objectionable basic features, had demonstrated what powerful means of action—financial and otherwise—a unified labor organization might have at its disposal.

The attempt to merge Socialists, Communists, and Catholics in one trade union organization was made in six Continental countries: Austria, Belgium, France, Germany, Holland, and Italy. The results are significant.

From the outset, unification failed in three countries among the six. To facilitate the merger of the unions, the Dutch Social Democratic party allied itself with religious groups holding socially advanced views and thereby clearly marked its intention of opening its doors wide to non-Marxians or anti-Marxians. It even dropped its old name and called itself the Party of Labor. Nevertheless the religious unions refused to merge with the Socialist-led movement and maintained the division of Dutch trade unionism. In Belgium, the Socialist-led unions, which had in the past followed somewhat the British pattern and had been collectively affiliated with the Belgian Labor Party, now separated from the party in the hope that this move would make it possible for the Catholic unions to merge with them. This hope was not realized. Similarly, the French Christian Unions rejected without hesitation the invitation to join the Confédération Générale du Travail (C.G.T.).

In Italy, the attempt was at first successful. Unified trade unions were established to combine workers of differing social and political views. Yet from the outset each unified union was, so to speak, a federation of differing political groups, which maintained a sort of existence as well-organized factions within the union and strove to gain control over the entire body. At the Congress [of unions] the various factions submitted resolutions designed primarily to test their relative strength within the "united" organization. The membership of the Executive Committee of the Confederation was carefully divided among the various factions according to their numerical representation at the Congress as demonstrated in the vote on the resolutions submitted. Even in this first stage, the so-called unity barely concealed the division of the organization over political and social issues. Each of the factions, needless to say, represented a political party.

Even this "sham unity" did not last very long. First the Catholics (1948), then the anti-Communist wing (1949) of the Socialists and the Republicans broke away. One group of the Republicans merged with the Catholics, another is engaged in an attempt to remain independent. Without too much difficulty, it is possible to see in this threefold division a reflection of the threefold split of Italian socialism into the pro-Communist Nenni group, the right-wing Saragat Socialists who are coöperating with the Catholics in the government, and the independent Socialists led by Romita and Silone.

Germany and Austria thus offer the only examples of successful attempts at unification on the basis of "nonpartisan" labor action. But closer examination would indicate that in these countries, too, political groups contrive to exist within the unified trade unions. The official publication of the Austrian trade union confederation, in its reports on discussions of the governing bodies of the confederation, carefully indicates the political affiliation of each speaker. A rough system of proportional representation for the various political factions in the governing union bodies is used in both countries.

"Political" unionism, it would seem, remains the fate of European labor, for better or for worse. It "fits" Europe clearly in the same sense in which, according to Selig Perlman, "pure and simple" trade unionism "fitted" American labor. In its philosophy, as well as in its methods, European labor remains intensely "political," at least in the usual meaning of the term. Thus, in most countries the unions continue to coöperate closely with particular political parties and to rely largely upon them for the satisfaction of some major demands. Among these parties the Socialists, the Communists, and the Catholics continue to be the most important.

In these respects the over-all picture does not show any basic alteration, but the relations of the political parties with which the unions are allied have undergone considerable and significant changes. The most notable are concerned with Socialist-Communist conflict.

The liberation of Continental Europe from German occupation was accompanied by a semirevolutionary trend, although neither of the major advancing armies favored a fully revolutionary development. The result was an impressive growth of the Socialist and Communist movements and, on the whole, closer coöperation between the two. To a large extent this reflected the wartime alliance of the Soviet Union with the Western powers. A series of well-known events profoundly disturbed the Socialist-Communist harmony: the absorption of the Socialist parties in Eastern Europe by the Communists; the radical divergence of the attitudes taken by Socialists and Communists toward the Marshall Plan; the rapidly growing tension between the Soviet Union and the Western nations.

This evolution has been clearly reflected in the international organization of the unions. At the height of the wartime alliance in World War II the old International Federation of Trade Unions (I.F.T.U.) appeared more and more anachronistic. Not only had it lost, by the advance of the Nazis, its strongest battalions on the Continent, it had also excluded the trade unions of the Soviet Union on one hand and the C.I.O. on the other, each representing vital elements in the chain of resistance to the Axis powers. By almost irresistible pressure the Russians and their friends succeeded in forcing the reluctant British trade union leaders—who held key positions in the international trade union movement—to abandon the I.F.T.U. In its stead was set up a new organization, the World Federation of Trade Unions (W.F.T.U.), which united all major labor organizations of the world except the American Federation of Labor. The basis of the W.F.T.U. was Socialist-Communist co-operation. As soon as this was endangered, the W.F.T.U. was doomed.

After prolonged negotiations the unions of the West finally left the W.F.T.U. and established in December, 1949, the International Confederation of Free Trade Unions (I.C.F.T.U.). With this step the division between Socialists and Communists was re-established. Indeed, in some ways it was more complete than ever before.

During the interwar period the Socialist movement was divided into two main currents, the reformist Right Wing and the Marxian Center. These were in some ways the continuation of pre-World War I divisions of the Socialist movement. While the Communists had absorbed most of the former extreme leftist groups, the Right Wingers continued the traditions of the Revisionists, and the Marxian Center more or less continued those of the old Radicals. In particular, the leaders of the Center maintained consistently that the Socialist-Communist split was only a passing phenomenon and that the reunification of all currents in one large Socialist party was the indispensable condition for the final victory of socialism. As long as the division persisted, one wing would emphasize the immediate tasks at the expense of the future, and the other would sacrifice present-day interests of the workers for the sake of their future victory. Only a united movement, combining the best features of both Reformists and Communists, could provide for the proper distribution of emphasis between the immediate and the future tasks of the movement and thus ensure victory.

It is, perhaps, the most significant fact in the recent evolution of Socialist labor in Europe that this faction has, for all practical purposes, ceased to exist. Its main leaders (Léon Blum, Otto Bauer, Friedrich Adler) have disappeared, and postwar events seem to have convinced the great majority of the European Socialists that the reunification of the movement is neither desirable nor possible. The Socialist-Communist split is being accepted as permanent.

Perhaps the most widely accepted analysis of this change of attitude is that it is impossible for the Socialists to unite with the Communists on the basis of a loyal understanding. The violence and trickery employed against the Socialists of Eastern Europe, both before and after their merger with the Communists, and the gradual disappearance of the Socialists from the leadership of the united party seem to have finally convinced most of the Socialists that Moscow demands submission rather than loyal coöperation. Tito's rebellion against the Kremlin greatly accentuated the feeling that true unification was impossible, as did the growing conviction that communism is not only a method of social transformation, but also a means of national oppression.

The policy of the Marxian Center had been based upon the conviction that the objectives of Socialists and Communists were identical and that the divergence concerned merely the methods of achieving the common end. This belief seems to have been shaken on two counts. Socialism was to be a free society with a controlled economy —yet more than thirty years after the great Russian Revolution the Soviet dictatorship shows no signs of relaxing its iron grip. Also, instead of being a brief transitory phase in the development of socialism in Russia, the dictatorship of the proletariat seems fiercely resolved to remain as a dictatorship over the proletariat. On the other hand, democratic socialism, perhaps warned by the example of the Soviet dictatorship, is setting its sights considerably lower than in the past. For a whole period at least it is aiming at what has been labelled a mixed economy, combining a substantial nationalized sector of the economy with another sector left to private enterprise. The Socialist-Communist split, it becomes increasingly clear, concerns not only methods, but also objectives.

This growing realization of the gulf separating Socialists and Communists is furthered by the greater emphasis which Western Socialists are placing upon democracy and civil liberties. Not that Socialists at any time failed to realize that their ultimate aim was a society of democracy and fully developed civil liberties, but a number of Socialist parties—particularly the French and the Austrian—had at times expressed the view that a temporary dictatorship of the proletariat would become inevitable since the bourgeoisie would not give in without unconstitutional resistance to a Socialist majority engaged in constructing the bases of a new society. Such unconstitutional resistance on the part of the bourgeoisie (the 1926 Linz program of the Austrian Socialists pointed out, for instance) would compel the Socialist majority to resort to dictatorial methods for a period of transition. The experience of Nazi oppression and probably even more the struggle against the establishment of a Communist dictatorship has changed the Socialist attitude to one of unconditional allegiance to democracy and civil liberties. This does not necessarily imply that a Socialist party would never be willing to associate itself in time of war or civil war with emergency measures which might temporarily suspend civil liberties or democratic rights. That change implies, instead, a shift in emphasis, so far as the education of the party members is concerned, to an unconditional belief in the value of democratic methods.

This shift has been accompanied by a rapid, perhaps not very profound but nevertheless significant, re-examination of Marxian theory. Differing in this respect from British Labour, Continental Social Democracy has been deeply imbued with the spirit of Marxism. Unlike American journalists, the Continental Socialists have never identified Marxism and communism, but have rather disputed the Communists' claim to be the true descendants of Marx and Engels. The Socialists have described themselves, rather than the Communists, as the true disciples of Marx. Indeed, fear of Communist vituperation often compelled Socialists to profess publicly a belief in Marxian theories which they did not hesitate to criticize privately. The postwar years have produced the first open signs of a change of attitude. Leaders of the German Social Democratic party, once a stronghold of real or professed belief in Marxism, have publicly admitted that the party has opened its doors to Marxians and non-Marxians alike. Although the intellectual productivity of the Socialist movement since the end of the war has not been very great, its intellectual activity has indicated a readiness to revise and re-evaluate accepted notions, which contrasts strongly with the prewar dogmatism. There is, in particular, great emphasis on "voluntarism" as opposed to the "inevitability" of the prewar version of Marxism, on human choice among alternative courses of action, and consequently on moral and humanitarian values. Indeed, one of the significant intellectual developments is the search of the Socialist movement for its ethical, humanitarian, and often religious sources. The stronger the opposition to the Communist belief that the end justifies the means, the greater the emphasis on the moral value of Western civilization.

As a result, the Socialist-Communist opposition has become much sharper than it has been at any time since the beginning of the Popular Front period in the 1930s. The main issue in the battle between the two is the control of the trade union movement; the principal battlefields are France and Italy.

West of the line from Lübeck to Trieste which divides Europe into two halves, democratic socialism is in almost full control of the labor movement—with two major exceptions—France and Italy. In these two countries the trade unions are divided along politico-philosophical lines, and the Communists are in control of the majority of the unions. It is here that the great, and in many ways decisive, battles between socialism and communism are being fought. On their outcome a good deal of the future orientation of European labor is likely to depend.

Northwestern Europe—Great Britain, Scandinavia, and in some respects Belgium and Holland—is the stronghold of democratic socialism. It is at the same time the outstanding example of the reformist current in European labor whose leadership has passed more and more into the hands of British labor. Full employment, the nationalization of certain parts of industry, and a more equal distribution of income by means of taxation represent the main planks of British Labour's policy. Similar ideas are guiding the activities of most other labor movements of Western Europe.

These and related policies have brought a number of new issues to the fore. The labor parties of Northwestern Europe are government parties. The policies of the administration are worked out in close coöperation with the unions, but the labor parties represent vastly larger parts of the electorate than do the unions. What is the status of unions under such conditions? While they are closely associated with the government they must at the same time retain a large measure of independence from it. Has a permanent form yet been found for this peculiarly ambiguous relationship of intimacy and independence?

A similar problem arises in the nationalized industries. Nationalization has been to a large extent the result of union pressure. The unions feel a certain sense of responsibility toward the nationalized enterprises. But, at the same time it is the duty of the unions to represent their members' interests as against those of the enterprises themselves. Two main patterns have evolved in Western Europe in the attempt to solve this contradiction: the British "public corporation," with a board on which former trade unionists represent the spirit of labor without being delegated by labor; the French tripartite board, in which delegates of consumers, the government, and the union are supposed to coöperate in such a way that out of the clash of interests a wise compromise emerges.

Full employment has placed the unions in a strategic position favorable to a rapid increase of money wages. If the unions were to take full advantage of their opportunity, inflationary tendencies would inevitably result. Once again, labor is confronted with a difficult choice torn as it is among its national responsibility and its loyalty to its membership; its political responsibility and its pressure group tradition.

Basically, this dilemma is part of the normal life of democracy. The conflict between group interests and the interests of the com-

munity at large is inevitable, not only in a class society, as the traditional Marxian view leads one to believe, but in any social organization with a developed division of labor, and perhaps even one with
different temperaments and inclinations. It is the everyday business
of democracy to find compromises for such issues which will be
acceptable to the majority of its citizens. Perhaps it is not excessive
to say that democracy is firmly established only when conditions and
traditions are such as to make compromises continuously possible
between group and community interests.

Any theory of the European labor movement must take into account the fact that European labor has grown up in a society in
which the tradition of democratic compromise has been conspicu-
ously lacking—moreover, in a society in which clear lines of demarcation separated class from class. The feudal tradition of a strictly
hierarchical society allocated to everyone a distinct status. Every
effort was made to impress on each subject a sense of this status, its
rights and even more its duties and its relative place in the social
structure. The worker in industry did not need much education in
class consciousness. It was impressed upon him by the powers that
be and by his daily experience. It was this social and political dis-
qualification, far more than his economic exploitation, which shaped
the European worker's mind. Almost fully insulated from the life of
the upper classes, he was the object of politics. Whether or not governments were friendly or unfriendly toward the worker, they always
represented a different class and did not conceal this fact either by
their hostility or by their patronizing benevolence.

Socialist unionism thus essentially only articulated the class division and an awareness of the social hierarchy which the worker experienced. But, undoubtedly, the separation was accentuated by this
awareness of his place in society and of its structure. The growth of
Socialist unionism, the power which it acquired, particularly after the
turn of the century, and the gradual progress of democracy made this
existence of what was almost a nation within a nation a serious issue
for society. The continued existence of this bloc within society to
which other blocs were sharply opposed presented a problem somewhat similar to that which monopolies create for a competitive market
economy. The use of the power contained in this bloc in the way
pressure groups are inclined to employ it, threatened to become incompatible with the functioning of democracy. Indeed in the great
depression which sharply intensified the opposition of the power blocs,

democracy, where it was not firmly established, broke down in a wave of totalitarian dictatorships.

The great task to be performed was that of reintegrating this power bloc into society. But this could no longer be done on the basis of the place which labor formerly held in the social hierarchy. Labor was demanding a far higher place. The new status of labor in society has become the basic social issue of the West. The Russian Revolution shows the explosive qualities of this problem. The British Labour government is an example of an attempt to solve the problem within the framework of Western democracy. It requires for its success that the power bloc which claims leadership in society acquire not only the qualities, but also the sense of responsibility, which go with leadership. The pressure group must transform itself into a real political party. It must concern itself with all the great issues which confront society. It must be willing to integrate the particular interests of the group which it represents with the general interests of the community. If democracy is to survive, labor must not only accept, but must formulate for itself the compromises that democratic government requires.

It is in this light that the postwar issues of Western Europe, and labor's attempts to solve them, must be examined. Has labor acquired the maturity and the statesmanship which its new power in society requires? Much more may depend upon the answer to this question than the success or failure of labor in Western Europe. Success may mean the revival of Western Europe, giving new meaning and a new lease on life to the civilization of the Old World. Failure would throw Western Europe into social disorganization, which would seriously impair its power of resistance and its chances of survival.

No doubt these considerations could not be applied to the American scene without substantial qualifications and modifications. The belief that American labor is in some way following, with a certain time lag, the example set by British labor has little foundation in fact. It overlooks the tremendous differences between the social and political history of this country and that of the Old World (and clearly also the significant differences among the various European labor movements). Indeed, it might be said with at least equal justification that in some respects European labor is following the example set by the brethren on this side of the Atlantic.

I am referring particularly to the complex of union activities to which Professor Perlman has given the label of "control of job opportunities." With political democracy as firmly established in many countries of Western Europe as anything can be in the twentieth century, European unions have devoted increasing attention to the problems of "economic democracy"—the participation of the unions in the determination not only of wages, but also of job opportunities and working conditions. The French Joint Shop Committees (Comités d'Entreprise) reflect this trend as much as does the emergence of the "closed shop" issue in Great Britain and some recent developments of labor relations in Scandinavia.

It is perhaps a symbol of these developments that coöperation between the unions of the United States and those of Western Europe has reached an intensity which few would have believed possible twenty years ago. It is sufficient to read Samuel Gompers's unhappy reflections on his meetings with European labor leaders during World War I to measure the distance which labor has traveled on both sides of the Atlantic.

61 · ORGANIZED LABOR AND POLITICS IN LATIN AMERICA*

Robert J. Alexander

REVOLUTIONARY ROLE OF LABOR

Labor's role in Latin American politics is revolutionary. The entry of the organized labor movement into the political life of the Latin American countries means a fundamental altering of the rules by which the political game is played in Latin America, for it means bringing the lower and hitherto despised social elements of the various nations into an active role in their civic life. It also brings to politics a civilian element able to challenge the age-old tradition that the armed forces should have the last word in the making and unmaking of governments.

* *Government and Politics in Latin America,* edited by Harold E. Davis. Copyright 1958 The Ronald Press Company.

Social Revolution

The appearance of more or less strong trade union movements in virtually all of the Latin American countries during the past quarter-century is part of that vast socio-political upheaval which, for lack of a better title, we may call the Latin American Social Revolution. The changes which it embraces result in large measure from modern industrialism.

Labor and Politics Before World War I

During the nineteenth century most of the people of the region lived by means of a primitive subsistence agriculture and were thus permitted only a very low level of material well-being. Large-scale manufacturing industry virtually did not exist in most of the countries. The only "working class" elements were railroad workers, scattered groups of miners, and the handicraftsmen of the cities, who still made most of the locally-produced "manufactured" goods. Although there was some semblance of trade union organization among these elements—and in a few countries such as Argentina, Uruguay, and Brazil they were increasingly vocal and were growing in influence—in no Latin American nation did they play a major role in the political life.

Power rested firmly in the hands of the landowning aristocracy and their allies and associates, the merchants of the coastal cities, engaged largely in the export-import trade. The source of the aristocracy's power lay in its control of the economy by virtue of its monopoly of the ownership of land, the principal natural resource then under exploitation, and in its control of the trade in products of the land.

The great majority of the people were semi-serfs, working on the landed estates of the aristocracy under conditions suggestive of Europe in the later Middle Ages. These peasants were ignorant, miserably poor, and were concerned principally with the problems of keeping body and soul together on a subsistence level. They had neither time for, nor interest in, politics. Furthermore, their patriarchal loyalty to the *patrón* made them little more than pawns, politically speaking, in the hands of their landlords.

Except for certain turn-of-the century trends in Chile, Uruguay, and Argentina, politics during the century preceding World War I was a game played by the landholding elite. The vote was a privilege of the educated, who were a small proportion of the total population.

Social issues played little part in the quarrels among contesting parties. The chief political importance of the economic issues raised appeared in the Church–state controversy, and this controversy became acute partly because of the landowners' interest in acquiring the Church's lands. This conflict provided the principal issue in the politics of pre-1914 Latin America, and the victory of the anti-clerical forces reinforced the dominant position of the landholding elite. If the majority of the people, the peasants, had been consulted, the result might well have been the opposite, a resounding victory to the forces of ultramontanism.

Only in the closing years of this period did the problems of the lower classes begin to play a role in the political life of the more economically advanced of the Latin American countries. In Argentina, Chile, Uruguay, and Brazil, socialist parties and anarchist labor movements appeared among the city artisans and the rising industrial working class laboring on the railroads, on the docks, and in the mines of these countries. In Mexico, a revolution which began as a political contest between elements of the aristocracy quickly got out of hand and gave the peasants and urban labor groups an opportunity to play the dominant role.

THE WORLD WARS AND THE GROWTH OF LABOR

World War I

But the cases just discussed were exceptions. It was not until World War I gave a sudden impetus to industrialization that for the first time the urban working class began to play a significant role in the political life of many of these countries. The textile industry, in particular, owes its first firm foundations to World War I. Cut off from their sources of supply in Europe and the United States, the Latin American peoples found that they themselves had to provide clothing and the goods from which it is made. Some other industries, too, received a considerable impetus from this world-wide conflict. To the incipient metallurgical industry it was a shot in the arm; then, too, the processing of some foodstuffs prospered, and the construction materials industry also felt the impact of Latin American wartime isolation. The upshot was that by the early 1920's the weight of the workers in the new manufacturing industries was beginning to be felt, and the urban working class was beginning to become much more vocal.

Between the Wars

Nowhere were these trends more evident than in the labor organizations themselves. The prewar labor movement had been largely anarchist in ideology, following a philosophy which seems to be peculiarly congenial to the small craftsman and artisan but not very attractive to the factory worker.

After World War I the influence of anarchists in the Latin American trade union movement declined sharply. By 1930 it had been virtually obliterated, except in such isolated cases as that of Uruguay, where some anarchist elements still exist in the nation's labor movement. The socialists, communists, and, a little later, various indigenous groups took over political leadership of the trade unions.

The Great Depression gave a further impetus to industrialization and hence to the trade union movement. Furthermore, in the political unrest arising from the Depression, the labor movement began for the first time to play an important, if subsidiary, role in the making and unmaking of governments. Since the Depression, industrialization has become the well-accepted creed of most politically thinking Latin Americans and the policy of most of the governments. During the economic crisis, the Latin American countries were forced to produce many of the things which, owing to lack of foreign exchange, they were not able to buy from abroad.

World War II

Once again, during World War II, the Latin Americans were thrown to a considerable degree upon their own resources, pushing industrialization to the fundamental step of heavy industry. Governments found it necessary to adopt a more positive attitude toward industrialization. During the past fifteen years virtually every country in the region has established some sort of development corporation, whose job it is to plan for and stimulate the construction of new industries. Tariffs, exchange controls, and other methods of giving protection to the rapidly developing manufactures have also been generously used by the various governments.

The result of this emphasis on industrialization has been that the industrial working class—taken in its broadest sense to include not only those employed in manufacturing but those who work for railroads, airlines, steamship lines and ports, mines, and even great modern agricultural enterprises producing the "desert crops" and industrial raw materials for the United States and Western Europe—has grown by leaps and bounds. This increase in the size of the working class has been reflected in the growth of Latin American cities. Mexico City, for instance, has more than quadrupled its population since the beginning of the Revolution in 1910. São Paulo, Santiago, Medellín, and scores of other towns have enjoyed equally phenomenal growth since World War I.

GROWTH OF LABOR ORGANIZATIONS

. . . . .

Changing Political Attitudes

The growth in labor organization has brought a change in the nature of Latin American politics. Politicians and governments, realizing full well the potentialities of this new force for the political life of their nations, have sought both to encourage and to control the new trade union movements.

That the attitudes of Latin American politicians have been influenced by a variety of factors was brought home to the author of this chapter by a discussion of this problem with the late President Arturo Alessandri of Chile. When President Alessandri was asked why he sought to enact a labor code in the early 1920's, an effort finally successful in September, 1924, he replied that he was motivated by two considerations. First of all, he said, he knew the miserable conditions under which most of the urban and mining workers of Chile lived, and he felt that something should be done to improve their situation. In the second place, Chile had recently become a member of the International Labor Organization, which recommended certain minimum requirements in labor legislation. If Chile were to be a full-fledged member of this new international group, he said, she must fulfill her obligations by adopting some or all of the measures recommended by the ILO, including official recognition of the trade union movement.

No doubt these two motives, genuine sympathy for the plight of the new industrial workers and the necessity for "keeping up with the international Joneses," have induced more favorable attitudes in many of the Latin American governments and among politicians toward the organized workers and their demands.

Other motives, however, have also played an important part in this development. Latin American politicians have undoubtedly realized that their own fates lie in the hands of the organized workers. If a politician gains the support of this important new group, it can be of great value to him, for in those nations where governmental change is brought about by ballot rather than bullet, organized workers represent an important bloc of votes. Where cruder methods of altering the administration are the rule, the ability of the trade union movement to paralyze much of the national life by resort to partial or general strikes is peculiarly useful, whether the politico favored by the unions is in power and finds his regime in danger, or whether he is out of power and wishes to seize the government by force. In the latter case, the organized workers may be a source of civilian soldiers for the politician who has won labor sympathy.

The tendency of certain army officers to cultivate labor support in recent years, because of the importance of industrialization for a modern army, has also been noted in a previous chapter.

For these various reasons many politicians, civilian and military alike, have shown unexpected sympathy for the trade union movement. At the same time, because they have realized the potential dangers of the movement, they have sought to hedge legal recognition and other workers' benefits with a kind of government control which the labor movements of the United States and most Western European countries would not permit.

GOVERNMENT AND THE UNIONS

Political Supervision

Thus we find that many of the labor codes provide for government supervision of trade union elections and for some type of control over the use of labor funds. These restrictions usually prohibit the use of funds for political purposes, a prohibition more honored in the breach than in the observance. Often the labor codes specify the structure of the trade union movement and provide government supervision of collective bargaining. They usually exclude certain kinds of workers, particularly government employees and agricultural workers, from legal trade union organization.

Labor Dependence on Government

For their part, the workers have usually welcomed whatever help they could obtain from the government or from particular groups of politicians. In the first place, this help provides legal recognition, almost eliminating in Latin America in recent years the kind of strike which was so common in the United States before the National Labor Relations Act—the strike for union recognition. In the second place, in actual collective bargaining negotiations the unions have frequently appealed to friendly politicians, often to the president, to force employers to grant their demands. In doing so, the unions have been fully aware of their own political importance to the government and the politicians.

Finally, the unions have needed the financial help received from a close alliance with politicians and the government. Most Latin American industrial workers are still very poor by any standard and have little money to spare for the payment of union dues. But, despite this poverty of their members, Latin American unions need considerable funds. They need money for organizing, for the costs of transportation, for the costs of collective bargaining. Like unions elsewhere, they need full-time, or nearly full-time, officials. Hence, they have been more than willing to accept the support of middle-class politicians willing to offer their financial backing, or that of the government if they are in power, in order to gain labor loyalty.

LABOR AND POLITICAL PARTIES

The consequence of this political and financial dependence has been to wed the average Latin American trade union firmly to one or another political party and to deprive it of the independence of the government usually considered healthful. Few Latin American trade union groups escape control by a political party. Unfortunately, this has frequently meant that the trade union is sacrificed when the party is in difficulty. A growing trend toward union independence of the government and politicians will be discussed later in this chapter, but it may be noted here that organizations really independent in the sense that they are in the United States are a small minority.

The growth of the labor movement has, of course, brought numerous new political parties which appeal particularly to organized workers. Some of the older parties have also been transformed in their efforts to gain the support of the trade unions by including labor demands and aspirations in their programs.

・　・　・　・　・

LABOR, A NEW POLITICAL FORCE

The impact of the rise of organized labor on Latin American politics is not confined, however, to new political parties and the alteration of old ones. Of equal or more importance, in the long run, is the fact that the trade union movement presents the Latin American republics, for the first time in a century and a quarter of national existence, with a potential rival to the armed forces as the ultimate determinant of power in political life.

The potency of the Latin American unions as a power factor is likely to increase as industrialization proceeds. The power of a labor movement is strictly limited in an economy in which most of the people grow their own food, make their own clothing, and construct their own houses. Although it may be able to damage individual urban employers or mining interests through strikes, it cannot cripple the entire economic life of the nation. The great majority of the people will continue to live more or less normally, despite anything the labor movement might be able to do. In a more highly industrialized economy, however, the situation is entirely different. In such an economy there is great interdependence. No individual or family group is self-sufficient, economically speaking. Large cities must be fed by a constant inflow of agricultural produce from the interior. The power of labor is increased by the fact that a general strike can bring the life of a community virtually to a standstill. Furthermore, as the organized urban working class becomes larger and larger, it tends to become an important pool of recruits, already accustomed to the discipline of factory life and trade union activities, for participation in armed rebellion.

In recent years Latin America has provided a number of striking examples of the power of this new political force. Three nations in which labor has thus gained considerable power will be discussed.

The earliest development was that of Mexico. As far back as 1915, Venustiano Carranza and his advisers, then engaged in civil war with the forces of Pancho Villa and Emiliano Zapata, became aware of the military and political potentials of the trade union movement. Carranza made an agreement with the still weak Mexican labor movement, granting the workers freedom to carry on their activities behind the lines of the Constitutionalist Army, in return for which they agreed to provide badly needed battalions for Carranza's hard-pressed forces. These Red Battalions, as they were called, played a key role in the triumph of Carranza's forces over his two rivals.

Twenty years later, President Lázaro Cárdenas, pushing hard for the completion of his land reform and the nationalization of the Mexican economy, began to doubt the political dependability of the army, previously loyal to ex-President Plutarco Elías Calles, who had now become a political opponent. In this situation, Cárdenas fell back on the organized labor movement and armed the organized peasantry to strengthen his regime against attempts at subversion by the military.

Not only did Cárdenas and his lieutenants unify most of the hitherto badly divided Mexican trade union movement into the Confederation of Mexican Workers (Confederación de Trabajadores de México), but he also provided arms to his labor cohorts, encouraging the formation of a labor militia under the control of the new Confederation. Thus the government had at its command a powerful force able to paralyze the economic activity of the urban centers and able also, if necessary, to enter the field against any potential military foe. Organized labor thus greatly strengthened the hand of the Cárdenas regime. In return labor received many benefits in the form of labor laws and wage increases.

A spectacular exhibition of the power of the trade unions vis-à-vis the armed forces was furnished by the Argentine workers in October, 1945. At that time Perón had already become the idol and boss of the trade union movement, but was temporarily overthrown by a faction of the army opposed to his personal ambitions. The workers in the unions loyal to Perón went out on a virtually spontaneous general strike throughout the country, thus hampering the efforts of the new regime to re-establish order. At the same time, laborers from Buenos Aires and its suburbs, led by the packing-house workers from nearby La Plata and Avellaneda, marched on the capital city. Within a few days of Perón's overthrow, the streets of Buenos Aires were in the hands of his labor supporters. Although the army could probably have put down this insurrection, the cost in lives of Argentine workers would have been great, and great hatred would have been inspired in the masses of the urban population. The army did not think it worth this price to prevent Perón's continuance in power and hence it permitted him to return from the prison island of Martín García on the night of October 16. The next day he triumphantly addressed his supporters from the balcony of the Casa Rosada.

From October 17, 1945, until June 16, 1955, Perón governed with the support of organized labor and the armed forces, the latter held in check by the menace of a repetition of the nightmare of October 17. This power structure lasted until the labor movement was caught off guard by the naval mutiny of June 16, 1955. The army, by remaining "loyal" to Perón and suppressing the revolt, was able to seize the upper hand once more in Argentine politics. The unions were strangely quiet in the events of September, 1955, which drove Perón from power.

Peronista leaders in the labor movement subsequently received at least temporary setbacks. They attempted a revolutionary general strike against General Pedro Aramburu a few days after he seized the government from General Lonardi in November, 1955. Aramburu crushed the general strike and proceeded to "intervene" in the CGT and all of its constituent unions, placing army, navy, and air force officers in charge of union affairs until elections could be held throughout the labor movement.

A third example of the power of the trade union movement may be seen in the April, 1952, revolution in Bolivia. That conflict began as an insurrection of the National Police in alliance with the outlawed MNR party, but was turned into a struggle of the organized workers of La Paz and the mining centers against the national army when the National Police seemed to be beaten in the fighting two days after it began. The trade union forces, led by the tin miners' chief Juan Lechín and Hernán Siles, decided to continue the struggle and in the end they were victorious. They triumphed over the armed forces, placing Víctor Paz Estenssoro and the MNR in power. The MNR regime thus rested squarely on the trade unions. After the beginning of the agrarian reform in 1953, the growing forces of the peasantry, anxious to defend their newly acquired land, came to share power with the workers.

Failures to Use the Power of Labor

Events of recent years have also provided at least three examples in which ruling political groups that commanded the support and loyalty of the trade union movement were unable or unwilling to bring its weight to bear in defense of their regimes. These failures occurred in Venezuela, Cuba, and Guatemala, and can be briefly summarized as follows.

In November, 1948, President Rómulo Gallegos of Venezuela was unwilling to call upon the nation's trade union movement to defend his regime against the attempt of the army to oust him. Although the intentions of the top military officers were widely known throughout the country for at least three weeks before his ouster, President Gallegos insisted on trying to settle the problem "without violence."

As a result, although sporadic strikes in defense of the regime occurred in different parts of the country, they proved futile because they received no encouragement from the presidential palace. Had Gallegos used the radio to call upon the workers to declare a general strike and to join with military elements still loyal to the regime, he might well have saved his government, according to competent observers, thus sparing Venezuela the experience of the military dictatorship which followed.

President Carlos Prío Socorrás of Cuba showed the same kind of vacillation on March 10, 1952, when faced with the military coup of General Fulgencio Batista. Prío made no attempt to notify the trade union leaders, virtually all of whom were his loyal supporters, that a military movement against the government was afoot. Although the trade unionists called a nationwide general strike when they learned of the coup at nine o'clock on the morning of March 10, it was already too late. The strike fizzled out because it had no support from the president. Both trade union and student leaders offered to fight for the regime if Prío would give them arms which he still had in his control. Here again, had Prío acted with decision, calling the workers to a general strike and arming his labor and student supporters, he could probably have snuffed out the Batista coup.

Finally, there is the case of Guatemala. Here, too, the trade unions, though of less importance than in Venezuela or Cuba, were loyal to the government of President Arbenz. His failure to bring to bear either the economic or military potential of the labor movement, was one of the principal causes of his overthrow by the forces of Carlos Castillo Armas in 1954. Communist influence in the Arbenz regime made the situation in Guatemala different from those in Venezuela and Cuba, but the lesson is the same.

LABOR'S FUTURE POLITICAL INFLUENCE

What of the future influence of labor in Latin American politics? Conflicting tendencies are presently at work. The labor movement will undoubtedly play an increasingly important direct role in those countries which have not yet experienced revolutionary social changes, or where these changes have temporarily been thwarted. One can expect more examples of the power of labor such as those of April 9, 1952, in Bolivia and October 17, 1945, in Argentina. So long as the Latin American social revolution has not occurred in a given country, one of the principal tasks of the trade union movement will continue

to be the achievement of fundamental changes in the social and political structure of the nation. And the labor movement will continue
to be a force of tremendous revolutionary political potential.

Paradoxically enough, however, once the social revolution has occurred in a given country, we may expect a lessening of the direct
political importance of the labor movement. Forces which are at work
will make the trade unions turn increasingly in the direction of economic rather than political activity. As Latin American industrialization continues, as the living standards of the workers rise, and as
workers become more capable of paying the costs of their trade union
movements, labor unions will acquire increasing political independence. They will rely less on the government and politicians, more
on their own resources. As they become stronger financially and more
independent politically they will become increasingly concerned with
the basic economic problems of wages, hours, working conditions,
and productivity—less directly concerned with the political framework
within which these economic problems are to be resolved.

There are evidences of this trend toward political independence
in some of the Latin American countries. In Mexico, since 1950
unions have increasingly demanded the checkoff of union dues, the
compulsory deduction by employers of dues which are then paid
directly to the union. Increasingly, the unions depend on members'
contributions for their finances. At the same time, the unions are
increasingly concerned with day-to-day collective bargaining. Collective contracts are becoming long and more detailed, tending to
include seniority rights, grievance procedures, and other such provisions which are still alien to most of the Latin American unions.

In Cuba the trade union movement has acquired considerable
political independence during the period since 1952. As a result of
the armed truce between the Batista government and labor, the trade
unions have turned more and more to economic issues. The demand
for the checkoff is growing, and the unions are gaining a financial
independence never before enjoyed.

Finally, in Colombia, the rise of the Colombian Workers Union
(Unión de Trabajadores de Colombia) since 1946 has presented a
new phenomenon. The UTC is not politically affiliated with any party.
It has, in fact, had to fight off attempts by Conservative party politicians to infiltrate and take over control of the organization. The
UTC is largely financed by the dues of members and has been anxious
to be granted the checkoff. It has attempted to build up in the ranks

of its members a consciousness of being good trade unionists first and members of one or another political party second.

CONCLUSIONS

One should not overstate the case, of course. Latin American labor legislation over the years has tied the unions more closely to the ministry of labor than is customary in the United States or Western European countries, so that traditionally in Mexico, Cuba, and Colombia the unions tend to take their difficulties to the government for solution to a much greater degree than in the United States. However, the evidence of the Mexican, Cuban, and Colombian labor movements would seem to indicate that the trade unions in those countries, at least, are becoming more like those of the United States than has been true in the past.

As this new trend continues, the trade unions will undoubtedly find that they must supplement their collective bargaining activities by participation in politics. They will want friends in the government and in the halls of congress in order to protect themselves from legislation unfavorable to labor. But these political activities are likely to be subordinated to their collective bargaining functions, as they become principally economic organizations rather than partisan political groups.

In those countries in which an extensive social revolution has been taking place, factors other than the tendency of unions to concentrate on economic rather than political matters will reduce the direct political importance of Latin American trade unions. In Mexico and Bolivia, for instance, the increasing political role of the peasantry will lessen the relative importance of the votes of urban workers. The growth of the middle class as a result of industrialization will have the same effect.

Thus emerges a picture of the Latin American trade unions playing a key role in the social, economic, and political revolution now under way. As compact organized bodies in the principal centers of population these unions are playing a role out of all proportion to their size or to the wealth or individual influence of their members. Organized labor is truly a revolutionary force in Latin America, promoting further industrialization, altering the relationship of classes, increasing the pressure for the democratization of political life, giving rise to new political parties and profoundly modifying some of the old. Yet if present trends continue, the labor movement is likely to

play in the future a role of somewhat less direct political importance
in those countries which have experienced the social revolution, although it will continue to be of great importance in the preparation
for this transformation.

Agriculture

62 · ALCOHOL AND POLITICS IN FRANCE *

Bernard E. Brown

Large-scale state intervention in the alcohol market in France dates
from World War I, when the government committed itself to encourage the production of alcohol. Two chief reasons then lay back
of this decision: a huge supply of alcohol was needed for the manufacture of gunpowder, and the devastation of the beet-growing regions
of the north had severely limited production of beet alcohol, thereby
throwing the domestic market out of balance. A law of June 30, 1916,
adopted under emergency procedure, established a state agency empowered to purchase alcohol. At the end of the war, a decree of 1919
accorded the government the right "provisionally" to maintain the
state monopoly. In 1922 the beetgrowers and winegrowers gave their
support to the principle of a state monopoly which, in effect, reserved
the industrial market for beet alcohol and the domestic market for
viticulture. In 1931 the state was authorized to purchase alcohol distilled from surplus wine. The interests of *betteraviers* (beet growers)
and *viticulteurs* were thereby happily gratified, but the state soon
found itself in possession of huge stocks of alcohol. As a means of
providing an outlet for the surplus, the government in 1923 had re-

* Bernard E. Brown, "Alcohol and Politics in France," *The American Political Science Review*, LI (December, 1957), 976, 980-984. Reprinted by permission of The American Political Science Association. The footnotes in the
original version are omitted here.

quired oil refineries to add a specified amount of alcohol to gasoline. A decree-law of July 30, 1935 modified previous legislation and decrees with respect to alcohol and confirmed the absolute monopoly of the state. In the language of a decree of April 21, 1939, "the economic *régime d'alcool* is the keystone of French agriculture." After World War II beet production was again stimulated by the Monnet Plan, on the assumption that beets would be used in the manufacture of much-needed sugar, and also that beet cultivation would render the soil productive and help prevent erosion. The purpose of this paper is to investigate the policy and pressure group ramifications of these successive steps in governmental intervention.

• • • • •

THE ALCOHOL LOBBY

An astonishing number of people in France derive a livelihood from alcohol or are at least vitally interested in its production, transport and sale. One and a half million persons are engaged in viticulture, and 150,000 in beet culture; perhaps 500,000 are employed in related industries, such as bottling, canning and transport; and there are three and one half million *bouilleurs de cru* (home distillers). In addition, there are those who own or are employed by 450,000 *débits de boissons,* along with numerous distilleries and apéritif firms. It would appear that between four and six million Frenchmen profit in some manner from alcohol.

In fact, however, there is no single "alcohol lobby" that coordinates the efforts of all those so interested. Of course, all alcohol groups have a common goal in wishing to maintain the *régime d'alcool.* As Eugène Dubois said in addressing an emergency meeting of the *Union Nationale des Groupements des Distillateurs d'Alcool* in September 1954: "the measures taken today against the beetgrowers can be envisaged tomorrow against apples and cider, and the day after tomorrow against wine." But collaboration seems to be limited to the beetgrowers and the distillers who, with the support of twenty-one less important organizations, have created the *Institut Français d'Alcool.* The IFA puts out a monthly journal, *Alcools et Dérivés,* in an attractive and expensive format. Viticulture and the *bouilleurs de cru* have no apparent links with the IFA.

The Betteraviers. Beet cultivation has been encouraged by the French state since the time of Napoleon in order to provide alcohol for the manufacture of gunpowder, and to increase the fertility of the soil. Since World War I beets have been grown in France to be made into either alcohol or sugar. The state has established a parity of price for beets destined alike for sugar refineries or distilleries. Since distilleries are less costly to run than sugar refineries, they can afford to guarantee crop purchase early in the season, so that beets tend to be sent preferably to distilleries. Economic links also appear to exist between certain wealthy *betteraviers* and distilleries.

The beetgrowers have been able to maintain their privileged position by exerting powerful pressure on the administration and the parliament. The 150,000 members of the *Confédération Générale des Planteurs de Betteraves* are among the most prosperous farmers in France. The concentration of beet culture in the northern departments makes it necessary for all political parties to take the demands of the *betteraviers* into account. Furthermore, the CGB receives the closest possible support from the *Fédération Nationale des Syndicats d'Exploitants Agricoles*. M. Blondelle, when president of the FNSEA, regularly attended the *betteraviers'* annual assemblies, and spoke frequently in favor of the *régime d'alcool*. His successor, Jean Lépicard, was in fact president of the *Syndicat Betteravier*—which assured rather close ties between the beetgrowers and the national farm organization.

According to the officers of the CGB, it is in the public interest to encourage beet cultivation (primarily in order to maintain soil fertility), but it is uneconomic to make sugar out of beets. It appears that 500,000 tons of sugar, out of a total average production of 1.7 million tons, have to be stocked and sold at a loss each year on the world market, because the world price of sugar is lower than the purchase price of beets. Said Henri Cayre, secretary-general of the CGB: "We are obliged to state that it is more profitable to make alcohol than sugar, even if we make jump out of their seats certain *maîtres* who condemn us in the name of production of meat and milk, for which the world market is not very promising either." Therefore, conclude the beet spokesmen, the state must support beet production by purchasing at least four million HL of alcohol each year. Any surplus alcohol can conveniently be disposed of by requiring the addition of *two* million HL annually to gasoline (an operation that would cost the state about 15 billion francs).

Bouilleurs de Cru and Viticulteurs. One of the "achievements" of the French Revolution was an Act of the National Assembly suppressing taxes on all beverages. Even though the exigencies of the public finances required reestablishment of the taxes shortly there-after, the Act of 1790 has become part of the "mythology" of the home distillers. It was decided by the Consulate to require a license of *all* distillers, "for reasons of economic order, but also in the interest of public morality and health." In 1808, an exemption was accorded the *bouilleurs de cru*—the beginning of the "privilege" that has played such an amazing role in French politics.

The privilege conferred upon *bouilleurs* by statute consists in being able to produce ten liters of pure alcohol each year, exempt from tax and also from supervision by the *Service des alcools*. Anyone owning fruit trees or a vineyard can ask the commune for a certificate enabling him to benefit from the statute. The number of *bouilleurs de cru* (or "petits récoltants," as they prefer to call themselves) in France has increased from 90,000 in 1862 to 3,650,000 in 1954. It is extremely difficult for the state to supervise home distillation, particularly in the West. The Economic Council has estimated the *bouilleurs'* annual fraudulent production at 200,000 HL of pure alcohol (approximately as much as is legally permitted). According to Dr. May: "The alcohol distilled by the *bouilleurs de cru* represents, after the excessive production of wine, the great cause of alcoholism in our country. The privilege of the *bouilleurs de cru,* originally conceived to permit farmers to consume small quantities of alcohol from their own harvest, has become, bit by bit (because of the weakness of the public powers) a vast organization that not only cheats the Treasury, but also diffuses (in rural households first, then in all of France), increasingly great quantities of alcohol."

The *bouilleurs* are organized in a *Syndicat National des Bouilleurs de Cru,* which was reactivated after the Liberation (mainly through the efforts of André Liautey) to secure the abrogation of a Vichy decree suppressing certain privileges of the *bouilleurs*. Membership dues are insignificant. Financial support seems to come primarily from the distillers who travel throughout the *bouilleur* departments. The SNBC publishes a monthly newspaper, the *Bouilleur de France;* the travelling distillers publish their own journal, *La Défense des Distillateurs Ambulants et des Bouilleurs de Cru*. The strength of the *bouilleurs* obviously resides in their numbers, not their financial resources.

The third large group within the "alcohol lobby" consists of the *viticulteurs*. Out of 1,570,000 persons engaged in wine cultivation in metropolitan France, 94 per cent (1,480,000) produce less than 100 HL annually, accounting for 44 per cent of the total production. Thus, a huge number of relatively poor electors are interested in protection for the wine industry, while a small number are able to furnish financial aid. Inasmuch as viticulture is the mainstay of whole regions (especially the Midi), it is inconceivable for a deputy with a "wine" clientele to criticize the Alcohol Statute. All deputies, regardless of party affiliation, from l'Aude, l'Hérault, Gard, Pyrénées-Orientales, Var and la Gironde, are firm defenders of viticulture. The most vigilant among them come from regions where bad wine is cultivated for the express purpose of being distilled into alcohol.

The increasing sensitivity of French opinion to the agitation of alcoholism issues has created a serious public relations problem for the alcohol groups. The *betteraviers* and distillers, *bouilleurs de cru* and *viticulteurs* all contend that "alcoholism" is primarily an invention of selfish foreign interests. The beetgrowers argue that the so-called "alcohol crisis" became acute only when the sturdy French peasantry was successful in producing enough alcohol to make feasible a "national" carburant. The president of the CGB has hinted that a plan was hatched in Washington during the war (an oblique reference to M. Monnet) to suppress the creation of a French national carburant for the benefit of oil importers. Those who resist the just demands of the beetgrowers are therefore serving the interests of foreign oil companies and Arab nationalism to the detriment of France. The wine growers have also suspected the existence of a vast conspiracy by foreign companies to attack French mores and customs. The viticulture press has given considerable publicity to the fact that the Pepsi-Cola Company of Casablanca recently awarded prizes for essays having as their theme "the liberation of Algeria from French imperialism." The *bouilleurs* have likewise discovered that French alcoholism was "invented" by the Anglo-Saxons, who thereby hope to sell their fruit juices, soda and whiskey in place of French alcohol.

Insofar as alcoholism is admitted to be a problem, each alcohol group blames the other for the "fléau." The beetgrowers contend that "industrial" alcohol is in no way responsible for alcoholism. The *bouilleurs* assure the public that their sole concern is to defend the Revolutionary principle of "liberty" (the right to "bouillir" being one of the precious gains of the Revolution) and the interests of the "little man" against alcohol trusts and foreign companies. The viticulture groups indignantly deny that wine could possibly cause alcoholism, and have even recently established a correlation between consumption of water and the incidence of cancer. "To drink water may be dangerous," proclaims *Le Moniteur Vinicole* of November 10, 1956, "fight against cancer by drinking alcohol."

. . . . .

63 · LAND REFORM IN THE POSTWAR ERA*

Kenneth H. Parsons

Land reform has again become a major policy issue in this century, after several decades of comparative quiet. This was inevitable, no doubt, as national independence and devotion to national economic development spread so widely over the globe. This happened in Europe as the old agricultural order gave way to the new industrial regime. But now, due to the contest of ideologies, land reform and related matters are issues of international politics and diplomacy.

Land reform programs are directed toward changing the form of man's relation to land, particularly the status of the cultivators. Through land reforms the cultivators acquire the ownership of the land they till, becoming owner-cultivators; or their tenancies become more secure and less costly; or they become members of cooperative or collective farms and so on. The variety of possibilities is very wide; what happens in any country is a matter partly of the particular circumstances of the agricultural economy and partly of the dominant ideas and political philosophy.

Amidst the nearly limitless variety of problems and situations which have produced land reform programs in recent years, a few common elements are to be found. There is the nearly universal fact that peasant cultivators live in poverty or near poverty, regardless of how hard they work. Technological and economic advance of recent centuries has largely by-passed peasants.

It is not only that the peasants have remained poor, it is quite likely that most of them have become poorer generation after generation,

* Kenneth H. Parsons, "Land Reform in the Postwar Era," *Land Economics*, XXXIII (August, 1957), 213-215. This excerpt from the original article is reprinted by permission of Kenneth H. Parsons and *Land Economics*.

for the past two or three centuries. This decline may have been arrested or even reversed in several spots by the educational and development programs since World War II. However, there are enormous influences weighting the peasants down—especially the deterioration of soil and the increase in numbers. The peasants have been the mudsills, so to speak, upon which the social structure of Asia has rested. The dislocations of the village economies due to the intrusion of factory products and modern methods since the 17th century have resulted in pushing the artisans of obsolete crafts and their descendants back upon the land resources of the villages.

Most of the countries which have neither industrialized nor developed a predominantly commercial type of agriculture—now called underdeveloped—entered the 20th century with a feudal type of economic and social system, or a tribal system still more primitive. Such feudal arangements varied widely. In some countries there were enormous holdings of land: in prerevolutionary Russia, Hungary, parts of Italy, Egypt and many others. But of greater importance was the fact that social, economic and political power accrues "naturally" to a relatively few families in old societies as land acquires a value from prospective sales of products, as lending becomes secured by pledges of land, as property rights become securely defined and national governments take shape. This is a feudalism of economic, political and social power, not merely of land holding alone.

If there is a constant within these diverse situations it is in the attitude and culture of the peasants themselves. There is a deep belief among peasants, whose ancestors may have lived for centuries from particular lands, that the lands and waters which have sustained them so long are somehow theirs—in a rightful sense. . . . To the individual peasant family their hold on the land has long been both the hallmark of their status and the elementary basis of their survival. With sufficient land of their own, some have lived well; without land countless millions have suffered literal starvation. The peasants' attachment to land is not a mere whim or prejudice; it reflects solid judgments of the requirements for survival which have matured through centuries of precarious and rugged living.

It is with such situations as these, or worse, that the leaders of underdeveloped countries must cope if their countries are to move toward economic development—the strengthening of the national economy and the reduction in poverty. What the leaders attempt is very likely that to which their general political or philosophical viewpoints lead them. In some countries the leaders are still trying to hold the lid on; in others, revolutionaries have had, or are having, their day. In more, devoted patriots are trying to make progress through gradual alleviation of the most glaring injustices, inefficiencies, and inequalities.

The land reform programs are among the ways of implementing these basic philosophies of government. It is meaningful, therefore, from the perspective of the American experience to gauge the agricultural policies and recent land reform programs against some of the basic ideas of Western liberalism which have affected our own land policies so profoundly. The Marxist-communist view is one of repudiation—of the basic importance of individual man as well as of the productivity of freedom. In this view, the owners of property in land, including owner-cultivators and small proprietors are considered enemies of the state—to be swept aside making way for the triumph of technology through collective farms. There is a correlative reliance upon bureaucratic administration rather than the rule of law, as we know it. These views have not been applied without qualification in the communist countries; Russia, Jugoslavia, China and the satellite states. But the restraint is evidently attributable to practical rather than ideological considerations. Russia has permitted at least some members of the collective farms to have little dooryard gardens and pastures. Jugoslavia is backing out of the collectivization of agriculture and returning to a more traditional type of peasant farming. China has not yet moved wholly into the collectivist pattern; individual peasants still have their allotments of land but their control is far short of private ownership. However, the eradication of private ownership of land and the collectivization of agriculture, with the thorough subordination of the individual cultivator to the will of the state, are evidently fundamental ingredients of the Marxist-communist policy toward agriculture.

In general, the noncommunist states affirm the historic liberal view that free men are stronger than slaves and that liberty is made secure through the rule of law, mostly through some variety of property rights. This view leads toward increasing the number of owner-cultivators, attempting to assure tenants security of occupancy with fair rents, and so on—in the belief that the independent farmer on a modest-sized farm is a good citizen and an efficient operator, or can be made efficient through education, agricultural credit, cooperatives and other sustaining measures.

It is for such reasons that land reform has become a battleground issue between communist propagandists and their adversaries in so many of the underdeveloped areas of the world. The Marxist-communist line is simple: the economic progress of peasants requires the elimination of the feudalistic landlords and an end to their exploitation. There is enough evidence of inequalities of income and status as well as a sufficient number of grievances in almost any old agrarian society to give this propaganda an effective appeal to the plain people. Such propaganda, fully illustrated by the experiences of former land owners in Russia and China, has undoubtedly stimulated the undertaking of land reform programs in several countries.

In effect, the peasants are courted by all political factions, or parties, in underdeveloped areas, through appeals to what used to be called the land hunger of the peasants. It is well known that communists have ridden to power in several countries by their promises of land to the peasants, which land they so devoutly want. Similarly, the slogan of "land to the tiller" has been used with great effect in Asian politics. The policy of land to the cultivator is one of the cardinal principles of the India Congress Party as well as of the party of the late President Magsaysay of the Philippine Islands.

The demands of the peasants for land of their own have erupted into open revolution on many occasions over recent centuries—the seizing of land by the peasants in Mexico following 1911, for example. More recently there have been sporadic threats and seizures of villages by the embittered peasants in several countries; in Italy, India and the Philippines, and elsewhere. It would be a mistake however to consider contemporary peasant societies as seething with unrest. To the casual visitor the peasant villages of Asia appear calm and even lethargic. Nevertheless, especially under the nationalistic awakenings, the potential is there for unrest with explosive dynamic force, particularly as school graduates return to the villages with little or nothing to do. In fact the fear of the masses, in the cities and in the villages, by the political leaders of Asia evidently serves to give public opinion a very great influence in the halls of government even where genuinely democratic elections are not held.

Military

64 · THE MILITARY AND POLITICAL POWER

E. William Steele

The mobilization of political power by the military leadership in the United States is more a product of time and circumstance than of intensive ratiocination. History has provided neither authority nor guidelines for an activist role by a collective military group in the American political system. Having observed the politicians and the milieu in which they operate, most professional military men have scorned politics. Budget-cutting congressmen and civilian cabinet secretaries have presented an image to the American military man that has encouraged him to shun the very term "politics." Such an attitude has been fortified by an often repeated aphorism heard in camps and bases since the Civil War: "When the army gets into politics, politics will get into the army."

Political generals there have been; men such as McClellan and Miles were, in the sight of their brother officers, led astray by popular adulation. There have been other generals—Taylor and Grant— who forsook the less glamorous, more boring, peacetime occupation of the professional soldier. But these have been exceptions, and the military services have taken pains to dissociate these personal decisions from the realm of the soldier's oath, "Duty, God, and Country."

The twentieth century bears witness to a new development. An enduring defense posture has catapulted the military leaders to positions of power and influence. Today, admirals and generals command attention and respect, not merely for their qualities of leadership on the battlefield but also for their leadership and service in peacetime in laboratories and offices in Washington, Paris, Ankara, Tokyo, and Berlin. The careers of Admiral Hyman Rickover, General Bernard Schriever, and General Lauris Norstad are examples of the change.

Furthermore, as national security has become America's greatest business enterprise, its managers have increasingly achieved new positions of strength and prestige.

No clandestine plots move military leaders in the United States to achieve power. In fact, their current historically unparalleled influence in policy formation has been modestly exercised. A future chronicler of these times might well write of the military, "Never have so many sought so little so reluctantly." But they do make decisions, however reluctant they may be and however quietly such decisions may be carried out. Often, the choices reflect civilian abdication of responsibility in the more sensitive areas of governmental administration. If American foreign policy today has a "military definition of reality," it is less the result of conscious civilian deliberation than of political timidity and accident. The words of Irwin Shaw may be taking on a chillingly literal meaning today: "We live in a confused age and we will be saved by confused heroes."

The fruits of military choices have drawn much attention—and criticism—to the prominent role of military leaders. When criticized, they have fought back, not in defense of an unwarranted usurpation of power but rather in defense of the validity of their advice. The battle has not been easy, for to defend decisions that have a one-dimensional character invites oversimplification. Such a condition has produced an occupational case of schizophrenia. The challenge is whether the military leaders should seek to be better informed and prepared for their actual role—and this means becoming quasi soldiers, quasi statesmen—or whether they should seek allies. The two approaches are by no means mutually exclusive, but each represents a distinct approach by emphasis and degree. The latter course has been emphasized by some thoughtful American students, particularly C. Wright Mills. The former approach, however, has been the one that time, circumstance, and professional objectives most frequently dictate.

The expediter, the catalyst of myriad details into a meaningful mosaic, the manager of a huge business enterprise, the uniformed synthesizer at a table surrounded by other uniformed figures—these are the realistic images of American military leaders today.

In all these roles, the military leaders must deal with the problems of pride-ridden nationals of many tongues; with sensitive congressmen whose constituents face the loss—or gain—of a naval depot, an air base, or a missile site; with corporate managers intent on developing or building nose cones, nuclear-powered submarines, jet fighters, and Arctic personnel carriers.

As the roles and the responsibilities have increased, so too have the demands for greater competence on the part of military men. Today, the military man's area of discretion needs greater breadth and depth than ever before; matters involving foreign affairs and industrial mobilization have become, for better or for worse, a part of his interest and of his working existence. The importance of participation in the process of government at one of the focal points of the military organization was revealed in the following dialogue between Congressman George H. Mahon, the Chairman of a House of Representatives Subcommittee on Department of Defense Appropriations, and Admiral Arthur W. Radford, Chairman of the Joint Chiefs of Staff at the time of the following exchange.*

> MAHON: I am seeking to discover the force and influence, if any, of the Joint Chief of Staff on our military spending, on the Budget, and on our military program.
>
> RADFORD: I would say the work of the Joint Chiefs of Staff and the Joint Staff is almost the heart of the Defense Department operation, because the forces that we maintain stem largely from the strategic and logistics planning originated by the Joint Chiefs of Staff. In other words, we make the strategic plans, and then we recommend the forces of the various services that are necessary to carry out those plans. Of course, in doing that we take into account the approved national policy and the commitments we have as a Government around the world. In the operation of building a budget in the Defense Department the Chiefs have to come up with their recommendations before the budget can really be started.
>
> MAHON: The Joint Chiefs of Staff are due great credit for past military program planning, or they are due discredit, whatever the facts may be; and that is applicable to the present operations of the Joint Chiefs of Staff?
>
> RADFORD: Yes, sir. We are in the position of being advisers. In fact, under the law we are the principal military advisers to the Secretary of Defense, the National Security Council, and the President. Of course, they can accept our recommendations and advice or they can disagree.
>
> MAHON: That brings up my next point. To what extent during your tenure as Chairman of the Joint Chiefs of Staff have the recommendations of the Joint Chiefs of Staff been accepted?

* Dept. of Defense Appropriations for 1957, 84th Congress, 2nd Session, Jan. 30, 1956. Government Printing Office, Washington, D.C., 1956.

RADFORD: I would say almost 100 per cent.

MAHON: In other words, you and your group have really written the military policies and programs of the Government?

RADFORD: To a large extent I would say that is true.

MAHON: Do the Joint Chiefs of Staff give consideration to political factors in arriving at the budget?

RADFORD: Not political factors, if you mean domestic political factors. We do give consideration to political factors as they affect our foreign policy. I would say the politico-military factors that we give consideration to are largely those that stem from our foreign commitments of one kind or another, and also estimates of the situation in various countries which very often take into consideration the domestic political situation in those countries.

In their attempt to meet the demands of the quasi-military, quasi-political roles, the services have entered new avenues of preparation or have intensified and broadened old ones. The service academies and postcommission training establishments increasingly stress studies in international politics, languages, and area specialization. New schools and programs—for example, the Industrial College of the Armed Forces—emphasize the areas of industrial mobilization, international economics, and resource and geographic studies. Individual officers are encouraged to seek advanced degrees and graduate training in specialized areas that embrace language studies and the physical, biological, and social studies fields.

The trend is clearly toward the training of a more broadly schooled and highly skilled corps of military men, men able to exercise skill and judgment in fields which, until recently, were felt to be beyond the concern of military duty. In the process, of course, the increased and broadened competence may be channeled into areas which have, in the past, been reserved exclusively for civilians. The meaning of the very term "military," as well as the profession itself, has become broadened both by events of the last twenty years and by the character and skill of the men involved. What the impact may be—both for the nation and for the military personnel—is still unclear, but that *there is an impact* and a *dilemma* for these mobilizers of political power, the military, can be seen nowhere more clearly than in the following statement by a former Chief of Staff of the United States Army, Maxwell Taylor:*

* From a speech at a Founders' Day Dinner, West Point Society of New York, March 17, 1956. Quoted in *Army,* Vol. 6, No. 10, May, 1956, pp. 14-15.

Never before in our history has such responsibility been placed in the hands of military men as at present. For this reason, never has there been greater need for men of integrity, selfless men without ambition, disdaining political advantage and personal preferment. *Only such men of character can make their voices heard at the council tables of our nation, where sound and responsible military views are so important in guiding our national policy.* In the last analysis, the requirement for character in our military leaders arises from the awfulness of *the weapons which they now control.* Only men of the highest principles and standards of conduct should be allowed to make these decisions which may involve the destiny of all mankind. (Editors' italics.)

65 · THE SUPREME COURT AND THE MILITARY

A · THE SUPREME COURT AND THE MILITARY

LYMAN JAY GOULD

An activist and powerful military is a political fact of life common to many countries. In these nations the politically oriented and sophisticated soldier is no stranger to the society. The civilian reaction has been twofold: to attempt repeatedly to return the uniformed politician to the barracks, or to accept fatalistically his non-martial role while seeking to channel and use his political power. Neither approach has yielded consistent success.

The American experience has been of a different nature. Historically confined to the barracks by legal and emotional barriers, the professional soldier in the United States has broken bounds in the face of the strong tradition insistent upon civil supremacy over the military. It is this context that shapes, and continues to limit, the claims, explicit and implicit, made by the military upon contemporary decision-making. Thus the implications and complexities of the present escape from the barracks cannot be fully appreciated without an understanding of the tradition.

Much has been written on the subject, but perhaps the proper voice to give expression both to the tradition and the difficulties involved in applying it is that of the Supreme Court. The tenor of recent opinions of the Supreme Court indicates that it has taken the lead in protesting what it views as military ursurpation of civil, i.e., judicial, authority. These recent decisions, however, do not represent a late awakening by the Supreme Court to the problem. The Civil War, as the forerunner of modern total war, thrust upon the nation the actuality of military tribunals. Although evading the issue in *Ex Parte Vallandigham* (1864), the Supreme Court belatedly rapped presidential and military knuckles in the landmark case of *Ex Parte Milligan* (1866). Justice Davis not only emphasized the right of civilians to be tried by civil court and a jury, but also narrowly defined the scope of martial law by denying it constitutional existence "where the courts are open, and in the proper and unobstructed exercise of their jurisdiction." The import of this decision was not vitiated by a subsequent withdrawal from the issue, upon jurisdictional grounds, in *Ex Parte McCardle* (1869).

The Second World War presented the Supreme Court with a series of cases raising questions of military authority. In *Hirabayashi* v. *United States* (1943) and *Korematsu* v. *United States* (1944) the Supreme Court acquiesced in what was essentially a military decision to evacuate American citizens of Japanese ancestry from the West Coast of the United States. Then, perhaps in a fit of conscience, the justices held in *Ex Parte Endo* (1944) that the detention program was not authorized by law. By incorporating the "Milligan rule" into the Organic Act of Hawaii, the Supreme Court invalidated, albeit again belatedly, martial law in the Islands in *Duncan* v. *Kahanamoku* (1946).

More recently the Supreme Court has had to deal with cases resulting from the Uniform Code of Military Justice in its application to civilians. In *Toth* v. *Quarles* (1955) the attempt by the Air Force to try a discharged airman for a crime committed while in the service was declared unconstitutional. This was followed, after an initial hesitancy in *Kinsella* v. *Krueger* (1956) and *Reid* v. *Covert* (1956), by a number of decisions restricting military jurisdiction over civilians. Peacetime military trials of civilian dependents of the members of the armed forces overseas in capital cases (*Reid* v. *Covert,* 1957), of civilian dependents in non-capital cases (*Kinsella* v. *Singleton,* 1960), of employees of the armed forces overseas in capital cases (*Grisham* v. *Hagan,* 1960), and of employees of the armed forces overseas in non-capital cases (*McElroy* v. *Guagliardo* and *Wilson* v. *Bohlender,* 1960), were all struck down as unconstitutional.

Thus it can be seen, at least since 1946, that the Supreme Court has made meaningful the concept of the Constitution as a symbol of restraint. In the process, it has restated and underscored the American tradition of the military being "on tap rather than on top." As such, the Supreme Court has emerged as a possible major obstacle to an expanding military voice in our national life. The two selections that follow illustrate both the basis and the feasibility of such a role for the Supreme Court. The opinion by Justice Black states the American tradition, whereas the one by Justice Jackson frankly confesses to the bitter practical truth found in the maxim: *inter arma silent leges*.

B · JUSTICE BLACK ON THE MILITARY *

The tradition of keeping the military subordinate to civilian authority may not be so strong in the minds of this generation as it was in the minds of those who wrote the Constitution. The idea that the relatives of soldiers could be denied a jury trial in a court of law and instead be tried by court-martial under the guise of regulating the armed forces would have seemed incredible to those men, in whose lifetime the right of the military to try *soldiers* for any offenses in time of peace had only been grudgingly conceded. The Founders envisioned the army as a necessary institution, but one dangerous to liberty if not confined within its essential bounds. Their fears were rooted in history. They knew that ancient republics had been overthrown by their military leaders. They were familiar with the history of Seventeenth Century England, where Charles I tried to govern through the army and without Parliament. During this attempt, contrary to the Common Law, he used courts-martial to try soldiers for certain non-military offenses. This court-martialing of soldiers in peacetime evoked strong protests from Parliament. The reign of Charles I was followed by the rigorous military rule of Oliver Cromwell. Later, James II used the Army in his fight against Parliament and the people. He promulgated Articles of War (strangely enough relied on in the Government's brief) authorizing the trial of soldiers for non-military crimes by courts-martial. This action hastened the revolution that brought William and Mary to the throne upon their agreement to abide by a Bill of Rights which, among other things, protected the right of trial by jury. It was against this general background that two of the greatest English jurists, Lord Chief Justice

---

* Reprinted from the opinion of Justice Black in *Reid* v. *Covert*, 354 U.S. 1, 23-32, 39-41 (1957). Footnotes in the original are omitted here.

Hale and Sir William Blackstone—men who exerted considerable influence on the Founders—expressed sharp hostility to any expansion of the jurisdiction of military courts. For instance, Blackstone went so far as to assert:

"For martial law, which is built upon no settled principles, but is entirely arbitrary in its decisions, is, as Sir Matthew Hale observes, in truth and reality no law, but something indulged rather than allowed as a law. The necessity of order and discipline in an army is the only thing which can give it countenance; and therefore it ought not to be permitted in time of peace, when the king's courts are open for all persons to receive justice according to the laws of the land."

The generation that adopted the Constitution did not distrust the military because of past history alone. Within their own lives they had seen royal governors sometimes resort to military rule. British troops were quartered in Boston at various times from 1768 until the outbreak of the Revolutionary War to support unpopular royal governors and to intimidate the local populace. The trial of *soldiers* by courts-martial and the interference of the military with the civil courts aroused great anxiety and antagonism not only in Massachusetts but throughout the colonies. For example, Samuel Adams in 1768 wrote:

". . . (I)s it not enough for us to have seen soldiers and mariners forejudged of life, and executed within the body of the county by martial law? Are citizens to be called upon, threatened, ill-used at the will of the soldiery and put under arrest, by pretext of the law military, in breach of the fundamental rights of subjects, and contrary to the law and franchise of the land? . . . Will the spirits of people as yet unsubdued by tyranny, unawed by the menaces of arbitrary power, submit to be governed by military force? No! Let us rouse our attention to the common law,—which is our birthright, our great security against all kinds of insult and oppression. . . ."

Colonials had also seen the right to trial by jury subverted by acts of Parliament which authorized courts of admiralty to try alleged violations of the unpopular "Molasses" and "Navigation" Acts. This gave the admiralty courts jurisdiction over offenses historically triable only by a jury in a court of law and aroused great resentment throughout the colonies. As early as 1765 delegates from nine colonies meeting in New York asserted in a "Declaration of Rights" that trial by jury was the "inherent and invaluable" right of every citizen in the colonies.

With this background it is not surprising that the Declaration of Independence protested that George III had "affected to render the Military independent of and superior to the Civil Power" and that Americans had been deprived in many cases of "the benefits of Trial by Jury." And those who adopted the Constitution embodied their profound fear and distrust of military power, as well as their determination to protect trial by jury, in the Constitution and its Amendments. Perhaps they were aware that memories fade and hoped that in this way they could keep the people of this nation from having to fight again and again the same old battles for individual freedom.

In light of this history, it seems clear that the Founders had no intention to permit the trial of civilians in military courts, where they would be denied jury trials and other constitutional protections, merely by giving Congress the power to make rules which were "necessary and proper" for the regulation of the "land and naval Forces." Such a latitudinarian interpretation of these clauses would be at war with the well-established purpose of the Founders to keep the military strictly within its proper sphere, subordinate to civil authority. The Constitution does not say that Congress can regulate "the land and naval Forces and all other persons whose regulation might have some relationship to maintenance of the land and naval Forces." There is no indication that the Founders contemplated setting up a rival system of military courts to compete with civilian courts for jurisdiction over civilians who might have some contact or relationship with the armed forces. Courts-martial were not to have concurrent jurisdiction with courts of law over non-military America.

On several occasions this Court has been faced with an attempted expansion of the jurisdiction of military courts. Ex parte Milligan (US) 4 Wall 2, 18 L ed 281, one of the great landmarks in this Court's history, held that military authorities were without power to try civilians not in the military or naval service by declaring martial law in an area where the civil administration was not deposed and the courts were not closed. In a stirring passage the Court proclaimed:

"Another guarantee of freedom was broken when Milligan was denied a trial by jury. The great minds of the country have differed on the correct interpretation to be given to various provisions of the Federal Constitution; and judicial decision has been often invoked to settle their true meaning; but until recently no one ever doubted that the right of trial by jury was fortified in the organic law against the power of attack. It is *now* assailed; but if ideas can be expressed in words, and language has any meaning, *this right*—one of the most valuable in a free country—is preserved to everyone accused of crime who is not attached to the army, or navy, or militia in actual service."

In Duncan v Kahanamoku, 327 US 304, 90 L ed 688, 66 S Ct 606, the Court reasserted the principles enunciated in Ex parte Milligan and reaffirmed the tradition of military subordination to civil authorities and institutions. It refused to sanction the military trial of civilians in Hawaii during war-time despite government claims that the needs of defense made martial law imperative.

Just last Term, this Court held in United States ex rel. Toth v Quarles, 350 US 11, 100 L ed 8, 76 S Ct 1, that military courts could not constitutionally try a discharged serviceman for an offense which he had allegedly committed while in the armed forces. It was decided (1) that since Toth was a civilian he could not be tried by military court-martial, and (2) that since he was charged with murder, a "crime" in the constitutional sense, he was entitled to indictment by a grand jury, jury trial, and the other protections contained in Art III, Sec. 2 and the Fifth, Sixth, and Eighth Amendments. The Court pointed out that trial by civilian courts was the rule for persons who were not members of the armed forces.

. . . . .

It is urged that the expansion of military jurisdiction over civilians claimed here is only slight, and that the practical necessity for it is very great. The attitude appears to be that a slight encroachment on the Bill of Rights and other safeguards in the Constitution need cause little concern. But to hold that these wives could be tried by the military would be a tempting precedent. Slight encroachments create new boundaries from which legions of power can seek new territory to capture. "It may be that it is the obnoxious thing in its mildest and least repulsive form; but illegitimate and unconstitutional practices get their first footing in that way, namely, by silent approaches and slight deviations from legal modes of procedure. This can only be obviated by adhering to the rule that constitutional provisions for the security of person and property should be liberally construed. A close and literal construction deprives them of half their efficacy, and leads to gradual depreciation of the right, as if it consisted more in sound than in substance. It is the duty of courts to be watchful for the constitutional rights of the citizen, and against any stealthy encroachments thereon." Moreover we cannot consider this encroachment a slight one. Throughout history many transgressions by the military have been called "slight" and have been justified as "reasonable" in light of the "uniqueness" of the times. We cannot close our eyes to the fact that today the peoples of many nations are ruled by the military.

We should not break faith with this nation's tradition of keeping military power subservient to civilian authority, a tradition which we believe is firmly embodied in the Constitution. The country has remained true to that faith for almost one hundred seventy years. Perhaps no group in the nation has been truer than military men themselves. Unlike the soldiers of many other nations, they have been content to perform their military duties in defense of the nation in every period of need and to perform those duties well without attempting to usurp power which is not theirs under our system of constitutional government.

Ours is a government of divided authority on the assumption that in division there is not only strength but freedom from tyranny. And under our Constitution courts of law alone are given power to try civilians for their offenses against the United States. The philosophy expressed by Lord Coke, speaking long ago from a wealth of experience, is still timely:

"God send me never to live under the Law of Conveniency or Discretion. Shall the Souldier and Justice Sit on one Bench, the Trumpet will not let the Cryer speak in Westminster Hall."

C · JUSTICE JACKSON ON THE MILITARY *

Korematsu was born on our soil, of parents born in Japan. The Constitution makes him a citizen of the United States by nativity and a citizen of California by residence. No claim is made that he is not loyal to this country. There is no suggestion that apart from the matter involved here he is not law-abiding and well disposed. Korematsu, however, has been convicted of an act not commonly a crime. It consists merely of being present in the state whereof he is a citizen, near the place where he was born, and where all his life he has lived.

Even more unusual is the series of military orders which made this conduct a crime. They forbid such a one to remain, and they also forbid him to leave. They were so drawn that the only way Korematsu

* Dissenting opinion of Justice Jackson in *Korematsu* v. *United States*, 323 US 214, 243-248 (1944). The footnote in the original is omitted here.

could avoid violation was to give himself up to the military authority. This meant submission to custody, examination, and transportation out of the territory, to be followed by indeterminate confinement in detention camps.

A citizen's presence in the locality, however, was made a crime only if his parents were of Japanese birth. Had Korematsu been one of four—the others being, say, a German alien enemy, an Italian alien enemy, and a citizen of American-born ancestors, convicted of treason but out on parole—only Korematsu's presence would have violated the order. The difference between their innocence and his crime would result, not from anything he did, said, or thought, different than they, but only in that he was born of different racial stock.

Now, if any fundamental assumption underlies our system, it is that guilt is personal and not inheritable. Even if all of one's antecedents had been convicted of treason, the Constitution forbids its penalties to be visited upon him, for it provides that "no attainder of treason shall work corruption of blood, or forfeiture except during the life of the person attainted." But here is an attempt to make an otherwise innocent act a crime merely because this prisoner is the son of parents as to whom he had no choice, and belongs to a race from which there is no way to resign. If Congress in peace-time legislation should enact such a criminal law, I should suppose this Court would refuse to enforce it.

But the "law" which this prisoner is convicted of disregarding is not found in an act of Congress, but in a military order. Neither the Act of Congress nor the Executive Order of the President, nor both together, would afford a basis for this conviction. It rests on the orders of General DeWitt. And it is said that if the military commander had reasonable military grounds for promulgating the orders, they are constitutional and become law, and the Court is required to enforce them. There are several reasons why I cannot subscribe to this doctrine.

It would be impracticable and dangerous idealism to expect or insist that each specific military command in an area of probable operations will conform to conventional tests of constitutionality. When an area is so beset that it must be put under military control at all, the paramount consideration is that its measures be successful, rather than legal. The armed services must protect a society, not merely its Constitution. The very essence of the military job is to marshal physical force, to remove every obstacle to its effectiveness, to give it every strategic advantage. Defense measures will not, and often should not, be held within the limits that bind civil authority in peace. No court can require such a commander in such circumstances to act as a reasonable man; he may be unreasonably cautious and exacting. Perhaps he should be. But a commander in temporarily focusing the life of a community on defense is carrying out a military program; he is not making law in the sense the courts know the term. He issues orders, and they may have a certain authority as military commands, although they may be very bad as constitutional law.

But if we cannot confine military expedients by the Constitution, neither would I distort the Constitution to approve all that the military may deem expedient. That is what the Court appears to be doing, whether consciously or not. I cannot say, from any evidence before me, that the orders of General DeWitt were not reasonably expedient military precautions, nor could I say that they were. But even if they were permissible military procedures, I deny that it follows that they are constitutional. If, as the Court holds, it does follow, then we may as well say that any military order will be constitutional and have done with it.

The limitations under which courts always will labor in examining the necessity for a military order are illustrated by this case. How does the Court know that these orders have a reasonable basis in necessity? No evidence whatever on that subject has been taken by this or any other court. There is sharp controversy as to the credibility of the DeWitt report. So the Court, having no real evidence before it, has no choice but to accept General DeWitt's own unsworn, self-serving statement, untested by any cross-examination, that what he did was reasonable. And thus it will always be when courts try to look into the reasonableness of a military order.

In the very nature of things military decisions are not susceptible of intelligent judicial appraisal. They do not pretend to rest on evidence, but are made on information that often would not be admissible and on assumptions that could not be proved. Information in support of an order could not be disclosed to courts without danger that it would reach the enemy. Neither can courts act on communications made in confidence. Hence courts can never have any real alternative to accepting the mere declaration of the authority which issued the order that it was reasonably necessary from a military viewpoint.

Much is said of the danger to liberty from the Army program for deporting and detaining these citizens of Japanese extraction. But a judicial construction of the due process clause that will sustain this order is a far more subtle blow to liberty than the promulgation of the order itself. A military order, however unconstitutional, is not apt to last longer than the military emergency. Even during that period a succeeding commander may revoke it. But once a judicial opinion rationalizes such an order to show that it conforms to the Constitution, or rather rationalizes the Constitution to show that the Constitution sanctions such an order, the Court for all time has validated the principle of racial discrimination in criminal procedure and of transplanting American citizens. The principle then lies about like a loaded weapon ready for the hand of any authority that can bring forward a plausible claim of an urgent need. Every repetition imbeds that principle more deeply in our law and thinking and expands it to new purposes. All who observe the work of courts are familiar with what Judge Cardozo described as "the tendency of a principle to expand itself to the limit of its logic." A military commander may overstep the bounds of constitutionality, and it is an incident. But if we review and approve, that passing incident becomes the doctrine of the Constitution. There it has a generative power of its own, and all that it creates will be in its own image. Nothing better illustrates this danger than does the Court's opinion in this case.

It argues that we are bound to uphold the conviction of Korematsu because we upheld one in *Hirabayashi* v. *United States,* 320 US 81, 87 L ed 1774, 63 S Ct 1375, when we sustained these orders in so far as they applied a curfew requirement to a citizen of Japanese ancestry. I think we should learn something from that experience.

In that case we were urged to consider only the curfew feature, that being all that technically was involved, because it was the only count necessary to sustain Hirabayashi's conviction and sentence. We yielded, and the Chief Justice guarded the opinion as carefully as language will do. He said: "Our investigation here does not go beyond the inquiry whether, in the light of all the relevant circumstances preceding and attending their promulgation, the challenged orders and statute *afforded a reasonable basis for the action taken in imposing the curfew.*" 320 US at 101, 87 L ed 1786, 63 S Ct 1375. "We decide only the issue as we have defined it—we decide only that the *curfew order* as applied, and at the time it was applied, was within the boundaries of the war power." 320 US at 102, 87 L ed 1787, 63 S Ct 1375. And again: "It is unnecessary to consider whether or to what extent *such findings would support orders differing from the curfew order."* 320 US at 105, 87 L ed 1788, 63 S Ct 1375. [Italics supplied.] However, in spite of our limiting words we did validate a discrimination on the basis of ancestry for mild and temporary deprivation of liberty. Now the principle of racial discrimination is pushed from support of mild measures to very harsh ones, and from temporary deprivations to indeterminate ones. And the precedent which it is said requires us to do so is *Hirabayashi*. The Court is now saying that in *Hirabayashi* we did decide the very things we there said we were not deciding. Because we said that these citizens could be made to stay in their homes during the hours of dark, it is said we must require them to leave home entirely; and if that, we are told they may also be taken into custody for deportation; and if that, it is argued they may also be held for some undetermined time in detention camps. How far the principle of this case would be extended before plausible reasons would play out, I do not know.

I should hold that a civil court cannot be made to enforce an order which violates constitutional limitations even if it is a reasonable exercise of military authority. The courts can exercise only the judicial power, can apply only law, and must abide by the Constitution, or they cease to be civil courts and become instruments of military policy.

Of course the existence of a military power resting on force, so vagrant, so centralized, so necessarily heedless of the individual, is an inherent threat to liberty. But I would not lead people to rely on this Court for a review that seems to me wholly delusive. The military reasonableness of these orders can only be determined by military superiors. If the people ever let command of the war power fall into irresponsible and unscrupulous hands, the courts wield no power equal to its restraint. The chief restraint upon those who command the physical forces of the country, in the future as in the past, must be their responsibility to the political judgments of their contemporaries and to the moral judgments of history.

My duties as a justice as I see them do not require me to make a military judgment as to whether General DeWitt's evacuation and detention program was a reasonable military necessity. I do not suggest that the courts should have attempted to interfere with the Army in carrying out its task. But I do not think they may be asked to execute a military expedient that has no place in law under the Constitution. I would reverse the judgment and discharge the prisoner.

66 · ARMS AND POLITICS IN LATIN AMERICA*

Edwin Lieuwen

Essential to a deeper understanding of the social significance of the resurgence of militarism is a closer examination of the role of the military leaders. For, as might be expected, Latin America's twentieth-century economic, social, and political metamorphosis was clearly mirrored in the officer corps. The dramatic struggles that occurred between the old and the new, between farm and city, between vested interests and newly organized labor, resulted in institutional upheavals in the armed forces as far-reaching and profound as those that occurred in civilian society.

After World War I there began to appear in the lower echelons of the officer corps representatives of the rising urban middle groups. The sons of industrialists, bureaucrats, and urban professional men began to acquire the educational background and the modern, progressive outlook that made them superior cadets in the military academies. As in the past, men who chose a career in arms continued to come from the middle class, but the military representatives of these new urban groups, unlike the traditionally rural-oriented officers, had no ties with either the landed oligarchy or the church hierarchy. Consequently, they had, at least initially, little enthusiasm for perpetuating the role of the armed forces as a guarantor of the traditional social order.

The social identification of the new-type officer with the urban groups where he originated was probably the fundamental cause of the junior-officer uprisings that occurred in Latin America's armies in the second quarter of the twentieth century. In general, the ideological conflict was between the old and the new generation, between the generals, on the one hand, and the majors, captains, and lieutenants on the other, with the colonels often pulled in both directions. Such cleavages were nothing new in Latin America; what was new was their origins in social conflict.

* Edwin Lieuwen, *Arms and Politics in Latin America* (New York: Praeger. for the Council on Foreign Relations, 1960), pp. 125-132. Copyright © 1960 by the Council on Foreign Relations, Inc. Reprinted by permission of the Council on Foreign Relations, Inc. A footnote in the original version is omitted here.

Almost invariably, Latin America's popular revolutions of this century were led by the young officers. They became the sponsors of fundamental change and reform, the underminers of traditional institutions, the proponents of public-welfare measures. Democratic political institutions were of less concern to them. Indeed, they were often the leading advocates of militarized, authoritarian government and were apt to speak scornfully of "decadent" democracy. Their revolutionary zeal was by no means entirely altruistic, for changes in the make-up and role of the armed forces meant unparalleled opportunities for promotion. Militarization of government and extreme nationalistic policies meant new and important jobs for them, as well as expansion and enrichment of the state apparatus upon which the military was dependent for its income.

The new militarism, therefore, went much deeper than in the past. It was much more complex, as new social forces (labor and middle groups) and new military factors (politically influential navies and air forces) were added. Thus, those who stood for the old-type military dictatorship, backed only by the landed oligarchy and the upper clergy and often favored by foreign commercial or financial interests, had to face an entirely new, modern type of military competitor for political power.

Generally speaking, the new leader did not create the new sources of power. More often than not, the environment called forth the man, who rode to power at the head of a popular reform movement. A typical example was that of Arbenz in Guatemala. The new social philosophy was not primarily the brain child of the leader himself. His articulate expression of popular demands, demands in which he himself probably did not believe, was a weapon, a technique utilized for the enhancement of his personal power.

The new leader's relationship to the armed forces, the institution out of which he rose to power, was a curious one. He did not rise to be the head of a revolution by his own individual initiative, as had the *caudillos*. Rather, he represented a substantial cross section of the junior or middle-rank army leadership, concentrated in a conspiratorial clique, like the Group of United Officers in Argentina or the Patriotic Military Union in Venezuela. These young officers thought of themselves as enlightened members of a new, modern generation. Regarding the generals as unimaginative and behind the times, they sought to bring the armed forces into more sympathetic relations with the rest of the society. They were also interested in power, which could be had by gaining popular support, by playing the role of saviors of the downtrodden masses.

To win his battle against the oligarchy, the revolutionary leader had to pose as a representative of the lower- and middle-income groups. He had to make them believe that the enhancement of his power would lead to a parallel advancement of their interests. If the people responded to his vilification of the old regime and his Messianic promises, he was well on the way to the establishment of a kind of plebeian dictatorship, whether or not he had the majority of the people behind him. Opposition leaders could be effectively handled by simply condemning them as enemies of the people. Particularly troublesome elements, such as the conservative press, could be suppressed by organized violence, generally by police or security forces acting in "the people's" interest.

Every successful new leader announced a revolutionary reform program reflecting popular demands. The people supposedly would rule; they were the state; their new leader was its representative. He proposed to rebuild the national economy along modern lines, gave at least lip service to demands for agrarian reform, promised to curb the power of the landlords and the foreign capitalists, and pledged greater benefits to workers and peasants in the form of higher wages, better housing, and expanded social security.

In a typical case, the beneficiaries of these material gains were content with the vicarious enjoyment of political power through identification with the military dictator; but his colleagues were not. They had originally brought him to power; he was still dependent upon them. To decrease this dependence and thereby enhance his own power, he appealed even more to the people. Generally, to this end he built up organized labor as a counterpoise to potential rivals in the armed forces. The alliance with labor, the technique used by Perón, Arbenz, and others, was often as essential to the cause of fundamental reform as it was to the leader's drive for power. For in the frequent cases where his military colleagues began to lose their enthusiasm for drastic change soon after the revolution succeeded, labor was caught in a dilemma. Unless it shared in the aspiring dictator's drive for supreme power, achievement of its material and social demands was impossible. Generally, the lower classes chose to go along with him, as the only hope for more "economic democracy."

The first of these new-type military rulers, officers who rose to power as leaders of popular reform movements, was General Car-

ranza in Mexico, who in 1915 appealed to the new social forces and
gave lip service to—but did not fulfill—their demands. His successors,
Generals Obregón and Calles, were more attentive to such demands.
Prior to 1930, Major Ibáñez of Chile was the only other leader of
the new type on the Latin American scene. Between 1930 and 1957,
eleven of the fifty-six military men who held the presidential office
in the twenty Latin American republics for as long as a year might
be so described: Major Ibáñez (1930-1931), Colonel Perón (1945-
1955), Colonel Rafael Franco (1936-1937) of Paraguay, Colonel
Busch (1936-1938) and Major Villaroel (1943-1946) of Bolivia,
General Rojas Pinilla of Colombia (1953-1957), Colonel Remón of
Panama (1952-1955), Colonel Arbenz of Guatemala (1950-1954),
General Cárdenas of Mexico (1934-1940), Sergeant Batista of Cuba
(1933-1944), and Major Osorio of El Salvador (1948-1956). In
three countries young officers who had conducted revolutions sustained reform-oriented, civilian-led regimes in power. This was the
situation in Brazil under Vargas (1930-1945), Venezuela under Be-
tancourt and Gallegos (1945-1948), and Ecuador under Velasco
Ibarra (1944-1947).

Generally opposed to the military "reformers" were the senior officers. Their god was stability, and as its defenders they frowned upon
social and political experimentation. They might be more partial to
democratic institutions than their younger rivals, but this was likely
to be the narrowly based "democracy" which had been allowed to
function within the traditional order. Their political philosophy was
understandable. Having arrived at the top of their profession, they
were affected by the conservatism that came with rank, age, status,
and the attainment of comfortable material circumstances. The exalted rank of general enabled them, unlike the junior officers, to enter
politics without sacrificing their professional position.

In the events of the years 1947-1957 already described, every one
of the reformist military regimes was overthrown, usually either by
conservative army officers or by young officers, originally leaders of
the revolution, whose zeal for reform had withered before the winds
of labor-leftist extremism. Reactionary movements brought to the
fore officers whose mission it was to halt the social revolution, although they were never completely successful, for the changes wrought
by the reform regimes were generally too fundamental to be undone.
In most cases labor-leftist political activity was sharply curtailed or
prohibited, and although most of the social and material gains already

attained were preserved, no new ones were forthcoming. In economic policy, however, the military leaders of the counterrevolution generally stole much of the industrializing, modernizing, and nationalistic programs of their predecessors.

It is difficult to make reliable generalizations about the socio-political attitudes of the officer corps in a single country, let alone in Latin America as a whole. Some military leaders did not conform to any type. The lines between groups were fluid, and there was seldom any permanent resolution of the struggle among those vying for power. Sometimes revolutionary young officers would win control, only to lose it to their more conservative seniors, as in Chile between 1925 and 1932. Sometimes senior officers would attempt a liberating revolution, as in Colombia in 1953. Sometimes junior officers originally liberal would turn conservative, as in Brazil between 1930 and 1945 and in Venezuela between 1945 and 1948. Sometimes the same officers that originally sponsored a military dictatorship would later bring it to an end, as happened when Perón and Rojas Pinilla were ousted.

Struggles within the officer class were complicated by ideological cross-currents and fierce personal and professional rivalries. Many officers in the lower ranks who talked of social reform really wanted increased pay and more rapid promotion. At times some of the senior officers, convinced of the inevitable political triumph of the new social forces compromised with them in order to preserve their own positions. This occurred, for example, in Guatemala in 1944. In the larger countries, generals interested in keeping pace with modern military technology in order to improve the capabilities of the armed forces, sometimes supported the new nationalism and industrialization.

Sometimes the three services were split along divergent political lines. The situation in Argentina under the Perón regime, for example, was most complex. There the army was the most powerful and the most politically inclined of the three branches of the armed forces. Within the army, whose officer corps had a middle-class background, there were two groups: one—the dominant—was nationalistic, socialistic, and politically minded; the less powerful group was more democratic in its outlook, inclined to accept the *status quo,* and relatively nonpolitical. A similar division characterized the navy, whose officers came from the upper middle class and the landed aristocracy. But in the navy, the democratic rather than the nationalist group held sway. Consequently, Perón never really had the navy on his side. To compound the confusion, the air force was split about evenly. Only the police force, built up by Perón himself, revealed no broad internal divisions.

Throughout Latin America the armies were the strongest and the most politically active of the three services. They reflected social tensions most accurately, and therefore they were more seriously wracked by internal splits. Air forces had no significance in Latin America until World War II and have not yet achieved a major political role. Navies (important only in Brazil, Argentina, Chile and Peru), though less politically minded than armies, usually remained unified, fundamentally conservative institutions. A naval career, consequently, carried more social prestige.† The aristocratic tendencies of naval officers, however, often were moderated by the democratic views of the British and United States officers who were their professional advisers. Conversely, before World War II, authoritarian attitudes of some Latin American armies were reinforced by the influence of German, Spanish, and Italian military missions.

67 · BURMA'S NEW DEAL FROM THE ARMY— IS IT A PATTERN FOR ASIA? *

Albert Ravenholt

Why have one third of Asia's new nations turned within the past two years to military management of their governments? Are Western-style representative political institutions unworkable for these countries newly emerged from colonialism, or only temporarily discredited? What inhibited the undisputed ideal of democracy from finding a more workable form? Such questions are asked today not only by curious observers. Perceptive Asians are themselves re-examining their political assumptions. Goaded by Red China's monumental disciplining of its 670 million citizens, some leaders in neighboring lands are becoming impatient for more effective means of getting things done at home.

† This was not true in Colombia, however.

* Albert Ravenholt, "Burma's New Deal from the Army—Is It a Pattern for Asia?," *American Universities Field Staff Reports Service* (Southeast Asia Series—Volume VII, Number 12), pp. 1-4, 7-11, 13-14. Reprinted by permission of Albert Ravenholt and the American Universities Field Staff, Inc.

When approached from this perspective Burma offers revealing insights even though in the various countries of Southeast Asia the military role differs with each social and historical setting. Joined to Communist China by a 1,000-mile common but disputed border, the Burmese are linked through Buddhism to much of South and East Asia and by a heritage of British education and administrative experience to the Western World. In this eleven-year-old nation the Army has been in power now for seven months. The compulsions that made the Commander in Chief of the Army, General Ne Win, assume the premiership and the neat legal manner in which this was achieved tell much about the attitudes of Burmese, that here as elsewhere are so vital a part of political institutions. The young colonels who now run the Government have shown both what the Army can and can not do. In their hands they hold not only the fate of Burma, but, by example, the chances for an open and free society among their neighbors who are searching for a workable formula.

The immediate reason for the Army's assumption of new authority was a controversial "split" in the ranks of the Anti-Fascist Peoples Freedom League that had ruled Burma since independence. But the root causes go far deeper. Burma was left more totally shattered by World War II than any other Asian country except the Philippines. . . .

The material cost of allied liberation was dwarfed by the human toll, due mainly to disease and malnutrition. Old suspicions between the lowland dwelling Burmans and the hill folk—Shans, Karens, Kachins, Chins and others—erupted into bitter fighting as the British and Americans outfitted the minorities, some of whom were Christians. When hatred for the Japanese military led the Burmese revolutionaries to side with the Allies, the British were slow to face political realities. So even victory and VJ-Day had a bitter quality that brought only peace of sorts.

Independence which was won from the British by negotiation with the Labour Government almost became a mirage soon after the Union of Burma was established on January 4, 1948. The previous summer the gifted and dynamic recognized leader of the country, U Aung San, and six of his colleagues in the Executive Council had been assassinated. Burma thereby lost the most talented of her leaders just when they were needed. Soon the land was beset by insurrections and rebellions that for a time limited the new Government's effective authority to Rangoon and its environs. White Flag or Stalinist Communists followed the lead of the 1948 Calcutta resolutions to stage uprisings in Burma as they did in Malaya and Indonesia. Trotskyites, known as Red Flag Communists, armed their followers and tried to seize territory for themselves. Equally serious was the civil war launched by the Karen National Defense Organization, well equipped with wartime British arms and in control of the Tenasserim coast adjoining Thailand and much of the rice granary in the delta. As the Communists overran China in 1949, remnant Chinese Nationalists retreated across the border to occupy Kengtung in the Eastern Shan States. There they survived on the opium trade and banditry after one abortive foray into Yunnan, while outfitting their forces with American-made arms brought from Thailand and fighting a running war with the Burmese Army.

This internal struggle crippled Burma's reconstruction. The bounty from the high prices for rice exports during the first postwar years was needed to outfit the military and maintain essential services when more of it might otherwise have been invested in national improvements. Guerrillas, employing a favorite trick of implanting dud Allied bombs of a thousand pounds or more under the railways and detonating them when a train passed overhead, made reconstruction of communications an endless task. The rich mines that before the war shipped tin, silver, tungsten and rubies to earn much of Burma's foreign exchange were usually kept closed or prevented from transporting their wealth to Rangoon. Extraction of teak from the extensive forests was only slowly resumed as special forest guards were trained and armed to protect both loggers and elephants.

Socialism as the ideological watchword of officials in the new Government encouraged some odd economics. The Burmese were understandably determined to be rid of the Indian money lenders who held much of the richest land, even though this meant eliminating an important source of rural credit. Likewise, in order to "guide" development they insisted upon joint Government partnership with the chief foreign capitalists, including British interests in oil and the two largest mines. But the new ideology also brought costly investments such as a steel mill to process the scrap war had left behind. It now faces an uncertain future since Burma has no large known deposits of iron ore. Like so many of the new nations in Asia, Burma's imagination was captured by the dream of rapid industrialization before the facilities for a solid tax base, transportation, administration, and a sound agriculture had been achieved. A Marxian suspicion of private capital combined with a Burmese lack of entrepreneurial experience and traditional resentment of Chinese and Indian businessmen to inhibit economic recovery.

More disastrous was the decay in public morality left as a heritage of war and abetted by inflation and the disorganization of civil strife. In an early post-independence move the Burmese Government drastically cut salaries of senior officials to a fraction of the formerly munificent and prestigious sums they were paid under the British. For a man with the ascetic habits of ex-Premier U Nu, this worked no particular hardships. But innumerable politicians and officials with less abstemious tastes and with family responsibilities found themselves unable to support the standard of living to which they wanted to become accustomed. This proved true despite the fact that unlike Thailand, the Philippines, and other neighbors, Burma is a land where conspicuous consumption by officials is publicly frowned upon. Colonel Tun Sein, the dashing 240-pound new Army administrator of the Rangoon Corporation, caustically describes the modes of his civilian predecessors. "Socialism for those politicians was an excuse for accepting bribes from a property owner on promise to remove squatters from his place. Then, the same official turned around and collected bribes from the squatters to let them stay. People came to think socialism meant they could move onto anybody's property, including government sites and parks, and remain there however long they wished."

．　．　．　．　．

Government by the Military

The days that followed [the assumption of power by the military] were unlike anything Burma had experienced. The chronic hedging, bickering and shying from responsibility that had characterized rule by the politicians now was supplanted by swift and firm action. While naming only two military men to the Cabinet along with a large majority of civilians, the new Prime Minister placed officers in each Government agency whose function was critical. Colonel Kyi Win moved in to push agriculture and rural development. Another colonel, Chit Khaing, stepped in to the Directorate General of Labor, a favorite instrument for accumulating political influence during the previous administration. Colonel Ba Than took over information and psychological warfare. In all, roughly a score of officers hold key positions today—they have been put in next to or above the civilian heads of agencies. These colonels, a few lieutenant colonels, a squadron leader from the Air Force and a Navy captain, who average 38 years of age, meet weekly, and oftener in smaller groups, to hammer out operational problems. When they are confronted with a major policy issue it is referred to the Cabinet for decision.

Their first concern has been national security and a national house cleaning. Since November the campaign against the insurgents has been pushed with greater vigor than ever before, and with results. . . .

Political Innovations

Ordinary citizens throughout Burma are being enlisted in this campaign to re-establish order and responsible government in a way that recalls the methods of the late Philippine President Ramon Magsaysay. *"Warazein,"* meaning "lighting from the sky," has become the watchword for a nation-wide system of public informants. Telegrams are addressed to *"Warazein"* and telephone calls are made to this code name giving tips on both insurgents and public malefactors. In the hinterland, locked steel boxes controlled by the military have been set up where the villagers drop notes that have become an important source of intelligence as the people gain confidence in the Government's capacity and determination to protect them. Some 1600 politicians including seven members of Parliament have been jailed on charges of corruption and conniving with the insurgents, and the new administration is steadily finding more tainted officials as it screens strongholds of the former leaders.

Throughout the villages and larger towns, citizens are being formed into "Solidarity Councils," in which politicians, significantly, are barred from membership on executive committees. These public bodies serve as liaison between the people and the District Security Council wherein the military have joined with their opposite-number civilian officials to plan regional needs. The local "Solidarity Councils" provide supplies of firewood if it is short in the community; guard against flood threats; and organize village self-defense. Their motto is "courage" and their symbol is a lion. The members are being told: "We had ten bad years. Whatever government comes into power, be sure the councils remain." And there is the added admonition: "Remember, so long as the Union of Burma exists the Army will exist and be a watchdog for you. And we will not stand for a return to old conditions."

This mobilization of the Army of the people to overcome former political abuses and guard against allied gangster terrorism is matched by an intensive psychological warfare effort. Communists have been classed as "deep red," "red," "pink," and "pink-washed," and a strategy has been designed to deal with each category. Now a campaign is under way to inform the Burmese people of local Communist attacks upon Buddhism and the desecration of temples and pagodas recently recovered by the Army. . . .

The Burmese economy is coming in for an equally thorough overhaul, with the new emphasis upon practical and immediate results. Under the energetic direction of Brigadier Aung Gyi, specialized agencies of the Army are forcing improved performance. In a move that is speeding an exodus of Indian and Pakistani middlemen seventy per cent of the country's imports have been taken over by co-operatives, the Civil Supplies Board, Joint Venture Corporations, and other Government-controlled combines. Prices are being stabilized in part by limiting retailer markups, often to 10 per cent. Activities of foreign banks, particularly those backed by Red China, are being curbed by tighter supervision. The Electrical Supply Board is being reorganized, as is the administration of railways, docks, and inland water transport. Although selling its export rice in a buyers' market where the competition includes the United States Surplus Commodity Disposal Program, Burma's State Agricultural Marketing Board is moderately optimistic about disposing of last year's crop. But the Burmese have been reluctant to cut their prices to competitive levels since not only are such sales the chief source of foreign exchange but also the Government derives much of its internal revenue from the differential between the price paid the farmer and that received from exporting nearly two million tons of rice annually.

Among the more consequential new enterprises is the expanding role of the Defense Services Institute. In addition to maintaining commissary facilities for the armed forces, it operates a press, controls a large English-language newspaper, and owns Rangoon's biggest book store. DSI is now starting an egg and milk supply business, establishing stores where drugs can be sold at reasonable prices, and organizing the fishing industry. In keeping with the new Government's policy of cultivating ties with Israel a bi-national shipping venture, the Five Star Line, has been launched. The Institute has formed a partnership with *Solel Boneh,* the construction branch of the Israeli General Federation of Labor, to engage in large-scale building. The

Burmese Army's new agricultural resettlement projects in the under-populated and newly pacified delta are patterned on the Israeli pioneer communities, as will be the projected settlements of retired soldiers along the lands bordering China and India. The Israeli Army's education system is being taken as a model for giving young Burmese in uniform technical competence and enhancing their sense of national identity. Several hundred Burmese officers and technicians have studied within recent years in Israel and in June it was General Ne Win's destination on his first trip abroad as Premier. Burmese are impressed with the Israeli capacity for evolving a program which is essentially their own while accepting outside economic help and technical skills. They are equally attracted by Israel's blend of private initiative and socialism, which fits well with Burma's desire to evolve a society that avoids some of the features of uninhibited private capitalism they find unattractive.

The face lifting that is following the Army's advent into civilian administration is perhaps nowhere more dramatically presented than in the capital. Despite the gold-sheathed Shwe Dagon Pagoda and other equally delightful if less spectacular Buddhist shrines that adorn its hill- and lake-studded expanse, Rangoon had become as shoddy as any metropolis in Asia. Refugees had erected squatter slums of rusty tin, scraps of tenting and bits of boards. Here filth bred disease and trouble. Garbage accumulated in huge heaps on the streets as city drivers sold their gasoline instead of hauling refuse and contractors responsible for collection bribed officials to avoid performance. In heavy rains garbage-blocked gutters became gushing fountains. Mangy dogs roamed the streets and created a health hazard while the politicians refused to destroy them because of Buddhist scruples against taking life, and argued about whether male and female dogs should be resettled on separate islands. Like the streets, where holes were left unfilled, the municipal water supply was miserably maintained.

Today the campaign to "clean Rangoon with our sweat" has brought a transformation. The streets are clean and being rapidly repaired. Fifty thousand dogs have been disposed of and more than 10,000 crows. Most noticeable has been elimination of the unsightly slums. When the new Army administrators took office they were determined to at least rid the capital of its squatters. Three new satellite cities were surveyed on the rice paddies outside of Rangoon. Within four months nearly 150 miles of streets and roads were built, water lines laid to each block and even some street lights erected. Each squatter family was registered, assigned a lot in the new cities and given a deadline for moving out of Rangoon. The Army insured that private trucks were available for hire at a reasonable price to move squatters. Train loads of bamboo, boards, and roofing materials were shipped in and sold at cost. Flooding in some new communities is still a problem—last month I saw the monsoon bring six inches of rain in one 48-hour period. But now that they are in possession of a lot with a 30-year lease and hopes for a 90-year renewal, many families once living in miserable shacks have built themselves two-story homes. In all, 170,000 squatters have been moved out of Rangoon and those remaining are scheduled for transfer by autumn.

It is in trying to initiate change through the civil service that the Army encounters a more obstinate problem. Schooled originally in the rigid British tradition of exemplary, though leisurely, administration these career services suffered sadly at the hands of the officials. But a considerable number of able Burmese, who scorned the post-independence crop of politicians, remained in the service. Not all or even the ablest are ready overnight to set aside their accumulated status and experience and gladly accept dictation from younger Army officers, despite the inadequacy of the bureaucracy's performance on many counts. Like almost every underdeveloped country in Asia, Burma has a government structure designed for maintaining performance at near present levels, rather than engineering speedy progress. And Burma's new Army leaders have yet to think through this problem and come up with workable answers. They seem to sense, as do a few aware officials elsewhere, that the peasant's ways, which must be altered so radically to permit serious development, cannot be changed by ramming suggestions at him through the bureaucracy. While Burma has an abundance of plans for the future the instruments that promise fulfillment in the crucial area of revolutionizing agriculture are not in evidence.

Revolutionaries in Uniform

The Burmese military who are engineering these vital changes today consider themselves something special—a revolutionary army. And this quality has been critical for their efforts toward preserving the Union of Burma during its early years. The movement from which present leadership among the military emerged had its origins chiefly in the University of Rangoon during the 1930's. There the most politically conscious youth of Burma were nurtured on an intense nationalism that demanded independence and a modern recreation of ancient cultural traditions that had been submerged when the British overran the Kingdom of Ava at Mandalay in the late 19th century. The ideology of these young people was confused—they studied Fabian socialism and other versions of Marxism, were impressed by Mussolini and Hitler, and hungered for an Asian political rebirth.

. . . . .

The Army's role in the bitter struggle for national survival despite civil war has been crucial. As brother fought brother in the successive insurgent unheavals, the Army's unique capacity to foster a loyalty superseding that of the family made it the effective competitor of the Communists for such dedicated devotion to a larger nonpersonal goal. Officers and men both tended to feel themselves part of an elite largely uncontaminated by the corruption of the civilian politicians. Like the military establishments of some other new nations, the Burmese Army has had difficulty in harmoniously amalgamating officers of differing backgrounds. Those who retreated with the British to India during 1942 as part of Burma's regular military forces, which were weighted heavily with minority Karens, Shans, etc., seem to have been shunted aside in favor of men who emerged from the Burmese revolutionary tradition. And resentments generated by the issue of the political status of the minorities, now incorporated into separate States of the Union encouraged some critical defections when the insurgent revolt was at its height. But through it all the Army repeatedly has been toughened, tested, and now increasingly unified.

The roughly one hundred thousand officers and men in the Defense Services of the Union of Burma, aside from twenty thousand in the police, are fast developing the traditions of a professional corps. Although the Navy and Air Force are judged vital services, primary emphasis is upon the Army with better than thirty regular battalions; the first fully constituted division is now being raised. It is a volunteer service army where men enlist to serve for ten years and at present those who have completed their tour are not readily released because "the country needs them." Today the private soldier, who receives the equivalent of twelve dollars monthly plus free rations, quarters, medical care, uniform, etc., is achieving a steadily rising status in Burmese life, in contrast to his prewar low estate. The new military academy just graduated its first class of thirty-four officers. But an officers training school continues to bring in men from the ranks and civilian life. Field grade officers must graduate from the Staff College. A National Defense College is now being organized where strategic problems will be explored. While Burma manufactures its own small arms, ammunition, etc., it still depends substantially upon outside sources for heavy equipment, including some provided quietly by the United States. With an annual defense budget of almost one hundred million to be spent in a land with some twenty million citizens whose economy is primarily agricultural, the Defense Services inevitably affect the lives of Burmese in more than the military sphere.

Political Goals

. . . . .

Once they are out of political office the determined and patriotic-minded young Army leaders can be expected to continue to exert a far greater influence in civilian affairs than before. The phrase heard most often is that they will "monitor" the civilian politicians to protect the interests of the people and the nation. This still requires that the Army set itself up as judge of events and raises the inevitable question as to whether the military will continue to merit public confidence in their assumption of this role. The answer will depend primarily on whether the Army remains united and uncorrupted. To escape both of the erosions which have undermined the military rule in the public esteem of neighboring Thailand and Indonesia, the Burmese Army officers will need to remain a "priesthood unto themselves." They cannot afford to permit their members to become involved with contending political factions, each seeking to enhance its opportunities for gaining advantages by cultivating the military. It will also be necessary for the Army to continue to enlarge its program of giving officers and men the decent housing and other facilities that insure their maintenance of equal status with other leading groups in the society. But most decisive of all will be the extent to which the Burmese military leaders are enabled to broaden and deepen their own education so as to "see themselves in perspective" and cope effectively with the innumerable problems confronting the Union.

. . . . .

Church

68 · THE POLITICS OF RELIGION

Lyman Jay Gould

The inclusion of organized religious groups among the mobilizers of political power is an analytic necessity beset by emotional pitfalls. To reject the conclusion that spiritual societies have secular interests demanding political action is to deny the obvious. At the cost of much blood and pain, it has been demonstrated vividly throughout history that the distinction between that which is Caesar's and that which is God's is at best artificial. The advent of modern representative government has not eliminated church participation in politics, but rather has succeeded in altering, and even disguising, its nature. Yet any discussion of the topic draws what are almost conditioned responses in terms of intensity and subjectivity. Some people, carrying the folksy warning about "politics and religion" *ad absurdum,* deny the existence of this political phenomenon altogether. Others, while accepting the fact, immediately translate a discussion of church politics into a discussion of church dogma, as for example, when they convert anti-clericalism into anti-Catholicism. Finally, even if they avoid these extremes, many approach the subject hobbled by prejudices, articulated or otherwise. Nevertheless, despite the difficulties, the politics of religion must be recognized as a fact.

A comprehensive survey of the political church in all lands would be the best and safest course, but since such a survey would require a separate volume, if not several volumes, the approach here is limited to the American and Latin (more particularly Spanish and Spanish American) experiences.

The Latin recognizes, with no difficulty at all, the fact of political activism by organized religious bodies. Born into a society where it is an integral circumstance of everyday political life, he is constantly exposed to it, expects it, and reacts to it. The church militant in politics is merely another weight in the national power scales. However, it is important to note two basic facts. To the Latin, church is taken to mean the Roman Catholic Church. Other denominations, struggling as they are to maintain their precarious foothold in the society, are too weak to pretend to a political role. If they appear on the scene at all it is as pawns in the larger contest between the clerics and the anti-clerics. Thus the Protestant groups are of significance only as symbols of a drive for religious toleration, religious freedom or both. More extreme was the case of Mexico in the 1920's with the creation of a short-lived "National" Catholic Church (*La Iglesia Ortodoxa Católica Apostólica Mexicana*). Here the government encouraged the schismatic group as a countermeasure in its struggle with the Roman Catholic Church.

Secondly, given this focus upon the activities of the Roman Catholic Church, it must not be assumed to be a monolithic body pursuing identical policies and programs in all Latin countries. Though there is, of course, agreement as to fundamentals, this by no means precludes adjustments to each particular national situation. What may be tactically or strategically feasible in one country may be political suicide in another. Thus the Church in Spain is able to demand, and receive, a privileged status, while the Church in Mexico, living under the shadow of a violently anti-clerical constitution, is prepared to settle for the position of a "free church in a free society." Furthermore, like any body politic, its attitudes are shaped and influenced by the composition of its members. Differences in education and outlook inevitably produce differences, however great or minute, in political orientation as well.

Spanish history has been witness to a symbiotic relationship between church and state. The two have been so intertwined as to defy easy separation. The intense religiosity of the Spaniard, the crusading fervor engendered by the many centuries of the *Reconquista* (reconquest of Spain from the Moors), and the mutually beneficial support given the one by the other, made the Roman Catholic Church in Spain more than merely the spiritual arm of the secular state. The result, as Clarence Haring has put it, was an "indissoluble union of the altar and the throne." This congruence of interest accompanied the Spaniard as he colonized and administered his New World domain. The clergy served in the colonial government, provided needed social services (schools, hospitals, orphanages, etc.), and, in general, were a primary bulwark of the crown. In return it received a monopoly in regard to spiritual matters and a guarantee of privileges. Yet the association was not one of actual peers, for the *real patronato de las*

Indias (royal patronage of the Indies) allowed the crown a control of ecclesiastical affairs not equalled in other Catholic lands. Through the *patronato,* the crown not only acquired the "right of presentation" (nomination to church office) but also control over the number and migration of the clergy to the New World, as well as church construction, ecclesiastical taxation, the publication and dissemination of Papal bulls and briefs, and, to some extent, church discipline. Thus the union of church and state in the Americas, although intimate, was ordered in such a way as to leave ultimate authority residing in the crown. This relationship, both in Spain and in Spanish America, was not without its frictions, but in the final analysis the differences were family differences.

This politico-religious balance, so carefully nurtured and developed over the centuries, was rudely disturbed by the Napoleonic assault upon Spain. In the New World this event proved to be the catalyst that precipitated the independence movements, while in Spain it unleashed the forces of liberalism. In both instances, one end product was a new political posture for the Roman Catholic Church. No longer was it assured the unqualified support and protection of the state in its activities. The Church found itself on the defensive in that it now had to protect its power, position, and prestige from question and challenge by an ever burgeoning anti-clerical faction. Unlike the situation in the Reformation, the threat poised was essentially a secular one. Thus the Roman Catholic Church responded, not with the intellectual and moral armament that had characterized the Counter-Reformation, but in a purely secular fashion. It plunged headlong into the national political fray in the hopes of preserving the *status quo.*

The issues in conflict were many, varying in intensity, time and nature from country to country. Of basic concern was the legal and constitutional status to be afforded the Roman Catholic Church. Was it to be accorded the prerogatives of an established religion, or was it to exist in a forced independence created by the separation of church and state? Corollary to this was the question of religious dissent. Just how much freedom would and could be allowed the heretic and the apostate? Another problem, even where the Church retained a privileged status, was that of its wealth and property. The bequests of the faithful, its ability to meet the "banking" needs of those seeking liquid capital (particularly in colonial America), and other factors had made of the Roman Catholic Church a sizable landowner and a financial power. The anti-cleric not only resented this accumulation but viewed the increase of land in *manos muertos* (mortmain) as a barrier to national economic development. In the process the anti-cleric lost sight of the fact that the church needed at least some of these riches in order to pay for its charitable, educational, and social operations.

Peripheral but crucial were the issues of the number of clergy and of monasticism. In a sense these two (and the question of abolishing the Inquisition) were legacies from an earlier period. The presence of an excessive number of clerics and religious orders had drawn hostile reactions prior to the nineteenth century. Thus, with the advent of significant anti-clericalism, they easily became centers of controversy and criticism. Finally, where separation or restricted privilege gained in ascendancy, the Church has fought a rear-guard battle over such matters as secularized cemeteries, civil marriage, divorce, and education. These matters have become the pivotal issues of the twentieth century. Monasticism, Church wealth, religious freedom, and even separation, have been, except possibly in Spain, for the most part resolved, and thus, are fading as vital issues from the political front. But the questions of morals and education remain pertinent and prominent as it is in these matters that the Roman Catholic Church still demands recognition and authority.

Not all the issues have arisen in all the countries, nor have they arisen at the same time. Adjustments in the existing politico-religious structure have been made relatively peacefully in some nations, whereas in others they have been accompanied by extensive violence. The nature of the adjustments has varied as have the emotional reactions thereto. Yet one factor remains constant throughout. The Roman Catholic Church has attempted to mobilize political power in order to preserve and protect what it considers to be its vested interest. This mobilization of political power has ranged from the crude and simple device of raising and leading its adherents in the field, e.g., the *curas guerrilleros* (fighting priests) of the Carlist Wars in Spain (1833-1840; 1870-1876), to the more sophisticated tactics of a pressure group operating through its devout followers.

The Church, while powerful, could not stand alone. Thus political necessity begot political alliances. These were found, where possible, with other power groups, namely the landed aristocracy and the military, who also possessed a vested interest in the *status quo*. In the process, the Church, to a great degree, exchanged social action for social reaction. Interestingly enough, since the mass of the populace was politically impotent, the nineteenth century anti-cleric was also drawn from the same power groups to the extent that some of their number were influenced by the tenets of liberalism. In fact, except to a small rising industrial class, liberalism came to mean republicanism and anti-clericalism; and for some the latter was not only a shibboleth but the *raison d'être* for their liberalism.

The contemporary Hispanic world still encounters a political church. Yet, except for Spain, where the hierarchy seem intent upon pursuing a reactionary road, there has occurred a transformation, however subtle and gradual, in its policies and tactics. The original political alliance of Church, landed aristocracy, and military no longer stands firm and unbroken. Like the younger army officers, the clergy in many Latin lands have become quite sensitive to the rising social revolution. Taking their cue from the social encyclicals of Pope Leo XIII (*Rerum Novarum*) and Pope Pius XI (*Quadragesimo Anno*), they have abandoned the *status quo* for a voice, and perhaps even leadership, in the tide of change. This action has been facilitated by a partial accommodation to the legal status produced by nineteenth century anti-clericalism. That is to say, apart from the questions of morals and education, such issues, separation of church and state, religious freedom, monasticism, etc., no longer rouse fervid political action. Finally while still a mobilizer of political power, the Roman Catholic Church must now share the political arena with a great many more groups. The traditional power blocs of church, military, and landed aristocracy have been joined by the party, industrial and agricultural labor, and the middle class. One immediate result has been a diminution of the relative strength of the Roman Catholic Church vis-à-vis the total political complex. However, if for no other than symbolic and prestige reasons, the Roman Catholic Church is still a force to be reckoned with in Latin politics.

Any analysis of the "church in politics" in the United States encounters the command of the First Amendment to the Constitution (made applicable to the states by its incorporation into the Fourteenth Amendment) that "Congress shall make no law respecting an establishment of religion." As interpreted by the Supreme Court:

> Neither a state nor the Federal Government can, openly or secretly, participate in the affairs of any religious organizations or groups and *vice versa*. In the words of Jefferson, the clause against establish-

ment of religion by law was intended to erect "a wall of separation between Church and State."

This clause reflects the needs of a pluralistic society founded by religious dissenters. To the extent that it eradicates competition among religious groups for the favor of the state, it also serves as an essential bulwark to the guarantee of religious freedom. As such it has passed into American constitutional tradition and political mythology. This should not be taken to mean that Americans have succeeded in achieving a purely secular brand of politics, totally divorced from religious influences. On the contrary, organized religion has been quite active and vocal, often unintentionally breaching the wall of separation under the guise of insuring that the state be not hostile to religion.

The First Amendment has spared Americans divisive controversy over established religion, the principle of religious freedom, and many of the other issues that have plagued the Latin for more than a century. Furthermore, taken as an article of faith, it has set loose ground rules which limit the play of church politics. Thus, there have been no formal affiliations between political parties and organized religions, nor are candidates advanced as the standard bearers of this or that religious group. But the limitation has gone only this far and no further. Political parties, through the "balanced ticket" and the platform, appeal to the voter on religious grounds. The basic assumptions underlying the democratic process itself assure participation to all groups and all interests. It is through this door that religion enters American politics and the churches become mobilizers of political power.

Church political activism is not a recent phenomenon in the United States. One can, by scanning American history, find such pertinent examples as the role played by Protestant groups (particularly missionary interests) in American imperialism; the labors of the Methodist, Baptist, and Presbyterian churches in securing prohibition; the activities of members of the Roman Catholic hierarchy on behalf of Irish independence, and, more recently, the work of Jewish rabbis in the Zionist cause. Contemporary American politics experience church influence in such matters as education (released time, religious education, school buses, etc.), divorce laws, Sunday Observance laws, birth control, and censorship. Since under our Federal system these issues are handled mainly by the state police power (power to regulate for the health, safety, welfare, and morals of the citizens), there is a concentration of church effort at the state and local level. However, the focus can shift to the national forum if the Federal government is the agency concerned, as, for example, in the case of dissemination of birth control material and information to under-developed nations. The political tactics of the churches are neither crass nor clumsy. Basically, they operate either indirectly by influencing their communicants as voters, or directly as pressure groups, appealing to the legislative and executive branches of the government. Since all groups—Protestant, Catholic, and Jewish—participate, they are obviously most powerful when united as to objectives. They have available to them the pulpit and the religious press. Their strength emanates from their position in the community, and, by the same token, is limited thereby. Their status and prestige afford them leadership and guarantee that they will be heard. However, this initial advantage may be weakened or lost if the clergy should trespass into areas not normally associated with their office. In other words, the churches are most effective politically when engaged in moral and social questions, and least effective when they wander afield. One might note that education falls into a "twilight zone," since the secular tradition in American public education acts as a counterweight to the belief held by many that spiritual values are essential to the children's development.

The author is a member of a community action group that draws part of its strength from the support given it by the churches. An act of discrimination against a Negro college student by a local motel owner precipitated a desire to secure the passage of a state public accommodations law and to form an organization that would concern itself with community relations, more particularly those involving minority groups. A Committee on Community Relations was formed, having on its Executive Committee, among others, a Congregational minister, a Presbyterian minister, and a Catholic priest. The parent committee includes, in its membership, representatives of all the religious groups in the city. The presence of the clergy not only eased matters before the legislature (although it was not crucial since the temper of the state was such that the bill met with no outward opposition) but also provided an avenue of communication to community leaders. Furthermore, the committee has discovered that the existing church congregations are effective vehicles for mobilizing public opinion. This experience, however microscopic, is illustrative of many similar projects occurring daily across the nation. While meeting resistance within their own ranks and congregations to political activity, the churches nevertheless pursue such a course, perhaps of necessity, when the state undertakes or is in a position to regulate that which the religious groups consider vital.

69 · CONSTITUTIONAL STATUS: IRELAND—UNITED STATES—MEXICO

CONSTITUTION OF IRELAND

In the Name of the Most Holy Trinity, from whom is all authority and to Whom, as our final end, all actions both of men and States must be referred.

We, the people of Eire,

Humbly acknowledging all our obligations to our Divine Lord, Jesus Christ, Who sustained our fathers through centuries of trial,

Gratefully remembering their heroic and unremitting struggle to regain the rightful independence of our Nation,

And seeking to promote the common good, with due observance of Prudence, Justice and Charity, so that the dignity and freedom of the individual may be assured, true social order attained, the unity of our country restored, and concord established with other nations,

Do hereby adopt, enact, and give to ourselves this Constitution.

· · · · ·

Article 6

1. All powers of government, legislative, executive and judicial, derive, under God, from the people, whose right it is to designate the rulers of the State and, in final appeal, to decide all questions of national policy, according to the requirements of the common good.

· · · · ·

THE FAMILY

Article 41

1. 1° The State recognizes the Family as the natural primary and fundamental unit group of Society, and as a moral institution possess-

ing inalienable and imprescriptible rights, antecedent and superior to all positive law.

2° The State, therefore, guarantees to protect the Family in its constitution and authority, as the necessary basis of social order and as indispensable to the welfare of the Nation and the State.

2. 1° In particular, the State recognizes that by her life within the home, woman gives to the State a support without which the common good cannot be achieved.

2° The State shall, therefore, endeavour to ensure that mothers shall not be obliged by economic necessity to engage in labour to the neglect of their duties in the home.

3. 1° The State pledges itself to guard with special care the institution of Marriage, on which the Family is founded, and to protect it against attack.

2° No law shall be enacted providing for the grant of a dissolution of marriage.

3° No person whose marriage has been dissolved under the civil law of any other State but is a subsisting valid marriage under the law for the time being in force within the jurisdiction of the Government and Parliament established by this Constitution shall be capable of contracting a valid marriage within that jurisdiction during the lifetime of the other party to the marriage so dissolved.

RELIGION

Article 44

1. 1° The State acknowledges that the homage of public worship is due to Almighty God. It shall hold His Name in reverence, and shall respect and honour religion.

2° The State recognizes the special position of the Holy Catholic Apostolic and Roman Church as the guardian of the Faith professed by the great majority of the citizens.

3° The State also recognizes the Church of Ireland, the Presbyterian Church in Ireland, the Methodist Church in Ireland, the Religious Society of Friends in Ireland, as well as the Jewish Congregations and the other religious denominations existing in Ireland at the date of the coming into operation of this Constitution.

2. 1° Freedom of conscience and the free profession and practice of religion are, subject to public order and morality, guaranteed to every citizen.

2° The State guarantees not to endow any religion.

3° The State shall not impose any disabilities or make any discrimination on the ground of religious profession, belief or status.

4° Legislation providing State aid for schools shall not discriminate between schools under the management of different religious denominations, nor be such as to affect prejudicially the right of any child to attend a school receiving public money without attending religious instruction at that school.

5° Every religious denomination shall have the right to manage its own affairs, own, acquire and administer property, movable and immovable, and maintain institutions for religious or charitable purposes.

6° The property of any religious denomination or any educational institution shall not be diverted save for necessary works of public utility and on payment of compensation.

THE CONSTITUTION OF THE UNITED STATES

Amendment I
Congress shall make no law respecting an establishment of religion, or prohibiting the free exercise thereof. . . .

EVERSON V. BOARD OF EDUCATION *

Mr. Justice Black delivered the opinion of the Court. . . .

The "establishment of religion" clause of the First Amendment means at least this: Neither a state nor the Federal Government can set up a church. Neither can pass laws which aid one religion, aid all religions, or prefer one religion over another. Neither can force nor influence a person to go to or remain away from church against his will or force him to profess a belief or disbelief in any religion. No person can be punished for entertaining or professing religious beliefs or disbeliefs, for church attendance or non-attendance. No tax in any amount, large or small, can be levied to support any religious activities or institutions, whatever they may be called, or whatever form they may adopt to teach or practice religion. Neither a state nor the Federal Government can, openly or secretly, participate in the affairs of any religious organizations or groups and vice versa. In the words of Jefferson, the clause against establishment of religion by law was intended to erect "a wall of separation between Church and State."

* 330 US 1, 15-16.

POLITICAL CONSTITUTION
OF THE UNITED MEXICAN STATES

Article 3

The education that the State—Federation, States, Municipalities—imparts shall tend to develop harmoniously all the faculties of the human being and shall encourage in him, at the same time, love of country and the consciousness of international solidarity, independence, and justice.

I. Freedom of belief being guaranteed by Article 24, the criterion that shall orient said education shall be maintained completely free from any religious doctrine and, based on the results of scientific progress, shall struggle against ignorance and its effects, servitudes, fanaticisms, and prejudices. . . .

IV. Religious corporations, ministers of faiths, stock companies which exclusively or predominantly engage in educational activities, and associations or societies connected with the propagation of any religious creed, shall not intervene in any form in institutions in which is imparted primary, secondary, or normal education, and in that destined for workers and peasants.

Article 5

. . . The State cannot permit the execution of any contract, pact, or agreement having as its object the diminution, loss, or irrevocable sacrifice of the liberty of man, whether for reason of occupation, education, or religious vow. Therefore, the law does not permit the establishment of monastic orders, whatever the denomination or ostensible purpose of their establishment.

Article 24

Every man is free to profess the religious belief which is most pleasing to him and to practice the ceremonies, devotions or observances of the respective creed, in places of public worship or in his private residence, provided they do not constitute a crime or misdemeanor punishable by law.

Every religious act of public worship must be performed strictly within the places of worship which shall always be under the supervision of the authorities.

Article 27

. . . Legal capacity to acquire ownership of lands and waters of the nation shall be governed by the following prescriptions:

. . . . .

II. Religious associations known as churches, whatever their creed, shall in no case have legal capacity to acquire, possess, or administer real property, or capital invested therein; all such property held at present, directly or through an intermediary, shall revert to the Nation, the people having the right to denounce property so held. Presumptive evidence shall be considered sufficient to declare the denunciation well-founded. The places of public worship are the property of the Nation, as represented by the Federal Government, who shall determine which of them should continue in that capacity. The bishoprics, rectories, seminaries, asylums or schools of religious associations, convents, or any other building, built or destined for the administration, propagation, or teaching of a religious creed, shall pass immediately, as a matter of law, to the direct domain of the Nation, to be devoted exclusively to the public services of the Federation or of the States within their respective jurisdictions. All places of public worship hereafter erected shall be the property of the Nation;

III. Public or private charitable institutions, which have as their aim the aid of the needy, scientific research, the diffusion of knowledge, the mutual aid of their members, or any other lawful purpose, shall not acquire more real property than what is indispensable to their immediate purpose or directly intended thereto; but they can acquire, hold, and administer capital invested in real property, provided the terms of the investment do not exceed ten years. In no case shall institutions of this character be under the patronage, direction, administration, charge, or supervision of religious corporations or institutions, nor of ministers of religious sects, or similar persons, even though the former and the latter may not be exercising their ministry.

Article 130

The federal Powers shall exercise the supervision required by law in matters relating to religious denominations and external discipline. Other authorities shall act as auxiliaries of the Federation.

The Congress cannot enact laws establishing or prohibiting any religion.

Marriage is a civil contract. This and other acts of a civil nature concerning persons are within the exclusive competence of the civil officials and authorities, in the manner prescribed by law, and shall have the force and effect defined by said law.

The simple promise to tell the truth and to fulfill obligations that are contracted binds the one who so promises, and in the event of failure to do so, he shall be subject to the penalties prescribed by law.

The law does not recognize any personality in religious groups called churches.

The ministers of religious sects shall be considered as persons who exercise a profession, and shall be directly subject to the laws enacted on such matters.

Only the legislatures of the States shall have the power to determine the maximum number of ministers of religious sects necessary for local needs.

To practice the ministry of any sect in the United Mexican States, it is necessary to be a Mexican by birth.

The ministers of religious sects may never, in a public or private meeting constituting an assembly, or in acts of worship or religious propaganda, criticize the fundamental laws of the country, the authorities in particular, or the Government in general; they shall not have an active or a passive vote, or the right to form associations for political purposes.

Permission to dedicate new places of worship open to the public must be obtained from the Secretariat of Government, with prior consent of the government of the State. There must be in every place of public worship a representative who is responsible to the authorities for compliance with the laws on religious discipline, in said place of worship, and for the objects pertaining to the worship.

The representative of each place of worship, in conjunction with ten other residents of the neighborhood, shall immediately inform the municipal authority as to who is the person in charge of the place of worship in question. Any change must be reported by the departing minister in person, accompanied by the new incumbent and ten other residents of the neighborhood. The municipal authority, under penalty of removal from office and a fine of up to one thousand *pesos* for each offense, shall see that this provision is complied with; under the same penalty, he shall keep one registry book of the places of worship, and another of the representatives in charge. The municipal authority shall give notice to the Secretariat of Government, through the Governor of the State, of every permit to open a new place of worship, or of any change in a representative in charge. Donations in the form of movable objects shall be held in the interior of places of worship.

No privilege shall be granted, or for any reason confirmed, or any other step taken which has as its purpose to give validity in the official course of studies to studies pursued in establishments devoted to the professional instruction of ministers of religions. The authority who violates this provision shall be criminally responsible and the privilege or step referred to shall be void and shall thereby cause the nullification of the professional degree for the attainment of which the violation of this provision was made.

Periodical publications of a religious character, whether they be such because of their program, title, or merely because of their general tendencies, may not comment on national political matters, or report on acts of the authorities of the country or of private persons directly related to the functioning of public institutions.

The formation of all kinds of political groups, the name of which contains any word or indication whatsoever that connect it with any religious denomination, is strictly prohibited. Meetings of a political character may not be held in places of worship.

A minister of any denomination may not himself, or through an intermediary, inherit or receive by any title any real property occupied by any association for religious propaganda, or for religious or charitable purposes. Ministers of denominations are legally incapacitated to be testamentary heirs of ministers of the same denominations, or of any private person who is not related to them within the fourth degree.

The acquisition by private parties of personal or real property owned by the clergy or by religious associations shall be governed by Article 27 of this Constitution.

Trials for violation of the above provisions shall never be heard before a jury.

70 · THE ATTITUDE OF THE CHURCHES
TO POLITICS *

Canon H. M. Waddams

In 1958 the Church of England, as the national Church, neither
retains nor claims the exclusive voice in national affairs which at one
time seemed to be hers by right. The political presuppositions which
lie behind the conception of a national Church and the identification
of Church and Nation have long ago been discarded, and the possession of seats in the Upper House by certain diocesan Bishops of the
established Church is no more than a hangover from a former time,
however useful it may be.

· · · · ·

The Free Churches

The Free Churches have moved a long way from the position
which they held in politics at the beginning of the present century.
They have had a strong and close link with the Labour Party, as is
well known. This link still exists though it has been much changed
and weakened. There is little doubt that much of the change has been
the result of the weakening of Free Church religious influence in the
country as a whole, a development which is paralleled in the established Church. The time when the nonconformist conscience had an
immediately powerful effect on politics has passed, though in certain
fields it still carries influence and helps to form the opinions of Christians on certain subjects, such as gambling.

The attitude of Free Church people to politics has been affected by
two main developments. The first affects other Christians too, but
is especially applicable to them, namely, the change in the aims of
politicians themselves. There were at the beginning of the century
fearful wrongs to be righted, and frightful conditions of housing and
poverty to be overcome. The moral impetus of the reformers had the
full support of the Free Churches and was for many identified first

* H. M. Waddams, "The Attitude of the Churches to Politics," *The Political
Quarterly*, 30 (January-March, 1959), 34, 36-43. Reprinted by permission of the
editors of *The Political Quarterly*. The footnotes in the original version are
omitted here.

with the Liberal and later with the Labour Party. There are still wrongs to be righted and conditions to be improved, but in 1958 there is no party which does not loudly proclaim its intention to deal with these shortcomings. This has brought a radical change, for, instead of a simple question of who is on the side of right, a much more difficult question is posed, namely, whether the political parties are honest in their professions, and, still more difficult, which of the parties is most competent to put its professed aims into effect. Thus, instead of being a moral issue, the question becomes technical in the political sense, and when this happens there can be as many differences of opinion among Christians as among any other section of the population.

The Declining Use of Moral Judgment

It is at this point that the main change of attitude towards politics on the part of Christians can be seen. In one sense it might be claimed that the nonconformist conscience has won its victory. The aims of the political parties are all highly moral. It would be unthinkable for them to be anything else. Christian principles of social and international life are accepted by all.

There are some difficult spheres, such as marriage, where the state and Christian opinion are not always at one. But, even here, the state has not been able or willing to go further than it thought could be justified by appealing to high moral principle. There has been no attempt to escape from such principles. The same thing is seen in the argument over the question of legislation affecting homosexual practices. The difference of opinion is confined to the question as to the most effective method of dealing with the problem: it is not a dispute between a Christian and non-Christian point of view.

The second development affecting Free Church attitudes to politics has been the radical change in the relations of the Free Churches to the established Church in England. (In all these matters the Church of Scotland occupies a position of its own which does not altogether fall within the generalisations. But by and large it has been influenced by the same changes of atmosphere.) At the beginning of the century there was bitter feeling against the Church of England on the part of the Free Churches, especially over the subject of education, in which the established Church was thought to be exercising an unfair and discriminatory monopoly. Free Church opinion, therefore, often identified itself with the party (in this case the Liberals) which was prepared to right what they thought to be a wrong. Since that time, however, although echoes of the struggle are still heard, the introduction of agreed syllabuses and other compromises has removed most of the bitterness. In almost all fields there is now co-operation in place of rivalry.

There would seem to be three more or less distinct areas of opinion among Christians towards politics and policy. There is, first, the attitude of the Bishops in the House of Lords to political questions of the day; secondly, the outlook of those Church representatives who work in the headquarter offices of their Churches or who play a part in common consultation on representative bodies of the British Council of Churches; thirdly, a mass of Church lay and clerical opinion in the country as a whole.

The Nonconformist Conscience

Let us take the third division first. It is difficult to make any useful comments about the attitude of the laity in general, as Christians. Their views reflect the views of the country as a whole, though among them there may be a higher sense of responsibility in those who are politically conscious. It would seem probable that members of the Free Churches contain a higher proportion of Christians who consciously try to approach politics from a Christian point of view. This is due to several factors, some of which have already been noticed. The nonconformist conscience has been a political force in the fairly recent past and is not forgotten everywhere. But there is also the factor that the Free Churches are better organised than the Church of England for serious study purposes since their structures are simpler and are more concentrated under London headquarters.

Several of the Free Churches have their own departments for social responsibility, or similar subjects, whose purpose is to try to discover the duty of the Christian citizen in public life in applying his faith to industry or politics. These departments provide study material for local groups, who are thus encouraged to take a lively interest in political events.

The socially conscious and intelligent Christians have all some time ago reached a common mind as to the need for making a specifically Christian contribution to the policy of their country in internal and in external affairs. This attitude is summarised in a short extract from the Report of the relevant Committee of the 1958 Lambeth Conference of Anglican Bishops from all over the world: "The Christian will be seeking to do God's will, and to be loyal to his vocation, not only in religious activities, but in the doing of the job in which he earns his livelihood during the week. That is an essential expression of his share of the priestly ministry of the whole body. Not everything in the Christian life is specifically and technically religious; but for the Christian nothing can ever be merely secular."

"Technical" Problems Outside the Church's Jurisdiction

This quotation brings out another characteristic of the present attitude, namely, the importance of the individual member of the Christian Church putting into practice his Christian principles in the sphere in which he himself is expert. And the equally important negative corollary that it is not the business of ecclesiastics or of ecclesiastical assemblies to try to deal with the technical problems of any particular field. Principles must be stated without trespassing on technical problems, whether of diplomacy or of politics. It is true that there are some ministers and clergymen who play an active part in one or the other of the political parties, but the majority opinion in the Churches thinks it unseemly from a Christian point of view for a minister of religion to adopt a party line, since it is probable that, if he does so, he will not be able to minister effectively to those members of his flock who belong to other parties.

But there seems to be little cynicism in the Christian attitude towards the parties. Most politically conscious Christians feel it incumbent upon them to exercise their votes and to exhibit a sense of responsibility in the field of civic life.

In the spread of serious discussion about social and international topics the emphasis is put upon a Christian's duty to make his influence felt in these affairs. It is a matter for regret that recent developments in local government tend to reproduce national party lines. Such developments make it more difficult for those with responsible positions in local Churches to take any leading part in local government without becoming identified with one of the main political parties.

Organised Co-operation Among the Churches

The second area of interest is that represented by the Brtish Council of Churches and its departments, and similar Councils and committees of the constituent Churches themselves. Over a wide field the non-Roman Churches have come together in practical work and consultation, chiefly through the British Council of Churches, formed in 1942. Here representatives of the various Churches meet to consider together matters of public importance in which Christian interests or principles are involved. Its various departments cover the main fields of such interest, namely, education, social responsibility, international affairs, and aid to refugees and the needy. The members of the departments come from the denominational circles which are wrestling with the same problems from their narrower point of view.

These departments have a double duty. On the one hand, they must try to formulate in a coherent manner the views of the better informed Christians on the topics under discussion; and on the other they must stimulate thought and study on these matters among the rank and file of Christians. Their action therefore provides some sort of link between the ordinary lay person and the heads and ruling Councils of the Churches through a two-way traffic. One of the activities is frankly educational, stimulating Christians to take an intelligent interest and to play their part in the life of their country by the light of their faith.

. . . . .

The Christian Approach to Politics

Christians, of course, differ widely on many political problems and are not encouraged to think that there is one Christian programme which ought to be adopted by all. There is even difference on moral problems as was shown by the variety of the speeches of the Bishops in the House of Lords on the subject of capital punishment. But the work of the Christian Social Movement of the last century, carried on in this by such men as Scott Holland, Gore, and William Temple, has worked a great change in the Christian outlook on politics. The main principles for which these men fought are now generally accepted, and may be summarised in the words of Archbishop William Temple, who defined the lines on which a Christian approach to political problems should be based: "(1) the claims of sympathy for those who suffer; (2) the educational influence of the social and economic system; (3) the challenge offered to our existing system in the name of justice; (4) the duty of conformity to the 'Natural Order' in which is to be found the purpose of God."

This quotation may perhaps be supplemented by a quotation from a recent article by the present Archbishop of Canterbury, Dr. Geoffrey

Fisher: "It must, however, never be forgotten that Christians and Christian statesmen do not make the conditions in which they work nor have they the power always (or often) to do just what they would of themselves wish to do. We can only try to make the best out of our conditions, recognizing the limitations imposed on our freedom of action by the facts or by the obstinacies of other men or by conflicting responsibilities. For this reason Christians will always be patient with one another since, in the application of Christian principles to the raw and sinful facts of the world, there is a large room left in which a Christian citizen or statesman may make mistakes of detail (and especially of technical detail) either in his judgment or in his motives or in his methods of expression. It is hard to 'have a right judgment in all things.' The ordinary Christian citizen can never be in such a good position to judge as the statesman. But he can and should watch to see where the statesmen seem to be diverging from the true path or the best path, and must, by the power of sympathy and prayer and, where necessary, by ordinary or even extraordinary political methods, try to help them to keep to or return to the true course. That is an exacting task in itself, and will take all our powers of spiritual insight and energy within the context of a spiritual purpose on which all Christians can agree."

Christian Political Parties Rejected

Without accepting Dr. Fisher's exposition as altogether free from obscurity and ambiguity, it can be said to represent the attitude of many influential Christians of today in its temper. And this temper demonstrates why all Christians in Britain dislike the idea of Christian political parties, as they are known on the Continent of Europe, and consider themselves very fortunate to have escaped such developments at home. Christians in Britain have adopted as desirable the penetration of all political parties by the Christian spirit rather than the attempt to commend any particular political programme as more Christian than another. They are happy to know that all three parties contain a high proportion of practising Christians among their Members of Parliament.

The importance of the House of Lords and the Bishops' position in it has diminished as other means of expression have been found. Unhappily there are few Bishops who sit in the House who appear ready to take a part in the debates, except on very rare occasions. It is true that ill-informed episcopal utterances would do far more harm than good, and that if the Bishops have nothing to say, it is better that they keep silence. Yet the House of Lords can still be used as an important platform for the Church, as was amply demonstrated by the late Bishop George Bell of Chichester. His courageous opposition to mass bombing during the war did not gain him popularity in England, but it redounded to the glory of Britain on the Continent and helped to make him the best-known and best-loved Churchman of his generation. In a world where liberty was so widely quenched, the freedom of Britain was demonstrated in a way which struck the imagination of the world.

Bishop Bell would have echoed the words of Bishop Hensley Henson, and in doing so would have fairly represented the views of the Bishops today: "As a spiritual peer, I ought to speak on an issue which does assuredly raise the question of moral obligation."

Students

71 · POLITICS AND THE UNIVERSITY *

Richard W. Patch

Peru has not yet attained the Platonic distinction of rule by a philosopher king, but its new cabinet, appointed this month, approaches the ivory eminence of government by university professors. . . .

The cabinet appointments throw a new handful of straws into the wind, giving fresh material to the coffeeshop pundits. The epigram makers see a myriad of portents in the changes, but one peculiar facet of the new cabinet went unremarked by press, pundit, or punster. Five of the nine civilian ministers of the new cabinet are

* Richard W. Patch, "Politics and the University," *American Universities Field Staff Letters* (Peru-RWP-5-'58). Reprinted by permission of Richard W. Patch and the American Universities Field Staff, Inc.

professors of the University of San Marcos. The Foreign Minister, Raul Porras Barrenechea, is a distinguished professor of colonial history. His specialty dovetails nicely with that of Minister of Education, Jorge Basadre, who teaches and writes about the history of Peru since the formation of the republic. The Minister of Government and the Minister of Justice are appropriately both professors of law. The Minister of Labor founded the university's Institute of Human Relations, and teaches industrial psychology. Such an invasion of the Government by the professors might provoke talk in the United States, but Peruvians, untroubled by a word for "egghead," seem undismayed by the prospect.

Fact is that faculty members of universities are considered distinguished persons. They are intellectuals, and the country respects intellectuals—a phenomenon familiar to Europeans but strange to many North Americans.

A professor at San Marcos is a national personage, respected for his learning, and expected to state and defend his position on national issues as a matter of course. It is natural that he make known his political feelings, and not unknown for him to form his own party. If his abilities and inclinations so lead him, he may assume the responsibilities of his convictions by participation in the Government. The University itself is a political training ground and forum for both professors and students. Much of the students' time is devoted to intricately organized student groups which pressure not only the University authorities but, more often, the Government itself. Professors and students alike busy themselves in the affairs of political parties, taking charge of doctrine but also vigorously interesting themselves in strategy.

The universities do not, however, entirely spontaneously produce the large number of political leaders who apparently spring from classroom to congress and cabinet. Actually many aspiring politicians seek a professorship, or even student status, for the prestige which accompanies it, and its nearness to the heart of civilian political movements.

The University of San Marcos has a long if not always distinguished history. It was founded by a royal proclamation signed by *Doña* Juana, mother of Charles V, in Valladolid on May 12, 1551. This was a scant sixteen years after the founding of Lima as the capital of the new vice-kingdom of Peru. The first Rector of the

University was the Prior of the Dominican Convent, *Fray* Juan Bautista de la Roca. Courses taught were theology, canon law, and Latin. But as early as 1571 the Royal Audience authorized the professors of the University to elect a lay rector. Courses taught during the seventeenth century were theology, sacred writings, pontific law, civil law, Saint Thomas, medicine, philosophy, metaphysics, the Quechua language, and moral theology. In the eighteenth century Lima was the intellectual capital of the Spanish colonies, and the University contributed to the peculiar climate which developed through reforms intended to emphasize the Peruvian qualities of the institution, as distinct from its Spanish qualities. The University's revolutionary role began in the nineteenth century, when it found itself in the awkward position of urging independence from Spain in the colony which was the most determined of all the colonies of South America to retain its ties with Spain. Spanish troops were finally driven from Peru in 1826, not by Peruvians, but by Bolivar and José de San Martín. San Marcos students still take pride that the University was the only one in the vice-kingdom to receive San Martín (in 1822) and Bolivar (in 1826). Since then such an official reception has carried a special meaning. In spite of this proud moment, San Marcos had declined in the last years of the eighteenth and during the first half of the nineteenth century to a position of merely certifying the degrees conferred by separate colleges which had taken over San Marcos' teaching functions. Not until a national education reform in 1856, which assigned the University responsibility for studies beyond primary and secondary instruction, did it gradually resume actual teaching. The University was re-organized in 1941, and at present is made up of colleges of law, medicine, arts, sciences, economic sciences and commerce, pharmacy and biochemistry, dentistry, education, chemistry, and veterinary medicine.

The Administration of San Marcos is divided into the hierarchy of a University Assembly, made up of the eighteen senior faculty members, and empowered only to elect a rector and a vice rector and to accept or reject their resignations; a University Council, made up of the rector, vice rector, deans of the colleges, and a delegate elected by each of the colleges; and, finally, the rectorship. The University Council has powers similar to those of a board of trustees. It sets general policy, appoints administrative personnel not directly related to a college, prepares legislative bills which the President of the Republic refers to the legislature with his recommendation, fixes student tuitions and fees, examines University accounts, creates and abolishes professorships, determines the number of assistant professors, administers the wealth and income of the University, fixes salaries, may declare the rectorship vacant, and may "recess the University when circumstances do not admit a fruitful continuation of teaching." The rector is the immediate head of the University, and its official and legal representative. He must be a full professor (*Catedratico Principal Titular*), who has taught in his chair for not less than ten years. He is elected by the University Assembly for a period of five years. The rector convenes and presides over both the Assembly and the Council, and is responsible for carrying out the decisions of the council.

One of the principal problems of the faculty members is that the professorships are largely honorific. Salaries do not nearly meet living needs. The result is that all faculty members hold other positions which usually demand more time than the University appointment.

The student groups are strongly influenced by the political alignments of Peru: the *Apristas,* the Socialists, the followers of President Prado, supporters of Fernando Belaunde, Communists, Revolutionary Unionists, and so forth. Most of the students are *Apristas*—members of the party founded by Victor Raul Haya de la Torre—or Socialists of a Marxist bent, under the leadership of Luciano Castillo, professor of political economics; or they are independents. In the periods when *Apra* has been recognized by the Government its members have controlled most student organizations. *Apra* leadership is now being strongly contested by the Socialists, Communists, and Independents.

Students of each college have formed their own "Federated Center," and the Federated Centers are associated into the "University Federation of Students of San Marcos," the body which published a manifesto condemning the visit to the University of Vice President Nixon. It is a peculiar feature of the University Federation and also some of the Federated Centers that a large proportion of their leaders, while technically matriculated students, are older men already pursuing professional careers, who do not attend classes, but who present themselves at the University only for Federation meetings at which they defend the position of their particular parties. In the struggle for recognition and for a following among the students, the representatives of the various parties often fight for action on national issues far removed from the academic business of the University.

Other students simply are more interested in politics than in their studies.

On the other hand, the Federated Centers of the colleges are more concerned with the immediate teaching and student problems than is the University Federation. They organize special functions and also occasionally harass favored professors by asking them to give extra lectures, and to repeat lectures so that students who work during the lecture hour may attend. However, attendance at lectures is not obligatory and most professors find themselves lecturing to a small fraction of the students registered for a course.

Classes are poorly attended because many students work, often at full-time jobs. According to a recently published census of students, over 20 per cent of the 10,500 students received all of their funds from their own work.* A third of all students live and study on less than $10 a month. Two-thirds live and study on less than $30 a month. In Lima the smallest and most sparsely furnished room rents for between $5 and $10 a month.

The Federated Centers of the colleges have delegates for each of the class years. A delegate for the first class year, corresponding to the freshman class, must normally be in political agreement with the delegates of the upper class years in order to secure their help in a campaign for election by the members of his own class and college. But once he has been elected the delegate often is re-elected in the second and succeeding years. He is likely to attach less importance to academic work than to the affairs of the Center and its dominant political party.

The University Federation, supposedly the voice of the students and as such a power in national politics, is controlled by a junta. The junta is elected by the votes of only the delegates of the several Federated Centers, and not directly by the students. Furthermore, a large part of the members of the University Federation are not bona fide students of the University. They are, as previously explained, often long-time student politicians who have graduated but who reenrolled in graduate studies—where they may remain, fulfilling only nominal formalities—in order to retain membership in the influential University Federation. For these reasons there may be a wide divergence between the pronouncements of the Federation and what the majority of full-time students actually think.

* Universidad Nacional Mayor de San Marcos, *Censo del Alumnado,* Comision Coordinadora de la Reforma, Lima, 1957.

At present the Federation is dominated by the *Apristas,* as it often has been, during the periods when the party has been legal. In 1956 *Apra,* outlawed at the time, supported Manuel Prado and provided the balance of votes which elected him president. Prado legalized the party, appointed *Apra* members to his cabinet, and the party began a period of "coexistence." The trouble is that Prado represents the landowning class and the banking interests of the country, being a member of a wealthy family which controls, among other things, the *Banco Popular del Peru. Apra* destroyed much of its image as a defender of the Indians and champion of the working class by joining the Prado Government. Now the entrenched *Apra* leaders in the University can no longer inspire the hot-eyed following they once did. The parties which are gaining among the students are the "independents," and the Socialist and Communist groups. The Socialist Party, under Luciano Castillo, hews to a dogged Marxist line which I find difficult to distinguish from that of the smaller Communist Party. The first goal of the Socialists and Communists in the University is to replace the *Apra* leaders. In this they are supported by the Christian Democrats and the followers of Fernando Belaunde (Popular Action). The political interests of the Federation are apparent in the composition of the assemblies which it calls periodically. When the subject of the assembly has to do with internal matters of the University it is attended by a number of interested students who are not members of the Federation, while many of the members are absent. The opposite takes place when an assembly is convened to discuss a national political issue: members appear in force, but few other students are attracted. Partly in order to create larger audiences for the latter type of assembly the Federation sometimes calls for worker-student assemblies, which are largely attended by persons who have no connection with the University. For many reasons the declarations of the Federation, which are given wide circulation in Lima newspapers, bear little relation to the sentiments of the University students.

The University has many problems which are of concern to students with whom I have talked. Chiefly the students feel that courses are hastily put together and indifferently taught by professors who often miss lectures and sometimes disappear for weeks together while engaged in other activities. But the professors are physically unable to spend a major part of their time in teaching when that teaching provides them with only a small part of their income. Students in the

Arts College also complain that teaching is largely in terms of theory and doctrine. Few professors have time for their own research, much less for supervision of student research. Some courses are nothing more than the exposition of a book or a writer, without ventured interpretations and comments. A few courses are taught by unofficial student assistants.

None of the students who talked with me had any notion of a university education as a broadening, maturing, humanizing experience which would serve them no matter what career they finally chose. Practically all students come from families of modest circumstances, and they view higher education in the immediate light of providing them with a profession which will justify the financial sacrifice involved. For example, students of "economic science" by and large hope to become accountants, and they are sometimes frustrated by the theoretical orientation they receive. Students are encouraged to work outside the University in the mechanics of accounting, and in order to give them time to do this classes are given between seven and nine A.M. and from six to nine P.M. Students with broader interests and greater resources go overseas to study. On the other hand few foreign students come to San Marcos. Of 10,442 students at San Marcos, only 92 are foreigners.

But in spite of the students' attitude, it would be far from the truth to suppose the University produces only narrow professionals taught by professors biding their time for a political career. The students are serious, and eager for new ideas. Some professors are not only nationally but internationally distinguished in their fields.

• • • • •

The nation is acutely sensitive to the political doctrines which arise in the universities. The Government, well aware of its own vulnerability to attack from the University, has in the past taken strong measures to control the expression of University criticism. It was only ten years ago—October 1948—that the Government used Army tanks to force its way into the University to arrest students. That was after the disastrous and unsuccessful *Aprista* uprising in Callao on October 3 against the Government of Bustamante. Bustamante declared *Apra* illegal (although *Apristas* had been members of his Cabinet) and the Rector of the University, Luis Alberto Sánchez, an *Aprista* leader, was forced to take political asylum in the Paraguayan Embassy. After three weeks of unrest, the University Federation (*Aprista* dominated) protested the actions of the Government. *Aprista* students entrenched themselves in the patios of the thick-walled University. San Marcos was surrounded by troops that in the night of October 26 attacked with tanks, tear-gas bombs, and carbines, soon reducing the students to submission. But then General Odría attacked the Bustamante Government, forced him to leave the country, and began his own war against *Aprismo*.

In the face of these attacks, *Aprismo* flourished, openly or clandestinely, among the always present revolutionary students. It is only now—with *Aprismo* not under attack, but rather sought by the Government to support its own compromise and ad hoc policies—that *Apra* has lost its appeal to the young and disenchanted.

The decline of *Apra* in the university is apparent in the elections which are now being held to choose delegates of the Federated Centers of the colleges. Three of the ten colleges: medicine, pharmacy, and law; have already held elections in which 57 delegates have been chosen. Only 11 of the delegates are *Apristas*. This reverses the hegemony which the *Apristas* have enjoyed. The reversal in the University, political bellwether of the nation, bodes ill for the future of *Aprismo*. Equally significant is the way the realignment is taking place. The students have formed three groups by means of deals among individual parties. The Popular Action and Social Democratic parties, along with some genuine independents, formed the Independent Student Front. The Socialists, Communists, and Social Progressives formed the Revolutionary Student Front. The *Apristas* chose to call themselves the Reform Student Front. The purpose of the first two groups is mainly to remove the *Apristas* from power. At this stage the most successful vote getter is the Independent Student Front, which has elected 43 of the 57 delegates that have been chosen so far. The Socialists, Communists, and Social Progressives trailed in with three lonely delegates. But there is an unhappy possibility under the surface of this apparently encouraging picture. The most successful single party is Popular Action. Members of Popular Action speak, if at all, in terms of a loosely knit, ill-defined, and sometimes contradictory platform based on the pronouncements of Fernando Belaunde, a Lima architect. Belaunde was an eleventh-hour candidate for president in the 1956 elections, and the party was formed as his personal vehicle. Belaunde trounced the Government candidate, Lavalle, and came within striking distance of Manuel Prado, who was finally elected only after accepting the votes and terms of *Apra*.

Belaunde may have drawn a lesson from old-pro Prado, because his flamboyant speeches have carefully avoided a position on the Communists. It is my opinion that if Belaunde again runs for president in 1962, he will accept Communist support. The present common goal of Popular Action and the Communists in attacking university *Aprismo* may be a foreshadowing of what will happen in 1962—or sooner if Manuel Prado does not complete his constitutional term.

In Peru a political party with an established platform and a continuous life apart from a single founder-leader is the nearly unknown exception to the rule of short-lived parties organized to fit the immediate needs of an individual. A professional politician who can consistently and honestly live by his profession is about as unlikely a figure as an African-born governor of Georgia. In the absence of stable political organizations and in a situation where politics offers only a most precarious career, the University has come to exercise the function of a political microcosm. It furnishes the training, the career, and the prestige which are lacking in other institutions—with the ominous exception of the army.

The University is the living core of civilian political life. Both students and professors are involved—not only by choice but by the necessity of some organism to provide leadership. The internal politics of the University has more significance than is usually attributed to student polemics and professorial proclamations. The changing alliances provide, in miniature, a barometer for the future climate which it is well not to ignore. At present the indicator predicts the decline of *Apra* and a rising level of activity of the Marxists and Communists. New independent parties are gaining popularity, but they may accept Communist support in order to dislodge *Apra,* which will be a long time fading away.

Scientists

72 · FREEDOM AND INFLUENCE: OBSERVATIONS ON THE SCIENTISTS' MOVEMENT IN THE UNITED STATES *

Edward Shils

I

In 1944 there began a new current of thought and action among American scientists. It originated within the Manhattan project and arose from the depths of a troubled concern about the application of their scientific work. It raised no moral question about the rightness of their own actions in the realization of the atomic bomb, but it insisted that their will be consulted about its applications. For about two or three years there pulsated with an intensity, which varied with institutions, age, and the state of international relations, a current of anxiety, political alertness, and the desire for original and courageous action to prevent the harmful use of the achievements of science.

Its novelty lay not only in the considerable scale on which it touched the life of American scientists but also in its content. The earlier interest of American scientists in the social repercussions of their work had been not only isolated and scattered, but it was part of a radical, more or less Stalinist, criticism of American society; it was less interested in the integrity of science than in the derogation of the existing social order. The American Association of Scientific Workers which embodied this tendency never found an echo in the sentiments of American scientists. The new movement, organized in the Federation of American Scientists and expressing its views in the *Bulletin of the Atomic Scientists,* though it swept or drew into its ranks many who

* Edward Shils, "Freedom and Influence: Observations on the Scientists' Movement in the United States," *Bulletin of the Atomic Scientists,* XIII (January, 1957), 13-15. This excerpt from the original article is reprinted by permission of Edward Shils and the *Bulletin of the Atomic Scientists.*

had once shared the Leninist-Stalinist view and some who still did, did not concern itself with a radical criticism of America. Whereas the A.A.Sc.W. had complained of the suppression of science by capitalism, the new movement was impelled rather by the fear of the ways in which science had been and might be applied. Most of their leaders had had no contact with public life previously, and their desire to call to the attention of the public and its constituted authorities consequences which might arise from the presence of nuclear weapons was not the product of any doctrinal prepossession. The gradual realization of the bomb, and then the two detonations in Japan had shaken them into a worried conviction that they alone possessed an awful knowledge which, for the common good, they must share with their fellow countrymen and, above all, with their political leaders. Free from the technocratic fringe of left-wing scientism, the movement which emerged never had a program which would make rulers out of scientists. It accepted the general structure of government and of scientists in it and sought only in an informal way, and amateurishly, to transmit to legislators, administrators, publicists, and civic leaders the awareness which their scientific experience had given them.

Beginning with the campaign for the development of a feasible scheme for international control of the uses of atomic energy and the elimination of its military application, and at the same time the civilian control of atomic energy, the scope of their interest gradually broadened as new issues arose. What was first conceived as an emergency, in which a few specific problems required resolution, established itself as a chronic condition. Loyalty and security policies, the genetic consequences of atomic bomb and hydrogen bomb tests, and the political desirability of such tests, the estimation of the destructive power of nuclear weapons and the possibilities of civil defense, the nature of nuclear warfare and the possibilities of maintaining peace in the age of nuclear weapons, the economic development of backward areas of the world and the contributions of science to this, and, increasingly, the discovery of the optimal relations between scientists, scientific work and institutions, and the rest of the community, provided a natural agenda for the movement.

Problems had to be pursued into areas of social life which might have appeared earlier to be unconnected with the interests of responsible scientists. The interest in the international control of atomic energy, which was at first their exclusive concern, and which, in fact, is the original contribution of the movement to public discussion, led to the study of the more general features of disarmament and then to the whole range of foreign policy. The study of the significance of atomic bombs has led the scientists' movement to attend to matters of military technology and military strategy and planning; the concern with civil defense has led into the problems of industrial location and the psychology of the family; the development of atomic power has forced the scientists' movement to consider the advantages of private as compared with public enterprise, of monopoly and competition; the desire to protect the integrity of science and the status of scientists has required reflection about the status of intellectuals and intellectual activities of all sorts in modern societies, liberal and totalitarian. So, the simple and urgent problems of ten years ago have become knottily involved with nearly every aspect of society. The decision of the *Bulletin of the Atomic Scientists* to add to its title "A Magazine of Science and Public Affairs," and even to consider changing its title to *Science and Public Affairs,* accurately recorded the broadened scope and permanence of the emergency once considered to be no more than a transient and grave distraction.

The clamorous flood of problems and the limited resources of the scientists to deal with them gave little time for thought about fundamentals or a general philosophy. There is no trace of a political affiliation in the American scientists' movement although there is probably a disposition in the direction of the Democratic party. The movement has scarcely had an ideology—such ideology as it has, has nothing to do with any prevailing current of political ideology. Here and there one or another of its leaders might have expressed the belief that the scientific mode of thought provided a specially valuable preparation for public life and for judgment on questions of public policy and that therefore scientists had more than their distressing knowledge to contribute to American politics. The scientists' movement has, however, been remarkably free from the delusions of "scientism," from the scientific variant of the idea of the "philosopher-king." Every issue has had to be confronted on its merits, and the humane and flexible viewpoint, at once liberal and realistic, which emerges from the pages and deeds of the scientists' movement is the precipitate of numerous discrete actions. No principles to govern the relations of science and society have been promulgated, nor are they likely to be promulgated in the near future; instead, a more differentiated judgment has been schooled, and a more realistic understanding of the obduracy of the facts of social and political life has been developed.

II

The Federation of American Scientists, with its headquarters in Washington and its local branches and affiliates at a few universities and national laboratories, and the *Bulletin of the Atomic Scientists* are the products and generators of this movement. They have lived from hand-to-mouth for a decade. They have been run by amateurs who have remained scientists and scholars, on scant time, grudgingly torn from their own scientific and academic work. Unlike the trade unions of scientists, they have never interested themselves in questions of salaries, hours or tenure, or conditions of work. When they have spoken on behalf of the rights of the scientific profession, it has always been for its right to pursue the truth, and to be free from irrelevant intrusions in doing so.

The small groups or cluster of groups which constitute the scientists' movement in the United States are bound together only in a loose and ill-coordinated organization. The two major organs have no formal connection. The real link which binds the two organs together and which binds the small network of the more intensively and actively interested with the sympathetic matrix of the scientific profession is an informal consensus. The movement is neither a party nor a sect, nor has there ever been any serious effort to turn it into such. It is the more articulate expression of a widespread mood of scientists who are unable to give literary form to their sentiments or who grudge the time required or who lack self-confidence for the public representation of their views on questions of policy relating to science. Those at the center of the movement know that they are the objects of the hope, the projection of the aspirations of many with whom they have no contact, and this sustains them.

The center, the actual life and work of the movement, draws on a very small number of persons with very small funds and very little time and energy at their disposal. Active collaboration in writing, editing, organizing, making representations, raising funds, investigating, etc., is probably the product of the efforts of little more than one hundred persons, with active but less intensive support from not many more. Despite its epoch-making novelty and its eminently meritorious achievements, the movement has not succeeded in enlisting the vigorous participation or even the explicit attachment of the scientific profession in the United States.

III

What have been its accomplishments? The movement has definitely made a mark on American life. The Federation of American Scientists and, even more, the *Bulletin of the Atomic Scientists*—even though they can claim only a few specific victories (and no complete victory on any major problem)—can justly declare that they have installed themselves into the conscience and intelligence of the upper levels of American public life, and that, through the latter, their influence has radiated outward toward the whole politically interested population. The most important publicists of press, radio, and television who write and speak on matters connected with science heed with some measure of respect what the scientists say through their two organs. Many Senators and Representatives, especially those on the relevant congressional committees, turn an interested and sometimes even hospitable ear to what the scientists associated with or sympathetic to this movement have to say. The Executive Branch of the government, although it seldom obeys, listens with discomfort and respect to what the organs of the scientists' movement say, and it feels the need to reply and to adapt its conduct to render it less vulnerable to the scientists' criticism. When the Gray Committee decided that Dr. Oppenheimer was a security risk, it also felt it had to defend itself against the kinds of criticism which would come forth from the scientists' movement. When, during the 1956 Presidential election, the Republican administration wished to support its present position on hydrogen bomb tests, it recognized that it had to appear to have the support of leading figures in the scientific community in order to undo the impression created by other members of the scientific community. In vital matters of national policy, the support of scientists was sought by both of the contending parties.

In brief, the scientists' movement in the United States—and the stirrings in the great professional scientific associations which these two groups, by their incessant and dignified activity, occasionally engender—has introduced a new element into American public life. On almost every issue which has aroused the interest of our scientists' movement, something arising from the efforts of the scientists has stuck and deflected the course of political or administrative action toward what was almost always a more reasonable course—through prodding, reminding, pointing out, through the embodiment of an outlook or state of mind which reasserted the values of detachment and generosity of judgment, of freedom from tyrannous passion, and of the desirability of objective inquiry and of calm reflection.

To the educated public, the *Bulletin of the Atomic Scientists* has brought assurance and support. The small circulation—15,000 including foreign subscriptions and gifts—has sent its ripples far beyond the zone of its regular readership. The resonance which it has found in the American and foreign press has helped to imprint in the American public an awareness of its independence, its detachment, its reasonableness. Many who would otherwise have been more reconciled to iniquities, have been stiffened in their inner resistance by the feeling that there was someone who was thinking on these problems; some few were even encouraged to act with more courage and to express their views in public places. Backbones have been stiffened and hearts have been cheered in many quarters by the scientists' movement, and many minds have been made more thoughtful on all the issues of public policy in which science is involved.

SUGGESTED READINGS

LEADERSHIP

Gouldner, Alvin (ed.). *Studies in Leadership: Leadership and Democratic Action.* New York: Harper, 1950.

Hunter, Floyd. *Community Power Structure: A Study of Decision Makers.* Chapel Hill: University of North Carolina Press, 1953.

Lasswell, Harold D. *Power and Personality.* New York: W. W. Norton, 1948.

Lerner, Daniel (with the collaboration of Ithiel de Sola Pool and George K. Schueller). *The Nazi Elite.* Hoover Institute Studies, Stanford: Stanford University Press, 1951.

Lippmann, Walter. *Essays in the Public Philosophy.* Boston: Little, Brown, 1955.

Mosca, Gaetano. *The Ruling Class.* Translated by Hannah D. Kahn. Edited and revised with an introduction by Arthur Livingston. New York and London: McGraw-Hill, 1939.

North, Robert C. (with the collaboration of Ithiel de Sola Pool). *Kuomintang and Chinese Communist Elites.* Hoover Institute Studies, Stanford: Stanford University Press, 1952.

Park, Richard L., and Tinker, Irene (eds.). *Leadership and Political Institutions in India.* Princeton: Princeton University Press, 1959.

Salter, J. T. *Boss Rule: Portraits in City Politics.* New York: McGraw-Hill, 1935.

Santayana, George. *Dominations and Powers.* New York: Scribner, 1951.

Spitz, David. *Democracy and the Challenge of Power.* New York: Columbia University Press, 1958.

Tugwell, Rexford G. *The Art of Politics.* Garden City: Doubleday, 1958.

Zink, Harold. *City Bosses in the United States.* Durham: Duke University Press, 1930.

POLITICAL PARTIES

Alexander, Robert J. *Labor Parties of Latin America* (L.I.D. Pamphlet Series). New York: League for Industrial Democracy, 1942.

Bailey, Sydney D. (ed.). *Political Parties and the Party System in Britain.* New York: Praeger, 1952.

Bone, Hugh A. *Party Committees and National Politics.* Seattle: University of Washington Press, 1958.

Duverger, Maurice. *Political Parties.* Translated by Barbara and Robert North. New York: Wiley, 1954.

Kantor, Harry. *The Ideology and Program of the Peruvian Aprista Movement.* Berkeley: University of California Press, 1953.

Karpat, Kemal H. *Turkey's Politics; The Transition to a Multi-Party System.* Princeton: Princeton University Press, 1959.

Key, V. O. *Politics, Parties, and Pressure Groups.* 4th edition. New York: Crowell, 1958.

Leiserson, Avery. *Parties and Politics.* New York: Knopf, 1958.

Michels, Robert. *Political Parties.* Translated by Eden and Cedar Paul. Glencoe, Ill.: Free Press, 1949.

Neumann, Sigmund (ed.). *Modern Political Parties.* Chicago: University of Chicago Press, 1956.

Overacker, Louise. *The Australian Party System.* New Haven: Published for Wellesley College by Yale University Press, 1952.

Stevenson, John Reese. *The Chilean Popular Front.* Philadelphia: University of Pennsylvania Press, 1942.

Truman, David B. *The Congressional Party.* New York: Wiley, 1959.

Weiner, Myron. *Party Politics in India.* Princeton: Princeton University Press, 1957.

BUREAUCRACY

Blau, Peter M. *The Dynamics of Bureaucracy.* Chicago: University of Chicago Press, 1955.

Cole, Taylor. *The Canadian Bureaucracy.* Durham: Duke University Press, 1949.

Gaus, John M. *Reflections on Public Administration*. University, Ala.: University of Alabama Press, 1947.

Hyneman, Charles S. *Bureaucracy in a Democracy*. New York: Harper, 1950.

Marx, Fritz Morstein. *The Administrative State*. Chicago: University of Chicago Press, 1957.

Mises, Ludwig von. *Bureaucracy*. New Haven: Yale University Press, 1944.

Parkinson, C. Northcote. *Parkinson's Law*. Boston: Houghton Mifflin, 1957.

Robson, William A. (ed.). *The Civil Service in England and France*. New York: Macmillan, 1956.

Rosenberg, Hans W. *Bureaucracy, Aristocracy and Autocracy*. Cambridge: Harvard University Press, 1958.

Simon, Herbert A. *Administrative Behavior: A Study of Decision-Making Processes in Administrative Organization*. New York: Macmillan, 1947.

Waldo, Dwight. *The Administrative State*. New York: Ronald Press, 1948.

White, Leonard D. *The Federalists 1789-1801; A Study in Administrative History*. New York: Macmillan, 1948.

———— *The Jeffersonians 1801-1829; A Study in Administrative History*. New York: Macmillan, 1951.

———— *The Jacksonians 1829-1861; A Study in Administrative History*. New York: Macmillan, 1954.

White, Leonard D. (with the assistance of Jean Schneider). *The Republican Era 1869-1901; A Study in Administrative History*. New York: Macmillan, 1958.

BUSINESS

Berle, Adolf A., Jr., and Means, Gardiner C. *The Modern Corporation and Private Property*. New York: Macmillan, 1933.

Bisson, T. A. *Zaibatsu Dissolution in Japan*. Berkeley and Los Angeles: University of California Press, 1954.

Brady, Robert A. *Business as a System of Power*. New York: Columbia University Press, 1943.

Catton, Bruce. *The Warlords of Washington.* New York: Harcourt, Brace, 1948.

DuBois, Josiah E. (in collaboration with Edward Johnson). *The Devil's Chemists.* Boston: Beacon Press, 1952.

Haas, Ernst B. *The Uniting of Europe.* Stanford: Stanford University Press, 1958.

Hamilton, Walton. *The Politics of Industry.* New York: Knopf, 1957.

Lilienthal, David E. *Big Business: A New Era.* New York: Harper, 1953.

Lynch, David. *The Concentration of Economic Power.* New York: Columbia University Press, 1946.

Maurer, Herrymon. *Great Enterprise: Growth and Behavior of the Big Corporation.* New York: Macmillan, 1955.

Mayo, Elton. *The Social Problems of an Industrial Civilization.* Boston: Division of Research, Graduate School of Business Administration, Harvard University, 1945.

Prothro, James W. *The Dollar Decade.* Baton Rouge: Louisiana State University Press, 1954.

Quinn, T. K. *Giant Business: Threat to Democracy.* New York: Exposition Press, 1953.

Russell, Oland D. *The House of Mitsui.* Boston: Little, Brown, 1939.

Stocking, George W., and Watkins, Myron W. *Cartels in Action.* New York: Twentieth Century Fund, 1947.

———— *Cartels or Competition?* New York: Twentieth Century Fund, 1948.

United States Department of State. *Report of the Mission on Japanese Combines.* Part I. Washington, D.C.: Government Printing Office, 1946.

Whyte, William H., Jr. *The Organization Man.* New York: Simon and Schuster, 1956.

LABOR

Bakke, E. Wright; Kerr, Clark; and Anrod, Charles W. *Unions, Management, and the Public.* 2nd edition. New York: Harcourt, Brace, 1960.

Chamberlain, Neil W. *Sourcebook on Labor.* New York: McGraw-Hill, 1958.

Childs, Harwood L. *Labor and Capital in National Politics.* Columbus: Ohio State University Press, 1930.

Clark, Marjorie R. *Organized Labor in Mexico.* Chapel Hill: University of North Carolina Press, 1934.

Fawzi, Saad Ed Din. *The Labour Movement in the Sudan, 1946-1955.* New York: Oxford University Press, 1957.

Hardman, J. B. S., and Neufeld, Maurice F. (eds.). *The House of Labor.* (Prepared under the auspices of Inter-Union Institute, Inc.) New York: Prentice-Hall, 1951.

Karson, Marc. *American Labor Unions and Politics, 1900-1918.* Carbondale: Southern Illinois University Press, 1958.

Kornhauser, Arthur; Sheppard, Harold L.; and Mayer, Albert J. *When Labor Votes—A Study of Auto Workers.* New York: University Books, 1956.

Laski, Harold J. *Trade Unions in the New Society.* New York: Viking Press, 1949.

Marquand, Hillary A. (ed.). *Organized Labor in Four Continents.* London and New York: Longmans, Green, 1939.

Mills, C. Wright. *The New Men of Power.* New York: Harcourt, Brace, 1948.

Spiro, Herbert J. *The Politics of German Codetermination.* Cambridge: Harvard University Press, 1959.

Sturmthal, Adolf F. *The Tragedy of European Labour, 1918-1939.* 2nd printing. New York: Columbia University Press, 1951.

AGRICULTURE

Benedict, Murray R. *Farm Policies of the United States, 1790-1950.* New York: Twentieth Century Fund, 1953.

Blaisdell, Donald C. *Government and Agriculture.* New York: Farrar and Rinehart, 1940.

Dove, R. P. *Land Reform in Japan.* London: Oxford University Press, 1959.

Hardin, Charles M. *The Politics of Agriculture*. Glencoe, Ill.: Free Press, 1952.

Hicks, John D. *The Populist Revolt*. Minneapolis: University of Minnesota Press, 1931.

McCune, Wesley, *The Farm Bloc*. Garden City: Doubleday, Doran, 1943.

――― *Who's Behind Our Farm Policy*. New York: Praeger, 1946.

Mitrany, David. *Marx Against the Peasant*. Chapel Hill: University of North Carolina Press, 1951.

Pomfret, Joan E. *The Struggle for Land in Ireland: 1800-1923*. Princeton: Princeton University Press, 1930.

Roberts, Henry L. *Rumania: Political Problems of an Agrarian State*. New Haven: Yale University Press, 1951.

Royal Institute of International Affairs. *Agrarian Problems from the Baltic to the Aegean*. London: Royal Institute of International Affairs, 1944.

Saloutos, Theodore, and Hicks, John D. *Agricultural Discontent in the Middle West*. Madison: University of Wisconsin Press, 1951.

Shannon, Fred A. *American Farmers' Movements*. Princeton: Van Nostrand, 1950.

Sharp, Paul F. *The Agrarian Revolt in Western Canada*. Minneapolis: University of Minnesota Press, 1948.

Simpson, Eyler N. *The Ejido: Mexico's Way Out*. Chapel Hill: University of North Carolina Press, 1937.

Tomasevich, Jozo. *Peasants, Politics, and Economic Change in Yugoslavia*. Stanford: Stanford University Press, 1955.

Whetten, Nathan L. *Rural Mexico*. Chicago: University of Chicago Press, 1948.

MILITARY

Andrzejewski, Stanislaw. *Military Organization and Society*. London: Routledge and Kegan Paul, 1954.

Craig, Gordon A. *The Politics of the Prussian Army, 1640-1945*. Oxford: Clarendon Press, 1955.

Howard, Michael. *Soldiers and Governments: Nine Studies in Civil-Military Relations*. Bloomington: Indiana University Press, 1959.

Huntington, Samuel P. *The Soldier and the State*. Cambridge: Harvard University Press, 1957.

Huzar, Elias. *The Purse and the Sword*. Ithaca: Cornell University Press, 1950.

Janowitz, Morris. *The Professional Soldier*. Glencoe, Ill.: Free Press, 1960.

Liddell Hart, B. H. (ed.). *The Red Army*. New York: Harcourt, Brace, 1956.

Lieuwen, Edwin. *Arms and Politics in Latin America*. New York: Council on Foreign Relations, 1960.

Lory, Hillis. *Japan's Military Masters*. New York: Viking Press, 1943.

Maxon, Yale C. *Control of Japanese Foreign Policy: A Study of Civil-Military Rivalry, 1930-1945*. Berkeley: University of California Press, 1957.

Millis, Walter (with Harvey G. Mansfield and Harold Stein). *Arms and the State*. New York: Twentieth Century Fund, 1958.

Pool, Ithiel de Sola, and others. *Satellite Generals*. Stanford: Stanford University Press, 1955.

Rockefeller Brothers Fund. *International Security—The Military Aspect*. New York: Doubleday, 1958.

Sapin, Burton M., and Snyder, Richard C. *Role of the Military in American Foreign Policy*. Garden City: Doubleday, 1954.

Smith, Louis. *American Democracy and Military Power*. Chicago: University of Chicago Press, 1951.

Taylor, Telford. *Sword and Swastika*. New York: Simon and Schuster, 1952.

Turner, Gordon B. (ed.). *A History of Military Affairs in Western Society Since the Eighteenth Century*. New York: Harcourt, Brace, 1953.

Vagts, Alfred. *A History of Militarism*. New York: W. W. Norton, 1937.

———— *Defense and Diplomacy*. New York: Kings Crown Press, Columbia University, 1956.

Wheeler-Bennett, John. *The Nemesis of Power: The German Army in Politics, 1918-1945*. London and New York: Macmillan, 1953.

Wright, Quincy. *A Study of War*. 2 volumes. Chicago: University of Chicago Press, 1943.

CHURCH

Acton, Baron John E. E. D. *Essays on Church and State.* New York: Viking Press, 1953.

Binchy, Daniel A. *Church and State in Fascist Italy.* London: Oxford University Press, 1941.

Brenan, Gerald. *The Spanish Labyrinth.* New York: Macmillan, 1943.

Callcott, Wilfred H. *Church and State in Mexico, 1822-1857.* Durham: Duke University Press, 1926.

———— *Liberalism in Mexico, 1857-1929.* Stanford: Stanford University Press, 1931.

Curtiss, John S. *The Russian Church and the Soviet State, 1917-1950.* Boston: Little, Brown, 1953.

Ebersole, Luke E. *Church Lobbying in the Nation's Capital.* New York: Macmillan, 1951.

Fogarty, Michael P. *Christian Democracy in Western Europe, 1820-1953.* Notre Dame: University of Notre Dame Press, 1957.

Mecham, J. Lloyd. *Church and State in Latin America.* Chapel Hill: University of North Carolina Press, 1934.

Moody, Joseph N. (ed.). *Church and Society, Catholic Social and Political Thought and Movements, 1789-1950.* New York: Arts, Inc., 1953.

Pfeffer, Leo. *Church, State, and Freedom.* Boston: Beacon Press, 1953.

Stokes, Anson P. *Church and State in the United States.* 3 volumes. New York: Harper, 1950.

STUDENTS

There are no definitive, book-length treatises on the role of students as mobilizers of political power. Recent student political activity in Japan, Cuba, Turkey and other nations leads one to expect more detailed, scholarly investigation in the immediate future. In the meantime, the interested student is advised to consult professional journals, particularly those in political science and sociology. There is a rapidly growing body of newspaper, magazine, pamphlet, and monograph material on this subject. Such material does provide the reader with excellent descriptions, if little analysis, of student political activity.

SCIENTISTS

Barber, Bernard. *Science and the Social Order.* Glencoe, Ill.: Free Press, 1952.

Bush, Vannevar. *Modern Arms and Free Men.* New York: Simon and Schuster, 1949.

Dupree, A. Hunter. *Science in the Federal Government.* Cambridge: The Belknap Press of Harvard University, 1957.

Goudsmit, Samuel A. *Alsos.* New York: Henry Schuman, 1947.

Knebel, Fletcher, and Bailey, Charles W., II. *No High Ground.* New York: Harper, 1960.

Kramish, Arnold. *Atomic Energy in the Soviet Union.* Stanford: Stanford University Press, 1959.

Price, Don K. *Government and Science.* New York: New York University Press, 1954.

Thomas, Morgan (in collaboration with Robert M. Northrop). *Atomic Energy and Congress.* Ann Arbor: University of Michigan Press, 1956.

United States Atomic Energy Commission. *In the Matter of J. Robert Oppenheimer: Transcript of Hearing Before Personnel Security Board.* Washington, D.C.: Government Printing Office, 1954.

Vucinich, Alexander S. *The Soviet Academy of Sciences.* Stanford: Stanford University Press, 1956.

CHAPTER VI

The Transfer of Political Power

Man's quest for political certitude is persistent, but doomed to failure, for change is the only constant in politics. What has been written in the preceding pages has perhaps already become obsolete. Politics never remains static. Change within the total political environment is as inevitable and inexorable as are the proverbial death and taxes.

Yet even as a constant, change is no simple concept. It has the quality of mercury—easily observed but virtually impossible to grasp. This is particularly apparent in the transfer of political power. Alterations in the form and substance of governments are the bone and marrow of history. Some of these alterations, however, are merely formal; that is, the focus of power may be transferred from one group to another with no significant change in structure or policy resulting from the transfer. This type of change may occur through either violent or nonviolent techniques. What is important to note here is that the techniques of transfer do not necessarily determine the nature of the change in terms of substance; nor, indeed, do they certify that any substantive change has taken place at all. Conversely, very fundamental and extensive changes may occur in a society *without* any real or apparent resort to violence. It is therefore imperative always to look beyond the mere fact and techniques of transfer to what may or may not be the substantive significance of the transfer.

Examples of mankind's capacity to alter his political environment may be seen all around us. Each alteration inevitably involves some transfer of political power. Sometimes it occurs with incredible rapidity and under conditions of violence; at other times and elsewhere, it takes place very slowly and subtly, with neither violence nor the threat of violence anywhere in evidence.

The techniques employed permit of no easy classification, but for purposes of clarity the editors have treated them under two broad headings—violent and non-violent.

The techniques of violent transfer, which ordinarily furnish the most dramatic incidents, often appear simple and obvious, but are in fact highly complex and sophisticated. Revolution as the radical alteration of a society involves change that reaches to the very core of the body politic. Because revolution is so fundamental an alteration, both its causes and its results are extraordinarily involved. Neither the words nor the actions of the participants ever fully articulate the total meaning of "the revolution."

It would be a gross oversimplification to assume that all violent transfers of political power can be categorized as revolutionary. As Stokes' article admirably illustrates, there are a great many possible methods, including such "in-between" types as the coup d'état and the barracks revolt. Each of these is suited to a particular time and circumstance, and each requires its own careful analysis.

Among most American students, the non-violent methods of transferring political power are both familiar and, often, taken for granted. This is not surprising since the most obvious and frequent method of non-violent transfer is the one that occurs at the polls, through elections. Yet as a closer examination of the electoral process quickly reveals, even this well-tried and seemingly simple technique involves a great many intricate and subtle arrangements.

One of the newer insights into the problem of the transfer of political power is noted in the selection by Douglass Cater. As Cater shows, there are powerful instruments for altering the structure of power even within existing governments themselves. A government's policy on information, for example, may strongly condition the climate in which its performance will be judged as a whole. This is possible because the careful selection or inclusion of data enables those responsible for a government's information policy to create and destroy public images to whatever extent a particular country's laws and political morality may countenance. The more complex political life becomes, the more important is the question of how and by whom information on public issues is selected for circulation. Today, in contrast to times past, a completely free market in the information required for the exercise of political judgment simply can no longer be taken for granted.

Finally, the editors have concluded with a previously unpublished address by a twice-defeated Presidential candidate. It gives some sense of the process whereby formal political power is regarded as transitory and suggests an idea about the competition for the right to make political decisions and to exercise power. That idea is the importance of being able to lose and yet live to fight another day— the certitude of uncertainty itself, which leads the victor to recognize the victory as temporary. There is a renewable option—but it is only an option.

The meaning to be found in the transfer of political power lies not in the methods employed but, rather in the implications of the act of transfer. The variety of fighting faiths and the weapons used, whether Mexican machete or Gandhian fast, are ultimately the reflection of man's persistent dissatisfaction with the *status quo*. It is this quality that gives man his personal tragedy and his enduring nobility.

Techniques of Violent Change

73 · VIOLENCE AS A POWER FACTOR IN LATIN-AMERICAN POLITICS *

William S. Stokes

Violence seems to be institutionalized in the organization, maintenance, and changing of governments in Latin America. The methodology of force is found in advanced and in backward countries, in Indian, *mestizo,* and white republics, in the large states and in the small ones, in urban and in rural areas, in agricultural and in industrial organization, in the beginning of the twentieth century, in the present period, and in the early, middle, and late nineteenth century —in a word, wherever and whenever Hispanic culture is to be found in the Western Hemisphere. . . .

Force is a unifying factor in Latin-American political culture, yet the fact of geographical and ethnic differences and of varying rates of social and economic development leads to the logical inference that the mobilization of violence for political purposes is not likely to revolve around one simple formula. This is, however, exactly what is done when the general term "revolution" is employed to describe all use of force in Latin-American politics. Violence is, instead, a highly developed technique for obtaining power. Direct action procedures include *machetismo, cuartelazo, golpe de estado,* and revolution. The monopolization of the power factors of the state by a single political leader, a group, or a class sometimes renders unnecessary the direct employment of violence, and in such cases the methods of *imposición, candidato único, continuismo* and election (in the Anglo-American sense) may be selected. These are, of course, outwardly

* William S. Stokes, "Violence as a Power Factor in Latin-American Politics," *The Western Political Quarterly,* V (September, 1952), 445, 447-452, 456-458, 461-465. Reprinted by permission of *The Western Political Quarterly.* The footnotes in the original version are omitted here.

peaceful methods of obtaining and maintaining power, but they rest upon a foundation of force.

. . . . .

"MACHETISMO"

Machetismo is a crude, primitive method of mobilizing violence primarily in local, rural politics but occasionally in national, urban areas as well. The term emanates from the word "machete," the general utility knife employed widely throughout Latin-America. In an extractive, agricultural economy guaranteeing little more than subsistence to the majority of the people, poverty is seldom or ever so great as to deny the rural resident his machete. It is a major implement in the construction of habitation, the production of foodstuffs, and in the establishment of political power. To survive, the rural inhabitant must develop proficiency in its use, and the process of becoming expert begins as a child. Whoever can command the authority represented by the machete in rural areas possesses political power of an important nature and automatically constitutes a factor to be recokoned with in the affairs of government.

If it could be demonstrated that no political leader has exercised sufficient discipline over the rural masses to employ their collective strength in direct action, then it might be possible to argue that *machetismo* no longer characterizes Latin-American rural politics. However, leadership of a highly personal nature can readily be observed in Latin America. The matters that vitally concern the rural resident include distribution of government patronage, rights to water holes and grazing areas, military service to the central government, road building in lieu of payment of taxes, and adjudication of social disputes. In many instances, the leader who exercises authority and issues judgments on such issues is the *alcalde, jefe de operaciones militares, comandante de armas,* or official in the church hierarchy. But on the other hand the political leader might very well possess no official position at all. That his power exists there is no denying; his authority is so well known that almost anyone in the area of his jurisdiction can identify him as *el que manda* (the one who commands). This kind of absolutist personal leadership is local, rural *caudillismo.*

Many writers, Latin-Americans included, have associated *caudillismo* with the violent struggle for leadership among the generals in the early independence period, and hence terms such as the "Age of the *Caudillos*," and "Men on Horseback" are common in historical literature. It is correct to define *caudillismo* as a principle of personal leadership in politics, but it cannot be restricted to any one age or period in Latin-American history. Indeed, its origins are to be traced in part at least to the feudal institutions of Spain and Portugal and to the nature of government in the colonial period. *Caudillismo* as personal authority, as a substitute for direction and control by institutional means, such as law, is to be found in all periods of Latin-American development, including the present. Nor is it accurate to think of the *caudillo* solely as a man on horseback, for he may be a civilian, such as Carlos Antonio López of Paraguay, García Moreno of Ecuador, Estrada Cabrera of Guatemala, and Fulgencio Batista of Cuba (who although a sergeant in the army did not even learn to ride a horse until after he had first achieved power!).

· · · · ·

Although Latin-American rural communities are frequently isolated by poor communication facilities, the local *caudillos* are thrown into contact from time to time (to divide the spoils of government, for example), and occasionally, in activities such as drinking, card playing, carousing, and brawling a man so stands out that the others automatically accept his authority and extend to him their loyalty. When this occurs for an area as large as a province or a department, institutional means for resolving major issues of public controversy have been created which frequently may be entirely disassociated from the formal structure of government. The sectional *caudillos* are usually the group from which "available" presidential candidates are to be found. When a sectional leader commands the loyalty of all other major *caudillos* in the country, than a *jefe máximo* (or *caudillo supremo*) is recognized, and if he wants the presidency he will have it: he assuredly will determine who *will* have it. This procedure for the establishment of executive power is one that is essentially based upon violence, because any leader at any time may challenge the hierarchy of power, with immediate local, sectional, or national conflict resulting. Indeed, case studies of *machetismo* can be discovered somewhere in Latin America at all times, although most frequently in the local areas.

Widespread evidence of *machetismo* at the national level can still be observed among backward and advanced countries alike from time to time. . . . When no one *caudillo* can peacefully subjugate existing opposition, when one or more challenges claim to "supreme power," *machetismo* becomes a costly and time-consuming methodology for establishing authority. Among seventy nation-wide examples of *machetismo* in Colombia in the nineteenth century, one conflict alone took approximately 80,000 lives, and the struggle which covered the years 1899 to 1903 took about 100,000 lives.

. . . . .

The *caudillo supremo* produced by *machetismo* may govern by means of harsh measures including *estado de sitio* (state of siege), but on the other hand, his stature may be such that no challenges of importance may be directed against him, and he might well become *un presidente simpático*. In any event, it is doubtful that a *caudillo* can long maintain himself in power, no matter how mechanized and up-to-date his military and police systems, unless he has a large body of popular support (*tiene gente*). . . . For the *caudillo* is, above all else, a man who can command (he is *muy hombre,* or *un presidente macho,* literally, a stallion president). . . . The *caudillo* thinks and acts in terms of absolutes, and in active politics "for" or "against" are sole choices. In the language of speeches, and in day-to-day communication words like "inflexibly," "inexorably," "unchangeable," or "instantly" appear frequently. The president refers to his "supreme power"; he is not merely president but *el Presidente Constitucional;* all the symbols of power and status he puts forth openly; if he has a Ph.D. degree he is "doctor"; and if he is a general as well, he will be *El Presidente Constitucional de la Republica de* _____ *el doctor y general* _____. The *caudillo* meets situations with lordly equanimity; he can't be an ordinary president; he heads a "Restoration Movement" (for example, General Odría of Peru, 1950); he is a regenerator, *benemérito,* restorer, defender of the constitution, pacificator. Government by *caudillo* tends to be authoritarian, intolerant (law of *desacato* of Argentina), personal ("my government," "my administration," "my people," nepotism, graft), antiscientific, and violent. But it should also be pointed out that in most instances it probably tends also to be representative of majority opinion.

"CUARTELAZO"

Cuartelazo (sometimes called *sargentada* or *golpe de cuartel*), a more highly developed, complex method of organizing and changing governments than *machetismo,* has its focus in the barracks (*cuartel*). Its classic pattern is the treason of a single barracks, the *pronunciamiento, manifiesto* or *grito,* the march on centers of communication, sites of military supplies, the exchequer, government headquarters, and ultimately the capital itself, the announcement to the populace that the government has changed hands, and finally the appoinment of a patriotic *junta* to guide the country in the interim period. Even the most cursory examination of illustrative *cuartelazos* reveals that it is a mistake to think of the technique as involving massive, overpowering military force repressing the legitimate desires of the people. To be successful the *cuartelazo* requires consummate skill in the selection of leadership, the drafting of a program, the equating of the power factors, the technical problems of logistics, and the drafting of at least a temporary series of policies to meet the most pressing problems of government when power is obtained. He who would play barracks politics must know his fellow officers and men well indeed to suggest that they follow his leadership in a calculated plan of treason. Betrayal by a single officer or soldier means at least ignominious failure in the venture and possibly death by firing squad.

The *cuartelazo's* success depends upon capturing the support of other centers of military power as well as that of public opinion. This is a problem which effectively deters all but the most well prepared politician. Many Latin-American armies, particularly those in the South American area, have been trained by German technicians, whereas the navies have been trained or inspired by the British. In the century of air power, the plane must be considered, and as a competing unit with the older vested interests in the area of defense, it can constitute a delicate source to be placated. Even assuming that a barracks has been captured and that it is able to obtain sufficient support from other segments of the armed forces to justify some optimism for success, what about the civilian *caudillos* in both the rural and urban areas? As has already been demonstrated, they also command power in politics, including from time to time the authority to plunge an entire country into civil war. Thus, it usually develops that the successful *cuartelazo* involves substantial support from the sectional leaders, the leading university and professional men, and the leaders of several of the principal political parties in the country.

When the politics of the *cuartelazo* have been organized with skill, the change in governments is likely to occur with a minimum loss of life or property. Excellent illustrations of well-planned and maturely executed *cuartelazos* include those of Argentina in 1930 and 1943. General José F. Uriburu combined a section of the army with strong civilian groups and announced to the acting president on the morning of September 6, 1930 that he was marching on the capital. When he reached the *Casa Rosada* that evening about six o'clock, the acting president resigned and fled. Then General Uriburu demanded the allegiance of the military commanders who had not participated in the *cuartelazo* (which he promptly received), issued a manifesto detailing his general policies, dissolved the legislature, and issued a decree making himself provisional president. The major details of the *cuartelazo* of June 4, 1943, are known, but this classic should be studied in complete detail. General Pedro P. Ramírez, war minister in the government of President Ramón S. Castillo, hoped to advance to the presidency through party nomination and election. This aspiration was put in jeopardy by the open hostility of the president, and Ramírez then conspired with his friends in the important *Campo de Mayo cuartel* about twenty miles outside Buenos Aires for organization of a *cuartelazo*. President Castillo learned of the conspiracy, called a cabinet meeting at about 2:00 a.m., and ordered the arrest of Ramírez. This was the signal for General Ramírez to call for the march, and General Rawson began leading about 8,000 troops from *Campo de Mayo* to the *Casa Rosada*. Although the *cuartelazo* was superbly executed, it appears that the head of the Navy's Mechanical Training School either was not advised of the plan or refused to affiliate himself with it, for he offered a defense, and in the resulting military action forty lives were lost. The first troops from the *Campo de Mayo* arrived in the capital about 7:00 a.m. and surrounded the *Casa Rosada;* by noon they had occupied the central police barracks, the *Banco de la Nación* and other government offices. By three o'clock in the afternoon the troops controlled the radio stations, and in the evening of June 4, General Rawson announced to the crowds that he was president. Communiqués indicated that Colonel Juan D. Perón (the leader of the "colonels" group in the *cuartelazo*) was made chief of staff of the Army. By eight o'clock in the evening, the excitement was over, the streets were cleared, and it was evident that the *cuartelazo* was successful. Former President Castillo and his cabinet had taken refuge on a mine sweeper.

• • • • •

"GOLPE DE ESTADO"

The *golpe de estado,* frequently called the coup d'état, and sometimes referred to as *golpe militar,* with the noun *derrocamiento* being occasionally employed along with the descriptive phrase *desplazar del poder,* is the fastest, the most difficult to plan and implement successfully (short of genuine revolution), and potentially the most dangerous of the forceful methods of establishing and changing governments in Latin America. The *golpe* is a direct assault on power—almost always personal in Latin-American countries—which means the immobilization of the president either through assassination or detention. The possibilities of success are obviously enhanced if the president's cabinet, high-ranking members of the armed forces, and the head of the police system can be seized when the assault on the president is consummated. The *golpe de estado* is distinguished from the *cuartelazo* by the fact that professional military experience is less needed, and by the procedure of attack which bypasses the *cuartel* entirely. Whereas considerable military skill is required to capture the loyalty of troops and lead them successfully against a major *cuartel,* even a civilian with literary, professional or scholarly training can, assuming ingress to the *casa presidencial,* blow out the president's brains and proclaim a change in governments. The *golpe,* then, is a forceful method of organizing and changing governments which definitely permits, even encourages, civilian participation.

Inherent in the technique is ecstatic excitement for leaders and masses alike, for the *golpe* guarantees that a "bad" *caudillo* can be replaced by a "good" one, that "justice" can be substituted for "injustice" *immediately,* without the time-consuming and demoralizing limitation of such institutional restraints as law or constitutions. To the predilection toward extremism in politics in Latin America is added the factor of extreme speed and flexibility. The leader can ascertain easily and quickly the extent to which public opinion has been conditioned to the kind of change in administrations he is attempting. Politically, his status might well be nothing one moment, everything the next; his *golpe* might be rejected upon its announcement and he, himself, put to flight or captured and subject to penalties that might include death.

Yet the *golpe* is not spontaneous combustion in the field of organizing and changing governments. As with the *cuartelazo,* mastery of the elements of politics within the environmental framework of each

Latin-American country is required by the successful politician (some of whom have participated in many *golpes* during a lifetime). The first step in the process is almost invariably the organization of the cadre of leaders and sub-leaders. To cement loyalty and guarantee incentive, the *jefe supremo* of the proposed *golpe* is likely to appoint his key personnel in advance. Sometimes there is no need to carry on any propaganda whatever prior to the assault; public opinion might be favorably disposed toward a change by the ineptitude of the incumbent. If this is not the case, however, then media of communication are required to attack the government, more frequently than not (unfortunately for the research scholar who faces the task of separating objective evidence from falsification), through lies, slander, and license. As insurance against failure, the *caudillo* should have an airplane, an automobile, or other means of locomotion ready for immediate departure. Recognition by the United States and other major powers is no longer a primary determinant, if it ever was, for the existence of a government, yet it is undeniably true that immediate recognition of a new regime might have a positive effect on public opinion in the Latin-American country concerned. The leaders, therefore, endeavor to plant competent diplomats in the several capitals to negotiate speedy recognition. Timing is of the utmost importance, and although circumstances vary from country to country, Sundays and holidays, when the official offices are closed and the president probably is separated from his major supporters, are to be preferred. . . .

The recent political history of Bolivia provides excellent case studies of the *golpe de estado*. Eight different men occupied the presidency from 1930 to 1943. One resigned under pressure, one committed suicide or was murdered, two transmitted power peacefully, and the others were forcibly ejected. . . .

Other examples of successful *golpes* based upon personal assault include the well-organized effort of the Argentine minister of the interior and the commander of the *Campo de Mayo cuartel* who forced President Pedro P. Ramírez ("with a gun leveled at his head") to resign February 24, 1944, in favor of General Edelmiro Farrell, who had been vice-president under Ramírez. On August 23, 1947, Colonel Carlos Mancheno obtained entrance to the *casa presidencial* in Ecuador and forced President Jóse María Velasco Ibarra to resign (at gun point) in his favor. At the time of the assault the Army and the police supported Mancheno, and public opinion appeared conditioned to the *golpe* by the unfavorable publicity given President Velasco Ibarra's alleged preparation for the *imposición* of Mariano Súarez Veintimilla.

. . . . .

REVOLUTION

The history of Latin America from independence to the present time is a history of violent struggles of "ins" versus "outs," but it is not a history of revolutionary movements designed to remold the institutional bases of Latin-American life. By "revolution" I mean ". . . fundamental change in the nature of the state, the functions of government, the principles of economic production and distribution, the relationship of the social classes, particularly as regards the control of government—in a word, a significant breaking with the past." Revolution so defined is rare in Latin America, and even mass participation in violence is only occasionally found. It is an obvious and inescapable fact that revolution is too big and too difficult a power mechanism to employ in Latin America with any frequency. Problems of leadership, ideology, policy, planning, logistics, and timing are all maximized in genuine revolution.

Profound institutional transformations have taken place in Uruguay since the first decade of the twentieth century, but such changes have not occurred in an atmosphere of revolution, despite the ferocious violence of the nineteenth century. The Liberal revolution in Central America which began in the 1870's dramatically established in theory the doctrines of the liberal-democratic state and attempted some institutional changes, such as relations between Church and State. But the revolution lacked sustained vitality and continuity, and its effect was shadow rather than substance. Systematic research might well reveal that revolutions have been under way in various Latin-American countries in recent times, such as in Brazil from 1930 to 1945, in Argentina since 1943, and in the Dominican Republic from the 1930's to the present. . . . But I would also argue that the only clear-cut illustration of revolution in Latin America since independence is the Mexican revolution, which began in 1910-11 and which continues to exist as the dominant characteristic of Mexican economic, political, and social life today. Despite the difficulties of mobilizing violence in revolution, of all the forceful methods of organizing power in Latin America, it is probably the most democratic. Revolution is the only method which invites mass participation and renders imperative the formation of decisions on basic issues of public policy by virtually all members of the state.

"IMPOSICIÓN"

Imposición is a nominally peaceful method of organizing power in which the dominant political element in the state hand-picks a candidate and then rigs the election to guarantee victory. Its major principle is the presupposition of success for the privileged candidate. That being the case, the opposition must never become convinced that an *imposición* is operating because then there logically is no further premium in maintaining peace and force is likely to result. The conditions under which *imposición* enjoys maximum possibilities for development include: (1) the existence of a *caudillo* of such stature, power and personal popularity that no opposition dares stand against him; (2) a government firmly in power; (3) the principal parties or major elements of political strength in the country in agreement on the same candidate for supreme power. Even under the most favorable conditions, however, *imposición* is exceedingly difficult to exploit, and only the most mature, prepared, and experienced individuals or groups have been able to utilize it successfully.

A firmly established, confident government can, of course, openly announce support for a particular candidate and successfully carry through a campaign. On the other hand, such a course invites the opposition to unite and opens the way to charges of official unfairness which might result in undesirable violence. The typical *imposición* usually begins, therefore, with an official announcement from the highest sources in the state that the government is neutral and will guarantee free, fair elections. These protestations of impartiality and fairness are repeated continually throughout the campaign through all the media of communication. The president frequently will issue an impressive order to all government personnel calling attention to the principles of representative democracy and outlining specifically the provisions of the electoral law relating to proper conduct by government employees.

The government is likely to encourage a large number of candidates to offer their names in the election. The politically ambitious *caudillo* can reason thus: if the election is really fair, perhaps the vagaries of public opinion will favor his candidacy; if an *imposición* is under way perhaps he is the chosen candidate of those who are manipulating power. All during the campaign the perpetrators of the *imposición* carefully select and sharpen for effective use the methods required to insure success, whether they be control over the nominating machinery, registration fraud, appointment of key personnel at the polls, intervention in the *escrutinio* (official check of balloting), or cruder techniques involving purchase of votes or employment of violence through party workers, the police, or the armed forces.

If the election in an *imposición* is adroitly rigged, power will be maintained or changed peacefully, and the press and even scholars will hail the experience as a final demonstration of the democratic aspirations of the country. On the other hand, long experience has made most Latin-American politicians and the politically conscious citizenry exceptionally sensitive to fraud, and an *imposición* has to be very ably executed to forestall violence.

. . . . .

"CANDIDATO ÚNICO"

Candidato único, or an election in which there is but one candidate running, occurs occasionally when a *caudillo* develops who is so overwhelming in stature that no other political figure dares oppose him. An excellent illustration is General Manuel Odría of Peru who obtained power by *cuartelazo* in October, 1948, then developed his position so strongly that he was able to run for the presidency on July 2, 1950, without opposition. It is true that General Ernesto Montagne offered his name as an opposition candidate, but the National Electoral Board refused to accept it, and the general wisely did not persist in his presidential aspirations. President Felipe Molas López of Paraguay achieved power in a *candidato único* election of April 17, 1949. When so employed, however, it becomes an open, blunt repudiation of representative democracy and opens the administration to attack at home and abroad. More frequently the astute *jefe supremo* of the country will select *imposición* as a more subtle, mature method of realizing his objectives. For an outstanding *caudillo* it is a relatively simple matter to persuade a respectable, distinguished man to run against him, with the understanding that the dummy candidate will receive enough votes to make the campaign appear authentic and to maintain his honor.

Candidato único is used much more frequently when one major party is unified, the other hopelessly fragmented. When victory for the latter seems utterly impossible it commonly will refuse to campaign, and will count its strength by the number of people who stay away from the polls. . . . In instances in which it appears that neither of two *caudillos* will give way *candidato único* may be resorted to in order to preserve the peace by awarding the presidency to a third man.

"CONTINUISMO"

Continuismo is a peaceful, constitutional methodology for maintaining a chief executive in power beyond the legal term of his office. From time to time a *caudillo* will discover at the termination of his tenure that no one wishes to challenge him. He might even be approached by representatives of major power groupings in the country with the appeal that he continue in office. If the constitution prohibits re-election, then *continuismo* must be embraced. This usually involves amending the constitution, drafting a new document (in which the major change will be a section providing for temporary abrogation of the no-re-election article), enactment of legislative statute, plebiscite, or judicial interpretation. . . .

ELECTIONS

Finally, the electoral method of organizing power has been employed at least once in all of the Latin-American countries. It is my hypothesis, however, that elections in the Anglo-American sense for the determination of executive leadership are resorted to mainly in Latin America when more satisfactory methods have for one reason or another proved inadequate. Election under such circumstances is not likely to produce a strong, popular leader, but the technique may provide time for reassembling and again bringing into play the more fundamental bases for determining political power.

If the assumption of force in Latin-American politics possesses validity, the question quite fairly can be raised: Why have elections at all? The reasons include the following: (1) The need for the friendship and financial assistance of the United States dictates at least superficial respect for the idiosyncrasies of that country in the field of organizing and changing governments. (2) Elections have a public-opinion role to perform for the government. Through the media of communication the government can help to strengthen the conviction that it has chosen the right candidate. (3) Elections are also useful to the opposition which can employ the campaigns to build up moral justification for revolt. (4) There is the belief that the electoral technique of the liberal-democratic state should be developed as the most satisfactory procedure for organizing and changing governments.

74 · UPHEAVAL*

Anita Brenner

There were no hurrahs for President Wilson among the revolutionaries. The only thing marked "Made in the U.S.A." they wanted was guns, with which to do the job on Huerta themselves.

First among them—but by courtesy only, and just because he had been the first to issue a formal call against Huerta in the name of the Constitution—was the white-bearded Venustiano Carranza of Coahuila. He controlled the northeast corner of Mexico, which included the most convenient gun-running territory, and was near the strategic junctions of the railroads to the capital and to the oil-fields. His leading brain truster was Luis Cabrera, who believed that American capital should be curbed by stiff competition from other sources and that all foreign capital should leave a sizable slice of the benefits in Mexico. He wanted the revolution to cut into monopoly, curb the church as Juárez had done, destroy the remains of feudalism, and back a new strong middle class—business men, industrialists, professionals, and small farmers. Carranza had been a senator in the Diaz days. He was a cold-eyed, sensual, stubborn old patriot who believed himself to be the only possible savior of his country, a superman. He gave himself the title of First Chief and fought implacably to enforce it.

To the northwest, in Chihuahua and Durango, was Pancho Villa, the former cattle rustler and pack driver. Sometimes he obeyed Carranza, sometimes he didn't. He had rolled up a phenomenal record of victories since the fight against Diaz had begun and by now had a little council building him up as the future Strong Man. He had a foreign affairs department in the person of George C. Carothers, President Wilson's agent. He had a financial adviser who, it was as-

* *The Wind That Swept Mexico* by Anita Brenner. Copyright 1943 by Anita Brenner and George R. Leighton. Reprinted by permission of Harper and Brothers.

sumed, was in touch with the Terrazas clan and with Hearst and other interested Americans. As a counsellor of policy and teacher of Clausewitz, Villa had General Felipe Angeles, who hoped that law and order might be established not too far to the left. General Angeles had attachés of his own, including the artist, Francisco Goitia, whose job was to paint, as he went along, the triumphs and agonies of revolution. Above all, Villa had the feared and famous—it seemed invincible—Dorado cavalry.

To the southwest, in Morelos and Guerrero, was Emiliano Zapata, called "The Attila of the South" by the newspapers of Mexico City. He operated in complete independence of the other revolutionaries and his council had no middle grounders at all. With him were an eloquent lawyer, Antonio Diaz Soto y Gama, and the Magaña boys who had agitated the college students, and the village schoolteacher Otilio Montaño, who had written in grim clumsy rhetoric the first formal revolutionary program—Zapata's *Plan de Ayala,* derived from Molina Enriquez' ideas and preaching complete, immediate expropriation of lands and other productive holdings for the benefit of the poor. The slogan "Land and Liberty" didn't mean the acquisition of these things gradually and in the future; it meant land and liberty by direct action right now.

The only military chief who was his own brain trust was a ranchero and ex-mechanic from Sonora in the northwest, the plump and agreeable Alvaro Obregón. His personal followers were the fiercest fighters in Mexico, Yaqui Indians. He considered himself a socialist and was unique among the guerrillas in the way he ran campaigns. Before each major move he talked things over with his staff, taking stock of details in his remarkable photographic memory. Political matters he worked out with friends such as the other "socialist" generals—Hill, Alvarado, and Calles—and civilians who were mostly labor organizers and a few intellectuals connected with unions in some way. What Obregón decided to do was always a combination of desirables with practicables, in terms of the circumstances and people involved —that is, a shrewd immediate political adaptation of the boys' radical demands.

These four men, with their armies and retinues, were the great guerrilla chieftains. In addition there were scores of other chieftains who, with a few hundred followers, acknowledged bigger leaders only provisionally, and there were still others trooping independently who recognized no overlordship whatever. The first and indispensable requirement of a chief was that he have proved himself without fear in battle. The second was that he be a winner, and the third, that he be generous with the proceeds. They campaigned like tribes, each chief with his bunch of boys, sometimes allied loosely with other chiefs, sometimes following super-chiefs, picked according to their successes and the material returns on these. The battle cry was *"Que Viva Villa"*—*Que Viva* whoever the chief might be, followed by a hoarse, growling, shrilling *"Que Viva la Revolución!"*

There was no agreement binding the revolutionaries. There was only a common enemy—Huerta—and a common drive to get a satisfactory place in life. And as the revolutionary wave began to roll— "Death to Huerta, down with the foreigners, Mexico for the Mexicans"—there was revealed also an unarticulated set of common hates which could be seen operating when a revolutionary army came to town.

First the jails were opened and the prisoners invited to join. Next a loan was levied on the local rich, except in the rare case of a rich man who was also a sympathizer. Goods were taken from the stores, too, and here the line drawn was between Mexicans and foreigners, but in exact reverse of the distinction made in Diaz days. Some chiefs issued receipts for what was taken and conducted the disgorging of stores and warehouses in a formal systematic way. Mostly, however, it was done with a yell—"That one's a Spaniard!"—and the stuff was taken by whichever soldiers were there first, enthusiastically helped by the store's former customers. Food and liquor went at once in long, hilarious parties with music; songs about love, hunger, jail, and exile, punctuated with shots at times, to decide impromptu who was brave and who wasn't. You could sometimes tell whose soldiers they were by the songs. *Villistas* tore loose about *Adelita,* "green as the sea were her eyes . . ." *Carrancistas* strung bawdy rhymes about politics and women to the chorus of *La Cucaracha,* the cockroach who couldn't travel any more. Zapata's men sang in melting tenor to *Valentina,* breaking to sudden ear-piercing whoops with "If I am to die tomorrow, let them kill me right away . . ." The next day was a town fair: a bunch of ostrich plumes exchanged for a Christ Child out of a church perhaps, or a good cursing parrot for a mother-of-pearl-incrusted gun.

The fighting style of the troops became a projection of each region's kind of daily life. Some were ranchero units, based on the farm owned by the chief, or perhaps on a captured ranch, or on a hideout in the sierra neighborhood. Each had started round a core of the home-town or home-farm boys. In Guerrero for instance the Almazán brothers, medical students of ranchero family, led off a unit of the local farm hands. In the village of Jiquilpan in Michoacan young Lázaro Cárdenas, who had a little job as some sort of court clerk, opened the village jail and took its single prisoner away with him to find or make the nearest guerrilla troop. In some of the most arid places a few parish priests, perhaps remembering that the revolutionary heroes of generations past had been such men as they, unfrocked themselves and joined their rebel congregations. As a rule the general staff of each segment or troop or division consisted of two kinds of people; rancheros or independent peasants, and professionals—the young doctors, lawyers, writers, artists, druggists, telegraphers, engineers—who had sat smoldering on the discounted plaza bench.

The Zapatistas were a revolving peasant army, based on their own homes. The soldiers went back from time to time to look after their corn and chili patches. A detachment could often, if in a bad military spot, simply evaporate, each man becoming again a soft-eyed, vague-talking peasant by just slipping off his cartridge belt and putting it with his gun in a cache. It was impossible to defeat them, difficult even to find them, as they materialized only when they were ready to attack; and knew, besides, all the shortcuts in their mountain country and the tunnels and caves used by runners, soldiers, and spies since before Moctezuma. They wore ordinary peasant white, except the chiefs, who dressed in ranchero clothes; in Zapata's case symbolic, theatrical dead-black, skintight and set off with startling silver. Under the great hat his face was small, Asiatic, sensuous. Mandarin mustaches drooped over his full red lips and his soft cat eyes looked out, as in a mask of skin, from the death's head of his skull. The first act on raiding an hacienda or municipal center was sharp and symbolic; they got to the safe and destroyed all papers dealing with land titles, and then invited the neighborhood peasants to homestead on the hacienda lands.

The northern revolutionaries had a more military look. They wore uniforms, or parts of them—khaki bought in the United States, and broad-brimmed Texas hats—supplemented with job-lot accessories. One division wore magenta socks; there was a battalion with silk bandannas and a brigade in orchid shirts. The cavalrymen wore mostly tight ranchero pants and military tunics. There were some troops of sierra Indians, braves in loincloths with a hawk look on their faces, carrying six-foot bows.

The main battles were along the railroads, with advance attacks often carried out in combination with railroad men who had waived their payroll and pension rights and had come in as revolutionaries. A locomotive might be speeded ahead, heavily armed, moving fast into a town like a tank; or an old engine or a handcar might be turned into a torpedo by loading it with explosives and sending it crashing into a Federal train.

When these armies moved it was like a mass migration. They carried families, three layers deep: some inside the boxcars, some on top, and others, mostly the boys and young men, in hammocks slung between the wheels. Tortillas were ground and baked on fires in oil cans along the whole top of the train, and dogs and babies accommodated themselves in the warmest corners inside. The age span for soldiering was from about seven to seventy. Boys under ten were usually buglers, drummers, or couriers, and did sentry duty too. Beyond twelve no one questioned their place as full-fledged soldiers. The women, though their job was foraging, cooking, and looking after the wounded, pitched in and fought if they felt like it. If a woman's husband was killed she could either attach herself to some other man or take over his uniform and gun herself. Almost every troop had a famous lady colonel or lady captain, a husky earringed girl armed to the teeth, and among headlong reckless fighters one of the first. All these people, Zapatistas, followers of Obregón or Carranza, painters and buglers, Yaqui Indians and mule drivers, were known as Constitutionalists—opposed to the Federals whose reluctant bayonets upheld Huerta. Within a year, despite all international calculations to the contrary, they had wiped the Federals out in three-fourths of Mexico.

* * * * *

[*Peace did not come to Mexico with the defeat of Huerta. The revolutionaries could not agree on either policy or leadership. Civil war and anarchy resulted*—EDITOR'S NOTE.]

. . . The battleground was everywhere, and every inhabitant became accustomed to living provisionally, and to being ready to migrate fast, in the wake of one army or away from another, to get food. There were nearly two hundred kinds of worthless paper money.

The orthodox private-property men who were Carranza's chief advisers found seizing funds and other necessaries a disorganized way of running an army; which, besides, set a dangerous example. So a printing press traveled with the general staff to make money, and thus, explained the theoreticians, "all the people shared the opportunity of financing the revindicating Constitutionalist revolution." This struck a great many other chieftains as a good idea, so they issued currencies too; Zapata näively had his official pesos hacked out of pure gold and silver bullion. The moment a general took a town only his scrip was legal tender, good for just the time he held on. Buying anything and everything became the frantic occupation of troops and non-combatants, prices ballooned grotesquely and food or any goods could be coaxed only through barter, or with gold or gun in hand. The *bola*—guerrilla fighting—was now the only way to get ahead; and many thousands more whose jobs and wages now meant nothing, attached themselves to whatever troop swept through.

The railroads, prime military objectives, were torn up and patched and blown up and fixed and torn again. A mountain of scorched and buckled scrap rose in the central yards at Aguascalientes. The tinted walls on almost any street in every town were pocked with bullet holes, and the best houses gaped roofless, and quail or coyotes nested inside. The spatter of rifle-fire disposing of some hacendado or other rich man who had hidden himself or his money was a familiar sound of the night, like an owl's cry. Hanged men hung desiccated, tattering like scarecrows, in many wooded spots, and Sunday sightseers strolled out to look and sometimes enterprising villagers put up refreshment stands. Typhus, as in most wars, killed many more than bullets; and the diseases endemic among the forgotten 80 per cent became epidemics. Life had to be used today, like the paper money. Yet for most people the mood was not, strangely perhaps, fear, but a mixture of resignation and simmering excitement; for life was a fast lottery and the day held equal chances of drawing the red instead of the black.

Mexico City was No Man's Land. Generals swept in and out and no one could be sure at any time who was supposed to be sitting in the presidential chair, and most of the time no one was. Villa had his picture taken lolling in it, with Zapata beside him, sitting as if he were made of springs. But the Zapatistas drifted away as they had drifted in, somberly, silently, leaving the townspeople dazed because they had expected a murderous sacking and nothing had happened. When there was no food in the markets the Zapatistas knocked timidly on people's doors and in roundabout gentle Indian style asked for a little something to eat. They were seen in the palace and the museum walking carefully through the salons, looking at things in each place with curious, respectful interest. Obregón proved to be a much greater terror, for when he occupied the city he levied taxes and issued stringent rulings to sequester food and money, some for the army and some for relief of the faminestricken poorer population. Severely worded reprimands for his rough handling of business and the clergy were wired from Washington, which Obregón tabled, remarking, "Those gentry seem to believe that it suffices a starving man if you speak to him in a foreign language. . . ."

The decisive military duel developed between Obregón and Villa, with the odds at the start on Villa's side. He and the generals friendly to him held over two-thirds of the country, and outnumbered the Carranza forces perhaps five to one. They had the main railways, quickest access to ammunition, and a friendly press and support of other kinds in the United States. The upper classes and clergy in Mexico preferred Villa too—if they had to choose among bandits. Carranza against this had the oil regions, the best gun-running border territory, and he had, because Obregón was his commander-in-chief, mobile yet unified military method. Against Villa's massive cavalry attacks Obregón's strategy was to advance very fast; stop at some good fortifiable point; set up barbed-wire entanglements; and lay out trenches, in open-loop shape, in which he put chiefly the Yaqui troops who were the core of his personal army. They had been fighting for generations, trained to win or commit suicide.

When the fight began the Yaquis each lay in a trenchhole with his wife and children, who kept handing him a reloaded gun as fast as one was finished; and if he was wounded or killed, they continued firing. Cavalry issued to charge head-on into the Dorados, and then to run, apparently routed, into the open loop, where the Yaquis caught the pursuing Dorados in murderous cross-fire. They massacred the first wave, and the second, and sometimes a third. The Dorados, accustomed to being invincible, were not so good at a fourth try, and the same sort of trap closed on them in battle after battle. In short quick pushes Obregón herded Villa northward. The mere fact of retreat began to crumble Villa's army. Its Waterloo was a three-day fight in Celaya, followed by Santa Rosa, in which bloody clash Obregón's right arm was blown off by a grenade. By the middle of

1915 Villa was corralled in the northern deserts, and the United States somewhat dubiously recognized Carranza.

75 · FEBRUARY 27, 1917 *

Leon Trotsky

How scant are the records of the mass fighting in the February days—scant even in comparison with the slim records of the October fights. In October the party directed the insurrection from day to day; in its articles, proclamations, and reports, at least the external continuity of the struggle is recorded. Not so in February. The masses had almost no leadership from above. The newspapers were silenced by the strike. Without a look back, the masses made their own history. To reconstruct a living picture of the things that happened in the streets is almost unthinkable. It would be well if we could recreate at least the general continuity and inner order of events.

The government, which had not yet lost hold of the machinery of power, observed the events on the whole even less ably than the left parties, which, as we know, were far from brilliant in this direction. After the "successful" shootings of the 26th, the ministers took heart for an instant. At dawn on the 27th Protopopov reassuringly reported that, according to information received, "part of the workers intend to return to work." But the workers never thought of going back to the shops. Yesterday's shootings and failures had not discouraged the masses. How explain this? Apparently the losses were out-balanced by certain gains. Pouring through the streets, colliding with the enemy, pulling at the arms of soldiers, crawling under horses' bellies, attacking, scattering, leaving their corpses on the crossings, grabbing a few firearms, spreading the news, catching at rumours; the insurrectionary mass becomes a collective entity with numberless eyes, ears and antennae. At night, returning home from the arena of struggle to the workers' quarter, it goes over the impressions of the day, and sifting

* Leon Trotsky, *The History of the Russian Revolution*, translated by Max Eastman (Ann Arbor: The University of Michigan Press, 1957), I, 117-128. Reprinted by permission of the University of Michigan Press.

away what is petty and accidental, casts its own thoughtful balance. . . .

In the morning the workers streamed again to the factories, and in open meetings resolved to continue the struggle. Especially resolute, as always, were the Vyborgtsi. But in other districts too these morning meetings were enthusiastic. To continue the struggle! But what would that mean to-day? The general strike had issued in revolutionary demonstrations by immense crowds, and the demonstrations had led to a collision with the troops. To continue the struggle to-day would mean to summon an armed insurrection. But nobody had formulated this summons. It had grown irresistibly out of the events, but it was never placed on the order of the day by a revolutionary party.

The art of revolutionary leadership in its most critical moments consists nine-tenths in knowing how to sense the mood of the masses. . . . An unexcelled ability to detect the mood of the masses was Lenin's great power. But Lenin was not in Petrograd. The legal and semi-legal "socialistic" staffs, Kerensky, Cheidze, Skobelev, and all those who circled around them, pronounced warnings and opposed the movement. But even the central Bolshevik staff, composed of Shliapnikov, Zalutsky and Molotov was amazing in its helplessness and lack of initiative. In fact, the districts and barracks were left to themselves. The first proclamation to the army was released only on the 26th by one of the Social Democratic organizations close to the Bolsheviks. This proclamation, rather hesitant in character—not even containing an appeal to come over to the people—was distributed throughout all the city districts on the morning of the 27th. "However," testifies Yurenev, the leader of this organization, "the tempo of the revolutionary events was such that our slogans were already lagging behind it. By the time the leaflets had penetrated into the thick of the troops, the latter had already come over." As for the Bolshevik centre—Shliapnikov, at the demand of Chugurin, one of the best worker-leaders of the February days, finally wrote an appeal to the soldiers on the morning of the 27th. Was it ever published? At best it might have come in at the finish. It could not possibly have influenced the events of February 27. We must lay it down as a general rule for those days that the higher the leaders, the further they lagged behind.

But the insurrection, not yet so named by anyone, took its own place on the order of the day. All the thoughts of the workers were concentrated on the army. "Don't you think we can get them started?" Today haphazard agitation would no longer do. The Vyborg section staged a meeting near the barracks of the Moscow regiment. The enterprise proved a failure. Is it difficult for some officer or sergeant-major to work the handle of a machine gun? The workers were scattered by a cruel fire. A similar attempt was made at the barracks of a Reserve regiment. And there too officers with machine guns interfered between the workers and soldiers. The leaders of the workers fumed, looked for firearms, demanded them from the party. And the answer was: "The soldiers have the fire-arms, go get them." That they knew themselves. But how to get them? Isn't everything going to collapse all at once to-day? Thus came on the critical point of the struggle. Either the machine gun will wipe out the insurrection, or the insurrection will capture the ma-chine gun.

• • • • •

There is no doubt that the fate of every revolution at a certain point is decided by a break in the disposition of the army. Against a numerous, disciplined, well-armed, and ably led military force, unarmed or almost unarmed masses of the people cannot possibly gain a victory. But no deep national crisis can fail to affect the army to some extent. Thus along with the conditions of a truly popular revolution there develops a possibility—not, of course, a guarantee—of its victory. However, the going over of the army to the insurrection does not happen of itself, nor as a result of mere agitation. The army is heterogeneous, and its antagonistic elements are held together by the terror of discipline. On the very eve of the decisive hour, the revolutionary soldiers do not know how much power they have, or what influence they can exert. The working masses, of course, are also heterogeneous. But they have immeasurably more opportunity for testing their ranks in the process of preparation for the decisive encounter. Strikes, meetings, demonstrations, are not only acts in the struggle, but also measures of its force. The whole mass does not participate in the strike. Not all the strikers are ready to fight. In the sharpest moments the most daring appear in the streets. The hesitant, the tired, the conservative, sit at home. Here a revolutionary selec-tion takes place of itself; people are sifted through the sieve of events. It is otherwise with the army. The revolutionary soldiers—sympathetic, wavering or antagonistic—are all tied together by a compulsory discipline whose threads are held, up to the last moment, in the officer's fist. The soldiers are told off daily into first and second files, but how are they to be divided into rebellious and obedient?

The psychological moment when the soldiers go over to the revolution is prepared by a long molecular process, which, like other processes of nature, has its point of climax. But how determine this point? A military unit may be wholly prepared to join the people, but may not receive the needed stimulus. The revolutionary leadership does not yet believe in the possibility of having the army on its side, and lets slip the victory. After this ripened but unrealised mutiny, a reaction may seize the army. The soldiers lose the hope which flared in their breasts; they bend their necks again to the yoke of discipline, and in a new encounter with the workers, especially at a distance, will stand opposed to the insurrection. In this process there are many elements imponderable or difficult to weigh, many cross-currents, collective suggestions and auto-suggestions. But out of this complicated web of material and psychic forces one conclusion emerges with irrefutable clarity; the more the soldiers in their mass are convinced that the rebels are really rebelling—that this is not a demonstration after which they will have to go back to the barracks and report, that this is a struggle to the death, that the people may win if they join them, and that this winning will not only guarantee impunity, but alleviate the lot of all—the more they realise this, the more willing they are to turn aside their bayonets, or go over with them to the people. In other words, the revolutionists can create a break in the soldiers' mood only if they themselves are actually ready to seize the victory at any price whatever, even the price of blood. And the highest determination never can, or will, remain unarmed.

The critical hour of contact between the pushing crowd and the soldiers who bar their way has its critical minute. That is when the grey barrier has not yet given way, still holds together shoulder to shoulder, but already wavers, and the officer, gathering his last strength of will, gives the command: "Fire!" The cry of the crowd, the yell of terror and threat, drowns the command, but not wholly. The rifles waver. The crowd pushes. Then the officer points the barrel of his revolver at the most suspicious soldier. From the decisive minute now stands out the decisive second. The death of the boldest soldier, to whom the others have involuntarily looked for guidance, a shot into the crowd by a corporal from the dead man's rifle, and the barrier closes, the guns go off of themselves, scattering the crowd into the alleys and backyards. But how many times since 1905 it has happened otherwise! At the critical moment, when the officer is ready to pull the trigger, a shot from the crowd—which has its Kayurovs and Chugurins—forestalls him. This decides not only the fate of the street skirmish, but perhaps the whole day, or the whole insurrection.

The task which Shliapnikov set himself of protecting the workers from hostile clashes with the troops by not giving firearms to the insurrectionists, could not in any case be carried out. Before it came to these clashes with the troops, innumerable clashes had occurred with the police. The street fighting began with the disarming of the hated Pharaohs, their revolvers passing into the hands of the rebels. The revolver by itself is a weak, almost toy-like weapon against the muskets, rifles, machine guns and cannon of the enemy. But are these weapons genuinely in the hands of the enemy? To settle this question the workers demanded arms. It was a psychological question. But even in an insurrection psychic processes are inseparable from material ones. The way to the soldier's rifle leads through the revolver taken from the Pharaoh.

The feelings of the soldiers in those hours were less active than those of the workers, but not less deep. Let us recall again that the garrison consisted mainly of reserve battalions many thousands strong, destined to fill up the ranks of those at the front. These men, most of them fathers of families, had the prospect of going to the trenches when the war was lost and the country ruined. They did not want war, they wanted to go home to their farms. They knew well enough what was going on at court, and had not the slightest feeling of attachment to the monarchy. They did not want to fight with the Germans, and still less with Petrograd workers. They hated the ruling class of the capital, who had been having a good time during the war. Among them were workers with a revolutionary past, who knew how to give a generalized expression to all these moods.

To bring the soldiers from a deep but as yet hidden revolutionary discontent to overt mutinous action—or, at least, first to a mutinous refusal to act—that was the task. On the third day of the struggle the soldiers totally ceased to be able to maintain a benevolent neutrality toward the insurrection. Only accidental fragments of what happened in those hours along the line of contact between workers and soldiers have come down to us. We heard how yesterday the workers complained passionately to the Pavlovsky regiment about the behaviour of its training squad. Such scenes, conversations, reproaches, appeals, were occurring in every corner of the city. The soldiers had no more time for hesitation. They were compelled to shoot yesterday, and they would be again to-day. The workers will not surrender or retreat; under fire they are still holding their own. And with them their women—wives, mothers, sisters, sweethearts. Yes, and this is the very hour they had so often whispered about: "If only we could all get together. . . ." And the moment of supreme agony, in the unbearable fear of the coming day, the choking hatred of those who are imposing upon them the executioner's role, there ring out in the barrack room the first voices of open indignation, and in those voices —to be forever nameless—the whole army with relief and rapture recognizes itself. Thus dawned upon the earth the day of destruction of the Romanov monarchy.

· · · · ·

One after another, from early morning, the Reserve Guard battalions mutinied before they were led out of the barracks, continuing what the Fourth Company of the Pavlovsky regiment had begun the day before. In the documents, records, memoirs, this grandiose event of human history has left but a pale, dim imprint. The oppressed masses, even when they rise to the very heights of creative action, tell little of themselves and write less. And the overpowering rapture of the victory later erases memory's work. Let us take up what records there are.

The soldiers of the Volynsky regiment were the first to revolt. As early as seven o'clock in the morning a battalion commander disturbed Khabalov with a telephone call and this threatening news: the training squad—that is, the unit especially relied on to put down the insurrection—had refused to march out, its commander was killed, or had shot himself in front of the troops. The latter version, by the way, was soon rejected. Having burned their bridges behind them, the Volyntzi hastened to broaden the base of the insurrection. In that lay their only salvation. They rushed into the neighboring barracks, of the Litovsky and Preobrazhensky regiments "calling out" the soldiers, as strikers go from factory to factory calling out the workers. Some time after, Khabalov received a report that the Volynsky regiment had not only refused to surrender their rifles when ordered by the general, but together with the Litovsky and Preobrazhensky regiments—and what is even more alarming, "having joined the workers"—had wrecked the barracks of the political police. This meant that yesterday's experiment of the Pavlovtsi had not been in vain: the insurrection had found leaders, and at the same time a plan of action.

In the early hours of the 27th, the workers thought the solution of the problem of the insurrection infinitely more distant than it really was. It would be truer to say that they saw the problem as almost entirely ahead of them, when it was really nine-tenths behind. The revolutionary pressure of the workers on the barracks fell in with the existing revolutionary movement of the soldiers to the streets. During the day these two mighty currents united to wash out clean and carry away the walls, the roof, and later the whole groundwork of the old structure.

Chugurin was among the first to appear at the Bolshevik headquarters, a rifle in his hands, a cartridge belt over his shoulder, "all spattered up, but beaming and triumphant." Why shouldn't he beam? Soldiers with rifles in their hands are coming over to us! In some places the workers had succeeded in uniting with the soldiers, penetrating the barracks and receiving rifles and cartridges. The Vyborgtsi,* together with the most daring of the soldiers, outlined a plan of action: seize the police stations where the armed police have entrenched themselves; disarm all policemen; free the workers held in the police stations, and the political prisoners in the gaols; rout the government troops in the city proper; unite with the still inactive troops and with the workers of other districts.

The Moscow regiment joined the uprising not without inner struggle. Amazing that there was so little struggle among the regiments. The monarchist command impotently fell away from the soldier mass, and either hid in the cracks or hastened to change its colours. "At two o'clock," remembers Korolev, a worker from the "Arsenal" factory, "when the Moscow regiment marched out, we armed ourselves. . . . We took a revolver and rifle apiece, picked out a group of soldiers who came up (some of them asked us to take command and tell them what to do), and set out for Tikhvinskaia street to shoot up the police station." The workers, it seems, did not have a moment's trouble telling the soldiers "what to do."

---

* *Vyborgtsi* means the men of the Vyborg District—the Workers—just as *Pavlovtsi* means men of the Pavlovsky Regiment. In the singular, *Pavlovets*. [Trans.]

One after another came the joyful reports of victories. Our own armoured cars have appeared! With red flags flying, they are spreading terror through the districts to all who have not yet submitted. Now it will no longer be necessary to crawl under the belly of a Cossack's horse. The revolution is standing up to its full height.

Toward noon Petrograd again became the field of military action; rifles and machine guns rang out everywhere. It was not easy to tell who was shooting or where. One thing was clear: the past and the future were exchanging shots. There was much casual firing; young boys were shooting off revolvers unexpectedly acquired. The arsenal was wrecked. "They say that several tens of thousands of Brownings alone were carried off." From the burning buildings of the District Court and the police stations pillars of smoke rolled to the sky. At some points clashes and skirmishes thickened into real battles. On Sampsonievsky boulevard the workers came up to a barrack occupied by the bicycle men, some of whom crowded into the gate. "Why don't you get on the move, comrades?" The soldiers smiled—"not a good smile," one of the participants testifies—and remained silent, while the officers rudely commanded the workers to move on. The bicyclists, along with the cavalry, proved to be the most conservative part of the army in the February, as in the October revolution. A crowd of workers and revolutionary soldiers soon gathered round the fence. "We must pull out the suspicious battalion!" Someone reported that the armoured cars had been sent for; perhaps there was no other way of getting these bicyclists, who had set up the machine guns. But it is hard for a crowd to wait; it is anxiously impatient, and quite right in its impatience. Shots rang out from both sides. But the board fence stood in the way, dividing the soldiers from the revolution. The attackers decided to break down the fence. They broke down part of it and set fire to the rest. About twenty barracks came into view. The bicyclists were concentrated in two or three of them. The empty barracks were set fire to at once. Six years later Kayurov would recall; "The flaming barracks and the wreckage of the fence around them, the fire of machine guns and rifles, the excited faces of the besiegers, a truck load of armed revolutionists dashing up, and finally an armoured car arriving with its gleaming gunmouths, made a memorable and magnificent picture." This was the old, Tzarist, feudal, priestly, police Russia burning down, barracks and fences and all, expiring in fire and smoke, spewing out its soul with the hiccough of machine-gun shots. No wonder Kayurov, and tens, hundreds, thousands of Kayurovs, rejoiced! The arriving armoured car fired several shells at the barracks where the bicyclists and officers were barricaded. The commander was killed. The officers, tearing off their epaulets and other insignia, fled through the vegetable gardens adjoining the barracks; the rest gave themselves up. This was probably the biggest encounter of the day.

The military revolt had meanwhile become epidemic. Only those did not mutiny that day who did not get around to it. Toward evening the Semenovsky regiment joined in, a regiment notorious for its brutal putting down of the Moscow uprising of 1905. Eleven years had not passed in vain. Together with the chasseurs, the Semenovtsi late at night "called out" the Izmailovtsi, whom the command were holding locked up in their barracks. This regiment, which on December 3, 1905 had surrounded and arrested the first Petrograd soviet, was even now considered one of the most backward.

The Tzarist garrison of the capital, numbering 150,000 soldiers, was dwindling, melting, disappearing. By night it no longer existed.

After the morning's news of the revolt of the regiments, Khabalov still tried to offer resistance, sending against the revolution a composite regiment of about a thousand men with the most drastic orders. But the fate of that regiment has become quite a mystery. "Something impossible begins to happen on that day," the incomparable Khabalov relates after the revolution, ". . . the regiment starts, starts under a brave, a resolute officer (meaning Colonel Kutyepov), but . . . there are no results." Companies sent after that regiment also vanished, leaving no trace. The general began to draw up reserves on Palace Square, "but there were no cartridges and nowhere to get them." This is taken from Khabalov's authentic testimony before the Commission of Inquiry of the Provisional Government. What became of the punitive regiments? It is not hard to guess that as soon as they marched out they were drowned in the insurrection. Workers, women, youths, rebel soldiers, swarmed around Khabalov's troops on all sides, either considering the regiment their own or striving to make it so, and did not let them move any way but with the multitude. To fight with this thick-swarming, inexhaustible, all-penetrating mass, which now feared nothing, was as easy as to fence in dough.

Together with reports of more and more military revolts, came demands for reliable troops to put down the rebels, to defend the telephone building, the Litovsky Castle, the Marinsky Palace, and other even more sacred places. Khabalov demanded by telephone that loyal troops be sent from Kronstadt, but the commandant replied that he himself feared for the fortress. Khabalov did not yet know that the insurrection had spread to the neighbouring garrisons. The general attempted, or pretended to attempt, to convert the Winter Palace into a redoubt, but the plan was immediately abandoned as unrealizable, and the last handful of "loyal" troops was transferred to the Admiralty. Here at last the dictator occupied himself with a most important and urgent business: he printed for publication the last two governmental decrees: on the retirement of Protopopov "owing to illness," and on the state of siege in Petrograd. With the latter he really had to hurry, for several hours later Khabalov's army lifted the "siege" and departed from the Admiralty for their homes. It was due only to ignorance that the revolution had not already on the evening of the twenty-seventh arrested this formidably empowered but not at all formidable general. This was done without any complications the next day.

Can it be that that was the whole resistance put up by the redoubtable Russian Empire in the face of mortal danger? Yes, that was about all—in spite of its great experience in crushing the people and its meticulously elaborated plans. . . .

Techniques of Non-Violent Change

76 · DRAMA AT THE SEASHORE *

Louis Fischer

Gandhi was a reformer of individuals. Hence his concern for the means whereby India's liberation might be achieved. If the means corrupted the individual the loss would be greater than the gain.

* *The Life of Mahatma Gandhi* by Louis Fischer. Copyright 1950 by Louis Fischer. Reprinted by permission of Harper and Brothers.

Gandhi knew that the re-education of a nation was a slow process and he was not usually in a hurry unless prodded by events or by men reacting to those events. Left to himself, he would not have forced the issue of independence in 1930. But now the die was cast; Congress had decreed a campaign for independence. The leader therefore became an obedient soldier.

During the weeks after the stirring New Year's Eve independence ceremony, Gandhi searched for a form of civil disobedience that left no opening for violence.

Gandhi's monumental abhorrence of violence stemmed from the Jainist and Buddhist infusions into his Hinduism but, particularly, from his love of human beings. Every reformer, crusader, and dictator avows his undying devotion to the anonymous mass; Gandhi had an apparently endless capacity to love the individual men, women, and children who crowded his life. He gave them tenderness and affection; he remembered their personal needs and he enjoyed catering to their wants at the unnoticed expense of his limited time and energy. H. N. Brailsford, the humane British Laborite, explains this by "the fact that female tendencies were at least as strong in his mental make-up as male. They were evident, for example, in his love of children, in the pleasure he took in playing with them, and in the devotion he showed as a sick-nurse. His beloved spinning wheel has always been a woman's tool. And is not Satyagraha, the method of conquering by self-suffering, a woman's tactic?" Maybe. But maybe Brailsford is being unfair to men and too fair to the fair. Like Brailsford, everyone will interpret Gandhi's lovingness according to his own experience. It wrapped the Mahatma's iron will and austerity in a downy softness; one touch of it and most Indians forgave his blunders, quirks, and fads. It ruled out anything that could lead to violence. In the successful Bardoli Satyagraha in 1928, for instance, there was no violence, but there might have been. The peasants might have allowed themselves to be goaded into the use of force. The civil disobedience campaign of 1930, Gandhi felt, had to preclude such potentials, for if it got out of hand no one, not even he, could control it.

Rabindranath Tagore, for whom Gandhi had the deepest veneration, was in the neighborhood of Sabarmati Ashram and came for a visit on January 18th. He inquired what Gandhi had in store for the country in 1930. "I am furiously thinking night and day," Gandhi replied, "and I do not see any light coming out of the surrounding darkness."

The situation made Gandhi apprehensive. "There is a lot of violence in the air," he said. The British government had altered the exchange rate of the rupee so that India might import more from Lancashire; the Indian middle class suffered. The Wall Street crash of October, 1929, and the spreading world economic depression hit the Indian peasant. Working-class unrest was mounting for all these reasons and because of the government's persecution of labor organizers. Again, as in 1919 to 1921, a number of young Indians saw an opportunity of striking a bloody blow for freedom.

Civil disobedience in these circumstances involved "undoubted risks," but the only alternative was "armed rebellion." Gandhi's confidence remained unshaken.

For six weeks, Gandhi had been waiting to hear the "Inner Voice." This, as he interpreted it, had no Joan-of-Arc connotations. "The 'Inner Voice,'" he wrote, "may mean a message from God or from the Devil, for both are wrestling in the human breast. Acts determine the nature of the voice."

Presently, Gandhi seemed to have heard the Voice, which could only mean that he had come to a decision, for the February twenty-seventh issue of *Young India* opened with an editorial by Gandhi entitled "When I am Arrested," and then devoted considerable space to the iniquities of the salt tax. The next number of the magazine quoted the penal sections of the Salt Act. And on March 2, 1930, Gandhi sent a long letter to the Viceroy serving notice that civil disobedience would begin in nine days.

It was the strangest communication the head of a government ever received.

Dear Friend, Before embarking on Civil Disobedience and taking the risk I have dreaded to take all these years, I would fain approach you and find a way out.

My personal faith is absolutely clear. I cannot intentionally hurt anything that lives, much less human beings, even though they may do the greatest wrong to me and mine. Whilst, therefore, I hold the British rule to be a curse, I do not intend harm to a single Englishman or to any legitimate interest he may have in India. . . .

And why do I regard the British rule as a curse?

It has impoverished the dumb millions by a system of progressive exploitation and by a ruinous expensive military and civil administration which the country can never afford.

It has reduced us politically to serfdom. It has sapped the foundations of our culture. And by the policy of cruel disarmament, it has degraded us spiritually. . . .

I fear . . . there never has been any intention of granting . . . Dominion Status to India in the immediate future. . . .

It seems as clear as daylight that responsible British statesmen do not contemplate any alteration in British policy that might adversely affect Britain's commerce with India. . . . If nothing is done to end the process of exploitation India must be bled with an ever increasing speed. . . .

Let me put before you some of the salient points.

The terrific pressure of land revenue, which furnishes a large part of the total, must undergo considerable modification in an Independent India . . . the whole revenue system has to be so revised as to make the peasant's good its primary concern. But the British system seems to be designed to crush the very life out of him. Even the salt he must use to live is so taxed as to make the burden fall heaviest on him, if only because of the heartless impartiality of its incidence. The tax shows itself still more burdensome on the poor man when it is remembered that salt is the one thing he must eat more than the rich man. . . . The drink and drug revenue, too, is derived from the poor. It saps the foundations both of their health and morals.

The iniquities sampled above are maintained in order to carry on a foreign administration, demonstrably the most expensive in the world. Take your own salary. It is over 21,000 rupees [about $7,000] per month, besides many other indirect additions. . . . You are getting over 700 rupees a day against India's average income of less than two annas [four cents] per day. Thus you are getting much over five thousand times India's average income. The British Prime Minister is getting only ninety times Britain's average income. On bended knee, I ask you to ponder over this phenomenon. I have taken a personal illustration to drive home a painful truth. I have too great a regard for you as a man to wish to hurt your feelings. I know that you do not need the salary you get. Probably the whole of your salary goes for charity. But a system that provides for such an arrangement deserves to be summarily scrapped. What is true of the Viceregal salary is true generally of the whole administration. . . . Nothing but organized non-violence can check the organized violence of the British government. . . .

This non-violence will be expressed through civil disobedience, for the moment confined to the inmates of the Satyagraha [Sabarmati] Ashram, but ultimately designed to cover all those who choose to join the movement. . . .

My ambition is no less than to convert the British people through non violence, and thus make them see the wrong they have done to India. I do not seek to harm your people. I want to serve them even as I want to serve my own. . . .

If the [Indian] people join me as I expect they will, the sufferings they will undergo, unless the British nation sooner retraces its steps will be enough to melt the stoniest hearts.

The plan through Civil Disobedience will be to combat such evils as I have sampled out. . . . I respectfully invite you to pave the way for the immediate removal of those evils, and thus open a way for a real conference between equals. . . . But if you cannot see your way to deal with these evils and if my letter makes no appeal to your heart, on the eleventh day of this month I shall proceed with such co-workers of the Ashram as I can take, to disregard the provisions of the Salt Laws. . . . It is, I know, open to you to frustrate my design by arresting me. I hope that there will be tens of thousands ready, in a disciplined manner, to take up the work after me. . . .

If you care to discuss matters with me, and if to that end you would like me to postpone publication of this letter, I shall gladly refrain on receipt of a telegram. . . .

This letter is not in any way intended as a threat but is a simple and sacred duty peremptory on a civil resister. Therefore I am having it specially delivered by a young English friend who believes in the Indian cause. . . .

I remain

Your sincere friend,

M. K. Gandhi.

The messenger was Reginald Reynolds, a British Quaker who later wrote a book on beards. Clad in khadi and a sun helmet, he entered the Viceroy's house and delivered the letter to Irwin who had flown back from the polo matches at Meerut to receive it.

Irwin chose not to reply. His secretary sent a four-line acknowledgment saying, "His Excellency . . . regrets to learn that you contemplate a course of action which is clearly bound to involve violation of the law and danger to the public peace."

This law-and-order note, which disdained to deal with matters of justice and policy, caused Gandhi to say, "On bended knee I asked for bread and I received stone instead." Irwin refused to see Gandhi. Nor did he have him arrested. "The government," Gandhi declared, "is puzzled and perplexed." It was dangerous not to arrest the rebel, and dangerous to arrest him.

As March eleventh neared, India bubbled with excitement and curiosity. Scores of foreign and domestic correspondents dogged Gandhi's footsteps in the ashram; what exactly would he do? Thousands surrounded the village and waited. The excitement spread abroad. Cables kept the Ahmedabad post office humming. "God guard you," the Reverend Dr. John Haynes Holmes wired from New York.

Gandhi felt it was the "opportunity of a lifetime."

On March 12th, prayers having been sung, Gandhi and seventy-eight male and female members of the ashram, whose identities were published in *Young India* for the benefit of the police, left Sabarmati for Dandi, due south from Ahmedabad. Gandhi leaned on a lacquered bamboo staff one inch thick and fifty-four inches long with an iron tip. Following winding dirt roads from village to village, he and his seventy-eight disciples walked two hundred miles in twenty-four days. "We are marching in the name of God," Gandhi said.

Peasants sprinkled the roads and strewed leaves on them. Every settlement in the line of march was festooned and decorated with India's national colors. From miles around, peasants gathered to kneel by the roadside as the pilgrims passed. Several times a day the marchers halted for a meeting where the Mahatma and others exhorted the people to wear khadi, abjure alcohol and drugs, abandon child marriage, keep clean, live purely, and—when the signal came—break the Salt Laws.

He had no trouble walking. "Less than twelve miles a day in two stages with not much luggage," he said. "Child's play!" Several became fatigued and footsore, and had to ride in a bullock cart. A horse was available for Gandhi throughout the march but he never used it. "The modern generation is delicate, weak, and much pampered," Gandhi commented. He was sixty-one. He spun every day for an hour and kept a diary and required each ashramite to do likewise.

In the area traversed, over three hundred village headmen gave up their government jobs. The inhabitants of a village would accompany Gandhi to the next village. Young men and women attached themselves to the marching column; when Gandhi reached the sea at

Dandi on April fifth, his small ashram band had grown into a non-violent army several thousand strong.

The entire night of April 5th, the ashramites prayed, and early in the morning they accompanied Gandhi to the sea. He dipped into the water, returned to the beach, and there picked up some salt left by the waves. Mrs. Sarojini Naidu, standing by his side, cried, "Hail, Deliverer." Gandhi had broken the British law which made it a punishable crime to possess salt not obtained from the British government salt monopoly. Gandhi, who had not used salt for six years, called it a "nefarious monopoly." Salt, he said, is as essential as air and water, and in India all the more essential to the hard-working, perspiring poor man and his beasts because of the tropical heat.

Had Gandhi gone by train or automobile to make salt, the effect would have been considerable. But to walk for twenty-four days and rivet the attention of all India, to trek across a countryside saying, "Watch, I am about to give a signal to the nation," and then to pick up a pinch of salt in publicized defiance of the mighty government and thus become a criminal, that required imagination, dignity, and the sense of showmanship of a great artist. It appealed to the illiterate peasant and it appealed to a sophisticated critic and sometime fierce opponent of Gandhi's like Subhas Chandra Bose who compared the Salt March to "Napoleon's march to Paris on his return from Elba."

The act performed, Gandhi withdrew from the scene. India had its cue. Gandhi had communicated with it by lifting up some grains of salt.

The next act was an insurrection without arms. Every villager on India's long seacoast went to the beach or waded into the sea with a pan to make salt. The police began mass arrests. Ramdas, third son of Gandhi, with a large group of ashramites, was arrested. Pandit Malaviya and other moderate co-operators resigned from the Legislative Assembly. The police began to use violence. Civil resisters never resisted arrest; but they resisted the confiscation of the salt they had made, and Mahadev Desai reported cases where such Indians were beaten and bitten in the fingers by constables. Congress Volunteers openly sold contraband salt in cities. Many were arrested and sentenced to short prison terms. In Delhi, a meeting of fifteen thousand persons heard Pandit Malaviya appeal to the audience to boycott foreign cloth; he himself bought some illegal salt after his speech. The police raided the Congress party headquarters in Bombay where salt was being made in pans on the roof. A crowd of sixty thousand assembled. Hundreds were handcuffed or their arms fastened with ropes and led off to jail. In Ahmedabad, ten thousand people obtained illegal salt from Congress in the first week after the act at Dandi. They paid what they could; if they had no money they got it free. The salt lifted by Gandhi from the beach was sold to a Dr. Kanuga, the highest bidder, for 1,600 rupees. Jawaharlal Nehru, the president of Congress, was arrested in Allahabad under the Salt Acts and sentenced to six months' imprisonment. The agitation and disobedience spread to the turbulent regions of the Maharashtra and Bengal. In Calcutta, the Mayor, J. M. Sengupta, read seditious literature aloud at a public meeting and urged non-wearing of foreign textiles. He was put in prison for six months. Picketing of liquor shops and foreign cloth shops commenced throughout India. Girls and ladies from aristocratic families and from families where purdah had been observed came out into the streets to demonstrate. Police became vindictive and kicked resisters in sensitive parts. Civil resistance began in the province of Bihar. Seventeen Satyagrahis, including resigned members of Legislative Councils, were sentenced to periods of from six months to two years in prison. A Swami who had lived in South Africa received two and a half years. Teachers, professors, and students made salt at the sea and inland and were marched to jails in batches. Kishorlal Mashruwala, a faithful disciple of Gandhi, and Jamnalal Bajaj, a rich friend of Gandhi's, were sentenced to two years' incarceration. In Karachi, the police fired on a demonstration; two young Volunteers were killed. "Bihar has been denuded of almost all its leaders," Mahadev Desai wrote, "but the result has been the opening of many more salt centers." Congress distributed literature explaining simple methods of producing salt. B. G. Kher and K. M. Munshi, leaders of the national Congress, were arrested in Bombay. Devadas Gandhi was sentenced to three months' imprisonment in Delhi. The salt movement and the arrests and imprisonments spread to Madras, the Punjab, and the Carnatic (Karnatak). Many towns observed hartals when Congress leaders were arrested. At Patna, in Bihar, a huge mass of thousands moved out of the city to march to a spot where salt would be made. The police blocked the highway. The crowd stayed and slept on the road and in the fields for forty hours. Rajendra Prasad, who was present and told the story, received orders from the police officer to disperse the crowd. He refused. The officer announced that he would charge with cavalry. The crowd did not move. As the horses galloped forward, the men and women threw themselves flat on the ground. The horses stopped and did not trample them. Constables then proceeded to lift the demonstrators and place them in trucks for transportation to prison. Other demonstrators replaced them. Mahadev Desai was arrested for bringing in a load of salt. In villages, millions of peasants were preparing their own salt. The British pressed local officials to cope with the problem. The officials resigned. Vithalbhai Patel, the speaker of the Legislative Assembly, resigned. A large group of prominent women appealed to Lord Irwin to prohibit the sale of intoxicating beverages. At Karachi, fifty thousand people watched as salt was made on the seashore. The crowd was so dense the policemen were surrounded and could make no arrests. At Peshawar, the key to the volatile northwest Frontier Province, an armored car, in which the Deputy Police Commissioner was seated, first ran full-tilt into a crowd and then machine-gunned it, killing seventy and wounding about one hundred. In parts of Bengal, in the United Provinces, and in Gujarat, peasants refused to pay rent and the land tax. The government tried to place all nationalist newspapers under censorship, whereupon most of them voluntarily suspended publication. Congress provincial offices were sealed and their property and office paraphernalia confiscated. Rajagopalachari was arrested in Madras and given a nine months' sentence. The wild Afridi tribe, in the northwest frontier Tribal Area, attacked British patrols. In the city of Chittagong, Bengal, a band of violent revolutionists raided the arsenal to seize arms. Some were killed.

The Viceroy, says Irwin's biographer, "had filled the jails with no less than sixty thousand political offenders." Estimates ran as high as a hundred thousand. "A mere recital of the action taken by him during this time," the biography affirms, "belies once for all the legend that he was a weak Viceroy. Those who were responsible for executing his orders testify that his religious convictions seemed to reinforce the very ruthlessness of his policy of suppression. . . ."

A month after Gandhi touched salt at the Dandi beach, India was seething in angry revolt. But, except at Chittagong, there was no Indian violence, and nowhere was there any Congress violence. Chauri Chaura in 1922 had taught India a lesson. Because they treasured the movement Gandhi had conjured into being, and lest he cancel it, they abstained from force.

May 4th, Gandhi's camp was at Karadi, a village near Dandi. He had gone to sleep on a cot under a shed beneath the branches of an old mango tree. Several disciples slept by his side. Elsewhere in the grove, other ashramites were in deep slumber. At 12:45 A.M., in the night of May 4th to 5th, heavy steps were heard. Thirty Indian policemen armed with rifles, pistols, and lances, two Indian officers, and the British District Magistrate of Surat invaded the leafy compound. A party of armed constables entered Gandhi's shed and the English officer turned the flashlight on Gandhi's face. Gandhi awoke, looked about him, and said to the Magistrate, "Do you want me?"

"Are you Mohandas Karamchand Gandhi?" the Magistrate asked for the sake of form.

Gandhi admitted it.

The officer said he had come to arrest him.

"Please give me time for my ablutions," Gandhi said politely.

The Magistrate agreed.

While brushing his few teeth, Gandhi said, "Mr. District Magistrate, may I know under which charge I am arrested. Is it Section 124?"

"No, not under Section 124. I have got a written order."

By this time, all the sleepers in the compound had crowded around the shed. "Please, would you mind reading it to me?" Gandhi asked.

The Magistrate (reading): "Whereas the Governor-in-Council views with alarm the activities of Mohandas Karamchand Gandhi, he directs that the said Mohandas Karamchand Gandhi should be placed under restraint under Regulation XXXV of 1827, and suffer imprisonment during the pleasure of the Government, and that he be immediately removed to the Yeravda Central Jail."

At 1 A.M., Gandhi was still cleaning his teeth. The officer told him to hurry. Gandhi packed some necessities and papers in a small bag. Turning to the officer, he said, "Please give me a few minutes more for prayer."

The officer nodded in assent, and Gandhi requested Pandit Khare to recite a famous Hindu hymn. The ashramites sang. Gandhi lowered his head and prayed. Then he stepped to the side of the Magistrate who led him to the waiting motor truck.

There was no trial, no sentence, and no fixed term of imprisonment. The arrest took place under an ordinance, passed before a British government existed in India, which regulated the relations between the East India Company and Indian potentates.

77 · GOVERNMENT BY PUBLICITY *

Douglass Cater

To study the publicity process in government means to study the ways and means by which government explains itself to the people. It also means necessarily to study the news-forming habits and techniques of the press, radio, and television, which transmit most of the public explanation of government. It means to examine the definition of news itself. Just as individual man cannot communicate thoughts that lie beyond the limits of his vocabulary to express, so it might be said that the vocabulary of the press delimits the thinking of men in organized society, particularly on matters as remote to their daily experience as their national government.

It is strange that the political scientist has so long neglected the study of the interaction between government and the press. The American Fourth Estate operates as a *de facto,* quasi-official fourth branch of government, its institutions no less important because they have been developed informally and, indeed, haphazardly. Twelve hundred or so members of the Washington press corps, bearing no authority other than accreditation by a newspaper, wire service, or network, are part of the privileged officialdom in the nation's capital. The senior among them claim a prestige commensurate with their continuing power. For Presidents come and go but press bureau chiefs are apt to remain a while.

The power they exercise is continuing and substantive. They are the articulators of those events of government which they and their bosses deem worthy of note. Their strength stems from their ability to select—to define what is news and what isn't. In Washington on an average day, a good many hundreds of thousands of words are spoken, tens of dozens of "events" occur. The press decides which of those words and events shall receive the prompt attention of millions and which, like timber falling in a deep and uninhabited forest, shall crash silently to the ground.

The reporter in Washington has prerogatives belonging to jour-

* Douglass Cater, *The Fourth Branch of Government* (Boston: Houghton Mifflin Company, 1959), pp. 13-21. Copyright 1959 by Douglass Cater, Jr. Reprinted by permission of Douglass Cater and Houghton Mifflin Company.

nalists in no other capital. He has access to the Chief Executive. At the White House press conference, he determines by his questions which matters shall be brought to the President's attention and in what way. The reporters, not the President, ultimately decide which of the President's utterances are headlined to the nation, which given lesser treatment, and which pretty well ignored.

The President, of course, gives the ritual of the press conference its basic content. But the reporters largely determine the form. It is a source of continual amazement to the uninitiated how loosely defined are the ground rules for interrogating our head of state.

The reporter serves as one systematic channel of communication between Congress and the Executive which continues to function when others have broken off. Through him the opposition as well as lesser members of the President's own party can bring their queries to the President's ear with some certainty of a response. Conversely, select reporters enjoy an intimacy with the congressional leaders that few members of the White House staff ever share.

In times of critical congressional debate, when the hour for voting draws near, the rooms outside the chambers become a beehive of whispered consultation between press and politician. News tickers in the Capitol and White House lobbies transmit the last-minute communiqués. The hastily torn off teletape rushed to the Senate floor is a familiar sight during the final frenzied assaults on the enemies' strongholds. As each congressional fight reaches its crisis, one is made sharply aware of the pervasive influence of news and newsmen.

No one who has been in on the development and growth of a major policy is likely to minimize the publicity consciousness which must guide its course every step of the way. At a gathering of newsmen to pay honor to him for his famous Plan, General George C. Marshall gave an unsolicited testimonial to this. "I found as in everything I touched almost, particularly in military operations, it is not so hard to make a general plan; the great problem is how to put that thing over; how you carry it through, and that was the case in this instance." Marshall went on to spell out those problems of putting across the Marshall Plan which have lingered in his memory. He told of his concern at the time of his speech at Harvard in June 1947, lest the conservative Middle West rise up to veto the Plan before it had got off the ground. What he had not anticipated and what proved to be a tremendous boon to the Plan was the immediate response of the European leaders to his speech. "The result of Messieurs Bevin and Bidault's anticipation of the Plan provoked so much reaction that the Middle West was forgotten for a month and a half," Marshall declared.

Of course, the Middle West was not forgotten at all, least of all by the people in the Middle West. But what really happened was that the great floodlights of the press were concentrated on the European news events rather than searching out, and perhaps stimulating, news events from Ohio.

This tendency for the development of news to influence reactively the development of the events on which it feeds should not be minimized. It is a force that cannot be precisely charted. It can be a result of pure chance. It can, as modern practitioners of the art of public relations appreciate, be made the object of manipulation. It can even be a product of conscious cooperation from the press. At the gathering in Marshall's honor, Paul Hoffman paid glowing tribute to certain members of the Washington press corps. "We would have never gotten the dollars," said Hoffman, "if it hadn't been for the support of the reporters of the Overseas Writers Club." The tribute was duly accepted by the members present, including representatives of the passionately objective wire services. There are many moments in a reporter's workday when he silently accepts the fact that the formulation of news is not exactly a scientific process foreign to the reporter's thoughts and feelings and ambitions.

The reporter works within limits. News is a vaguely definable commodity recognized more by instinct perhaps than by copybook maxims. One of the perennial sources of astonishment for the nonprofessional is to attend a congressional committee hearing and witness the row upon row of reporters seated at the press tables as they lift their pencils and lay them down with almost ballet corps precision while the flow of testimony moves along. The skilled reporter's measurement of "news" is not simply defined by what goes into the total story. It can be charted by which chunk goes into the "lead," which is buried in the tail, and which, with squirrel-like foresight, it tucked away for the "overnight." The dogmas of what is "news" help determine the priorities of what is communicated to the public about its government.

News standards go to the very core of policy formulation by officials. As a program moves from the tentative planning stage in the Executive department through the long wearisome process of legislative enactment, appropriation, further enactment, and still further appropriation, there is an inevitable tendency to accentuate those aspects which are newsworthy and to de-emphasize—sometimes causing atrophy—those aspects which are not newsworthy.

The competitive news advantage of one policy over another has great bearing on the comparative ease with which each survives the legislative process. Under the vast panoply of our foreign aid programs, military assistance with its newsworthy qualities—its marching troops, long lines of tanks, and low sweeping planes—has a publicity appeal which aids greatly its continuation. On the contrary, a worthy program like economic aid requires tremendous exertion to seek out its newsworthy traits, vast oversimplification, and the mammoth efforts of private groups who zealously exploit the small news potential in order to develop political support. Congressional ardor in approaching these two programs bears a direct relationship.

It is impossible to chart precisely the conforming influence of publicity upon policy. A few who were privy to the initial formulation of the Marshall Plan discovered that publicity requirements as much as anything else dictated its evolution from a program directed against "hunger and want" to one aimed more concretely at Communism. It was perhaps a subtle shift of emphasis but far-reaching in its effect.

It is useful to examine the basic conflict of interest that exists between government and the press. Here I would simply point out that the official and the reporter are moved by fundamentally different compulsions. The official's first response to a newsworthy event is assimilative. He attempts to relate it to the broad body of record on which he precariously builds his policies. The reporter's first impulse, on the other hand, is distributive: he seeks to communicate the newsworthy event as speedily and widely as possible.

Inside the Executive Branch official cables, coded and decoded, lag by vital hours and sometimes days the dispatches of the press. On a weekend in 1955 the Undersecretary of State, acting in his superior's absence from the city, learns through a press report that Chinese Communist leader Chou En-lai has made a bid for negotiation on the Formosa Straits dispute. He knows, too, that the American public has been similarly informed. The press stands ready to take down, even insistent on receiving his response. The Undersecretary has not received an official report from the field evaluating the proposal, but he does not want to give the "publicity play" to the Communists over the weekend. He drafts a hurried reply summarily knocking down the Communist bid. It turns out that he has not had time to gauge the full import of Chou En-lai's proposal or to conceive a skillful answer. The Secretary, on his return, makes an effort to rectify the blunder. In this case, the priorities of the press have hustled the procedures of government.

The official must think in terms of finding the lowest common denominator of agreement. For him the business of policy making is a matter of accommodation. Particularly as it reaches the topmost levels of government, there is need to fuzz over disagreements in the quest for a sense of unanimity. Regular participants at meetings of the National Security Council, the nation's highest strategic body, testify that the problem frequently reduces itself to finding the phrase of appropriate subtlety to bridge unnecessary conflicts. The official, as Dean Acheson has remarked, remembers the words of Justice Holmes: "Some things have got to be stated obscurely before they can be stated clearly."

For the reporter, the basic quest is to discover and high-light traces of disunity. As a government official once complained, the reporter is Hegelian. He thinks in terms of thesis and antithesis. It is his premise that progress comes through controversy and that truth, as has been said, is generated by encounter as fire is made by rubbing together two sticks.

The official acts on the premise that premature publicity can be a destructive force if it undermines the effort to reconcile diverse interests and causes the hardening of fixed positions. The reporter believes in the purifying powers of publicity. He is the sworn enemy of secrecy. He holds firm in the faith that "public opinion" must have an opportunity to express itself while policy is still malleable and has not been molded into unchangeable dogma.

Arthur Krock, columnist of the *New York Times,* has summed up succinctly the conflicting mandates of newspaperman and official:

> Our obligations are merely these in deciding whether to go into print with information: Is it true? Has it been legitimately acquired? Is it fit to print—public property or a private matter? These satisfactorily settled, the facts are ready for their bath of printer's ink.
>
> But the statesman has other considerations. Is it premature? Will publication make the going more difficult? Will publication tend to confuse, rather than to clarify, the popular mind? These are some of the problems before him, particularly if he is President of the United States in a catastrophic hour, forcing the innermost fibers of his body and the full resources of his spirit into his colossal task.

It is interesting to note that in the Soviet Union there is no such dichotomy between the reporter and the commissar. By Communist definition, the press is an instrument of state and party for the "education" of the people. News can be held in a state of suspension for weeks or months without losing its newsworthiness when the decision to publish is finally made. Despite its lip service to a philosophy of dialectical materialism, the Soviet press has invented a whole new vocabulary to describe its government in nondialectical terms. Socialist progress as reported in *Pravda* is a straight-line proposition. The Soviet reporter will admit of no conflict of interest between government and the press.

But for American government, this conflict is very real. On Dean Acheson's last day in office as Secretary of State, he was paid a visit by James Reston, Washington correspondent for the *New York Times*. The purpose of Reston's call was to ask quite bluntly why the Secretary and he had not enjoyed better working relations. Underlying his question was the unhappy conviction that Acheson, who brought unusually high talents to the office, had been unwittingly caught in the riptides of publicity. The Secretary's effectiveness had been gradually eroded by failures of communication.

Secretary Acheson answered equally bluntly that what Reston suggested would have been impossible, since there was a basic conflict of purpose between the two of them. A Secretary of State, Acheson said, has to germinate new policies and to nurse them along until they have reached the stage of development when they can withstand the battering assaults of the political arena. The reporter's primary purpose, on the other hand, is to get news for his paper no matter what the effect on policy.

Reston stoutly denies that the conflict can be defined in quite these terms. He admits it is the duty of the reporter to get at the news while it is still news. In government today, when so many policy decisions are made in the closed precincts of the Executive departments, the press would be abdicating its function if it were to sit by until these decisions are formally announced. But Reston argues that Secretary Acheson failed to understand and make use of the creative power of the press to muster public support for sound policy and, alternatively, to gauge the full extent of public reaction to unsound or unrealistic policy.

This dialogue between the Secretary and the reporter—both able and earnest men, both anxious that democratic government should be effective government—reveals a dilemma of government and the press in a free society. It is a dilemma more recognizable in the United States than in the parliamentary democracies where the press does not play so intimate a role in the scheme of things. It afflicts Republican and Democratic administrations alike for it has nothing to do with partisan affiliations of government or the press.

There are other dilemmas. With the growth of big government and of modern mass techniques for communicating the news about government, there has been a parallel growth in the subtle art of manipulating the flow of information. To a remarkable extent, the public trust nowadays is afflicted with an acute public relations sense. The tendency to "manage the news" on the part of those having a particular interest in it disturbs and frequently confounds the best of reporters.

· · · · ·

Certainly, the institutions of both government and the free press in America are equally ancient and inviolable. Much of the tension between the two is part of the healthy unrest of democracy.

Yet both need to be examined to discover how much or how little they contribute to a continuing disorder in democracy which results in weakness rather than strength. It is a failure for democracy when government fails to explain itself clearly and candidly to the citizens. It is equally a failure when the press fails to communicate intelligibly the news of government or when that news becomes a propaganda weapon employed by self-seeking interests to frustrate effective leadership in a democracy.

78 · INTIMIDATION AND PUBLIC ORDER *

W. J. M. Mackenzie

1 · Pressure on Individuals
An individual may be influenced in his vote by threats of personal violence to himself or those to whom he is attached, or by threats of

* From *Free Elections: An Elementary Textbook* by W. J. M. Mackenzie. © George Allen & Unwin Ltd., 1958. Reprinted by permission of Holt, Rinehart and Winston, Inc., New York, and of George Allen & Unwin Ltd.

economic and social sanctions such as boycotting. Private violence, or the threat of it, is a crime under any system of law worthy of the name, and requires no special electoral legislation. Other sanctions are usually not forbidden in general terms; indeed the boycott and the strike are held to be weapons of the under-dog rather than of the powers that control physical resources of wealth and weapons, and complete prohibition of organizations using such sanctions is one of the marks of dictatorship. In spite of this difficulty, it is easy enough to legislate that the use of any threat designed to influence the vote of an individual is improper: and most electoral codes include such a provision.

The difficulty is to enforce it. How can one frame a law in terms precise enough to justify action by the police and the courts? For instance, it was well understood in eighteenth- and nineteenth-century England that the tenant of a farm should vote in his landlord's "interest"; some landlords were tolerant, but most expected and secured obedience. Was this due to "improper" pressure? Most tenancies were from year to year, and could be terminated quite legally on short notice: how was the law to distinguish the landlord's use of discretion in managing his own property from his use of property to influence votes? Explicit sanctions of this sort merge imperceptibly into a general system of social sanctions and social conformity. Certain pressures make it inconvenient for permanent civil servants in Britain to be avowed members of the Communist Party, which is not an illegal organization; other pressures make it difficult for a working coal miner to be an avowed Conservative. Such social pressure is rarely directed so specifically to the question of voting that electoral law can be brought into play.

There are, however, three things which may help a little to redress the balance. One is provision for the secret ballot: its power is real, even though it only defends the individual who is prepared to defend himself by dissimulation. A second requirement is that there should be independent courts freely open to individuals strong-minded enough to use them, and that the courts should take a strict view in any case when there is an allegation of improper pressure. In the third place, if parties exist which compete on a national scale, each of them gives countenance and support to possible sympathizers isolated in a milieu unfavourable to them. A combination of these three factors gives reasonable scope to the dissenter: but they cannot in themselves protect him completely. It is idle to think that there can be the same degree of independence in a society of village communities as there is in a great metropolis. Electoral law cannot create a higher degree of individual responsibility than the nature of society permits: the most it can do is to strengthen a trend towards individual decision in face of forces which tell against it.

2 · Mass Intimidation

In a sense, any large organization is alarming. The scale of modern political parties dwarfs the individual, and the mere existence of great parties discourages the efforts of smaller ones. But large parties (or parties ambitious to become large) have open to them a choice of tactics. They may seek to be persuasive, or they may seek to be imposing.

The rules of action for a party which seeks to impose itself are now familiar. Those which would generally be accepted as legitimate are the summoning of large meetings in public open spaces, processions through the streets with banners, a large expenditure on posters, the wearing of badges and the display of window cards by supporters. These things make possible a display of strength, sometimes on a very large scale, but they do not threaten formally the state's monopoly of force. Threats to create a state within a state were the mark of Fascism and Nazism during their rise in the 1920s, and in most countries such action is now illegal. Examples of it are the adoption of party uniforms which travesty military or police uniforms: the creation of para-military organizations within the party; public demonstrations in military order; the organization of squads of stewards which assume sole responsibility for order at meetings. The Fascists and Nazis went on to use such organizations to provoke riots and street-fighting; other parties were so placed that they must either seem ineffectual or reply in kind, and both lines of action were disastrous to electoral democracy.

Resistance to Fascism failed in Italy and Germany partly because there was tacit sympathy between police and army on the one side, the Fascists on the other: this was what Fascists and Nazis wished the public to believe, and unfortunately it was in substance true. In such circumstances, free elections are in the end impossible: but if police and army are loyal to the idea of a state founded on consent, the control of para-military organizations is not difficult. Party armies are amateurish at best, and cannot stand against professionals acting in earnest. Similarly, it is easy to defeat attempts by parties to replace the police by their own squads of stewards and strong-arm men if the official police are adequately financed and resolutely led, and have sufficient professional pride to regard with disgust the efforts of self-appointed "auxiliaries."

These principles of control are better understood now than in the days of the Ulster Volunteers and the Irish Volunteers, or of Mussolini's *squadristi* and Hitler's first "storm-troopers." Any competent government can now stop threats of this kind before they become serious: the question at present is whether governments have become so cautious that they discourage all public demonstrations of party strength lest they become a threat to public order. It is not easy to draw the line between defence of public order against a show of force through numbers, and defence of the existing government against a rising party which wishes to replace it. Opposition, even Communist opposition, in Western countries has for some time been very docile; the problem of control of mass parties following "charismatic" leaders is one that principally troubles "colonial" governments during the process of transferring power to local people. To introduce elections in a traditional society involves also the introduction of new mass organizations: the process by which such organizations are created is more delicate and dangerous than the electoral process itself. The British have on the whole been judicious (or fortunate) in India, the Gold Coast and Nigeria; but elsewhere—in Malaya for instance and in Kenya—nascent political parties have attempted to establish themselves by violence directed largely against their own countrymen, and have been checked by armed forces brought in from outside.

3 · Polling-Day

All these questions come to a head on polling-day, which may be a serious test of police organization if the public is excitable and party leaders are reckless. On the whole, elections in the West are so much a matter of course that the risk of disorder is very small: in countries where elections are new they are generally treated with great respect, and the public itself maintains good order as an indication of its political maturity. But it is not difficult to distort the results of an election, or even to wreck it completely, by organized violence: quite a small number of people, working to a common plan, can create by pre-arranged outbreaks an atmosphere of general uneasiness, and the position may deteriorate quickly if the election is closely contested.

To handle such dangers is a matter of police tactics rather than of political science. To the layman the secrets of success appear to be adequate information, adequate communications, and adequate concentration of force. It is usual to post a policeman in or near each polling station, as a symbol of authority and an immediate support for the presiding officer. But one man is of little value in a crisis unless he can summon support quickly, and effective control depends on the mobility of police reserves. If they are known to be at hand, the risk of violence is greatly reduced.

It may in certain circumstances be useful to spread a general election over several days, so that limited police reserves can be used successively in different parts of the country, and this may also be useful in deploying limited resources of trained clerks. This idea of a general election spread over a period is sanctioned by a British tradition ended only in 1918, and it is hard to see any objection to it in principle. It is, however, best to avoid it, if possible, in countries where there are adequate mass communcations, because the progress of the election in the first constituencies to poll becomes known throughout the country, and may affect the voters elsewhere: *how* it affects them is difficult to say—some may climb on the "bandwagon" of the winners, others may see a new danger and vote against it—but the mere fact that some constituencies poll first may lead to endless arguments. These difficulties might be met by delaying the count, or the announcement of results, for the first constituencies to poll: but such a remedy creates other problems.

4 · Conclusion

What has been said above is directed mainly to the question of how public force may be used to exclude private force from intervention in elections. Everyone knows that public force may itself be a danger to freedom: if public force is identified by public opinion with the government in power, the government's claim that it is using force to maintain order will in itself be a threat to its opponents. In the last resort, therefore, the system of free elections depends on a certain separation of powers between administrators (or policemen) and politicians: there must be some public sense that police and administration serve the public, not the party leaders.

The Marxist view of the situation is that this cannot happen, and that the pretense that it can happen is a mere fraud. The doctrine of Marxist elections, in which the choice is between voting for the government and seeking to subvert the regime, follows consistently enough from these premises. The theorists of free elections would answer that a class view of society is a limited view: class domination exists and is important, but the existence of strong semi-independent groups within society is also important, and the idea of established professions of administrators, soldiers and policemen partly independent of the politicians is no more paradoxical than the idea of professions of doctors, lawyers, scientists and engineers, exercising within their own spheres great power subject to public responsibility. The debate between these two points of view is too complex for serious discussion here: all that need be said is that the effective organization of free elections presupposes the tradition of a public service independent within its own professional sphere.

79 · A FUNNY THING HAPPENED TO ME ON THE WAY TO THE WHITE HOUSE *

Adlai E. Stevenson

A funny thing happened to me on the way to the White House. Let me tell you something about it all.

While I did not carry many states, I seem to have run way ahead in the fourth estate, excluding, of course, you publishers. I can think of no state I would rather have carried, and perhaps I should begin by apologizing to those of you who work for a living and who thought I was out in front, somewhere beside Mississippi, Britain and France. The fact was, of course, that the General was so far ahead we never saw him. I was happy to hear that I had even placed second.

It is apparent that I was not the first choice of a great many. But no one will say, I trust, that I snatched defeat from the jaws of victory. Which reminds me that four years ago, occupying the seat I occupy tonight, was another great governor—excuse me, the Governor of another great state—some say the second greatest state in the Union. What has just happened to me had just happened to him. In fact, it had just happened to him for the second time. But did he despair? He did not. He said to himself—if I may take a newspaperman's license to tell you what a man says to himself—he said: "If

---

* Reprinted by permission of Adlai E. Stevenson.

I cannot be President myself, I can at least make somebody else President." Which, blast his merry heart, he proceeded to do. . . .

. . . four years ago the newly-elected Governor of Illinois sat down there with you common people—which reminds me that I rather enjoy talking over your heads—at last! [Stevenson was speaking from a rostrum raised above the level of the other diners.] I was happy and carefree and had nothing to worry about; nothing except the organization of a new administration to clean up the state of Illinois after the long years of the usual Republican misrule. (And now I don't even have that to worry about!)

I, a Democrat, had just been elected Governor by the largest majority ever received in Republican Illinois. And here I am, four years later, and just defeated by the largest majority ever received in democratic America.

Wasn't it Jim Watson who said that he entered the Senate with almost no opposition from the people of Indiana, and that he left the Senate with none? I feel a little the same way. But I wonder if I'm not entitled to some kind of record. Did anyone starting from scratch ever enter our public life with such widespread approval and then leave, with such widespread approval—all in the space of four years? Frankly, I think that the chroniclers of our times have overlooked the meteoric beauty and brevity of my political career.

Well, I had not planned it that way. I had wished to continue as Governor of Illinois, there to erect and fortify a shining temple of administrative purity and political probity. But the gods decreed otherwise—after meeting in the Chicago stockyards. Mindful of the Chinese maiden's philosophical acceptance of unwanted and aggressive attentions, I concluded to accept my fate gallantly and joyfully, with consequences that were regarded by most of you publishers— also joyfully!

Now I content myself that it is all for the best. After all, didn't Socrates say that the duty of a man of real principle is to stay out of politics? So you see I'm delighted that the sovereign people have put an even higher value on principles than I did.

Yes, I have much to be thankful for and it would be out of character if I didn't frankly confess my happy state of mind, even here, surrounded by my late executioners.

As you all know, I just love to make speeches. Especially light-hearted speeches. For laughter most of all distinguishes us from the lower—or untaxed—animals, and I was much relieved that the Republicans evidently decided not to prohibit humor in politics by Federal law. Maybe they are going to leave it to the states to deal with this newest threat to the Republic?

I am happy that almost 27,000,000 voted for me. I was a little baffled by the emergence of that word "egghead," to describe some of my supporters—a word which I am glad to bequeath to the nation's vocabulary. It seems to have been first used to describe the more intelligenziac members of that lunatic fringe who thought I was going to win. I am happy to note that you refrained from saying of the eggheads that the yolk was on them!

That figure, 27,000,000, still staggers me. But I need a much stronger word to describe what the still larger number of those who liked Ike does to me!

I have not compared notes with the President-elect on how he enjoyed the campaign. Indeed, now that the affair is over, I hope some time to know him, which recalls many editorials and articles you gentlemen wrote last spring about how I wanted to run against Senator Taft but not the General who was my old friend. It has seemed to me odd that the simple truth that I did not want to run against anyone had so little news value.

I would tell him that for my part I enjoyed the campaign—in spots. There were times, I confess, when I was afraid I wouldn't die, times when I felt I wouldn't do it to a dog. Let me add, by the way, that like every red-blooded American patriot, I own a dog. It was not a campaign contribution. And I think the General would say to me that there are times when he wishes he was in my shoes—you see I had them fixed.

A lot of wonderful things happened to me during the campaign. People shook hands (have you ever shaken 4,000 hands, one after the other, with a happy smile and a bright word for the owner of each hand?). They even shouted: "Good old Ad-lie!" If any of you gentlemen run for public office and have a slightly unusual name, let me advise you either to change it before you start, or be prepared to take other people's word for it.

I travelled. In San Francisco a woman in the crowd shook hands with me through the car door and shortly announced that she had lost a diamond ring. I travelled tens of thousands of miles, up and down this vast country, on such a sightseeing tour as few men are privileged to make, and all free! Free, that is, if blood and sweat, money and deficits, don't count?

I got several hours of sleep a night; they fed me pretty regularly; I got a little tired of cheese-on-rye sandwiches and coffee in cardboard containers. And I frequently thought unhappily of Froude's line in his *Life of Bunyan:* "The excitement of perpetual speech-making is fatal to the exercise of the highest powers." I became very familiar with the sound of my own voice. I hope the Recording Angel will note that I did not say the "sound of my own *words*"—although, if you want to raise this ghostly subject, I should be quite willing to open my speech-writing books, if the Luce publications and the Readers Digest will open theirs?

And, speaking of books, although I clearly won the bosom-baring and public-stripping contest of last fall, I am now prepared to go a step farther and disclose my pre-nomination expenditures in full!

Before nomination:

Item 1. 3-cent postage stamps to explain, mainly to
the press, why I was not a candidate for the
nomination $150.00

After the convention commenced in Chicago, a large number of persons took up their residence on the street and lawns around my house —and you know who they were—and the following expenditures were incurred before I could escape:

Item 2. 68 cases of beer—for the press $272.00
  3. 16 cases of nonalcoholic beverages for the
press 34.00
  4. 8 cases of other beverages—for the press.... 480.00
  5. Hire of truck from house to Convention Hall
—for the press 30.00
  6. Hire of bus from house to Convention Hall—
for the press 50.00
  7. Special police assigned to protect house *from*
the press 500.00
Total $1,366.00

There is a further item, not yet available, for restoring lawns destroyed, if not permanently scorched—by the press.

The eggheads present, if any, will identify and understand, why I think of those words, "How sharper than a serpent's tooth it is to have a thankless—press."

Of course, I make this further and positively final revelation with no expectation of political reciprocity, but merely to suggest, with characteristic delicacy, that the A.N.P.A. can send the check to me.

And now that the tumult and the shouting have died . . . how does the vanquished hero feel, and what of the future?

Well, gentlemen, there are certain pleasurable aspects of defeat. Although there seemed little perceptible editorial enthusiasm for me during the campaign, except in some of the better papers, I have been stirred by the virtues which so many essayists discovered in me the moment it became clear that the outs were in. Much of this comment seemed to suggest that it couldn't have happened to a nicer guy. . . .

Then there were the letters. We gave up counting before long and began to weigh them. So many of them were from people who voted for the General, and evidently felt that they owed me an explanation; curious why people will go to all that trouble to write a long letter when a little X in the right place would have been so much easier. But I am grateful to them all, and I wish there was some refined way befitting my station to explain to each of them that we spent a lot of money we didn't have, etc. But I suppose if I did they might write again, in less friendly vein, and say: "Just like a Democrat."

As to my future. Well, there are those like the man who changed the sign on his car after the election from "Switched to Stevenson" to "Switched, Bothered, and Bewildered," who feel that I should devote my classic talents to the welfare of mankind by frequent talking; then there is another smaller group who insist that God, and/or the election, has appointed me the scourge of the Republican party; and finally there is the much smaller group that feel that it is not wholly unworthy or improper to earn a living. My sons are numbered in the latter group.

But despite anything you may have read or written, there are some future plans of action I have definitely rejected. I have declined an invitation to become president of the National Association of Gag-writers. And I will not go into vaudeville. . . .

. . . . .

But, whatever happens to the Republicans, the Republic will survive. I have great faith in the people. As to their wisdom, well, Coca Cola still outsells champagne. They may make mistakes. They do sometimes. But given the time they correct their mistakes—at two or four-year intervals. I have faith in the people, and in their chosen leaders: men of high purpose, good will, and humble hearts, men quite prepared to stand aside when the time comes and allow even more humble men to take over.

As to you, the press, a last word. It is the habit of journalists, as of politicians, to see the world in terms of crisis rather than continuity; the big story is turmoil and disaster, not the quiet spectacle of men working. I trust that there will be none among my party who will hope for just a small, dandy little catastrophe to vindicate us. I am aware of the thesis that bad news sells papers. But neither politicians nor publishers have the right in this age to hope for the worst. Every newspaperman has talked at one time or another of how to handle the story of the end of the world; but who will be around to buy the extra?

Every lesson of history is that democracy flourishes when speech is freest. No issue is more important—and more troublesome—in this time of conflict with massive repression than preservation of our right, even to bore each other. (I was flattered, by the way, by an unsigned letter last week that said: "Please start talking again, Governor, or we'll be bored to death before we're starved to death.") Never was the responsibility of the majority press greater to make clear that it is concerned about the freedom of all Americans, and not merely about its own liberty to agree with itself. Your typewriter is a public trust. Its sound may be the most beautiful noise you know, but it has meaning and justification only if it is part of the glorious symphony of a free society.

I am grateful . . . to all of you for your courtesy and patience with me.

To the minority among you, I say "Chins up!" and

"There, there, little mink coat, don't you cry,
For you'll be a teapot by and by."

SUGGESTED READINGS

TECHNIQUES OF VIOLENT CHANGE

Aristotle, *Politics*.

Brinton, Crane. *The Anatomy of Revolution*. Revised edition. New York: Prentice-Hall, 1952.

Brogan, Denis William. *The Price of Revolution*. New York: Harper, 1952.

Burns, Cecil Delisle. *The Principles of Revolution: A Study in Ideals*. London: Allen and Unwin, 1920.

Chorley, Katherine Campbell. *Armies and the Act of Revolution*. London: Faber, 1943.

Edwards, Lyford P. *The Natural History of Revolution*. Chicago: University of Chicago Press, 1927.

Gross, Feliks. *The Seizure of Political Power in a Century of Revolutions*. New York: Philosophical Library, 1958.

Hunter, Robert. *Revolution: Why, How, When?* New York: Harper, 1940.

LeBon, Gustave. *The Psychology of Revolution*. Translated by B. Miall. New York: Putnam, 1913.

Lenin, Vladimir Ilich. *Selected Works*. Moscow: Foreign Languages Publishing House, 1952.

Machiavelli. *Discourses on the First Decade of Titus Livius*.

Malaparte, Curzio. *Coup d'État, The Technique of Revolution*. New York: Dutton, 1932.

Mao Tse-tung. *Selected Works*. New York: International Publishers, 1956.

Pareto, Vilfredo. *The Mind and Society*. Edited by Arthur Livingston; translated by Andrew Bongiorno and Arthur Livingston, with the advice and active cooperation of James Harvey Rogers. New York: Harcourt, Brace, 1935.

Ravines, Eudocio. *The Yenan Way*. New York: Scribner, 1951.

Selznick, Philip. *The Organizational Weapon—A Study of Bolshevik Strategy and Tactics*. New York: McGraw-Hill, 1952.

Sorel, Georges. *Reflections on Violence*. Translated by T. E. Hulme and J. Roth. Glencoe, Ill.: Free Press, 1950.

Wolfe, Bertram D. *Three Who Made a Revolution*. New York: Dial Press, 1948.

TECHNIQUES OF NON-VIOLENT CHANGE

Bartlett, F. C. *Political Propaganda*. New York: Cambridge University Press, 1940.

Berelson, Bernard, and Janowitz, Morris (eds.). *Reader in Public Opinion and Communication*. Glencoe, Ill.: Free Press, 1950.

Bernays, Edward L. (ed.). *The Engineering of Consent*. Norman: University of Oklahoma Press, 1955.

Bondurant, Joan V. *Conquest of Violence*. Princeton: Princeton University Press, 1958.

Clapp, Gordon R. *The TVA*. Chicago: University of Chicago Press, 1955.

Friedrich, Carl J. *The New Image of the Common Man*. Boston: Beacon Press, 1950.

Gallup, George. *A Guide to Public Opinion Polls*. Princeton: Princeton University Press, 1944.

Kelley, Stanley, Jr. *Professional Public Relations and Political Power*. Baltimore: Johns Hopkins University Press, 1956.

Kuper, Leo. *Passive Resistance in South Africa*. New Haven: Yale University Press, 1957.

Kuper, Leo, Watts, Hilstan, and Davies, Ronald. *Durban: A Study in Racial Ecology*. London: Jonathan Cape, 1958.

Lasswell, Harold D. *Politics: Who Gets What, When, How?* New York: McGraw-Hill, 1936.

Lerner, Daniel. *The Passing of Traditional Society*. Glencoe, Ill.: Free Press, 1958.

Lippmann, Walter. *Public Opinion*. New York: Harcourt, Brace, 1922.

Lowell, A. Lawrence. *Public Opinion and Popular Government*. New York: Longmans, Green, 1914.

Rodgers, Lindsay. *The Pollsters*. New York: Knopf, 1949.

Steinberg, Charles S. *The Mass Communicators*. New York: Harper, 1958.

17-401

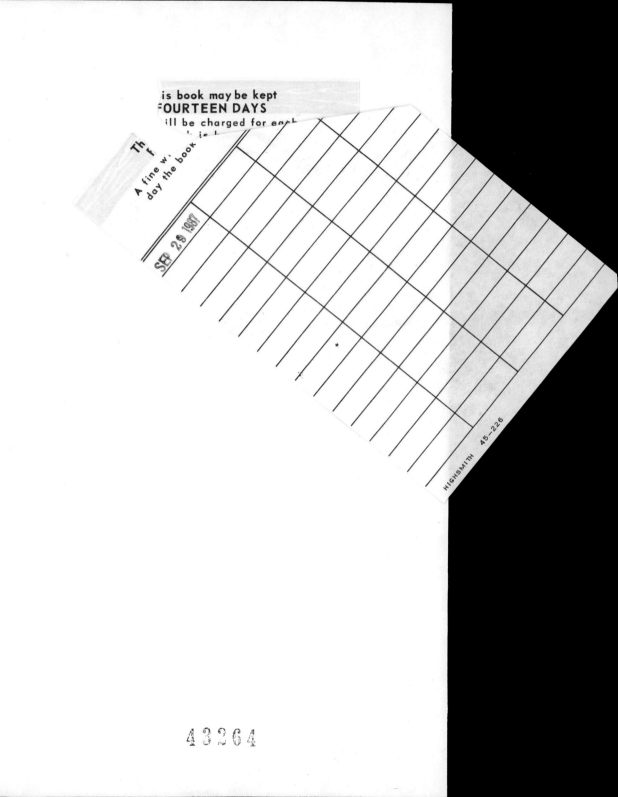

is book may be kept

FOURTEEN DAYS

ill be charged for ea

Th

A fine w.
day the book

SEP 29 1987

HIGHSMITH 45-226

43264